D0295367

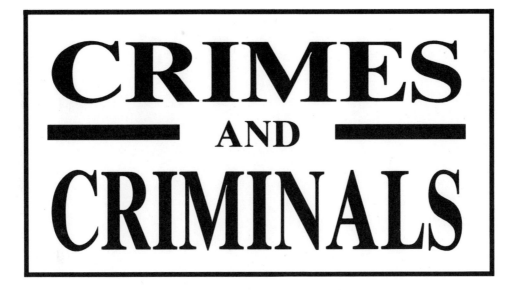

CRIMES AND CRIMINALS

BLACK CAT

INTRODUCTION

What causes our universal fascination with stories of crime – even, if not especially, amongst the most respectable and law-abiding of citizens? Is it the thrill of seeing how others dared to flout society's conventions? . . . the spice of a dash of controlled horror? . . . or even the fascinating insights into human psychology and behaviour that they provide?

The tales of crimes of all types collected together in this volume provide all these facets of fascination . . . and more! From the gruesome stories that inspired the Vampire legends and the terrifying accounts of witchcraft – and the way society dealt with so-called witches – to classic crimes of jealousy like that of Ruth Ellis, the last woman to be hanged in Britain, and contemporary accounts of the 'big-business' of organized crime and gang warfare.

There are also sections of the book devoted to the less sensational aspects of crime, such as the stories of the pitiful victims and how their lives are changed by the criminal act, the painstaking police work that has gone into solving some of the great crimes and scandals of recent times, the work of the highly professional lawyers – such as the celebrated Sir Edward Marshall-Hall – and the often lengthy and engrossing trials that have resulted, and, in many cases, changed the course of legal history.

What is patently revealed to be true is that at the heart of the fascination of crime and criminals is the fact that they usually provide us with really good stories. Moreover, they need not all be grim tales of blood-lust and violence. Few readers will be able to resist a smile at the tale of Victor Lustig, arguably one of the world's greatest confidence tricksters who managed to sell the Eiffel Tower to an unsuspecting dupe not once, but twice!

Copyright © Macdonald & Co (Publishers) Ltd, 1990

The material in this book originally appeared in *Crimes and Punishment*
© Phoebus Publishing Co/BPC Publishing Ltd 1973/4/5/6

first published in Great Britain in 1990
by Macdonald & Co (Publishers) Ltd.
under the Black Cat imprint

Reprinted 1991

All rights reserved.
No part of this publication may be reproduced, stored in a
retrieval system or transmitted in any form or by any means
without the prior permission in writing of the publishers, nor be
otherwise circulated in any form of binding or cover other than
that in which it is published without a similar condition
including this condition being imposed on the subsequent
purchaser.

Macdonald & Co (Publishers) Ltd
Orbit House
1 New Fetter Lane
London EC4A 1AR

A member of Maxwell Macmillan Pergamon Publishing Corporation

ISBN 0-7481-0295-7

Printed and bound in Czechoslovakia by Aventinum

50829

CONTENTS

AP, UPI

PERVERTED KILLERS

The "Baby-faced Beast" of Coatesville, Pennsylvania, has never been forgotten in his home town, such was the brutal nature of his crime. Pink-cheeked Alexander Meyer was just 20 years old when he knocked down 16-year-old schoolgirl Helen Moyer (right) in his truck, carried her off unconscious, raped and finally killed her.

THE baby-faced, pink-cheeked youth who drove along a quiet road near Coatesville, Pennsylvania, did not look like a killer. But when he set out in his green Ford truck that afternoon of February 11, 1937, he had killing on his mind—and rape.

It was just after 3.30, when the children came out of high school. He passed several girls, but there were always other people around, or other cars on the road. Then he saw, far ahead, a solitary female figure on a lonely stretch of road. Without hesitation, he swerved the truck and struck her, knocking her down. The truck went over her body. The youth jumped out, picked up the unconscious girl and dumped her in the back.

He drove to a deserted farmhouse and carried the girl inside; there he stripped her and raped her. The schoolgirl seemed to be dead—or so the attacker later claimed. He carried the naked body to the well outside and threw her down it. After that he went home and ate a good dinner. Two days later he returned to the farm with a stick of dynamite, which he threw down the well. The explosion partly covered the body with rubble.

Obsessional neurosis

The police who were confronted with the disappearance of 16-year-old Helen Moyer were at first baffled. They found her shoes and schoolbooks close to the spot where she had been knocked down. The shoes had been split open, and the shattered glass of a headlight suggested that she had been the victim of a hit-and-run driver. But where was she?

When the news of the girl's disappearance became known two people contacted the police. One was a scrapyard worker,

and it seemed possible that he had actually seen the "accident" from a distance. At least, he had seen a green truck swing across the road and hit a telegraph pole. It backed, turned, and hit another pole. Then it had driven off fast.

Helen Moyer's next-door neighbour, a 15-year-old schoolgirl, also came forward. Six days before Helen's disappearance she had accepted a lift from a young man in a green truck; he had a "baby face" and wore dirty overalls. He pulled up in a quiet lane and tried to undress her; the girl fought back, and he hit her with a wrench. She had managed to jump out of the truck and run towards a house, and the man drove off.

Police examined the telegraph poles and found flakes of green paint—the same type of paint they had found on Helen's shoes. They began tracing and questioning the owner of every Ford truck in Chester County, and when the Philadelphia police discovered that 20-year-old Alexander Meyer was the owner of a green Ford truck they realized suddenly that this might be their man.

Three years before, Meyer had been sentenced to an indeterminate sentence for firing at two Philadelphia girls with a rifle. He was the son of a well-to-do coal broker from Downington, 12 miles from the place where Helen had disappeared. The medical report from the reformatory said he was a "constitutional psychopathic inferior, the victim of his own retarded mentality, insensible to pain . . . sadistic and slightly effeminate".

Meyer was arrested as he was driving his milk truck—the green Ford—and taken in for questioning. At first he denied all knowledge of the girl. Then, when the police pointed out that dents on his truck corroborated the scrap-man's story, and that the paint matched that found on the schoolbooks, he admitted that he *had* knocked Helen down, but said it was an accident. Finally, he told the true story of the attack and the rape, and led the police to the well. There the body was dragged to the surface—minus a leg torn

off by the blast. Medical evidence revealed that the girl had been alive when she was thrown in, and that she died by drowning.

Meyer went to the electric chair in April 1937. More than a quarter of a century later the "Baby-faced Beast" has still not been forgotten in Coatesville.

The horror of the story drives us to ask: why do such things happen, and how can they be prevented? There is no simple answer to either question. Meyer was a "pervert", like Jack the Ripper, like Peter Kurten, like Harvey Glatman, who indulged his sadistic fantasies by tying up his female victims and photographing them as they struggled before he finally choked them to death. In psychological terms these men were suffering from "obsessional neurosis". One idea dominated their minds to the exclusion of all others.

Most of us have to make a considerable effort to concentrate on a particular subject for more than a fairly short period; we are distracted by things that happen around us. A child may be watching television, but if someone brings him a new toy, he will instantly forget the programme to play with the toy. An older child or a teenager might well finish watching the programme, then examine the toy; it has decided to take one pleasure at a time.

This is sensible—but not entirely desirable, for people who "take life as it comes", and enjoy the pleasure of the moment spontaneously, are often healthier and happier than more "sensible" people. An obsessional sense of duty often produces ulcers. We all have to learn to balance our sense of purpose with the ability to just "open up" and enjoy the present moment. This is something the "obsessional" cannot do.

An obsessional is *not* necessarily a pervert. Some women are obsessed with cleanliness in the home. Many patients in mental homes wash their hands every time they touch something. Obsession is what happens when the sense of purpose gets wildly out of hand. But if the obses-

VICTIM TURNED CAPTOR. Pretty Lorraine Vigil fought back when Harvey Glatman attacked her. After a struggle she grabbed his gun, called the police.

Both AP

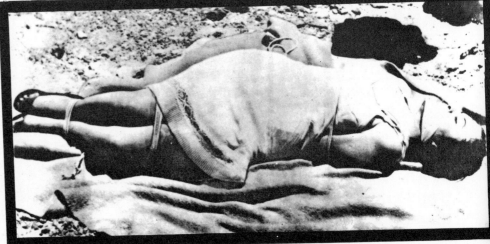

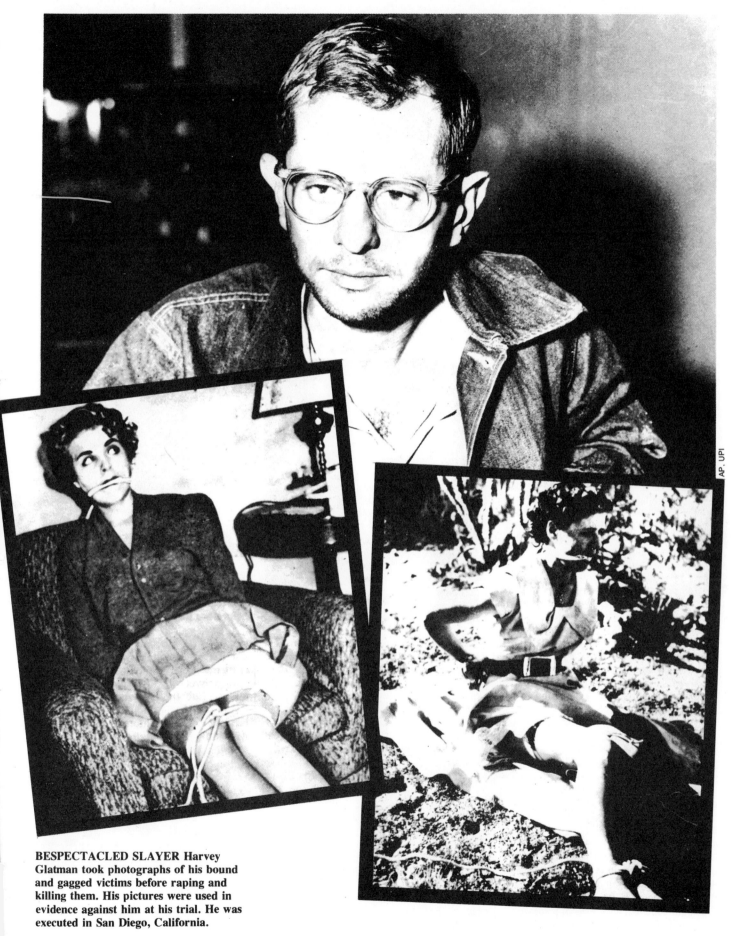

AP . UPI

BESPECTACLED SLAYER Harvey Glatman took photographs of his bound and gagged victims before raping and killing them. His pictures were used in evidence against him at his trial. He was executed in San Diego, California.

sion happens to be sexual, then the community has reason for concern.

Freud's explanation of the obsessional type was that it represented: "the outstripping of libidinal development by ego development"—which means simply that a child's "ego"—his sense of his own importance—grows faster than his "sense of pleasure"—"libido" does not refer only to our "love energies" but to *all* kinds of enjoyment, from playing football to eating an ice cream—but Freud's *definition* only *describes* the obsessional, without explaining him.

One thing is clear: the pervert is essentially immature. All babies want their own way, and see no reason why they shouldn't have everything they want. If the family background involves a great deal of love and security they soon begin to learn to give—and to give way. They recognize that having their own way in everything would give pain to those they love. So one basic answer to the problem of the obsessional is lack of love in childhood.

Love has the same effect on the personality as sunlight on vegetation: it causes it to grow and ripen. Without love the obsessional sees no need to "ripen", to try to grow up. Perhaps his parents denied him many things he wanted in childhood, so he harbours a deep feeling of resentment. Later, he feels that society is denying him many things he wants; and so he is prepared to grab it when society is off its guard. The result is behaviour like that of Alexander Meyer, where another human being is treated purely as a dispensable object, like a throwaway handkerchief.

The remorseless ego

In his book *Sex Perversions and Sex Crimes* Dr. Melvin Rheinhardt describes the temperament in two words: the "remorseless ego". The characteristics are always the same: a completely self-enclosed state of mind in which the other person is unreal. The California rapist Harvey Glatman kidnapped models, spent hours—sometimes days—raping them, then killed them.

In 1953 a middle-aged pervert named Carl Folk "hi-jacked" a trailer containing a man and his wife—Raymond and Betty Allen—tied up the husband, then spent a whole night raping and torturing the wife, who finally died. Folk was so preoccupied that he did not notice the husband's escape, and was startled when Raymond Allen pulled open the door and shot him in the stomach. But it was too late to save Betty Allen. When Raymond Allen shot him, Folk was about to drench the caravan with petrol, to burn the Allens and their baby. He treated them as "throwaways", whose sole purpose was to provide him with pleasure.

THE ILL-FATED BRIDE . . . Betty and Raymond Allen on their wedding day. Betty was tortured to death by Carl Folk (inset), before her husband could save her.

In a sense such perverts are insane. They have allowed their obsession to dominate them until it becomes their sole aim. Yet to call them insane is to evade the central issue. There is undoubtedly an element of *free will* in all this. The pervert *chooses* to be "insane".

This can be seen in one of the grimmest cases of "compulsion" on record, the murder of Alice Porter by Donald Fearn near Pueblo, Colorado, in 1942. Fearn was a 23-year-old railway mechanic, a mild-looking, bespectacled little married man. He was fascinated by stories of the Pueblo Indians and their capacity to bear pain. In an adobe church out in the desert members of an Indian sect called the Penitentes had tortured, and sometimes crucified, one another.

Fearn began to spend a great deal of time in the adobe church, 50 miles outside Pueblo. He was particularly ob-

sessed by the bloodstained altar. No doubt a writer of weird tales, in the H. P. Lovecraft tradition, might suggest that he was "taken over" by the spirits of the Penitentes. But the explanation is simpler. By brooding on thoughts of torture he brought a flash of intensity into his otherwise dull life, and he dreamed of kidnapping a girl and taking her to the adobe church. "Ever since I was a young boy I have wanted to torture a beautiful young girl".

He put his fantasy into practice on April 22, 1942, when his wife was in hospital, having their second baby. Seventeen-year-old Alice Porter, a pretty student nurse, was walking home from evening classes at 9.30 in the evening. Fearn jumped out of his car, pointed a gun at her and ordered her to get in. She screamed, and a nearby resident looked out in time to see a blue car driving away.

Fearn drove Alice Porter to the adobe church and then proceeded to put his sadistic fantasies into practice. He bound her, undressed her, then placed her on the altar and tortured her in a manner that has never been fully reported; it involved binding her with red-hot wires. Fortunately she lost consciousness long before Fearn had finished. Finally, he raped her and, like Meyer, threw her body down a well.

Driving home through a storm, his car bogged down in the mud. He had to find a local farmer to haul it out with his tractor, and then he went back to Pueblo to visit his wife in hospital. The baby had been born the day before. When the police finally searched the adobe church the burnt remains of the girl's clothes and the "torture kit" convinced them they had found the site of the murder. They soon located her body in the well, the head battered with a hammer.

There were fingerprints on an awl which had obviously been used in the killing, but they were not of any known sexual offender. Routine investigation led police to the farmer who had hauled Fearn's car out of the mud. He told them it was an old Ford sedan. The detectives eventu-ally located it in a Pueblo garage. Fearn's fingerprints matched those on the awl. When details of the murder came out, mobs gathered and there was talk of lynching. Fearn was taken away to jail in Canon City for his own safety. On October 22, 1942, he was executed in the gas chamber there.

It is worth making one purely practical point about this case. If Alice Porter had screamed and run it is possible that Fearn might have shot her, but the chances are that he would not have killed her. Rape cases reveal this basic truth: that girls who refuse to allow themselves to be forced into cars escape without harm more often than girls who submit, hoping to "get it all over quickly".

As in the case of Alexander Meyer, the girl who fights and tries to escape stands a good chance of survival. This is not invariably true, of course; a girl *may* escape more serious injury if she submits to her attacker. But in innumerable cases involving rapist *killers*, it is the girls who have fought who have lived to identify their attackers; it seems to be partly a question of "victimology". The question is not simply how to prevent people like Donald Fearn from becoming possessed by sadistic obsessions but also how to prevent girls like Alice Porter from making it too easy for them.

It is true that cases like the ones described above produce a certain feeling of helplessness: that there is absolutely nothing that doctors or criminologists can do about perverts like Glatman, Meyer and Fearn. But it would be a mistake to allow this feeling to paralyse our sense of balance and logic. To begin with, when we study such cases we begin to see the emergence of an over-all pattern. And to see a pattern is to begin to understand a thing *scientifically*. And that is the first and most difficult step in solving any problem.

For example, we see that men like Harvey Glatman, Peter Kurten, Donald Fearn are not exactly a "modern" phenomenon. Krafft-Ebing describes the "girl-stabber of Bozen", a case of 1829 – a young soldier with violently sadistic impulses. "Gradually, the thought came to him how pleasurable it would be to stab a young girl in the genitals, and take delight in the sight of blood running from the knife". After several attacks on girls he was arrested.

In 1867, at Alton, in Hampshire, a clerk named Frederick Baker, "a young man of great respectability", spoke to three small girls who were playing in a meadow and offered one of them, Fanny Adams, a halfpenny to go with him into a hollow. He led her away, crying. Late that evening searchers found the child's head in a hop garden. Other parts of the body were scattered about the garden.

I don't know what I'm doing

After Baker's arrest his diary was found, with an entry: "Killed a young girl today. It was fine and hot." He was hanged in December 1867. In 1880 a 4-year-old child named Louise Dreux vanished from her home near the Tuileries, Paris. The following day neighbours reported to the police the foul black smoke that was issuing from the chimney of a retarded 20-year-old youth named Louis Menesclou, who lived on the top floor of the same house.

The police burst in and searched Menesclou; they found the child's fore-arms in his pockets, and parts of her body half burned in the stove. He admitted luring the child to his room with sweets, where he violated her, then killed her. In his pocket the police found a poem by Menesclou that ended: "In my blind fury, I don't know what I'm doing." He admitted sleeping on the corpse on the previous night. He was executed.

TORTURE FANTASIES were acted out in real life by Donald Fearn, killer of student Alice Porter. Fearn, seen below at police HQ, went to the gas chamber.

In Manhattan, in February 1961, a four-year-old girl named Edith Kiecorius vanished from outside her home; the uncle who had been keeping an eye on her had gone off to buy cigarettes. There was a massive police search. Police finally looked into the recently vacated room of an alcoholic dishwasher, 34-year-old Fred Thompson, and found the child's violated body hidden there. Thompson was caught in Tom's River, New Jersey. He was an electronics expert, but he had been in and out of sanatoriums many times for alcoholism.

These killers all have one thing in common: they are outcasts, men living alone without real social contact. The American psychologist William Glasser has said that before he can start to cure a patient the patient needs to have one real "contact" with another person; without such a contact there can be no cure. Thompson, Menesclou, Baker, Fearn, Meyer all lacked this contact. They were living in modern civilization like hermits in the desert.

This is the foundation of the problem: Karl Marx's "alienation". And this once again suggests immediate grounds for optimism. Marshall McLuhan, the "communications expert" who is the author of the best-seller *Understanding Media* (1964), has pointed out that the various forms of alienation were the outcome of the invention of printing, and of other mechanical devices—like the wheel and the radio—that became extensions of man and produced a new environment. People felt "cut off", like a child lost in an engineering factory.

Television is again changing the world into a "global village". It is bringing all kinds of people into other people's homes; and the smallness, the lack of definition in a TV picture means that children "scan" it for meanings in the same simple way that an African tribesman might scan it. They do not "follow" it, as a literate adult follows a cinema film or reads a novel. So McLuhan believes that some of the basic effects of "alienation" will wear off; we shall again have a society of non-alienated people who communicate directly with one another.

McLuhan may be over-optimistic, but his ideas suggest that these new mass media—TV, pop records and so on—might be used in some purposeful way to bring people closer together, to educate at a partly unconscious level. His most famous assertion—that "the medium is the message"—means that it doesn't matter whether television is showing gangsters shooting each other or Mickey Mouse: it is the medium itself, not what it "says", that has the really important *subliminal* effect. If this is true it suggests new and interesting approaches to the increasing problem of crime.

It is, admittedly, difficult to see how a McLuhanized criminology could do anything about the real perverts—for example, about a man like the Hungarian Sylvestre Matushka, a "company director" who needed to see a train crash in order to achieve full sexual satisfaction, and dynamited a number of trains in the early 1930s. On Saturday, September 12, 1931, as the Budapest-Vienna express was crossing a viaduct near Torbagy station, there was a tremendous

A MURDERER MEETS THE PRESS. Fred Thompson (below), an alcoholic dishwasher, abducted 4-year-old Edith Kiecorius (below right) and killed her.

explosion, and part of the train plunged into the abyss. Twenty-two people were killed. It had been detonated by an electrical device.

One of the "passengers" who sued the railway company for injuries was Matushka; but when the police began to investigate his background they could find no one on the express who had actually seen him—although he had undoubtedly been at the scene of the explosion. Further investigation revealed that Matushka had bought dynamite. He was arrested, and finally confessed that the Bia-Torbagy explosion was his third attempt on a train.

He had also been responsible for an unsuccessful attempt to derail the Vienna-Passau train near Ansbach on New Year's Day 1931, and for the derailing of the Vienna express near Berlin on August 8, 1931, in which 16 people were injured. Matushka was tried several times, the juries being unable to agree on his sanity. Matushka explained that a spirit called Leo had ordered him to wreck trains. He was finally sentenced to hang; but appeals led to the commutation of the sentence to life imprisonment. The crime writer Paul Tabori has reported that he was subsequently freed by the Russians, and went to work for them as an explosives expert.

It may ultimately be impossible even for the most highly skilled "social engineering" to eliminate madmen like Matushka. But it *could*, undoubtedly, do a great deal to reduce the "alienation-level" in our society. In so doing it could not only reduce the number of sadistic perverts, but also have decisive effects in lowering the crime rate. This is an aim well worth the deepest consideration of all criminologists and social workers.

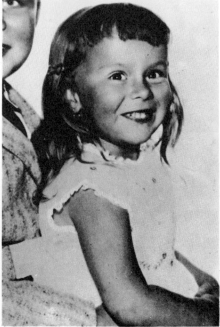

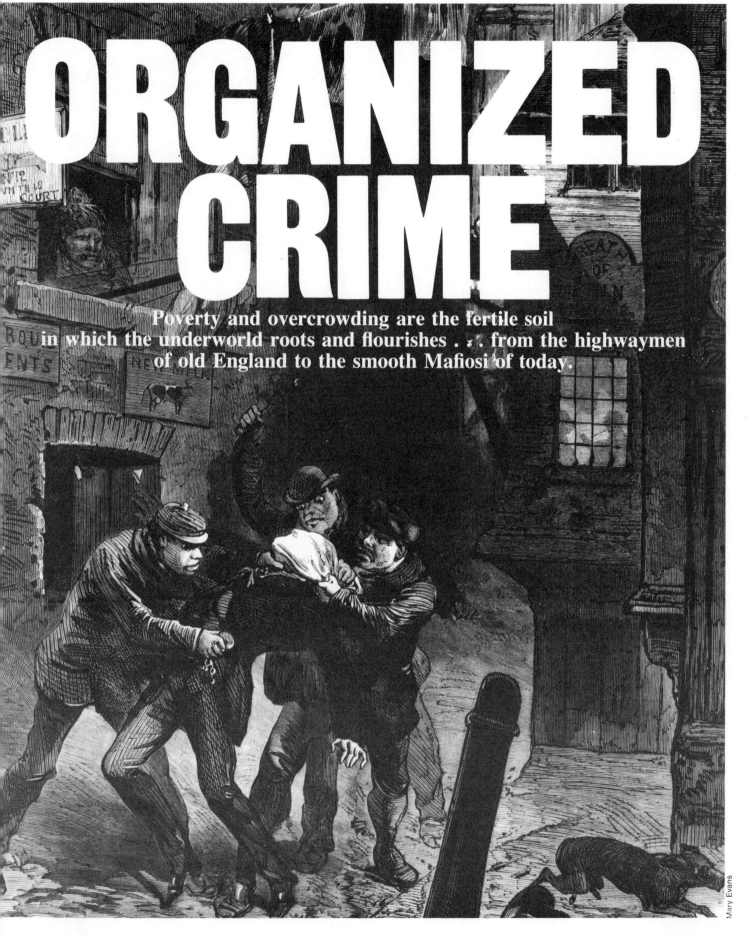

ORGANIZED CRIME

Poverty and overcrowding are the fertile soil in which the underworld roots and flourishes . . . from the highwaymen of old England to the smooth Mafiosi of today.

Mary Evans

JAMES ISLAND is a half square mile of territory out in Chesapeake Bay; and, apart from a U.S. quarantine station, its inhabitants are mostly Sika deer. It was in 1956 that a scientist named John Christian went to study the deer. Five of them had been transported from the mainland in 1916; 40 years later they had increased to a herd of 300.

And then, two years after Christian's arrival, a strange thing happened. The deer began dying off at an astounding rate—more than half of them died in three months. By the middle of 1959 there were only about 80 deer on the island. Then the deaths stopped.

What was so puzzling was that there appeared to be no obvious reason for their deaths. They looked healthy and well-fed. Christian had shot a number of deer when he first arrived on the island and made a detailed study of their internal organs. The only obvious difference between these and the more recent deaths was that the animals that died in 1959 and 1960 had enlarged adrenal glands—in some cases nearly twice as big as in the shot deer. The adrenals are the glands that flood the system with the hormone adrenalin when confronted with a crisis.

Christian's observations indicated that the deer had died of stress due to overcrowding. Yet in realistic terms they were not overcrowded: around one to an acre. All the same, that was enough to produce a condition of continual stress that caused haemorrhages of the glands, brain and kidneys. It was nature's way of controlling the population.

Rapists and cannibals

The deer is a non-aggressive animal; its response to overcrowding is to "give up" and die—one writer on ethology noted that the same thing affected some American prisoners in Korea; they would become dull and lethargic, and die of convulsions; it became known as "give-up-itis". In more aggressive species the response to overcrowding is crime—violent and often pointless aggression. The researcher John Calhoun observed that overcrowded rats became rapists and cannibals.

When slum areas of cities become overcrowded a certain proportion of their inhabitants—usually about 5%—develop

THE TONG WARS . . . the first truly organized crime. New York scenes show the consequences of such weapons as the Tong hatchet (held by detective, far left).

All UPI

15

a kind of "alternative society", a way of life that is based on crime, and which is taken completely for granted as a social norm: an "underworld" develops.

It is an interesting observation that the "underworld" of a city seems directly related to its population. Before the 1917 revolution the Russian port of Odessa had a flourishing underworld, and it is described—humorously—in stories by the writer Isaac Babel. By comparison modern Russia has no underworld, and this is only partly due to the totalitarian system, which reduces crime by reducing the freedom of the individual. The basic cause is the fact that, as the Russian population expands, a new city is built in the wilderness to house the overflow.

Russia has well over 200 cities with populations of over 100,000. By American—or even English—standards these are little more than villages. Consider, on the other hand, that New York has a population of more than twelve million, that Hong Kong has more than four million, and Calcutta nearly five million —and that these cities, crammed into a relatively small area, also have the highest crime rates in the world. One statistician calculates that by the end of the present century Calcutta may have as many as sixty million inhabitants—it is currently expanding at the rate of a million every three years. If this actually happens, Calcutta will be one immense seething hotbed of crime.

Anti-climactic

It is necessary to understand all this if we are to understand the frighteningly steady growth of the "underworld" in the twentieth century. In the 1850s a sociologist named Henry Mayhew undertook an enormous study of the habits of the London poor and produced four big volumes describing them. If we turn to the sections on London's underworld, they seem absurdly anti-climactic compared with modern organized crime.

There are accounts of prostitutes and their "bullies", pickpockets, shoplifters and thieves. Types of robbery described include stealing from street stalls, stealing from clotheslines, breaking shop windows, and child-stripping—enticing a child into a dark alleyway and stealing its re-saleable clothes. This "underworld" was run on a strictly amateur basis. The real professionals, it seemed, were the "fences" who bought the stolen goods.

The last real attempt to organize crime had been made more than a century earlier by the notorious "thief-taker" Jonathan Wild, who was basically a highly successful fence. Wild had been executed in 1725, in the days when the commonest crime in England was highway robbery. By half-way through the nineteenth century a fairly efficient police

force had made the highways safe; besides, the great majority of travellers now went by rail. So crime had contracted again into the heart of the great cities—Glasgow, Liverpool, London.

But it sprang out of poverty rather than from any anti-social resentments. The same was true of most of the great crime cities of the world, including Paris, Berlin and New York. In these cities there was no room for a "crime explosion", for the police knew most of the habitual criminals.

Sheer cunning

In Paris the Sûreté was even *run* by an ex-convict, Vidocq, and when he began work as a police-informer, around 1809, Paris had a number of gangs of efficient thieves; by sheer cunning and skill, Vidocq broke up most of these. On one occasion he joined the gang run by a man called Constantin, posing as an escaped galley-convict from Toulon; when the

gang arrived back from a burglary Vidocq had the police waiting for them.

It was America that gave birth to the first truly organized crime: the Chinese tongs, which originated in the gold fields of California in the 1860s. They were originally intended as protection societies for the Chinese, who were hated by the white Americans, as were the Mexicans. Inevitably they began to live off their own people, and "protection" took on its modern meaning—extortion. There were plenty of gangs of desperadoes in all the major cities—New York, San Francisco, Chicago—but they usually controlled a small area, perhaps only a single street.

Then in the 1870s the Italians began to create their own secret societies—or, rather, they brought them from Italy. In Italy societies like the Camorra had been formed for the protection of citizens, since the police were underpaid and subject to political pressures.

In America the Camorra became the Black Hand, then the Mafia. It began an organized despoliation of the Italian community. New Orleans was one of its major breeding grounds. After the murder of police chief David Hennessy in 1890, and the subsequent acquittal of the nine accused, the irate citizens rose up, broke into the jail and lynched the malefactors; and for the time being the power of the Mafia in America was broken.

It soon revived, however, this time in New York. In 1902 and 1903 there was a sudden wave of murder in the Italian colonies of New York City. Bodies were found in sacks, barrels and boxes. In many cases the tongues had been slit in two, indicating that this was a gang murder whose aim was to impose silence. The victims had been "talkers". The gangs' code of conduct was harsh and brutal; Giuseppe Morello, a Sicilian gang-leader, had his own 18-year-old stepson kidnapped and tortured to death because the

boy had let slip some of his stepfather's secrets. Most of Morello's large income came from a counterfeiting ring whose products went out all over the United States.

The downfall of the Morello gang occurred shortly after this. Its most feared members were Morello himself and two lieutenants known as Lupo the Wolf and Petto the Ox. On April 13, 1903, a woman strolling past a lumber pile on the edge of the Italian section of the lower East Side saw a barrel—with an arm and leg protruding from it.

Powerful slash

When the police opened it they found the body of a man whose head had been almost severed with one powerful slash of a razor. The fact that his ears had been pierced suggested that he was a Sicilian. He wore a watch chain but no watch. A detective who saw a photograph of the murdered man recognized him as an "unknown" who had been seen in the company of the Wolf and the Ox in an Italian restaurant run by Pietro Inzarillo; the detective had been shadowing the Wolf and the Ox.

Good detective work soon led them back to the Italian restaurant. The barrel, with sawdust in the bottom, scattered there to soak up the blood, had contained onion skins and butts of Italian cigars. It was traced through the manufacturer to a wholesale grocer, who had supplied it to Inzarillo's restaurant.

A brilliant Italian operative, Joseph Petrosino, was assigned to the case. He went to Sing Sing to interview a convict named de Priemo, an ex-member of Morello's gang, now serving time for counterfeiting. When de Priemo saw the photograph of the murdered man he wept. It was his brother-in-law, Beneditto Madonia. Mrs. Madonia later identified her husband's body.

Detectives went to question Lupo at his wine shop. Lupo instantly pulled a stiletto, and was about to plunge it into the throat of a detective when another policeman grabbed his arm and dragged him to the floor. Lupo was arrested; so were Petto the Ox, Morello, Inzarillo and several other suspects. In Morello's house the police found a letter, written to him by Madonia shortly before his death, saying that he was tired of this dangerous work of distributing counterfeit money and intended to return to his family in Buffalo. It was clear he had been killed because he knew too much.

But the inquest on Madonia revealed

GANGSTER Giuseppe Morello (far left) was tracked down by brilliant New York detective Joseph Petrosino . . . who was gunned down by the Sicilian Mafia on the steps of the Palermo Court of Justice.

Both UPI

something of the power of Morello and his Black Hand. Madonia's son was asked to identify his father's watch. There was an ominous shuffling of feet in court, and a man rose to his feet and placed his finger to his lips. Madonia's son stammered and was suddenly unable to swear that the watch was his father's. Mrs. Madonia also seemed to lose her memory when the shuffling began. De Priemo was brought from Sing Sing to testify, and he declared with an air of apparent frankness that he was certain the Ox had *not* killed his brother-in-law because the Ox was one of his oldest friends.

And so all the suspects went free. However, the New York police were determined to get them behind bars. Not long after, Morello and the Wolf were arrested and charged with counterfeiting. And although the evidence seemed thin, a judge sentenced them to 25 and 30 years respectively. Inzarillo was picked up on a charge of altering his citizenship papers and sent to prison for a longer term than the offence warranted. In fact, reading between the lines of the account given by ex-Deputy Inspector Arthur Carey, it looks as though the police stretched the letter of the law to get the killers of Madonia behind bars.

Unknown intruder

Petto the Ox moved to Browntown, Pennsylvania. But in October 1925 he stepped into his back yard and was cut down by five shotgun blasts. Coincidentally, de Priemo, the man who had sworn to get the killer of his brother-in-law, had recently been released from Sing Sing, his term of imprisonment commuted for exemplary conduct. When Inzarillo came out of prison he opened a pastry shop; shortly afterwards he was also killed by an unknown intruder.

It became increasingly clear to the American police—and politicians—that the problem of organized crime started in Italy. A member of a committee from Congress was told by the police chief of Palermo that Sicily had very little crime. He asked why, and was told seriously: "Most of our criminals have gone to America." In 1907 Joseph Petrosino went to Palermo to see what could be done about close co-operation between the Sicilian and American police. On the day of his arrival he was shot down in broad daylight outside the Palazzo Steri, the court of justice, by the head of the Sicilian Mafia, Don Vito. Vito, of course, had an unshakable alibi and was never charged with the murder. That round of the fight had definitely gone to the Mafia.

Ever since the 1870s America had been convulsed by violent labour disputes. In many ways this is understandable. The accounts by Jack London of his own early days as a stoker make it clear that labour was ruthlessly exploited. The American "success ethic" meant that an employer had no pangs of conscience about keeping a man on a starvation wage, and dismissing him and allowing his wife and children to starve if he could get someone at an even cheaper rate.

The commercial world was a jungle—the title Upton Sinclair gave to his great novel of corruption in the Chicago stockyards. With fighters like Sinclair, Jack London, Clarence Darrow and Eugene Debs, organized labour slowly began to make some headway against the big corporations, although strikes were often long and bloody, and imported strikebreakers were sometimes ambushed and murdered by angry workers.

And as organized labour finally began to establish its right to exist, the thugs moved in. In New York all the major industries were controlled by gangs—the docks, the garment industry, the gambling houses and brothels. The "protection racket", which had developed in New Orleans in the 1870s, was now a recognized and established business. The gangs fell into three clear groups: the Jews, the Irish and the Italians—the Chinese, who had once been New York's leading racketeers, had long ago been forced into a minor position.

In the autumn of 1912 East Side clothing workers went on strike. At least, most of them did; some were not militantly inclined and continued to work. Labour leaders, who were always hand-in-glove with racketeers, approached a Jewish gangster, Dopey Benney Fein, to send some strong-arm boys over to persuade these recalcitrants to join the strike.

However, the clothing bosses had also bought "protection" from a couple of gang leaders named Tommy Dyke and Harry Lenny, an ex-prize fighter. It was an absurd situation, with both sides of labour represented by mobsters. Dopey Benney's chief lieutenant was an Irishman named Joe Miller, who, to demonstrate his freedom from racial prejudice, had re-named himself Jew Murphy. Murphy was told to interview Dyke and Lenny and order them to withdraw their protection from the clothing bosses.

One of Dyke's men punched Murphy in the face and threw him out. Murphy swore revenge. A month later, at the opening of the six-day bicycle race at Madison Square Garden, shooting started between the two gangs. Luckily only one Lenny henchman was injured. Commissioner Arthur Woods, who had recently been installed in office, realized that next time the innocent bystanders might not be so lucky.

He proved to be an accurate prophet. Trouble came on the evening of an annual ball given by the Dyke and Lenny gang

AMERICA votes for Prohibition—and missing her last chance to beat organized crime. In effect, the Capones and Schultzes were elected by the people, to their lasting regret.

at Arlington Hall, near St. Marks Place. As Dyke and Lenny were about to swagger up the steps of the hall to meet a respectful reception committee, firing suddenly broke out behind them. They leapt up the steps and into the hall. For the next ten minutes the air was full of bullets. And when the shooting stopped a man lay dead on the pavement: Frederick Strauss, a court official.

No police allowed

Woods was furious. The gangs were going too far. Not long before, he had had to send in whole contingents of police to the Car Barn district on the East River because the Car Barn Gang had put up notices declaring that no police would be allowed in the area. The Car Barn gang had been broken up; now he was determined to do the same for the Dopey Benney Mob and the Dyke and Lenny Association. His first problem was to find out how the Fein mob had managed to get hold of guns.

Most of them were known to the New York police and were likely to be stopped at any hour of the day or night. If they were found in possession of a hidden weapon it usually meant at least a year in jail, so Woods was reasonably sure that they had not gone to Arlington Hall carrying guns. The underworld grapevine brought him his answer: a girl named Annie Britt had carried seven guns in her handbag. She was one of the first "gun

molls" on record.

Woods ordered the arrest of seven members of Fein's gang, including Annie Britt. The trial was a fiasco. Most of the testimony came from gangsters and it conflicted so much that the accused men were acquitted. Nevertheless, police harassment had its effect. During Woods's administration the gangs almost disappeared. Dopey Benney's gang broke up as a consequence of the case. Woods had proved that the police *could* break this new kind of organized crime if they simply harassed enough.

Then America entered the First World War. Many of the gangsters went off to fight, and New York crime dropped. When the soldiers came back home there was a crime wave—there usually is after a war—but the police showed themselves able to cope. For a while it looked as if the pattern of organized crime in America might be broken.

Unfortunately for America there were powerful forces at work in support of crime—forces that believed themselves to be on the side of law and order. The Temperance Movement began in America as long ago as 1770, when a member of a Quaker meeting in Philadelphia protested that he was "oppressed by the smell of rum" from his fellow Quakers. Rum was one of the most popular medical remedies of the time.

By the 1830s "Temperance" had become a powerful movement in England as well as America. Dramas like *The Drunkard* and *Seven Nights in a Bar Room* brought in massive crowds in the 1840s and 50s. But England, with its usual genius for compromise, declined to embrace strict Temperance; the Americans, as usual, preferred to do things the hard way. Hot gospel revivals had always been an American speciality; now the Anti-Saloon League, represented at national level by Senator Andrew Volstead, succeeded in declaring all forms of alcoholic liquor illegal in the United States as from January 17, 1920.

Prohibition had arrived—and with it America's last chance, in the twentieth century at least, of beating organized crime. The story of Johnny Torrio, Al Capone, Dutch Schultz and the other gang-leaders of the bootleg era has been told many times. The problem was that they had the average American citizen on their side, that the man in the street thought it was stupid that his democratically elected government should deny him his finger of whisky or gin. In effect Capone and Schultz were *voted* into office by the people. Organized crime gained the stranglehold that it has held ever since. It may yet prove to be the most serious challenge America will have to face in the last quarter of the twentieth century.

SEX SCANDALS

Indecent disclosure, particularly when it involves politicians, is a feverish obsession of the British. "Kinky" spanking or flogging is known in Europe as "the English Vice". Member of Parliament Lord Lambton and prostitute Norma Levy (below) whipped the public into a prurient frenzy.

Syndication International

"THERE IS a rich old banker in Broad Street who has arranged with the head-mistress of two girls' schools, one in Hackney, one in Stratford, to pay them a large weekly sum each for a most peculiar entertainment. At the time of his weekly visits at each school, the children receive their accumulated punishments. The old man stands in an adjacent room and watches through an aperture while the girls, one after another, are brought in, bared behind, and chastized with the rod."

This extract from a book published in 1792 – *The Cherub or Guardian of Female Innocence* – pinpoints one of the more curious aspects of the psychology of the English: the strong element of *voyeurism* that seems to be part of the national character. Ivan Bloch, the German sexologist, makes the same point at considerable length in his classic *Sexual Life in England*, where he also remarks that the English taste for flogging and spanking is so well-known on the Continent that it is referred to as "le vice Anglais".

Masochistic pleasure

Both obsessions find expression in the peculiar English love of sex scandal. Most countries are inclined to hush-up the sexual indiscretions of their public men; the English seem to take a masochistic pleasure in displaying them to the whole world. In 1825, a high-class prostitute named Harriette Wilson wrote an indiscreet volume of memoirs in which the Duke of Wellington figured prominently. When she offered to let him buy his way out, the duke made the celebrated remark "Publish and be damned". She did, and became rich on the proceeds.

Nearly a century and a half later, the public displayed the same voracious and morbid interest in the divorce proceedings of the Duchess of Argyll, which had all the ingredients that delight the British press: aristocracy, political scandal (most of it carefully suppressed, but these things leak out), lots of promiscuity and even dirty photographs showing the duchess in compromising positions. A Sunday newspaper bought the duchess's memoirs at a record price.

And then, overnight, everyone forgot her; the headlines were occupied with more important matters. International crises? The moon rocket? No, merely the saga of an indiscreet Cockney named Christine Keeler, who had not only slept with a cabinet minister, but also with a diplomat from the Russian embassy.

The rest of the world saw it as a storm in a tea cup; nobody believed for a moment that the minister had disclosed state secrets to Miss Keeler, who had then passed them on to the Russians. But the British public were not willing to take this *blasé* attitude. They wanted their scandal, their indecent disclosures; and the press

saw to it that it got them: for month after month, ad nauseam.

Why *are* the English so obsessed by sex? There are two reasons: the basic puritanism of the English character, and sexual frustration. It is true that the Americans are also puritanical, being Anglo-Saxon in origin, but America is always in some kind of violent ferment; the latest political scandal, the latest mass murder, provides plenty of material for headlines.

England is a quieter country. It is also a small, crowded country, where everybody tends to know everybody else's business – particularly in working-class areas. The teenager who gets herself pregnant, the youth who gets into trouble with the police for carnal knowledge of a girl under sixteen, is likely to remain the subject of gossip for months. In this atmosphere of scandal and disapproval, sexual desires become repressed.

The English attitude to sex can be seen mostly clearly in the music-hall joke, with its endless *double entrendres* and the Blackpool dirty postcard, with its hen-pecked little husbands casting longing glances at bosomy blondes in bikinis. A number of Sunday newspapers cater for this desire for scandal; the headlines and the tone of the stories are full of moral

DESTROYED . . . for the love of Kitty (below). The British weakness for scandal knows no bounds. It could even be used to blight the career and life of the great Irish leader Charles Stewart Parnell.

disapproval – "Should This Beast Have Been Allowed Out of Jail?" – but they take care to report every shocking detail – "He placed one hand over my mouth, and tore at my panties with the other . . ."

For various reasons, sexual attitudes on the Continent of Europe have always been more candid and uninhibited. The English schoolboy who reads *The Three Musketeers* finds it startlingly unlike the romances of Henty and Rider Haggard; Dumas simply takes it for granted that his heroes have love affairs with married women. As to the Scandinavians, they seem to take a healthy, almost sterile attitude to sex that the English find repellent. If sex isn't rather wicked, surely you lose half the fun . . .?

Unscrupulous opponent

The result of this outlook is that, in England, sex scandal has become the ideal weapon for ruining political opponents. The Duke of Wellington could afford to say "Publish and be damned"; as a result of the battle of Waterloo, he was a national hero. Besides, a soldier is allowed his love affairs. But later politicians discovered just how deadly a weapon British public opinion can be when used by an unscrupulous opponent.

Charles Stewart Parnell was one of the most remarkable Irishmen ever to shake the foundations of the British government. Inspired to become a politician by the execution of the "Manchester martyrs" in 1867, he soon became the most powerful advocate of Home Rule for Ireland in

Radio Times Hulton

Mary Evans/Radio Times Hulton

VORACIOUS and morbid interest . . . the duchess was shown in compromising positions, and the press revelled in it. Publish and be damned? The duke was hardly likely to have been consulted.

the British House of Commons. He forced Parliament to listen to him by "filibustering"—talking for hour after hour to prevent a debate being wound-up.

The British government tried accusing him of provoking political crime in Ireland and had him put in prison; he became more powerful than ever. After the Phoenix Park murders—when two British diplomats were killed by Irish patriots—*The Times* published the facsimile of a letter, purporting to have been written by Parnell, condoning the murders. For a while, it looked as if Parnell was ruined—until he was able to prove, in court, that the letter was actually forged by a man named Richard Pigot, who subsequently committed suicide. Parnell emerged from the case more influential than ever.

Challenged to duel

And then, in 1889, an old friend and colleague of Parnell's—Captain O'Shea—cited Parnell as co-respondent in a suit for divorce. O'Shea had known about his wife's adultery with Parnell since at least 1881—eight years earlier—when he had challenged Parnell to a duel, but subsequently O'Shea acted as Parnell's agent, and in 1885 Parnell got him elected Member for Galway. So it was, to say the least, highly convenient for the British government that O'Shea should suddenly decide to cite Parnell in his divorce case.

The divorce took place; Parnell married Kitty O'Shea; and his Irish party declared they would stand by him. But his English supporters, including Gladstone, hounded him out of office. His fall broke Parnell; he died a year later. In Ireland, his own party divided into those who regarded him as a martyr, and those who found his

Both Mirrorpic

adultery too shocking to accept; the dispute split the party for many years.

The techniques that destroyed Parnell proved equally successful a quarter of a century later against another Irish rebel, Sir Roger Casement. Casement had been granted his knighthood for his services to the British government — he had been in the consular service, and investigated atrocities in the Belgian Congo and in the Putumayo, South America. During this period, Casement kept diaries that seem to indicate that he was homosexual — although, by modern standards of frankness, the entries seem mild and discreet enough: "Gave [medicine] to [Indian servant] and rubbed it over his lovely body, poor boy . . . After dinner spoke to steward Indian Cholo about frejot and he got some for me and then another thing. It was huge and he wanted awfully."

The entries — interspersed among much other material — showed that Casement was obsessively interested in male sexual organs. "Steward showed enormous exposure after dinner, stiff all down left thigh." The native loincloths gave him full opportunity to indulge his curiosity.

There are many entries mentioning money given to the Indians, and cryptic references which seem to refer to orgies: "0 14$. A 10$ and beer . . . Olympio first at Big Square, then Polvoro and followed and pulled it out and to Marco when in deep." Casement obviously took advantage of his position; but in the Congo or the Putumayo most white men did the same. Casement merely happened to prefer the native men to the women.

Condemned to die

In 1912, he left the consular service, returned to Ireland, and became increasingly involved in Nationalist politics. What he wanted, quite simply, was for the Irish not to get involved in the war that was obviously looming over Europe. On the contrary, he saw it as an opportunity for Ireland to make the break with England. He went to America as a Nationalist propagandist, and then, in 1914, to Germany, where he tried to persuade Irish prisoners of war to fight for Ireland, and to persuade the Germans to send an expeditionary force to Ireland.

They were not interested; but Casement returned to Ireland in a German submarine, escorting a ship with arms to help the rebellion — which, of course, took place in Easter, 1916. A British patrol boat captured the ship; Casement landed near Tralee, but was captured and taken to London.

Now clearly, the British had a perfectly fair case for executing him as a traitor; Eire was then part of Great Britain, and Casement had been prepared to let in the Germans. On the other hand, as his friend Bernard Shaw recognized, Casement was only trying to do what Parnell had tried to do. He had failed. With luck — and British justice — he might escape with a term in jail.

Shaw advised Casement not to defend himself, but to make a rousing speech about Irish nationalism — Shaw even offered to write it for him. Casement was too discouraged to try. His defence confined themselves to the argument that Casement had not technically committed "treason", since treason involves being in the King's realm at the time, and Casement was in Germany. It failed, and Casement was condemned to die.

Even so, there was a strong body of opinion in favour of a reprieve. Influential Americans were on Casement's side; Bishop Henson, a friend of King George V, was also known to be in favour of reprieve. But just as many influential men wanted to see him hanged — among them, F. E. Smith — later Lord Birkenhead — who prosecuted Casement. Casement's diaries had been found in his London lodging, and Smith realized this was what he needed. The "pornographic" sections were copied or photographed, and secretly shown to anyone who might be inclined to support a reprieve — Bishop Henson, the King, influential Irishmen and Americans.

Sexual degeneracy

Sir Ernley Blackwell, legal adviser to the Home Office, wrote disgustedly: "Of late years he seems to have completed the full cycle of sexual degeneracy, and from a pervert has become an invert — a woman or pathic, who derives his satisfaction from attracting men and inducing them to use him". His memorandum was circulated among members of the government. This, and the diary excerpts, served their purpose; the movement for a reprieve was stopped in its tracks.

In those days, it was only necessary to whisper the word "homosexual" to arouse memories of the trial of Oscar Wilde, in 1895, on charges of indecent behaviour with males. Until that time, many Victorians had never even suspected the existence of such a vice; Wilde became a symbol of something unutterably evil and perverse, that must be suppressed and forgotten as soon as possible.

And now Casement was raising the spectre all over again. To reprieve an Irish patriot was one thing; to reprieve a "moral invert" was another. So Casement was executed in Pentonville prison on August 3, 1916.

But he was not forgotten; as Blackwell had predicted, he became an Irish martyr, one of the names that inspired the uprising of 1921, which led to the independence of Eire. Casement's defenders alleged that the British government had forged the diaries, but this was unfair.

THE GREATEST SEX SCANDAL of the 1960s involved the Soviet Naval Attaché and the British War Minister. They shared the same mistress, Christine Keeler (left).

They were published in America in 1959, and their authenticity is clear on every page. What is equally clear is Casement's basic decency and honesty; it seems strange that such a man should have been executed for a genetic peculiarity over which he had no control.

It might be supposed that the "permissive society" has produced some basic changes in the English attitude to sex scandal. In fact, this is not so; it is something too deep to be easily eradicated. In the early months of 1973 there was every sign that something like the Christine Keeler scandal was about to be repeated; a Sunday newspaper announced that it had evidence that a government minister was involved with a prostitute.

For the next ten days there was feverish speculation, which ended abruptly when the Prime Minister announced the resignation of Lord Lambton. He had been paying regular visits to a call girl named Norma Levy; the call girl's husband had taken secret photographs, which he had offered for sale to the newspaper. In this case, there was no possibility of official secrets being involved; in fact, some newspapers had the courage to say that it was Lord Lambton's private life, and therefore nobody's business but his own.

But it would have been politically impossible for a man who frequents prostitutes to remain a member of a government whose attitude towards sex is definitely conservative. Lord Lambton made public apologies, and vanished out of the political limelight. Norma Levy, an Irish nurse who specialized in "kinky" clients with a penchant for being beaten, fled to Spain with her husband at the time of the resignation, and the British public was cheated of its revelations of high life.

Dressed in leather

But when she returned a few months later, a "girly" magazine, *Alpha*, immediately ran a long interview with her, showing her dressed in black leather and holding a whip, and she spoke frankly of her life as a prostitute. *This* is what would have been impossible in the mid-sixties: the open discussion of her activities in a magazine. It is an interesting example of the double standard in British society: the conservative majority, shocked that a minister should have an extra-marital sex life, and the sophisticated minority, who take it for granted that some men like to be beaten by girls dressed in black leather. How long it will take for the minority attitude to percolate through to the majority is a question of considerable

Mirrorpic

sociological interest.

Although it is difficult to generalize about a country as big as America, it would be safe to say that, in most parts, the transition took place many years ago. In the 19th century, America was as puritanical as Victorian England. Its attitudes can be gauged from the famous Beauchamp tragedy, the great *cause célèbre* of 1826; in the nationwide interest it inspired, the Beauchamp affair could be compared to England's Red Barn murder, which took place in the following year.

In Frankfort, Kentucky, a prominent lawyer named Colonel Solomon P. Sharp had a love affair with Ann Cooke, a woman in her early thirties. She became pregnant; there was no question of Sharp marrying her—he was already married—so she retired to her family's farm near Bowling Green, where she bore a still-born child.

Kill the seducer

The scandal was a nine days' wonder, and it fascinated an 18-year-old law student, Jereboam Beauchamp, who came from the area. When he returned to Bowling Green, he persuaded his sisters to introduce him to Miss Cooke. He fell in love with her, and asked her to marry him. She agreed—on condition that he killed her seducer, Colonel Sharp—although in Beauchamp's confession he asserted that the murder was *his* idea.

Beauchamp agreed. He met Colonel Sharp in the street, slapped his face and

OPEN DISCUSSION of Norma Levy's activities would have been impossible ten years ago. Now she promotes her own biography. In America, pornographic slides of local schoolgirls in a millionaire's flat provoke little national indignation.

challenged him to a duel; Sharp declined. Then Beauchamp and Miss Cooke plotted to lure the Colonel to her farm, where he could be murdered; he accepted the invitation, then became suspicious and changed his mind. Four years went by; Beauchamp married Miss Cooke, but this did nothing to reduce his morbid obsession with the "seducer". In the early hours of Sunday, November 6, 1825, Beauchamp knocked on Colonel Sharp's door at two in the morning, claiming to be an acquaintance. The Colonel let him in and Beauchamp stabbed him in the solar plexus. The Colonel died a few hours later, and Beauchamp was arrested. A court found him guilty and sentenced him to death.

In his confession, Beauchamp declared that his death would serve the purpose of causing seducers to "pause in their mad career" and think about retribution. His wife was allowed in his cell. On the day of the execution—July 17, 1826—both took opium, then stabbed themselves. Mrs. Beauchamp died; Beauchamp, half dead, was dragged to the gallows and hanged.

To our own age, it seems clear that Beauchamp was possessed by a mixture of envy and sexual repression; the very

thought of "seduction" filled him with violent emotions, which he mistook for moral indignation. The interesting thing is that the rest of America felt the same. The Beauchamp tragedy became the subject of endless sermons, newspaper articles, popular ballads. Ten years later, it inspired a play by Edgar Allan Poe—*Politian*—and as late as 1842 was turned into a novel by William Gilmore Simms. The idea of illicit sex fascinated everybody, in a country where morality was still as rigid as in the days of the Pilgrim Fathers.

By the turn of the century, this attitude was slowly changing. Sensational journalism was virtually invented by one man: William Randolph Hearst; when he discovered that stories about love nests and vice dens would sell a million copies, he made sure that his newspapers featured them prominently. The result was that the American public gradually became *blasé* about sex scandal, assuming—usually correctly—that it was being blown up out of all proportion. J. Edgar Hoover talked angrily of the "public apathy and moral deterioration of our population".

A typical example can be seen in the case of a scandal which erupted in June 1955, when the Massapequa Farmers' Market in Long Island burned down. The market also contained the luxury apartment of a well-known millionaire. In the burned-out rubble, firemen found rolls of 16 mm. film, which when examined proved to contain shots of various young girls, engaged in obscene acts. Their ages ranged from 11 to 17, and they were local schoolchildren.

Unsuspecting parents

It became clear that, for several years, the millionaire had been luring young girls to his apartment and holding orgies with them. In some cases, the unsuspecting parents had given their children permission to go to the home of the "nice millionaire", who was regarded as eminently respectable. There were more than twenty girls on the film, and they were obviously just a fraction of the total.

In England, the man would have been locked up, and the Sunday newspapers would have spent the next year detailing the life stories of every girl involved. The American court, while indignant, felt no such morbid curiosity; he was allowed free on a $100,000 bail, and promptly vanished to Latin America; he has not been heard of since.

No doubt it is a pity he escaped the penalty; on the other hand, the American public escaped being bombarded with sordid details that might have inspired more attacks on children. Hoover may be right about moral deterioration, but there are times when there is a great deal to be said for public apathy.

All UPI

der & Mitchenson Collection. Associated Newspapers/Quartet

THE 'POWERFUL PERVERTS' MYSTERY

Beautiful dancer Maud Allen was a sensation on the London stage during the First World War. She played "Salome" in Oscar Wilde's play, produced by J. T. Grein (below left). But the fanatical Noel Pemberton Billing (below right) accused her of being the head of a "Cult of the Clitoris". . . .

NOT even Charlie Chaplin at his most maniacal could have reduced a courtroom to such a shambles. The Old Bailey in London – normally a scene of sombre dignity, rigid tradition, and measured words – had turned into a madhouse. A preposterous charlatan held the stage with a mixture of threats, abuse, innuendo, and audacity. A motley collection of witnesses paraded through the witness box with stories so fantastic they had virtually tongue-tied Prosecuting Counsel. Interrupted at almost every other sentence, the Judge banged his gavel in a hopeless attempt to restore order to a trial that had lost all contact with reality.

Courtroom carnival

But then, what could one expect? The whole case had begun with a crackpot allegation that no person in his right mind could have taken seriously. From there it had escalated into a full-dress courtroom carnival, with a cast of clowns, con-men, liars, and lunatics.

Right in the centre was one of the biggest frauds ever thrown up by a country rich in eccentrics – Noel Pemberton Billing, independent Member of Parliament for East Hertfordshire. Patriotism, rather than politics, was Pemberton Billing's big drum – and the mighty whack he had given it a few months earlier had reverberated round Britain.

The year was 1918 and victory seemed further away than ever. All the early optimism had evaporated in the face of the appalling death-toll on the Western Front – where an advance of a yard was measured in thousands of lives. The British public, unused to the spectre of defeat, had reached a stage of fear and desperation where they were willing to believe that some sinister force was working against them; that some weakness or corruption in high places was sabotaging every effort. What they yearned for, above all, was a scapegoat, someone on whom the blame could be fastened.

Noel Pemberton Billing, part-time inventor, professional patriot, witch-hunter, and rabble-rouser, had found one . . . or rather, 47,000 of them. In his magazine *Imperialist* – founded to promote "purity in public life" – he revealed the evil force that was sapping Britain's energy. It was that old friend of professional puritans, sexual vice. And not the good, old-fashioned variety, either. But perverted and unnatural vice, which had left 47,000 of the country's leading figures open to blackmail by German agents.

What's more, the names were all on record in a shameful "Black Book", kept under lock and key by a high German official. Under the heading "THE FIRST 47,000", the magazine's anonymous informant wrote:

"There exists in the *Cabinet Noire* of a certain German prince a book compiled by the Secret Service from the reports of German agents who have infested this country for the past 20 years, agents so vile and spreading debauchery of such a lasciviousness as only German minds could conceive and only German bodies execute.

"The officer who discovered this book while on special service outlined for me its stupefying contents. In the beginning of the book is a precis of general instructions regarding the propagation of evils which all decent men thought had perished in Sodom and Lesbos.

"The blasphemous compilers even speak of the Groves and High Places mentioned in the Bible. The most insidious arguments are outlined for the use of the German agent in his revolting work. Then more than a thousand pages are filled with the names of 47,000 English men and women. It is a most catholic miscellany. The names of Privy Councillors, youths of the chorus, wives of Cabinet Ministers, dancing girls, even Cabinet Ministers themselves, while diplomats, poets, bankers, editors, newspaper proprietors and members of His Majesty's household follow each other with no order of precedence."

However, the *Imperialist* was a cranky magazine with a small circulation, and only a handful of Britons slept uneasily in their beds that night. What was clearly needed to inflame public opinion was a recognizable symbol of moral decadence, someone around whom fear and prejudice could crystallize. The unlucky person appeared right on cue, in the shapely form of Maud Allen, the celebrated dancer and aesthete.

According to newspaper advertisements, Maud Allen had agreed to give two private performances at the Royal Court Theatre of Oscar Wilde's play, *Salome*, including her famous rendering of the Dance of the Seven Veils. The climax of the dance, with the artiste kissing a wax model of Jokaanan's head, had already horrified some local authorities, and one had insisted on her substituting a dish of gravy. The Sunday performances, for subscribing members only, were being promoted by Mr. J. T. Grein, a respected ballet critic and entrepreneur.

It was a gift for Pemberton Billing. Here was a man with a German name defiling the British Sabbath with a noxious play by a known pervert, and starring a

OSCAR WILDE and Lord Alfred "Bosie" Douglas. Later, "Bosie", a defence witness in the Billing libel case, attacked his former friend as a "power for evil".

Mansell

licentious dancer who had received her training in Germany. In the stifling atmosphere of Edwardian Britain Maud Allen had certainly asked for trouble. She had defied prudish convention, dancing in bare feet, dressed in what some critics had described as "a wisp of chiffon".

Scandalous advertisement

Her sensual image had been heightened by the purple and panting prose of her publicity handouts—which told how she was in "artistic sympathy" with those Latin races whose voluptuous bodies and acute passions had brought about the greatest *crimes passionnel*; how she was perfectly made, with slender wrists and ankles; how her skin was satin-smooth, crossed only by the pale tracery of delicate veins that laced the ivory of her round bosom; how her naked feet beat a sensual measure while the pink pearls slipped amorously about her throat and bosom; how the desire that flamed from her eyes and burst in hot gusts from her scarlet mouth infected the very air with the madness of passion; how she was such a delicious embodiment of lust that she might win forgiveness for the sins of such wonderful flesh.

Maud Allen's forthcoming appearance contained all the elements upon which Pemberton Billing could capitalize. In one stroke he could appeal to philistinism,

THE TOILET OF SALOME as seen by artist Aubrey Beardsley. According to Pemberton Billing, the play was "evil and corrupt" and Maud Allen "obscene".

patriotism and popular prejudice—and ensure a wave of public acclaim which could make him a national hero.

Under the headline "The Cult of the Clitoris"—a sentence many people would have regarded as far more obscene than any of Maud Allen's cavortings—Pemberton Billing reprinted the advertisement for the performance in full, adding the comment: "If Scotland Yard were to seize the list of subscribers to these performances I have no doubt they would secure the names of several thousand of the First 47,000."

This time the response was instantaneous. There was a public outcry. And Maud Allen instituted proceedings for criminal libel. Pemberton Billing's "smokescreen" defence, which hid the fact that he had no defence at all, was that *Salome* was "an open representation of degenerate sexual lust, sexual crime and unnatural passions", and its performance would attract many of the "easy victims of pressure" whose names were listed in the Black Book. The result would be "highly deleterious and prejudicial to public morality and to the interests of purity in the public life of this country

generally".

The Judge was the light-hearted Mr. Justice Darling, whose constant stream of witticisms from the Bench had endeared him to the public and earned him the undying animosity of every advocate at the Bar. From the moment the trial opened, however, the jocular Judge was to be reduced to the position of stooge.

Almost before counsel had taken their seats, Pemberton Billing—conducting his own defence—was on his feet, objecting to being tried by Mr. Justice Darling. "My reason," he explained, "is that I have, in my position as a public man and as a Member of Parliament, on many occasions criticized Your Lordship's administration of justice in this country. I have referred both in the columns of the Press and in a book I have written and on public platforms to the atmosphere of levity which Your Lordship has frequently introduced into cases you have tried."

"No hint of vice"

For once the Judge didn't have a merry riposte to cover the situation. Casting the objection aside, he commented snappily that he had never read any of Pemberton Billing's criticisms. Falling over backwards to prove his impartiality, the Judge invited the defendant to step down from the dock and conduct his case at a table in front of the Bench. It was Mr. Justice Darling's first mistake. Never a man to be satisfied with an inch when he could snatch a yard, Pemberton Billing was to take advantage of the Judge's extraordinary latitude time and again, until the entire courtroom became his soapbox.

With the supercilious disdain with which only the British can reduce poetry to banality, Pemberton Billing read passages from *Salome* to illustrate that it was "evil and corrupt". He dwelt at length on the kissing scene at the end of the Dance of Seven Veils, and in the stilted courtroom atmosphere the prose sounded more over-heated than ever . . .

"Ah! thou wouldst not suffer me to kiss thy mouth, Jokaanan. Well! I will kiss it now. I will bite it with my teeth as one bites a ripe fruit. Thy body was a column of ivory set on a silver socket. It was a garden full of doves and silver lilies. Thy voice was a censer that scattered strange perfumes . . . I love ye yet. I am athirst for your beauty. I am hungry for thy body; and neither wine nor fruits can appease my desire."

There were disapproving mumbles from the court—memories were stretching back to the homosexual scandal of Oscar Wilde 23 years earlier—but Mr. Ellis Hume-Williams K.C.. Prosecuting Counsel, argued that there was no hint of unnatural vice in *Salome*. There was nothing but "the straightforward passion

Radio Times Hulton

of a woman for a man".

With unworldly innocence, Maud Allen claimed that Salome's love of Jokaanan was "the awakening of her soul to the voice of God" — a lofty interpretation that provided Pemberton Billing with an excuse for quoting more of Wilde's exotic rhapsodizing . . .

"Thy mouth is redder than the feet of those who tread the wine in the wine-press. Thy mouth is redder than the feet of the doves who haunt the temples and are fed by the priests. It is redder than the feet of one coming from a forest where he hath slain a lion, and seen gilded tigers."

Judge: Gilded tigers?

Pemberton Billing: Yes, gilded tigers.

Judge: Go on.

Pemberton Billing: "It is like the Bow of the King of the Persians, that is painted with vermilion, and is tipped with coral. There is nothing in the world so red as thy mouth." Before we go any further . . .

Hume-Williams: Let us go no further.

Maud Allen: She would not have been the first woman who has asked to kiss a man's mouth.

Judge: But, gentlemen, that is hardly the question. She is the first woman who has talked about the gilded tiger!

Maud Allen: Not as an Oriental, I do not think. Besides, it is her fantasy; I think her imagery is very great. It is quite uncustomary for a Westerner to understand the imagery of the Oriental people.

Judge: Do you think that Oscar Wilde understood it?

Maud Allen: He may have understood it and written it down. I do not understand Oscar Wilde, because I did not know the gentleman.

At this, Pemberton Billing snapped shut

DEATH IN THE TRENCHES . . . Pemberton Billing claimed that Britain's victory was being delayed by the activities of men in power, blackmailed by Germany.

Salome and turned to a far more explosive volume, the infamous Black Book. The time had come to relegate Maud Allen to the wings and introduce the depraved 47,000. It needed all Billing's unscrupulous cunning and barefaced effrontery to use the courtroom as the platform for his campaign. For there was one awkward obstacle to be overcome. Despite all the wild claims of his witnesses, the Black Book could not be produced.

If the trial was like a scene from a farce, then Mrs. Villiers Stuart was undoubtedly the female comedian. Her haughty and piercing cries of "It's in the book!" were to convulse the court and make Mr. Justice Darling speechless. She mounted the witness-box with aristocratic aplomb, and launched into a bizarre tale of an evening when two Army officers took her — for no apparent reason — to a remote lakeside inn called The Hut Hotel. Over a calming cup of tea she was shown the perfidious Black Book. It contained the names of some of the highest people in the land. The two officers, she hinted darkly, had been "put out of the way".

"It's in the book!"

The story was too much for Mr. Justice Darling. He turned to Pemberton Billing and ruled that nothing more could be said about the Black Book unless the volume could be produced. With a wild gleam in his eye Billing turned to the bristling Mrs. Villiers Stuart.

Pemberton Billing: Is Justice Darling's

name in that book?

Mrs. Stuart: It is, and that book can be produced!

Judge: It can be produced?

Mrs. Stuart: It can be produced; it will have to be produced from Germany, and it can be, and it shall be. Mr. Justice Darling, we have got to win this war, and while you are sitting there we will never win it. My men are fighting — other people's men are fighting . . .

Pemberton Billing: Is the Prime Minister's name in the book?

Mrs. Stuart: It's in the book!

Pemberton Billing: Is his wife's name in the book?

Mrs. Stuart: It is! It is!

Pemberton Billing: Is Lord Haldane's name in the book?

Mrs. Stuart: It's in the book!

Judge: I order you to leave the witness box!

For an hour after this incredible exchange the court echoed with abuse, accusations and applause, with Pemberton Billing in the centre, inflaming the mood of hysteria like some mad magician. The following morning a procession of advocates appeared, representing the famous people slandered in the Black Book. "My client wishes to disclaim the completely unfounded allegations made in court" became a daily refrain throughout the trial.

If Mrs. Villiers Stuart's story had been barely credible, then Captain H. S. Spencer's account of the Black Book aspired to an entirely different level of fantasy. Captain Spencer, it turned out, had been the author of the original article exposing the 47,000 in the *Imperialist*. He was also the unnamed officer who,

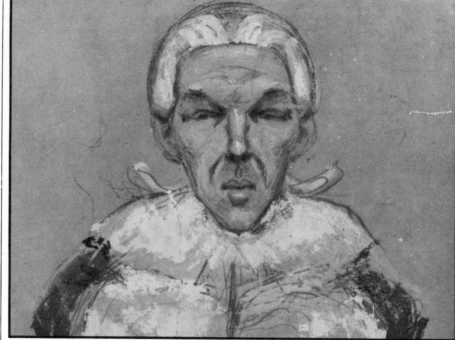

TWO VIEWS of Lord Justice Darling. Normally noted for his keen wit in court, Darling was outdone by Pemberton Billing, who turned the trial into a shambles.

Mansell, National Portrait Gallery

while working as *aide de camp* to the German Prince William of Wied, had been shown the dreaded Black Book at the Palace of Durazzo in 1913.

"It was," he said, "a list of names of people who might be approached, and the method in which they could be approached, to obtain information."

That was just about the only coherent sentence in his testimony. From there the Captain rambled off on a tortuous story about a secret mission he had undertaken to the Balkans, which had been thwarted at every turn by mysterious forces. "An attempt was made to silence me by the military authorities because I knew too much," he claimed. He eventually found himself locked in a small hut with another man, who got up after a while, held out his hand and said, "Goodbye, old chap. They are shooting me at three o'clock."

Certain nasty suspicions which had been germinating in the minds of the spectators seemed to be confirmed when Captain Spencer went on to describe how Army doctors had told him he was suffering from "unusual hallucinations". However, this was merely another plot to prevent him telling the truth to the British public. "The doctors put me in a room in an old orphan asylum," he said, "but I escaped in the uniform of a medical orderly. After further medical examination I was maliciously invalided out of the service."

Where are your notes?

It was with some trepidation that Mr. Hume-Williams rose to cross-examine. As it turned out, he had every reason to be nervous. Counsel tried to unravel a statement by the Captain that he had seen the book three times, and had taken some notes. Slowly, Counsel became enmeshed in the witness's vague and meandering answers.

Counsel: What has become of the notes?

Spencer: I put them in another book, a book of Albanian personalities, with their failings and vices.

Counsel: What did you do with your notes?

Spencer: The whole thing was cabled for and given to Commander Cozens-Hardy, of Naval Intelligence. I put everything in a trunk. It was all I took out of Durazzo, with the exception of a toothbrush.

Counsel: What did you do with your notes when you got to Rome?

Spencer: I put them in a small steamer-box or trunk.

Counsel: What became of the steamer trunk?

Spencer: I cannot trace it. I do not know.

Counsel: Did you lose it?

Spencer: I do not know what became of it. I was ordered on special service. If you communicate with Commander Cozens-Hardy you might find the notes.

Counsel: Did you say he found the trunk?

Spencer: He cabled, and got all the papers.

Counsel: In whose care did you leave the notes?

Spencer: I did not leave them in any-body's care.

Counsel: Then how did Commander Cozens-Hardy get them?

Spencer: I do not know. It is hearsay evidence.

Counsel: Then you do not know he got them?

Spencer: Yes, I know he got them because I saw them at his office at the Admiralty.

Counsel: Did you examine them?

Spencer: I did not.

Counsel: Did he tell you he had got the notes?

Spencer: He told me he had received what he was trying to get.

Counsel: Did he tell you he had your notes?

Spencer: He did not specify notes; it was a packet of papers and books.

Germany at work

The ultimate incredulity came when the Captain tried to involve Mr. Hume-Williams in the impenetrable cloud of conspiracy surrounding the Black Book. The Captain had claimed that British secret agents were "marooned on Greek islands" when they got to know too much.

Spencer: The agent is ordered to an island, and then kept there.

Counsel: And he is sometimes shut up as mad?

Spencer: Yes.

Counsel: When he is not?

Spencer: Yes.

Counsel: And that is the English system?

Spencer: No, it is a German system, practised in England. It is Germany working in England.

Counsel: So that the people who are

able to get Secret Service agents marooned by the orders of the British government are in the German service?

Spencer: Yes, I think I told you that privately. Do you never remember meeting me at dinner, and my talking to you?

Counsel: I? Never!

Spencer: When I came back from Albania you met me at dinner at a house, and we had a conversation together.

Counsel: I never met you before!

Spencer: I expected you to say that.

Counsel: Because it is the truth!

Spencer: You were never at the Clitheroes?

At this point Mr. Justice Darling threw a lifebelt to the struggling advocate. "At this rate," he quipped, "I expect one or other of you will get marooned!"

After Pemberton Billing had shepherded a collection of priests and doctors into the witness box—including a physician who maintained that it would have been impossible for Maud Allen to have played the part of Salome as Oscar Wilde had intended "without her being a sadist herself"—there burst through the doors one of the most familiar figures in British litigation. It was Lord Alfred Douglas, Oscar Wilde's former boy friend "Bosie", now a repentant sinner and professional witness, without whom no British libel trial of the time was complete.

In the 18 years since Wilde had died Lord Alfred Douglas had lost no opportunity to condemn or denigrate his former lover. Confident that everyone in court —and outside it—sympathized with his new role as moral guardian, Lord Alfred Douglas gave full vent to his bitterness on the subject of Wilde and *Salome*.

"I think Wilde was the greatest force for evil that has happened in Europe during the last 350 years," he said. "He was a man whose whole object in life was to attack and sneer at virtue and to undermine it in every way by every possible means, sexually and otherwise. I do not think he ever wrote anything which had not got an evil intention, except perhaps a stray poem or two; but if you take the whole of his poetry, it is inspired by evil intention. It is the same with his plays and books. He was studying Krafft-Ebing when he wrote *Salome,* which he intended to be an exhibition of perverted sexual passion. Whenever he was going to do anything particularly horrible it was always disguised in the most flowery language and always referred back to Art."

Mr. Hume-Williams approached cautiously and read out a complimentary review of the play which Lord Alfred Douglas had written at Oxford.

Counsel: Is that your opinion of *Salome*?

Lord Alfred: It is exactly the same opinion as *your* witnesses now have about it. The only difference is I have escaped from the influence and your witnesses are still under it!

It was the fifth day of the trial, and Pemberton Billing was still parading his witnesses like a circus ringmaster. Some were coming round for the second time— like the formidable Mrs. Villiers Stuart, who provided a grand finale by imitating the witness box technique of the fanciful Captain Spencer. According to her, the Black Book, though still unobtainable, had moved a little nearer the Old Bailey. It was now lying in the former British Embassy in Berlin.

Pemberton Billing: Had you mentioned this book to anyone before this trial?

Mrs. Stuart: Yes. I mentioned it to a prominent public figure. I described it as a dangerous state of affairs, but the man advised me that there were too many people involved to make a personal sacrifice to expose it.

Pemberton Billing: Who was this man?

Mrs. Stuart: Mr. Hume-Williams K.C.!

But it was left to Mr. Justice Darling— roaring back into form as one of the biggest buffoons on the British Bench—to give the whole travesty of a trial its punchline. Five days too late he decreed that all the evidence concerning the Black Book had been "irrelevant". Pemberton Billing's comment that "If Scotland Yard were to seize the list of subscribers I have no doubt they would secure the names of several thousand of the First 47,000" had not been defamatory in itself. The charges rested on the headline, with its imputations against Maud Allen.

Pemberton Billing, however, was almost dancing with delight. He had achieved his object and used the court as a vast megaphone for his own self-promotion. In his final speech he crowed: "I am a libeller. I have libelled public men for the last two and a half years. I have libelled them in the Press; I have libelled them on public platforms; I have libelled them in the House of Commons." He finished with a sinister warning note. "There is an influence, a mysterious influence, which seems to have dogged our footsteps throughout the whole conduct of this war campaign. Gentlemen of the jury, I assure you there must be some reason for all the regrettable incidents of this war!"

The bewildered figure of Maud Allen —who had almost forgotten why she was there—heard Mr. Hume-Williams try to inject some reality into the last few minutes of the trial.

"Almost the only person of whose personal honour nothing disparaging has been dsaid has been Miss Allen," he said. "But I fear it is in vain. If you are going to return a verdict in this case which shall clear the character of Maud Allen I confess it will take some courage. The defendant has created a sort of atmos-

VOLUPTUOUS Maud Allen lost her case against Pemberton Billing, who turned the court into a platform for his odd views.

phere, by his friends in the gallery and his followers outside, calculated to intimidate the jury if he can do it."

When, an hour and a half later, the jury returned a verdict of Not Guilty there was uproar in court. A jubilant crowd surged towards Pemberton Billing. Above the pandemonium the defendant smiled wolfishly at the Judge and made an enquiry about costs. "You have nothing to say, sir," snapped Mr. Justice Darling, out of humour for once. "You are discharged!" Grim faced, the Judge stalked from the court as the news of Pemberton Billing's acquittal spread to the crowds waiting outside the Old Bailey. The cheers were deafening.

It was a victory only for the blind and the bigoted. The following day the *Daily Mail* reported scathingly, "The proceedings in court constituted nothing less than a libel on the nation. A weak Judge, a feeble counsel and a bewildered jury combined to score for the defendant a striking and undeserved success."

In a statement a few days later the Foreign Secretary disowned Captain Spencer as a secret agent. "He had not been entrusted with any special mission," he said, "nor had he made any special confidential reports." Even the Germans disclaimed all knowledge of the dashing Captain. Prince William of Wied denied ever having heard of him.

And the unspeakable Black Book? The Germans admitted that they would have loved to have compiled a list of 47,000 high-ranking perverts who might be open to blackmail. But no such list ever existed, and they were at a loss to explain how the rumour ever came about.

One German official, however, worried about the mystery for years. Long after the war had ended he came up with an explanation. Far from being a record of degenerates who "practised evils which all decent men thought had perished in Sodom and Lesbos", the Black Book had merely been a pre-war list of potential British customers for Mercedes cars.

Mander & Mitchenson Collection

THE MAD MUDSLINGERS

A girl is washed up on a beach . . . in life she had been unknown, and now she is gone for ever. But the name of Wilma Montesi is about to burst on to every front page for many weeks. She will rub shoulders with the rich, glamorous and powerful, and play the lead in a tragi-comedy which brings Italy to the verge of civil war.

THE wildly dramatic case which became known as the "Montesi Affair" began with the sad but unremarkable death of a 21-year-old girl, washed up one morning on the beach at Tor Vaianica, 15 miles south of Rome. Fed by gossip and speculation, the affair swelled into a resounding political scandal. By the time the cloud of rumour drifted away, reputations had been wrecked, a senior government official had resigned and the government itself faced accusations of corruption and demands for its resignation; it was Wilma Montesi's misfortune to die at exactly the right time.

Wilma Montesi, a dark, attractive girl, had left her home in Rome on the afternoon of April 9, 1953, apparently to visit the Ostia lido only 30 minutes from the capital. She was never seen alive again. Thirty-six hours later—at dawn on April 11—her body was found at Tor Vaianica, 10 miles further down the coast. Her stockings and suspender-belt were missing.

Secretly destroyed

A post-mortem indicated that she had been having her period at the time and a routine police inquiry concluded that she had fainted while paddling and her body had been carried down the coast to Tor Vaianica by the wind. Her suspender belt, it was assumed, had been removed by the friction of water and sand. That was where the pathetic story of Wilma Montesi should have ended. But, in fact, it was only just beginning.

A few weeks later, a Rome scandal-sheet dropped a vaguely-worded hint that Wilma's suspender-belt had been secretly destroyed by the police after being handed in by the son of an influential government Minister; with its whiff of scandal in high places and government corruption, the idle piece of title-tattle was a gift to the Communists, ever eager to seize a chance of embarrassing the right-wing Christian Democrat party.

This was election year and Rome—like the rest of Italy—was governed by the Christian Democrats. Social reforms had ground to a standstill, corruption was widespread and there had been a series of scandals implicating the government. Riots had broken out all over Italy, the grossly underpaid Southern workers were campaigning for better pay and conditions, and the whole political future of the country was in the balance. The Montesi Affair couldn't have happened at a more propitious moment.

In January 1954, the scandal broke. Writing in the weekly newspaper

WILMA MONTESI: Goings-on at the hunting lodge? There were stories about degenerate parties and drug-taking. And a government minister was implicated.

Attualita, a journalist named Silvano Muto linked the death of Wilma Montesi with "goings on" at a hunting-lodge called Capocotta, only a short distance from where her body was found. Capocotta was owned by a syndicate consisting of some of Rome's most illustrious names. There were heavy-handed hints about dengerate parties, drugs, girls and orgies. In time-honoured fashion, the readers were left to draw their own conclusions.

However reluctant they may have been to reopen the Montesi case, the authorities had no alternative. On January 28, Muto appeared in court charged with "publishing falsehoods likely to disturb the public peace". The first "Montesi Trial" had started.

Muto lost no time in hurling the mud around. In reply to the judge's first questions, he offered to produce witnesses who would testify that Wilma Montesi had been taken ill after experimenting with drugs during a party at the Capocotta hunting lodge. She had died and her body had been taken away in a car and dumped on the beach. According to Muto's informants, the lodge had been the scene of drug orgies.

Shaken, the Judge adjourned the hearing for five weeks for Muto to produce his witnesses. The balloon was up. The Left-wing Press hurled itself into a frenzy of speculation and condemnation. The government was branded as decadent and corrupt. The police were accused of suppressing evidence. Ugo Montagna—named in court as the head of the Capocotta syndicate—was hounded by reporters.

Unita—the Communist party daily—ran a story alleging that, a few days after Wilma Montesi's death, "a famous film star" had telephoned Piero Piccioni, son of the Italian Foreign Minister, and said: "What sort of a mess have you got yourself into this time? So you knew her, did you? Well, what are you going to do now? And what does Ugo think about it?"

Decline in morality

By the time the trial was resumed on March 5, the whole of Italy was agog to hear the evidence of Muto's witnesses, Adriana Bisaccia and Anna Caglio, two aspiring young actresses. They were in for a disappointment with Adriana Bisaccia. She was recovering from barbiturate poisoning and answered every question with a numb "I am in no condition to remember." But Anna Caglio—who admitted to being Ugo Montagna's mistress—gave much better value.

Anna Caglio's testimony was long and detailed, and delivered with verve and relish. She alleged that Montagna and Piero Piccioni had conspired with government officials to hush up the whole affair. According to Caglio, Piccioni had telephoned Montagna a few days after Wilma

Montesi's death and pleaded with him to intervene with the Chief of Police.

Together, Caglio and Montagna drove to the Cabinet Office, where they met Piccioni. They were inside for half an hour and when they reappeared Piccioni looked agitated but Montagna appeared calm and satisfied. "Now everything's fixed up," Montagna had said. When Caglio commented, "If Piero Piccioni has slipped up, he ought to pay for it even if he is the son of a Minister," Montagna became angry and shouted at her. When he calmed down, he told her, "Look here, old thing, you know too much. It's time you had a change of air and went to Milan."

After that Caglio frequently used to wake up in the middle of the night to find Montagna awake and staring at her, as if he had been listening to her talking in her sleep. On one occasion, Montagna had told her "before they arrest me, I'll let them know about twenty other people"

Anna Caglio claimed that Montagna's money came from drug-trafficking and that there was frequent talk of "orgies" among his circle of friends. A few weeks after the rendezvous at the Cabinet Office, Montagna had shown her round a flat which, he said, had been bought for Tommaso Pavone, the Chief of Police, "for services rendered".

Testimony of mistress

Anna Caglio's evidence was sensational and the repercussions were immediate. Newspapers beat their breasts about the decline in national morality. Angry crowds besieged the law courts. In Parliament, the Communists accused the Christian Democrats of being "pimps and spies". Montagna sued Muto for libel and on March 13 Police Chief Tommaso Pavone resigned. Three days later, Foreign Minister Piccioni tendered his resignation, only to have it turned down.

In her first big dramatic role, Anna Caglio—the aspiring TV starlet—had almost succeeded in toppling the government. But the trial of Muto wasn't yet over, and the most startling development was yet to come.

While the hearing was still going on, Signora Marri—Anna Caglio's landlady—told the press that Anna had written the name of the person responsible for Montesi's death in a letter and handed it to her. There was pandemonium. The landlady was hauled to court and ordered to produce the letter. "Impossible," she replied, "Anna asked me to post her back the letter, which I did this morning."

The Judge immediately suspended the sitting and ordered the police to find the letter at all costs. With sirens wailing, squad cars raced through the streets to the letter-box where Signora Marri had posted the letter. It had been cleared.

AP

DRAMATIC FLAIR enlivens the court testimony of the starlet Anna Caglio (struggling with photographers, right), alleging orgies and dope. But drugs, ironically, have left fellow actress Adriana Bisaccia (inset) "numb" and unresponsive. The tales told by "his girls" will land journalist Muto (left) a libel suit.

The cars roared on to the Rome sorting office, and the police began sifting every letter posted that day. After an hour, they found it. With motor-cycle escorts clearing the way the police cars screamed back to the courtroom, where the hearing was resumed.

Dramatically, the judge held up the envelope. "We have in our hands an envelope," he said. "We tear it open along the top. We take out a plain sheet of white paper, we unfold it and we read: 'Do not believe any other letter I may have written, only this one. All the others have been extorted from me. My Christian principles are too strong for suicide but because I know the character of Ugo Montagna and Piero Piccioni, I am afraid of disappearing and leaving no trace behind. Alas, I know that the head of the gang of drug-traffickers is Montagna. He is responsible for the disappearance of many women. He is the brain of the gang, while Piero Piccioni is the murderer . . .'"

As the riot squad formed up in a solid cordon round the Law Courts, the Judge adjourned the trial of Muto indefinitely and ordered the authorities to prepare criminal charges against Montagna and Piccioni and any others suspected of being involved in Wilma Montesi's death. The investigations, and interrogation of witnesses, were placed in the hands of Raffaello Sepe, the respected President of the Instruction Section of the Court of Appeal. Two-and-a-half years and 92 volumes of evidence later, the trial opened in Venice under the distinguished judge, Mario Tiberi. It had been decided not to hold the trial in Rome, as the risk of public demonstrations was too great. Piero Piccioni was charged with culpable homicide. Ugo Montagna and Saverio Polito — a top police official — were charged with complicity in Piccioni's crime and all three were charged with conspiracy.

Piccioni, a 35-year-old jazz musician, denied ever having met Wilma Montesi. "The first I ever heard of her was the day her death was reported in the newspapers, like everybody else." He did know Anna Caglio, however. She went to him for singing lessons.

Modest in everything

Polito, the former police boss, now bent and aged, cut a pathetic figure. "They have embittered the last years of my life and sought to destroy me," he told the Judge. "You know, Mr. President, to go from the chair of the *Questore* of Rome to the dock is a terrible thing. It is an intolerable burden and there is nothing against me; nothing, nothing, nothing. Do you understand, Mr. President? Forgive me this outburst."

Montagna, a large, striking-looking man, with a smooth, sophisticated manner, told the court: "I proclaim my innocence with all my strength!"

Rodolfo Montesi, Wilma Montesi's father, took the stand next, and launched into a passionate defence of her honour. "Wilma was a good girl, religious, respectful and modest," he said. "It angers me that newspapers say she used to be out at night with men. When I went to the police station to report her disappearance and when I told them she was a good and honest girl, the officer said to me, 'You say that because you're her father', and began to consult the register of prostitutes. I thought I would die of shame and anger. I deny that my daughter had a double life. She was modest even to her clothes, as in everything else."

That Wilma had, in fact, been a virgin was one of the few points on which the parade of expert medical witnesses agreed. The other was that she had drowned. From then on, each doctor stuck to his own theory. One said she had been murdered. Another claimed she had committed suicide. The third plumped for accidental death.

None of the witnesses pushed harder than Anna Caglio, making her triumphant return to the witness stand. This time, she got off to a shaky start.

Judge: You have already said too many things that have nothing to do with the trial. In this place, you must only refer to the Montesi Affair. Now, what did Montagna tell you about the affair?

Caglio: Immediately after the death of the girl, he told me that Piccioni was very depraved and that he'd had an accident, but that it was nothing to do with him and that if anybody tried to push him inside, he'd let them have twenty names first.

Public Prosecutor: When you speak of the disappearance of a lot of women, what do you mean?

Caglio: One was Montesi, another would have been me, if they'd killed me. And then Muto told me about the other women.

Public Prosecutor: So the source of this information was Silvano Muto?

Caglio: Well, partly, yes.

After the efforts of the aspiring actress, it was the turn of an established star to take the stage.

Alida Valli had been identified as the "famous star" who was alleged to have telephoned Piero Piccioni after the death of Wilma Montesi. She quickly knocked the bottom out of any sinister implications the conversation might have had.

Judge: When you were talking to Piccioni, did you mention the Montesi Affair?

Valli: I have already told Dr. Sepe that,

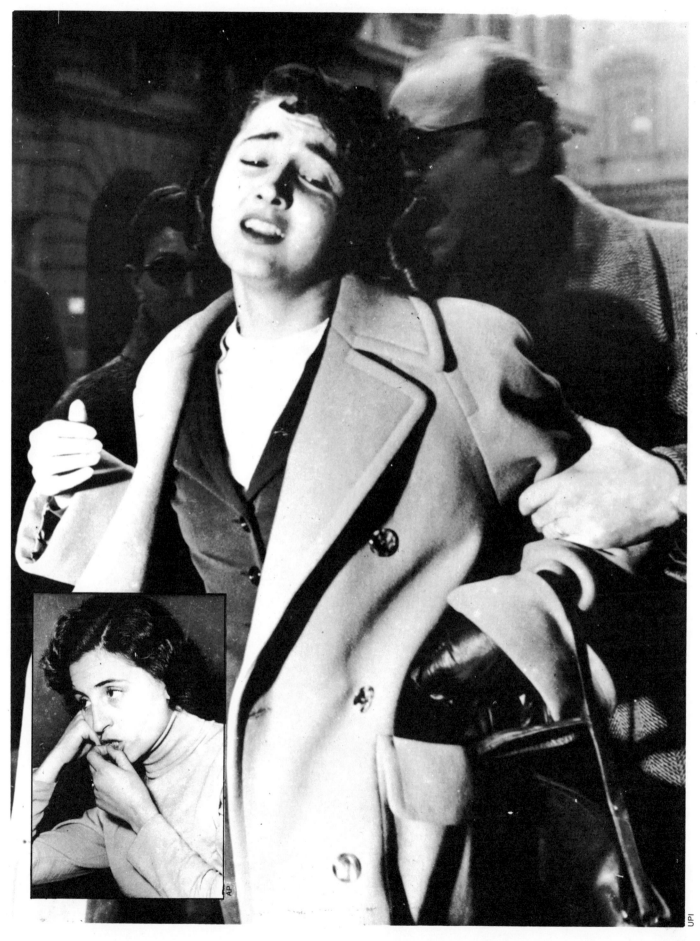

L'Agenzia Ansa

ILLUSTRIOUS NAMES linked to scandal at Capocotta Lodge (below) included minister's son Piero Piccioni (circled left) and businessman Ugo Montagna, in court.

if any reference to the affair was made, it was with regard to the news that had already appeared in the papers.

Judge: Do you remember saying 'What have you done? What has happened to that girl? So you knew her, and what are you going to do?'

Valli: As I have already said, if I did refer to the affair at all, it was only on the basis of what I read in the papers.

Public Prosecutor: Do you deny having uttered the phrase 'And now look what a fix that idiot's got himself into', in the bar?

Valli: I do deny it. I never talk to myself.

Methodical alibi

Far from piling up, the evidence against the accused seemed to be getting thinner and thinner. Piero Piccioni's brother swore that on the night Wilma Montesi disappeared, Piero had been in bed with tonsilitis. There was no doubt about the date. "My brother is very methodical," said the witness. "He even has a file with 'Health' written on it, where he keeps the results of analyses, prescriptions and X-rays on himself."

The alibi was borne out by a procession of doctors and nurses, along with a policeman on duty at the house that evening who had given Piero injections to relieve the discomfort.

It was at this point that the most preposterous character in the entire cast burst upon the court in a blaze of innuendo . . . Gianna la Rossa, or Red

Jenny, a figure straight from the pages of melodrama. She first appeared in a letter to the investigator, Dr. Sepe:

"I know all about the events of April 1953 and the death of Wilma Montesi. Since I was horrified at the cruelty of Montagna and Piccioni, I tried to get in touch with the drug traffickers who operate in the province of Parma, at Traversetolo, and I tried to make a big purchase from them, while keeping the police informed at the same time, so that they could be arrested.

"But the Parma police pigeon-holed it and wouldn't act. A few months before, while I was preparing to do this, I deposited a letter with the priest of a little village near Traversetolo. He is a priest who is qualified as an engineer. I knew him at the university. I was almost certain that if I were found out I should end the same way as poor Wilma. The priest will hand over the letter if you give him the torn-off half of a ticket which I enclose. The other half is with the letter.

"I will only come forward if I have adequate guarantees for my personal safety. Montagna's money and Piccioni's contacts could be my ruin, even if I were protected by the police. My skin is not worth much, but it is all I have."

There was no problem in tracing the priest with the other half of the ticket. He was Don Tonin Onnis, the 30-year-old parish priest of a small village called Bannone di Traversetolo. The two halves

were exchanged in true cloak-and-dagger fashion and Dr. Sepe read the second letter from Red Jenny:

"When these lines are read, I shall be dead. I wish it to be known that I have not died a natural death, but have been done away with by the Marquis Montagna and Piero Piccioni. I ask God's pardon for my life, and I hope that men also will pardon me. I have been drawn into a whirlpool against my will. I wish these things to be known so that other poor girls may not meet my end. I have found that it is impossible, or at any rate very difficult, to do anything to avoid this evil. I live from moment to moment under the threat of ending up like poor Wilma, and I know that human justice can be bought with the money and the contacts that those two have. Poor people like us just have to suffer in silence and then, when we are no longer useful, or become dangerous to them, they do away with us with such monstrous ease."

Bizarre situation

Red Jenny repeated her determination to set a trap for the drug traffickers by acting as a go-between with the police, and ended:

"I have no one to say good-bye to, because no one in the world has ever loved me. I ask pardon once more from God."

For a humble parish priest, Don Onnis seemed to have a knack for finding himself

L'Agenzia Ansa

in bizarre situations. He told Dr. Sepe that, in August 1953, he was going to Parma on his motor-scooter when he was stopped by a man who asked him to carry a package into town. Luckily for him, Don Onnis refused, for as soon as he reached the city, he was waved down by police. At the police station, Don Onnis was told that the police had received a letter which said that, during the day, a man of "irreproachable character" would try to smuggle a packet of drugs into the town on a motor-scooter bearing the priest's number-plate.

It seemed that Don Onnis had unwittingly found himself in the centre of a vast and sinister conspiracy. Nor was its baleful influence confined to the priest. A few days after the Bishop of Parma, Monsignor Evasio Colli, had taken Don Onnis aside to ask him to behave with greater decorum, he received a threatening letter from Red Jenny.

Nationwide search

If Dr. Sepe suspected there was more than a hint of the greasepaint about the whole Red Jenny affair, he didn't show it. A nationwide search was conducted for her but, to nobody's surprise, Red Jenny remained elusive. In court, it was the hapless Don Onnis's task to pluck Red Jenny from the pages of imaginative fiction and clothe her in flesh and blood.

After describing how Red Jenny came into his sacristy and borrowed his typewriter to write her letters, he was questioned by the Judge.

Judge: How was she dressed, this woman?

Don Onnis: She was a woman of about 30, dressed in a decent manner. She was educated, spoke without any noticeable accent. She was tall, had a good figure, her hair was fair or light brown and she had an oval face.

Judge: Yes, but how was she dressed?

Don Onnis: I don't know exactly how to say. She had a leather bag and hung it on her chair by a strap. Her suit was perhaps brown or rust colour. I don't know much about these things. I remember she had a car key with a lucky charm.

Public Prosecutor: Why did you ask her name and address?

Don Onnis: I wanted to know who she was.

Public Prosecutor: But when she went out, you weren't interested enough to follow her?

Don Onnis: I thought perhaps she was a woman in trouble, that she might have done something silly.

Francesco Carnelutti (Piccioni's counsel): Did you think of anybody who Red Jenny might have been?

Don Onnis: I did name two or three people; people who might have done it to harm me.

Judge: But you didn't know the woman who came into your sacristy?

Don Onnis: She might have been sent by them.

Carnelutti: But what harm could she have done you with this letter?

Before Don Onnis could reply, Defence Counsel Augenti chipped in with the thought that had already begun to surface in many minds: "People might have thought he was Red Jenny himself."

Decently buried

There were more sarcastic asides as Don Onnis floundered through his account of the drug-carrying incident.

Public Prosecutor: Did anybody else know that you were going to Parma on the morning of August 27?

Don Onnis: Only my mother.

Public Prosecutor: You realize that, because of the letter to the police, at least one other person besides you *must* have known you were going?

Don Onnis: I don't understand.

Public Prosecutor: What do you mean? Surely you tried to find out who wrote that anonymous letter?

Don Onnis: No, I didn't try to find out. I guessed.

Question by question the parish priest sank deeper below the surface of credibility.

Judge: Did you go back to the police in Parma after this occasion?

Don Onnis: They had told me to come back to hear how the affair was going on.

Both AP

Keystone

Once I went on my own accord, but there was an official I didn't know. I told him the story of the packet of drugs all over again and he said to me, 'Go home and don't worry. The packet has been confiscated. Don't think any more about the whole affair.'

Public Prosecutor: You have described Red Jenny and have told us that she wore strong perfume. I don't suppose you know the names of perfumes?

Don Onnis: What do you think?

Public Prosecutor: Do you know that the day after your talk with the Bishop of Parma, he received a letter?

Don Onnis: I have heard of it. My Bishop talked to me about it in a general way but I have only recently seen a photostat of the letter and seen that it was signed "Red Jenny".

Public Prosecutor: And what do you think about it?

Don Onnis: That there is some brainless person who is trying to get between me and my Bishop.

Public Prosecutor: Well then, explain the coincidence of the signature.

Don Onnis: What can you expect? Everybody was talking about Red Jenny by then.

Public Prosecutor: But did you tell anybody about your talk with the Bishop?

Don Onnis: Certainly not. I told nobody.

Public Prosecutor: Then there is a little devil stealing your thoughts. You have to go to Parma and the little devil goes and warns the police. You have a talk with your Bishop and the little devil tells Red Jenny, who writes a threatening letter.

Carnelutti: Was it a nice talk you had with the Bishop?

Don Onnis: Talks with one's superiors are always nice.

Judge: Did the Bishop rebuke you?

Don Onnis: What do you mean by rebuke? It was simply a clarification. We informed each other.

And so, with good humour all round, Red Jenny was decently buried and the court turned to more serious matters. Slowly, the whole tone of the trial was changing. As the earlier, wild allegations were knocked down one by one, the atmosphere began to clear. Even the three defendants started fading into the distance, particularly when the various members of the Montesi family began following each other into the witness box. What had begun as a national scandal was contracting into a typically Italian family feud. The first hint that all was not well in the Montesi family came when Wilma's aunt, Ida Montesi, was giving evidence:

"I remember that when she was a child Wilma was playing one day in the water on the beach at Fregene. She was 5 and I was 12. At one moment, she slipped in deep water and disappeared. I ran up and pulled her out of danger and helped her back to the beach. She was quite lost. My sister-in-law told me that Wilma often remembered that episode and said 'If Ida hadn't pulled me out, it would have been a good death. The water is beautiful'."

Public Prosecutor: Why have you not said all these things before today?

Ida Montesi: Originally my sister-in-law didn't want anybody to mention her fear that Wilma had committed suicide, but I thought that she herself would talk about it sooner or later.

The uneasy feeling that somebody, somewhere, was hiding something was heightened by the appearance of Giuseppe

DEFTLY DEFUSED: but no verdict. Rossana and fiancé Giuseppi — and the rest of the Montesi clan — have nothing but tears to show for their ordeal . . .

Montesi, Wilma's 30-year-old uncle. On the day Wilma disappeared, he had left work early. At first, he denied this, but his story floundered when he was confronted with Leonelli, the Chief Compositor of the printing firm where he worked.

First, the Public Prosecutor asked Leonelli: "Did Montesi tell you that he was having an affair with a girl who would sleep with him the day before her marriage?" "Yes," replied Leonelli. Then the two men faced each other.

Change of story

Leonelli: On April 9, you went out shortly after five and you said you were going to Ostia, where you boasted that you had a *pied-à-terre*.

Giuseppe: Ask the witness if he has a criminal record!

Judge: That doesn't concern us. You tell us whether you went out of your office on April 9 in the afternoon.

Public Prosecutor: Listen, Montesi. We are not accusing you of anything. We only want to know where you were between 6 and 11 on the evening of April 9. There are certain moments in one's life when one has to admit things that one would rather keep quiet.

Giuseppe: I am sure you are not accusing me, but I still say that I was at the printing works.

Judge: Did you go to Ostia?

Giuseppe: I did not.

Public Prosecutor: Then where did you go?

Giuseppe: I don't know.

Counsel: He had better say, for his own good.

Giuseppe: I can't say!

This was too much for the Judge; Giuseppe was clearly trying to conceal something. The court was cleared and Giuseppe was pressed again on the events of April 9. Without the embarrassment of the public hanging on every word, Giuseppe changed his story. Yes, he admitted he had left early; for some time he had been having an affair with his fiancée's sister, Rossana Spissu. On April 9, she had phoned him and they had driven to a lonely spot in the Via Flaminia and made love. Rossana had subsequently borne his child.

The Public Prosecutor still wasn't satisfied and Giuseppe was charged with perjury, on the basis of his first version of the story. The Public Prosecutor was determined not to let Giuseppe off the hook. He savaged Rossana Spissu, who rather lamely supported Giuseppe's alibi. Then he turned again to Giuseppe.

Collapsed in tears

Public Prosecutor: You've invented all this business afterwards, but you've invented it badly. And so what did you do that evening?

Giuseppe: As usual, we went along the bank of the Tiber and we had a coffee in one bar and a brandy in another, and then we went to our usual place, out along the Via Flaminia.

Public Prosecutor: You've cooked up this version with Rossana, but you've forgotten to put the lid on the pot. Why did you need to see each other so urgently, if you met every day?

Giuseppe answered limply that, on this occasion, he hadn't seen her for two days and felt a desire to take her to the Via Flaminia.

Public Prosecutor: On the evening of April 9, you did not go home before 11 o'clock, and that is a very suspicious circumstance. You are not telling the truth this time, either. Perhaps there is a third truth, and of course it may have nothing to do with the disappearance of your niece. Perhaps you went to a place or with a person you don't want to be known, but we must make it clear to you that we have absolute proof you are not telling the truth today either.

Overcome by the cross-examination, Giuseppe could barely croak "But I am telling the truth! I have never been subjected to such an examination!"

Day after day, the grilling of Giuseppe continued. Repeatedly accused of lying, Giuseppe jumped to his feet and bellowed: "This is the last time I shall repeat that I know nothing! I know nothing of the death of Wilma Montesi. I don't know how Wilma died. Perhaps her father knows, or her mother or her sister,

but I don't know anything!" At the end of one interrogation, he clutched his head and shouted, "No, no, no!"

When he wasn't facing the Public Prosecutor, Giuseppe was confronted with other witnesses who challenged his evidence, like the journalist Luciano Doddoli:

Doddoli: Look in my eyes! You told me that you often saw your niece!

Giuseppe: What are you insinuating, 'saw'?

Doddoli: This. When we spoke of a man in Wilma's life, I said to you: 'Signor Montesi, you are that man.'

Giuseppe: You are lying. You are lying in a completely barefaced manner!

Doddoli: And you were afraid and said: 'For God's sake don't bring my name in! I'll help you in any way I can.'

The same heat was turned on Rossana.

Public Prosecutor: Signorina Rossana, tell the truth!

Rossana: But I have told it! I swear on the head of my child!

Public Prosecutor: Leave your child alone. Do not bring innocence into this room! Tell the truth and stop crying! Tears are useless. Tell us why Giuseppe did not recognize the child at first.

Rossana: He will.

Public Prosecutor: But why has he waited so long?

Rossana: That doesn't come into it.

Public Prosecutor: It does come in. Why has he decided now to recognize the child? Perhaps his recognition of his son is tied up with your evidence?

By now, the Judge and Prosecutor between them had screwed the tension to screaming-point with their highly-charged combination of machine-gun questioning and dramatic confrontation of witnesses. Every day, the court was packed with spectators, their emotional reactions mirroring the moods of the witnesses . . . anguished, outraged, defiant, downcast.

When it seemed that nothing more could be squeezed out of Giuseppe and Rossana except further tears, the prosecution produced two surprise witnesses whose evidence destroyed the "Via Flaminia" alibi. Mr. and Mrs. Piastra swore that, on the evening of April 9, Rossana Spissu was with them at Rome Central Station, seeing off Mrs. Piastra's mother. They produced a marked book of concessionary railway tickets to prove it. Rossana denied going to the station, but faced with the implacable Piastras, she collapsed in tears.

"Tell me, Signor Piastra, why you want to harm me?" she pleaded. "You know I was not at the station." The whole courtroom sobbed with her as her shoulders rose and fell. The Public Prosecutor, as usual, was made of sterner stuff.

"Rossana," he intoned, "perhaps you are afraid that if you tell the truth you will do a great deal of damage. Giuseppe

Montesi is not accused of anything. He has chosen you as his shield, but the shield has failed him."

It was a relief to see the pressure lifted from Giuseppe and Rossana—there was nothing more they could say and it was useless baiting them any further—and on the last day, a parade of picturesque witnesses entered the court for the "grand finale".

Wilma Montesi's fiancé turned out to be a rather simple-minded policeman who referred to the girl throughout as "this Wilma Montesi". He did not appear the most inspiring lover and the Public Prosecutor couldn't resist commenting that Wilma used to put on two coats of lipstick to prevent him kissing her. A furious row broke out between two witnesses—punctuated by shouts of "Scum!" and "Liar!"—and an elderly Fascist who volunteered to give evidence ended up hitting everyone in sight and having to be restrained by two policemen.

It was a fitting conclusion to a trial that had started as a national sensation and ended in family recrimination.

Deftly defused

On May 20, the Public Prosecutor made his final speech. He maintained that Wilma Montesi had indeed gone to the beach, not at Capocotta but Ostia, and with a man, though there was no evidence to show it had been Piccioni. He added darkly, "There is the possibility of finding out in the future who this man was." After defence counsel had made their pleas, the Judge and his two colleagues retired for seven hours to consider their verdict. The result was hardly a revelation. Piero Piccioni was acquitted for "not having committed the crime", and Ugo Montagna and Saverio Polito were also acquitted, "as there had been no crime".

The "Montesi Affair" was right back where it started from, but at least it had shed the hysterical atmosphere of witch-hunting fermented by the press and the politicians. Outside Italy, observers wondered how all the half-baked witnesses and ramshackle evidence ever got as far as a courtroom.

But sophisticated Italian analysts of the political scene knew that the truth was subtle. To have refused to hold a trial on the grounds of insubstantial evidence would have left the Christian Democrats wide open to accusations of corruption and suppression. As it was, Italy was almost on the brink of civil war and the Communists were baying for blood.

By taking a chance and allowing the Montesi Affair to take its own course, the situation had been deftly defused and the rumours exposed for the nonsense they were; if there was any political conspiracy at all in the entire Montesi Affair, that was it.

CON-MEN

They prey on "mugs" and "suckers", their bait is greed. They have "sold" the Eiffel Tower and Brooklyn Bridge and even conned Henry Ford himself . . .

Acme, Culver, Bettmann Archive/Quartet

WOULD you believe that a car could be run on water instead of gasoline? Before you answer No, consider the incredible case of the inventor Louis Enricht. In the year 1916, the world was gripped by an oil crisis. One April morning, New York's reporters were invited to call at a house in Farmingdale, Long Island, to witness a demonstration which, they were assured, would be spectacular. The few reporters who turned up found a big, grey haired man with an impressive face and a foreign accent, who introduced himself as Louis Enricht, and explained that he had invented a cheap substitute for gasoline. The reporters yawned, and looked bored.

Enricht led them to a small European car, pointed out that the gas tank was empty, and asked the reporters to examine it closely to see that there was no supplementary fuel tank. They weren't experts, but it certainly didn't look as if Enricht was deceiving them. Enricht then asked a reporter to fill a bucket at the tap. When the man returned with the water, the inventor produced a bottle full of a green liquid. He told the man to empty it into the bucket — warning him that the stuff was deadly poison.

The reporter poured the bucket into the gas tank, and Enricht asked the driver to try the engine. After a few splutters, it started, and a smell of almonds pervaded the air. Enricht offered each of the reporters a ride around Farmingdale. If there *was* a concealed gas tank — which is the obvious hypothesis — then it must have been large, for the car trips went on for at least an hour.

The next day, the story made the front pages, and Enricht was besieged with letters, phone calls and reporters. He declined to see them. A Harvard professor declared sourly that no possible combination of chemicals could turn water into a combustible fuel, but Enricht declined to comment. His next visitor was

FOOLING THE FAMOUS . . . there is no doubt that Enricht was sufficiently clever to unnerve many of the leading lights of the car industry — even Ford . . .

Henry Ford himself. Ford examined the car carefully, and since he was one of the world's leading experts, he was pretty thorough. He watched Enricht mix his green liquid with water, and then went for a ride in the car.

Enricht admitted that the smell was cyanide, but said it had been put in to conceal another smell. His process was absurdly simple, he said, and until his lawyer had devised a way to patent it, he wasn't dropping any hints.

Ford was so impressed that, even when the *Tribune* printed a story revealing that Enricht had been a fake company promoter, Ford ignored it. The evidence of his own eyes assured him that the car had run on water, and he gave Enricht a cheque for $10,000 on account.

When this news was leaked to the papers—by Enricht—Hiram P. Maxim, son of the inventor of the Maxim gun, offered Enricht a million dollars, and offered to build him a laboratory for further research. In fact, Enricht received only $100,000; he was to receive the rest when he handed over the formula—which, Maxim agreed, should not be until he had patented his discovery.

Penny-a-gallon fuel

Ford was infuriated, but since Enricht had returned his cheque, there was nothing much he could do. Then America came into the First World War, and Maxim was so busy making munitions that he agreed to call off the whole thing; he had more than recovered his invest-

ment in the upward-turn taken by his company's shares when his deal with Enricht was announced.

The man who decided to take over from Maxim was a rich banker named Yoakum. He also gave Enricht $100,000, accepting a sealed envelope which was supposed to contain the formula. Yoakum told President Wilson that he intended to present the secret of penny-a-gallon fuel to the American people, and Wilson was delighted. But Enricht launched delaying tactics, and Yoakum hired the Pinkerton detective agency to investigate him.

PRESIDENT WILSON (foreground) was fooled by Enricht, a friend of Von Papen (far left). Enricht used a formula known to Edison (centre) to con Maxim (right).

Acme Photo The Bettmann Archive Culver Pictures

He was flabbergasted to discover that Enricht had been seen consorting with Von Papen, the German military attaché, before the outbreak of war, and that the "inventor" was suspected of being a German spy. Then Yoakum opened the envelope that was supposed to contain the formula—and found only a few liberty bonds. But there was no way to get Enricht into a court of law.

Yoakum had broken his own undertaking by opening the envelope. Talk about trying Enricht for treason dragged on until Yoakum died, and Enricht was

HENRY FORD pictured in an early automobile. He gave Enricht a cheque for $10,000 as a down payment on the con-man's "miracle" fuel.

once again in the clear.

At the age of 75 Enricht was still a man of restless imagination. In 1920, he announced that his continued experiments in the manufacture of gasoline had led him to conclude that the easiest and cheapest way was to distil it from peat. Such was the magic of his name that investors again rushed to thrust cheques into his hand, and he may have received as much as a quarter of a million dollars.

But the Nassau County District Attorney decided it was time someone brought Enricht's career to an end. The D.A. examined Enricht's bank accounts until he found a cheque for $2000, handed over by an investor and promptly endorsed to pay a bookmaker. That was fraud, since he was a limited company, and all money

was supposed to benefit other investors. At the age of 77, Enricht received seven years in gaol for grand larceny. Paroled after a few years, he died at the age of 79 without revealing to anyone the secret of his formula for cheap gasoline.

The formula

How did he do it? The answer may lie in a formula discovered by Thomas Edison. He found that a mixture of acetone and liquid acetylene *will* drive a car if mixed with water. If cyanide is added, it hides the very distinctive nail-varnish smell of acetone. The mixture costs more to make than gasoline, and it also had the disadvantage of corroding the engine after a while. But this is probably the answer to the enigma.

Undoubtedly, the most remarkable con-man of them all was the Scotsman, John Law. Born in Edinburgh in 1671, Law had no need to work: his father, a successful goldsmith and moneylender, left him two estates. But Law was immensely ambitious. Besides, he was driven by another itch that characterizes many of the great con-men: the passion for beautiful women. At 23 he went to London where his success in love became as legendary as his success at cards. He packed more experience into the next five years than most men in a lifetime. Then his luck turned: he killed a man in a duel, was tried and fled to the Continent.

There he continued to gamble and seduce: but he also became a fascinated student of high finance. It seemed to him that the secret of wealth was a perfectly simple one. All businesses run on credit, and the more money they make, the more they borrow in order to expand. But in those days, money was made of gold or silver, and there was a limited amount of it to go round. The answer, said Law, was to print paper money instead — which could be instantly redeemed for gold merely by walking into a bank.

But so long as the customers trusted their paper money, why should they demand gold instead? And in that case, the government could issue any amount of paper money, and use it to increase trade. So long as there was no sudden panic, it was a foolproof way of increasing credit and prosperity.

Law returned to Scotland — which at the time had its own government, so that he was safe from arrest — and tried hard to persuade his fellow countrymen of the value of a national bank that would issue paper money. He was ignored. And when Scotland discussed union with England, he decided it was time to return to the Continent. In 1708 he went to Paris, and found it the most exciting

GREATEST CON-MAN of all. John Law's "paper money" scheme caused riots in the streets of Paris when it crashed ruining hundreds of rich investors.

Mansell, Viollet

capital in Europe. Everyone gambled. Soon Law was known in the most exclusive drawing-rooms in Paris, and the size of his stakes made him famous.

He met the Duc d'Orleans, and convinced him of his financial genius; for a while it looked as if he would get his opportunity to print paper money. Then the police began investigating him; D'Argenson, lieutenant of the Paris police, had received hundreds of complaints from losers who doubted Law's honesty. Law was driven out of France.

In 1715, Louis XIV died. Law could hardly believe his luck when he heard that his old friend the Duc d'Orleans had been appointed Regent of the young king, and was virtually dictator of France. He hurried back to Paris, and this time the Duke allowed him to put his schemes into effect.

To begin with, he gave Law permission to open a private bank and to print his own money. Law had built up a

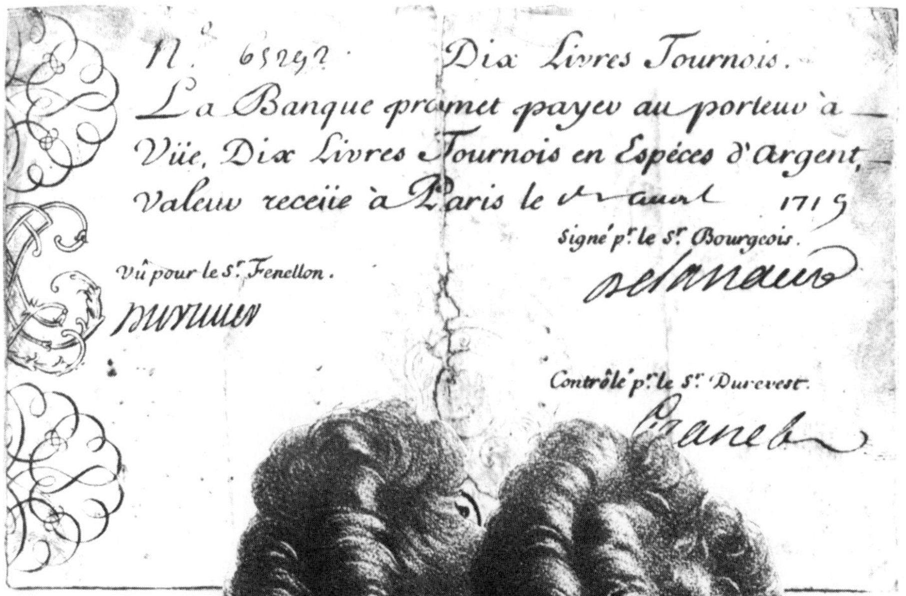

THE DUC D'ORLEANS was Law's most powerful patron (right), though Law's banknotes bankrupted aristocrat D'Argenson (left). Law died a pauper.

fortune of eighty thousand pounds, so he had the gold to back his notes—to begin with. He started out cautiously, aiming to create confidence. He lost money, but people came to feel that his notes were as safe as gold.

By 1718, Law's bank was making so much money that the Duke transformed it into a Royal Bank. Law could print as much money as he liked.

Now obviously, this was a very dangerous game. It is true that money makes money. But if there is a slump or sudden panic, a bank must have enough money to change all its notes into gold—or collapse. In theory, Law had all the money he needed; it was now time to use it to make more money: real money. The answer lay across the Atlantic, in Louisiana—which belonged to the French.

Viollet, Mansell

QUINQUENPOIX

'T GECKE HUYS

'T ARMHUYS

Mary Evans

TWO BUBBLES. The Mississippi Bubble (above) and the British "South Sea" Bubble were both con-tricks, and both were savagely caricatured in print.

Mansell

Louisiana consisted of thousands of square miles of swamps and uncultivated land; Law set himself to persuade the French people that it was full of gold, silk and valuable minerals, and that all they had to do to double their money was to invest it in Louisiana bonds. The money flowed in, Law cornered the Canadian fur market, and made huge profits.

But he was now aware of the dangers of this incredible game of confidence. As the money poured in, share prices rose; speculators could make fortunes overnight. Everything went faster and faster—and Law had to keep running faster than anybody, always making sure he had the gold to meet all demands. If Louisiana was to make money, he had to persuade emigrants to go there. Law hired men to go throughout France, telling stories of the wealth of Louisiana.

From the government he purchased the right to collect taxes, and made a vast fortune that way. He bought trading companies in the Far East. He cornered Virginia tobacco. The money kept flooding in. His office in the narrow Rue Quincampoix was besieged by crowds day and night; any shares he deigned to sell could be resold within minutes for

twice their price. Moneylenders nearby lent money at one per cent *per hour*, and their customers still made a fortune.

Soon there wasn't enough gold to go round; the Duc d'Orleans had to be persuaded to pass laws forbidding goldsmiths to make gold articles weighing more than a few ounces. Confidence slumped, and the rush came. At first the bank would only cash one hundred livre note per person; soon this was reduced to ten livres. And in December 1720, two years after he had become head of the Compagnie de l'Occidente, Law decided it would be safer to flee the country.

For the next few years he lived quietly in London. His old skill as a gambler had not deserted him; when he had only a thousand pounds left, he staked it all on a bet that he could throw six double sixes one after the other: he won. But his luck turned—perhaps due to the curses of thousands of Frenchmen whom he had ruined. He remained on friendly terms with the Duc d'Orleans to the end; the Duke had remedied the bankruptcy by the simple expedient of burning every paper connected with the Royal Bank. But when Law finally died in Venice, in 1729, he was again a pauper.

In the year of the collapse of Law's Compagnie de l'Occidente, England was having its own grave financial crisis, the bursting of the South Sea Bubble. The full details of the dealings of the South

Sea Company are even more complex than those of Law's Royal Bank; but the parallels are otherwise very close. Law needed the permission of the Regent to start his company; the directors of the South Sea Company got their permission for their vast dealings by offering to take on the English National Debt—the money the government owes investors in government stocks.

Their equivalent of Louisiana was Peru and the South Seas. Between 1711 and 1720, millions of pounds changed hands, and fortunes were made. All kinds of other schemes swept to success on the tail of the South Seas comet: a scheme for making a "wheel of perpetual motion", a scheme for making a soft metal out of mercury. One speculator even launched a scheme "for great advantage, but nobody to know what it is", and made two thousand pounds in one morning.

The South Sea directors had to take legal action against these other companies, and in doing so, they started the panic slide that led to the crash. In this case, some investors got back at least some of their money, for the government seized part of the assets of the directors of the Company.

The Eiffel Tower

The classic "con" case of modern times is undoubtedly that of Count Victor Lustig's sale of the Eiffel Tower —not once, but twice. Like John Law, Lustig came from a respectable middle-class family, and he too loved gambling and women. Some time before the First World War, he left his home in Czechoslovakia and moved to Paris. Lustig was only one of two dozen aliases that he

used at different times; he learned the techniques of confidence trickery from the gambler Nicky Arnstein.

Lustig was in Paris when he saw a newspaper item reporting that repairs to the Eiffel Tower would cost thousands of francs. Some days later, several rich financiers received letters from a government department inviting them to a secret conference at the Hotel Crillon. The "director deputy-general" who received them was actually Victor Lustig. He began by assuring them that this business was classified as top-secret—hence the hotel suite instead of his office.

The government has decided, he told them, that the Eiffel Tower is too expensive to maintain; it is to be sold for scrap metal . . . They gaped. "Would you gentlemen care to submit your bids to me?" He had already noted the man who was the obvious "mark", Andre Poisson, a man who clearly felt socially inferior to the others. A few days later, Lustig rang him and told him that his bid was the highest—several million francs—and that if he would bring a certified cheque to the hotel, the deal

could be concluded. Poisson was not entirely happy—until Lustig apologetically asked for a bribe, to ensure that negotiations would go smoothly.

That convinced Poisson that this was a genuine government official; he handed over the cash. And later, when it became clear he had been swindled, he was too ashamed to go to the police and make himself the laughing stock of France. The result was that Lustig was able to repeat the same trick a few years later.

The second part of Lustig's life was an anticlimax—an observation that applies to most confidence tricksters. In America in the early 1930s, he turned to the distribution of counterfeit money; the F.B.I. finally caught up with him, and he was sentenced to twenty years in gaol, dying in Alcatraz in 1947. The Federal agent mainly responsible for his capture, James P. Johnson, wrote the classic book on his career under the title *The Man Who Sold the Eiffel Tower*.

It is a saddening book, for it underlines the strange romanticism that leads brilliant and imaginative men to become confidence swindlers.

UPI, Barnaby's, NW Daily News

CLASSIC CONS. Gambler Nicky Arnstein (above) taught "Count" Victor Lustig (right) the art of conmanship. Later Lustig sold the Eiffel Tower—twice.

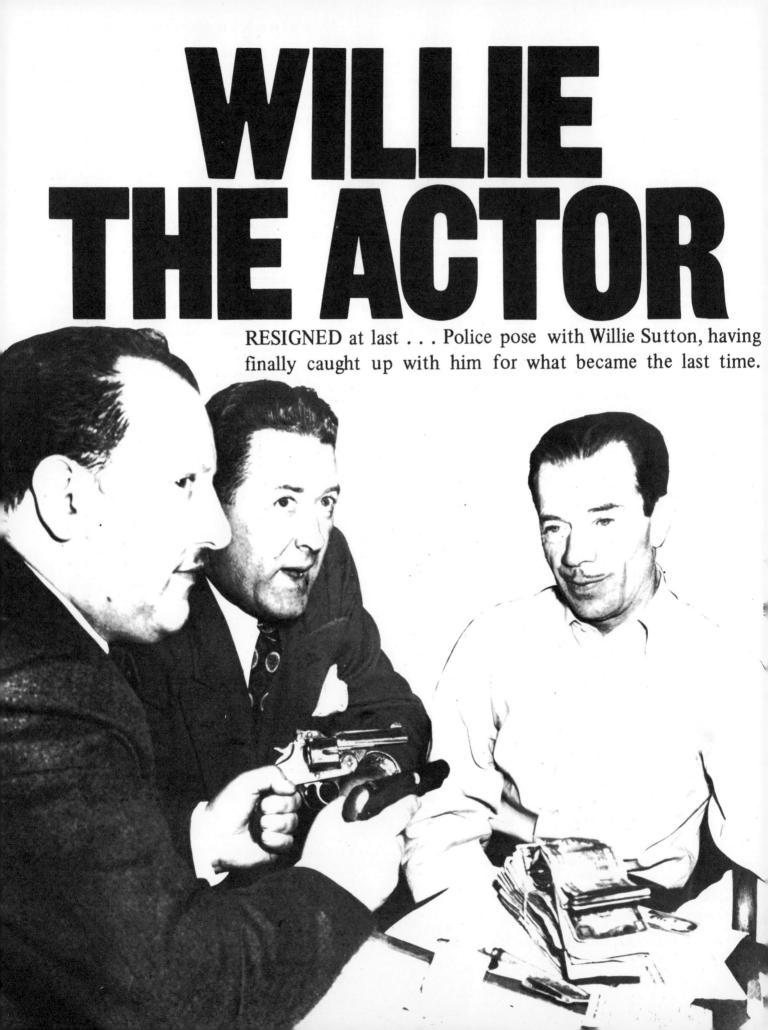

WILLIE THE ACTOR

RESIGNED at last . . . Police pose with Willie Sutton, having finally caught up with him for what became the last time.

THE Waverley School of Drama could be proud of its star pupil, Willie Sutton. He had studied hard for the part, paying particular attention to the make-up. He had flattened his nose, puffed out his cheeks with cottonwool, heightened his complexion. His costume of a bank messenger had been selected with great care. He was word-perfect.

Willie Sutton was about to make his acting debut in a dramatic role which would bring in probably the highest-ever fee for a single performance.

His opening line, "I've got a telegram for the boss," was perfectly timed. It was 8 a.m. and the sleepy doorkeeper of the bank at Jamaica, Long Island, took the familiar-looking Western Union yellow envelope and started to sign. With both the doorman's hands occupied, Willie deftly lifted the revolver from the man's holster and told him, "Now be a good boy and you won't get hurt."

The man was flabbergasted. Raising his hands, he backed into the bank while Willie's accomplice, Jack Bassett, slipped in and shut the door. One by one, the bank staff arrived for work. With Willie's gun prodding him from behind, the doorkeeper followed his usual routine and let them in. Jack Bassett lined up half a dozen chairs against the wall and each employee was forced to sit down with his hands in the air. With the arrival of the manager at 8.30 Willie's first-night audience was complete.

"All I want you to do," he told the manager, "is to open your vault. It would be very silly of you to refuse. If you do, nothing will happen to you but I promise you that the lives of your employees here will be jeopardized."

Polished performance

The line of clerks looked at their manager imploringly. It was a cunning move. With a gesture of resignation, the manager unlocked the vault. Inside was $48,000 in new banknotes, which Willie dropped into his "messenger's" briefcase.

It was 9.40—only 20 minutes before the bank was due to open for business—and Willie Sutton's meticulous dress rehearsals had already shown that there would probably be a few early customers waiting outside.

But the actor had his audience exactly where he wanted them. "We're leaving now," he told the seated employees. "But I have a third man outside. If anyone goes through this door in the next five minutes, he will be shot."

There was no third man, but Willie Sutton knew his threat would keep them glued to their chairs for at least a minute, and that was all the time he needed to make his escape.

He and Jack Bassett slipped out of the door and melted into the crowds hurrying

WILLIE'S WOMEN . . . what his relations were with the two women in his life is unclear. But they certainly adored him.

to work along Jamaica Avenue. It was a polished performance and one which was to be repeated many times to stunned audiences all over the east coast of America. Willie the Actor, the prize—indeed, the only graduate—of the Waverley School of Drama, had arrived.

The Waverley School was one of Willie's most inspired inventions. A few weeks before the bank robbery, he had had imposing notepaper printed with the name and address of the non-existent college. With a contrived story about a college drama production, he had been able to get his bank messenger's uniform from a theatrical costumier. Obtaining the second important "prop"—the Western Union cablegram—had been easy. He

merely wired one to himself, steamed it open and inserted the bank manager's name behind the cellophane window.

It was detailed planning like this, coupled with a genius for make-up and disguises, that earned him the title of Willie the Actor. "I thought of it all as a drama with myself as the director and lead actor," he once said.

Character sketches

If ever there was a frustrated Thespian, it was Willie. Right from the start of his career as America's most successful bank robber, he had been fascinated by make-believe and impersonation.

He learned to put corks in his nostrils to flatten his nose and pads in his cheeks to broaden his face. He dyed his hair or powdered it to make himself look older. He altered his appearance with wigs and moustaches and increased his height with built-up shoes. In an extraordinary series of "character sketches" – policeman, postman, messenger, railwayman, window-cleaner – he cleaned up more than $2,000,000 and became the most wanted man in America. Beneath all his disguises, his real face was such a mystery that he once stood underneath his own "Wanted" poster without being recognized.

Constant temptation

Yet the strange truth about Willie Sutton was that the man of a thousand faces really *was* faceless. Somehow, his own character became swallowed up in his disguises. A mild-mannered and often lonely man, he enjoyed nothing more than reading and gardening.

Girl-friends knew him as gentle and rather diffident. On the run in the 1940s, he worked for two years at an old folks' home, where his sympathetic manner endeared him to the nurses and inmates.

His flaw was that he just couldn't resist robbing banks. Other people's money stuck to his fingers. Some men cannot resist drink, drugs, women or gambling. Willie Sutton's constant temptation was the door to a bank or jewellery store. Every one was a challenge that made his eyes light up. Even passing a bank on a stroll, he automatically sized up its potential and calculated its risk.

It wasn't always the money that fired his compulsion. He once robbed a bank with $40,000 already in his pocket. Although hardly a consolation to his victims, he just couldn't help it.

In the end, he paid a crucifying price for indulging his obsession. So did his friends. For there was a jinx on Willie.

Perfect crime

Although non-violent himself – he never fired a shot in his whole career – nearly every person whose path he crossed met a violent end. Some were shot evading arrest. Others were gunned down by gangsters. Suicide, madness, blindness, the living death of life imprisonment, the voodoo of Willie Sutton touched almost all who knew him. And a succession of pathetic, trusting women discovered too late that life with a fugitive is measured in days, not years.

The inevitability of Willie Sutton's rise to big-time crime – from the day in 1908 when, aged eight, he stole 50 cents from his mother's purse – has a theatrical touch to it, like one of those old Warner Brothers gangster movies, with James Cagney in the leading part.

Born in the rough Irishtown quarter of Brooklyn . . . as a child, progressed from shoplifting to breaking into stores after

dark . . . during the First World War gave up a secure job to earn big money in a munitions factory . . . with the fat pay-packet, a taste for natty suits, silk shirts, fast cars and faster women . . . then the Depression and unemployment . . . the "easy money" lure of organized crime . . . and the apprenticeship, working as a collector for racketeers like Arnie Rothstein, "Dutch" Schultz and "Legs" Diamond.

Willie's solution to any problem was to put his fingers in the till. At 17, he fell in love with Bessie Hurley, daughter of a Brooklyn shipyard owner. They eloped to Poughkeepsie, a romantic adventure financed by $16,000 he had stolen from her father's wages-office. They were hauled back, but Mr. Hurley's influence saved him from a jail sentence. He never saw Bessie again.

So far, Willie had only hovered on the fringes of the underworld. It was a "doctor" who finally provided the prescription for the perfect crime, and who unerringly set him on the path to being Willie the Actor.

Eddie "Doc" Tate had studied science at Chicago University and now employed his formidable knowledge in a way which would have amazed his professors. He was America's top safebreaker, a perfectionist who disdained vulgarities like oxy-acetylene and dynamite, relying entirely on his sensitive fingers, which he protected by white gloves during off-duty hours. The most fiendish locks melted like butter in his hands.

"Doc" Tate's motto was "Plan every detail in advance" and among his golden rules for safer safebreaking was "Always use ordinary tools and leave them all behind when you finish a job, except for your jemmy. Keep that with you until you are clear. Never overlook the possi-

UPI/Quartet

bility of locked doors barring your escape. If you have your jemmy with you, no door is locked against you."

Tagging on to the cutaway coat-tails of the elegant Doctor, Willie embarked on a series of spectacular break-ins. On their first combined effort, they looted four shops in two hours, netting more than $10,000. As a sign that the evening's work was over, the Doctor sportingly left his jemmy on the window-sill of a nearby police-station.

Tip-off

Willie was a star pupil, his skill soon rivalling that of "Doc" Tate. Gradually, the character of Willie the Actor was taking shape. His girl-friend was Adeline "Atchie" Rao, a Broadway showgirl. Sitting in her dressing-room before a performance, he discovered how make-up could completely alter a person's appearance. Fascinated, he watched actors mould their faces like putty, saw them grow younger or age before his eyes.

But it was a chance walk down Broadway that provided the final inspiration. He noticed two uniformed security guards ringing a bell outside a locked store. They were immediately admitted, with barely a glance at their faces. It wasn't only a jemmy that opened all doors, he realized, but a uniform. Quickly checking through a classified telephone directory, he found dozens of theatrical costumiers who specialized in providing convincing uniforms of all kinds. It was better than being handed a key.

CAPTURED AGAIN . . . Willie is brought back into custody after escaping from Sing Sing. Left: Eastern State Jail and the mask Willie made there for escape.

The opportunity to put his theory into practice came quicker than Willie expected. "Doc" Tate decided to take off for a long holiday in California. "You don't need me any more," he told Willie. "You've learned about all I can teach you." It was time for Willie the Actor to take the stage.

Willie Sutton was 24, but it was to be another six years before he could make his debut. From 1925 to 1929 he was a "guest artiste" at Sing Sing and Dannemora jails. Following a tip-off by an informer, he had been arrested and sentenced for burglary. It was in Sing Sing that Willie met Jack Bassett and together they achieved Willie the Actor's first great coup, the robbery of the bank at Jamaica, Long Island, in 1930.

After the robbery, Willie returned home to his wife, Louise. The sudden appearance of $24,000 needed some explaining, but Willie's "training" with the Waverley School of Drama saved the situation. "You'll never guess what has happened," he told her. "My rich Uncle William has died in Ireland and left me all this money. I've just collected it from his lawyers."

Using one disguise after another—but never the same one twice running—Willie went on a rampage of robbery. "Uncle William's legacy" was boosted by the proceeds of 14 break-ins within a few

months. At the Rosenthal jewellery store on Broadway—where Willie used the Western Union messenger trick again—the manager was so terrified that he forgot the combination of his own safe. At the point of a gun, they forced the negro porter to phone the proprietor at his home and ask for the combination—using the flimsy explanation that the manager hadn't turned up. The result was $130,000 of gems . . . and another prison sentence.

The trap they hadn't foreseen was Jack Bassett's love-life. Jack's wife, Kitty Bassett, found out about his string of mistresses and in revenge betrayed him to the police. Under third-degree interrogation, Bassett confessed to the Rosenthal break-in and 13 other jobs, implicating Willie Sutton. As "Doc" Tate had said years earlier in one of his homilies, "Women, whisky and work don't mix."

Steel doors

Willie was a tougher nut to crack. For five days, police beat him with rubber hoses until his entire body, except for his face, was deep purple. Fearing that they might extract a confession under delirium, Willie tore open the roof of his mouth with his fingernail and started spitting blood. He convinced the prison doctor that he had sustained internal injuries and the beating stopped. But his kidneys had been so badly damaged that he passed blood and urine for five months.

Willie's skill at make-up and disguise paid dividends at an identification parade, where victims of nearly all his robberies were asked to pick him out. Nobody recognized him. One victim shook his head and said, "No, the guy who robbed me had a flat nose." Another laughed and said, "This skinny fellow? The man who took my stuff had fat cheeks. I remember it clearly." A third victim was even more impatient. "Don't waste my time," he said. "The man who grabbed my jewellery must have been 60. This fellow is just a kid." For a moment, Willie the Actor thought he had fooled them all. Then the negro porter at Rosenthal's jewellery store stopped in front of him. "That's the man," he said.

Willie went to Sing Sing for a year. Actually, the judge sentenced him to 30 years, but in December 1932, Willie picked four steel "escape-proof" doors in quick succession, climbed over the wall on a ladder hidden by another prisoner and drove off in a car left by an outside accomplice. He was in business again.

A one-man crime wave hit New York. Robbery after robbery bore Willie the Actor's fingerprints. Disguised as a policeman, he took $18,000 from one bank. At a 5th Avenue jewellery store, a fireman turned up and asked to inspect the premises to check if there were any violations of the city fire-prevention laws. When the proprietor, Mr. Isadore Wiatre, recovered consciousness, diamonds worth $45,000 were missing. Posing as an impatient postman whose package was too big to go through a bank's letterbox, he persuaded the caretaker to open the door. Within five minutes, the bank was lighter by $160,000.

But despite these huge hauls, Willie's

SALESMAN Arnold Schuster caught a great deal of publicity after giving police the tip-off about Willie Sutton. He died shortly after: shot in the eyes.

AI. UPI. Quartet

life had become furtive and deprived. By a quirk of irony, the one thing Willie the Actor could never achieve was recognition. A fugitive afraid of voices, shadows, and footsteps, his money melted as he flitted from bolthole to bolthole.

The more notorious he became, the

FORMER convict John Mazziotta was strongly suspected of having taken the underworld's revenge on Arnold Schuster.

more he was rejected as an outcast. He could never return home, although his wife had had a baby daughter. In his search for superficial and safe companionship, he mingled with the crowds at the Roseland dance-hall, where for a dime you could dance with one of the hostesses.

SLAIN in the street . . . Photograph indicates the scene of the Schuster murder and the route of the escaping gunman. Was Willie responsible or not?

After buying a few dollars' worth of companionship, he would return to his lonely apartment and go to bed with a book.

His jinx had already started to cast its shadow. "Dutch" Schultz had died, victim of a gangland killing. Johnny Eagan, one of his partners, had been slain by hoodlums. Another partner, Eddie Wilson, was blinded by a police bullet. Jack Bassett was to spend 32 of his 52 years behind bars and "Doc" Tate choked out his last breath in a prison infirmary. In every way, Willie the Actor was a dangerous man to have around. But not for long. For the law was catching up with him again.

Solitary confinement

The police had picked up Joe Pelango, one of Willie's accomplices in the $160,000 Philadelphia bank robbery. They worked him over and he talked. At breakfast a few days later, Willie Sutton was reading newspaper accounts of Adolf Hitler's accession to power in Germany when there was a knock on the door. He found himself staring into the muzzle of a police tommy-gun. On February 4, 1934, he walked through the gates of the Eastern State Penitentiary—one of the toughest jails in America—to begin a 25-50 year sentence.

If there was one thing Willie prided himself on more than getting into a place, it was his skill in getting out. The prison officers knew it, and for 18 months he was kept in solitary confinement before being transferred to the top-security "7th Gallery". Alert guards, stone walls and thick steel doors weren't the only obstacles to escape. The prison was riddled with informers out to curry favour with the parole board. There wasn't a

chance . . . but Willie the Actor still started working on his first plan to "Exit, left".

It almost ended in disaster. Using a map slipped to him by another prisoner, Willie managed to get into the underground sewage system. After crawling 200 feet, he reached a second conduit full of water and refuse, with a steel door at the end. He plunged into the sewage and swam underwater for 15 feet, his hands groping for the handle of the door. But it was automatically operated—and immovable. Willie's lungs were bursting and there was not room to turn round. As he pushed himself backwards from the door, he could feel himself beginning to black out. Then his head broke the surface. Staggering back along the 200-ft. main conduit, he picked up his clothes, climbed into the prison cellar and got back into his cell. Thirty seconds later, the guards started making the roll-call.

Face mask

Two years dragged by before Willie tried again. With materials smuggled into his cell by fellow-prisoners, he made a plaster of Paris mask of his face and hand. Again, his make-up skill proved useful. He pulled hairs from his head to make eyebrows and a moustache. He fashioned a wig from cord salvaged from his cell-mops. He tinted the mask's cheeks and pencilled in details of eyes, nose and mouth. When friends smuggled in some rope, a grappling hook and a hacksaw blade, he was ready.

On a wet and chilly night, he hunched up his bedclothes, placed the mask on his pillow and let the hand peep from under the blanket. He had already sawed through most of the bars and it only took a few minutes to finish the job. Squeezing on to the window-ledge, he waited for the hoot of a nearby factory whistle which coincided with the change of guard. In the few minutes while the guards were handing over their duties, all he had to do was throw out the grappling hook and haul himself over the prison wall.

Isolation block

But instead of the expected whistle, the prison alarm suddenly sounded and the whole place was alive with guards, shouts and searchlights. Willie had picked the very moment when another group of prisoners had tried to stage a breakout.

Feeling uncomfortably like a figure in a French farce, Willie scrambled back off the freezing window-sill, replaced the bars, hid his tackle, mask and plaster hand and tumbled into bed. "What's going on?" he asked innocently as a warder flashed his torch into the cell. "Two damn fools tried to go over the wall," the man replied.

The most immediate result of the escape

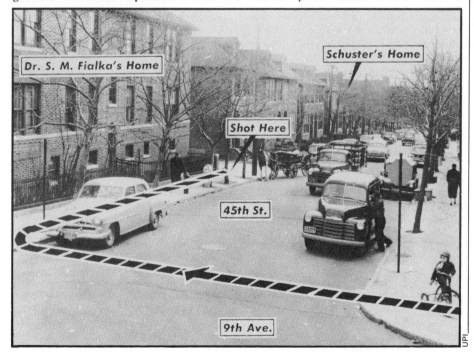

Dr. S. M. Fialka's Home

Schuster's Home

Shot Here

45th St.

9th Ave.

UPI

attempt was an all-round tightening of security. The following morning, a routine search in Willie's cell uncovered his getaway kit and he was committed to the isolation block for two years.

Willie used the time to learn shorthand, typing and Spanish, eventually being allowed to act as secretary to the prison psychiatrist. The work interested him, and he was deeply affected by the letters to the doctor from former prisoners who had been successfully rehabilitated.

"What about me?" he once asked the doctor. "I've been here 10 years now. Don't you think I have learned my lesson?" The doctor's reply was evasive.

"I don't know, Willie. Every time you see a bank, it appears to present a challenge you can't resist."

Willie pressed on. "You don't think I can ever be a useful member of society?" Again the doctor wouldn't give a straight answer.

"Only you can answer that, Willie."

Freedom tunnel

Willie knew his life was slipping away. Outside the penitentiary, the world had changed. Prohibition had been repealed. President Franklin D. Roosevelt had been elected President, served and died. Hitler had come and gone. The Second World War had been fought and won. In the year Willie was arrested, the latest weapon had been the tommy-gun. Now it was the atom bomb.

Towards the end of 1945, Willie and 12 other prisoners—each one with little hope of parole—started digging a tunnel to freedom.

The plan called for backbreaking work. A 30-foot shaft had to be sunk from a cell occupied by a forger named Clarence Kliney, followed by a 97-foot tunnel and an upwards shaft leading to the street on the other side of the prison wall. Yet six months later, it was finished.

The break-out was timed for just after breakfast. One by one, the men lowered themselves into the tunnel and crawled the 120 feet to the end. Only 24 inches of earth separated them from street level. The remaining rubble and tarmac were hacked away and then men burst out, scattering in all directions.

Willie leaped from the hole . . . and ran straight into the arms of two policemen.

"Put your hands up or I'll shoot!" one of them shouted.

"Go ahead then, shoot!" cried Willie in despair. All the men were rounded up and Willie found himself once more in the isolation block, with 10-20 years added to his original sentence.

Incredibly, Willie Sutton still clung to his dream of escape, strengthened by the knowledge that he now had nothing to lose. The first glimmer of hope came in August, 1946, when he and four others were transferred to Holmesburg County Prison, near Philadelphia. After 18 months, an outside accomplice managed to smuggle in a ·38 revolver in a vegetable-delivery lorry. Friends in the prison machine-shop obtained hacksaws and blades, and Willie and the others started sawing slowly through the bars of their cell doors. On February 9, 1947, Willie Sutton was ready for his fourth and most desperate escape bid.

At 10 minutes before midnight on a wild, snowy night, Willie cut through the last threads of his bars and joined the others in the centre of the cell-block. They crouched outside the steel door to the guardroom, set in the hub of the star-shaped prison complex. Every night, the door opened for a few seconds to allow one of the armed guards to slip out and patrol the corridors.

Their only chance was to force their way in the instant the door opened.

They heard the key turn in the lock, followed by a knife-edge of light as the door began to open. Together, they hurled themselves into the guardroom so quickly that the guards didn't have time to reach for their guns. Covering the officers with the .38, they carried on to the engine-room, where ladders were stored.

Using the guards as a shield, and partly obscured by the swirling snow, they carried the ladders across the prison yard. As the officers were placing the ladders against the wall, a trigger-happy sentry in a watchtower let off a burst of machine-gun fire. With presence of mind, one of the convicts shouted, "Stop it! Can't you see we're guards?"

The sentry walked forward to get a closer look, shielding his eyes against the snow, but the convicts shinned up the ladder and dropped over the wall. They raced to a spot three blocks away where a getaway car should have been waiting. It wasn't there. Luckily, a milk-delivery lorry lurched round the corner and they commandeered it. As the lorry rattled towards Philadelphia, the convicts toasted their escape in milk. At his fourth attempt in 13 years, Willie the Actor was free.

The others were quickly recaptured, but Willie had long practice at keeping one step ahead of the law. He scanned the "Situations Vacant" columns of the newspapers, searching for the kind of low-paid, anonymous job where you almost merged into the wallpaper, and where board and accommodation were included. One vacancy was made to measure—hospital porter at Farm Colony, an old folks' home on Staten Island. The New York City authorities had provided the perfect hideout, and under the name of "Edward Lynch", Willie signed on for his $20 a week job and simply evaporated.

Willie enjoyed working at the home and a strange and touching relationship grew up between the fugitive who sought anonymity and the old people who craved company. Lonely, frequently disabled and virtually waiting for death, their plight was worse than his. He listened to their stories, comforted and fussed over them. Willie was so highly regarded by the staff that he was "promoted" to the main women's ward. "I was completely happy there," Willie recalled later, "and I felt humble before the low-paid dedication of those nurses."

Ashen tint

For once, it looked as though Willie the Actor had turned his back on crime and was playing a useful part in life, the part of "Eddie Lynch". Maybe the prison psychiatrist had been wrong all those years earlier, and he *was* capable of rehabilitation. Encouraged by favourable reports from the patients, one of the nurses, Mary Corbett, took him in as a lodger. For the first time since 1931, he had a home. He started going to church.

But there was one profound difference between Willie and the old folk he tended. Their past life was gone, finished, almost beyond recall. Willie's was waiting to catch up with him.

The sense of security he created so carefully was shattered one day in August, 1949, when a voice behind him in the ward suddenly boomed, "Hello, Willie Sutton!" No feat of make-up could have captured the ashen tint that spread across his face as he turned around. But he still retained his composure. "Willie Sutton? Who's that?" he asked.

Gertrude Horgan, one of the nurses, handed him a copy of that day's *Daily News*. Every time a bank was raided, the newspapers cried "Willie Sutton strikes again!" This time, they had used a picture. "You must admit, it looks just like you," laughed the nurse. "You're right," said Willie. "Only if I were Willie Sutton, I wouldn't be working here for $80 a month." They all laughed the incident off. But it had shaken Willie to the soles of his shoes.

He decided to leave Farm Colony. Mary Corbett was enthusiastic. "I always knew you could do better for yourself if you tried," she said. Willie brushed up his typing and shorthand and went the rounds of the employment agencies. The answer was the same in each one: "Sorry, but you're too old." At 50, the normal life which had never begun was already over.

Years earlier, Willie had hidden $18,000 in a buried jar in a field near Laurenton, Long Island. He dug it up, intending to use the money to start his own little business. But his past life was now on his heels. One afternoon, he just happened to walk past Manufacturers' Trust Company Bank, in the New York City suburb of Sunnyside. Like a long-dis-

used combination lock suddenly manipulated by sensitive fingers, his mind started automatically clicking into place. Almost unconsciously, it registered the entrance, the condition of the roof, the number of people going in and out. Willie walked inside and noted the position of the cages, the alarm system, the number of employees. The old compulsion had not died. He visited the bank several times, mentally photographing vital details. It was vulnerable and he knew it.

Fatal compromise

Willie was torn in a cruel mental struggle. Everything in him rebelled against returning to crime, yet he knew he could crack that bank. In the end, he made a fatal compromise. He passed on his information to a gang of cracksmen. A few weeks later, the bank was robbed of $64,000 in a "carbon copy" of one of Willie's operations. Once again, the papers were filled with Willie the Actor's picture and he was back on the run, with nowhere left to run to.

On February 18, 1952—two years after the Sunnyside robbery—24-year-old Arnold Schuster, a salesman working in his father's clothing factory, was sitting in a New York subway train. The man opposite seemed familiar and Schuster looked at him for a long time.

Then it dawned on him. It was the same face that he had seen staring out a hundred times from the warning leaflets the police had distributed to every clothing store in the city. Leaflets which said: "If this man tries to hire a uniform or costume from you, contact the police immediately." It was Willie the Actor.

Willie had noticed the way young Schuster had been watching him and got out at Bergen Street station. Schuster followed him as far as a garage, then went to tell the police.

Willie Sutton was tinkering with his car battery—it refused to start—when the two policemen loomed over him. At first, they just asked to see his licence. But they returned with a detective.

"You'd better come along to the station with us," one of them said. "You look like Willie Sutton." Desperately, Willie insisted it must be a case of mistaken identity, but when they checked his fingerprints at the police station he knew there was no longer any hope of concealing his identity. His shoulders drooped and he looked like a tired old man. "I might as well be dead now," he said. "You can kill me for all I care."

The first public reaction to Willie's arrest—except among those he had robbed—was a tinge of regret. The law had finally caught up with a colourful character who had become a legend in his lifetime. On Sunday, March 9, the public mood abruptly changed to revulsion. While walking home to his father's store, Arnold Schuster was ambushed by an underworld trigger-man and shot in each eye—the ritual form of killing for an informer. Willie's jinx had claimed another victim. Although he disclaimed all knowledge of the crime—and there was no proof that he was connected in any way with the killing—he instantly forfeited all public sympathy. It was a tragic way to bring home the lesson that, for all his non-violence, Willie still belonged to the brutal and degenerate world of the professional criminal.

Willie Sutton was charged with the

IRRESISTIBLE . . . That was how Willie Sutton thought of the Manufacturers' Hanover Trust Bank. He just had to check out the possibilities for robbery.

robbery of the Manufacturers' Trust Bank at Sunnyside. Throughout the trial, he vehemently protested his innocence, sticking to his story that he had merely passed on the information.

Was Willie innocent? Or deep down, was he just ashamed to admit that he had failed himself; that after attempting to go straight, he had finally been unable to control the criminal urge; that in the end, he had confirmed the prison psychiatrist's conclusion that he would always be an habitual thief?

Several witnesses testified that he had led the gang which raided the Sunnyside bank, but he claimed they had been "conditioned" to recognize him after seeing so many pictures in the newspapers.

It could be the ultimate irony that, after 32 successful robberies, Willie the Actor was convicted for the one crime he didn't commit. The point is academic. At 52, Willie Sutton was sentenced to 30-years-to-life. Taking into account sentences still outstanding, it meant he would be behind bars until the year 2087. "They said I was the best," he told the court sadly. "But what is the result? I'm 51, I've spent most of my adult life in prison or in hiding and now I haven't a penny."

But there was still a flash of the old humour. When the suit he was wearing at his arrest was searched, $7000 in cash was found in the pockets. Asked why he hadn't banked it, Willie replied laconically, "It's never safe in a bank."

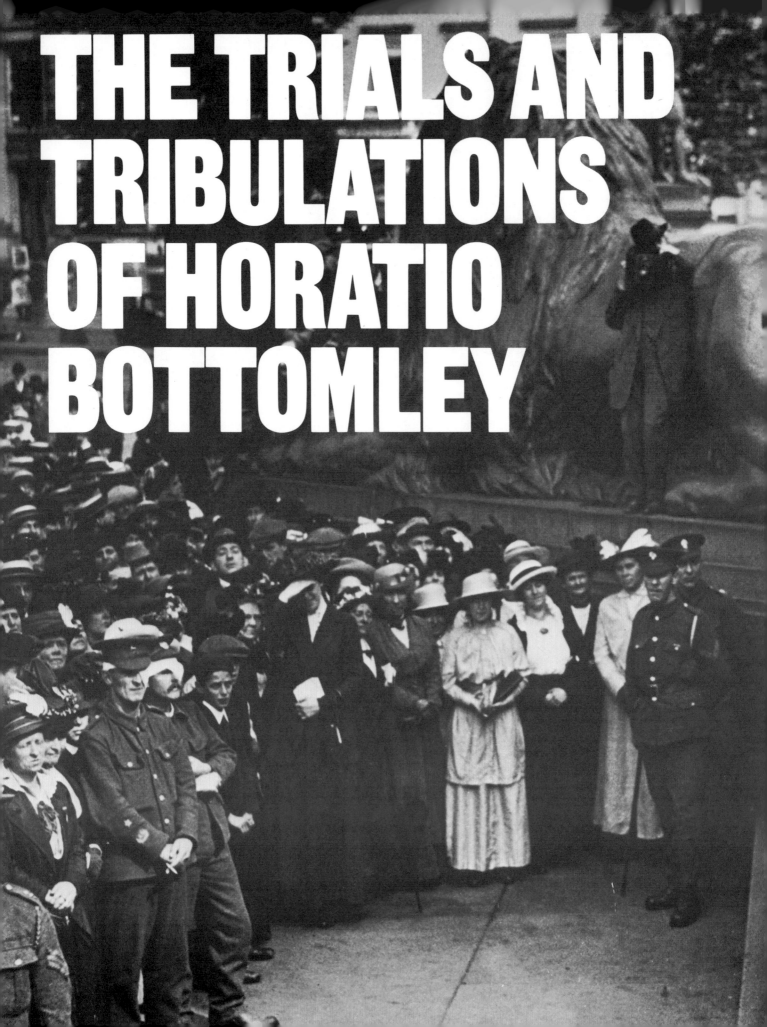

THE TRIALS AND TRIBULATIONS OF HORATIO BOTTOMLEY

Syndication International

2ⁿᵈ Batt. LONDON REGT.
·ROYAL FUSILIERS·

GOOD RECRUITS WANTED
JOIN US – DO IT NOW

HEADQU

2ⁿᵈ
·L·
RE
(ROYAL
9 Tuft
Westm

HARANGUING the crowd in London's Trafalgar Square in an attempt to recruit army volunteers. It was not so very patriotic; Bottomley was paid well.

FAINT connections with Charles Bradlaugh (above and right) were enough to give Bottomley the idea of posing as the celebrated atheist's illegitimate son.

Mansell Collection

ONE OF the most colourful characters ever to appear in the dock of the Old Bailey was Horatio William Bottomley, Member of Parliament, financier, company promoter, journalist, public orator, newspaper and magazine proprietor, theatrical backer, racehorse owner, gambler and bankrupt. He was twice acquitted in spectacular trials in which he was charged with fraud and conspiracy, and in another trial the magistrate refused to convict him of promoting an illegal lottery, in spite of the evidence.

It was the fourth and final trial, which opened at the Central Criminal Court before Mr. Justice Salter on May 18, 1922, that proved his undoing. This time he was accused on 24 counts of fraudulently converting to his own use more than £150,000, entrusted to him by members of the public for investment in his so-called Victory Bond Club and three other enterprises.

Mr. Travers Humphreys, perhaps the greatest criminal lawyer of his time in England, led the prosecution. Bottomley, as usual, conducted his own defence.

By this date, the 62-year-old defendant looked bloated and dissipated. "In truth, it was not I who floored Bottomley," said Humphreys after the trial. "It was drink. The man I met in 1922 was a drink-sodden creature, whose brain could only work on repeated doses of champagne."

Both Bottomley's parents died when he was a child and in consequence he was placed in an orphanage school. He ran away from the school to become successively an errand boy, a clerk in a solicitor's office and a shorthand reporter in the Law Courts, where he acquired considerable legal knowledge as well as forensic skill.

For many years he pretended to be the illegitimate son of the celebrated atheist Charles Bradlaugh, whom he strikingly resembled; actually his father was a tailor's foreman who ended his life in a lunatic asylum. But he did have a somewhat tenuous connection with Bradlaugh through his mother who was a sister of Bradlaugh's friend George Holyoake, the founder of the Co-operative Movement.

His first business venture, a small suburban weekly newspaper, ended in bankruptcy and prosecution for fraud. He was acquitted and the judge who tried the case was so impressed with his conduct of it that he advised him to become a barrister. As an undischarged bankrupt, however, he was unable to obtain admission to any of the Inns of Court, so that he turned instead to the shadier occupation of promoting Australian gold mining companies.

Recklessly extravagant

By the time he was 37, it was estimated that Bottomley had made £3 millions in this way. However, his companies failed regularly, and in the first five years of the present century he was served with no less than 67 bankruptcy petitions and writs. At the same time Bottomley was recklessly extravagant in his personal expenditure. He started a racing stable, and although he won the Cesarewitch and other prizes on the turf, he squandered large sums on various theatrical enterprises, besides a luxurious flat in London, a large country house in Sussex, where he kept his racing stables, and a villa in the south of France.

He posed as a philanthropist and this helped to secure his election to Parliament as Liberal MP for South Hackney in 1906. Three years later he was again charged with fraud and acquitted. But shortly afterwards he was made bankrupt for a second time so that he had to resign his seat in Parliament.

The outbreak of war in 1914 provided Horatio Bottomley with a fresh opportunity for self-advancement and, incidentally, self-enrichment. He told his friends he would break with his "sordid past", in which he had latterly been involved in the organization of gigantic lotteries and sweepstakes. He now became a recruiting officer for the armed forces and stomped the country making patriotic speeches — for not less than £50 a time — exhorting the young men to join the colours.

These speeches, along with a series of propaganda articles which he wrote for the *Sunday Pictorial,* for which he was likewise well remunerated, made him a nationally known figure. He was thus able to pay off his old creditors and to obtain his discharge from bankruptcy.

At the General Election in 1918 he got back his old parliamentary seat in South Hackney, this time as an Independent. Shortly afterwards the Government floated a Victory Loan, in which the smallest bonds were of a nominal value of £5 and were issued at £4 5s. Bottomley conceived the brilliant idea of forming a club, so that the "little man" and the "little woman" could share in the loan by subscribing smaller sums; with these Bottomley would buy Victory Bonds or National War Bonds in the club's name. Interest on the club's holding of stocks, and the bonuses, represented by the Government's annual redemptions, were to be combined in a fund which would be distributed by lot among the subscribers; and the subscribers would also be entitled to withdraw their subscriptions at any time and get their money back in the same way as Government Premium Bond holders can do today. Bottomley invited the public to subscribe in units of 15s 6d, which represented the purchase price of a £1 share, the proceeds of which he would incorporate in the club's funds.

Defamatory pamphlet

The public fell for the scheme in a big way. Between June 1919 and the end of the year, Bottomley received subscriptions to the amount of nearly half a million pounds. Some of this he handed over to the Treasury Department, but much of it—so it was alleged—Bottomley applied to bolster up various companies in which he was interested, or else barefacedly transferred to his own pocket.

In October 1921 the Chancery court appointed a receiver to examine Bottomley's enterprises. At the same time he quarrelled with an associate named Reuben Bigland, who proceeded to publish a defamatory pamphlet about him in which he described the Victory Bond Club as Bottomley's "latest and greatest swindle" and told how he "gulled poor subscribers to invest one pound notes" in the Club. Bottomley replied by prosecuting Bigland for criminal libel.

Bigland put in an elaborate written plea of justification, but in the event he was not called upon to prove his accusations, since Bottomley abandoned the prosecution and Bigland was formally acquitted. This made Bottomley's own prosecution inevitable.

Since Bottomley was still an M.P., the normal practice would have been for the Crown to be represented by one of the Law Officers. But such was the legend of Bottomley's invincibility in the courts that Mr. Lloyd George's Government, which was highly nervous about the proceedings, declined to instruct either the Attorney-General or the Solicitor-General. They offered Humphreys any K.C. he might choose to lead him, however, but Humphreys declined. Though he had no specialized knowledge of accountancy, he put aside all other work to prepare the prosecution case, had an extra table brought into his chambers in the Temple, and worked for weeks with the government accountants, so that he eventually became as familiar with the questioned figures as Bottomley himself.

Two favours

The preliminary proceedings took place in March 1922 at Bow Street Magistrates' Court. On his way to the court, Bottomley waylaid the prosecutor's clerk and asked for a few minutes' interview with his master. Humphreys consented provided his junior counsel was present.

Bottomley asked for two favours at the interview. First, he wanted a short adjournment each day at 11.30, so that he could have a pint of champagne, which he said he simply could not do without if he was to get through the morning. He added that he would call it his "medicine" to the magistrate. Humphreys agreed provided that the magistrate had no objection, and this was conceded.

Secondly, Bottomley wanted Humphreys to suppress the name of a certain lady into whose account, which he had opened for her in the same bank, he had paid various Victory Club subscriptions. Humphreys agreed provided Bottomley would state that the account was his own private one. If there was any attempt at prevarication, said the prosecutor, the lady would be put into the witness box. In the event the hearings before the magistrate went according to plan, and Bottomley was duly committed for trial.

In his opening speech to the jury at the Old Bailey, Humphreys showed how very large sums from the Victory Bond Club had passed to its founder. For example, there was a payment of £5000 for the upkeep of racing stables in Belgium, and another to a wine merchant for over a hundred dozen bottles of champagne, while a company which was merely an alias for Bottomley benefited by £20,000.

Many thousands more went to one of his numerous lady friends who acted as another go-between. Altogether over £150,000 in cheques drawn on the Club's account had been diverted in this way. Books dealing with the Club accounts were absent, there were never any Club trustees except Bottomley, and there was never any regular audit.

Since the Club's affairs had been taken over by the Receiver, 85,000 persons had written in claiming back their money, but of course it was impossible to call these people as witnesses. But the fraction Humphreys did put into the witness box could be taken as a fair cross-section of the whole.

Central Press Ltd/Popperfoto/Syndication International

PARTNERS who fell out . . . Reuben Bigland (above) quarrelled with his former associate, Bottomley (left), and pilloried him. Centre: Bottomley's home.

A colonel who said he was a regular reader of Bottomley's weekly *John Bull*, in which the attractions of the Victory Bond Club were extensively puffed, stated he had lost £10,000 which he had invested in it. At the other end of the scale were domestic servants, unemployed, needy widows and the like who had been persuaded to part with a few pounds, amounting sometimes to all their savings. Many were deluded by the following advertisement:

> "A New Road to Fortune
> £1 gives you an opportunity of
> winning £20,000."

One woman, named Mrs. Alice Twichett, said she sent £10 to Bottomley after reading the advertisement. In April 1921, she wanted her money back. She wrote four letters and eventually forwarded the certificates. But she never got a penny back. Another woman witness who had invested £5 eventually received a letter giving the result of the draw, after she had asked to have her £5 returned.

"You did not get a prize?" asked Humphreys.

"No," replied the witness.

Only one witness, a retired naval officer, who was also a regular reader of *John Bull*, admitted when cross-examined by Bottomley that he had no grievance against him, and that he did not charge him with the fraudulent conversion of the £4 he had invested in the bonds. But this witness also admitted that he had been asked to subscribe for a French Premium Bond, although he had not parted with any more money. This was a new scheme of Bottomley's by which Victory Bonds could be exchanged for French Government Bonds, Bottomley making a profit on each exchange.

Pertinent question

A stockbroker gave evidence to the effect that Bottomley had owed him £10,000 since 1912 and that eventually the debt had been settled through an arrangement by which Bottomley gave the broker scrip of National War Bonds for that amount.

"In exchange for the £10,000," Bottomley asked the witness in cross-examination, "did I claim against you a considerable number of shares?"

"Yes, under the settlement," the broker agreed.

"On very favourable terms, as it happened?" Bottomley continued.

"I should think so, undoubtedly."

Humphreys asked the witness one extremely pertinent question on re-examination. "Just tell me the name of the company in which those shares were?"

"John Bull Limited." This was, of course, Bottomley's magazine company. By that time *John Bull*, though still edited by Bottomley, had been taken over by Odhams Press.

Subscriptions or not?

An official of the Midland Bank, who had been employed by Bigland to make investigations, gave particulars of the Victory Bond account and the account of another Bottomley concern, the Northern Territory Syndicate. A cheque for £25,000 drawn on the Victory Bond account was paid into the Northern Territory account, and shortly afterwards the sum of £5,000 was withdrawn from the latter to purchase Belgian francs in order to defray the expenses of Bottomley's racing stable at Ostend.

"Are you satisfied," Bottomley asked this witness, "that considerable sums of money, other than subscriptions, were paid into the Bond Club's account?"

"The bank would not know whether the credits were or were not subscriptions to the club," replied the bank official. "Considerable sums were paid into the Victory Bond Club account which were cheques drawn in your name." He added that the bank would know nothing of the ins and outs of the account. The cheques were simply paid in.

Bottomley went on to ask the witness whether he could say from his investigation of the Victory Bond Club account how many debits represented repayments to subscribers for their money. The reply was that he had not totalled them up, but there were a large number of small items.

"I suggest that they came to nearly £50,000?"

The witness said he could not accept or deny that, but on being pressed by Bottomley he admitted he should have thought they were quite £50,000.

Emotional appeal

"Do you say," Bottomley went on, "it is or is not wrong to draw on a trust account, assuming that the monies you draw out were due to you?"

"I think that is a lawyer's question and not a banker's question," was the cautious reply. "A great deal would depend as to whether the bank was suspicious."

"Take the £25,000 transferred from the Victory Bond Club to the Northern Territory account. Would that appear

COLOURFUL and well-known, Horatio Bottomley's name was rarely out of the news. He fostered the belief that he was a true patriot helping the war effort.

Syndication International

SUNDAY PICTORIAL

THE WAR UP TO DATE

MARCH 14, 1915

WHY I BELIEVE IN PROSPECT OF EARLY PEACE.

By HORATIO BOTTOMLEY (Editor of "John Bull.")

Mr. Horatio Bottomley is the Editor of "John Bull." One of the most eloquent and human speakers in Great Britain, he has since the war began proved himself a powerful agent for gathering recruits to the colours, and stimulating the patriotism of the country. As speaker, a journalist, a politician, and a lay lawyer, Mr. Bottomley is a public character of untiring energy.

AM one of the few individuals who are predicting that we are now witnessing the beginning of the end, and that the month of June, if it does not mark the technical finish of the war, will find hostilities suspended pending discussion of the terms of peace. I do not propose to base this view upon any special expert military or naval knowledge. I suppose no man has had experience and opportunities has accumulated a more profound store of ignorance of such matters than have I. But these considerations do not count so much as others which I propose to refer.

These impressive phenomena are not the outcome of diplomatic intrigue. None of the Allied Governments has stooped to cajole or intimidate an independent nation. Such forces as may gather to our aid will come freely to the defence of freedom. By her gross violation of international right, followed by the cynical repudiation of every article in the civilised code of war, Germany has contrived to array against herself every force in Europe which makes for liberty and righteousness, and if (I am not certain that it is so), as Napoleon declared, the moral factor in war is to the material as three to one the...

THREE FACES of a con-man . . . Horatio Bottomley seen (left to right) as a young man, a respected and successful politician, and after his spell in jail.

Mansell Collection/Syndication International

a suspicious transaction?"

"It would all depend. I don't say it would be."

At this point the judge, who was well nicknamed "Drysalter," broke in. "Is it a question for the witness to say what he suspects? Is it not rather a question for the jury?"

Before opening his defence, Bottomley asked the judge to say if he was entitled to call 100,000 members of the Victory Bond Club, if necessary, to prove that they had had their money back in full, by way of rebutting the few witnesses called by the prosecution. Mr. Justice Salter refused to give any ruling but contented himself with saying that he would listen to any evidence and objections placed before him. He then directed Bottomley to proceed with his opening, which the defendant did with a strongly emotional appeal to the jury.

Shady financial transactions

"You may have entertained a great opinion of me," he said, "and thought that, whatever my faults in days gone by, I have endeavoured to do my duty to my King and country. Now you are asked to change your opinion, and to say that all the time I was an arrant humbug and scoundrel." The only question for the jury, he went on, was whether he had dealt fraudulently with the funds and securities of the Victory Bond Club.

"You have got to find," he declared, "that I had the intention to steal the money of poor devils such as ex-soldiers who subscribed to the club. You have got to find that Horatio Bottomley, editor of *John Bull*, Member of Parliament, the

man who wrote and spoke throughout the war with the sole object of inspiring the troops and keeping up the morale of the country, who went out to the front to do his best to cheer the lads—you have got to find that that man intended to steal their money. God forbid!"

"I swear before God," he concluded, "that I have never fraudulently converted a penny of the Club's money." But this in effect was just what Travers Humphreys's searching cross-examination revealed. Even his "patriotism" was financially rewarding. "Were you not paid for your patriotic speeches during the war?" the prosecutor asked him.

"Never a farthing for my recruiting meetings," answered Bottomley. "But later on, as lecturer on the war, I got certain remuneration." He was a bankrupt at the time, he added, and had to get his living. Pressed for details, he agreed that his lecture receipts for a time averaged between £300 and £400 a week. In fact he had made £27,000 out of his speaking campaign.

"So the war did you pretty well?" queried Humphreys.

"No, it did not," replied Bottomley angrily. "As a professional journalist and lecturer, I delivered a large number of lectures, as distinct from attending a large number of recruiting meetings. I was most desirous of clearing off my liabilities and getting back into Parliament. I am not at all ashamed of my work as a professional lecturer . . . I think it is rather unfair to introduce this."

There was, however, nothing unfair about the way the prosecutor took Bottomley through the tangled web of his

shady financial transactions, in which there was an occasional gleam of humour. For instance, his friend the eccentric Independent M.P. Pemberton Billing had bought the captured German submarine *Deutschland* for £5,500 and sold it to *John Bull* for £15,000 paid out of the Victory Bond Club account. But it did not become the property of the Club, since at that time the Club owed him (Bottomley) more money than the submarine cost.

"They could have the vessel now, if they liked," Bottomley added amid laughter. The *Deutschland* was to be taken round the country on exhibition, but before she was ready an explosion took place on board injuring several people. The exhibition when it was mounted resulted in a considerable loss.

At a loss for a reply

Questioned about a meeting of Club members he had called in the Cannon Street Hotel in January 1920 for the purpose of explaining the position to them, Bottomley said about 200 were present. "Did they all speak?" asked Humphreys.

"Many of them at the same time," said Bottomley, and his reply raised a laugh.

At the same time Bottomley had circulated a report in which it was stated that the stock of the Club consisted of £500,000 in bonds.

"Was that true?"

"Well," said Bottomley, "it is not quite the phrase I should have used myself." Nevertheless he admitted responsibility for the report, in which it was also stated that the bonds were held by the Club's bank. In fact, those left had been transferred to Bottomley's private account with the Credit Lyonnais in Paris.

It was practically the same thing, said Bottomley. Yet by February 1921 all the remaining stock had been sold. "Is that practically the same thing as remaining with the Club's bankers?" For once Bottomley was at a loss for a reply.

Guilty on all accounts

In his defence Bottomley called two former members of his staff to prove that £3500 had been repaid to Victory Bond subscribers. But not a single one of the 100,000 people whom Bottomley had stated had been repaid their subscriptions in full appeared in the witness box.

In his final speech to the jury, Bottomley again reached the height of his characteristic rhetoric. "You will not convict me," he fulminated. "The jury is not yet born who would convict me on these charges. It is unthinkable." He then pointed to the large sword suspended above the Bench.

"The sword of justice will drop from its scabbard if you give a verdict of Guilty against me," he went on. "I say it with a clean conscience. I say it without one thought of fear or misgiving. I know my country and my country's people, and knowing you, and knowing myself, and knowing the truth about this matter, without one atom of hesitation, one atom of fear . . . I know by the mercy of God and the spirit of justice you will liberate me from this ordeal." He thereupon burst into sobs, so affected was he by his own oratory.

But the jury was not impressed when they heard the judge's scrupulously fair summing up of the evidence. In less than half an hour they found Bottomley guilty on all accounts, except one which was withdrawn on the judge's direction. Meanwhile, the sword of justice remained securely in its scabbard.

"Horatio Bottomley," said the judge to the man in the dock, "you have been rightly convicted by the jury of a long series of heartless frauds. These poor people trusted you, and you robbed them of £150,000 in ten months. The crime is aggravated by your high position, by the number and poverty of your victims, by the trust which they reposed in you. It is aggravated by the magnitude of your frauds and by the callous effrontery by which your frauds were committed. The sentence of the Court upon you is that you be kept in penal servitude for seven years."

Expulsion from the House

"I was under the impression, my Lord," said the prisoner, "that it was sometimes put to an accused person, 'Have you anything to say before sentence is passed upon you?' "

"It is not customary in cases of misdemeanour," replied Mr. Justice Salter.

"Had it been so, my Lord," observed Bottomley, "I should have had something rather offensive to say about your summing up!"

With that remark Bottomley was taken to the cells below and thence to Wormwood Scrubs prison. A few days later he was formally expelled from the House of Commons, after he had apologised, in a letter to the Speaker, for the slur he had brought upon it. His expulsion, he wrote, was "a punishment far greater and more enduring than any sentence of any Court of Law . . . But I have myself to blame, and all I can do is to ask Members of the House to judge me as they knew me".

After serving just over five years of his sentence, Bottomley was released on licence. A Sunday newspaper paid him £12,500 for a series of articles on his prison experiences, a considerable sum for those days. Some old friends, mostly money lenders who had done well out of him in the past, rallied round with more money, and he started a magazine which he called *John Blunt*.

A pathetic end

It was a failure from the start, as were his other journalistic ventures at this time. He was again made bankrupt and had to part with "The Dicker", his large country house near the Sussex Downs. He was eventually driven to applying for the Old Age Pension, which was granted and then for some reason immediately withdrawn.

His wife died, and in his last days he was cared for by an ex-musical comedy actress named Peggy Primrose, whose shows he had backed in more prosperous times. Finally, he made a pathetic series of appearances at the Windmill Theatre, but after a few days he collapsed and was admitted to Middlesex Hospital. He died in May 1933. "What a wasted life," commented Travers Humphreys when he heard the news. "What a pity!"

GRIM-FACED but confident, Bottomley leaves court during the Bigland hearing. The politician later withdrew his action, only to face prosecution . . .

Syndication International/Quartet

THE MASS MURDERERS

The demented features of slayer Richard Speck stare from a prison authority photograph, taken after his capture in July 1966. Speck methodically murdered eight student nurses in a Chicago hostel. But a ninth girl escaped and later identified him. Fleeing the police, the killer holed up in a skid-row hotel—pictured in the background—and attempted suicide.

BETWEEN June, 1918 and April, 1926 the district of Rudraprayag in northern India was terrorized by a savage killer who despatched his victims by tearing their throats out. He claimed 126 lives. Yet when the man who finally shot him saw the body, he was surprised.

"Here was no fiend, who while watching me through the long night hours had rocked and rolled with silent fiendish laughter at my vain attempts to outwit him, and licked his lips in anticipation of the time when, finding me off my guard for one brief moment, he would get the opportunity he was waiting for of burying his teeth in my throat."

The deadly killer was only an old leopard, whose muzzle was grey and whose lips lacked whiskers. Yet over a period of eight years he had brought more terror to Rudraprayag than Jack the Ripper brought to Whitechapel, or Peter Kürten to Düsseldorf. The hunter Jim Corbett ended the reign of terror with a single bullet through the shoulder.

Why is it, then, that we feel no horror when we read of the man-eater? Because, as Jim Corbett said: "This was the best-hated and most feared animal in all India, whose only crime — not against the laws of nature but against the laws of man — was that he had shed human blood, with no object of terrorizing man, but only in order that he might live."

Beasts of prey

This goes to the heart of the matter. When killing is performed in this clean, natural way, we feel no horror, because there is no *evil* involved. It is the human capacity for evil, for cruelty, that frightens us. And here we face a strange paradox. The worst modern criminals, from Jack the Ripper to Richard Speck and Dean Corll, *are* beasts of prey, in the most precise sense. They stalk through modern cities like a hungry tiger, completely indifferent to the fear and sufferings of their victims. Their only desire is to satisfy an appetite.

A typical case is that of Jerry Thompson, who was not a mass murderer, but simply a rapist. His one and only murder victim was found on the morning of June 17, 1935, in a ditch in the cemetery at Peoria, Illinois. She was a pretty girl, and her white dress had been pulled up under her armpits; her torn underwear lay nearby. The medical report revealed that she had been raped and strangled. She was identified as 19-year-old Mildred Hallmark, a waitress, who had vanished the evening before, shortly after leaving the cafeteria where she worked. When the police appealed for information, several girls came forward, and disclosed that they had also been raped. The attacker was a good-looking young man who had offered them a lift, then driven them to a quiet

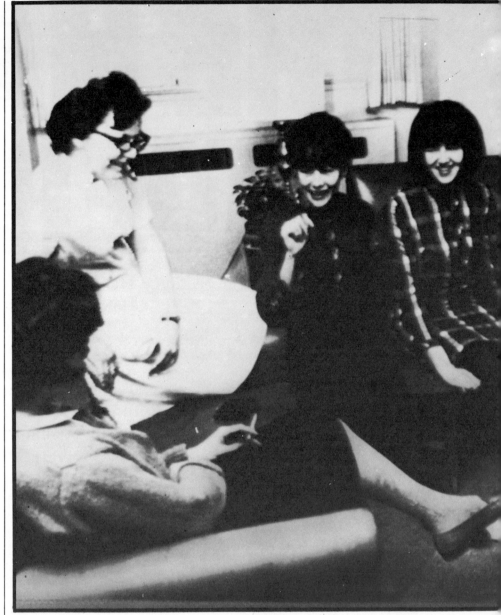

place and forced them to submit.

The police decided to make a general appeal through the newspapers, asking for all women who had been attacked to come forward, with a promise of complete anonymity. They hoped that one of these women might be able to give them some clue to the identity of the rapist. The response startled them. More than 50 women came forward, and it became clear that the police were looking for a highly successful sex-maniac.

In many cases he had stopped beside a girl walking along a lonely street and dragged her into the car. If she resisted or screamed, he silenced her with a violent punch on the jaw or in the stomach. He would drive to a lonely place, undress the girl, and commit rape. Then he would take out a camera, and take photographs of her naked, sprawled in obscene positions. He would tell the girl that if she told the

HAPPIER DAYS. A week after this photograph was taken, five of the six women shown were dead. Judith Dykton, seated in left background, was not in the dormitory when killer broke in. Right, police remove a shrouded corpse.

police her name would appear in the newspapers, and everyone would know what had happened to her. There are few girls who do not prefer privacy to revenge.

Five days after the discovery of Mildred Hallmark's body the police had the break they needed. A girl named Grace Ellsworth told them that she had been picked up by a clean-cut, well-spoken young man who had offered her a lift. In an empty road, he stopped the car, and tried to kiss her. When she slapped his face, he hit her on the jaw, then beat her up so viciously that she was incapable

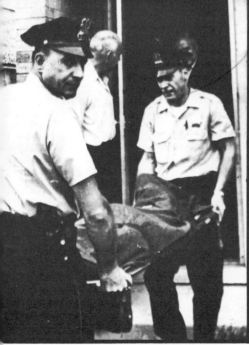

of resisting as he undressed her. Afterwards, he dragged her into the headlights of the car, took photographs of her with a box camera, and warned her that if she reported him to the police the pictures would be sent to her friends and relatives.

And then, some weeks later, a man had been introduced to her at a dance. She was certain this was the rapist. When she asked him if they hadn't met before, he denied it. But *she* was sure. The man had been introduced to her as Jerry Thompson. The police had no way of tracking down Jerry Thompson. But they suspected that Mildred Hallmark had known her killer. She was a shy girl who would never get into a car with a stranger. They went to her father, who worked in a tractor factory in East Peoria, and asked him if he knew a Jerry Thompson: he did. Thompson worked in the machine shop, and was a neighbour of theirs.

Ripped underwear

Thompson proved to be a handsome young man in his mid-twenties, who was engaged to be married. He flatly denied being the rapist; but Grace Ellsworth picked him out from a line-up, and a lie detector test revealed that he knew more than he would admit about the murder. The detective in charge of the case shocked a confession out of him by throwing Mildred Hallmark's ripped underwear into his lap.

Thompson broke down, he confessed to picking up Mildred, offering her a lift, and taking her to the cemetery. She had resisted, and he had struck her under the chin and throttled her into unconsciousness before tearing off her clothes and raping her in the back seat. Then, he said, he realized she was dead. In his room, police found dozens of photographs of the naked women he had raped, and a diary detailing dozens of rapes that he had committed since he was 16. He was electrocuted on October 15, 1935.

The Thompson case is interesting because we can see that he was living by the "law of the jungle". *All* healthy young men, particularly the "dominant 5%", would like to be able to make love to dozens of pretty girls. No doubt it is partly fear and caution that prevents them from becoming Jerry Thompsons. But it is also, perhaps, a sense of decency; they do not *want* to hurt another human being, any more than they would want to set fire to a haystack or torture a cat. So desire is outweighed by revulsion.

Jerry Thompson was obviously a man of exceptionally strong sexual desires; but his photograph, with its cold eyes and slightly cruel mouth, also reveals that he lacked the human warmth that would have led him to restrain these desires. He may not have been evil or cruel by nature, but after the first few rapes he would begin to

think of himself as a criminal, a lone beast of prey, and so develop this aspect of his personality.

Thompson's rapes were committed between the mid-1920s and 1935. This was the "Age of Sex Crime", especially in America. During the Second World War, the rate of sex crime rose steadily—which is to be expected when thousands of men are away from home, deprived of their wives. But it continued to rise after the war. Why? Because men who thought they were coming home to a new world where they would be treated like heroes found themselves in the same old ruthless mechanized civilization, where they were mere cogs in a wheel.

Such a civilization produces the effect which Karl Marx called "alienation", the feeling of not belonging. The mass murderers of the fifties and sixties were all "alienated men", "outsiders": Haigh, Heath, Christie, Richard Speck, Howard Unruh, Charles Manson, Charles Whitman, Ian Brady.

Not all these men were sex criminals; Haigh was motivated by money. Unruh and Whitman and Manson by paranoid hatred of society; but the sense of alienation meant that they had no fellow feeling for their victims. And the Richard Speck case shows something even more disturbing: the alienation turning into cruelty. *Not* sadism; Speck did not actually torture any of his victims; but he took pleasure in terrorizing them.

Speck's orgy of murder came to light at just after 5 a.m. on Thursday, July 14, 1966, when a girl rushed out on to the balcony of a nurses' hostel on the south side of Chicago and began screaming. Two patrolmen who rushed into the building found a nauseating scene. In various rooms there were the naked bodies of eight women. Most of them had been strangled, and also stabbed many times. Their hands had been tied behind them. None of them had been raped, but a perverted sexual attack had been made on one of them, Gloria Davy.

The one survivor, a Philippino girl named Corazon Amurao, told how there had been a knock on her bedroom door sometime after midnight. She opened it, and found herself facing a man who smelt of alcohol and held a gun. He had a pockmarked face and blond hair. This was Richard Speck, a 25-year-old seaman. Speck rounded up six girls into one dormitory bedroom, and tied their hands with sheets that he cut up with a knife. He kept explaining that he needed money to get to New Orleans, and promised not to hurt them.

This indicates that, in spite of his intention of committing murder, he still maintained some "fellow feeling" for the intended victims. Three more nurses came home late; Speck took their money, and tied them. Finally, Speck took one of the girls out of the room. A few minutes later he took another, and they heard a cry.

Corazon Amurao was a courageous girl, more "dominant" than the others; she urged them to free themselves and try to "jump" the man. They replied that he didn't appear to be violent, and that they had better sit still. Miss Amurao decided to roll under a bed, where she hid. The man continued to come in and out for hours. Then all was quiet. When an alarm clock went off at five o'clock, Miss Amurao rolled out from under the bed, crawled on to the balcony, and began to scream for help.

A sultan with his harem

Speck had left fingerprints all over the place, and Corazon Amurao was able to give an exact description of him, even to a tattoo on his arm, with the words "Born to raise hell". From the seaman's knots that bound the dead girls, the police guessed that the man was a sailor. There was a labour exchange much used by sailors not far away. The police soon established the identity of the man they were seeking, and half an hour past midnight, on the following Sunday, Speck was taken into the Chicago Cook County Hospital, his wrists slashed in a suicide attempt. The doctor who attended him saw the tattoo, and called the police.

Psychiatrists who examined Speck learned that he had been known at school as a "sulky loner" who hated his stepfather. He drifted from job to job—labourer, garbage collector, truckdriver and seaman. At the age of 20 he married a 15-year-old girl, and they had a baby daughter, whom he adored. But after five years of fighting, they divorced.

He drank heavily, and took drugs—yellow jackets, red-birds—amytal and seconal drugs that can cause hallucinations. In Dallas, Texas, earlier in 1965, he had attacked a young girl as she was parking her car, holding a carving knife to her throat. Sentenced to 18 months in prison, he was soon released on parole—which he instantly skipped. To drinking companions he was known as a braggart who boasted about all the women he had slept with, but who never seemed to be able to date a girl.

In April, 1966, when Speck had returned to Monmouth, Illinois, where his relatives lived, a barmaid named Mary Pierce vanished from a tavern where Speck drank; her naked body was later found in a hog house behind the tavern. Speck had often asked her for a date. After leaving Monmouth, Speck had worked on Great Lakes ore boats, but had been rushed into hospital for an appendix operation in early May.

He began to date a nurse there; she found him gentle, but full of hatred of society. He talked vengefully of two people in Texas he wanted to kill, and he told someone else that he intended to return to Texas and kill his ex-wife Shirley; significantly, the only Chicago nurse who was sexually assaulted closely resembled his wife. On the day before the murders, he had been drinking heavily in Chicago bars.

Chicago was in the midst of a heat wave, and there were riots when negro children turned on fire hydrants to bathe and police tried to stop them. Towards midnight, drunk and drugged, Speck approached the hostel that he had often passed—the building that was full of young girls. He was like a fox creeping into a chicken house. And the length of time he took to kill eight girls suggests that he was enjoying every moment of it: for a few hours he was a sultan with absolute power over a harem of girls.

It was two years after Speck had been sentenced that the police of Salem, Oregon, realized that they were dealing with another sex killer who had claimed several victims. Linda Slawson, of Aloha, vanished in January, 1968; Jan Susan Whitney, 23, had vanished from McMinnville in November, 1968; 16-year-old Stephanie Vilcko, who vanished in July, 1968, was found in March, 1969, on the banks of Gales Creek, her body so decomposed that the cause of death could not be established.

An ordinary transvestite

On April 23, 1969, Linda Salee, 22, vanished when she was out shopping for a birthday present for her boyfriend, and on May 10 a fisherman on the bank of the Long Tom River, near Corvallis, saw a body floating below the surface. It proved to be female, half clothed, without bra or panties, and had been held down by a heavy car-part. It was Linda Salee, and she had been raped and strangled. Not far away, the police found another body, 19-year-old Karen Sprinker, who had vanished on March 27. Her underclothes were also missing; she had been raped and strangled, and was held down by part of a car engine.

In April, a 15-year-old schoolgirl had been grabbed by a man who tried to force her into a car, but she managed to break away. Not long after, two schoolgirls had seen a man dressed in women's clothes in the car park of a big store; the police thought it possible that he was an ordinary transvestite—a man who dresses in women's clothes because he wants to be a woman. However, soon after the finding of the two bodies, the police had a break.

A girl student from Oregon State University told them of a date she had had with a strange man. He had claimed to be a Vietnam veteran, had spent an evening with her in the lounge of her dormitory, and had told her she ought to "be sad" on account of the girls who had been killed. He seemed a gentle, quietly spoken man, and it was only afterwards that she began to wonder if it was worth telling the police. It was one of hundreds of tips, but they checked it.

It led them to a mild, 30-year-old married electrician and photographer named Jerry Brudos, and they were soon convinced that this man, who made a habit of telephoning girls and claiming to be a Vietnamese veteran, knew something about the murders. He had a police record for stealing women's underwear, and for trying to force two girls to strip by threatening them with a knife. He had been caught near the women's dormitory of the Oregon State University carrying stolen women's clothing, and wearing a bra and panties.

Suspended from the ceiling

The police searched his home, near the State Hospital, to which he had been committed after the sexual charges. Brudos's wife seemed to have no suspicion that her husband had been leading a double life—her time was taken up tending to their two children—but she admitted that he spent much time in the photographer's dark room adjoining the house. In this dark room the police found what they were looking for—photographs of the dead girls.

It became clear that Brudos had kidnapped them, taken them to the studio, and there suspended them from the ceiling by their wrists while he had committed sexual assaults and photographed them. Brudos confessed to killing the four missing girls, though the death of Stephanie Vilcko, the 16-year-old, is still unsolved. He was sentenced to life imprisonment.

Comparing these three cases—Thompson, Speck, Brudos—we immediately note the violence and sadism of the more recent ones. Thompson, a typical killer of the "Age of Sex Crime", only wanted to possess attractive girls, with or without their consent. Speck and Brudos had a deep, psychopathic hatred of women.

It would not, of course, be true to say that torture murders were unknown in the "Age of Sex Crime". One of the grimmest cases on record is that of Donald Fearn, a 23-year-old railway mechanic of Pueblo, Colorado, who in 1942 kidnapped Alice Porter, drove her into the desert to an old adobe church used by the Indians, and whipped and bound her with red-hot wires. He killed her with a hammer after raping her and threw the body into a well;

LIFE IMPRISONMENT stretching ahead of him, sex killer Jerry Brudos leaves the courtroom for Oregon State Penitentiary. Linda Slawson (inset) was his first victim.

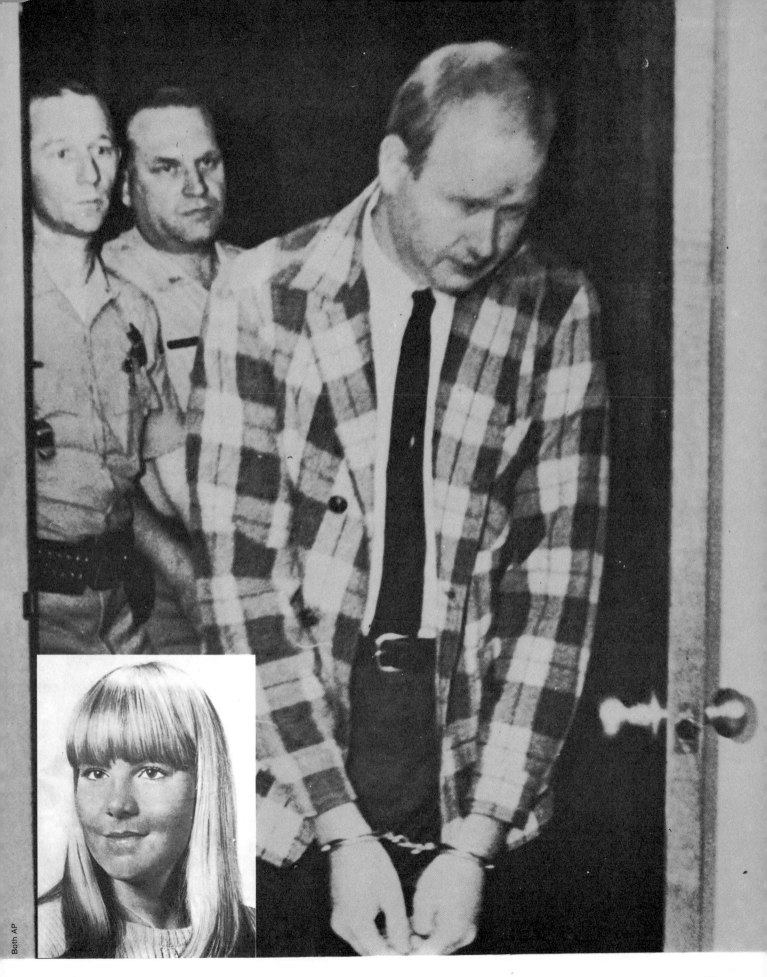

Both AP

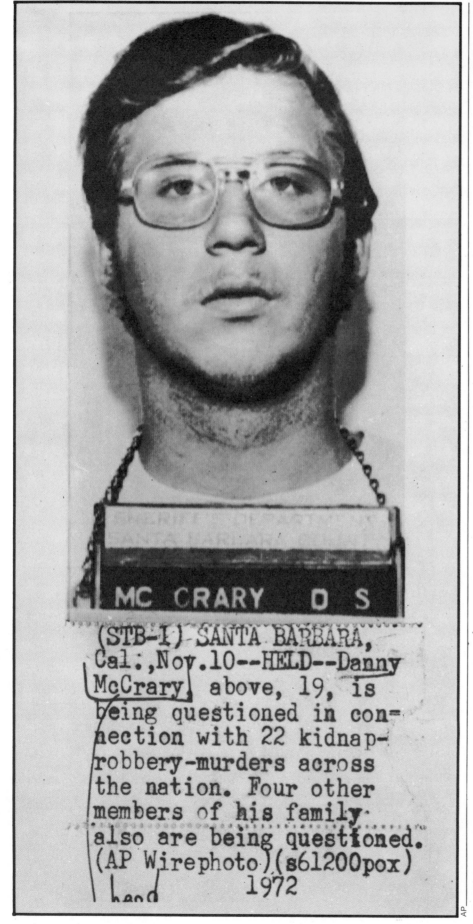

(STB-1) SANTA BARBARA, Cal.,Nov.10--HELD--Danny McCrary, above, 19, is being questioned in connection with 22 kidnap-robbery-murders across the nation. Four other members of his family also are being questioned. (AP Wirephoto)(s61200pox) 1972

he was executed in the gas chamber.

There was the mysterious "Moonlight Murderer" of Texarkana, Texas, who in 1946 attacked courting couples, and in two cases killed the man and then spent hours torturing and raping the girl before killing her.

A burnt-out car found near the murder site suggests that the murderer destroyed the evidence—police had tyre tracks of the murderer's car—and then committed suicide by flinging himself under a train. However, crimes like these are solitary examples of sick perversion which stand out from the general pattern of crime as exceptions. The murders of Richard Speck fit all-too-neatly into a pattern of crime that is becoming increasingly familiar in our time.

Seen and not heard

There is a strange sense of *lack of motivation*. We are confronted with patterns of crime that would have baffled criminologists of the old school, like Lombroso or Ivan Bloch. In February, 1968, the bullet-riddled body of August Norry, a landscape gardener, was found on a hillside in San Mateo County, California. A few months later, a pretty 18-year-old pony-tailed blonde named Penny Bjorkland confessed that she had killed him "for fun"; he was a stranger who had offered her a lift, and she had suddenly felt the urge to shoot him—for no reason.

In June, 1972, Santa Barbara police arrested a man in connection with a supermarket stick-up. He was 47-year-old Sherman McCrary, and the investigation led police to arrest McCrary's wife Carolyn, his daughter Ginger, his son Danny and his son-in-law Carl Taylor.

And as the police investigated the itinerant family, they came to the conclusion that they had been, jointly, responsible for murdering more than 20 young women, mostly waitresses and shop assistants, who had been abducted and raped over the past two years. The women were apparently aware that their husbands were involved in orgies of robbery and rape, but felt that a housewife should be seen and not heard.

And so the mass murders continue: after Manson, John Linley Frazier, Juan Corona, Herb Mullin, the McCrarys, Edmund Kemper, Gerry Schaefer, Dean Corll. In all these cases there can be no doubt that the fundamental problem is "alienation". Karl Marx would have smiled grimly. But if he was still alive, he would have to admit that *Das Kapital* holds no solution to this most baffling and disturbing problem of our time.

FAMILY AFFAIR. Danny McCrary (left), his parents, sister and brother-in-law, were jointly responsible for the murder of more than 20 young women before capture.

THE SAVAGE KILLERS

They are sadists. They kill for kicks. And most stranglers have sex as a motive. Dentist Arnold Axilrod (left) fed his patients with "love pills" in order to knock them out before he raped them. And he killed one patient—Mary Moonen (below).

Both UPI

THE word "strangler" has a brutal ring: like "slasher" and "ripper", it conveys an idea of physical violence, and this is no linguistic accident. In fact, most stranglers have been violent and brutal men. The act of strangling suggests a deliberate savagery.

A man who kills with a gun wants to get it over as quickly as possible, and a man who kills with a knife may be possessed by a vindictive fury, his basic aim being to destroy, to extinguish the spark of life. But the strangler is a man who takes pleasure in close contact with his victim. It takes several minutes to kill someone by strangulation, and during that time the strangler holds the choice of life or death; by simply relaxing his grip, he can allow the victim to breathe again. So strangling is a more wilful and deliberate form of murder than most, and it is never free from a touch of sadism.

It is therefore not surprising that in the great majority of cases stranglers are motivated by sex. Christie, the rapist of Notting Hill, chose to strangle his victims after he had rendered them unconscious with a coal-gas "inhaler", and then stripped and assaulted them. It would have been just as simple to have smothered them with a pillow, or even to gas them; he preferred strangulation because it was another form of "rape".

Life of murder

Earle Nelson, the "Gorilla murderer", strangled and outraged 22 women during his incredible career of murder in North America and Canada; the word "outraged" here has a certain frightful accuracy, since he tore open some of the bodies with his bare hands. Peter Kurten, the Düsseldorf sadist, often grabbed women in dark streets and throttled them until he achieved a sexual climax. If he achieved the climax while the victim was still alive, he left her, and, strangely enough, some girls who went out with him more than once actually allowed him to throttle them as they had intercourse; Kurten told one who protested: "That's what love's all about."

It follows, then, that female killers seldom commit murder by strangulation. The very few known cases involve highly dominant women, and the sexual *motif* is usually present somewhere. There was Nina Housden, who lived near Detroit: a passionate, violent and neurotic woman who was pathologically jealous of her bus-driver husband Charles. In 1947 he left her. Just before Christmas that year, she invited him over for a drink "for old times' sake", got him drunk, then strangled him with a clothes line.

The next day, she dismembered him and wrapped the parts of the body in newspaper. But from then on, luck was against her. She set out with the parts of

the body in the car, intending to dispose of them in the Kentucky Hills. The car broke down in Toledo, Ohio, and the garage proprietor was surprised when the woman said she would wait in the car, even if it took a week to repair.

A garage mechanic looked into one of the evil-smelling parcels on the back seat while Nina slept, and discovered a human leg. She was sentenced to life imprisonment. Then there was Mrs. Stylou Christofi, who strangled her daughter-in-law, stripped her naked, and tried to burn the body on a bonfire in the back yard of her Hampstead home in London. The motive was sexual jealousy of her son's wife, and this is underlined by the stripping of the body.

Pathetic case

Perhaps the most pathetic case of a female strangler was the Scotswoman, Susan Newell, who, in June 1923, strangled the 13-year-old boy who brought her newspapers; her husband had deserted her, and she was living alone. The following morning, together with her 8-year-old daughter, Janet, Mrs. Newell took the body to Glasgow in a go-cart.

As she climbed out of a lorry that had given her a lift, the cart slipped, and a head and foot protruded from the wrapped bundle inside it. A woman who saw this from an upstairs window called the police. Mrs. Newell was found guilty, and in due course hanged. A psychiatrist had declared that she was not insane. It seems probable that the motive for the crime was sexual. Sex-starved women have often been known to approach young boys. He may have struggled or threatened to tell, and she strangled him.

There is no complex Freudian reason for this association of strangling with sex. It is simply that, of all forms of killing, strangulation is the one that most directly expresses resentment. And, as police officers know, there is usually *some* sexual motive concealed in a strangling case, even if it is not at once apparent. For example, when the strangled body of 35-year-old John Mudie was found in a chalk pit near Woldingham in Surrey, the police were at first inclined

WOMEN STRANGLERS . . . Nina Housden (left) and Stylou Christofi. Mrs. Housden murdered her husband and put his dismembered body in her car. Mrs. Christofi killed the wife of her son, Stavros (below). Then she tried to burn the girl's naked body on a bonfire. Her motive . . . sexual jealousy.

London Express

AP

to believe that the motive was robbery.

Letters in the victim's room led them to Thomas Ley, ex-Minister of Justice for New South Wales, Australia, and to John Smith, a foreman builder who had been hired by Ley to help murder John Mudie. It eventually transpired that Ley had been insanely jealous of Mudie, believing that he was the lover of Ley's ex-mistress, Mrs. Maggie Brook. The belief had no foundation whatever; but when Ley succeeded in luring Mudie to his house in Kensington, he administered a brutal beating, then strangled him.

Even in the case of the death of a woman, the sexual motive may not at once be apparent. When the body of 21-year-old Mary Moonen was found in a driveway in a fashionable quarter of Minneapolis in April 1955, there was at first nothing to suggest a sexual attack: Her red coat, black skirt and white blouse were untorn, and the skirt had been pulled well down over her thighs. Her panties were apparently undisturbed, the autopsy revealed no sexual attack.

A handbag underneath the body contained five dollars, so the motive was clearly not robbery. But Mrs. Moonen had certainly been strangled, and had had intercourse not long before her death. At her home in East 17th Street the police discovered that she was the mother of a 9-month-old daughter, and that she was living with her father, an elderly retired man in poor health. Her husband was in the army, in Korea.

Mystery lover

This offered the police their first real lead, for Matthias Moonen had been overseas for six months. And Mrs. Moonen was found to be three months pregnant. Who, then, was her lover? Here they seemed to encounter a dead end. Her father seemed certain that she had no lover. She was a good Catholic, deeply in love with her husband, devoted to the baby. She was a regular churchgoer. It seemed impossible that she could be having a secret affair.

Dentist's pill

The police questioned the victim's sister, Mrs. Donald Newton, a pretty girl in her mid-twenties. At first, she could provide no clue. Then, when the police told her that her sister had mentioned a dental appointment on the day of her murder, Mrs. Newton looked thoughtful. She was able to tell them the name of Mary's dentist: it was Dr. Arnold Asher Axilrod. He was a well-known figure in Minneapolis, having served as mayor during the war, and since then taken an active part in civic affairs.

He *had* been Mrs. Newton's dentist, but she had walked out one day and never gone back. Why? Because Axilrod had given her a pill that had knocked her

73

out for six hours. When she had wakened up, he had "talked suggestively", and on a later occasion he had made a pass at her. But that had not prevented her re-commending Axilrod to her sister when she needed a dentist. And the sister knew that Axilrod had given Mary the same "knock-out pill" on a number of occasions, and had to drive her home afterwards.

When the police called on Mary Moonen's doctor, the case suddenly be-gan to simplify. The doctor told them that Mary claimed Axilrod was the father of the unborn child. He had given her a pill that made her groggy, laid her on the couch and had sexual intercourse with her. Dr. Axilrod, a middle-aged man with dark hair and dark moustache, was brought in for questioning and quickly admitted killing Mary Moonen. He claimed that she had often visited him and accused him of being the father of the child, which he denied.

Wait in car

On the day of the murder she had again accused him of fathering the child. He had asked her to wait for him in his car, then driven off with her. She threatened that she would expose him; then, said Axilrod, he blacked out; and when he came to, he was alone in the car. "I guess I did it," said Axilrod, sighing. "No one else was there."

The police now discovered that they already had a complaint against Axilrod on file. Three weeks before the murder a 17-year-old schoolgirl had called at his surgery for treatment. He had given her a pill. When she woke up, six hours later, Axilrod was sitting beside her. She had no idea whether any assault had taken place, but she was angry at being kept in his office until the early hours of the morning. Axilrod drove her home, and she had reported the matter by phone.

The police found that Axilrod seemed to prefer female patients — he had few males on his books, and at least 20 women told of being put to sleep with a knock-out pill, and waking many hours later, lying on the couch. Newspapers talked openly of Axilrod's "love pills" — the laws of libel being less stringent in America than in Europe.

The prosecutor at his trial described him as an amorous philanderer who drug-ged his pretty victims so they could not resist his sexual advances. The defence confined itself to trying to show that the police had not proved their case against Axilrod: for example, the victim's clothes had not been properly examined, but had been left in a damp morgue for five months. They also called a surprise witness — the victim's brother-in-law, Donald Newton.

Newton was serving a three-month sen-tence for indecent exposure, and had

told a cell-mate that he could crack the case wide open. However, he only added to the confusion; when asked whether he had been at work on the evening of the murder, he replied that he must decline to answer the question "because it might incriminate me".

This naturally gave rise to specula-tion about whether he meant he had some connection with the murder — although, on balance, it seems more likely that he was referring to the crime for which he was serving a sentence. Another witness, a taxi driver, declared that he had seen Mrs. Moonen get out of Axilrod's car and drive off with two men. But the jury re-mained unconvinced. They found Axil-rod guilty of manslaughter, and he was sentenced to between 5 and 20 years in the State prison.

Aggressive impulse

This final ambiguity about the Axilrod case is characteristic of many strangula-tion murders. When a man seizes a woman by the throat, his intention may only be to silence her; alternatively, he may be expressing some aggressive impulse that intends to stop short of murder. This means that, in many cases, the real solu-tion should perhaps be in the hands of a psychologist rather than a policeman. The following case of Frederick Field may

THE CHALK PIT KILLERS . . . Ley (in front) and Smith are led into court. They killed John Mudie (inset) and left his body in a chalk pit (opposite).

be taken as a typical example.

On October 2, 1931, the almost naked body of a young woman was found in an empty shop in Shaftesbury Avenue, London. She had been strangled. It did not take the police long to identify her as a prostitute, 20-year-old Norah Up-church, who was well known in the area. Suspicion quickly came to rest on the man who had the keys to the empty shop, an electrician, Frederick Field, who claimed he had given them to a man who wanted to rent the shop.

The police could establish no obvious motive for the crime — why should anyone kill a prostitute for sex? So although both the police and the coroner were con-vinced Field was lying, a verdict of mur-der by persons unknown was returned. On the whole, robbery seemed the likeliest motive. In 1933, Field, now in the Royal Air Force, walked into a newspaper office and said he wanted to confess to the murder of Norah Upchurch. It soon be-came clear that, if Field *was* guilty, his confession was basically false.

For example, he said he had strangled the girl with his hands; but she had been

Press Association

strangled with a belt. It seemed likely that he had confessed to get money out of the newspaper, which had treated his story as an "exclusive" and talked to him for hours before informing the police. Field went on trial, and now withdrew his confession, saying he made it only because he was "fed up" and he was having trouble with his wife. The judge instructed the jury to find him Not Guilty.

Prostitute's body

Then, in April 1936, the body of a prostitute was found in her room in Clapham; she had been suffocated. She was identified as Mrs. Beatrice Vilna Sutton; but no one had seen her with her killer. That evening, Frederick Field, who had deserted from his unit, called on a girlfriend and told her mysteriously that she would soon read something interesting in the newspapers. The girl's mother, thinking Field looked insane, telephoned the police.

The deserter was arrested, and at the police station he suddenly confessed to the murder of Mrs. Sutton. His description of her room was circumstantial—

and nothing had yet appeared in the newspapers. At his trial, Field tried the same trick as before: repudiating his confession, declaring he had made it because he was "fed up", but it was obvious that this time he knew too much about the crime to be innocent. The jury found him guilty, and he was sentenced to death. Police suspected that he may have been responsible for the murder of at least four more prostitutes in the Soho area.

The Lucie Berlin murder investigation, which took place in 1904, certainly deserves a high place among epics of forensic detection. Lucie Berlin was a 9-year-old girl, well developed for her age, who lived in a slum tenement in Berlin. On June 11, 1904, a boatman on the River Spree saw a bundle floating in the river and pulled it out. It contained the headless and limbless torso of a child, who was soon identified as Lucie Berlin, who had been missing for two days.

It was definitely a sex murder; the child had been raped, and her parents declared that she had been told repeatedly never to go off with a strange man. This led the investigators to wonder if she had

been killed in the slum tenement at 130 Ackerstrasse. They questioned all the other tenants. On the floor above Lucie's parents lived a prostitute named Johanna Liebestruth. A man who was also in her room identified himself as Theodore Berger, and gave another address.

It was only later that the police discovered that Johanna had been in prison for three days—for insulting a client—at the time of the murder, and that Berger, her lover and pimp, had lived in her room during that time. They also learned that Berger was proposing to marry Johanna—which caused some remark among their neighbours, since he had been steadfastly refusing for the past 18 years.

More parcels, containing the missing head, arms and legs, were found in the ship canal. Berger was taken to view these remains, but he continued to insist that he knew nothing about the child's death. Johanna Liebestruth was taken to police headquarters and questioned; she had nothing to hide, and she was even frank about the reason Berger had finally agreed to marry her. On the day Lucie's body had been found, she had come home from gaol and had discovered that a wicker suitcase was missing.

Making love

Berger had admitted that he was responsible; he had taken a prostitute back to the room, and only after lovemaking had he admitted that he had no money. He gave the woman the suitcase instead. And to placate Johanna for his infidelity, he had agreed to marry her.

The police asked Berger about the suitcase, and he instantly denied knowing anything about it. A few days later, a bargeman handed the case to the police. The stains in the basket proved to be of human blood; so did certain spots on the floor of Johanna Liebestruth's room, and Berger was charged.

What had happened was pieced together at the trial. One day not long before the murder, Lucie had been in Johanna's room, standing on her head, and Berger had noticed how well formed her legs were. When Johanna was in prison, Berger became sex starved. He invited Lucie into the room and attempted indecent assault on her, but she struggled; he strangled her, raped her, then dismembered the body and transported it to the river in the wicker suitcase, which he then threw away. Berger was executed.

It is an interesting reflection that, although the Boston Strangler achieved more notoriety than any murderer since Jack the Ripper, few people can actually remember his name. Crime experts have always found it puzzling that it is the *idea* of strangling that seems to have a morbid fascination for the public, rather than the strangler himself.

THE VICTIM . . . prostitute Norah Upchurch. Airman Frederick Field (below) confessed to strangling her. But later he claimed he had made up the admission.

Popperfoto. London Express.

DEAD GIVEAWAYS

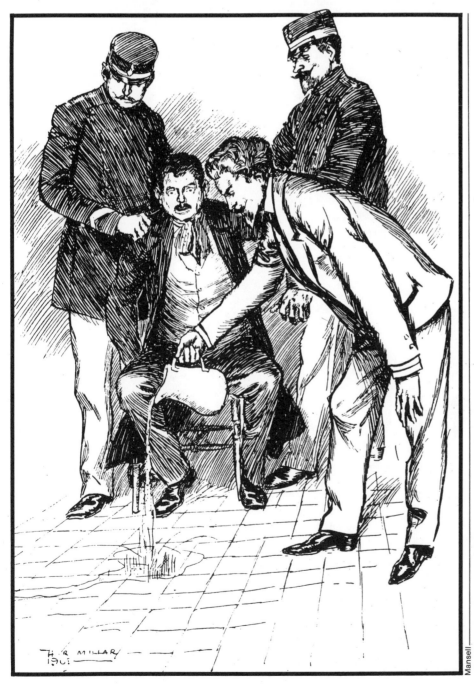

One little clue would bring mystery man Pierre Voirbo to the guillotine . . . straight from the room in which he had perpetrated his horrible crime and washed away (he thought) every last trace.

EDGAR WALLACE wrote a novel called *The Clue of the Twisted Candle,* in which an ingenious murderer succeeds in sealing a room by wedging a candle under the heavy latch of the door. As the candle gradually bends in the warmth of the room, the latch—inaccessible from outside—falls into its groove. Wallace was writing in the early days of forensic science, but, even so, his stratagem would have given little trouble to most experienced police officers. To begin with, some of the soft candle wax would inevitably have scraped off on the underside of the heavy latch, and the most stupid detective would have worked out the truth within minutes.

In real life, most "vital clues" are altogether less obvious. In the two hundred years or so since its beginnings, scientific crime detection has reached a high degree of efficiency. Even so, the kind of brilliant deduction practised by Sherlock Holmes plays little part in the solution of modern crimes. It is a matter of hard work, patience and luck.

We can see all three of these elements in the classic case of the demob suit, recounted by Superintendent Bob Fabian of the Yard. In the summer of 1946, Police Constable Arthur Collins attempted to detain five men who were trying to enter a building in Warwick. He was so badly beaten and kicked that for a time it was feared that he might die. The five men escaped, and the only clue was a small piece of cloth torn from the jacket of one of the men by the constable's wife—who had tried to come to the rescue of her unconscious husband. The Warwick police decided to ask the help of Scotland Yard, and Fabian was put onto the case.

The cloth was photographed, and the photographs sent off to tailors all over England. Then it was exhibited in the window of a local newspaper office. An ex-army officer was able to tell Fabian that it was undoubtedly from a demob suit. Fabian plodded to the nearest Ministry of Supply Depot in Birmingham; there, a check with a register showed that this pattern had been manufactured by a firm in Wellington, Somerset.

The police drove through the night—only to be told, at the factory, that this cloth had been enough for no less than five thousand suits. Moreover, soldiers often sold them to "wide boys" at the gates of the camp. However, they were able to give Fabian the address of two factories in Birmingham and one in Glasgow who had bought the cloth. Fabian drove back to Birmingham. Neither of the two factories had started using their consignment yet.

Fabian went on to Glasgow. There a supervisor looked at the torn fragment, and was able to tell, from the stitching, the name of the man who had made it into a suit. "Stitching is as distinct as handwriting," he said. Finally, the long-shot paid off. The workman looked at the cloth, and was able to recall that the suit was made for an exceptionally tall and broad man—it had had to be specially made, so he remembered it.

Foul well-water

The Ordnance Depot at Branston, near Burton-on-Trent, was able to give Fabian the name of the ex-soldier for whose demob they had ordered the suit, and the police found him at the Birmingham address to which the suit had been posted. When the police constable's wife identified him as her husband's assailant, the big Irishman (6 feet 2½ inches tall) broke down and admitted his part in the robbery. He received four years' penal servitude.

This same quality of incredible patience can be found in a case that certainly ranks among the epics of classic detection. It took place in 1869. During the January of that year, a restaurant owner in the Rue Princesse, Paris, noticed that the water from the well tasted foul. He investigated, and found a parcel floating in the water. When it was opened it proved to contain the lower half of a human leg. The horrified restaurateur sent for the police. A young detective named Gustave

Savage Attack On Warwick Police Officer
THEATRE STREET SCENE

POLICE continued the search over a wide area yesterday for the man who savagely attacked P.C. Arthur Collins, of Warwick, late on Sunday night and inflicted severe head injuries with the officer's truncheon.

P.C. Collins, who is in Queen Elizabeth's Hospital, Birmingham, was still unconscious when inquiries were made yesterday, although there had been a slight change for the better in his bodily condition.

He was preparing to go to bed at his home in Theatre Street, Warwick, ...ay, when, shortly before midheard suspic'... ...e dresse... ...chec...

A TORN FRAGMENT of cloth from the jacket of a policeman's assailant was the improbable key that unlocked the classic case of the demob suit.

Macé was placed in charge of the case. He looked down the well and found another parcel. In it was another leg, encased in a stocking.

Doctors told Macé the legs were almost certainly a woman's. Acting on this assumption, Macé obtained the files of 122 missing women and set about tracing them. It took him months, and finally there were only three left. Shortly after Macé had finally succeeded in tracing these remaining three, the doctors admitted that they could have been wrong. The legs were womanish, but could have belonged to a man. Macé heaved a sigh and started all over again.

He had two leads. On December 22 of the previous year, a policeman had met a man wandering along the Rue de Seine carrying a hamper. Because of the late hour, he asked the man what was in it. The man said he had just arrived in Paris from the country by train; unable to find a cab, he had been forced to walk with his hamper of country products.

He looked so honest that the policeman let him go, but his description—short, round-faced, with a black moustache—led Macé to suspect that this was the same man who had been seen a few days earlier

throwing lumps of meat into the River Seine. Someone asked him what he was doing, and he said he was baiting the river because he intended to fish the next day. Since then, large gobbets of meat had been fished out of the river—too big for the average fish to swallow.

The stitches on the parcel in which the first leg had been sewn had a professional look about them. Moreover, why had the murderer chosen the restaurant to dump the leg? It might, of course, be a dissatisfied customer who wanted to spoil the trade. Or it might be someone who had lived in the upstairs part of the house at some time. He asked the concierge if there was a tailor in the house. No. Had there *ever* been one? No. But there *had* been a tailoress. That sounded a long-shot, but Macé had no other lead. He interviewed the girl, who told him that she often did jobs for other tailors. Did any of them ever visit her at the house? Many of them did, she said; one in particular, M. Voirbo, was very kind and helpful. He often fetched water up from the well for her.

Strange habits

Voirbo was a tailor, and he knew the well: Macé asked the girl if this Voirbo had any special friends. There *was* one old man, she said, a M. Bodasse. She didn't know where he lived, but he had an aunt who lived in the Rue de Nesle. Macé didn't know the aunt's exact address, but compared to tracing a hundred or so missing women it was child's play to locate her, Madame Bodasse was able to tell Macé that her nephew lived in the Rue Dauphine. He was a retired craftsman who had been a tapestry manufacturer. Oddly enough, he hadn't been seen for some weeks now, but that wasn't unlike him. His habits were strange.

The concierge at old Bodasse's apartment startled Macé by telling him Bodasse was at home. She had seen the light in his flat the night before. But he wouldn't answer the door. He was an eccentric. Macé felt he had now discovered the identity of the victim. His guess was confirmed when Madame Bodasse identified the stocking—made of white cotton, with a man's sock sewn on the bottom—as belonging to her nephew. She also thought the legs were his.

As to the mystery man, Pierre Voirbo, he was a police spy, a man who pretended to be a rabid anarchist and attended left-wing meetings—only to make reports to the police. Macé broke into Bodasse's apartment. Everything looked neat, and an eight-day clock was still ticking. Macé decided to have the place watched, and borrowed a couple of men from the secret police. This proved to be a mistake; they knew Voirbo as a colleague, and when they saw him entering the building, they accosted him and asked him why they were supposed to watch him. Macé's quarry was alerted.

But Macé already had much valuable evidence. Bodasse's strong box was empty. But in the back of a watch Macé found a piece of paper with numbers of various securities written on it. Probing Voirbo's background, Macé discovered that, until a few months ago, he had lived in fairly cheap lodgings and had seemed to be poor. Then he had married and moved elsewhere, paying his rent with a five-hundred-franc share that could be cashed by anyone.

Macé hastened to the money-changer. He had kept the counterfoil of the share; the number tallied with one of those in the watch. Macé decided it was time to interview Voirbo. Now began the cat and mouse game. Voirbo was a plump, cheerful young man of 30, and he appeared to be a man of resourcefulness and character. Treating Macé as a friend—since they both worked for the police—he admitted that he had been worried about Bodasse's non-appearance.

He suspected that he might have been killed—in which case the murderer was an alcoholic butcher named Rifer, a petty crook, who had almost certainly been aided by three criminal acquaintances, whom Voirbo also helpfully pointed out. When Macé checked, he discovered that two of the three had perfect alibis: they had been in jail throughout December. And not long after, the alcoholic butcher had a fit of D.T.s and was taken to an asylum.

Macé decided he had to arrest Voirbo. It proved to be a wise decision, for Voirbo had a ticket to Havre in his wallet, and other indications showed he intended to embark for America. Voirbo seemed surprised and offended. What had he done that Macé should suspect him? They both knew there was no evidence.

Empty strong box

This, unfortunately, was true. Macé went to talk to Voirbo's wife, a quiet girl who obviously knew little of her husband's character and still less of his activities. Macé learned from her that she had brought her husband a dowry of 15,000 francs—about £600. Voirbo had gained the consent of her parents by telling them that he had 10,000 francs in securities; in fact, he had produced them before the wedding, but where were they now? The strong box was empty. Macé searched the house. Finally, in the cellar, he found Bodasse's securities; they had been soldered into a tin box, and suspended in a cask of wine.

Even that did not *prove* Voirbo a murderer. Macé now returned to Voirbo's old flat. A young couple had moved in, but they showed Macé precisely where the table had been when they first arrived. Macé was convinced this was where Bodasse had been killed; the cleaning woman had told him that Voirbo was notoriously untidy; yet on the morning of December 17—the day after Bodasse was last seen alive—his room had been

HE DISMEMBERED his victim's body in a room with a sloping floor. It took incredible patience on the part of a young detective to reconstruct Voirbo's crime and extract a confession. The case is another epic of classic detection.

WINDOW

HOLLOW IN FLOOR WHERE BLOOD COLLECTED

DOOR

STOVE.

WARDROBE ?

WASH STAND

TABLE

BED

HAT PEGS

Both Nigel Morland

polished and scrubbed. If Bodasse had been killed at the table, then he had probably also been dismembered there, and his blood must have run on the floor. This was perfectly clean; but it sloped a little towards the bed.

Macé staged his final scene with all the dramatic flair of a fictional detective. Voirbo was taken to his old room in the Rue Mazarin. He seemed calm and indifferent. Macé took a jug of water, poised it over the spot where the table used to stand, and poured it. The water flowed slowly across the floor, and formed a pool under the bed. Voirbo suddenly became restive. Macé sent for a mason, and ordered him to take up the floor tiles under the bed. The dark undersides were found to be coated with dried blood. Suddenly, Voirbo's nerve broke, and he made his confession.

A scoundrel in love

He had been tired of being a scoundrel, a petty crook, he said; he decided he wanted to settle down as a married man. He was in love with the gentle Mademoiselle Rémondé, but it was necessary to impress her parents that he also had money. He begged his friend Bodasse to lend it to him. When Bodasse refused, Voirbo decided he had to die.

He invited him to his room for tea, one day after they had dined together. Voirbo moved casually behind him, picked up a flat iron, and struck Bodasse on the head. Later, he dismembered the body and distributed the pieces around Paris, mostly in the river. After meeting the policeman who wanted to look into his basket—which contained bones and flesh—he decided to get rid of the legs by dumping them in the nearby well.

Voirbo was guillotined for the murder of Desiré Bodasse. But for one tiny mistake—sewing the leg into a piece of calico—he would have avoided suspicion. What is more, if he had kept his wits about him, he could have avoided detection even when the underside of the tiles showed traces of blood. He only had to deny that he knew where it came from, or declare that it was animal blood from a joint. In 1869 there was still no way of testing blood to determine whether it came from a man or an animal.

The story of how blood analysis was perfected is one of the great epics of scientific detection. Great scientists like Pasteur and Koch had discovered that if a human body is injected with *dead* germs, the blood will develop a resistance to living forms of the same germs; thus immunization was discovered. Twenty years later, in the 1890s, a German, von Behring, discovered that if a horse is injected with dead diphtheria germs, the serum from its blood—the clear liquid that separates out when blood is allowed

to stand—will actually help children who are suffering from diphtheria to recover: the serum develops "fighting" properties.

Around the turn of the century a chemist named Paul Uhlenhuth discovered that this same serum has even more remarkable properties. If a rabbit is injected with human blood, its blood serum develops a *resistance* to human blood. And if the serum is placed in a test tube, and the tiniest drop of human blood is introduced into it, it turns cloudy. It will not react at all to animal blood.

In 1901, shortly after Uhlenhuth had made this discovery, a travelling carpenter named Ludwig Tessnow was arrested on the Baltic island of Rügen, suspected of a particularly atrocious murder. Two small boys had been found in the woods, hacked and torn to pieces, scattered over a wide area. Three years earlier, Tessnow had been arrested on suspicion of killing two schoolgirls near the village of Lechtingen, near Osnabruck.

He had protested that certain stains on his clothes were of woodstain, not blood, and the police had had to release him for lack of evidence. Now he was questioned about a recently washed suit that showed slight traces of blood. Tessnow said that some of the almost obliterated stains were cattle blood, and that the others were woodstain. When the examining magistrate received the information from Osnabruck, he realized he was dealing with a man possessed of some insane desire to batter living creatures and tear them to pieces. A month before the two boys had been murdered, someone had attacked seven sheep in a field, cut them open and scattered the entrails all over the field. The shepherd had seen the man running away; he now identified Tessnow as the sheep butcher. But Tessnow denied everything.

Human bloodstains

Fortunately, the prosecutor had kept abreast of new developments in legal medicine, and had heard about Uhlenhuth's discovery. He sent Uhlenhuth the bloodstained clothing, and also the stone that had been used to batter the children. Uhlenhuth dissolved dozens of small stains in salt water and tested them all. He found 22 human bloodstains and half a dozen stains of sheep's blood. His

All Ullstein-Archiv

KARL HUSSMANN (far left) and victim posed for school photo . . . then quarrelled in the street (above). After the trial Hussmann was congratulated on his acquittal by his headmaster (right).

evidence convicted Tessnow, who was sentenced to death.

Not only would the serum distinguish human blood from animal blood; it would also distinguish different *types* of human blood: the groups A, B, O, and AB. This discovery did not provide sufficient evidence to hang a suspect in Gladbeck, Germany, in 1928, but a jury of sceptical burghers declined to convict on purely scientific evidence. The accused was 20-year-old Karl Hussmann, a dominant and violent student.

In the early hours of March 23, 1928, a youth named Helmut Daube was found dying in the street; his throat had been cut and his genitals slashed off. The police soon discovered that Daube's closest friend was his fellow-student Hussmann; when they went to Hussmann's house, they discovered that his shoes had been recently washed, and showed traces of

blood. His clothes were also blood-stained. Hussmann had completely dominated Daube, and the two had been lovers; but recently, Daube had realized that he preferred girls and had tried to break away.

At first Hussmann claimed the blood was that of a cat he had killed, but Uhlenhuth's test quickly revealed that it was human blood. Hussmann then changed his story and said he had had a nosebleed. The forensic laboratory at Bonn demonstrated that this was also impossible, for the blood on the shoes was type A — Daube's group — while Hussmann was type O.

The feeling of the court was that, while they were not convinced of Hussmann's innocence, they were by no means happy about convicting him on what, to them, amounted to purely circumstantial evidence, so Hussmann was acquitted. But the case drew wide attention to the use of testing for blood groups in criminal cases. Since that time, many criminals have been hanged on the evidence of a dried blood-spot on a wooden floor.

On humane grounds, perhaps the jury was right to disregard circumstantial evidence, for there is also the danger of hanging an innocent man. The case of Burton Abbott provides a thought-provoking illustration. Abbott was known to his neighbours in Alameda, California, as a quiet, rather intellectual man. He had never been known to be violent and had no police record.

On July 15, 1955, Abbott's wife was looking through old clothes in the basement when she found a wallet. It contained the identification card of 14-year-old Stephanie Bryan, some photographs, and an unfinished letter dated April 28, 1955. That had been the day when Stephanie had disappeared after coming out of school in Berkeley. She had never been seen since.

Georgia Abbott took the wallet upstairs and asked her husband how it had got there. He seemed as puzzled as she was, and they called the police. The next day, the police dug up Abbott's basement and found Stephanie's schoolbooks and her bra. Abbott pointed out that his garage had recently been used as a polling place, and that dozens of people had been in and out. However, a newsman went up to Abbott's summer cabin on Trinity Mountain with two dogs. The dogs led to a shallow grave. Stephanie Bryan's body was found in it; she had been strangled with her own panties, and the circumstances pointed to sexual assault.

Abbott was arrested and tried. He insisted that he knew nothing whatever about Stephanie or her clothes—and there was certainly no definite evidence

to connect him with her disappearance. But the jury convicted him. There were several stays of execution. The last one came just after 11.15 a.m. on March 14, 1947, but it arrived a few minutes too late; the cyanide gas pellets had been dropped under the execution chair at 11.15 precisely. Abbott persisted in denying his guilt to the end, although he is said to have told a doctor: "I can't admit it. Think of what it would do to my mother."

All the evidence suggests that Abbott was the killer of Stephanie Bryan. Yet there is an element of doubt: for example, he *could* have been framed by her real killer. The brilliant triumphs of scientific crime detection should never blind us to the fact that the word "clue" means an *indication,* and that, forensically, there is a vital difference between an indication and a final proof.

A REMOTE shallow grave yielded the body of 14-year-old Stephanie Bryan, after circumstantial evidence had led police to suspect Burton Abbott (right). But there is a vital difference between even the strongest clue and final proof....

All AP

THE COP KILLERS

Sergeant Mike McNeil was a careful cop. He always frisked his suspect thoroughly. But when he tried to arrest three at once, he slipped up . . . and even as he died, a colleague was being buried. It's total war—and war is hell.

THE London Metropolitan Police Force came into being in the year 1829. It was the brainchild of the Home Secretary, Sir Robert Peel; consequently, the new policemen became known as "bobbies". The nickname was not totally affectionate, however, for the people of London hated them. The old watchmen and parish constables who had kept order were just public employees, like rat-catchers and street sweepers. These uniformed men were "officials", whose business was to smell out offences against the law and put the offenders in jail; as a consequence, it was a risky job to be a policeman in the 1830s.

On June 29, 1830, Police Constable Grantham saw two drunken Irishmen quarrelling over a woman in Somers Town, north London. He tried to separate them and the men *and* the woman turned on him and knocked him down;

the men "put in the boot", kicking him brutally on the temple. He died shortly afterwards, thus becoming the first English policeman to die in the course of execution of his duty. The murderers walked off and were never brought to justice.

Six weeks later there was an incident that must have confirmed the London poor in their view that they were better off without the police. On August 16, Police Constable John Long accosted three suspicious-looking characters in Mecklenburgh Square, Grays Inn Road. One of them pulled a knife and stabbed Long to death. There was a hue and cry. A police constable who came on the scene saw a man running and grabbed him; the man protested that *he* was chasing one of the murderers.

A youth who was sitting on a doorstep was arrested by a police inspector; the youth protested that he was waiting for a friend, whereupon the police arrested the friend too. All three were taken into court, but the magistrate, reasoning that it was unlikely that a murderer would be sitting on a doorstep, discharged two of the defendants. But a tradesman's boy and a prostitute identified the remaining man as one of the policeman's assailants. No one asked the boy why, at an earlier stage, he had admitted that he had

not even seen the murder. The accused man—almost certainly innocent—was hanged. One has a feeling that the early police force felt it was better to hang the wrong man than nobody at all.

In May, 1833, a rather mildly revolutionary group called the National Political Union called for a public meeting of "anarchists and revolutionists" in Coldbath Fields, not far from the site of Constable Long's murder. Their "revolutionary" programme was hardly extreme; they simply wanted votes for the working man. The Home Secretary didn't like the idea; he told the Commissioner of Police to ban the meeting. The ban was ignored; a crowd gathered, and a speaker on a soap box asked the crowd to be orderly and peaceable.

Revolution and sedition

They had little alternative, being surrounded by about 800 policemen and troops. Other speeches were made, and a police spy slipped away to report that revolution and sedition was being preached. The man in charge of the police, Lieut.-Col. Charles Rowan, who had fought at Waterloo, ordered his men to advance slowly, holding their truncheons, and to halt frequently to allow "innocent" bystanders to get away. The police advanced—and were booed and pelted with stones.

This angered the Force, and they began hitting out wildly, knocking down women and children as well as men. Police Constable Robert Culley tried to capture one of the anarchist's banners, and hit the man with a truncheon. The man drew a knife, and stabbed Culley in the chest; he staggered a few yards and fell dead. Culley was a married man of 27 whose wife was about to have a baby.

The Coroner's jury that met to consider how Culley met his death were not disposed to sympathize with the police; they were mostly respectable tradesmen, and they felt that the police should have minded their own business, and permitted the traditional British right of free speech. They asked the police witnesses impertinent questions; then, when they were sent out to reach a verdict, told the Coroner they were unable to agree.

The Coroner did what was quite common in those days—told them that they would stay in the room without food or drink until they *did* agree. The result was that the angry jury produced a verdict that enraged the police and delighted the British public: that the man

THE VIOLENT DECADES in the war of "anarchists" and police included the bombing of a Paris police station (top left). —in retaliation for the brutality of May Day, 1891, at Clichy (left)—and in England, a shoot-out at Houndsditch (right).

Mary Evans/Viollet

ARMED BURGLARS IN THE CITY: THE TERRIBLE HOUNDSDITCH AFFRAY.

PHOTOGRAPHS BY TOPICAL, W.G.P., AND ILLUSTRATIONS BUREAU.

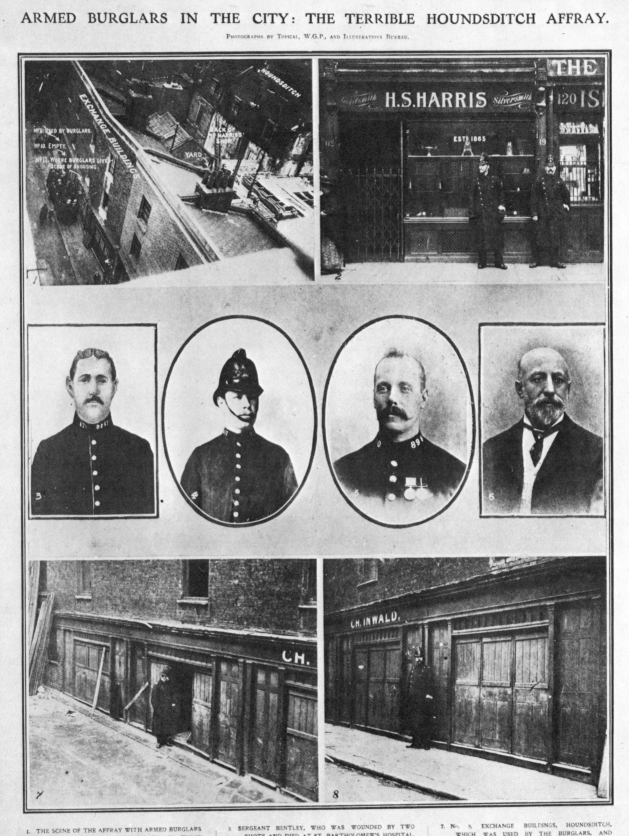

1. THE SCENE OF THE AFFRAY WITH ARMED BURGLARS WHICH RESULTED IN THE DEATH OF THREE POLICE OFFICERS: A PHOTOGRAPHIC DIAGRAM OF EXCHANGE BUILDINGS AND NEIGHBOURHOOD.
2. THE BURGLARS' OBJECTIVE: MR. H. S. HARRIS'S SHOP, WHICH BACKS ON No. 10, EXCHANGE BUILDINGS, AND IS SAID TO HAVE HELD BETWEEN £20,000 AND £30,000 WORTH OF JEWELS.

3. SERGEANT BENTLEY, WHO WAS WOUNDED BY TWO SHOTS AND DIED AT ST. BARTHOLOMEW'S HOSPITAL.
4. SERGEANT TUCKER, WHO WAS SHOT THROUGH THE HEART AND DIED A FEW MINUTES LATER.
5. POLICE-CONSTABLE CHOATE, WHO WAS WOUNDED BY SEVERAL SHOTS AND DIED IN THE LONDON HOSPITAL.
6. MR. H. S. HARRIS, WHOSE JEWELLER'S SHOP WAS THE OBJECTIVE OF THE ARMED BURGLARS.

7. No. 9, EXCHANGE BUILDINGS, HOUNDSDITCH, WHICH WAS USED BY THE BURGLARS, AND BEHIND WHICH A HOLE WAS BEING BORED THROUGH A BACK WALL INTO THE PREMISES OF MR. HARRIS.
8. Nos. 10 AND 11, EXCHANGE BUILDINGS, THE FORMER VACANT, THE LATTER RENTED BY THE BURGLARS, AND THE SCENE OF THE SHOOTING OF THE FIVE POLICE OFFICERS.

who had killed Constable Culley—and who had never been caught—was only guilty of justifiable homicide. The spectators in the court cheered. The jury were treated as heroes, and found themselves wined and dined for their defiance of the "bobbies".

This raises again the fundamental question: were the public simply protesting against this frightening new innovation, a police force? Or was it rather the expression of something deeper—that idealistic anarchism which is perhaps a profound and permanent part of human nature? For it is not only, for instance, "primitive" and peaceable societies such as the South Sea islanders who feel they have no need for civil authority. Slum dwellers in London's East End and country dwellers in tiny rural villages feel the same. The poor may fight among themselves; but they also help one another.

"Kill them like dogs"

In the poverty of Whitechapel and the Ratcliffe Highway there was a strong community spirit, which could be seen occasionally when a whole street hired a horse bus for an expedition to the country, or families went hop-picking to the fields of Kent, sleeping rough under hedges. As to country people, anyone who has ever moved from a city into a quiet country district has noticed the friendliness and warmth, and how a total stranger may go out of his way to offer help.

This is what had convinced nineteenth-century "peaceful anarchists" such as the Russians Kropotkin and Malatesta that men are good at heart, and that to subject them to the harsh processes of the law is an indignity to human nature. To some extent, it is undoubtedly the modern commercial metropolis, with its fairly well-to-do inhabitants living in flats, that has eroded this spirit of co-operation among ordinary people. No doubt Kropotkin, Bakunin, Proudhon and the rest were being absurdly idealistic when they imagined that a whole modern state could be run without the police, army or government. Yet they had grasped something about human nature that many people have lost sight of: that man is basically gregarious and prepared to help his fellow-creatures, because he needs help from them.

This explains some of the deep and widespread hostility to the police that persists even in our crime-ridden society. It is, of course, due partly to a kind of stupidity, to the confused reasoning of socially immature individuals, but it is more than that. There is also the obscure longing for a more innocent form of society, where the brotherhood of man is a reality. Many anarchists would agree that society needs law and order, because there are always people who may commit violent crimes.

But the answer, according to them, is to have police purely as guardians of the peace, like the sheriff of an old Wild Western town, whose business was to chase rustlers and stop visiting cowboys from shooting up the local saloon—not to go around looking for people who have parked their horse on double yellow lines.

This view actually offers a ray of hope in a society where the killing of policemen has become an increasing problem. (In America, more police are killed every year than have been killed in England since the beginning of the century.)

If the police killing is pure anti-social viciousness, then this is a reason for gloom. But if it also springs from some distorted impulse of defiance and human dignity, then a little intelligent thinking may provide some of the answers.

The outline of some of these answers can be seen in the subsequent history of the police force. In America, on the continent of Europe, and especially in Russia, the police continued to be regarded by most ordinary people as an instrument of oppression. "Police and militia, the bloodhounds of capitalism, are willing to murder!" declared a headline in the *Arbeiter-Zeitung*, the Chicago German-language anarchist daily.

On May 4, 1885, police moved in to break up a strikers' meeting in the Haymarket Square when someone threw a bomb into the police ranks. The explosion was terrific, and when the bleeding and screaming confusion died down, seven policemen were lying dead. In the following year, eight anarchists—arrested at random from the crowd—were sentenced to death for the killings.

It started a chain reaction of shootings, explosions, strike-breaking and the deliberate starvation of workers and their families, and the violence continued intermittently for nearly half a century. The execution of Sacco and Vanzetti in 1927 marked the end of this phase of militant anarchism in America.

Shot through the neck

On May Day, 1891, French anarchists were dragged into the police station at Clichy and beaten viciously. At their trial, one of them shouted: "If the police come, do not hesitate to kill them like the dogs they are . . ." On November 8, 1892, a bomb exploded in the police station in the Avenue de l'Opéra, Paris, blowing six policemen to fragments, including the one who had been rash enough to carry it, and once again there were explosions, assassinations, executions that continued for decades.

In 1922, anarchists robbed a train travelling from Paris to Lyons, and one

of them murdered an army officer who resisted. A few days later police arrested an anarchist called Jacques Mecislav Charrier, who had been overheard boasting of the robbery in a bar. Seven days after the robbery, acting on information forced from Charrier, police ambushed two men in the Rue des Ternes, Paris. Both men were killed; so was a police inspector.

Charrier declared in court: "I am a desperate enemy of society and I defy you to take my head." And although he screamed and pleaded for mercy as he was dragged to the guillotine, other French anarchists felt that the great war against the "bloodhounds of capitalism" was going on.

In England, however, the situation had changed in favour of the police. To begin with, the English have always been traditionally lenient towards political offenders; when Karl Marx fled to England in 1850, he was amazed that the English police were unarmed, and that the authorities did not seem particularly concerned about the "dangerous revolutionaries" in their midst. Anarchist and socialist clubs met openly, yet no one seemed worried. Jack the Ripper actually committed one of his murders—of Elizabeth Stride—in the backyard of one of these

GUNNED DOWN when he stopped a car, Detective Ian Coward (right) was the victim of a kind of casual violence rarely expressed in Britain. The killers, Sparrow (inset left) and Skingle, later burned the car—but got "life" anyway.

revolutionary clubs for foreign immigrants in 1888.

Marx was also astonished to find himself in a country where people seemed quite to like their policemen. The British bobby was usually an easy-going, kindly sort of man, and although there were still plenty of streets in London's East End where a policeman would never venture alone, no one actually regarded them as "capitalist bullies". Anybody who *wanted* to express that opinion was welcome to stand up on a soap box in Hyde Park and say so, while several bobbies looked benevolently on in case the crowd felt like attacking the speaker.

Two-hour chase

A number of violent incidents actually caused wide sympathy and support for the police. For example, there was the Tottenham outrage of 1909, when two young anarchists from the Baltic states tried to take a payroll from the men delivering it to Schurmann's rubber factory. The wages clerk struggled; shots were fired, and the two men fled. Unarmed policemen chased them. The first victim of the gunmen was a small boy, who fell dead. Next, a policeman named Tyler was shot through the neck and killed. The chase pounded on through back gardens and across allotments; more policemen were wounded.

In the Chingford Road, the men leapt on to a passing tram, and forced the conductor to drive it. An elderly passenger lost his nerve, and was shot in the throat. As the gunmen leapt off the tram, a milkman who ran towards them was shot in the chest. The men stopped a horse-drawn grocer's van and ordered the teenage driver to whip up the horse. Policemen on bicycles—one of them carrying a cutlass—hurtled after them.

Passing a policeman, one of the men fired, hitting him in the foot; the policeman blew his whistle and despite his wound joined in the chase. The anarchists leapt out of the van as their pursuers gained ground, and raced across fields again; at a fence, one of them fell. Before the police could reach him, he had shot himself through the brain, and he died later in hospital. Finally, the police cornered the other man in a cottage; two policemen burst into the child's bedroom where he was

David White

hiding, and shot him through the head. The chase had lasted two hours, and covered six miles; a policeman and a child had been killed, seven more policemen shot, and fourteen other people injured.

It was this kind of incident that rallied warm support around the British police. So did the shootings in Houndsditch a year later, when three policemen were killed and four more injured by a gang of foreign burglars; and when the Houndsditch affair culminated in the famous Siege of Sidney Street, everyone in England was delighted that the foreign desperadoes had been trapped. On the whole, the British public had decided that its police force was to be trusted.

Climate of violence

The situation in America is different. The high incidence of police-murders is due less to public hostility than to the general climate of violence, and the permissive American gun laws. Two typical cases of 1971 – one in England, one in America – will serve to underline the difference between the two countries.

On the evening of June 27, 1971, Detective Constable Ian Coward, 29, was driving through Reading when he noticed a white Morris that was swinging across the road in a manner that suggested the driver was drunk. When the car stopped in front of a restaurant, he got out and approached it. There were two men inside. He asked the driver for his identification and the driver, a young, unshaven man, got out to look for it. Coward went back to his own car, got into the driver's seat, and told the man to get in beside him.

At this moment, the other man approached the police car, pulled a gun, and fired nine bullets into Coward. As the policeman fell across the seat and through the open passenger door, the other man kicked him. Then both ran back to their car and drove off. Incredibly, Coward was still alive. He was rushed to hospital; but on July 23 he died.

Witnesses to the shooting were able to pick out the two men from the "rogue's gallery" of mug-shots; they were identified as Arthur Skingle, 25, and Peter Sparrow, 28. Both had criminal records, and Skingle, the gunman, had been released from prison – where he had served a sentence for robbery with violence – only ten days earlier. The men drove the white Morris to a spot a few miles away, and set it on fire with petrol. It was a routine matter for the police to pick up the murderers, who were both sentenced to full life terms.

On November 29, 1971, Sergeant Mike McNeil of Albany, New York, pulled in a car driver for questioning; his driver's licence did not correspond to the car's registration number. While the driver was being interrogated, at the section house, his three companions, who were waiting outside in the car, escaped.

Shot by a woman

McNeil went after them, caught them up a block away, and ordered them into his car. Before they climbed in, he frisked them. Even so, he missed a revolver in the pocket of Joseph Guerin, and when McNeil climbed into the driving seat Guerin shot him several times in the back of the head.

The killer ran off; the other two – a man and a woman – remained, and were able to give the police a lead that eventually led to Guerin's arrest. It was then discovered that Sergeant McNeil's killer was also wanted for grand larceny and robbery. He was sentenced to "life".

McNeil was the second Albany officer to die in three days. On the 26 November, Patrolman Edward Stevens was detailed to collect a woman and escort her to a mental home – where a court had ordered her to have treatment. As he knocked on her door, she fired through it with both barrels of a shotgun, killing him instantly.

So little suspicion

The contrast between the two countries is immediately obvious. The British policeman had so little suspicion of the men he had stopped that he invited one of them to get into his car while he was sitting down. McNeil did it the right way, frisking Guerin before climbing into the car himself; but he still died. What strikes the reader about so many American crimes involving policemen is their *casualness*. Obviously, the war between police and criminals is on an altogether deadlier level than in England.

Most sociologists would agree that, to some extent, Rousseau, Diderot, Kropotkin and the rest were right. To get the best out of human beings, you need to give them a chance to exercise their freedom. Perhaps the situation needs to be "defused" with sympathy and understanding. But it is also obvious that England has fewer police murders because it has fewer guns.

The police are not armed; neither are most criminals. It follows that the first step in solving America's problem could be simple; to pass logical and civilized gun laws.

A DEADLIER WAR for American policemen: the prevalence of guns means potential death in every routine call. As the victim below was buried, another died.

Mary Evans

SCARLET WOMEN

Who are the outrageous, sensual women whose lust for life carries all before them? What makes them thrive on wild passion, intrigue . . . and danger?

THE original Scarlet Woman was hardly a seductive siren. When she first makes her appearance, in the Book of Revelation, she has seven heads and 10 horns—it is not clear how the horns are distributed among the heads—and is drunk with the blood of martyrs and saints. This makes it fairly clear that what Saint John the Divine had in mind was not some Babylonian Mae West, but the city of Rome. And after the coming of Luther, Protestant theologians insisted that it was the Roman Catholic Church. It was a singularly un-promising beginning for what has become one of the great basic myths of the western world.

And it is, essentially, a modern myth. The ancient world experienced no feeling of morbid interest in the courtesan or prostitute. On the contrary, she was regarded as one of the foundation stones of a healthy society. The Babylonians took the view that every woman ought to

WICKED THOUGHTS? This nineteenth-century photograph depicts a high-class French prostitute brooding in the rather tasteless confines of her dressing-room.

have some experience of prostitution, so every woman in the land had to go to the temple of Venus—known as Mylitta—once in her life, and prostitute herself to a stranger.

The rule applied to everyone, from peasant girls to kings' daughters; in Phoenicia all virgins had to be ritually deflowered by a stranger before marriage. The inhabitants of Heliopolis, in Egypt, were so enraged when the Christian emperor Constantine put a stop to this custom that they burst into the temple, stripped the holy virgins naked, deflower-ed them, then disembowelled them, and encouraged the pigs to eat food from their stomach cavities.

In Cyprus a girl prostituted herself to

earn money for her marriage portion, and her husband took great pride in a wife who had earned him a small fortune. Early European travellers in Africa were shocked to discover that the tribal whore was regarded as an almost sacred figure. Such a girl would be bought in the slave market and ritually initiated into her trade in a public ceremony. After that, she was given a hut on the edge of the village and had to give herself to any man, youth or child who wanted her.

If she was exceptionally young or desirable there was a queue at her door for the first week or so, and she might have to satisfy a hundred men a day. Working at that pace, she inevitably lost her good looks, and then the demand dropped off. Most of these tribal pros-titutes died in a very short time of venereal disease, yet they were regarded as so essential to the well-being of the com-munity that a tribal overlord who wanted

this was a thoroughly unhealthy state. Society was becoming sex-obsessed, in the worst possible way. A prostitute could be ducked in a wooden cage until she was half drowned, or made to walk through the streets in a half-shift, while "respectable women" were allowed to slash and prick at her thighs. This clear division between "respectable women" and "loose women" was a product of a morbid attitude towards sex.

The Babylonians were altogether healthier when they made every woman prostitute herself once in a lifetime. This new obsession with respectability was really based on the notion that sex was a wicked activity that could only be disinfected by marriage, and that people who indulged in it without proper sanction were headed for damnation.

Dirty books

Boccaccio had an amusing story in *The Decameron* about a randy monk who seduces an innocent girl by telling her that her vagina is Hell, and that his penis is the Devil, and that he will show her how to please God by putting the Devil in Hell. But in the seventeenth century people really believed it; a man who entered a strange vagina was headed straight for Hell. Not surprisingly, the very fact that sex was forbidden gave it an unhealthy attraction.

It is significant that there was very little pornography before the eighteenth century. There were plenty of books that were *later* considered pornographic, like *The Decameron*, *The Heptameron* by Queen Margaret of Navarre, and the *Lives*

to punish a village only had to confiscate the village whore to reduce everybody to total subjection.

The explanation, obviously, is that in primitive societies there is no *idealization* of women. They are child-bearers, beasts of burden; the male's attitude towards her is thoroughly realistic, and this is how the women expect to be treated. But as a society becomes more "civilized" a new class of woman develops. Her hands remain white, because she has servants; her body remains attractive well into middle-age, because she is not worn out with childbearing and drudgery. To a large part of the population such aristocratic ladies become remote, glamorous creatures; and the idea of romantic chivalry develops.

In Europe this happened some time around the age of King Arthur—about the 7th century A.D.; and, significantly enough, the stories of King Arthur involve one of the first of the legendary Scarlet Women, the sorceress Morgan Le Fay, King Arthur's wicked sister. She is beautiful—she never looks more than 16—and has

PASSIONATE PHILOSOPHER . . .
Rousseau (inset) gave his contemporaries some new ideas on love—and practised them (above). Right: Fanny Hill. . . .

had a convent education; but she studied magic under Merlin—who, in some versions, she seduces. She also tries to seduce Sir Lancelot, and generally spends her time making trouble and mischief.

These legends of King Arthur began to crystallize out around the thirteenth and fourteenth centuries. At roughly the same time Boccaccio was writing his famous—and scandalous—work *The Decameron*. In *The Decameron* the women are healthy and down-to-earth, and even Mother Superiors of convents are capable of seducing young gardeners. Yet a few centuries later *The Decameron* was a "dirty book", banned in most countries. The old, carefree sexual morality of the Middle Ages had given way to something more rigid and puritanical. "Woman" was idealized. Consequently, the prostitute was regarded with a kind of horror.

Looking back on it, we can see that

of Gallant Ladies by the Sieur de Brantôme. But real "dirty books", written for sexually frustrated people—rather than people with a sense of humour—only started to appear in the mid-eighteenth century. John Cleland's famous *Fanny Hill* was one of the first of these, and Cleland was promptly offered a pension by the government if he would promise to write no more dirty books. The "establishment" obviously felt that pornography was a real menace to the state.

Now anybody who has ever read *Fanny Hill*, which is now quite easily obtainable, will realize why it caused so much alarm. Fanny is unashamedly a Scarlet Woman. In those days women were supposed to be sternly virtuous. The most popular novel of the day was Samuel Richardson's *Clarissa*, in which the virtuous heroine is kidnapped by the wicked Lovelace and finally drugged and raped; but she refuses to yield her virtue, or even to marry the villain, and when she escapes she eventually dies for her lost honour.

On the other hand, young Fanny Hill cheerfully allows herself to be seduced —admittedly by a man she loves—then to become an older man's mistress, then starts seducing handsome young lads for the pleasure of it. . . . It was more than just pornography. It was a deliberate jeer at the current idea of female virtue. Cleland was saying: most women enjoy sex just as much as men, and if they "lose their honour" they don't commit suicide; they make the best of it.

In 1761 Jean Jacques Rousseau created an even greater scandal with a book called *The New Heloise,* in which the pretty, virtuous heroine falls in love with her handsome young tutor and yields her virginity to him because she believes that when people are truly in love sex is no longer sinful. It is difficult now to understand the universal sense of shock caused by Rousseau's dangerous thesis. Less than two centuries earlier, Shakespeare's Antony and Cleopatra hopped into bed together without causing Queen Elizabeth any concern; but now the idea of female respectability was regarded as the bedrock of society.

Triumphant vice

It is also significant that the vilest and most sickening pornography ever written was produced in the final years of the eighteenth century by the Marquis de Sade, a French nobleman who spent most of his life in prison because of his sexual misdemeanours. De Sade is absolutely obsessed by this "virtuous" society that refuses to allow him to indulge his sexual inclinations as freely as he thinks he deserves, and the wickedest people in his works are always judges, priests and other pillars of society—who are invariably engaged in practising incest with their

daughters, or raping convent girls.

De Sade wrote the ultimate attack on the idea of the virtuous woman: *Justine,* in which, from the first page onward, the chaste and innocent heroine is raped, sodomized and beaten. And at the end, just as her misfortunes seem to be over, she is struck by lightning. De Sade then followed up this tale of injured virtue with a story of triumphant vice, *Juliette.*

Juliette is Justine's sister, and she is undoubtedly the most scarlet of all scarlet women. There is no vice or wickedness that she doesn't enjoy. She even seduces her own long-lost father, and then has him murdered; and at the end of the book she is rich and happy. It is not surprising that they kept De Sade in a lunatic asylum—though his sanity was never in doubt—until he died. The "virtuous society" had produced a man who rejected everything about it, who derided all its standards, and who insisted on trying to make it see its own face in a cracked distorting mirror.

Nausea of lust

The nineteenth century—the age of ultimate respectability—produced a non-stop flood of pornography. One of its most remarkable characters was a mystery man who is known to posterity only as "Walter". He was a "gentleman"; that is to say, he had enough money to devote most of his life to the untiring pursuit of sex.

He wrote the story of his endless sexual adventures in an astonishing document called *My Secret Life,* which is some 3000 pages long. It is instructive to compare this remarkable book with the famous *Memoirs* of Casanova, written a century earlier. Casanova also spends his life in seduction, but he regards it as one of the legitimate pleasures of life, and is interested in many other subjects—magic, philosophy and literature, for example. Walter, on the other hand, broods morbidly and single-mindedly on sex. He cannot see a woman without wondering what she is like without her clothes on, and if she is a working-class girl he always makes an effort to find out.

During the course of the book he possesses some hundreds of women, describing most of them in detail: whores, married women, virgins, even a 10-year-old girl. A phenomenon like Walter would not have been possible two centuries earlier. Men simply took sex more for granted; it was like drinking or hunting or falconry, one of the pleasures of life, not something that produced a kind of nausea of lust. The German psychologist Ivan Bloch wrote a famous *History of English Morals* in the early twentieth century, and it is mostly a description of the dozens of perversions that could be encountered in Victorian England.

BEAUTY is only one of the essential characteristics for a scarlet woman. She must also be intelligent and mysterious, like George Sand (top) and Lola Montez.

More recently Ronald Pearsall's remarkable book *The Worm in the Bud* has done the same thing. What is abundantly clear is that it was the Victorian obsession with morality and respectability that produced this explosion of morbid sexual obsession. In fact the Jack the Ripper murders were almost inevitable. The killer was undoubtedly some typical Victorian who had been brought up to think of sex as wholly sinful, and of prostitutes as an evil, degraded race. The truth, as we now know, is that most of the Ripper's victims were toothless, pathetic down-and-outs, and the only young one among them, Mary Kelly, was a strapping, boozy Irish doxy who could have knocked most men flat with a blow of her fist.

But for the average Victorian these women lived deliciously sinful lives. They even called them "daughters of joy". And the whores paid for their wicked pleasures with their horrible death at the hands of a satanic madman with a long knife. . . . Jack the Ripper, like Dracula, has become an archetypal figure of world mythology.

But even in the time of the Ripper things were changing. The puritanical sex-morality had exerted its stranglehold on European society for about two centuries, and it was time for something new. It began on the Continent, notably in France. Because of their political upheavals—the Revolution, Napoleon, the Second Empire—the French had always been less conventional than their luckier neighbours.

While Dickens, Thackeray and Trollope were writing novels for the Victorian family, Balzac and Dumas were writing about adultery and sexual intrigue, and their contemporary, George Sand—who was actually a woman—was shocking everybody by wearing men's clothes, smoking cigars and taking a succession of lovers. And in the second half of the century writers like Zola and Maupassant shocked even the French with their tales of adultery and prostitution. When an English publisher dared to issue a translation of Zola he was promptly thrown into jail.

Over indulgence

Amazingly enough, the breath of scandal was also blowing from across the Atlantic. It was in 1855 that a thin quarto book called *Leaves of Grass* was printed in Brooklyn. The author was a journalist named Walt Whitman, and his "free verse" celebrated the vastness of America —its many people, its rivers and cities— and also the sexual pleasures of healthy men and women coupling. No one could doubt Whitman's sincerity; yet this kind of frankness was almost frightening to the respectable Victorians, who even covered

INSIDE PFAFF'S Walt Whitman is greeted by an admirer. Left: George Sand in more conventional costume. Her lovers included de Musset and Chopin.

up table legs because the very mention of legs was enough to make ladies blush.

Whitman became a storm centre of controversy. His headquarters was a beer cellar beneath Broadway, run by a German called Pfaff. "Pfaff's" became the "bohemian" rendezvous of America. Everybody who visited New York in the 1860s looked in at Pfaff's, hoping to catch a glimpse of Walt Whitman—and also of a lady who was known as the Queen of Bohemia. Her name was Ada Clare, and she was beautiful, blonde, talented—and promiscuous.

She had begun her career, in the same year as the appearance of *Leaves of Grass*, by writing rather moving little love poems, devoid of literary merit, which were published in the New York weekly *Atlas*. Ada soon had a reputation as a fine poetess, and when she started coming to Pfaff's none of the male customers objected. She wrote a regular column in the newspapers. Now at this time one of the most sought-after males in America was a handsome young pianist called Louis Gottschalk. Women swooned at his recitals. He was also a composer, whose music is now once again becoming popular—his piano pieces in syncopated rhythms are said to be the true origin of jazz.

Louis was a Don Juan—in fact his early death was due to sexual over-indulgence. As soon as Ada Clare saw him she trembled with adoration. Gottschalk was never one to pass up an opportunity, and in no time at all he had made Ada pregnant. By the time her son was born, however, Gottschalk was giving concerts and seducing women at the other end of America. But Ada did not allow the disgrace to worry her. She continued to attend Pfaff's and to take lovers.

To begin with, she was in no way dependent on literature for her income — she owned property in the south. But she lost it in the Civil War, and from then on had to make her living by her pen — and also by stage appearances. She was not a good actress, but she was persistent. People streamed to see her because she had the reputation of being beautiful and wicked. She married an actor, and apparently settled down to becoming a faithful wife; but for her fellow-countrymen she remained the Queen of Bohemia, America's own Scarlet Woman.

Ada even wrote a novel describing her love affair with Gottschalk, and with Edwin Booth, the actor-brother of Lincoln's assassin. Then, in 1874, when she was 38 a tragic accident put an end to her career — and her life. She was sitting in a chair at a dramatic agency when a small dog leapt into her lap. She continued to talk as she caressed the dog; suddenly it jumped at her face and bit her through the bridge of the nose.

The wound was not — apparently — serious or disfiguring, and it began to heal after being sterilized. But Ada was convinced the dog had rabies, and she died on March 4, 1874. The owner of the dog said it was not suffering from rabies; so it could be that Ada's death was due to fatigue and hysteria.

PAINFULLY BEAUTIFUL, Eleonora Duse (below) excited men to frenzied passion and then left them heartbroken. She became a victim of poet D'Annunzio.

After Ada Clare, a series of scarlet women demolished the myth that women are innocent and sexless. There was Ada Mencken, the circus rider who rode in flesh-coloured tights that made her seem naked. On one occasion friends of the poet Swinburne decided that he needed a love affair, and paid Ada £10 to seduce him; but apparently the poet was overcome with nervousness and embarrassment, and he remained a virgin. There was Lola Montez, the adventuress who caused the downfall of the Bavarian throne. There was the young French actress and novelist Colette, who not only wrote scandalously frank books but openly flaunted her lesbian love affairs.

There were actresses like Eleonora Duse and Sarah Bernhardt, whose love

ETERNALLY MYSTERIOUS, actress Sarah Bernhardt broke almost every canon of conventional behaviour. She once took the role of Hamlet — with great success!

affairs were known all over Europe — Duse was known to be tragically in love with the Italian poet Gabriele D'Annunzio who, in true bohemian fashion, seduced and then deserted her. There was Isadora Duncan, the dancer, who bore a child to the actor Gordon Craig, and preached a fiery gospel of free love, and who also died tragically in 1927 when her scarf caught in the wheel of a car and strangled her.

But the woman who certainly did most to shatter the Victorian ideas on demure womankind was a pretty and voluptuous young woman called Marie Stopes. Born in 1880 of highly respectable parents, she was a brilliant student of science, and decided to become a doctor. In Japan, at the age of 27, she had an unhappy and unconsummated love affair with a Japanese professor. In America, in 1911, she

All Mansell

HIGHLY SENSUAL, but also a brilliant doctor, Marie Stopes (above) directed her frustrated energies into the writing of a pioneering work on sexual relations.

met Dr. Reginald Gates and married him — then found he was impotent, and divorced him on the grounds that she was still *virgo intacta*.

Since she was a highly sensual and dominant young woman, this long frustration made her intensely unhappy, and out of this unhappiness she wrote a book called *Married Love*, which at once became a best-seller and made her famous. She married a rich man — a founder of the Avro aircraft firm — and launched a campaign for birth control. She sued Dr. Halliday Sutherland for libel when he declared that her methods were dangerous. She was finally awarded a mere £100 damages, but the case made her name known to every newspaper reader in England and America. Towards the end of her life she had the satisfaction of seeing many of her measures for birth control advocated by the Church of England — which had bitterly opposed her in earlier days — at the Lambeth Conference in 1958. She died later in the same year.

Women's lib

We are now seeing the consequences of the work of Marie Stopes — and others like her. She may be regarded as the true founder of "Women's Lib"; she certainly did more than anyone else to bring about our modern "permissive society". It is too soon to know whether all this will produce a happier society; but it will certainly produce a less frustrated — and therefore healthier — one.

OPERATION MADAME KITTY

In its heyday the elegant building in Berlin's Giesebrechtstrasse enjoyed the rapt attentions of an endless stream of male visitors. This was Kitty Schmidt's kingdom, where she ruled over a bevy of the sexiest girls in all Germany. They had been chosen for their looks, their charms and their skill in the art of spying on their distinguished but unsuspecting clients . . .

Abelard Schuman/Quartet

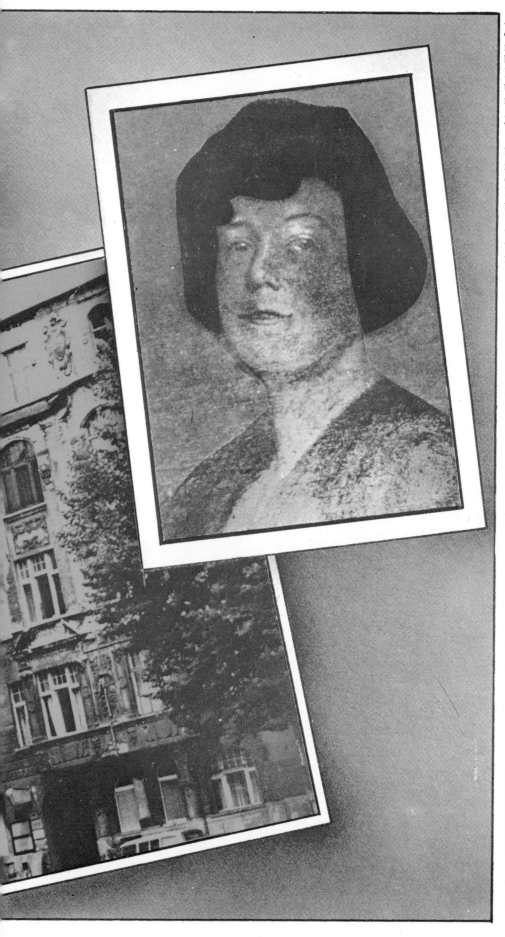

ACCORDING to city records, Kitty Schmidt owned the "Pension Schmidt", an anonymous-looking rooming-house at 11, Giesebrechtstrasse. Everyone in fashionable Berlin in the late 1930's, however, knew that the Pension was a front for the city's most luxurious and discreet brothel. At 57 Kitty was Berlin's most celebrated "Madame".

The Pension Schmidt was frequented by some of the most distinguished and influential figures in German society, by diplomats and government officials, by high-ranking officers, by famous names from the stage and movies.

They were catered for by the cream of the profession. Kitty's girls were trained to pander to every whim, to flatter, to flirt, sometimes just to listen patiently while their customers poured out their problems. Madame Kitty's fees were extremely high. What made it all worthwhile to the visitors who slipped in through the door of No. 11 was not the fine food and wines from her cellars, the expensive decor or even the all-embracing charms of the girls, but the atmosphere of absolute discretion which shrouded the establishment like the rich velvet curtains in Kitty's parlour.

Time to go?

But, for some time, Kitty had seen the writing on the brothel wall. The rise to power of Adolf Hitler had been reflected in a subtle change in her type of clientele. Roughnecks from the Brownshirts and SS had gradually replaced her favourite Jewish bankers and industrialists. The police, who for so long had turned a benevolent eye to the Pension Schmidt — indeed, the Chief of Police was one of her most devoted customers — had begun to harass her. Somehow, Kitty felt, there was no longer any room for her individual kind of trade in the new regime.

That was why she had started to salt away her takings in Britain. By 1939 she had transferred hundreds of thousands of dollars to bank accounts in London — mainly through the aid of Jewish refugees she had helped from Berlin. On June 28 she decided it was time to slip out of Germany and join her money.

Suave and devious

She had got as far as the frontier between Germany and Holland when a hand fell on her shoulder. Kitty spun round, to stare into the unsmiling face of a secret agent of the SD — the Sicherheitsdienst, the Nazi Central Security Organization. She had been followed from the moment she left the capital.

It took two weeks of softening-up in the cellars of the Prinz Albrechtstrasse — the Berlin headquarters of the Gestapo — before Kitty Schmidt was judged ready to meet the suave and devious head of the

SD, SS-Obersturmfuhrer Walter Schellenberg.

Schellenberg wasted no time on courtesies. "You're in trouble," he said icily. "Big trouble." He leafed through the dossier in front of him. "You realize the crimes you have committed?" Helplessly, Kitty Schmidt shook her head.

Schellenberg spread the fingers of one hand and ticked off the incriminating litany on each finger. "Helping Jews to escape—don't deny it, we have the evidence—illegally exchanging German marks for foreign currency, illegally transferring money out of the country, attempting to leave Germany without permission and travelling on a forged passport. I have no need to remind you of the penalties for such crimes?"

Ungovernable appetites

Kitty Schmidt had read the newspapers. She knew that the punishment for at least one of the offences was death, with a living death in a concentration camp for the others. So why the lecture? Kitty's intuition told her that there was more to it than that. Schellenberg drew slowly on a cigarette. "Of course," he said, "if you can do something for me, I may be able to do something for you. Are you willing to co-operate?" Kitty knew she had no choice. "Anything, Obersturmfuhrer," she said. "Anything you say."

Kitty Schmidt was a woman of the world. She had earned her money the hard way and in her long and lurid life she thought she had heard everything. But the proposition Walter Schellenberg proceeded to make caused even her hardened jaw to sag.

In exchange for her freedom, she was virtually to hand over her brothel to the SD. There were no explanations. Schellenberg pushed an "Official Secrets" form across the desk and ordered her to sign it. The first clause read, "Any attempt to divulge Classified Information will be punishable by death." Trembling, Kitty signed. "You can now go," said Schellenberg, "but report to my office every day."

Operation "Salon Kitty" had started. Later that day, Schellenberg marched briskly into the office of Gruppenfuhrer Reinhard Heydrich—head of the entire Gestapo network — snapped "Heil Hitler!" and saluted.

Reinhard Heydrich, later to achieve infamy as "The Butcher of Prague", was one of the most frightening administrators thrown up by the Nazi Party. Ruthless, intelligent, and ambitious, he had all the warmth of an icefloe and—according to Schellenberg — "ungovernable sexual appetites". He was also a man of few words. "Well?" he said. "Everything went perfectly," replied Schellenberg. "We can now go ahead with our plans to —ah, reorganize—the Pension Schmidt."

Heydrich twisted his features into a passable imitation of a smile. "Excellent, Obersturmfuhrer!" he said. Operation Salon Kitty had been Heydrich's idea from the start. For some time the Gestapo had been concerned about careless security leaks in high places. With Germany rapidly nearing a war footing, it was essential to stem idle chatter, and—even more vital—to identify the chatterers. There was nothing like wine and beautiful women to loosen a man's tongue, Heydrich had concluded. So what better than to infiltrate an exclusive brothel and use the girls as intelligence agents, reporting back to the SD any items of value they overheard?

It was Schellenberg who had added the extra refinements. Why stop there? he had asked. Why not take over the brothel completely and use it as a vast intelligence clearing-house? Security-leak suspects, and persons under surveillance, could easily be steered unawares to the brothel. It could also be used to glean information from visiting dignitaries, foreign diplomats, and embassy staff.

There was no need to rely on Madame Kitty's girls. They could install a team of girls, specially trained in intelligence techniques, who would encourage the customers to talk freely, watching out for any indiscretions. The girls would file immediate written reports as soon as the customers left.

Racial purity

But as a final safeguard—unknown to anyone except the highest security officials—all the rooms would be bugged, the wires leading down to a nerve-centre in the basement. Here, a team of agents working in shifts could monitor and record on disc every word uttered, confided, breathed, sighed, or exclaimed in the entire establishment. Schellenberg's electronic voyeurs could become the third ear of Nazi internal security.

Heydrich had given the go-ahead. Now the first stage in Operation Salon Kitty had been achieved. They had got their brothel. There was one monumental snag, however. They had not got the girls. That was the problem that landed on the desk of Unterstumfuhrer Karl Schwarz of the SD—the luckless agent delegated to organize the complete transformation of the Pension Schmidt.

Schwarz's first recruiting drive was a disaster. In what struck him as a brilliant stroke, he enlisted the services of the Lebensborn, the much-vaunted organization which undertook to bring together superb specimens of Aryan manhood and

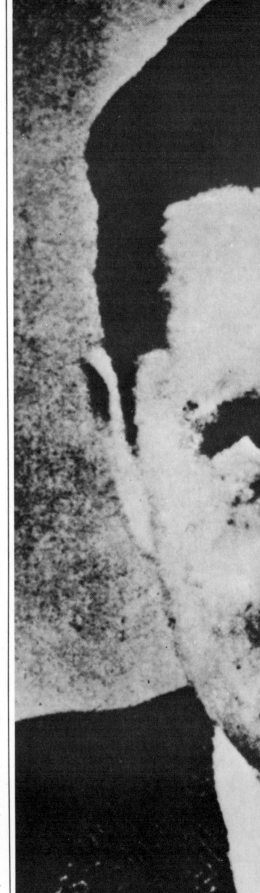

MASTER PIMP behind the "Salon Kitty" operation was Walter Schellenberg, who was subsequently promoted to SS Brigadefuhrer. The Allies arrested him in 1945.

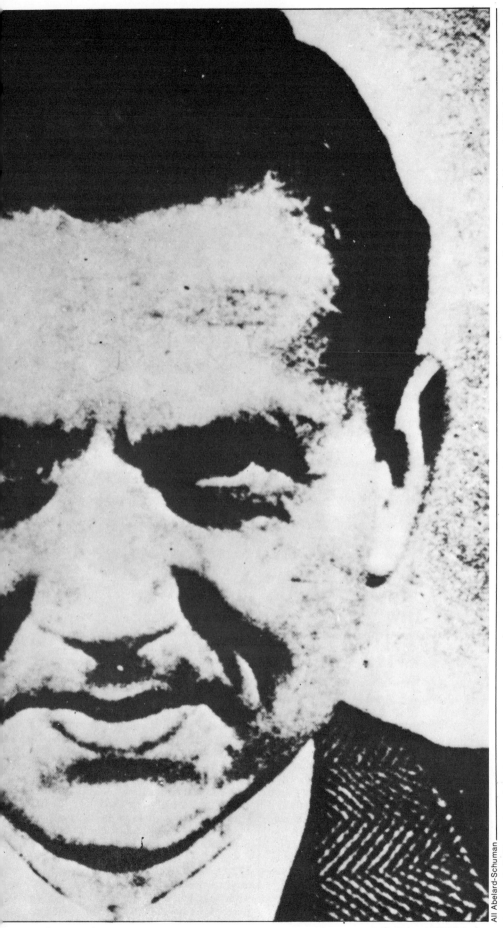
All Abelard-Schuman

womanhood for the purpose of breeding babies of undeniable racial purity. Schwarz's memorandum to the heads of the organization left little room for misconstruction.

"A situation has arisen," he wrote, "where we urgently need a group of women who are intelligent, attractive, have unwavering faith in the ideals of the Nazi Party and, preferably, possess a knowledge of foreign languages." The main qualification, however, was a liking for members of the opposite sex. The unspecified—but unmistakable—job would, he said, "be a wonderful opportunity for serving Fuhrer and Fatherland". There was not one reply. Breeding for the Fuhrer was one thing, soliciting was another.

Eye-stopping agents

Undismayed, Schwarz turned to the only other alternative. Since the amateurs weren't interested, he would have to try the professionals. During the next few weeks, the Berlin vice squad carried out an unprecedented number of raids on brothels, nightclubs, "dance bars", and other known haunts of prostitutes.

Hundreds of girls were rejected outright as being "emotionally unreliable". Many others were closely questioned by teams of investigators. Eventually, the "possibles" were winnowed down to a short-list of about 90. Schwarz himself, aided by a group of psychiatrists, doctors, language consultants, and university professors, made the final selection.

The 20 girls who emerged successfully from the seven days of non-stop tests and interrogation were certainly the most eye-stopping agents ever to write their names in invisible ink. A few days later, the girls were transferred to the officers' Academy at Sonthofen—where a sealed-off wing had been set aside for their training.

For seven weeks they underwent arduous courses in foreign languages, unarmed combat, home and foreign politics, marksmanship, economics, the use of codes and ciphers, and general intelligence techniques. Experts in cookery, make-up, and hygiene gave lectures. They had to memorize posters and wall charts illustrating military uniforms and decorations. Interviewers from German radio demonstrated how conversation could be used to draw out information. There was even a grim, severe-looking woman to instil the rules of etiquette.

Meanwhile, Untersturmfuhrer Schwarz was seeing to the "redecoration" of the Pension Schmidt. The entire place was gutted. Under the pretext of renewing the electrical wiring, microphones were installed in all the bedrooms, corridors, and reception rooms—with the leads joining in a multi-core cable which ran along the guttering and down a drainpipe to the listening-post in the cellar.

The cellar was completely rebuilt and bricked off, and contained five monitoring desks, each housing two record-turn-tables. Conversations in all seven bedrooms, Kitty's "reception" parlour, her own private room, and the kitchen could be recorded simultaneously on wax discs. On a tour of inspection, Walter Schellenberg was delighted. The place was as replete with bugs as a flophouse mattress. "I only hope," he said, "that the Salon Kitty lives up to expectations."

As it turned out, Operation Salon Kitty was to exceed their most audacious hopes. On March 25, 1940, Madame Kitty sat in the parlour of the magnificently re-furbished Pension Schmidt and waited for Untersturmfuhrer Karl Schwarz to reveal the part she was expected to play in the heady new life of the brothel.

"You will be told no more than is abso-lutely necessary," he began. "Business will carry on as before, and you will con-tinue to welcome all your old customers as if nothing had changed. If they enquire about the redecoration, you can explain that the place was getting a little shabby. Your existing staff of girls can stay, but there will be one small difference."

Schwarz reached into a mock-leather briefcase and pulled out a large album. It contained a selection of eyebrow-raising pictures of his 20 "horizontal agents", each girl identified by a typed list of personal details.

Unwitting client

"Every now and again, we will direct a certain customer to your premises," he said stiffly. "Under no account will you introduce him to one of your girls. You will show him this album, and when he makes his choice you will phone for the girl in question, and she will arrive within 10 minutes. You will not discuss the client with her, and she will leave immediately the man has gone."

Kitty Schmidt knew a set-up when she saw one, but she said nothing. "How will I recognize one of your special clients?" was all she asked. "Simple," said Schwarz with a self-satisfied smirk. "He will introduce himself with the code-phrase 'I come from Rothenburg'. As soon as you hear that, you know what to do."

The time had come to test the system. The unwitting test client chosen to "launch" the Salon Kitty was Wolfgang Reichert, a young SS officer on leave in Berlin. Steering him to the salon was pimp's play. "Just say you come from Rothenburg," Schwarz winked. "I can promise you an orgy of a time." So, on April 8, 1940, Schwarz and other high-ranking SD officers listened-in gleefully to the "opening performance" in the basement monitoring-room.

At first, Reichert was a disappointment.

As the microphones followed his pro-gress from parlour to bedroom, he babbled on about his home, his relatives, his friends in the SS, and his fervent regard for the Fuhrer. It sounded more like a recruiting advertisement than a security leak. Then the girl got to work. "I bet you want to see some real fighting soon . . ." she cooed. Reichert rose to the bait. To the horror of the eavesdroppers in the cellar, he started bragging about his unit's imminent transfer to Flensburg.

"If you ask me," he boasted, "the Fuhrer's got his eye on Sweden." "It works, it works!" cackled Schwarz, for-getting for the moment that the young officer had just let slip a vital piece of top-secret information. Salon Kitty was in business. Two hours later, the girl filed her written report, unaware that the entire conversation had already been recorded and forwarded to Gestapo head-quarters, and that her talkative companion was heading for court-martial.

Statuesque blonde

As more "Rothenburgers" were fed into the pipeline, Salon Kitty flourished as never before. Schwarz's 20 girls were soon loving round the clock. Shorter shifts were introduced as the monitoring teams slumped exhausted over their turn-tables. The attractions of the brothel were being increasingly touted among the country's high-ups, and Madame Kitty's guest-list read like an official reception for the Fuhrer.

When the Rothenburgers started out-numbering the genuine customers, Kitty complained that not only was the place running at a loss, she could no longer keep up with the demand for rationed food and alcohol. "Ignore the official rationing system," said Schwarz blandly. "We'll organize special supplies. As for money, put in your expenses for every Rothen-burg customer."

The customers, both contrived and genuine, poured in. In 1940, nearly 10,000 people climbed up to the third floor of No. 11 Giesebrechtstrasse. At its peak, the monitoring team were recording 3000 love-session discs a month. The "stars" of the records were some of the biggest names in international diplomacy.

Sometimes the listening team got more than they bargained for. The Italian-speak-ing female agent who slid between the sheets with the Italian Foreign Minister, Count Galeazzo Ciano, was treated to a blistering tirade on the inadequacies of Adolf Hitler as statesman, politician, soldier, lover, and family-man. In the basement, ears patriotically burned. Count Ciano then turned to Italy's pros-pects in the war, and scattered an in-credible amount of vital information before he remembered his reason for get-ting into bed. Schwarz was alerted, and a

transcript of the pillow talk was sent to Hitler. Relations between Germany and Italy were never the same again.

There was more embarrassment when the roistering, bucolic Major-General Sepp Dietrich—commander of the SS Leibstandarte, Hitler's private body-guard—bounced into the Salon Kitty, bellowing the "Rothenburg" code-word. "Don't show me one tart," he shouted jovially as Madame Kitty flipped through the album. "Bring the lot! I want to see them on parade!"

While a maid plied Dietrich and his companions with beer, Kitty frantically phoned the number given to her by Schwarz. "Round up as many of your friends as you can," she said, "we've got a party." In the bedroom, the monitoring team were impressed by Dietrich's per-formance, particularly his sweeping com-mand of sexual vocabulary, delivered in a thick Bavarian accent. But there were no dropped secrets. He fell asleep after an hour, the girl in one hand and a cham-pagne bottle in the other.

The "Rothenburg" password only slip-ped up once. One evening, a soldier appeared at the door and, after some pre-liminary mumbles, announced "I'm from Rothenburg". He didn't look as if he would know a secret if he tripped over one, but Kitty was taking no chances. The man thumbed through the album, eyes popping like wine corks. Eventually, he settled for Isolde, a statuesque blonde twice his size, who looked as though she had just stepped out of a Wagnerian opera.

The eavesdroppers in the basement were bewildered as the man revealed to the girl while undressing that he was a private in an infantry regiment on leave from the front. One banality followed another. However hard the girl tried, the only coherent sentence she could get out of him was, "How wonderful it will be to get back to the farm after all this is over." One of the monitoring team took off his earphones. "Who on earth sent this idiot?" he demanded. Months later, the truth came out. The man was a cowhand named Krebs . . . from Rothenburg.

Crackpot plan

Nobody was too important to be fun-nelled into Salon Kitty. On September 23, 1940, a telephone call warned Kitty Schmidt to be ready for a party of dis-tinguished guests. "Make sure you pick girls who speak Spanish," said the caller. Thirty minutes later, the bell rang. Stand-ing at the door were the German Foreign Minister, Joachim von Ribbentrop, his Spanish opposite number, Don Ramon

FELLOW CLIENTS . . . German Foreign Minister Joachim von Ribbentrop relaxes with his Italian counterpart Count Galeazzo Ciano. Both succumbed at Kitty's.

Abelard-Schuman

Serrano Suñer, and a group of Foreign Office officials. Kitty Schmidt had more important visitors than she realized, however. Down in the cellars, Walter Schellenberg himself had arrived to eavesdrop on the Foreign Minister. It was not a wasted hour. Locked in the parlour, Ribbentrop outlined a crackpot plan to Suñer involving the occupation of Gibraltar – which would have placed Germany under an impossible obligation to Spain.

Schellenberg scurried out of the building with the transcript and immediately telephoned his boss, Reinhard Heydrich. "It's monstrous!" said the Gruppen-fuhrer, secretly delighted at being handed fresh weapons to use in his long vendetta against von Ribbentrop. Heydrich reported the conversation to Heinrich Himmler, Hitler's head of the SS, who took steps to have the plan squashed instantly.

With his highly sharpened sexual tastes, it wasn't long before Heydrich yielded to desire and started visiting Salon Kitty, usually in the guise of a "tour of inspection". The inspection invariably took in several of the girls. "On these occasions," Schellenberg recalled in his *Memoirs,* "I was given special orders to turn off the listening and recording apparatus."

British agent

It was towards the end of the year that their most unwelcome guest almost literally stumbled across the existence of Salon Kitty. Lljubo Kolchev, a junior Press secretary at the Rumanian Embassy, chose to wander down Giesebrechtstrasse at the exact moment that Untersturm-fuhrer Karl Schwarz was supervising the re-routing of the monitor-wires to a new listening post at the SD headquarters at Meineckestrasse.

Kolchev almost tripped over the wires, and Schwarz involuntarily leaned forward to steady him. Kolchev took in the whole scene in a flash: the obvious SD man in civilian clothes, the workmen who looked more like soldiers, the multi-core cable running down the drainpipe, the general air of furtive hurry. He knew Salon Kitty was on the third floor of No. 11, and the "Rothenburg" password had already been bandied about the Rumanian Embassy.

"It's an Intelligence set-up!" he thought. "A love-and-listen centre." He was well qualified to judge. For Lljubo Kolchev was in fact Roger Wilson, a British Intelligence agent operating in Berlin.

It was fortunate for Wilson that he was handsome, and something of a sexual athlete. For Control in London ordered him to keep tabs on Salon Kitty without arousing any suspicion. "We will be sending you a technician to see if there is any possibility of tapping the wires for our own use," he was told.

Kolchev, alias Wilson, became a regular visitor to the salon, keeping his eyes and ears open even at the most ecstatic moments. Eventually, his communications expert arrived. Under cover of darkness, he managed to tap two or three of the individual leads in the multi-core cable. Now the bugs had bugs, and from the end of 1940 the British Secret Service was supplied with titbits from Salon Kitty.

But the golden days of Madame Kitty's speak-your-fate machine were waning. As Allied bombing raids on Berlin became more frequent, the flood of customers dried to a nervous trickle, and the monitoring teams had little to transcribe except for ardent and climactic monosyllables. Heydrich was also using the recordings more and more as ammunition in his inter-departmental feuds at Gestapo Head-quarters. In 1941, he ordered the monitoring centre to be moved to Prinz Albrecht-strasse, under his own control.

On July 17, 1942, the line from No. 11 went dead. The monitoring team tried everything, but they couldn't restore communications. Then the news was phoned in: "A bomb has just hit Kitty's." The indefatigable Untersturmfuhrer Karl Schwarz raced to the scene, his main concern being to spirit away the bugging equipment before anyone discovered it. The upper floors of No. 11 had been demolished. Kitty Schmidt's elegant furniture, carpets, and curtains were scattered all over Giesebrechtstrasse. Schwarz threw an army cordon round the building, and ordered his men to retrieve anything in sight and store it in the cellar.

Soot-blackened and awry, Kitty Schmidt stood watching as the firemen rolled up their hoses and the soldiers left the shell of No. 11. "Report to me tomorrow," said Schwarz as he climbed into his car. With a determined lift of his chin, he added, "Salon Kitty will rise again!"

When Schwarz had a problem, everyone associated with him shared it. Before the day was out, squads of workmen

arrived to convert the relatively un-damaged ground floor into a new salon. For 48 hours they struggled non-stop. On July 19 Salon Kitty reopened for boudoir business. Even Schwarz had to admit, however, that it was no longer possible to use electronic equipment to monitor the rooms. He had to rely on written reports.

But Salon Kitty had outlived its usefulness. The Nazi hierarchy had learnt that it was one huge megaphone, eager to amplify and transmit their innermost thoughts, for or against the Fuhrer. The diplomats, the officials and the officers drifted away, leaving it to soldiers on leave and old friends of Kitty's. Discipline began to slacken among the "Rothenburg" girls, and drunken parties – strictly forbidden by Schwarz – went on far into the night, to the sound of bombs, sirens, and anti-aircraft guns.

The salon had served its purpose. In the beginning of 1943 surveillance activities were officially wound up and the premises handed back to Kitty Schmidt, now 60, fat and haggard, and looking her age. Most of the "Rothenburg" girls had come to like the place, and they agreed to carry on as her normal "staff". Before the salon was returned to her, Kitty Schmidt had to sign a second form, swearing not to divulge anything she had seen, heard, or understood of "Operation Salon Kitty". The penalty for betraying this was death.

Extraordinary story

Within two years the Russians were at the gates of Berlin, now reduced to a wilderness of smoking rubble. The precious discs, so carefully stored in indexed filing cabinets at Gestapo headquarters, vanished. In 1954 huge crowds turned out for the funeral of Kitty Schmidt. She had honoured her word. To her dying day she never spoke about the secret of No. 11 Giesebrechtstrasse.

But the rumours about the hidden microphones, the highly trained girls, and the turntables in the cellar persisted. Only one man ever got on the right trail. For 25 years author Peter Norden investigated the extraordinary story of the love-nest-with-ears for his book, *Madam Kitty* (Abelard-Schuman). Only one thing eluded him: the whereabouts of the missing discs.

One day in 1963 he walked into a top-secret strongroom in the headquarters of the East German State Security Services in Communist East Berlin. And there they were, 25,000 of them . . . the silent graveyard of long-ago love, lust, and loose tongues.

Camera Press

THE PRISON CELLAR pictured was the monitoring centre for Salon Kitty. Heydrich (right) was pleased. He even managed to trap von Ribbentrop (left).

René Dazy/Quartet

Keystone/Syndication International

102

PICCADILLY CIRCUS in war-time. It was here that Evelyn Oatley was last seen alive, getting into a taxi with a young man. She was found brutally murdered.

THE WAR-TIME RIPPER

Night-time in London during World War II was dark and grim. But that didn't prevent the city's busy prostitutes from plying their trade. Under cover of darkness, however, another, more sinister, figure was at work—a horrifying sexual sadist!

WHEN 28-year-old Gordon Frederick Cummins, an aircraftman in the Royal Air Force, stepped into the prisoner's dock at the Old Bailey to stand trial for murder, the Crown believed it was bringing to justice a latter-day Jack the Ripper. Cummins might well have been the centre of as much publicity and notoriety as that most infamous of prostitute killers—except for one thing. This was March 1942, and blacked-out Britain was passing through one of the darkest periods of the Second World War. Attention on the home front was concentrated upon death almost nightly from German bombers.

Throat marks

Even so, Cummins made some headlines when his story had begun earlier that month at London's Bow Street Magistrate's Court—when he stood accused of six crimes: of the murder of Evelyn Hamilton, Evelyn Oatley, Margaret Lowe, and Doris Jouannet, and of the attempted murder of Greta Heywood and Catherine Mulcahy. To many in that courtroom he looked, at first sight, like a clean-cut young serviceman, with attractive green eyes and a fresh, boyish manner—the stuff, in fact, of which wartime heroes were made.

But the evidence showed another side to the apparently likeable young man. Detective Chief Superintendent Edward Greeno, of Scotland Yard, in charge of the murder hunt, stated that in the early hours of February 9, 1942, a woman's body had been found in the central London district of Marylebone. She had been strangled, and her silk scarf had been bound around her face, across the nose and mouth, as a gag. The body—apparently after the murder—had been dumped inside an air-raid shelter.

Greeno testified that the woman's empty handbag had been found in a nearby street, and the first indications were that she was the victim of a blackout "mugger", who had killed her when she attempted to resist him. She was identified as Miss Evelyn Margaret Hamilton, a 42-year-old qualified chemist who had recently been employed in Essex, and who was staying in London before moving on to a new job in Lincolnshire, in the north-east of England.

Only one clue, to what seemed to be an isolated murder, offered itself. It came from marks on the dead woman's throat which suggested to Chief Superintendent Fred Cherrill, of the Yard's Fingerprint Bureau, that they were made by the murderer's left hand. But the marks were bruises, and Cherrill was unable to find any fingerprints.

The following day, February 10, the body of 35-year-old Mrs. Evelyn Oatley was found in her apartment in Wardour Street, in the heart of the capital's "foreign" section, Soho. The naked corpse sprawled across a bed, as though it had been flung there, and the throat had been cut. The lower part of the body, near the sexual organs, had been ferociously slashed. By the side of the bed lay a bloodstained can-opener.

On the handle of the can-opener Cherrill had discovered faint impressions of fingerprints. He was satisfied that these had been made by a left-handed man. On a small piece of mirror, taken from the victim's handbag, he found a thumbprint, and that, he was convinced, came from a left thumb.

The court heard that Mrs. Oatley, separated from her husband, was a former showgirl who sometimes used the name of Nita Ward. She had taken to prostitution when wartime conditions had made it increasingly difficult for her to find theatre work. She had been last seen by friends on the previous evening, hailing a taxi in Piccadilly Circus in company with a young man.

The tale of death continued when—according to the police—three days later neighbours reported that they were worried about Mrs. Margaret Campbell Lowe—who appeared to be missing from her one-room flat in Gosfield Street, just off the West End's Tottenham Court Road.

Responding to the neighbours' alarm, detectives forced the door. Inside they found a room barely furnished except for a single bed, rug, and table. Near the foot of the bed lay a heap of woman's clothing, including a small pill-box-shaped hat with a feather in it. On the mantelpiece stood a glass candlestick and a half-emptied glass of beer.

Across the middle of the bed lay a "bulging" black quilt. When the quilt was stripped off detectives saw the naked body of Margaret Lowe. Around the neck was a tightly knotted silk stocking. As in the case of Evelyn Oatley, the lower part of the body had been obscenely mutilated. Scattered across the floor were a bread knife, two other knives, a poker, and a candle—all of which had been "used" on the victim.

Fashionable hotel

This time, Fred Cherrill testified, there was an abundance of fingerprints: on the candlestick and on the beer glass. Those on the glass were certainly of left-hand fingers and a left-hand thumb. Those on the candlestick were right-hand prints—but it was explained that a left-handed person might be expected, when removing a candle, to grasp the candle in his left hand and the candlestick in his right.

Mrs. Lowe, the court learnt, was 42, a tall, attractive woman who sometimes called herself Peggy Campbell, and who was known to many of her friends as Pearl. Before the war she had been the landlady of a boarding house in the coastal town of Southend. When the war put an end to that form of livelihood, she had drifted to London and into prostitution.

While detectives were still examining Margaret Lowe's body they received a message asking them to go immediately to Sussex Gardens, Paddington, in west London, where another dead woman had been found. This time the victim was 40-year-old Mrs. Doris Jouannet, the wife of the manager of a hotel in fashionable Sloane Square.

Mr. Jouannet said that, except on his days off, he slept each night at the hotel, and spent a few hours at home each evening with his wife. On the night of February 12 he had eaten supper with his wife at their flat; then she had walked part of the way back to the hotel with him.

"She wished me goodnight very sweetly, and her last words to me were, 'Don't be late to-morrow, darling,'" Mr. Jouannet continued. "I returned to the flat at seven o'clock on Friday night and was surprised to see that the milk had not been taken in. When I got into the flat I shouted out 'Doris', but there was no reply."

Sadistic frenzy

"On going into the sitting-room I found that the supper things from the night before were still on the table, and the curtains had not been drawn. I was worried, and when I found the bedroom door locked I knew something was amiss. I could not get any reply, so I went to the housekeeper and we sent for the police."

Police witnesses described the scene inside the bedroom—a scene they had advised Mr. Jouannet not to look at. Doris Jouannet's body lay across the bed, naked except for a bathrobe which had been dragged open at the front. Around her neck was a tightly knotted scarf, and, as in the other cases, the murderer had slashed at her body in a sadistic frenzy. Fingerprints were everywhere—but this time those that were identifiable belonged only to the dead woman.

But there had been another and, as it turned out, important event that same evening. It occurred when a young married woman, Greta Heywood, was in a Piccadilly bar-grill, waiting for a friend to join her for a meal. A good-looking young airman began chatting to her and eventually invited her to join him for a drink in a nearby pub.

Mrs. Heywood agreed, she said, on the understanding that it must be a "quickie" because of her appointment. They had

HANDSOME KILLER Gordon Cummins had no difficulty in persuading women to accompany him. They were flattered by his attentions and apparent good manners.

their drink, during which the man seemed charming and quietly pleasant. However, as they left the pub and came into the blacked-out street, the young airman suddenly said, "You must let me kiss you goodnight." He drew Mrs. Heywood into the doorway of an air-raid shelter. Then, without a word, he put his hands around her neck and began to throttle her.

In her fright she dropped the torch which, like most people in Britain, she carried to light her way. Its clatter as it fell to the sidewalk attracted the attention of a passer-by and the airman fled.

This incident, the court heard, provided the one decisive lead for which the police were seeking. When Mrs. Heywood reported the attempted attack, police officers who returned to the scene with her found that, in his frantic hurry, the assailant had dropped his service gas-mask, bearing his name and number. The name was Aircraftman Gordon Frederick Cummins.

Totally unperturbed

Evidence was then given on the routine checks with Royal Air Force authorities which speedily led the police to Cummins' billet in St. John's Wood, in north-west London. There Cummins was questioned about the attack on Mrs. Heywood and charged with assault. His fingerprints were taken and were compared with those found on the can-opener near Mrs. Oatley's body, and the candlestick in Mrs. Lowe's room. In each case the prints matched.

Meanwhile, the prosecution stated, there had been an attack on another woman, only two hours after the attempted killing of Mrs. Heywood. In the Piccadilly area Mrs. Catherine Mulcahy met a young airman and went with him by taxi to her apartment in Southwick Street, Paddington—only a few yards from Sussex Gardens, where the murdered body of Doris Jouannet still lay awaiting discovery.

At the apartment, Mrs. Mulcahy said, the man tried to strangle her. But she reacted too quickly for him. She screamed out, kicked, and hurt him with the boots she was wearing. He ran out of the apartment so fast that he left his R.A.F. belt behind him. Mrs. Mulcahy had been able to identify Cummins.

On his arrest, the police said, Cummins had made a statement in which he claimed that on the night Miss Hamilton was murdered he and a service friend spent the evening roaming around West End bars until, at about eleven o'clock, they picked up two women. They agreed to go off with the women separately and meet again later. They did meet, Cummins said, and rolled back drunk to their billet—where some of their fellow-airmen put them to bed.

Cummins' companion was interviewed,

the magistrate was told, but produced a story with quite a different ending. He said he returned to the billet, alone, at around 6 a.m., and Cummins was then already in bed. But, the police testified, small particles of brick dust found in Cummins' gas-mask case were tested. They were found to be identical with dust samples taken from the air-raid shelter in which Miss Hamilton's body was discovered. At his billet detectives unearthed a cigarette case and fountain pen which had belonged to Margaret Lowe and Doris Jouannet.

It was on the basis of this, and other evidence, that Cummins found himself in the prisoner's dock at the Old Bailey. He seemed totally unperturbed by the accusations made against him, and stared cheerfully around the court. In accordance with the normal practice of English law he had been charged with one murder only; that of Mrs. Evelyn Oatley.

His defence was one of complete denial—even though all the evidence, first given at the magistrate's court and then repeated at the Old Bailey, pointed indisputably to him. And it was the fingerprint evidence which led to a situation unique in British criminal courts.

As a set of fingerprints was being passed to the jury for inspection, Chief Superintendent Cherrill startled everyone by

MYSTIFIED detectives at the scene
of the murder of Evelyn Hamilton search
for clues. Cummins' identity was finally
revealed when his gas-mask was found . . .

Popperfoto/Robin Clifford

107

remarking quietly to the judge: "I think, My Lord, the jury has been handed a wrong exhibit."

On the judge's direction the prints were snatched from the jury and given to the sharp-eyed Cherrill, who was waiting in the witness-box to give his evidence. Cherrill studied the exhibit and immediately confirmed his own suspicions. The prints concerned one of the other cases for which Cummins was not being tried. The judge at once asked the jury to retire while he and the lawyers for Crown and defence discussed the legal implications of the mix-up.

When the jurors were finally ushered back into the courtroom, Mr. Justice Asquith told them: "It is possible, and very probable, that, from the exhibit before you, you might have drawn certain inferences which would have made it impossible for you to try this action properly. I know I can rely on you not to mention anything that has come to your knowledge from this exhibit."

His Lordship then appealed to newspapermen to "treat this matter with every discretion", and discharged the jury. A few days later the trial was re-opened with a new jury. Once more the evidence was repeated, and once more Cummins stuck to his "I am innocent" plea.

By the time the trial reached its end it took the jury only 35 minutes to find Cummins guilty. The judge, sentencing him to death, spoke of the slaying of Mrs. Oatley as "a sexual murder of a ghoulish type". Cummins himself seemed totally unmoved. In the brief smile that he gave to those nearby there was a hint of the charm that had proved so lethal.

Sexual escapades

Some people who knew him well, and who were in court for the verdict, recalled that he had been known as "The Count", and "The Duke", because of his educated speech and impeccable social manners. His highly respectable parents had provided him with every opportunity, but he had been a failure at school and at work. His interests were totally concentrated upon sexual escapades. The reasons for his sadism remained a mystery even to those who guarded him during his time in custody. Before his arrest no hint of his killer self had reached senior R.A.F. officers, for they had accepted him for training as a fighter pilot.

Cummins appealed against sentence, and was in relaxed and ebullient mood at the Court of Appeal as he sat between two prison officers. Several times he turned and smiled broadly at his young wife, who had stood bravely by him throughout his trial, and who was still convinced of his innocence.

But if Cummins genuinely felt that he might go free, he was to be disappointed. In dismissing the appeal, Mr. Justice Humphreys, the Lord Chief Justice, declared that "there was no scamping the evidence in this case". Superintendent Cherrill, he said, had been cross-examined in great detail, and the defence had called no witness to refute his evidence.

The Lord Chief Justice called fingerprinting "this peculiar but singularly conclusive form of evidence, because it is claimed nearly 600,000 persons have been identified without any error being known to have been made, and in no case have two people been found to have fingers or thumbs with identical marks".

Cummins was taken to Wandsworth Jail, in south London, to await execution. Despite the preoccupations of the war, there were many who felt that the circumstances of Cummins' conviction should be further examined. The People's Common Law Society collected 10,000 signatures pleading for a stay of execution.

Chief Superintendent Greeno was asked to prepare a special report replying to points raised in the petition. But, after considering that and taking other advice, Herbert Morrison, the Home Secretary,

THREE VICTIMS . . . Only ex-showgirl Evelyn Oatley (far left) could be said to be attractive. Evelyn Hamilton (left) and Doris Jouannet (below) were middle-aged. Why did Cummins choose them?

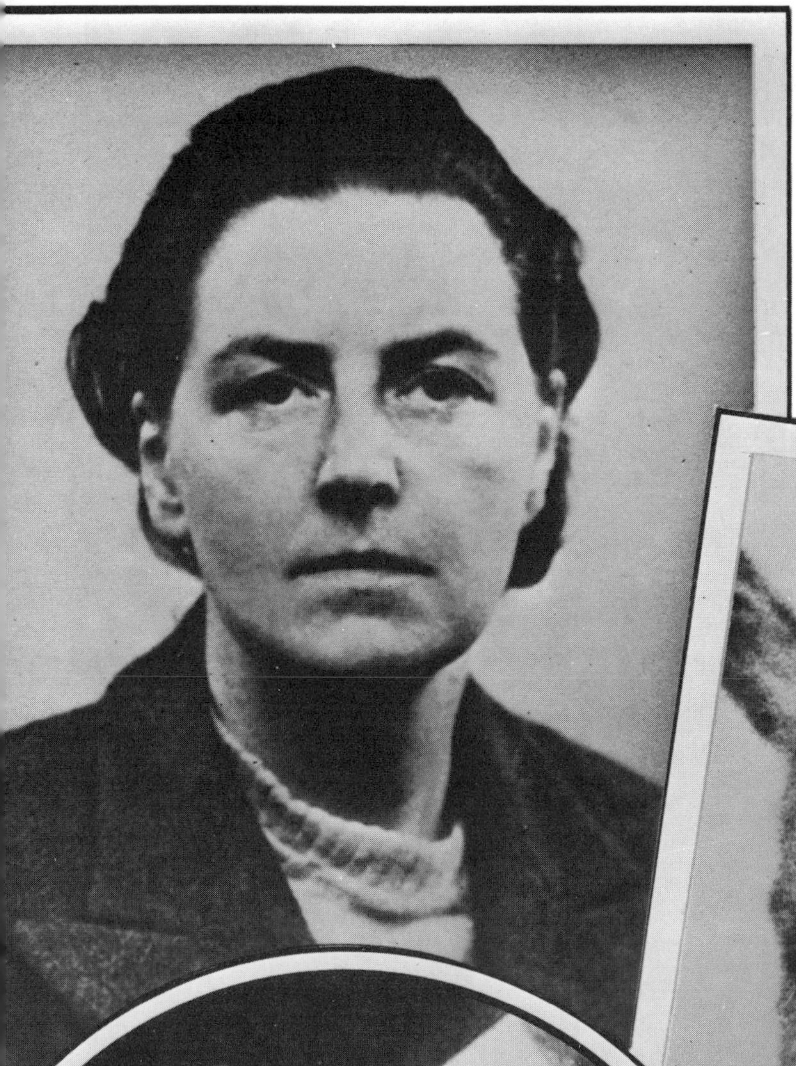

Syndication International

109

Robin Clifford/Quartet

announced that he found no grounds for a reprieve.

Shortly before eight o'clock on the morning of June 25, 1942, Gordon Frederick Cummins—dubbed by the press "The black-out Jack the Ripper"—walked, unmoved and unrepentant, to the gallows. The noise of the falling trapdoor mingled with the distant crump of explosions as Luftwaffe planes flew over London on a bombing raid.

The hanging of Cummins had a notable side effect on the "social" life of the capital. The thousands of prostitutes who had temporarily abandoned their operations—or confined them to well-known and trusted "regulars"—went safely back to work.

TERROR SEIZED London's good-time girls and prostitutes as one Cummins victim followed another. The killer's success was, of course, based to a large extent on his captivating personality. Women who would otherwise not dream of accepting the overtures of a strange man seemed to be mesmerized by him. Were there so many girls who felt lonely?

THE FIRERAISERS

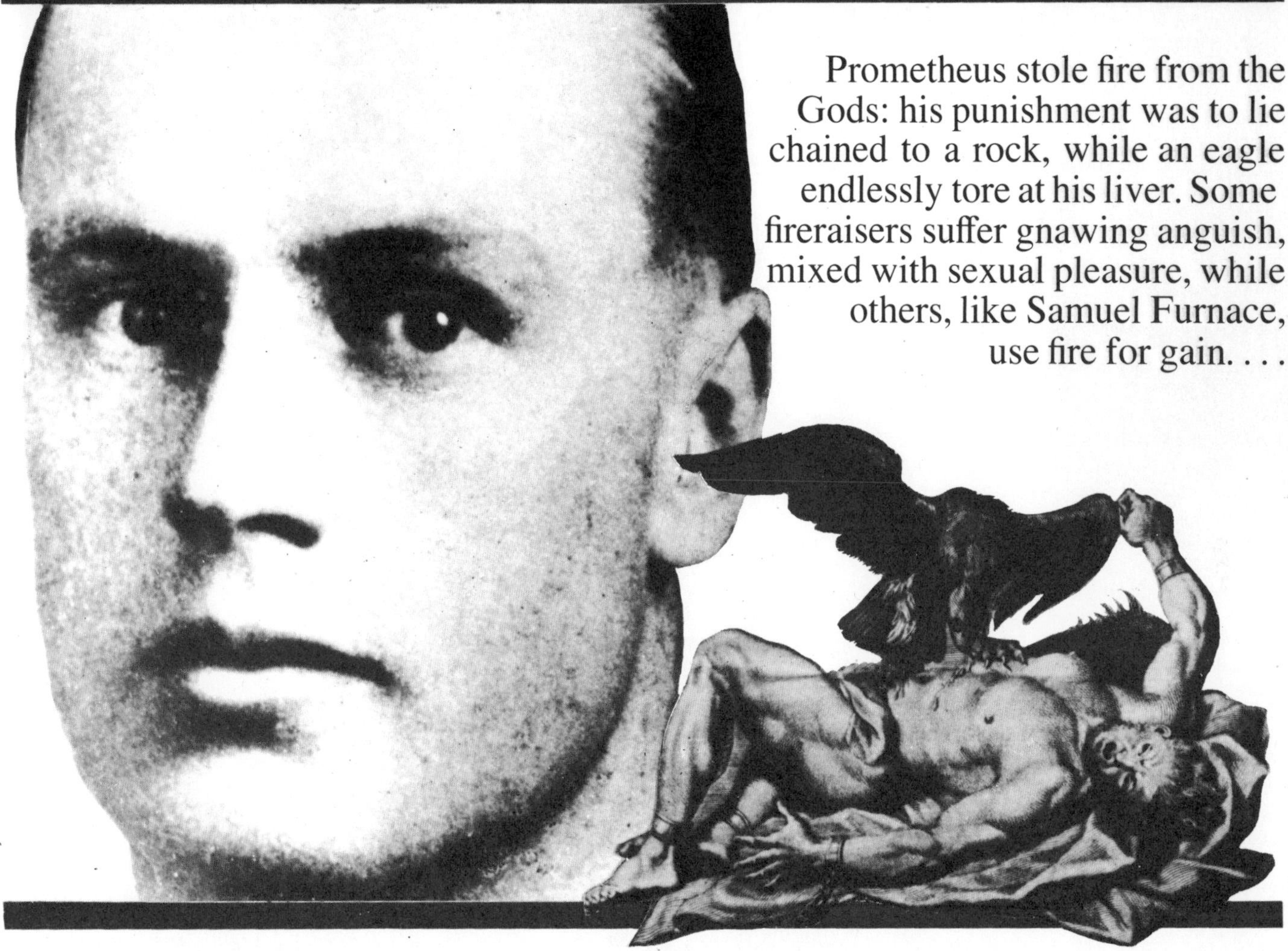

Prometheus stole fire from the Gods: his punishment was to lie chained to a rock, while an eagle endlessly tore at his liver. Some fireraisers suffer gnawing anguish, mixed with sexual pleasure, while others, like Samuel Furnace, use fire for gain. . . .

Syndication International

Mansell

"DURING the firing of the haystacks, the thought that human beings might be burnt added to the sensations that I experienced. I always watched the fires, usually from near at hand, so near in fact that I have been asked to give a helping hand. . . . The shouting of the people and the glare of the fire pleased me. During big fires, I always had an orgasm. If you see in my confession sometimes several arsons in one night, then I had no success with the first or the second. I also had an orgasm when I fired the woods. It was a lovely sight when one pine after another was consumed in the flames fanned by a sharp east wind . . . that was wonderful."

This extract is from the confessions of the arch sexual-pervert, Peter Kurten, the monster of Düsseldorf. And it introduces us to the most baffling of all sexual abnormalities: pyromania. Even today, little is known of this frightening urge. It is pointedly ignored in most textbooks of clinical psychiatry. Perhaps this is under-

standable. Anybody can understand a rapist or even a sadist, because there is a fragment of them in every one of us. But how can a normal human being understand someone who obtains sexual satisfaction from watching a fire?

We can obtain some insight into this complex process from a confession quoted by Dr. Melvin Reinhardt, in his classic study *Sex Perversions and Sex Crimes*. He cites the case of a 14-year-old boy who, with three other boys, was smoking cigarettes in a hay barn. Someone unintentionally tossed a cigarette butt into the hay; the barn caught fire, and all four ran away. The boy felt an odd compulsion to stop and watch; he stayed behind bushes, and observed the arrival of police and firemen. This *could*, of course, have been normal curiosity — most people like seeing a fire. But he also noted that he had vague sexual thrills from the sight of the flames. As he read about the blaze in the newspaper the next day, he

again experienced the same excitement, and a compulsion to go and start another fire. This time the thrill was even stronger. Finally, by the time he was watching his fourth fire, the intensity was so great that he masturbated. He was caught and sent to a reformatory.

There *are* other psychological elements here that we can recognize: for example, his delight as he read the newspaper headlines, and thought that no one but he knew who was responsible. This is straightforward ego-satisfaction, and it undoubtedly plays a part in pyromania. The psychiatrist Dr. Wilhelm Stekel has commented that most pyromaniacs are unhappy, drifting individuals, who feel themselves rejected by society. They often suffer from strong feelings of inferiority. Even so, this fails to explain how or why fire is associated with sexual feeling.

It becomes somewhat clearer in another case cited by Reinhardt, involving an

111

extraordinary, complex web of sexual emotions. The father of a family of three girls, all in their teens, had ceased to have sexual relations with his wife. His sexual desires became fixated on the 14-year-old daughter. One day, he met her out of school, drove her to a quiet lane, and had intercourse with her. The girl admitted in her statement to the police: "For two or three times, Daddy removed my panties . . . then I began liking it." Like many young girls, she was infatuated with her father.

For the next three years they continued to have sexual intercourse two or three times a week, and he also encouraged her to stimulate him orally. One night, the mother heard her daughter going to the father's bed. There was a violent quarrel, and she threatened to report him to the police. It was after this that he began to brood on killing his wife and one of the other daughters. (The third was away from home.) He then enlisted the aid of the incestuous daughter, who alleged: "He said he wouldn't interfere with me any more if I helped to pour gasoline on the floor."

On the afternoon of the murder, he met his youngest daughter, Ruth (age 13), in the kitchen and hit her violently in the stomach, knocking her unconscious. When his wife came in, he also struck her with his fists; he was obviously a powerful man, for three blows laid her out, too. The eldest daughter then came in; they both soaked the kitchen (and the unconscious wife and daughter) in paraffin. As they left, the man tossed a match into the room. As the place burst into flames, he drove off, went shopping, went for a swim, and then returned home, and found the fire engines there and the house burnt out. The empty paraffin cans gave the police the clue to the fire.

In this case, it would seem as if the fire was started as an attempt to cover up the crime. Understandably, no policeman of 50 years ago would have assumed there was any sexual element in the case. On the other hand, there is one highly significant point. In a carefully planned murder, the killer does not leave empty paraffin cans to suggest that the fire was started deliberately. However, every criminologist has observed that there are many cases of murder in which the killer seems to *want* to get caught. He does something that will provide an obvious clue: for example, parks his car near the scene of a murder, or leaves some article of clothing behind. This desire to expiate guilt happens most frequently in cases of sex murder.

APTLY NAMED Sam Furnace staged his own fake suicide by burning the body of a rent collector in his office. In jail he really killed himself with acid.

SAMUEL JAMES FURNACE,
Born 5/3/90.St.Neots.
5'10½"; comp: fair, hair
fair thin in front; eyes
hazel; full face;square
jaw; tooth missing upper
jaw front; gunshot wounds
left leg & both arms -
right bicep has long scar
shewing marks of 13
stitches.
Dress:- Navy blue suit,
new light blue shirt &
collar to match,lightish
brown overcoat,fully
belted,grey trilby hat
back band,straight rim,
light brown socks,black
shoes.

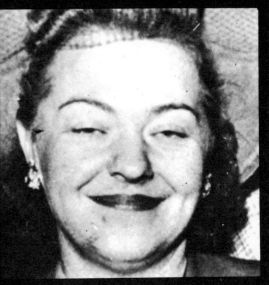

It appeared to apply to the present case, and was undoubtedly the reason that led Dr. Reinhardt to classify it with other examples of pyromania. After three years of sexual intercourse with his daughter, the father felt a burden of guilt, and the fire was a strange, twisted attempt to *burn away* the guilt. This could well resolve the otherwise inexplicable relation between sex and fire. Fire is a symbol of purity, and the self-divided pyromaniac simultaneously longs for purity and is sexually excited by it. This is confirmed by another curious observation made by many criminologists: that the pyromaniac often feels the need either to urinate or empty his bowels when he sees the flames.

In *The Sexual Criminal,* Dr. Paul de River mentions two female pyromaniacs —middle-aged, sexually frigid women— who felt a compulsion to stoop down and urinate as they watched the fires they had started, and a burglar who had to hide in bushes and empty his bowels after he had watched a fire. In all these cases, the criminal confessed to an immense feeling of relief *and purification* after the act—all of which seems to suggest the psychological explanation of this mystery.

Most people know what it's like to feel thoroughly oppressed by their everyday life, and to want to simply run away from problems. The inadequate personality feels like that *all* the time—which explains why, as Stekel says, he is often a drifter; he keeps on running away. There is an exhilarating finality about a fire; for example, if you burn old love letters or diaries, it is like watching your own past go up in flames. In a weak, vacillating person, flames may become

JEALOUSY drove Gerry Cornwell (left) to burn his ex-mistress Alice Franklin (above) and her lover to death. Below: the victim's burned sofa.

All UPI

associated with a feeling of delight and relief—just as the Russian physiologist Pavlov taught dogs to salivate when he rang a bell, because they *associated* it with dinner.

So the pyromaniac starts fires because each one brings this sense of relief, of a new start—as well as satisfying a basic resentment against the civilization that oppresses him. (The pyromaniac burglar cited by de River did not *always* set fire to the apartment; sometimes he only lowered his trousers and defecated on the carpet; this seems to prove the association between fire and resentment.) Finally, it is easy to understand how two completely different forms of relief—fire and sex—can become associated, in the same "Pavlovian" way.

This, then, is probably the basic psychology of the pyromaniac. There is evidence to suggest that, to some extent, it applies to *all* criminals who use fire as their "final solution". For some deep, atavistic reason, human beings have the feeling that fire can solve any problem whose solution seems to demand total destruction. This explains why witches and heretics were burned, and why the Nazis constructed ovens in their death camps. We can also see the same psychology at work in the case of Alfred Rouse, the English burning car murderer, and of the aptly named Samuel Furnace, whose crime was probably inspired by Rouse.

Numerous clues

In January 1933, Furnace, a builder of Camden Town, north London, killed a rent collector named Spatchett, stole £40 he was carrying, and then incinerated the body by setting fire to a shed that served him as an office. The corpse was assumed to be that of Furnace—until the pathologist noticed that it had been shot in the back of the head. A nationwide murder hunt for Furnace followed.

He wrote a letter to his brother-in-law, asking him to meet him in Southend-on-Sea, near London, and the brother-in-law informed the police. In prison, Furnace managed to poison himself by drinking a bottle of hydrochloric acid that he had sewn into the lining of his coat. A detailed study of the case reveals that Furnace was undoubtedly an "inadequate personality". To begin with, he was not (like Rouse) heavily in debt—only to the extent of £90. And his suicide revealed the same basic failure to face up to the consequences of his own actions.

This "psychology of inadequacy" can be seen in an otherwise somewhat commonplace murder that took place in Ypsilanti, Michigan, in 1931. Three ex-convicts had been drinking moonshine whisky, and then decided to go out and rob someone. They found four 16-year-olds in a car in a lovers' lane, held them up, and robbed them of two dollars. One of the girls was then dragged out of the car and raped. The others resisted, and all were battered to death or shot. The robbers next set the car on fire. Because of numerous clues they left behind, they were placed under arrest within a few hours. A court tried the case and sentenced them to life imprisonment in record time—there was a howling mob outside the courthouse, hoping to lynch the men.

A more recent American case makes the link between incendiarism and inadequacy even plainer. Gerry Cornwell was a 32-year-old mechanic, who lived in Oakland, California. Until a few weeks before Christmas, 1955, he had lived with his mistress, an ex-waitress, Alice Franklin, who was three years older than himself. Then Alice transferred her affections to a 27-year-old steelworker, Robert Hand. Cornwell quietly moved out of the apartment. He actually remained on fairly good terms with his ex-mistress and her lover, and on the night of the murder had been at a party with them.

He was drunk, and followed them back home to 5955 Telegraph Avenue; hiding outside the bedroom window, he watched them make love, then fall into an alcoholic slumber. He went to a nearby garage, bought three gallons of petrol, then walked into the bedroom—where the lovers snored on—and drenched the bed in petrol. As he went out, the pilot light of the stove ignited the petrol fumes. Firemen rushed the victims to hospital, but both died a few hours later. The police had no difficulty in locating Cornwell, who confessed. An interesting legal point arose at the trial—whether Cornwell could be charged with murder when he had not actually struck the match that ignited the petrol. The judge, however, pointed out that it was undoubtedly his intention to kill his mistress and her lover, and he was found guilty and sentenced to life imprisonment. Cornwell's inadequacy appears throughout: handing over the apartment to his rival, remaining friendly with the lovers, following them back to the apartment to watch them make love—a strong touch of masochism here—and the blind rage that is so typical of the inadequate personality when pushed too far.

No account of fire-raisers would be complete without some account of "the German Rouse cases"—although, in many ways, they fail to fit into the general pattern of pyromania. The first case actually took place a year before Rouse murdered an unknown tramp on the Northampton road. Kurt Erich Tetzner was also a commercial traveller, but in 1929 business was poor. One day, his mother-in-law told him she had cancer, and that her only hope was an operation; her chances of surviving it were only 50/50. Tetzner dissuaded her—for just long enough to insure her life for the equivalent of £500. (Because of her cancer, he was unable to make it more.)

Then he persuaded her to have the operation after all. His gamble paid off; she died three days later. Tetzner was amazed and charmed at the ease with which one could get money out of the insurance companies. He discussed with his wife how they could repeat the *coup*. She suggested a plan that was virtually the same as Rouse's: to get a body from a graveyard and burn it in his own car. Tetzner disagreed about the graveyard.

STARTLED CAT peers out from under a table in Mrs. Franklin's fire-stained apartment. A scorched Christmas tree hangs above . . .

"There must be blood around," he said.

He tried advertizing for a "travelling companion". A young man applied, but something in Tetzner's manner made him suspicious, and he changed his mind. Next, Tetzner picked up a hitchhiker on the road to Munich. The man's name was Alois Ortner, and he was an out-of-work mechanic. In a town called Hof, Tetzner gave him money to have a shave and buy himself a collar and tie. Then, outside the town, he asked the mechanic to check an oil leak under the car.

As soon as the man disappeared, Tetzner seized a hammer and an ether pad. If he had waited until Ortner's head appeared, and then hit him, while he was still under the car, Tetzner might have succeeded. But in his excitement, he allowed Ortner to emerge before he attacked him. The mechanic fought back fiercely, then ran away into the woods. But apparently he failed to report the incident.

On November 25, 1929, Tetzner picked up another hitchhiker, a thinly clad youth of 21, whose name Tetzner never found out. The youth complained of being cold, so Tetzner wrapped him in the travelling rug. When his arms were tightly pinioned, he grabbed a piece of rope and strangled the youth. Near Ettershausen, he crashed the car into a tree, put the body in the driving seat, and sprinkled it with petrol. Then he laid a trail of petrol back to the car and set it on fire.

Phone calls from Strasbourg

Tetzner was more fortunate than Rouse; he was not seen as he ran away. The burnt-out car was found; his wife identified the corpse as that of her husband, and it was buried. She now applied to the insurance company for the 145,000 marks for which Tetzner had insured his life (more than £13,000 in present-day terms).

However, the insurance officials were suspicious; to begin with, the slightly built corpse was not really like Tetzner. They contacted the Leipzig police, who kept a man on permanent duty watching Frau Tetzner. During the next few days, she was twice called to the telephone in a neighbour's flat. The neighbour told the police that the call was from Strasbourg and that the caller identified himself as "Herr Stranelli".

The police then asked their Strasbourg colleagues to check on a Herr Stranelli, who was probably thick-set, and had a pudgy face with pig-like eyes. When a detective from Leipzig arrived, the Strasbourg police already had "Stranelli" in custody. It was, as they had suspected, Tetzner.

Tetzner at first confessed to the murder, then withdrew the confession. His story in court was that he had accidentally knocked down the young man and

CAR-BURNING KILLER Alfred Rouse was seen sneaking away from the fire and soon had the police on his trail.

killed him. He had placed the corpse in the boot of his car, and gone for supper. During the meal, he suddenly realized he could now carry out his plan to disappear. . . . A forensic expert from Leipzig University supported his story, saying that injuries to the body suggested it had been run over. But the jury disbelieved it, and Tetzner was condemned to death. He was executed at Regenburg on May 2, 1931.

A young man named Fritz Saffran read about Tetzner's crime with great interest. He was manager of a large furniture store, Platz and Co., in Rastenburg. To all appearances, the store appeared to be prosperous. In fact, it was nearly bankrupt. Saffran had been selling the furniture on hire purchase, and during the depression his customers were simply not paying. Herr Platz, the owner, was perfectly happy to leave the management of the store in the hands of the brilliant young manager, for Saffran not only paid him a generous pension, but was also his son-in-law.

In fact, Saffran was having an affair with the girl who kept the accounts, a strong-minded young woman named Ella Augustin, and was planning on disappearing with her. He had also taken into his confidence the chief clerk, Erich Kipnik. The plan was to insure Saffran's life heavily, plant a body in the store, and set the store on fire. The problem was, where to obtain a body? Their original plan—of digging one up from a grave—was rejected. The three of them then set up camp in the Nicolai forest, and every morning Kipnik and Saffran would each drive off in his car, looking for a victim.

At their trial it transpired that they had made several unsuccessful attempts. One man who got into the car with all three of them said he had six children, so they let him go. On another occasion, Ella lost her nerve while Kipnik was

pounding a man with a life preserver, and allowed the person to go alive and free. Finally, they found a suitable victim, a young man on a bicycle—Saffran later said Kipnik had got out of the car and shot him, while Kipnik blamed Saffran. The corpse was duly taken to the store. For some reason, the conspirators delayed starting the fire.

The dead man—a dairyman named Dahl—was killed on September 12, 1930. But it was not until the evening of the 15th that a tremendous explosion shook the store. Many employees who were inside miraculously escaped safely. Kipnik, apparently in hysterics, declared that Saffran had rushed into the flames to try to save the account books. Later, a charred body was found.

Two weeks after the fire, a chauffeur named Reck was asked by Ella to call at her house and drive her mother to Königsberg. A man came out of the house, and the chauffeur recognized Saffran. He talked about this, and his gossip came to the ears of the police.

Their enquiries soon revealed the motive for the crime—that the store was nearly bankrupt. The manhunt for Saffran began. He was hiding in Berlin, with a relation of Ella Augustin's, a poor carpenter. In early November he stole the carpenter's identity papers, and boarded a train for Hamburg—from where he hoped to escape to America.

However, an old army acquaintance recognized him at the Spandau station, and notified the police. Saffran was arrested, and he, Kipnik, and Ella Augustin appeared in the same dock in Bartenstein, East Prussia, in March 1931. They pleaded for sympathy, begged the victim's wife tearfully for forgiveness, and tried to blame one another. The two men were sent to prison for life; Ella received five years.

A rare crime

Today, electronic fire alarms, fire-proof building materials, and automatic sprinklers are making arson one of the rarest of crimes. There is no reason why, in a civilized society, fire should not be stamped out like the bubonic plague. We may hope that the curious perversion known as pyromania may one day disappear of its own accord.

One thing, however, that is not in doubt is that when Prometheus, in Greek mythology, stole fire from the Gods and brought it to earth, he did not live up to his name—which meant Forethinker. He literally did not know the conflagration he was starting, and for his crime he was riveted to a rock by Zeus, who daily sent an eagle to tear out the prisoner's liver—which was renewed each night. A cruel, but, in mythological terms, just punishment.

THE SPY MASTERS

Soviet agent Rudolph Abel, posing as a bohemian New York artist, ran one of the most successful spy rings of all time—until he was jailed. Then American U.2 pilot Gary Powers was shot down over Russian territory and the two men were exchanged. Is this spying by international agreement . . . ?

Bettmann Archive

THE CORPSE that was dragged out of the icy waters of the Baltic Sea was still clutching two hefty books in its arms. The Russian captain of the vessel which found him was puzzled; why on earth should a sailor want to leap into the sea holding heavy books — and why hadn't he let go of them when he was drowning? The Russian was a novice in modern warfare; it was only September 1914, and most naval and military men were still naïve enough to believe that wars were fought only with soldiers. They knew little about spies and secret codes.

Coded messages

The captain's superiors in the Russian Admiralty were not much wiser. They recognized that they had captured German code books — handed by the captain of the sinking *Magdeburg* to one of his men, with orders to drop them into the sea. But it did not strike them as a particularly exciting discovery. A few days later, the Russian attaché in London called on Winston Churchill, the First Lord of the Admiralty, and told him that they had found the German naval code books. If the English would care to send a ship, they were welcome to them.

Churchill immediately appreciated their value. He sent the ship, and rushed the books to Admiral Oliver, head of Intelligence. Oliver handed them to one of his best men, an ex-teacher named Alfred

WOMAN'S WORK . . . Belle Boyd (top left) and "Rebel" Rose were confederate spies who, under the protection of Yankee chivalry, worked for Stonewall Jackson.

Ewing. Ewing knew all about codes: he had been trying to crack the German naval code for months.

He grabbed the latest batch of coded messages, picked up from radio signals sent out from the German naval base at Wilhelmshaven. Within a few minutes, he knew that fortune had presented him with a prize. It was possible for him to read

the secret orders of Grand Admiral Tirpitz and other senior commanders.

Two months later, in November 1914, Ewing was given a new boss — Captain William Reginald Hall, known as "Blinker" (because of a twitching eyelid). The new head of Naval Intelligence did not look in the least like a spy; he was short, rotund, and cheerful. In fact, he was one of the most brilliant spymasters in the history of espionage.

Tense wait

The first thing Hall wanted to know was whether the codes could tell them something useful. On December 14, 1914, Ewing decoded a report that announced that the German fleet intended to sail. Quietly, Hall moved his own ships into position in the North Sea. Two days later, Britain suffered its first naval bombardment, as ships of the German navy pounded the north-east coastal towns of Scarborough and Hartlepool with their heavy guns. Hall signalled his own battle cruisers, lying nearby, and told them to move in for the kill.

All day, Churchill and Hall waited tensely for news. When it came, it was disappointing. Fog and rain had swept down over the North Sea as the British navy moved in. There had been a few shots exchanged, and the Germans had vanished into the mist. Churchill was disappointed; but to his surprise, Hall

118

was looking jubilant. "There'll be a next time!" he cried. But that stoical reaction hardly explained his delight. He had been struck by a kind of vision. Modern warfare depended on *surprise*. The Germans had gained the element of surprise when they invaded Belgium. But ever since Marconi's discovery of radio in the 1890s, the surprise depended on a man with a transmitter and a code book. If he could find *all* the code books, it would be possible to anticipate every important move of the enemy. But how was he to do this? The two he had were important, but they were not the only ones.

For example, there were the strange signals coming from a transmitter in Brussels. Ewing had been working on the code for months, without success; Hall had a feeling it concealed important secrets. He ordered his spies to find out everything they could about the Brussels transmitter. This was not difficult; it had been there, in an office in the Rue de Loi, before the war. More inquiries revealed that it was

operated by a young man called Alexander Szek. "That name doesn't sound German," said Hall thoughtfully.

He made more inquiries—and suddenly knew that he was close to a solution. Alexander Szek, he discovered, was an Austro-Hungarian subject who had been born in Croydon, in south London. Members of his family were still living in England. Hall persuaded Szek's father to write Alexander a letter, begging him to work for the British. A British agent in Holland smuggled it to Brussels—and soon discovered that Szek was not par-

the code; a German Intelligence officer worked with him, and showed it to him when he needed it. But he could memorize it—a few figures at a time—and write it out.

In the early months of 1915, Szek began stealing the code. Every time he completed a page, he handed it over to the British agent. His nerve, however, was beginning to crack. He told the agent that he wanted to be smuggled to England as soon as he had finished copying the code. The agent pointed out that if he did that, the Germans would immediately change the cipher. But Szek was insistent.

Then, a short while afterwards, Szek was found dead in his room in Brussels. He appeared to have been killed by a burglar. The British later said he was a victim of the Germans. The truth, almost certainly, is that he was murdered by the British. Next, to their horror, the Germans suddenly discovered that their "surprise" moves were no longer surprises. Their European armies found they

AXIS POWERS celebrate signing of cooperation pact (above). Master spy Dr. Richard Sorge (top), however, knew all about their plans for World War II.

ticularly pro-German. The Germans had persuaded him to work for them because he was a good radio engineer. But neither was he a born spy; the idea of stealing the German secret code terrified him. The British hinted that his family in England might be put in prison if he refused: so, finally, Szek agreed.

Szek was not himself in possession of

were being outgeneralled because the enemy was able to anticipate their moves. The day of modern espionage, the espionage of the "cold war", had arrived.

During the American War of Independence, there were some notable espionage exploits. Nathan Hale, spying for the Americans, was captured and executed in the first year of the hostilities. He died saying, "I only regret that I have but one life to lose for my country"—the kind of sentiment that would make a modern spy snort cynically. Hale became a martyr; so did the British spy, Major John André,

who liaised with the infamous traitor Benedict Arnold. Women spies also came into their own during the war—since no one could tell *which* side a woman belonged to, and the officers of both nations were far too gallant to search one of the "gentle sex".

Important battle

Belle Boyd, a "rebel" spy, had Northern officers quartered in her house in Martinsburg, Virginia. She was thus able to gather all kinds of information about troop movements, which she promptly relayed to General Stonewall Jackson. (On one famous occasion, she got through the Northern lines and delivered a message that enabled Jackson to win a battle.)

The most amusing thing about her career is that the Northern officers were soon convinced she was a spy, but were forbidden by chivalry to take any action. She *was* finally arrested, when one of her dispatches fell into the hands of a Union agent—but she was exchanged for a Northern prisoner, and became a heroine in the South. The careers of "Rebel Rose" Greenhow and Pauline Cushman (a spy for the North) were equally remarkable, and now belong to American folklore.

Major industry

But it was under the Soviet regime that spying became the major industry we know today. The Russians always had their tradition of secret police; under the last of the Czars, it was called the Ochrana, and its chief business was to root out revolutionary activity. Trotsky's secret police, the "Cheka", soon became the dreaded G.P.U. ("Gay Pay Oo"). But after Lenin's death, the congenitally suspicious Stalin felt uneasy about the increasing power of the secret police. Its head, Yagoda, was executed in the purges

of 1937. It was fortunate for the Russian Intelligence Service that two of its greatest spies—Ernst Wollweber and Richard Sorge—were working abroad, out of Stalin's reach.

It is generally agreed by experts that Sorge was probably the greatest spy of all time. Born in Russia in 1895, his family moved to Germany when he was a child. As a student he became passionately left wing; he joined the German Communist Party, and eventually became its intelligence chief. He trained in Russia, then moved around Europe, building up spy rings in Scandinavia and Britain. (The British Secret Service spotted him fairly quickly; after that, Sorge always maintained that it was one of the best in the world.)

Ardent womanizer

In Russia in the late twenties, he was involved in clashes between the Army Secret Service and the Secret Police (G.B.), and his fate might well have been the same as that of Yagoda. Fortunately for him, the Communists decided that he would be useful in the Far East, specifically Japan. His instructions were simple, The Soviets were firmly convinced that the great threats of the future would come from Germany and Japan.

He was well qualified for the job. A highly intelligent man, who spoke several languages, he also had the perfect cover. He was an ardent womanizer. With so many shreds of scandal attached to his name, and a reputation for being an incorrigible philanderer, who could believe that he was also a spy and a top level Communist official? He didn't seem to be serious enough.

Nevertheless, in Japan, Sorge began to recruit agents. These included Agnes Smedley, a well-known author of books on

China, and a friend of Mao Tse-Tung; Ozaki, a Japanese correspondent; a Yugoslav pressman, Voukelitch. Methodically, Sorge also built up an intelligence network in China. Then, when Hitler came to power in 1933, he was given another task: to spy on the Germans in Japan. There was one important preliminary—he had to apply for membership of the newly-formed Nazi Party. Hitler's Intelligence system was so inadequate that Sorge was given a party card. Back in Tokyo, he then completed his own Japanese spy network with the addition of an American-Japanese, Miyagi Yotuka. Miyagi and Ozaki were ordered to form their own sub-network of Japanese spies.

Sorge's charm—and his cover as a correspondent for the *Frankfurt Times*—soon made him friends at the German embassy, among them a military attaché, Lieut-Colonel Eugen Ott. Meanwhile

Ozaki became a leading member of a "breakfast club" of Japanese intellectuals, with close connections with the cabinet. It was he who told Sorge in advance of Japan's projected attack on China: information which delighted the Kremlin, because while Japan was fighting China; it was unlikely to invade Russia.

Later, when Colonel Ott was appointed German ambassador, Sorge had sources of information about German and Japanese policies which made him the most important secret agent in the world. Sorge knew about the Japanese attack on Pearl Harbor—in December 1941—weeks before it happened. He knew the exact date when the Germans intended to invade Russia, and if it had not been for Stalin's complacency in ignoring his information, "Operation Barbarossa" would have been defeated within days.

The head of Japanese Intelligence, Colonel Osaki (not to be confused with the agent, Ozaki), knew there was a major spy network in Japan; his radio receivers picked up their coded messages, but he could not read them. Finally, he became convinced that Sorge was his man. He asked a German attaché to arrange a meeting with Sorge at a nightclub. Over a bottle of sake, he told Sorge about a beautiful girl who danced in the cabaret—about how many men were in love with her. Sorge was curious—and his curiosity was increased by the mask the girl wore. He began to spend every evening at the club, until finally the girl became his mistress. But she was an agent of Colonel Osaki's—an aristocratic Japanese girl who had been asked to sacrifice her self-respect for her country.

One night while driving her home, Sorge stopped his car, and started to make love to the girl. Then he asked her to come back and spend the night with him. Before deciding, the dancer asked him for a

UNDERCOVER AGENTS lead a dangerous life. Defector Gouzenko (far left) was forced to conceal his identity for fear of reprisal. Another defector was Reino Hayhanen (top). He revealed that Abel (below) used his studio (left) not only to paint but as a centre for espionage.

cigarette. Sorge took out his case—and a tiny roll of paper fell from it. He carefully tore the paper up, and threw the pieces out of the window. The girl made an excuse to get to a telephone, and rang Japanese Intelligence. Almost as soon as the car had driven away, Japanese agents were collecting the torn fragments of paper. The next morning, as Sorge lay asleep beside the girl, Colonel Osaki walked into the bedroom. He handed Sorge a section of the message he thought he had destroyed. The spy stood up and bowed. He knew he was defeated.

According to one account, Sorge faced his executioners—in November 1944—with complete nonchalance, smoking a cigarette. But there is no definite evidence that Sorge *was* executed. It is known that he claimed a reprieve on the grounds that he was a Soviet citizen, and that Russia was not at war with Japan. A British diplomat who knew Sorge claimed

that he saw him in Shanghai in 1947. And it was at about this time that the girl who had betrayed Sorge was murdered. So it seems possible that he ended his days behind a desk in the G.P.U. headquarters in Moscow.

After the war, Soviet Intelligence suffered a heavy blow when the attaché Gouzenko defected to the West, and took with him a complete list of Russian spies and their contacts. The result was that Russia decided to reorganize her spy system in the United States. The man who was chosen for the job was Colonel Rudolph Abel.

Abel was, in fact, already in New York when Gouzenko's defection led to the arrest of the Rosenbergs and the rest of their network. He had been a veteran of the secret service ever since Trotsky had founded it after the 1917 Revolution. Now, in 1948, on the collapse of the Soviet spy network in America, Abel

patiently set about rebuilding it.

The master spy established himself in an artist's studio in Fulton Street, Brooklyn. On the door was a notice: Emil Goldfus, Photographer. As well as film and cameras, the place was also full of radio equipment—Abel explained that he was a radio enthusiast, and supplemented his income repairing sets, which was true. His cover, like Sorge's, was almost perfect. A good-looking, intelligent, middle-aged man, he liked girls, played the guitar well, and was a more than passable painter. The artists who attended parties in his studio regarded him as a typical Bohemian with typical artistic activities.

In fact, he was busy contacting the remnants of Russia's spy ring in the United States, and putting them to work again. He also re-contacted various American embassy officials who had been blackmailed into aiding Russian Intelligence when they were stationed in Moscow. By 1953, the revitalized Russian spy ring was stronger than ever. The secrets that flowed to Moscow via Abel's transmitter included details of the American hydrogen bomb and atomic submarines.

Demoralized assistant

His downfall was a new assistant, Reino Hayhanen, a Russian Finn. Like many Finns, he was a heavy drinker. He was also unhappy about spying in a foreign country. Abel had Hayhanen's wife sent out to join him, but this proved to be a mistake. The couple quarrelled all the time, and Hayhanen became less efficient than ever. He resented his lack of contact with Abel; their meetings were often in public parks, or in the New York subway.

In 1955, Abel went to Russia; when he returned, he discovered that Hayhanen had been drunk for weeks. He told his demoralized assistant that it was time he journeyed to Russia for a holiday. Hayhanen was terrified; with his reputation as a drunk, it was a 50/50 chance that he would be eliminated. He travelled as far as Paris—then went to the American embassy, and explained that he wanted to defect. So one more Russian spy network collapsed. Abel was sentenced to 30 years in jail; but he spent only five there. In 1962, he was exchanged for the American pilot, Gary Powers. And Russia's greatest spy since Sorge returned after all to end his days in Moscow.

More and more the spy lives in a limbo between his employers and those whom he seeks to betray. In some cases—when the agent plays a double, or even treble, role—his life span can be calculated in terms of days rather than weeks, weeks rather than months. Ultimately, the spy finds himself with only one person left whom he can trust—himself. And when his own self-trust evaporates—as it eventually does—then he is as good as dead.

Tools of the trade

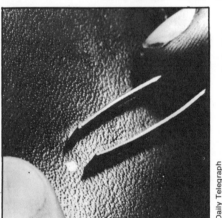

MICRODOTS . . . The process which turns documents into punctuation-size points; now considered unsophisticated.

PRIVATE EYE . . . This is a fully operational camera the size of a large wristwatch. Still a little obvious.

CUFF LINK . . . This can be wired to a tape recorder concealed in a pocket and is virtually impossible to detect.

CONVERSATION PIECE . . . The most useful of all spy weapons is the tape recorder now available in billfold size.

Camera Press

Daily Telegraph

Daily Telegraph

Daily Telegraph

ONE-WAY TICKET

The train shrieks into a tunnel that seems endless . . . and for some hapless travellers it is indeed a journey of no return. Shrouded in darkness, train murders are rarely easily solved—if at all.

Mary Evans

ON July 25, 1814, a strange contraption with iron wheels groaned and hissed into life, and dragged eight wagonloads of coal along parallel iron tracks. That first railway engine, christened "Blücher" and affectionately known as Puffing Billy, also dragged its inventor into the limelight of world history.

George Stephenson, the self-educated son of a Northumbrian miner, was not only an inventive genius; he also proved himself an inspired prophet when he told the British House of Commons: "People will live to see the time when railroads will become the great highways for the King and all his subjects . . ." What he did not foresee was that his great invention was inaugurating a new and fascinating chapter in the history of murder.

Oddly enough, the classic cases of "murder on the railway"—Müller, Dickman, the Merstham tunnel mystery, the Rock Island Express murder—now have a nostalgic fascination for students of crime. We can anticipate the day when railway stations will disappear and give way to airports—as they have already disappeared in many parts of America—and the thought of a steam engine chugging between green fields has all the charm of a pleasant daydream.

A run for his money

England's first train murderer was Franz Müller: Müller may well be the world's first train murderer, for he killed Thomas Briggs in 1864, and it was almost another ten years before Jesse James committed the world's first train robbery and brought a new kind of risk into the lives of railroad passengers. At least Müller had a run for his money. This was not true of England's second train murderer, Percy Mapleton, alias Lefroy, who seems to have been one of those unfortunate young men for whom nothing ever goes right.

He had a beaky nose, a low forehead and a receding chin, and his ambition was to make a living as a writer. His short stories were heavily sentimental, and the one he finished in mid-June 1881 was no exception. It was about a music-hall comedian, whose wife, Nellie, leaves him for a life of gaiety and sin, and finally returns, dying "of cold and want". Her husband naturally forgives her.

"'At last—Joe—darling husband—goodbye—', and with a sweet and happy smile, Nellie went down with the sun." Mapleton was a vain young man, and he liked to dress well. Short-story writing was obviously no way to a fortune, so on June 27, 1881, Mapleton took a decision that had been reached by the hero of Dostoevsky's novel *Crime and Punishment*: he would commit one remunerative crime, and use the proceeds to finance a career devoted to the

entertainment and betterment of humanity.

He was seen walking up and down the platform of London Bridge Station, peering into carriages. In those days, the corridor train was almost unknown; so once you were in a compartment, you stayed in it till the next station. Mapleton selected a compartment containing an old gentleman who looked rather well-to-do; he was, in fact, a retired merchant named Frederick Gold.

As the train was about to enter Merstham tunnel, between London and Brighton, passengers were startled by the sounds of revolver shots. At Horley, a village on the other side of the tunnel, several people in cottages near the line noticed two men struggling in one of the compartments as the train went by. A few miles farther on, at Balcombe tunnel, a door was heard to slam. When the train arrived at Preston Park, Brighton—where Mr. Gold lived—a young man climbed out, and his appearance attracted the attention of several passengers.

His face was blood-stained, his collar and tie missing, and he looked as if he had been in a fight. When the ticket

A BEAKY NOSE and receding chin made Percy Mapleton (top, inset) easy to find and capture after he killed an old man on a Brighton-bound train.

collector noticed a watch-chain hanging from his boot, he stopped him and asked him his name. The young man said Lefroy. He explained that he had been attacked in Merstham tunnel. According to "Lefroy", there had been two other people in his compartment: an old gentleman—Mr. Gold—and a rough-looking man of "rustic appearance".

In Merstham tunnel, said Lefroy, he had received a violent blow on the head. When he recovered consciousness, the other two passengers had vanished . . . The story was absurd; he was asking them to believe that the robber had first knocked him unconscious, then leapt out of the carriage with Mr. Gold. The ticket collector sent for a policeman, and Lefroy was arrested.

Not long after, the body of Mr. Gold was discovered in Balcombe tunnel—minus his watch and wallet: but his death was due to a violent blow on the head;

The Graphic

there were no gunshot wounds. With some dignity, Lefroy asked if he could go to his lodgings to change his clothes. The policemen agreed. Lefroy took them to a ladies' boarding school in Croydon, which, he claimed, was run by his aunts. He asked the police to wait outside; and, amazingly enough, they did. Lefroy vanished inside. Half an hour later, the police realized he was gone; he had walked out by the back entrance.

But Lefroy's appearance was too distinctive for him to remain at large for long. A *Daily Telegraph* artist made a sketch of him according to the description of witnesses—the first identikit picture. When it appeared in the newspaper, a landlady in a cheap Stepney lodging recognized it as a strange young man called Park, who kept his blinds drawn and stayed indoors all day. He had told her he was an engraver and needed quiet to work.

But when the police arrived, Lefroy, whose real name was Percy Mapleton, gave himself up quietly. At his trial he strenuously maintained his innocence. He also asked permission to be tried in a dress suit, convinced that no English jury

would sentence a "gentleman" to hang. He was mistaken. Before his death, he confessed to killing Frederick Gold. He was hanged on November 29, 1881. Oddly enough, the revolver was never found.

The next railway murder was unsolved. At 8.25 on the evening of February 11, 1897, a cleaner who entered a railway carriage at Waterloo Station saw a pair of legs sticking out from under the seat. The compartment was heavily bloodstained, and the body proved to be that of 33-year-old Elizabeth Camp, a barmaid from the East End of London. The motive was robbery; she had been carrying a silver-handled umbrella and wearing a rather flashy brooch—actually made of paste diamonds. She had also carried £16 in her handbag—which, like the umbrella and the brooch, was missing. She had been battered to death.

A blood-stained pestle

The compartment she had been travelling in was second class; her sister, who had seen her off at Hounslow Station at 7.42 that evening, had remarked that third-class compartments were safer for women; Miss Camp had replied that she preferred the class of people she met travelling second. Her murderer—who must have killed her very quickly, since the train halted every few minutes—was never caught. The only clue, a bloodstained chemist's pestle found on the line, led nowhere.

In 1901, a Mr. Pearson was shot in a tunnel near Wimbledon; a third passenger had been present, and the killer, a man named Parker, was quickly found and executed. But the next British train murder remains an intriguing mystery. On Sunday, September 24, 1905, at eleven o'clock at night, a gang of workmen who were about to carry out repairs to Merstham tunnel—the same tunnel in which Mapleton had attacked Mr. Gold—found a body lying by the railroad track. It had been badly mutilated by a train, and closer examination revealed it to be a young woman. The first assumption was that this was suicide. The head was smashed, the face unrecognizable, the left leg cut off, and the arm crushed.

Two facts soon convinced the police this was murder. A gag had been forced into the woman's mouth; and on the sooty side of the tunnel there were long marks indicating that she had jumped—or been thrown—out of a train. She had rebounded under the wheels of the train. The next day, a young dairy farmer named Robert Money viewed the body and identified it as his sister, 22-year-old Mary Sophia Money. Mary was a book-keeper who worked for a dairy at Clapham and lived on the premises.

And now the police encountered impenetrable mystery. Mary had been on

duty that Sunday. She had finished her work at seven o'clock, and told another woman, a Miss Hone, that she was going for "a little walk". Shortly after, she called at a confectioner's at Clapham Junction and told the man from whom she bought chocolates that she was going to Victoria. No other witnesses could be found who saw her after she walked towards the Victoria train at Clapham Junction.

But now a problem arises. There were only two trains from which Mary Money could have been pushed, and both of them ran from London Bridge to Brighton. Before Merstham tunnel, these trains both stopped at Croydon. So it seems that she went out from her lodging, claiming that she was going for a short walk, and had every intention of going to Victoria. Why? Almost certainly, to meet someone—a man. For some reason she then went on to London Bridge, or, possibly, Croydon. A guard who walked along the platform at East Croydon noticed a young man and woman in one compartment—No. 508—and they looked so "intimate" that another passenger, for whom he opened the door, went into the next compartment.

At South Croydon, the same guard—who seems to have had the instincts of a Peeping Tom—looked into the compartment again and saw they looked even more "intimate", having pulled up the arm-rest between them; they also looked guilty and furtive, as if they had been kissing. His description made the girl sound like Mary Money.

Altogether, then, the evidence suggests that Mary Money went off that evening to meet a male acquaintance at Victoria, intending to return to Clapham later the

A KISS and a cuddle on the train from Victoria—her date gets carried away, tries to rape her . . . and for pretty Mary Money the evening ends in death.

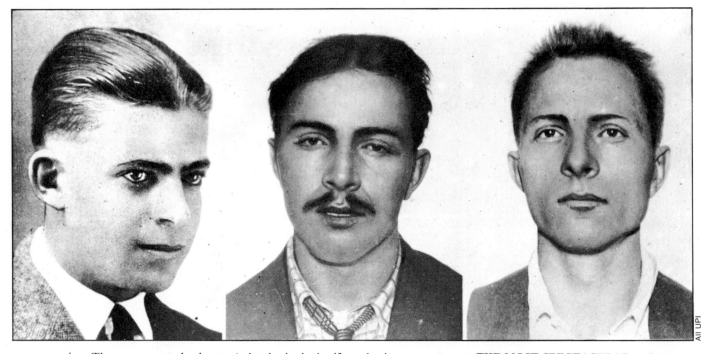

All UPI

THE MOST SPECTACULAR train murder in America: the DeAutremont brothers (from left, Hugh, Roy and Ray) dynamited a Southern Pacific mail train.

same evening. The man persuades her to get on another train to London Bridge or Croydon. Then he persuades her to take the train to Brighton with him. She is sufficiently infatuated with him to agree. They kiss and cuddle from Croydon to somewhere just before Purley Oaks; then the man gets carried away and tries to rape her. She screams; he forces a gag into her mouth—at which point he either decides to throw her from the train, or she opens the door and jumps.

In August 1912, the British press speculated about another possible solution after a sensational suicide case. A woman ran screaming from a room in a Brighton boarding house. Shortly after, there was a roar of flame, then the sound of shots. Firemen were called, and when they had extinguished the blaze, they found five charred bodies in the room: a man, a woman, and three children. In a vase there were twenty gold sovereigns, and a note saying: "I am absolutely ruined, so killed all that are dependent on me . . ." It was signed C. R. Mackie, but Mackie was soon identified as Miss Money's brother Robert, the man who had identified her body.

The woman who had run from the room was his mistress; the dead woman was her sister. Robert Money, it seemed, was a weak, vain man and an inveterate liar. He posed as "Captain Murray" and said his father was a barrister, although he was, in fact, a carpenter. He had lived with one of the sisters in Clapham, and given her two children, then run away with the other and given her a child, too. He married her, but later left her to return to his original mistress.

The circumstances that led him to despair are not clear; all that is known is that he invited wife and mistress—separately—to the room in Brighton, together with the children, then pulled out a revolver and tried to kill them all. The mistress escaped, wounded. Money had time to soak the bodies in petrol, throw a match on it, then shoot himself.

Was he the murderer of his sister? many journalists now asked in print. It seems possible but unlikely. What was his motive? Why should his sister go with him to London Bridge, then take the Brighton train? The tragedy of Robert Money only strengthens the possibility that Mary Money was murdered by a man with whom she was starting a liaison, for it suggests that brother and sister may have shared the same taste for "forbidden pleasures". Many leader writers at the time pointed out that railway murders could be stopped quite easily—by doing away with the old type of train in which the compartments are separate, and substituting corridor trains.

Baffling features

As an increasing number of corridor trains came into service, train crimes became rarer, and murders almost ceased—although as recently as the 1960s rapes have taken place in the old type of railway carriage. A case that occurred in 1914 has some of the same baffling features as the murder of Mary Money. On January 9, a boy travelling in a train from Chalk Farm to Broad Street noticed a leg sticking from under the seat.

It proved to be that of a five-year-old boy named Willy Starchfield, who had been strangled. Willy had lived in Chalk Farm with his mother, who was separated from her husband, John Starchfield. He had been missing since the previous

afternoon. Witnesses said they had seen a boy answering to Willy's description with a man on the previous afternoon, and the inquest brought in a verdict of wilful murder by the father.

But the witnesses were unreliable, and at his trial Starchfield was acquitted. He had no motive to kill his son—unless out of spite against the mother, which was never established. Not long before the murder, John Starchfield had been shot when he tackled a murderous maniac with a revolver, and he was awarded a "hero's pension" of £1 a week. It has been suggested that someone killed Willy out of "revenge" for his brave act, but this seems just as unlikely. The murder remains unsolved.

Another English railway murder occurred on March 13, 1929, when a Mrs. East was murdered when she was travelling between Kidbrooke and Eltham. However, the crime aroused little interest, and the murderer was never caught. Neither was the killer of a nurse on a London-Hastings train in January 1920.

America has had many rail murders, but most of them have been connected—as one might expect—with train robbery. The Rock Island Express murder of 1886 had, for a while, an interesting element of mystery. Kellogg Nichols was an Express Messenger, and on March 12, 1886, he was carrying over $22,000 from Chicago to Davenport, Iowa. Somewhere between Joliet and Morris a train hand named Newton Watt gave the alarm after a masked man had held him up.

Investigation of the mail car showed that Kellogg was dead, his brains beaten out.

The safe had been broken open. William A. Pinkerton, son of the famous detective, was called in. His suspicions soon fell on Watt, and on the brakeman, Fred Schwartz. Schwartz's hands were badly scratched, and the dead man had had skin under his nails, indicating that he had fought his attacker. Although no evidence could be found against the two men, Pinkerton was certain of their guilt—they had been several times overheard talking about large sums of money, and they talked of retiring from the railroad.

Finally, Schwartz made his mistake; he fell in love with an attractive young girl, Ella Washam, and married her. Since he already had a wife in Philadelphia, the police now had an excuse to arrest him, and while he was in jail, Pinkerton talked to Ella and got from her an admission that Schwartz claimed he had "found" a large sum of money. Confronted with her husband, Ella said: "Please tell them about the money you found . . ." Schwartz now alleged he had found $5000 in a package under a seat in the train on the day after the murder. A jury did not believe him, and although the evidence was entirely circumstantial, he and Watt were both sentenced to life imprisonment.

Cold-blooded shooting

Perhaps the most spectacular case of train murder in America took place in the autumn of 1922. Three brothers named DeAutremont—Hugh, Roy and Ray—held up the Southern Pacific mail train near tunnel 13 in Oregon. When E. E. Dougherty, the mail clerk, saw a man with a revolver approaching, he slammed the door, whereupon the gunman, Hugh DeAutremont, placed dynamite under the car and blew it apart, killing Dougherty. The driver was ordered to take the train into tunnel 13, but when it failed to move—because of the damaged mail car—both he and the foreman were shot down in cold blood.

When the bandits tried to get into the mail car, dense fumes drove them back, and they eventually fled. An envelope containing Hugh DeAutremont's name and address was found in a discarded pair of overalls near tunnel 13, and launched a manhunt for the brothers which lasted four years; Hugh was captured in the Philippines, where he was serving as a soldier; the twins Ray and Roy were captured in Steubenville, Ohio. All three brothers went to jail for life.

The name of Winnie Judd also deserves to be remembered in connection with railroad crimes, although her murders were not actually committed on a train. It was in October, 1931, at the Southern Pacific station in Los Angeles, that a baggageman noticed the strong smell emanating from two trunks which had been sent from Phoenix, Arizona. Blood was dripping from one. When a young man and woman came to claim the trunks, they were asked to open them; they said they didn't have the keys, and went off to get them.

When they failed to return, the baggageman forced open the trunks—and found

UPI

WINNIE JUDD (centre, with police matron) was ruled insane. After killing Hedwig Samuelson (above) and another roommate, she sent the bodies to herself by train. Murder scene (top) shows bloodstained rug.

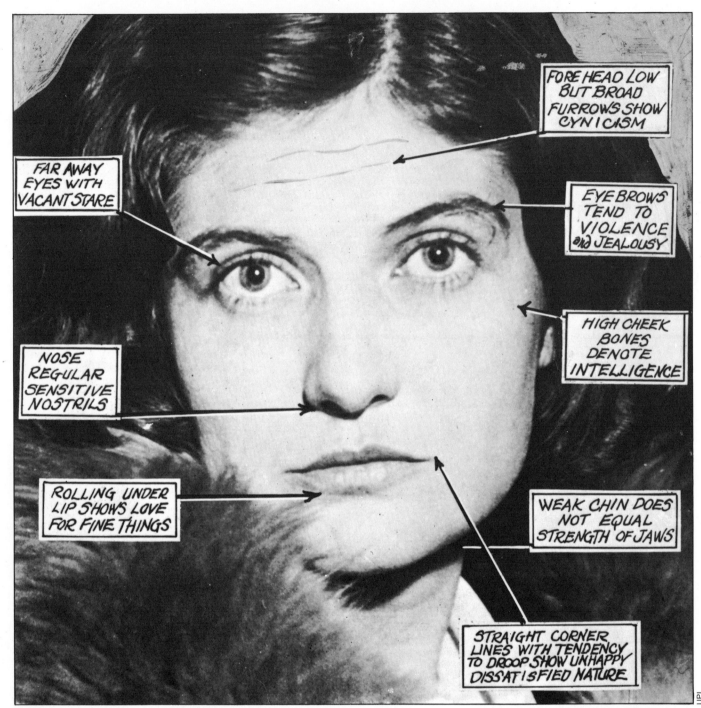

FORE HEAD LOW BUT BROAD FURROWS SHOW CYNICISM

FAR AWAY EYES WITH VACANT STARE

EYE BROWS TEND TO VIOLENCE and JEALOUSY

HIGH CHEEK BONES DENOTE INTELLIGENCE

NOSE REGULAR SENSITIVE NOSTRILS

ROLLING UNDER LIP SHOWS LOVE FOR FINE THINGS

WEAK CHIN DOES NOT EQUAL STRENGTH OF JAWS

STRAIGHT CORNER LINES WITH TENDENCY TO DROOP SHOW UNHAPPY DISSATISFIED NATURE

UPI

the bodies of two women, one dismembered. By now, Mrs. Judd, to whom the trunks were addressed, had vanished. The young man, her brother, had simply been asked to accompany her to the station— although, it appeared, she *had* finally admitted to him that the trunks contained bodies, and asked him to help her throw them in the sea. Her husband, a doctor, knew nothing whatever about the murders.

It transpired that Mrs. Judd had been in Phoenix for her health, and the two victims were her ex-flatmates, Hedwig Samuelson, 23, and Agnes LeRoi, 30. When Mrs. Judd finally gave herself up,

after a nationwide hunt, she alleged that they had quarrelled about men friends, and that Hedwig had tried to kill her with a gun, wounding her in the hand.

She had grabbed the gun, shot Miss Samuelson, then shot Agnes LeRoi when she attacked her, after which she dismembered Hedwig, packed both bodies in the trunks, and sent them by rail to Los Angeles. If Mrs. Judd had left them where they were, she would probably never have been suspected. As it was, she was found guilty but insane, and was not freed until December 1971.

When the train finally gives way to the aeroplane, no doubt we shall read books

SELF-DEFENCE was Winnie Judd's excuse: she said she and her two friends had quarrelled violently over men. Analysis of her facial lines by a criminal identification expert showed signs of mental disturbance and emotional coldness linked to a need for "attention at all costs".

on train murders with the same nostalgia with which we now read the Sherlock Holmes stories. In the meantime it may be as well to remember that most of them were exceptionally stupid and brutal. Perhaps they deserve to be recalled with interest; but never with regret.

PARENT KILLERS

ACCORDING to Freud, the crime of parricide – the murder of parents – is one of mankind's oldest established customs. He theorized that the earliest human beings lived in small hordes, consisting of one powerful male and several females. Naturally, the old male would want all the women to himself, and the only way the younger males could get their share was by rising up and murdering the old man. This, he said, is why man has always been haunted with legends of parricide.

He may have been right; but if so, he failed to explain why ancestor worship is among the oldest of mankind's religions. The ancient Egyptians, Chinese, Japanese, and Hindus worshipped their ancestors as gods, and many African tribes still do. Deep respect for the parents is the basis of Confucian religion – which is still, even in Mao's China, the foundation of morality. Since the earliest times, parricide has been treated as the worst of crimes. Take, for example, the grim and bloody story of the Cenci family.

The perfect murder

Francesco Cenci was one of the most vicious reprobates of history. The son of the Treasurer of Pope Pius V, he was the heir to an immense fortune that his father had accumulated by swindling.

Francesco soon discovered that his money gave him immunity. If he wanted to sleep with a beautiful girl, he didn't have to go to the trouble of seducing her; it was easier to have her kidnapped, then rape and sodomize her. When arrested, he simply bought his freedom. Altogether, he paid out over half a million pounds in fines at various times.

Cenci had 12 children by his first wife, and he hated them all. When the eldest two boys died, Cenci remarked that he wouldn't be happy until the others were buried near them. But as his youngest daughter, Beatrice, began to grow up, he found reasons for admiring her more than the others; with her pale skin and auburn hair, she was very beautiful. Cenci was so jealous of her that he transferred her – and his second wife – to a lonely castle near Naples called La Petrella. Francesco now decided to extend his repertoire of crimes to incest.

When a young, rich noble named Guerra – an abbé – made several proposals for Beatrice's hand, her father finally told him the reason for his refusal. "She is my mistress." Guerra thought he was lying, and spent three days trying to see Beatrice. Finally, he got his interview – and she admitted that it was true. "He deserves to die," said Guerra.

Beatrice, who was disgusted by her father's ill-treatment and avarice, agreed with him. Beatrice's stepmother joined in the plot; so did her brothers Giacomo and Bernardo. It was Giacomo who hired two *sbirri* – a kind of police officer – named Marzio and Olimpio. Marzio was infatuated with Beatrice, and Olimpio had already been her lover – and the keeper of the castle of La Petrella – before Cenci suspected and dismissed him.

On the evening of September 9, 1598, the two women mixed opium with the old man's wine. Always a heavy drinker, Cenci passed out and was carried to his bed. Then the two murderers entered. They took a large nail, hammered it through his eye and into his brain, and drove another nail deep into his throat. The writhing body was then hurled out of the high window, where it caught in the branches of a tree. When it was found the next morning, it was assumed that Cenci had leaned too far off the balcony when he was drunk, and fallen.

It looked like the perfect murder. Except that Cenci's death was a little *too* convenient. A few months after the murder, the wheels of justice began to turn

MACABRE BUNDLE containing the body of Francesco Cenci – murdered in bed.

slowly. The court of Naples sent a commissioner to investigate the affair. The only evidence he could find against the plotters was the deposition of a washerwoman, who admitted to washing a blood-stained sheet given to her by Beatrice – who claimed that the blood was menstrual.

Incredible courage

No one really mourned the dead debauchee; but the crime of parricide was too horrible for the authorities to contemplate. If the Cencis were allowed to get away with it, the whole fabric of society might collapse. The court of Naples decided on its favourite means of extorting confessions – torture. The Abbé Guerra heard about these plans, and hired two more *sbirri* to dispose of the murderers. They succeeded in assassinating Olimpio at Terni; but meanwhile Marzio was arrested. Under torture, he confessed. Beatrice, Giacomo, and Bernardo were all arrested. When Marzio saw Beatrice – the woman he still loved – he promptly withdrew his confession.

So the inquisitors thrust the Cencis into the torture chamber. Alexandre Dumas, who tells the story in his *Celebrated Crimes*, goes into gruesome detail. Beatrice was subjected to the *strappado*: that is, she was undressed, her wrists were fastened behind her, and a rope was tied to them. Then she was hauled into the air on a pulley. The effect was to dislocate her shoulders. With incredible courage, she denied everything. Weights were attached to her feet, and every time she fainted, she was lowered to the ground. Then, as soon as she opened her eyes, she was hauled up again. Her brother Bernardo showed less fortitude; he confessed. So did Giacomo, whose flesh had been torn from his body with red hot pincers.

Relatively law-abiding

Appeals were directed to the Pope, Clement VIII. He was sympathetic, and about to grant a reprieve, when news came of another case of parricide: the Marquis of Santa Croce had been stabbed to death by his son Paul. That settled it. Parricide was becoming an epidemic. The death sentences were confirmed. On September 11, 1599 – almost a year to the day after the murder – the Cencis went to the scaffold. Beatrice was the first to be beheaded, and the executioner displayed her head to the crowd. Next came Lucrezia. Giacomo was killed by having his head smashed with a mace. Only Bernardo received a last-minute pardon from the Pope, and a sentence of life imprisonment. (He was freed after a year.) Marzio had already died under torture. Guerra was the one conspirator who managed to escape; he fled from Italy, and was never heard of again.

The grim story has fascinated generations of historians, novelists, and playwrights; the poet Shelley made it the subject of his greatest play. Modern historians are inclined to reject the evidence that Cenci raped his daughter. But whether it is true or not, there can be no doubt that Francesco Cenci was guilty of far worse crimes than the one for which his children were executed.

Compared to the passionate and excitable Italians, the inhabitants of Britain are relatively law-abiding. Yet, surprisingly enough, England has produced a number of classic parricides. The case that invites comparison with the Cenci murder is that of Mary Blandy, executed in 1752 for the murder of her father. Ever since then, writers on crime have argued about whether she was guilty or not.

Mary was the daughter of Francis Blandy, an attorney of Henley-on-Thames. Her father was anxious that she should make a good marriage, and let it be known that she would have a dowry of £10,000 – a vast sum in those days. In fact, Blandy's total fortune was less than half that amount. The suitors came by the dozen, and were all rejected by Mr. Blandy. Time drifted by, and Mary was approaching 30. Then one day, at an aristocratic house, she met the Honourable William Cranstoun.

Gullible girl

He was short and bandy-legged, but his manners appealed to the amiable and placid Mary. One day, Cranstoun confessed that he was in love with her, and added that he was entangled with a mistress who claimed to be his wife. Mary agreed to marry him as soon as this problem was sorted out. This time her father agreed. Cranstoun may have been poor, but he was the son of a Scottish earl. He returned to Henley-on-Thames as a house guest of the Blandys, and his intimacy with Mary ripened.

Then came a setback. One of the captain's relatives wrote to tell Mr. Blandy that the "mistress" about whom Cranstoun had confessed was actually his wife. There were harsh words; but finally Cranstoun convinced the family that he was unmarried. For the next six months he lived with them, and Mary became his real mistress. Then the abandoned wife took him to a Scottish court, which found the marriage to be legal. This time, Mr. Blandy turned against his prospective son-in-law and told Mary to forget him.

In truth, Mary adored her father, and had always been an obedient daughter. But she was in love with Cranstoun. They continued to correspond, and one day it struck Cranstoun that the answer to his

Both Mary Evans

PLACID MARY Blandy helped her lover to poison her father. The lover fled; Mary (above) paid the penalty. Yet by all accounts she was a devoted daughter.

problems would be to remove Mr. Blandy. Accordingly, he hit upon a cunning plan. First, he gave Mary a powder which, he said, would make her father altogether more amiable. Mary put it into her father's tea, and it seemed to work; for a few days, he was less bad-tempered. So when

UPI

Cranstoun sent her more powder, Mary had no hesitation in putting it in her father's food and drink.

She seems to have been a singularly gullible girl. When she discovered that her lover had another woman in London, she forgave him. When one of the servants drank some of her father's tea, and immediately became ill, she still had no suspicion that Cranstoun's powder was to blame. She introduced the powder into oatmeal soup, and her father became ill as soon as he ate some. The cook tried the soup, and also became ill. The housemaid, Susan, had a small taste, and was sick for two days. Susan took the soup to the local chemist for analysis, and she warned Mr. Blandy that he was being poisoned.

Francis Blandy undoubtedly loved his daughter. He hinted at his suspicion so plainly that she was panic-stricken, and threw the rest of the powder on the kitchen fire. As soon as she left the kitchen, the cook rescued it, and took it to the chemist — who soon pronounced it to be arsenic. Mary drew the net more tightly around her when she wrote her lover a letter, warning him to be careful. She gave it to a clerk to post; he opened it, and handed it to the chemist.

On August 14, 1751, Francis Blandy died. He had told Mary that he thought she had poisoned him, and that he forgave her. When Captain Cranstoun heard of Blandy's death, he fled to France. Mary was arrested and charged with murder.

Love potion

The trial was chiefly of interest because of the detailed scientific evidence of the poisoning. Mary's defence was that she believed the poison to be a love potion to make her father change his mind. In retrospect, this seems to be true: why, otherwise, did she fail to get rid of the incriminating soup and tea? The jury disbelieved her, and she was hanged — asking the executioner not to hang her too high "for the sake of decency". Cranstoun died in poverty just over six months later.

There is an interesting sidelight on the case. When she was in prison, Mary Blandy heard about another woman condemned to death; Elizabeth Jeffries had plotted with her lover to murder her uncle. The novelist Horace Walpole wrote in a letter that the motive behind the murder was that the uncle had debauched his niece. Mary and Elizabeth Jeffries

BOMB KILLER John Gilbert Graham, the most callous parricide of all time. Graham killed his mother — and 43 other people — by planting a bomb in the hold of a DC-6B airliner in Denver. Motive: insurance fraud. Graham was executed in 1956.

entered into a sympathetic correspondence; but before her execution, Elizabeth finally confessed to her part in the crime. Mary was shocked, and wrote her a reproachful letter — which again seems to suggest that she was innocent.

In the present century, one of the most horrifying representatives of parent killers was undoubtedly John Gilbert Graham — who was responsible for the deaths of 43 other people as well as that of his mother. It happened when a DC-6B airliner exploded in mid-air shortly after its takeoff from Denver, Colorado, on November 1, 1955. The wreckage was spread over a five-mile area, and the smell of explosive convinced investigators that the crash had been caused deliberately.

Suicidal impulse

The bomb, it was discovered, had gone off in No. 4 baggage compartment — into which four cases had been loaded at Denver. The passengers who had boarded at Denver were checked. One of them was Mrs. Daisy King, a lady of considerable wealth. Her son, John Graham, a 23-year-old married man with two children, had taken out insurance policies on her life before she left Denver, but had forgotten to sign them. Detectives soon discovered that Graham had a police record for forgery, and his wife mentioned that he had put a "Christmas package" in his mother's suitcase shortly before she left home.

Under intensive interrogation, John Graham finally admitted that he had made a time bomb with dynamite, and hidden it in his mother's case. He was identified by a man from whom he had bought the timing device. Graham was found guilty, and executed at the Colorado State Penitentiary. He certainly ranks as the most spectacular and hard-hearted of all parricides.

Our own time has seen the emergence of another type of parricide who is both an immature and emotionally disturbed parricide. The central difference is this: that while the criminal-parricide plots his crime with every intention of avoiding its consequences, the psychologically-disturbed parent killer shows a complete lack of realistic foresight, fundamentally driven by a distorted suicidal impulse.

This can be seen in the case of Charles Whitman, the mass-killer of Austin, Texas. On July 31, 1966, Whitman went up to his mother's apartment at midnight, stabbed her, and shot her in the back of the head. In a note he wrote: "I love my mother with all my heart." Then he went home to his own apartment, stabbed his sleeping wife three times, and wrapped her naked body in a sheet. After this he continued his note, describing his hatred of his father — whom

his mother had left only a few months earlier — ending: "Life is not worth living."

This done, he took two rifles, a shotgun and three revolvers up to the observation tower of the University of Texas, and killed the receptionist with a blow from a rifle butt. A few minutes later, some people walked up the stairs. Whitman used the shotgun three times, slaying a 19-year-old youth and his aunt, and seriously wounding the boy's mother. Then, at 11.48 a.m., he began shooting from the top of the clock tower — shooting with a terrifying accuracy. The first victim was a pregnant woman, who collapsed with a bullet in her stomach; a classmate who bent over her was killed instantly. Six more people were shot, and many wounded, within the next half hour.

Police and Texas Rangers who surrounded the bell tower found the angle at which they had to aim impossible. The bullets only struck the walls. A light aircraft was chartered by the police, with a sharpshooter in the passenger seat; but Whitman's deadly fire drove it away. Finally, at 1.24, the police managed to burst into the observation tower, and kill Whitman. An autopsy revealed that he would have died anyway; he had a brain tumour. Sixteen people died as a result of his orgy of destructiveness.

Drug-induced delusions

But perhaps the most typical case of the suicidal parent-killer is that of Miles Giffard, a 26-year-old native of Cornwall. Giffard hated his father, who was clerk of the court to St. Austell magistrates. The two of them were always quarrelling about Giffard's dislike of work. On November 7, 1952, Giffard asked his father if he could borrow the car to drive to London to see his girlfriend; his father refused. That afternoon, while his parents were out, Giffard stayed at home and got drunk on whiskey.

At 7.30 he heard the car returning. He went down to the garage, and beat his father to death with a piece of iron pipe. He then went into the kitchen, and smashed his mother to the ground. When he was sure they were dead, he took the bodies, one by one, in a wheelbarrow, and dumped them over the cliff at the end of the garden. He then got into the car, and drove to London to see his girlfriend.

The bodies were found next day, the car quickly traced, and within 24 hours of killing his parents, Giffard was under arrest. At the trial, his doctor described him as an "idle little waster". And in spite of clear evidence that he was schizophrenic, he was sentenced to death and executed. A Cornish jury declined to accept the Freudian explanations of a psychiatrist called by the defence.

In recent years, there has been a

ACADEMIC
CENTRE

STUDENT UNION
BUILDING

ARCHITECTURE

BA
HIS
CE

marked increase in the number of parricides, particularly in the United States. This is due largely to the increasing use of drugs; in one recent case, a man suffering from drug-induced delusions decapitated his mother, and carefully placed her head on a church altar. Yet the increase is not great enough to support Freud's theory that the majority of people harbour some deep resentment of their parents.

If this was correct, the release of these inhibitions by drugs should have led to a staggering increase in parricide. That this has not occurred suggests that Freud was wrong, and that the Chinese philosopher Confucius was right: most people actually like their parents, and wish them nothing but health, happiness, and long and contented lives.

SHARPSHOOTER Charles J. Whitman, a student at Texas University, killed his mother and wife prior to climbing the University bell tower and spraying bullets into passers by on the campus

(above). In 90 minutes Whitman killed 14, wounded 33 and shattered glass in nearby windows before police gunned him down. Below, his signature in visitors' book, penned 3 days before.

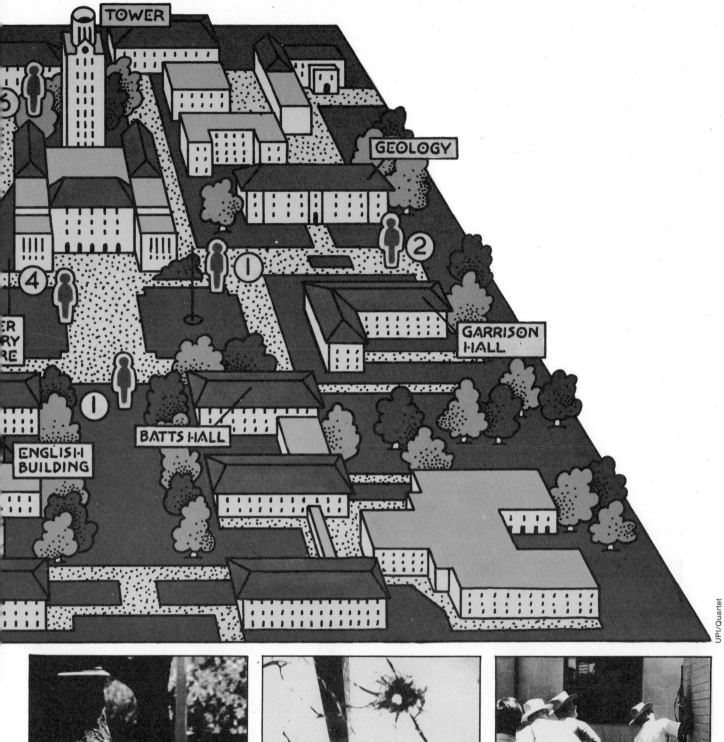

TOWER

GEOLOGY

GARRISON HALL

BATTS HALL

ENGLISH BUILDING

UPI/Quartet

All UPI

HE TOOK GOOD CARE OF

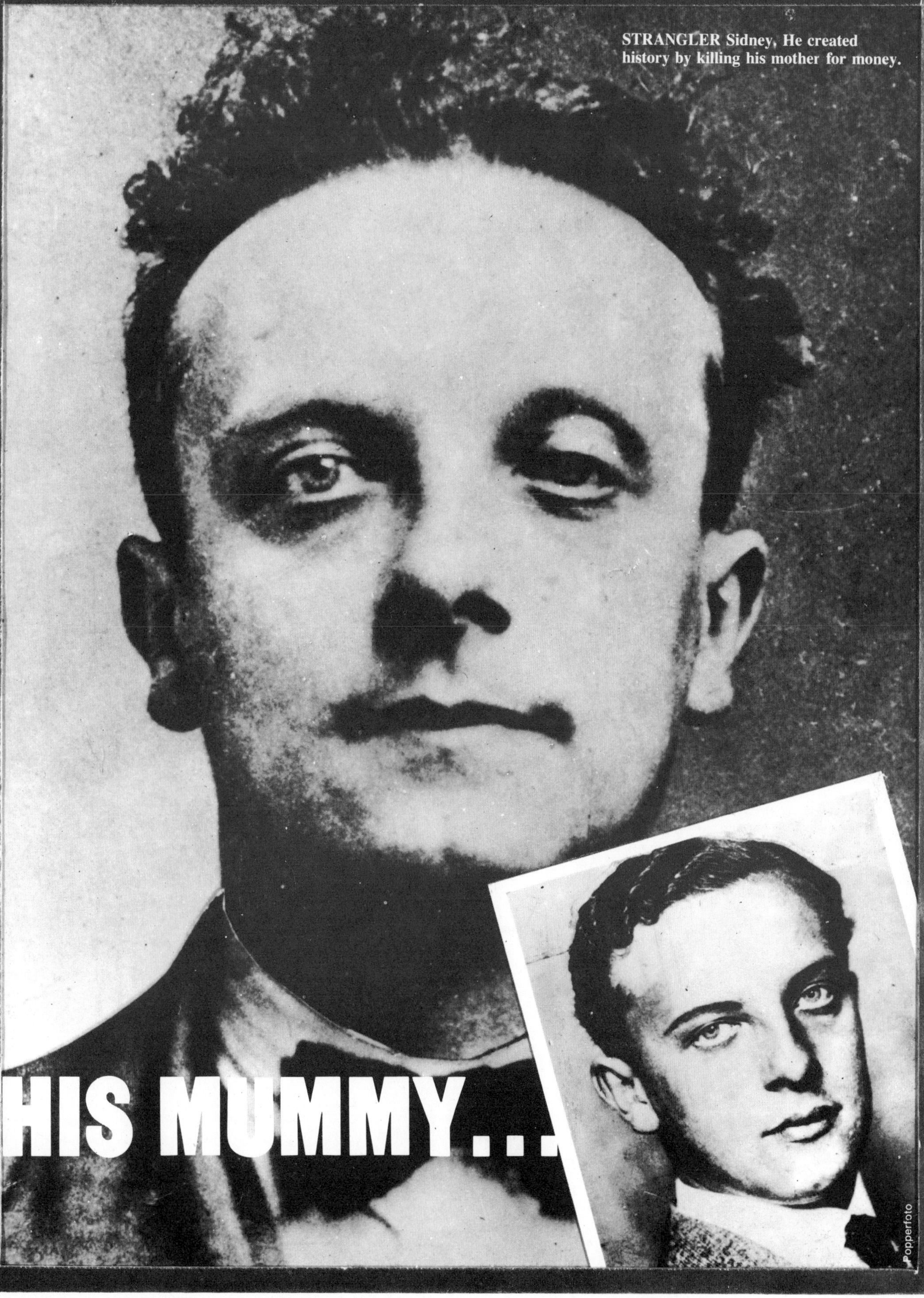

Both Syndication International

Popperfoto

STRANGLER Sidney, He created history by killing his mother for money.

HIS MUMMY...

137

Sidney Harry Fox was a professional crook who had formed a curious but successful partnership with his mother. Then he decided that she had outgrown her usefulness . . .

THE MOST striking feature of the man standing in the dock at the Sussex Assizes on March 12, 1930, was his drooping left eyelid. It hung like a half-open shade over his eye. But it was an appropriate feature, for Sidney Harry Fox was a shady character. Aged 31, he had behind him a long string of convictions for blackmail, theft, fraud, and forgery. Before a packed court in County Hall in Lewes, Fox pleaded "Not guilty" to the charge of murdering his 63-year-old mother. His trial was accompanied by a blaze of publicity, for it was the first case on record in Britain of a son murdering his mother for money.

Sidney Fox had lived by his wits all his life, and he took to petty crime in his teens. He was first gaoled at the age of 19 and was in and out of prison for the rest of his life. The youngest of Mrs. Rosaline Fox's four children, and said to be illegitimate, Sidney exerted a compelling influence over his mother. She became his partner in crime, and throughout the 1920's mother and son engaged in a life of fraud and deception.

Their method was simple. Moving from town to town and from hotel to hotel along the south coast of England, they left a long trail of unpaid bills and bad cheques. In this way they supplemented the ten shillings a week which Mrs. Fox drew on account of her eldest son having been killed in France in World War One, and the pension of eight shillings a week to which Sidney was entitled for a war wound. This odd couple, a shuffling, white-haired old lady with her devoted son by her side, charmed their way into debt and deceit.

No pleasure

Sidney compensated for any bad impression created by his drooping, shady eyelid, by exuding charm and plausibility. He had a notion of leading a "classy" life for which he affected an upper class accent, and he liked to be associated with parties and clubs. He variously posed as an Old Etonian, a Royal Air Force officer, and as Lieutenant Fox. Although not a member, he had letters addressed to The Honourable S. H. Fox at the Royal Automobile Club in Pall Mall, London.

In 1928 Fox, though a homosexual and proud of it, had an affair with a Mrs.

Morse in whose house he was staying at Southsea. Sidney was later cited as co-respondent in a divorce case – he admitted the adultery but denied any pleasure in it. But he did not forsake his true nature for nothing – he was about to turn his hand to more profitable work. He persuaded Mrs. Morse to insure her life for £6000 and then to make a will in his favour. His romantic approaches were shortly followed by more sinister occurrences when he stole some of Mrs. Morse's jewellery – and the seduced lady awoke to find her room mysteriously full of gas.

Worthless cheques

Fox was imprisoned for 15 months for the theft and while he was serving time, his mother went to the workhouse. On his release in March 1929, he collected his mother and they immediately resumed their round of fraud and deception. But Sidney's ambitions had not been blunted.

On April 21, Mrs. Fox made a will leaving all she had to her son. Her worldly possessions did not amount to much, apart from a small insurance which until recently had been in arrears. On May 1 Sidney insured his mother's life against accidental death. At the time he asked the insurance clerk, "Would this policy cover the case of drowning in a bath? Would it apply supposing a person was poisoned, let us say, by food at a restaurant?" If the clerk gleaned any clues about Fox's intentions from these questions, he kept them to himself.

During the next six months, mother and son scrounged their usual existence by passing worthless cheques and moving quickly from place to place. Leaving a thick wake of unpaid bills, they visited hotels in London, Canterbury, and Folkestone, ending up at Margate in Kent on October 16. The frail old lady and her dutiful son took rooms at the Hotel Metropole. They had no luggage – Sidney said it was "following later" – and only a few shillings between them.

A few days afterwards, Sidney went to London to make some further arrangements regarding his mother's life insurance policies. The cover, which totalled

DEFENCE counsel J. D. Cassels did his best to make inroads into the case presented by the prosecution. But his efforts were in vain. Fox was convicted.

£3000, was extended to midnight the following day, October 23. He returned to Margate, having borrowed money to pay the train fare. On the morning of October 23, Fox told the hotel management that he and his mother would be leaving the following day and he inquired about his bill. Mother and son dined together at the Metropole that evening, and Sidney ordered half a bottle of port for his mother as a "night-cap". At 11.40 p.m. Mrs. Fox was dead.

A few minutes before that a fire alarm was raised in the hotel by Fox himself: partly dressed, he rushed downstairs to the lounge shouting that there was a fire in his mother's room. A fellow resident, Samuel Hopkins, hurried to give assistance and followed Fox upstairs. Fox opened the door to his own bedroom and Hopkins rushed in only to be beaten back by the smoke. Sheepishly Fox then pointed to the room next door and said, "My mother is in there."

The area was full of dense smoke, through which could be seen the dull red glow of the gas fire. Hopkins covered his nose and mouth with a handkerchief and dived into the fumes. Mrs. Fox's half naked body was lying on the bed. He hooked his hands under her arms and, gasping for air, dragged her into the corridor. She was unconscious and her face was blue. Fox, who had made no attempt to help, cried, "My mummy, my mummy!"

Muddy water

Artificial respiration was applied without success. Two doctors had been sent for and the first to arrive was Dr. Cecil Austin. He pronounced Mrs. Fox—clad only in a dirty undervest—dead as a result of shock and suffocation. Dr. Robert Nichol, when he arrived, did not dispute his colleague's findings. In the meantime other helpers had put out the fire. They dragged out into the corridor an upholstered chair, the seat of which was burning furiously, and stamped out flames on the carpet where the chair had been standing. Dr. Nichol broke the news to Fox that his mother was dead. He was sobbing and still crying, "My mummy!" Fox, who was being soothed by the hotel manager's wife, asked the doctor to let him see his mother. "She is all I have in the world," he sobbed.

The death certificate was signed by Dr. Austin and at the inquest, the following day, a verdict of death by misadventure was brought in.

However, Sidney's grief was not too incapacitating, for he quickly persuaded a Margate solicitor to advance him £40 on account of the insurance policies he held on his mother's life. Then it was back to "work" again. Fox left Margate with his mother's body bound for Great

Fransham, her Norfolk birthplace. According to his custom, he neglected to pay the hotel bill.

Rosaline Fox was buried on October 29. The same day her son travelled to Norwich to make claims on the insurance policies. An official of the insurance company was suspicious. He wired head office: "Very muddy water in this business."

On November 2, Fox was arrested at Norwich and held on a charge of unlawfully obtaining credit. Meanwhile, Scotland Yard was called in and within a week Mrs. Fox's body was exhumed and Sir Bernard Spilsbury carried out a post mortem. The pathologist found no trace of carbon monoxide in the blood and no sooty deposits in the air passages. Mrs. Fox had evidently died before the fire started and it was Spilsbury's conclusion that she had been strangled. Fox was duly charged with murder. "It is absolutely untrue. I deny every word of it," he said.

Elaborate cunning

Mr. Justice Rowlatt presided at the trial and the Attorney General, Sir William Jowitt, led the prosecution. Fox—who was defended by Mr. J. D. Cassels—seemed quite unmoved by the proceedings, and freely admitted to telling lies in order "to impress".

The staff of the Metropole gave evidence which revealed Fox's elaborate cunning. When he arrived at the hotel, he had deposited a sealed envelope with the manager and with knowing nods conveyed the idea that it contained money. He spoke of escorting his mother to Flanders to visit the war grave of his brother and then of moving to a new house in the New Forest. Thus he established himself as a person of substance and a man of ideals. The hotel staff thought him "gentlemanly", "refined", and a "devoted son".

Apart from inspiring confidence, Fox was also busily preparing for his next move. He sent for a doctor because his mother was "a little bit run down". Dr. Austin attended Mrs. Fox and prescribed a tonic. Later, Fox told the hotel barmaid that the doctor ". . . was drunk when he saw my mother". He also questioned the prescription "for fear of an overdose". This was pure scene-setting so that in the event of his mother's death Fox could always refer to the doctor's visit and the medicine which he suspected at the time.

Out of sympathy for Mrs. Fox's poor health, the hotel management offered to move her to a more comfortable room. Consequently, the old lady moved to room 66, which had a gas fire and a connecting door to room 67, now occupied by her son. There was one further, incredible incident when Fox told one of the hotel staff that his mother was be-

ginning to feel a little better.

"We have been playing," he said. "We have had a sham fight, as we sometimes do when she feels well!"

Fox then entered the stand and told the court that on the night of the fire he took his mother up to her room about nine o'clock. "I lit the gas fire," he said, "and my mother, who sat in the armchair in front of the fire, asked for an evening paper which I fetched her." He explained how he helped his mother to undress down to her vest (like her son, she had no night clothes) and he wrapped her in the eiderdown taken from the bed. He then slipped out to get half a bottle of port. His mother drank half and he consumed the remainder.

"I kissed her goodnight," stated Fox, "and then went downstairs. I had a small glass of beer and read a newspaper in the bar." On retiring at 10.40 p.m. he said he went straight upstairs to bed.

"What was it that wakened you?" asked Defence Counsel. "I heard a rattling noise . . . I thought it was my window . . . I got out and pushed it up. I smelt some burning . . . I suddenly remembered that I had left my mother sitting by the fire, and wondered whether she had turned the fire out . . . I opened the communicating door and a volume of smoke met me, and I could not get into the room . . . obviously, there was a fire, and I needed help."

Bottle of petrol

The state of room 66, in which Mrs. Fox met her death, was of great interest. The old lady's body was found lying on the bed with the pillow on a nearby table. In answer to questions put by the Attorney General, the hotel chambermaid said, "When I called Mrs. Fox I always found her lying on the pillow. I had never before seen the pillow put on one side."

But the greatest mystery attached to the source of the fire. There was a gap of unburned carpet between the gas fire and the area of burnt carpet where Mrs. Fox's chair had stood. Dr. Nichol told the court, "There seemed to be no connection between the obvious source of the fire and the site of the fire itself." He went on to mention some charred paper found in the room which he associated with "the cause of the fire".

The armchair itself, as the Attorney General was careful to emphasise, was vitally important: "It is scorched and burnt on all sides, so that it seems plain that the fire must have concentrated under that chair." Margate Fire Brigade's Chief Officer gave it as his opinion that "the fire unquestionably originated directly underneath the armchair". He had carried out experiments and the only way he could start a fire of similar characteristics was with the aid of petrol. "Without using petrol he failed to burn the carpet," added the Attorney General emphatically.

"Do you know that a bottle of petrol was discovered in room No. 66?" the Attorney General then asked Fox. "I have heard it," replied the accused. "It was used for cleaning clothes." Prosecuting Counsel pressed the issue. "You see, Fox, if it had been difficult to start a fire it might have been handy to have a bottle of petrol near." In a matter-of-fact tone Fox answered, "I suppose it would, but I do not know anything about it, sir."

Fooling people was one of Fox's greatest accomplishments. But his bland performance in court did not carry much conviction. A clear picture of Fox, wily both by name and nature, getting his mother drowsy with port and then suffocating her on the bed with the pillow was beginning to form in the minds of the jury. Lighting the fire under the armchair with the aid of newspapers and petrol was literally a smoke screen. But the greatest drama was yet to come in the shape of pathologist Sir Bernard Spilsbury's evidence.

Spilsbury's post mortem report on Mrs. Fox had concluded quite simply, "Cause of death: asphyxia due to manual strangulation." However, there were no external marks of violence, which was highly unusual in a strangling case. The victim normally fights furiously to disengage the strangler's hands, but in the case of Mrs. Fox there was a complete absence of any bruises or scratches. The other unpleasant features of a strangling, the tongue forced out, blood flecks about the nose and mouth, and purple lips, were also absent. Dr. Nichol said that after death Mrs. Fox's face was composed and presented no special significance.

To explain his account of how Mrs. Fox died, Spilsbury produced in court a model of the human mouth and throat. "At the back of the larynx," he explained, pointing to the spot, "I found a large, recent bruise about the size of half a crown. It was then that I had the first indication of the conclusions to which I finally came, that death was due to strangulation." He also mentioned finding bruises at the back of the tongue and on the thyroid, and a small haemorrhage on the epiglottis.

Defence Counsel questioned Spilsbury about the fact that the hyoid bone in the larynx had not been broken: "It was very brittle?"

"Yes, it was. It does not require a great deal of force to break it," replied the pathologist.

"It is very important in this case, is it not, the absence of any fracture or damage to this brittle hyoid bone?" continued Counsel.

"Oh, yes, certainly."

"Would it have strengthened your opinion if the hyoid bone had been broken?"

"It would have made it more evident."

Fiery interchange

But the excitement really heightened when the defence medical witnesses gave evidence. Chief of these was Professor Sydney Smith, a scientist no less eminent than Spilsbury himself. Professor Smith and his colleague, Dr. Bronte, disagreed with Spilsbury's findings. They had been shown the various organs relating to the case at Spilsbury's laboratory. They looked for but could not find the bruise on the larynx—what they found was putrefactive discoloration. Spilsbury said: "It was there when I exhumed the body."

In court Professor Smith, who maintained that Mrs. Fox died of heart failure, came in for some intimidating questioning from the Attorney General. "Did you find any sign of injury of any part of the tissues . . . ?"

"No trace whatever."

"Were there any bruises at the back of the larynx?"

"No."

"Sir Bernard Spilsbury says that he saw a bruise the size of half a crown behind the larynx when he exhumed the body. What do you have to say to that?"

"I think it quite possible that it was a patch of discoloration from post mortem staining or putrefaction."

The Attorney General tried to get Smith to belittle Spilsbury. "Do you suggest Sir Bernard would not know the difference between the two?" he snapped. But Smith would not be bullied. He went no further than, "Nobody can tell merely by looking." It would be necessary to cut into suspected tissues, he explained.

"You are bound to accept the evidence of the man who saw the bruise?" demanded the Attorney General. "I do not think so," answered Smith quietly, "because if there was a bruise there it should be there now. It should be there forever. The larynx can be examined by anybody."

This ended the fiery, if somewhat academic interchange. What lingered in people's minds, and was the subject of much subsequent debate, was the authoritative tone of Spilsbury's testimony. "It was a bruise, and nothing else. There are no two opinions about it," he declared. But in the end it was not the unbroken hyoid bone or the debate about the bruise which sunk Fox, but his own admissions.

"Did you ever go into room 66 after the fire?" asked the Attorney General.

"Yes, I did on two or three occasions. The first was when I endeavoured to get in after the fire," replied Fox.

"Did you realise when you opened the communicating door that the atmosphere in the room was such as would probably suffocate anybody inside?"

"If I had stayed in three or four moments I should have been suffocated."

"So that you must have been greatly apprehensive for your mother?"

"I was."

"Fox, you closed the door."

"It is quite possible I did."

"Can you explain to me why it was you closed the door without flinging it wide open?"

"My explanation now is that the smoke should not spread into the hotel."

"Rather that your mother should suffocate in the room than that the smoke should get about in the hotel?"

"Most certainly not, sir."

Fox was squirming in the trap set for him. The vision of the accused carefully shutting the door to contain the asphyxiating smoke before going down to fetch help was overwhelming. After a lifetime existing on lies and deceit, Sidney Fox had to face the awful revelation that he was no longer believed.

In his summing up Mr. Justice Rowlatt said of Fox, "It may be that he is so perverted that even when an honest and innocent attitude could be taken up he takes this dishonest one." He was referring to the lies which Fox openly admitted telling Dr. Nichol about his mother's money only minutes after she was dead. The jury retired for an absence of an hour and ten minutes. They found the accused guilty and he was sentenced to death. Fox, reduced to a whisper, said, "My Lord, I never murdered my mother."

Perhaps "The Honourable" Sidney Harry Fox realised that he had told his last lie, for he is one of the few convicted murderers not to have appealed against sentence. He was hanged at Maidstone Prison in Kent on April 8, 1930.

DEATH CHAMBER . . . The room at the Hotel Metropole, Margate, where Fox arranged the "accidental" death by fire.

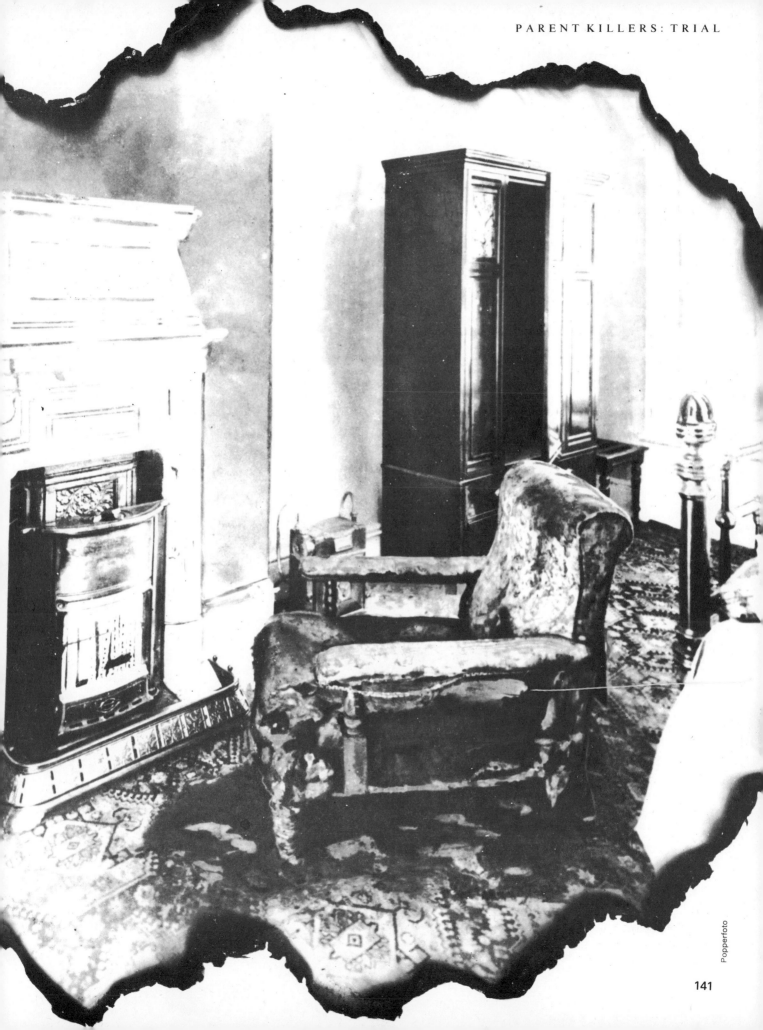

Popperfoto

THE HATCHET WOMAN OF FALL RIVER

Lizzie Borden was not a violent woman and, even though she hated her stepmother, she certainly adored her father. Yet who else had the opportunity to murder them both . . . ?

Lizzie Borden took an axe
And gave her mother forty whacks.
When she saw what she had done,
She gave her father forty-one.

LEGEND and folklore are the marginal notes of a good historical story, but the consummate enemies of historical truth. Lizzie Borden would testify to that. The actual charge against her was that she gave her stepmother—not her mother—20 blows with a sharp instrument, and her father 10. And, since she was acquitted, she even stands unjustly accused in the popular doggerel.

For all that, Lizzie deserves her place in folk-song. Her life-style, her mute, brooding family and the tight little community of Fall River, Massachusetts—in which she lived—were like the perfect setting for a play by Eugene O'Neill or Tennessee Williams. Lizzie Borden typified genteel, small-town, nineteenth-century America—and, in that, was almost as fascinating as the terrible crime which thrust her life and background under the microscope of history.

At 32, she did not rank among the beauties of Fall River. Her large, pale eyes protruded from a sallow complexion framed by curly red hair. She had few friends, although those few thought highly of her. Perhaps that was because Lizzie did not choose them for their social positions, for she was no snob, although she liked money. Unlike her father, she was generous and charitable, and her supporters were quick to point out all the good works with which she was associated as a Congregationalist.

Among the 50,000 New Englanders who lived in Fall River, the family of Borden was as celebrated as were the Medicis in Florence. No street was without its Borden. Andrew Borden, Lizzie's 70-year-old father, was among the most prosperous of the line; he had started his career as the town's undertaker, next turned property speculator, then invested his quick profits in the textile industry—whose mills provided Fall River folk with most of their work. By the time Lizzie was in her teens, Andrew Borden was worth half a million dollars, and was soon to be worth a lot more.

His meanness with money was a local legend. He took his own hens' eggs in a basket to market, and lived in a shabby, three-bedroom house at No. 92 Second Street that had hardly changed since the days of the Civil War. Curiously, he had two weaknesses that invariably caused his purse strings to open; they were his two daughters Emma, the elder, and Lizzie. Whatever else they might complain about, neither had reason to criticise the way their father kept their bank accounts healthy.

INVESTIGATIONS carried out by the local police proved highly inconclusive. They found the axe (below) which could have been the murder weapon — but proof was lacking. Neither was there any real proof that Lizzie Borden (right) was the killer — merely strong suspicion.

Culver/Herald News

The reason for this was Andrew Borden's desperate anxiety to buy peace within his family. Lizzie had given him many troubled moments — particularly when she had her "funny spells", which caused her to act totally unpredictably.

One of her turns

Once, during one of these turns, she had reported to her father upon his return from an outing that the bedroom of her stepmother Abby had been entered by a thief, who had ransacked the room and stolen a watch and trinkets. Mr. Borden called the police at once, and then dismissed them half-way through their investigations. His knowledge of the geography of the house, and the circumstances of the theft, had rightly convinced him that the burglary could only have been committed by Lizzie.

Then there was Lizzie's relationship with her stepmother. Whenever the two women were in the house, which was frequently, for Abby Borden rarely went out, the atmosphere was electric. It was obvious to all who knew them that Lizzie hated her stepmother, whom she called "Mrs. Borden". She never ate at table when Abby Borden was present, and spoke to her stepmother only when it was absolutely necessary to do so.

The breach between them had begun over a trifling incident — a decision by Andrew Borden to buy the house his wife's sister lived in and to put it in the name of his wife. It was an act which saved his sister-in-law from possible eviction. But in it Lizzie Borden saw a move on her stepmother's part to usurp her father's fortune.

In a small town like Fall River — where the affluent Bordens could afford to spend long, lacklustre summer days brooding in boredom over supposed injustices — the episode of the house was enlarged beyond all reason. And because the eye of envy distorts most vision, Lizzie Borden never forgave her stepmother for it.

Poor Abby Borden scarcely merited such fierce attention. She was a pathetic figure covered in rolls of fat, and had difficulty in moving her colossal boneless flesh around even her own house. Without friends, without ambition, and without avarice, Abby Borden was one of life's non-starters . . . only her husband had seen warmth and sympathy in her,

143

and had married her because of it.

The year of 1892 provided a rare 12 months of total summer; a period when New England sweated and suffocated. As the hot sharp sun cut the symmetrical streets, and made stiff shadows from the whitewood houses, several strange happenings disturbed the tedious routine of the Bordens' lives in Fall River.

Twice intruders broke into the outbuilding at the bottom of the Borden garden, where Lizzie, an animal fanatic, kept her pigeons. "They're after those birds," Andrew Borden said shortly. His remedy against the intruders was effectively simple: as if by some clairvoyant symbolism, he took an axe and decapitated the pigeons.

Small doses

Lizzie Borden's reaction to this extraordinary act was never recorded. Perhaps she said nothing, brooding on it beside the window in her bedroom. Perhaps she made a scene. Perhaps she simply stored up all the emotion it generated for the day of its total release, three months later, on the hottest day of the year and the most

momentous one ever in the town's history.

It was then, as summer scorched on, the local drugstore owners began to notice that Lizzie was asking regularly for small doses of prussic acid, a lethal poison. In fact, they noticed it so acutely that Lizzie was obliged to cut down on her drugstore shopping trips, and to make her inquiries more discreetly.

As none of the drugstores would sell the poison without a prescription, Lizzie's attempts to buy it cannot be related to

the stomach sickness which afflicted the entire Borden household at the end of July in that year. But oddly, Abby Borden was convinced that she *had* been poisoned after a long bout of vomiting. She made one of her rare outings—to the doctor's house across the road—and was afterwards soundly reproached by her husband for her "nonsensical" behaviour.

Andrew's view of it was supported by the doctor, who pointed out that the whole family seemed to be retching,

including Bridget the maid. As July gave way to August the summer's events had already established the Borden attitudes: there was hate in Lizzie's heart, fear in Abby's, and a feeling of growing irritation in Andrew's.

August 4 was the hottest day of all that hot summer; at first light Fall River already simmered. It was also the last day that Andrew and Abby Borden were to spend alive on earth.

Borden malady

Fortunately for her, sister Emma was out of town. Uncle John Morse, a guest in the house for the past few days, was up early. The Irish maid, Bridget Sullivan, followed him down and as she busied herself with her early morning chores she had to stop to be sick – the Borden malady still lay heavily upon her.

By 7.30 a.m. Abby and Andrew had dressed and were sitting at breakfast with

THE BLOODSTAINED bodies of Andrew Borden (below) and his wife Abby Borden (below left) were photographed by police. Left: the family house at Fall River.

Uncle John. Just over an hour later Uncle John left to go into town. Lizzie then came downstairs for a light breakfast, and Bridget went outside to clean the windows while Abby got on with the dusting and housework.

At about 9 am a young man walked up to the Bordens' front door, rang the bell, and delivered a message. The message, it was later assumed, was addressed to Abby, and indicated that she should leave the house to visit a sick friend. Either shortly before or shortly after this event, Andrew Borden set off for downtown. He waited outside the bank and then made up his mind to return home – where he arrived about 10.30.

While he was away, the arrival of another young man had been noticed by the neighbours. He was said to have hung about outside the Bordens' house, sometimes looking agitated. Then he disappeared, and was never identified.

Inside No. 92 Second Street horrific things had begun to happen. Someone crept up behind Abby Borden while she was dusting the guests' bedroom and, with a mighty, crushing blow, brought a

hatchet down upon her head – a blow that killed her instantly. Abby's barrel-like body collapsed on the bed, where more blows were rained upon it. When the murderer had finished this frenzied work, the room was awash with Abby's blood.

No noise had occurred to bring anyone running, and, if Lizzie, who was alone in the house, is to be believed, no one knew of the bloodsoaked corpse in the bedroom. Then, at half-past ten, the key turned in the front door lock and Andrew, hot and tired by his walk back from downtown, entered the house.

Stark horror

Again, Lizzie is the authority for what happened next. She helped her father settle himself for a rest on the sofa in the sitting room and then went outside to the outbuilding. She was away for 20 minutes; when she returned a scene of stark horror confronted her.

On the sofa lay the crumpled body of her father. Half his head had been cleaved away by blows from an axe and his blood, still piping from the hideous wounds, covered the floor and walls.

During the next few hours Lizzie was to summon up some remarkable resources of self-control, which could not fail to be missed when the day's events were later recounted in a hushed courtroom. She went first to a neighbour, who quoted her as saying, "Oh, Mrs. Churchill, do come. Someone has killed Father!"

Lizzie stated then that her mother had received a note asking her to go out and visit a sick person—she said, therefore, that she did not know where Mrs. Borden was. Even when the police and a doctor arrived, the corpse of Abby still lay unrevealed in the bedroom. It was found only after Lizzie had suddenly "remembered that she thought she had heard Abby come back from town", and an inquisitive neighbour went to look . . .

Double murder

Even with the hottest day of the year to constrain their movements, the people of Fall River flocked in droves down Second Street to the scene of the town's first ever double murder. While they gaped from a reverent distance at the hard wooden rectangle of the Bordens' front door, a man came up the street.

It was Uncle John, whose behaviour, like Lizzie's, was now remarkable. Instead of hurrying forward at the sight of the crowd surrounding his brother-in-law's front garden, he slackened to a loitering pace. When at last he reached the house he went first into the back garden, picked some fruit from a tree and munched it. With all the visible evidence of a disaster about him, Uncle John was in no hurry.

Once inside the house, however, his story gushed out like jackpot coins from a one-armed bandit. Uncle John remembered everything he had seen and done that morning. No detail, however insignificant, had escaped his suddenly prodigious memory. So perfect was his alibi that he became a leading suspect.

The swelling crowd around No. 92 Second Street, which had brought the town's traffic and work at the local mills to a standstill, had no doubts about Uncle John. When he ventured out a few nights later a thousand outraged citizens chased him back inside. After that, the police advised the family to stay indoors until they had decided whom to arrest.

Their deliberations were long and earnest before they plumped for Lizzie. For five days District Attorney Hosea Knowlton had resisted police requests for Lizzie's apprehension. "You don't have any evidence against her," he told the senior police officers. When he finally gave in the situation wasn't much better —it simply seemed more than ever evident that Lizzie was the only one who could have done the "bloody deed".

If the murders had been committed by someone outside the household, they reasoned, the murderer had relied upon an extraordinary set of coincidences to enable him to enter the house and get away twice. There was the unplanned absence of sister Emma; Uncle John's excursion into town; Bridget's morning spent washing the outside windows, and Lizzie's disappearance to the outbuilding long enough for murder to be done twice.

And where was this bloodstained axeman, if he existed? There was a large reward out for information leading to the arrest of a man who had presumably vanished into the shopping crowds of the closed Fall River community while stained red with blood from head to foot. No one came forward with even a hint of his existence.

Of the three connected with the household, Uncle John had an alibi which checked out, and Bridget had been seen by so many people while cleaning the windows that her every movement was accounted for. Lizzie had no corroboration as to how she had spent that morning.

"Why had she gone to the outbuilding?" she was asked. "To look for a piece of metal with which to mend a window screen", she replied; also to get some lead suitable for fishing weights (Lizzie was a keen angler). But detectives searching No. 92 found no broken screens, and no lead that could be used for fishing.

Where exactly did she go in the outbuilding? "Into its loft," she replied. But a policeman searching the loft afterwards thought it unlikely that the dust on the floor had been disturbed.

How long was she in the loft? "About 20 minutes," even though it must have been stifling hot. And, although she had a queasy stomach from the Borden sickness, she remembered eating three pears while she was there.

No fingerprinting

There was still plenty in Lizzie's favour to disquiet the District Attorney. In Fall River, although Lizzie had made no secret of her hate for her stepmother, her deep love for her father was well known. Of all the people who lived in that town, Lizzie Borden would have been the last to be suspected of parricide.

Then there was the murder weapon. A newly-broken axe handle had been found in the house, and, on a high shelf, its blade—rubbed with wood ash which bore no resemblance to the dust in the box in which it lay—suggested that there was no need to look further. But fingerprinting wasn't allowed in Fall River in the 1890s, so that the only thing which could connect Lizzie with the axe was that they both happened to be in the house.

Most puzzling of all was the absence of any bloodstained garment. If Lizzie killed her parents, she would have been soaked

---

"Why had she gone to the outbuilding?" she was asked. "To look for a piece of metal with which to mend a window screen," she replied; also to get some lead suitable for fishing weights . . .

---

in their blood, not once, but twice, at an interval of 90 minutes. Yet when the house was searched, all Lizzie's clothes were seen to be clean and spotless.

Later, when a friend of the Bordens, Miss Alice Russell, had moved into No. 92 Second Street to keep Lizzie and Emma company, it was announced that there would be another search, for the police were now convinced Lizzie was hiding something from them.

Was she, in fact? At Lizzie's trial nine months later, Alice Russell and Emma told an extraordinary story. They revealed how, before the second search was held, Lizzie began to tear up an old dress and burn it in the kitchen stove—"Because it was all faded and paint-stained".

But, Alice Russell testified later, she saw no paint on that condemned dress. Possibly with a deeper reason in mind for its destruction, she had declared, "I wouldn't let anybody see me do that, Lizzie, if I were you."

Innocence wronged

In the right hands that was a story which might have demolished the case for Lizzie Borden. But when Alice Russell spoke at the trial, there had been a dramatic volte-face in public opinion on the Borden case. Instead of the mob howling for her blood—as it had been in the murder week—all America was now loving Lizzie Borden. From every part of the country flowers poured in for her. Suddenly, she was innocence wronged, a maiden cruelly mistreated, a demure and heartbroken girl racked by the State on a charge that tried to make her a fiend.

The burnt dress? It couldn't possibly have been stained with blood, snorted her supporters, because no two people could agree what dress Lizzie wore on the day of the tragedy. The dress that she said she wore was unstained and unmarked.

By now Lizzie had a lot more going for her. The considerable fortune she had inherited from her dead father enabled her to brief the best lawyer in Massachusetts. He was George Robinson, a former Governor of the State. One of the three judges, Judge Dewey, was a man whom Robinson had elevated to the bench when he was Governor; Dewey, therefore, owed the defence lawyer a

LIZZIE'S STORY relied a great deal on her whereabouts at the time of the killings. Right: the exact location of the house and (inset) the Borden barn.

debt and he was aware of it.

It was certainly lucky for Lizzie that Judge Dewey refused to hear evidence about her attempts to buy prussic acid before the murders, citing it as irrelevant. And when, with a nice sense of timing, Lizzie fainted half-way through her trial, the emotional newspaper-reading public cried hysterically for an end to her torture.

They got their wish. The court shook with applause when, after a ten-day trial, Lizzie was found not guilty. That night she was guest of honour at a celebration party and laughed joyfully over the newspaper cuttings of the trial that friends had kept for her.

If Lizzie was innocent, then who was the guilty party? No one else was ever arrested for the Borden murders; indeed, no one else was ever seriously suspected. Was there ever such a person who, in the words of one of Lizzie's lawyers, had "a heart that was as black as hell"?

Peculiar turns

Who was the agitated young man seen outside the house? Did he, or someone else, dart in from the street that morning, kill Abby, strike again and make off undetected?

The idea of an intruder stumbles and collapses under a mass of facts. The front door was double locked and bolted all that morning. Even if the intruder had overcome that obstacle, it would have been impossible, in the small house, for him to have gone unnoticed by Lizzie.

Overwhelmingly the evidence points to the crime having been committed by someone who was alone in the house that morning—someone who could have only been Lizzie. What could have happened on the murder morning, says a modern American writer, Victoria Lincoln, was that Lizzie could have had an attack of temporal epilepsy—the medical term for what her family called her "peculiar turns".

They occurred in Lizzie, asserts Miss Lincoln in her book *A Private Disgrace*, about four times a year and were accompanied by menstruation. She goes on: "During a seizure, there are periods of automatic action which the patient in some cases forgets completely and in others remembers only dimly."

There was, suggests Miss Lincoln, a catalyst for the double tragedy of August 4. It was the note delivered to 92 Second Street just before Abby died. Uncle John Morse had come to stay at the Borden house to help arrange the transfer of another property to Abby at the bank on the morning of the murder. Naturally enough, the last person anyone wanted to tell about the transfer was temperamental Lizzie.

If Lizzie killed twice that day in an epileptic fit and believed that she did not

LIZZIE BORDEN.　　EMMA BORDEN.　　REV. MR. BUCK.　　MRS. C. J. HOLMES.　　MR. C. J. HOLMES.

THE PRISONER AND HER FRIENDS IN COURT.

THE TRIAL . . . Lizzie was lucky to have George Robinson, seen at work (below and right), as her defence attorney. He was both a good lawyer and a friend of Judge Dewey.

All Bettman Archive

kill, it would be one way of explaining her peculiar post-trial conduct. For although she then had wealth enough to keep several permanent servants, and enjoyed travelling, she went right on living in Fall River until the day she died.

But it was a different Lizzie Borden. She gave up church-going and quickly lost all the local popularity she had won during her ordeal. At first Emma lived with her; then, as the years passed, they became incompatible and Emma left.

Lizzie lived on alone except for her servants in a big, old-fashioned house she had bought in a better part of the textile town—a lonely, elderly woman about whom other elderly folk still whispered to the new, unknowing generation, when she passed in the street.

There, in 1927, she died; and there, in the town's graveyard, she was laid to rest. Her body lies in the family lot—along with Andrew and Abby. The family which made violent and lethal war within itself is now together in peace.

PRESERVED for all time, the murder exhibits can be seen by the public and include the two battered skulls of Andrew and Abby Borden and also the axe.

SABOTAGE

EXPLOSIONS rock the night air, ships disappear in mid ocean, mysterious fires spread death and havoc in factories and warehouses. It is all the work

IT WAS nearly noon on November 21, 1903, and the superintendent of the Vindicator silver mine, Cripple Creek, Colorado, set out on a routine check of the mine with his shift boss. They walked cautiously; for the past three months there had been constant trouble at the mine; the miners were on strike, the National Guard had been called in, and the night watchman had seen shadowy figures wandering around.

The two men reached the sixth level, and Charles McCormick gripped a handrail to steady himself. The sound of a revolver shot made them both fling themselves backwards; then there was a tremendous roar, and the mine collapsed around them, killing them both. Later, in the wreckage, investigators found the remains of a twisted revolver. Its trigger had been attached to the handrail with a fishing line, so that when anyone grasped the shaky rail, a bullet was fired into a bundle of dynamite sticks.

Union clash

The Cripple Creek mine explosion was one of the first acts of industrial sabotage in American history. But in those days it was not known as sabotage. The word only came into general use after a French railway strike of 1912, when railwaymen cut the shoes (or "sabots") of the railway lines to wreck trains. But sabotage, or industrial wrecking, had been preached by trade union organizations for more than 50 years; the first recorded instance of it occurred when Sheffield workers destroyed the tools of blacklegs (strike-breakers) in the 1860's.

That Cripple Creek mine explosion was not quite the first piece of industrial sabotage in American history. As early as 1892, there had been a clash between union and non-union miners at the Frisco mine at Gem, Idaho. Fifteen men died in the fight; then the strikers blew up the mine. Again, in 1899, a gang from Burke, Idaho, blew up the Bunker-Hill-Sullivan mine at Wardner, Idaho. These cases were not, perhaps, "sabotage" in the modern sense. But an explosion that occurred soon after the Cripple Creek incident *was*. On June 6, 1904, 26 non-union men from a mine at Independence, Colorado, were standing on the platform at a train depot after finishing their day's work. A sudden explosion turned the depot into matchwood, killing 14 of the men and seriously injuring the rest—some were crippled for life.

On November 17, 1904, Fred Bradley, ex-manager of the Bunker-Hill-Sullivan mine walked into the hall of his San Francisco home and lit a cigar; the next moment a discharge blew him straight out of the door. Although seriously injured, he recovered, and the San Francisco gas company subsequently paid

FRIENDLY FARMER Harry Orchard tends his chickens at Idaho State Prison Farm. But back in 1905 this smiling figure blew up the ex-governor of the state (above inset). His attempt to implicate union leaders was foiled by great criminal lawyer Clarence Darrow (right).

him nearly $11,000 in damages, assuming the explosion to be due to a faulty gas main.

On December 30, 1905, Frank Steunenburg, ex-governor of Idaho, opened his garden gate, and was hurled into the air by a blast of dynamite. His wife rushed out to find the snow stained with blood, and her husband unrecognizable—and dying. The police acted quickly. All roads out of the city were closed, and the hotels were searched. They were in luck; the proprietor of the Saratoga Hotel thought that one of his guests had been acting suspiciously; when the police called the next day, the man was still there. In his room, the police found potassium chlorate, and other explosive ingredients. He was a small, cheerful-looking Irishman with a round, red face, and he gave his name as Harry Orchard. Many people at the time recorded the impression that he didn't *want* to get away—that he sought out the notoriety and publicity that he felt were his due. And he got them.

Planted bomb

He confessed to a whole series of crimes. He had personally lighted the fuse that blew up the Bunker-Hill-Sullivan mine; he had planted the dynamite and revolver in the Cripple Creek mine; he had planted the bomb that blew up the railway station at Independence; he had blown up Governor Steunenburg, *and* Fred Bradley. The explosion that blew Bradley out of his own front door was not gas; it was pure coincidence that it took place as he lit a cigar.

Having got himself arrested, Harry Orchard—whose real name was Albert Horsley—proceeded to wriggle his neck out of the hangman's noose. The first thing he did was to implicate several leaders of the Western Federation of Miners Union, including William Haywood, George Pettibone, and Charles Moyer. He then had a religious "revelation", and declared himself to be a reformed man who had seen the light. He told reporters smugly that he had believed he was engaged in a class war, but that since God had enlightened him, he realized he had only been seeking revenge. His plan worked; he was sentenced to life imprisonment, and subsequently became a Seventh Day Adventist and a leading preacher in the penitentiary.

But if Orchard's conversion was unworthy of a revolutionary, his methods were an inspiration to labour saboteurs the world over. At the Independence railroad depot, a hundred pounds of dynamite had been placed under the floor. Detonating caps were placed on the dynamite. Above them, attached to a small wheel, was a bottle of sulphuric acid. A long wire fixed to the wheel meant that the acid could be tilted on to the caps

BLACK TOM promontory blazes furiously after violent explosions set off by saboteurs in 1916. Damage was estimated at $22,000,000.

at any time. Orchard was several hundred yards away when he tugged the wire that sent the station sky high.

He had got into Fred Bradley's home by becoming the lover of one of his servant girls. He used the same device—sulphuric acid on a kind of windlass. This time, however, the wire was attached to the door, so that the dynamite would explode when the door was opened. The same dynamite and acid-bottle device was used to blow up Mr. Frank Steunenburg.

There is one interesting point about Orchard's long confession. For all its pious expressions of repentance for his crimes, it is obvious that he enjoyed every minute of his strange manhunts. He had discovered a new sport that combined the adult's love of hunting with the child's delight in causing loud bangs. It is a characteristic that appears in many saboteurs.

Labour hero

In spite of Orchard's confessions, the accused Union leaders managed to escape largely due to the brilliant efforts of the great advocate, Clarence Darrow. Darrow became the hero of the American labour movement, and Pettibone, Moyer and the rest were regarded as near-martyrs. In retrospect, it seems more than

likely that the Union leaders *were* accessories. They were fortunate in that America's greatest criminal lawyer chose to defend them.

America suddenly discovered the full meaning of sabotage in World War I. The United States had a high population of immigrant Germans, many of them American citizens. Even before the United States entered the war, in April 1917, it was supplying England with arms and food. And then the explosions began. It was on a hot June evening in 1916 that a guard in the great freight yards of Black Tom—the promontory of New Jersey that faces New York City —was startled to see a fire burning under a railroad wagon loaded with munitions. Then he saw another fire a hundred yards away. He rang the fire alarm, but a quarter of an hour later tremendous explosions sent a column of smoke and fire into the air.

The whole freight yard, full of munitions for the Allies, went off like a giant bomb. The concussion was enough to have destroyed the skyscrapers of Wall Street, but the force of the blast went upwards; only two adults and a child were killed. A landlady subsequently reported that her lodger, a Hungarian named Michael Kristoff, had been pacing his room all night after the explosion groaning "What have I done?" An American agent actually got an admission of guilt out of Kristoff; then Kristoff disappeared. Ironically, he had been arrested for a civil offence, and put in jail, where

Brown Brothers

UPI

he stayed for the duration of the war.

On the other side of the country, in San Francisco, a German reported to the authorities that he had heard of a plot to blow up the Mare Island Navy Yard. Before the authorities could act, the yard erupted in flames and suffered explosions as violent as those at Black Tom. This time 16 children were among the dead.

The solution of the Mare Island explosion came by chance, after the outbreak of war in 1917. Although Mexico was neutral, there was much anti-Americanism there, and the Mexican police made no attempt to harass Germans who were obviously spies. Washington persuaded Paul Altendorf, a colonel in the Mexican army, to act as a counter-spy. In Mexico City bars, Altendorf made the acquaintance of Kurt Jahnke, who was suspected of being an enemy agent. Jahnke was a heavy drinker. One day, in a confiding mood, he told Altendorf that he was the patriotic citizen who had reported the plot to blow up Mare Island to the authorities—and also the man who had then blown it up. He had reported it because he knew that he would then be

the last person to be suspected of the explosion.

Jahnke was an explosives expert, who worked in combination with Lothar Witzke, another of Germany's most skilled saboteurs. Altendorf, pretending to be as anti-American as Jahnke, offered his aid in future projects. Jahnke said that Witzke needed help finding his way back across the Mexican border into the United States. Altendorf said that he knew the country intimately and would be glad to help. The consequence was that when Witzke arrived in Nogales, Arizona, he found American Secret Service men waiting to arrest him. He was subsequently sentenced to death, but reprieved and later allowed to return to Germany.

Beautiful spy

The end of the Witzke-Jahnke team was one of the triumphs that helped to put a stop to sabotage in World War I; the other was the capture of the beautiful German spy, Maria von Kretschman. This was due to a fortunate accident: a courier put two letters into the wrong envelopes. On the advice of British Intelligence,

SPY TRAPPER Paul Altendorf (right) in Mexican army uniform broke up the deadly team of Lothar Witzke (above top) and Kurt Jahnke (centre). Background picture shows Mare Island Navy Yard, one of Jahnke's "successes".

American agents were already watching an address on Long Island. A letter was duly intercepted, and the agents were puzzled. The envelope was addressed to a man—one of the German agents they were on the lookout for—but the letter inside was to a woman.

Chemical technicians tested the letter, and found another letter on the back, written in invisible ink. It was about the blowing up of munitions factories and mines. With excitement, the agents realized they had stumbled on a key figure in the sabotage network. But who was she? They traced the courier who had sent the letter—he had put his return address on the envelope—a sailors' lodging-house—but that didn't help much.

The man was simply a go-between who had agreed to post the two letters when he landed in New York. It was he who had removed the letters from their grubby old envelopes, and in re-addressing them, put them back in the wrong envelopes. He could even recall the address on the other envelope – but again the agents were frustrated. An old lady who lived there said she sometimes received letters for someone else, but she couldn't give any more information – except that she had once seen the name "Victorica" on one of them.

That didn't seem much to go on. The agents managed to find another cache of unopened "Victorica" letters at another *poste restante* address; but again the trail led nowhere. All they proved was that Victorica *was* involved in the series of explosions that were rocking American factories and dockyards every other week. The Secret Service then deployed dozens of agents to watch every person mentioned in the letters. They maintained their surveillance for weeks, and no one did anything suspicious. One weary agent reported to his chief that the young sister of one of the suspects seemed to be very religious – she never missed going to church. His chief looked up sharply. "In that case, follow her, you fool!"

Prayed briefly

His intuition proved to be correct. The next day, the agent saw the young girl kneel down in St. Patrick's Cathedral in Fifth Avenue, and place a newspaper on the seat; when she left, the newspaper was still there. Another man moved into the pew, prayed briefly, and left carrying the newspaper. The man went to a Long Island hotel, the Nassau, sat in the lounge for a few minutes. Then he walked out, leaving the newspaper behind. A tall, beautiful blonde woman in her thirties then sat down and casually picked it up.

A few days later, she was under arrest, the elusive Madame Victorica – whose real name was Maria von Kretschman. Under interrogation, she confessed – and told the agents how she had used religion to aid her activities as a key saboteur. She persuaded Catholic priests to help her in ordering religious statuettes from Zürich, in Switzerland. When the statuettes arrived, they would be full of chemicals vital to the detonating of explosives. The nervous strain had been telling on her; now that she was arrested, she cracked. (She died, a drug addict, a few years later.) With her capture, and the break-up of the Jahnke-Witzke partnership, the United States had eliminated the sabotage ring that had been causing so much damage.

The damage might have been worse if one of Germany's master spies – and saboteurs – had not been hamstrung by jealousy from bureaucrats at home. Franz Rintelen von Kleist – usually known simply as Von Rintelen – got into the United States on a Swiss passport in the month America declared war. His speciality was sabotage.

A German-American, Dr. Schlee, had invented a new incendiary device, no bigger than a fountain pen. It was divided in half by a thin copper wall. One half contained picric acid, the other half, sulphuric acid. When the sulphuric acid ate through the copper, a brilliant, hot flame shot out of the device. It was called a Thermit pencil. Von Rintelen contacted Schlee, arranged for the manufacture of hundreds of Thermit pencils, and passed them on to Irish dock workers who hated the British – and who dropped them into cracks on munition ships about to depart for England.

Soon there were fires at sea, and the British realized that a new master saboteur was at work. Another German inventor named Fay produced a kind of bomb that would explode as the rudder of a ship moved from side to side; it was attached by a magnet, like a modern limpet mine. The mysterious fires at sea were then supplemented by mysterious explosions that destroyed the ship's rudder.

Von Rintelen's brilliance was his own undoing. Congratulatory messages came from high sources in the Fatherland, and passed through the Washington Embassy. Jealousies and resentments flared. To Von Rintelen's alarm, the men who should have been protecting him began to commit indiscretions; one day, he actually received a letter addressed to him with his correct name (he was under an alias, naturally) and military title. As American agents closed in, he slipped on board a ship. All might have been well; but the ship stopped at Southampton. Although his passport said he was a Swiss citizen, Von Rintelen was questioned. Suddenly, the interrogator tried an old trick; he yelled in German: "Salute" – and Von Rintelen's heels automatically clicked together.

Greatest saboteur

Even then, he succeeded in escaping from custody, and was finally captured in Leicester. The great British spy chief, Admiral "Blinker" Hall, took advantage of his resentment about the German Embassy to get him to cooperate with British Intelligence. The man who could have been Germany's top saboteur of World War I was turned into a traitor by the petty envy and jealousy of his superiors.

The greatest saboteur of all time was also a German, although he devoted his life to working for Soviet Russia. Ernst Friedrich Wollweber was born in 1898, the son of a Hamburg miner. He was short, chunky, ugly, and driven by immense energy; later in life, he became an obese dwarf. It may have been some desire to compensate for his unattractive appearance that turned Wollweber into a revolutionary. In 1917, he joined the German navy; inspired by the Russian Revolution, he preached Socialism below decks. It was Wollweber's propaganda that helped stir the German fleet to mutiny in November 1918, and he personally hauled up the Red Flag on the

cruiser *Heligoland* at the entrance to the Kiel Canal—the signal for the revolt.

In Bremen, Wollweber led rioters on the Oslebhausen prison, and saw the prisoners set free. He hoped for a swift Communist triumph in Germany—but he was disappointed. Even in defeat, Germany was not ready for revolution. The Weimar Republic was formed in 1919 and Wollweber responded by leading another mutiny on board ship, and took the vessel to Murmansk, as a present for the Soviet regime. As a reward for this, he was appointed by Lenin as chairman of the International Seamen's Union. He sailed round the world, acting as an emissary of Communism in China, Japan, Italy, and the United States.

Undismayed

The Communists were shocked by the ease with which Hitler destroyed the German Communist Party when he came to power in 1933. But Wollweber was typically undismayed. He chose Copenhagen as his headquarters, and settled down to a career as a master saboteur. Ships left Denmark loaded with supplies for the Fascists in the Spanish Civil War. Wollweber's agents mixed TNT with the coal, and many of the ships failed to reach Spanish ports, or had their cargoes destroyed by fire.

One of Wollweber's great triumphs was the destruction of the German troopship *Marion,* which left Denmark for Norway in 1940. A shattering explosion sank the ship, and badly burned corpses floated ashore for weeks afterwards—4000 of them. When the Nazis invaded Denmark, Wollweber moved to Sweden. Although he was promptly arrested, he had already succeeded in organizing a sabotage ring there. His agent, Jacob Liebersohn, had

MUTINEERS MARCH through the streets of Kiel in November 1918. Their rising was carefully planned by master saboteur Wollweber (inset) as East German Security Minister.

MASTER SPY Von Rintelen was a victim of jealousy. His German superiors destroyed his cover— so he changed sides . . .

recruited two young waitresses, Erika Möller and Gunhild Ahman. They were ideal agents; no one suspected two women. They were responsible for the explosion that destroyed part of the freight yards at Krylbo, in central Sweden, on July 19, 1941—and detonated truckloads of German shells. There were many more fires and explosions before the counter-espionage branch of the Swedish Statspolisen arrested the two women and their accomplices, and sent them to prison.

The Swedes kept Wollweber in jail until the end of the war, in spite of Nazi demands that he be handed over. As soon as it was clear that the Nazis were losing the war, however, they allowed Wollweber to go to Moscow. There, he was treated as a Soviet hero, and entered Berlin not far behind Marshal Zhukov. Declining important political appointments, he went back to organizing an East German spy ring. He enjoyed undercover work. He may also have felt that a

public appointment would restrict his sex life—for he was known as an insatiable satyr.

Again, there were explosions on British and American ships—the fire on the *Queen Elizabeth* in 1953 was almost certainly Wollweber's work. But that was one of his last achievements in sabotage; in that year, he was appointed Minister of State Security in East Germany. There *was* a point in 1961 when it looked as if Wollweber's luck was at last running out; after a clash with Walter Ulbricht, the Secretary of the East German Communist Party ordered Wollweber's arrest. Wollweber contacted Moscow, and a telegram arrived: "Let Wollweber alone, he is a friend of mine." It was signed "Krushchev". So Wollweber died a natural death after all, in 1962.

It is the fate of the saboteur to live in an emotional no man's land, with no place that he can openly call his own. His existence—and psychological condition—is one of constant uncertainty, fear, and suspicion. He is like a man who has betrayed his wife *and* the mistress whom he has set in her place. He is his own worst enemy.

THE SLEEPWALKERS

The steamy stillness of a midsummer Kentucky night is shattered. A madman, guns blazing, has broken into the home of 16-year-old Jo Ann Kiger. But it's all a dream: Jo Ann wakes . . . she has shot and killed her father and brother. The unconscious is no respecter of law.

UPI, Mary Evans

ONE OF the most valuable assets any detective can have is the ability to imagine himself in the position of the criminal he is hunting. "What would I do if I were in his place?" That is the line of thought which brings success to so many crime investigations. "If I wanted to rob that bank . . . if I intended to kill that man . . . how would I set about it?"

Many detectives commit the crime, time and time again, inside their own minds. Some become so absorbed that their lives are dominated by their current cases. They work on the cases through the day. They mull them over as they drift into the limbo-land of sleep. And, just occasionally, there is a danger of them becoming obsessed.

Robert Ledru, a brilliant murder detective, did become a victim of his own dedication. It began to manipulate his mind—and it transformed him into a Sleep-Walking Slayer.

Courts of law, on both sides of the Atlantic, have returned "not guilty" verdicts on men and women accused of a wide variety of crimes—although the people concerned admitted the act and were seen committing it. These have involved allegations of dangerous driving . . . shop-lifting . . . money thefts. And of first-degree murder. Charges have been dismissed because the accused have convinced judges and juries that, at the time of the offence, they were fast asleep.

The innocent killer

Ledru provides one of the most dramatic examples of this phenomenon of somnambulistic crime, for he is the only man in recorded history who has tracked himself down as the innocent killer. But, before considering his extraordinary case, let us look at the broad picture of nightmares and sleep-walking crime.

When a man is sleeping the defences of his mind are relaxed; fears and violent emotions which he has suppressed through the day—or which he may not even know exist—are free to roam out of their dark corners. The subconscious, which still bears the imprints of our primeval ancestors, takes control, and the shackles of inhibition and convention are torn away.

That is why so many sleep-walkers display such startlingly uncharacteristic behaviour—why shy and respectable women wander naked through busy streets, and why gentle and compassionate men become savagely brutal killers. Sleep-walking, which usually starts an hour or two after falling asleep, is far more common than many people realize. Britain has half a million sufferers and America has two million. Children are more prone to it than adults, with 5 out of 100 sleep-walking at some time compared with the adult ratio of 2 in every 100.

Killings have been committed by sleep-

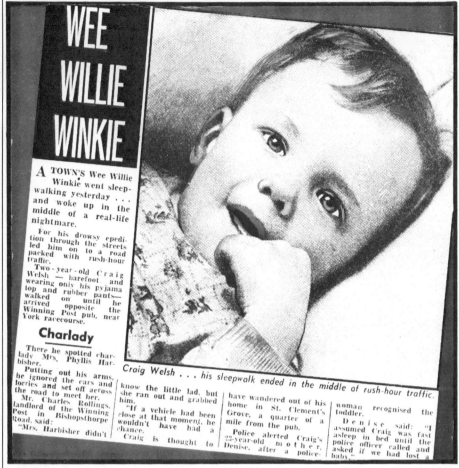

UPI

WEE WILLIE WINKIE

A TOWN'S Wee Willie Winkie went sleep-walking yesterday . . . and woke up in the middle of a real-life nightmare.

For his drowsy expedition through the streets led him on to a road packed with rush-hour traffic.

Two-year-old Craig Welsh — barefoot and wearing only his pyjama top and rubber pants—walked on until he arrived opposite the Winning Post pub, near York racecourse.

Charlady

There he spotted charlady Mrs. Phyllis Harbisher.

Putting out his arms, he ignored the cars and lorries and set off across the road to meet her.

Mr. Charles Rollings, landlord of the Winning Post in Bishopsthorpe Road, said:

"Mrs. Harbisher didn't know the little lad, but she ran out and grabbed him.

"If a vehicle had been close at that moment, he wouldn't have had a chance.

Craig is thought to have wandered out of his home in St. Clement's Grove, a quarter of a mile from the pub.

Police alerted Craig's 22-year-old mother, Denise, after a police woman recognised the toddler.

Denise said: "I assumed Craig was fast asleep in bed until the police officer called and asked if we had lost a baby."

Craig Welsh . . . his sleepwalk ended in the middle of rush-hour traffic.

A CHILD IS PUNISHED . . . and drowsy fantasies of escape take over. Most sleep-walking incidents have happy endings, like the adventure of little Craig Welsh.

walking children but, before we get to examples, let us look at a much simpler case—that of two-year-old Craig Welsh. In York, England, he was recently seen walking in his bare feet between rush-hour cars and lorries on one of the city's busiest streets—wearing just his pyjama top and rubber pants.

Analysis of the sleep-walking state reveals that the sleeper is invariably grappling with some problem. But a child of only two? What sort of inner turmoil could provoke him into somnambulism? The most common reason is that the child wants to escape from some situation which, while appearing trivial to an adult, seems intolerable to him. Possibly he feels he has been scolded or punished unfairly.

In his sleep he dreams of escaping from the unfairness, and so urgent is the need that he really acts out the escape. In Lancashire there was a far more serious case. A seven-year-old boy climbed into the cot of his baby sister and lay on top of her. She was suffocated and the coroner, after hearing that the boy was sleep-walking at the time, recorded a verdict of misadventure.

But what stimulated that misadventure? Unconscious jealousy of the newly-arrived "intruder"? A burning desire, normally buried in the boy's subconscious, to return to his old place as the pampered baby of the family?

Parents have also been killed by their own innocently sleeping children. Carl Kiger, a successful local-government official in Kentucky, a typical victim, was shot five times by his 16-year-old daughter Jo Ann. On August 16, 1943, Mr. and Mrs. Kiger and their two children—Jo Ann and six-year-old Jerry—went to bed early. Soon after midnight Jo Ann, who had a history of sleep-walking, had a vivid nightmare; a huge madman with wild eyes was easing his way into the house. She saw him creeping up the stairs and she was convinced he was going to murder the rest of the family. It was up to her to save them.

There is a popular but completely false belief that sleep-walkers tend to walk slowly with their arms protectively extended in front of them. In fact, the sleeper usually sits up quietly, gets out of bed and starts to move about in a clumsy and confused way; soon his movements become more co-ordinated and complex and the only clue to his somnambulistic state is the blank expression in his eyes.

This is how Jo Ann Kiger was on that

August night. She took two loaded revolvers belonging to her father and first went to the "rescue" of her little brother; one bullet went into his head, two more went into his body. He never woke.

But the "nightmare madman" was still amok in the Kigers' once-peaceful suburban house. Jo Ann chased him into her parents' bedroom and blazed away with both guns. Her father died almost immediately. Her mother, 49-year-old Mrs. Jennie Kiger, was shot in the hip. Suddenly Jo Ann woke up—still holding the guns and with the nightmare still lingering in her mind. She stared in horror at the body of her father and said: "There's a crazy man here who's going to kill all of us."

She was arrested on a charge of first-degree murder but, because of the sleep-walking defence, was acquitted.

Blemishes on the mind

What *really* caused that tragedy? Our most deeply-rooted motivations, of which we may not even be aware, are a complicated legacy of the past—as it has impinged on us and on our ancestors. Anxieties and irrational dislikes are often buried deeply because they are mental blemishes, "warts" on the mind, which people are too frightened or too inhibited to consciously recognize.

A man, for instance, may have repeated nightmares in which he is being strangled; this may not be a fear which worries him in the daytime and he may see no reason why it should haunt his nights. But, if it were possible for him to trace all his own history, he might well find that when he was a few days old he had almost suffocated in his cot. The incident has long gone into oblivion but the scar is still etched on his mind.

Legacy of dread

The same applies to the illogical fears and superstitions which we have unconsciously inherited from our long-dead ancestors; this is vividly demonstrated in the Fraser baby-battering case, described in detail in another article.

Our ancestors lived in terror of the beasts that prowled through the night. In their caves and rough huts they knew that death could be stalking them, that they might have to kill or be killed. Fraser, in a small and shabby house in 19th-century Scotland, wrestled through his sleep with that legacy of dread. The adrenalin surged through him in exactly the way it had done through his forebears. He jumped from his bed. He fought the monster and he killed it; and then he found it was his baby.

This common legacy of ours is still there, whether we realize it or not, and it forms a background tapestry to our thoughts; occasionally we make use of it and then we tend to talk about a "hunch"

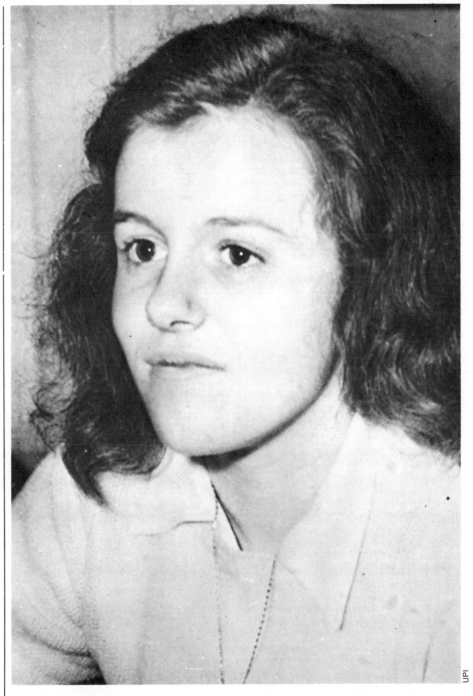

JO ANN KIGER was acquitted of murder because the law recognizes the somnambulist's inability to control his actions or to distinguish right and wrong.

or about "acting on instinct". The normal conscious mind, one not shadowed by mental sickness, is capable of keeping these mental blemishes in their proper perspective. But during sleep the conscious reasoning process is no longer in command—and so there are tragedies such as the one at the Kiger household.

The Kiger case was a classic demonstration of somnambulism being stimulated by insecurity, a motivation which psychiatrists know is immensely common among children. A child hears his parents quarrelling, perhaps, and hears them threatening to leave each other. This frightens him and the fear permeates his dream; he is going to lose one or maybe both of them, he is going to be robbed of their love and protection.

There does not have to be a row. This pervading sense of insecurity could be fuelled by a chance remark, by a wrongly-interpreted remark even, which festers in the sub-conscious.

Jo Ann Kiger deeply loved her family. The bond was so important to her that she had an obsessive fear that, in some way, she might be robbed of them, and although this fear may not have been in her conscious mind it was firmly lodged in her sub-conscious. She was an intelligent girl and, if she had been awake on that awful night and had really seen an intruder, she would probably have screamed and raised an alarm; it is most unlikely that she would have tried to tackle him single-handed. But, with reason suspended in her trance-like state, her response was purely emotional. She was going to lose her father, her mother and her brother. She alone was alive to the danger and she alone could save them.

Her brother was the smallest member of the family and so the most vulnerable. That was why her sub-conscious mental blemish took her initially to his room, and that was why he was the first to die. Children are more susceptible to sleep-walking than adults because they react more vigorously to most forms of mental stimulation. They have fewer inhibitions and have not learned the average adult's habit of self-control.

Their lips may tremble

There are ways to recognize potential sleep-walkers, even a day or so before they have set a foot out of bed. They often become quieter or more sullen, their lips may tremble a little or they may have unusual difficulty in pronouncing certain words. These are signs of some problem deep in the mind.

After a sleep-walking session the sufferer's heart usually beats faster than usual and the palms of his hands perspire more than normal. Most sleep-walkers, of course, wander harmlessly around. They may go downstairs or walk along corridors in blocks of flats and then return to their beds without realizing they have ever left them.

Some have killed themselves. One youngster, the son of a professor at Cambridge University, doused his clothing in turpentine and then set fire to himself. Another drank prussic acid. Many have fallen through windows or from great heights. In nearly every part of the world there have been cases of sleep-walkers who have woken up to find themselves in a state of acute embarrassment.

Back in 1954, for instance, there was a housewife who was found doing a Tarzan act, swinging completely naked from the branch of a garden tree. She had to be rescued by her husband and the fire brigade.

Many others find that in their sleep they have innocently broken the law. A 19-year-old apprentice bricklayer was charged with dangerous driving at Chesterfield, Derbyshire, and witnesses described how he was travelling at 60 miles an hour when he crashed into a car. The case was dismissed because the court accepted that he was fast asleep.

At Lymington, Hampshire, a 20-year-old girl admitted having taken more than £3 belonging to fellow servants in a large house. She was also found not guilty because she too had been sleep-walking. In February, 1970, a 51-year-old housewife appeared at South West London sessions accused of stealing a case and a calendar from a store. A store detective said that he followed her outside and shouted after her but "she didn't seem to hear". Again the defence of somnambulism was accepted.

Psychiatrists agree that these cases of "innocent dishonesty" again have their roots in our ancestry. Primitive man used to take what he wanted when he wanted it; to him this was absolutely natural. Through the centuries, for the majority of people, that sort of instinct has been repressed, and has become anti-social and unlawful, but the unconscious mind owes no particular allegiance to the laws of modern man.

The full potential horror of sleep-walking, however, is brought home most forcibly by the violent killings and the number of incidents which almost end in a violent killing. At Devon Assizes in February, 1952, consultant psychiatrist Dr. Hugh Scott Forbes emphasized the startling frequency of somnambulistic attacks. Giving evidence in the case of a 34-year-old Royal Navy lieutenant who was charged with attempted wife-murder, he described two other cases of somnambulists attacking their wives which, to his

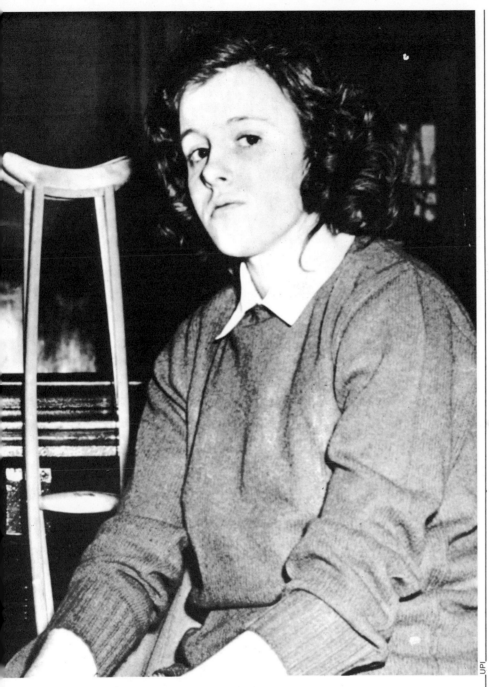

arm with his wife.

Some legal experts feel that somnambulism, if it can be established beyond doubt, provides such clear evidence of innocence that it is pointless to put a man through the ordeal of a formal hearing in a criminal court. That was the attitude the authorities adopted towards William Pollard, a 24-year-old chicken farmer of Arkansas after he became a Sleep-Walking Slayer.

Everyone in the district knew that Pollard was an habitual sleep-walker. One typical night, wearing his pyjamas, he loaded his wagon with chickens he intended to sell and started to make the journey to the nearby town of Little Rock; then he woke up, wondering why he was not in bed.

Nobody was very concerned about this type of escapade; his friends thought it was all a bit of a joke. "Wait till he nods off," they used to say. "He always works best when he's asleep." But in November, 1946, the joke exploded into horror.

Pollard had a nightmare in which he was being attacked by a strange man. He lashed out in self-defence and then awoke. That was all he could remember. Just a short and simple nightmare. But his four-year-old daughter was dead.

Strange and vacant look

Fuller details of that terrible night were given to a coroner's jury by Mrs. Pollard. She had been woken up by noises and had been aghast to see her husband, a strange and vacant look on his face, aimlessly playing a torch over an object on the floor; that object was their daughter Brenda and the back of her head had been crushed. Mrs. Pollard screamed hysterically but the child seemed beyond help.

Pollard had looked at her in a bemused way and shook his head hopelessly; he could not remember. He could not remember if he had dragged the child from her crib or not, he could not remember what he had hit her with or if he had hit her at all; he could not even remember where he had got the torch. All he could remember was the nightmare and how he had lashed out.

When he had collected his senses, Pollard rushed to get his father from next door and the two men took the child to a local hospital; she died within minutes of getting there. The authorities felt that, as Pollard's reputation as a sleep-walker was so well-established, he was not to be held responsible for any crime, so no charges were made.

Some people may feel that the slaying of little Brenda Pollard was no more than a gruesome psychological accident, one of those freaks of behaviour which cannot be explained, and this view might seem to be endorsed by the fact that Pollard was undeniably devoted to the girl. However,

THEIR FAMILY was close — too close? The Kiger case was a classic example of sleep-walking which is rooted in deep insecurity . . . with sometimes fatal results.

personal knowledge, had taken place in the previous eighteen months. One had tried to strangle his wife on two occasions and the other had injured his wife with his fists.

The lieutenant admitted that he had fractured his wife's skull with an axe and that he had woken up to find himself with his hands around her throat. His wife told the court: "Our married life has always been perfectly happy — always. We have never had a serious quarrel. At no time, apart from that night, has he ever used any kind of violence towards me."

The defending counsel, Mr. Dingle Foot, asked Dr. Forbes if a man in a state of somnambulism would have any conscious purpose.

The psychiatrist replied: "No, he is living out a dream. He is not fully in touch with reality. He is incapable of forming any logical purpose."

Dr. Forbes added that somnambulism was not a mental disease; it existed mostly as an entity in itself, without any other abnormality. It did not cause any form of mental deterioration and it never necessitated certification. It tended to recur. After a retirement of ten minutes the jury returned a verdict of not guilty, and the lieutenant left the court arm-in-there is a strong line of expert opinion which indicates that the cause of the tragedy was Pollard's survival instincts and those to protect his wife and child.

His sub-conscious reacted to the "nightmare intruder" and immediately propelled his body into action. Fright, in this raw and basic state, leads to one of two things, flight or fight. Pollard, aware of the need to defend his family, chose to fight.

The snatching of the child from the crib, even though he could not consciously remember it, could well have been a desperate attempt to pull her to safety. Then, if she had struggled in his arms, his imagination was almost certainly capable of transforming her into the person who was opposing him. So his daughter could become the enemy who was threatening the safety of the home and who had to be destroyed.

The sleeping strangler

A very different type of unconscious motivation would seem to have been behind the curious strangling of Jean Constable. The way she died, in England in 1961, is described in a separate article but here let us consider the psychological battle which must have raged in the mind of her sleeping strangler.

Staff Sergeant Willis Boshears had a marriage which was apparently normal and quite happy; but on New Year's Eve his wife and three young children were away visiting relatives and he was left all alone.

In the early hours of the following morning he was still asleep when he killed a girl who was sharing his bed. As he later explained to the jury: "There was no quarrel or argument. At no time did I make any overtures or sexual advances to her, nor did I have any desire to kill her or harm her in any way."

Other evidence seemed to confirm the truth of that statement; so why, then, did Jean Constable die? One of the most probable explanations is that Boshears' sub-conscious mind regarded her as a dangerous intruder. He wanted the company of his wife and this woman beside him had stolen his wife's place; there could be no hope of his wife and children returning to him while this girl was there. So the girl represented a threat to his marriage, and he had to get rid of her.

That may sound as if the killing had undertones of premeditation but this was certainly not the case; the subconscious cannot be indicted of premeditation.

The most bizarre case of a somnambulist killing was the one involving the French detective Robert Ledru. He was a man with a fine record of success which, to a great extent, he owed to his own lively imagination. He specialized in

CAN A SLEEP-WALKER have any purpose? asks Mr. Dingle Foot. The answer is no. The verdict: acquittal. Accused and "victim" left arm-in-arm.

murder and he would try to put himself inside the mind of the criminal; so, in his head, he executed murder after murder, perfecting a small point here, a tiny detail there. He was conscientious, perhaps too conscientious, and in 1888 his long arduous hours brought him a nervous breakdown.

He went to convalesce by the sea at Le Havre and, because the nights were cold, he got into the habit of wearing his socks in bed; one morning, after sleeping for twelve hours, he was perplexed to find that his socks were damp. There seemed no explanation but, then, it was not all that important; he shrugged, put on fresh socks, and forgot the matter.

A chill of recognition

Later that day he received a message from his chief in Paris: the naked body of a man called Andre Monet had been found with a bullet wound on the beach at nearby Sainte Adresse. Ledru's vast experience might prove useful to the local police and, although he was still on leave, would he be interested in helping? Ledru was delighted and, naturally, flattered.

The dead man had been running a small business in Paris and he had apparently gone for a night swim; his clothing was found in a neat pile near the body. As far as could be established, he had no particular enemies and he was not a rich man. So what possible motive could there be? There were two clues to the identity of the killer but the local police did not consider them to be useful.

In the sand, quite near the body, there were distorted footprints which had apparently been left by stockinged feet. Then there was the bullet which, it was estab-

lished by ballistics experts, had been fired from a Luger. It was so very little to go on; Lugers were such common weapons and, indeed, even Ledru himself had one.

But as Ledru examined the footprints through a magnifying glass he noticed a detail which sent a chill of horror through him; in each footprint there was something missing, the imprint of one toe. Ledru, as the result of an accident, had one toe missing from his right foot.

He pulled off his right shoe and pressed his foot into the sand; then he compared the prints and realized why he had woken with damp socks. His Luger was at his hotel and he found it had a discharged cartridge in the breech.

Robert Ledru had made up murders in his mind just once too often; they were fine and safe when his conscious mind kept his fantasies on a leash and made use of them, but when they percolated through into his unconscious mind they became a grim reality.

He surrendered himself to the authorities, but a court decided that he could not be held responsible. But, because doctors warned that he might kill again while asleep, he had to agree to report nightly to a Paris prison to be locked in. So until he died in his mid-eighties in 1939 he spent his days in freedom but, for the hours of darkness, he always submitted to captivity.

Nightmares in harness

However, no one should imagine that nightmares, in themselves, are dangerous; they can, in fact, be blessings in hideous disguise. Those grotesque fantasy creatures which trespass through your sleep can actually be harnessed rather like cart horses to work for you.

They can, for example, give you advance warning of imminent illnesses. British psychiatrist Dr. J. A. Hadfield reports a typical example. He had a patient who repeatedly had the same frightening dream—that he was paralyzed in the mouth and one arm; months later he did become partially paralyzed in the mouth and in one arm.

This man, Dr. Hadfield concluded, had been suffering mild attacks in his sleep, for the unconscious can pick up tiny symptoms from the body long before they penetrate the conscious mind, and translate them into dream form.

The most important function of nightmares, and dreams in general, is that they release tension. They let us indulge in refreshingly different fantasies, in amazing adventures and even in crimes which real life denies us. Only in the minority of cases is this release function ever likely to develop into tangible physical action. But from that minority come the pitiful ones who, usually unexpectedly, are identified as Sleep-Walking Slayers.

THERE'S A CORPSE IN THE CUPBOARD

Number 10 Rillington Place was a crumbling terrace house in London's Notting Hill. For more than a decade, and unknown to the police, a steady trickle of young women entered that house and were never seen again. Then a new lodger found the bodies. They were stacked neatly in an old cupboard!

Syndication International/AP

THE LATE Professor Francis Camps did not look in the least like a crime doctor. A cheerful, untidy man in baggy clothes, he might have been a farmer or auctioneer. He was, in fact, one of the most brilliant of English pathologists since the great Sir Bernard Spilsbury. On March 24, 1953, he became involved in an investigation into a death house murder case that received wider publicity than any criminal affair since Jack the Ripper.

Late that afternoon, he was contacted by the Criminal Investigation Department of Notting Hill Police Station in West London. They had received a five word message: "Woman's body found in cupboard." Camps packed his murder bag, and joined the murder squad detectives at a squalid, grimy-looking house at the end of a cul-de-sac. Its address, 10 Rillington Place, became as familiar to the British public as 10 Downing Street.

Earlier that evening the current tenant, Beresford Brown, had been tapping the wall at the end of the kitchen, looking for a place to put up brackets for a radio set. The wall sounded so hollow that he pulled off a strip of paper, and found a cupboard door with a corner missing. He shone a torch through the hole, and saw the naked back of a woman.

Well preserved

When Camps arrived, the police had stripped the remaining paper from the door, and opened it. The seated woman was not quite naked. She was wearing a suspender belt and brassiere, and also a jacket and pullover. These had been pulled up so that a strip of blanket could be tied to her brassiere, then fixed to the wall to prevent her falling forward. When the police removed the body, they spotted another victim, shrouded in a blanket and propped against the wall. They took it out, and came across a third body, also standing upright and wrapped in a blanket.

When the corpses were laid out in the next room, they proved to be those of three young women, all in their mid-twenties. A further search of the house revealed yet another corpse under the dining-room floor—this time of a woman in her fifties. She was soon identified as a previous tenant of the flat, Mrs. Ethel Christie. Her husband, John Christie, had left the place only three days earlier.

The corpses in the cupboard were remarkably well preserved; a constant stream of air had started to "mummify" them. Camps took vaginal swabs, and quickly established that the motive for the murders had been sexual; the girls had each had intercourse shortly before or after death.

But where was Christie? A nationwide alert went out for him. Surkov, head of the Russian writers' union, who was on a visit to England at the time, remarked contemptuously that the capitalist press seemed more interested in the bodies of women found in a cupboard than in political realities. But this was hardly fair. A mass murderer was apparently at liberty, and he might kill again. Camps recalled that there had been two other murders in the same house four years earlier—Mrs. Beryl Evans and her daughter Geraldine. The husband, Timothy Evans, had con-

HAPPY FAMILY? There seems to be nothing strange about this photograph of Christie and his wife. But when it was taken Christie was already a killer.

Syndication International

fessed to the crimes and been hanged. At one point, however, he had accused Christie of being the killer. No one had taken his accusation seriously, either in the police station or at the trial.

Now, as the police combed the death house, they discovered a human femur propping up the fence in the garden; digging uncovered two more skeletons — both female. Camps examined the other bodies at the nearby Kensington mortuary. The three bodies from the cupboard showed signs of carbon monoxide poisoning — coal gas — and they had been strangled.

The murder hunt for Christie ended a week later, when he was recognized by a policeman as he stood on Putney Bridge. He made no attempt to escape. He was a tall, thin, bald-headed man in his fifties. He seemed exhausted and confused; but he confessed to the murders.

When Camps examined Christie's shoes, he made a curious discovery; there were definite traces of semen on them. Christie had not only raped his victims; he had also masturbated as he stood above them. The enigma of Christie's mind began to fascinate Camps as much as the forensic details that emerged from his examination. And, as detectives slowly uncovered the evidence of Christie's past, he began to gain some insight into the motivations of this middle-aged, quietly-spoken monster.

The police investigation showed that Christie had committed eight various murders between 1943 and 1953 — including, most probably, that of the baby, Geraldine Evans. He had lured women to the house when his wife was away, killed and sexually assaulted them, and then concealed the bodies — except in the case of Mrs. Evans. He had disposed of his wife in December 1952, and followed this by a three-month "murder spree", slaughtering the women whose bodies were found in the cupboard.

Traumatic experience

Many sex murderers are subnormal men, who slay without considering the consequences of their acts. But Christie was a man who gave an impression of intelligence and control. He had appeared as a witness in the trial of Timothy Evans, and had been complimented by the judge on the clarity of his evidence. What had driven such a man to an orgy of killing, for which he was almost certain to be hanged?

Little by little, Camps pieced together the evidence of the strange life of John Reginald Halliday Christie. He had been born in Yorkshire in 1898, the son of a harsh, stern father, a carpenter. Christie was a born "loser" — weak, myopic, always ill. He was inclined to pilfering, and was usually caught; his father beat him brutally on these occasions. When he

MALE VICTIM of Christie's murder rampage was Timothy Evans (above). He was arrested for the murder of his own wife and child and "confessed".

lost a job as a clerk through petty theft, his father threw him out of the house.

At some time during his teens, he had a traumatic sexual experience. He took a girl out to lover's lane, and she led him on to have intercourse; at the crucial moment, his nerve broke, and he failed. The girl repeated the story, and he became known in the area as "Reggie-No-Dick", or "Can't-Do-It Christie". During the 1914 war he was mustard-gassed and blown up. How far he suffered a real disability is not known; but it encouraged his lifelong tendency to hypochondria. Periodically, he suffered from blindness and loss of voice due to hysteria.

At 22, he was married to Ethel, but it was two years before he was able to have sexual intercourse with her — the hysterical fear of failure remained. They had no children. Then, in 1934, he was knocked down by a car and suffered head injuries. Due to his handicaps, he earned low wages as an unskilled clerk. Yet he had a tendency to boast and show off. At one point he even became a member of the Halifax (Yorkshire) Conservative Association, and encouraged the rumour that he had been a rich man when he married, but had lost his money.

In 1939 he became a war reserve policeman. It was what he had always wanted — authority. But he abused it by acting as a petty tyrant, taking pleasure in issuing summonses for minor blackout

offences. He was still a constable in 1943 when he invited a woman called Ruth Fuerst back to his London home. But he was incapable of sex with a fully-conscious woman, even if she was willing. So he devised a way to render his "girl friends" unconscious. He claimed that he had an ideal remedy for catarrh and various nasal ailments — a mixture of Friar's Balsam and other ingredients, mixed with boiling water.

Sense of peace

The bowl had to be covered with a cloth, to prevent the steam escaping, and the patient had to breathe in the vapour. Christie then connected a rubber tube up to the gas tap, and allowed the gas to bubble through the hot liquid. When the girl was dizzy or unconscious, he carried her to the bedroom, raped her, and then strangled her.

When he had satisfied his desires — in a kind of frenzy that came from years of frustration — he knew he had to kill the girl, to prevent her from charging him. In this way, he killed Ruth Fuerst in 1943, and Muriel Eady — a friend of his wife's — in 1944 (also during his wife's absence). In 1949, his neighbour Timothy Evans who lived in the flat above, confided in Christie that his wife was pregnant again, and that he wanted to procure an abortion.

Christie immediately claimed that he was an expert abortionist, and agreed to do it one morning when Evans was at work. It seems fairly certain that when Christie saw Beryl Evans half-naked, he lost control of himself, beat her unconscious, and raped her. After this, he

165

killed her and the baby Geraldine.

Perhaps the strangest feature of the murder is that Christie then somehow persuaded Timothy Evans that his wife had died during the abortion, and that he, Evans, would be blamed unless he fled. Evans did so and the police assumed he was the murderer. When caught he proved to be mentally subnormal, and later, after questioning, readily confessed. No one will ever know what went on in Evans's mind when he discovered that Beryl and Geraldine had been strangled.

In 1952, Christie's violent urges again reached a climax; but his wife was there to prevent him realizing them. In December, he strangled her and buried her body under the floor. Then, early in January, he invited Rita Nelson, a prostitute, to the house. He went through his usual procedure of persuading her to inhale gas, then raped and strangled her. In all probability, he kept the body around for several days before putting it in the cupboard. A few days later, he raped and strangled another prostitute, Kathleen Maloney.

During these murders, he was like a starving man eating his fill for the first time; in a confession he later described the enormous sense of peace that came over him afterwards. But the danger of being caught was growing keener. Ethel's relatives were getting worried; Christie had no job; he had sold his furniture. He was going to pieces. There was one more victim, Hectorina McLennan, the mistress of an out-of-work Irishman. Christie had allowed them to sleep in the flat overnight, then he lured the woman back the next day and killed her. His final act in the death house was to pack the bodies of his victims in a cupboard and cover it with wallpaper.

Mummified body

Christie was executed for his crimes on July 15, 1953. Nineteen years later No. 10 Rillington Place was demolished together with the rest of the street (whose name had, by then, been changed to Ruston Close to discourage sightseers); it is now a truck park. But in the far corner of the park one can still see the outer walls and floor that once belonged to Britain's most notorious death house.

In his posthumously published book, *Camps on Crime,* Francis Camps has described another case of a body-in-a-cupboard, which was investigated by his friend Dr. Gerald Evans of Rhyl, North Wales. In May 1960, a widow of 65 named Sarah Harvey was taken into hospital for observation; during her absence, her son decided to redecorate her house, 35 West Kinmel Street. On the landing there was a large wooden cupboard that had been locked for many years. Mr. Harvey opened this, and

recoiled. On the floor there was a hunched shape covered with a sheet; a discoloured human foot grotesquely protruded from one corner of it.

The police were at once called, together with Dr. Evans. When the rotting cloth was cautiously pulled from the body, they saw a brown, mummified body, whose skin was as hard as granite. It seemed to be a woman. The mummy was placed in glycerine, to soften it, and then examined. There was a mark around the neck which could have been due to a ligature, and there were fragments of a stocking stuck to it.

In hospital, Mrs. Harvey explained that the corpse was that of an old lady named Frances Knight, who had come to live with her in 1940. One night, she said, Mrs. Knight died in pain. Mrs. Harvey then panicked and pushed her body into the cupboard. She continued to collect

£2 a week—due to Mrs. Knight as a result of a court order—for the next 20 years.

The presence of the stocking gave rise to suspicions of murder, and Mrs. Harvey was put on trial. The defence pointed out that many working class people have a custom of curing sore throats by wrapping an unwashed sock or stocking round the neck. Mrs. Knight could have done this, and accidentally strangled herself; or perhaps she had died of natural causes, and the neck had swelled after death, producing the mark on the flesh. The court gave Mrs. Harvey the benefit of the doubt. The trial was stopped after

PUBLIC SPECTACLE . . . The comings and goings of police and the removal of furniture from Christie's house provided plenty of local excitement (below). The garden (left) was searched extensively. (Right) Christie is taken into court.

three days; but she *was* found guilty of obtaining £2 a week for 20 years under false pretences, and sentenced to 15 months in prison.

The Christie case and the Rhyl mummy case make it clear why "murder houses" are so rare. It is true, of course, that many murders are committed in houses; but it is only under exceptional circumstances that the body is then kept in the house. It is not a wise thing to do, as Crippen discovered to his cost when he buried Belle Elmore in the cellar. When a man is suspected of murder, his house is the first place the police search. The consequence is that although horror stories are full of houses with corpses hidden under the floorboards and behind the walls, it very seldom happens in practice.

Really professional murderers understand the importance of disposing of the body as far as possible from home. The result is that not only were no bodies ever found at Landru's murder house in Gambais, but no bloodstains or other evidence was found either. Even the "calcined bones" reported by *The Times* proved to be an unfounded rumour.

H. H. Holmes, the master of "murder castle" in Chicago, discovered the most ingenious way of disposing of the bodies of his 20 or so victims. He hired a workman to strip off the skin, claiming that the people had died "normally" and that their corpses were intended for a medical school.

The village of Cinkota, near Budapest, can claim to possess a genuine death house, at 17 Rákóczi Street. Its owner had gone to the war in 1914, and was never to be seen again. In May 1916, the house was put up for sale by the local authorities, to pay for its back taxes. It was bought by a blacksmith, Istvan Molnar. Molnar became curious about seven large tin drums concealed behind a pile of old metal in the workshop. A few days later he forced one open—and recoiled when confronted by the naked corpse of a woman. The other barrels also proved to contain female corpses.

Detective Geza Bialokurszky, in charge of the case, found it baffling. He looked through the files of more than 400 missing women before he found one who seemed to fit. She was a 36-year-old cook called Anna Novak, and her ex-employer was still resentful because she had left without giving notice. Her trunk was in the attic, and in it the detective found his first clue: a newspaper advertisement: "Young man seeks female companion for walking tour in Alps; marriage possible."

It gave a P.O. Box No. 717. A search of Budapest newspapers revealed that advertisements involving Box 717 had appeared 20 times in two years. The box was apparently owned by Mr. Elemer Nagy, but the address was—17 Rákóczi Street, Cinkota. Nagy's handwriting was reproduced in newspapers, and a lady came forward to say that it was the handwriting of her fiancé, Bela Kiss; she had last received a postcard from him in 1914.

Baby sitter

Kiss had apparently been killed in battle. The police obtained a photograph from his regiment, and showed it around Budapest's red light district. They discovered that Kiss was a man of boundless sexual appetite—in fact, a satyr. He was well dressed, a "gentleman", and he paid well for his sexual pleasures. It was his physical drive which led him into the business of lady-killing; his advertisements lured spinsters with savings into his death house home. They ended up in metal drums, and their savings were spent on prostitutes. Kiss was never traced. He may have been killed in battle. One rumour has it that he changed identities with a dead soldier, killed in battle, and later emigrated to America.

In the United States the town of Plainfield, Wisconsin, also possesses a death house with a history as lurid as that of 10 Rillington Place or 17 Rákóczi Street, the residence of a gentle, quiet man named Ed Gein, whose obvious inoffensiveness made him a favourite baby sitter in the area. One afternoon in November 1957, a deputy sheriff, Frank Worden, called at the Gein farm. Worden's mother, who kept a grocery store in the area, had disappeared, leaving a pool of blood on the floor and a cash register showing that her last customer had been the mild-mannered Ed.

When Worden found that the farmhouse was empty, he looked into the wood-shed—and saw the corpse of his mother, naked and headless, hanging upside down from the ceiling. The body had been "dressed" like a carcass in a butcher's shop. He re-entered the farm and in the dining-room discovered a woman's heart in a dish; Mrs. Worden's head and intestines were in a box nearby. Gein, out at supper with a neighbour, was quickly arrested. He admitted committing the murder, but claimed he had been in a daze at the time.

Sexual passions

Detectives made a full-scale search of the farmhouse—which was indescribably filthy and untidy—and found no less than ten skins flayed from human heads, and a box containing noses. Human skin had been used to repair leather armchairs, and even to make a belt. Gein had been living on his own at the farmhouse since 1945 and from his admissions, the police constructed an incredible story. His mother had been violently religious, convinced that God was about to destroy the world because women wore lipstick. She in-

stilled into Gein a highly ambivalent hatred of "scarlet women". Gein's father died in 1940, his only brother in 1942. Old Mrs. Gein suffered a stroke in 1944, and Gein nursed her until she died a year later.

Then, alone in the house, he began to suffer from tormenting sexual passions. In 1942, he had called at a neighbour's house, and seen a woman wearing shorts; that night, a man had broken into the house, and asked the woman's son where his mother was. The intruder fled, but

the boy thought he had recognized Gein. Not long after his mother's death, Gein saw an announcement in a newspaper that a woman was being buried. That night, he drove to the graveyard, dug up the body, put it in his truck, then replaced the coffin and buried it carefully.

Waistcoat

Back at home, he at last had a woman to share his bed. "It gave me a lot of satisfaction," he explained. He found the corpse so sexually exciting that he ate part of the body, and made a waist-coat of the skin, so he could wear it next to his body.

At Christmas 1957, Gein was found insane, and confined for life in the Waupan State Hospital.

So the death houses—"castles", apart-ments, farms—stay where and sometimes as they are until they are renovated or razed. People live in the buildings, in the bedrooms and lounges in which the murders were committed, frequently without knowing the previous bloody his-tory of their homes. The death houses keep their secrets to themselves. Their walls may have ears, but they do not have tongues.

FARMHOUSE of death. Ten bodies, all horribly mutilated, were found on Ed Gein's farm (above). The killer (right) was found to be insane. His last victim was Mrs. Bernice Worden (top).

BLACKMAIL

When Sir Travers Twiss (below) married his charming and beautiful young wife, Marie, he accepted without question that she was of "respectable" social origins. He reckoned without the insidious menaces of a blackmailer . . .

"DO you feel a creeping, shrinking sensation, Watson, when you stand before the serpents in the Zoo, and see the slithery, gliding, venomous creatures, with their deadly eyes and wicked, flattened faces? Well, that's how Milverton impresses me. I've had to do with fifty murderers, but the worst of them never gave me the repulsion which I have for this fellow."

The speaker is, of course, Sherlock Holmes, and the man he is referring to is the blackmailer, Charles Augustus Milverton, "the worst man in London". The story of Milverton was first published in *Collier's Magazine* in 1904. The date is interesting because the slithery Milverton was probably the first blackmailer ever to make his appearance in fiction.

In fact, the crime itself was relatively new; a law against "threatening to publish with intent to extort money" was not passed until 1893, though the word "blackmail" dates back to the time of Queen Elizabeth I, when certain freebooting Scottish chieftains used to extort money from farmers along the Scottish border. This "protection money" was called black-mail, or black-rent, to distinguish it from the rent the farmer paid to his proper landlord.

This was not actually a crime—the law taking the view that if a farmer chose to pay black-rent, that was his own business. It was not until 1873 that the British parliament decided that "demanding money with menaces" was just as unlawful as pointing a gun at somebody's head and taking his wallet.

Medium dominance

It may seem curious that English law—and this also applies to America—took so long to take account of blackmail, but the reason can be seen in *Charles Augustus Milverton*. Milverton makes a living by buying up "compromising letters" written by ladies and gentlemen in high society, and threatening to send them to the husband or wife of the imprudent writer. Holmes is engaged to try to recover certain indiscreet letters written by a young lady to a penniless country squire; now she is about to marry an Earl, and the blackmailer threatens to send the letters to the future husband.

And, in fact, real-life Milvertons *were* making money in exactly this way. A century earlier, it would have been absurd; people in high society took mistresses—or lovers—all the time, and nobody gave a damn. Then Queen Victoria came to the throne, married a serious and religious German prince named Albert, and all that changed; in England, high society took its tone from the royal family. The Age of Respectability had arrived, and there were suddenly dozens of things that were just Not Done.

The "breath of scandal" could ruin a man—and totally destroy a woman; Queen Victoria turned violently and passionately against her own son when she heard he was having an affair with an actress, whereas her predecessors on the throne of England would have thought there was something seriously wrong with a son who *didn't* fornicate with actresses,

IRONICALLY, blackmail only blossomed as a crime when Queen Victoria turned licentiousness into a social offence . . .

Radio Times Hulton

chambermaids and ladies-in-waiting. But the First Lady of England, being a woman of only "medium dominance", was a romantic, one-man woman, who thought sex was rather dirty, and high society had to live up to her standards—or else.

The case that made the Victorians aware of the curious legal problems involved in blackmail took place in 1872. The lady in the case was called Lady Twiss; the blackmailer was a London solicitor named Alexander Chaffers. Lady Twiss was the wife of Sir Travers Twiss, a well-known Victorian advocate, and professor of International Law at King's College, London. She was regarded as thoroughly respectable—she had even been presented at Court to Queen Victoria. And now, to the horrified incredulity of British high society, she was accused by Mr. Chaffers of being a common prostitute.

Sir Travers Twiss had been a highly successful man of fifty when he had met a pretty Polish girl at his mother's house in 1859. Her name was Marie Van Lynseele, and she was the daughter of a Polish Major-General. Three years later, Sir Travers was in Dresden, and again met the pretty Pole. They fell in love, and married at the British Legation. On their return to England, Lady Twiss was presented first to the Prince of Wales, then to Queen Victoria.

ONE DAY in Kew Gardens (below) the cosy world of Lady Twiss and her eminent husband began to crumble—with a seemingly innocuous encounter . . .

Mary Evans

One day, when she and her husband were walking in Kew Gardens, a man suddenly raised his hat and said hello. Lady Twiss introduced him to her husband as a solicitor, Alexander Chaffers. Chaffers congratulated her on her marriage, and not long after, Lady Twiss received a bill for £46 from Mr. Chaffers "for services rendered". She ignored it. He sent another letter, this time asking for £150. Lady Twiss showed it to her husband, and explained that she really owed Chaffers some money for legal work he had once done for a maid in her employment. Whereupon Sir Travers Twiss arranged a meeting with Chaffers, and paid him £50, asking for a receipt. This was marked "in

HARDLY ELEMENTARY this time . . . Holmes and his friend Watson (above) were unused to tackling blackmailers.

full discharge".

But Chaffers was apparently not satisfied. He continued to ask Lady Twiss for money. He wrote a letter to the Lord Chamberlain—the Court official responsible for vetting the list of people who would be received by the Queen—telling him that Lady Twiss had been, to put it crudely, a French whore who had managed to worm her way into high society.

The Lord Chamberlain was baffled. Short of hiring a private detective, he couldn't think of any way of investigating the story, so he decided to treat it as a hoax and forget it. But he told Lord and Lady Twiss about the accusations. They were horrified, and confirmed his opinion that Chaffers was a madman. Chaffers certainly had the persistence of a madman. He had a writ for libel served on Sir Travers, claiming that Lady Twiss had been spreading all kinds of slanders about him, and then went to the Chief Magistrate at Bow Street to make a sworn statement of "the truth about Lady Twiss".

Made public

This statement declared that she was actually a prostitute named Marie Gelas, and that she had been intimate with Chaffers on several occasions in certain houses of ill-fame in Belgium. Now, as much as he disliked the idea, Sir Travers Twiss had to take action. In May, 1871, Mr. Chaffers appeared at Southwark Police Court, charged with having "published" various slanders against Sir Travers and Lady Twiss—in legal terminology, "published" means simply "made public". Mr. Chaffers' defence was that the "libels" were true.

Marie Van Lynseele claimed to be the daughter of a deceased Major-General,

Mansell Collection

and that she had been brought up in Poland and Belgium as the adopted daughter of a Monsieur Jastrenski. Marie admitted that she *knew* someone called Marie Gelas; according to her, Marie Gelas had been her chaperone when she first came to England in 1859 – the occasion when she had first met Sir Travers.

During that visit, Marie Van Lynseele had fallen seriously ill, and Marie Gelas had decided that her employer ought to make a will; she therefore sent for Mr. Chaffers, whom she already knew, and got him to draw up a suitable document. This, said Lady Twiss, was the full extent of her acquaintance with Mr. Chaffers, and he had been paid his £50 professional fee after the meeting in Kew Gardens.

Mr. Chaffers replied that there never *had* been a "chaperone" called Marie Gelas. Lady Twiss *was* Marie Gelas, and he had slept with her several times before she "struck it rich". Nowadays, this would be an open and shut case. Mr. Chaffers was admitting that he had tried to blackmail Lady Twiss by telling her husband about her past, and then, when that didn't work, trying to blackmail them both. But in 1872 there was no law against blackmail: only against libel.

Lady Twiss's problem was to prove that she was Marie Van Lynseele, daughter of a Major-General, not Marie Gelas. She called various witnesses to testify about her past, including a maid who swore on oath that Chaffers had tried to bribe her to support slanders against her mistress. Obviously Chaffers was a very nasty piece of work, and the judge made no attempt to hide his distaste.

Unsolved mystery

And then, quite unexpectedly, Lady Twiss surrendered. On the eighth day of the trial she decided she had had enough. Her counsel appeared in court to tell the judge that his client had left London, and decided not to continue the case. The judge had no alternative but to discharge Alexander Chaffers. He told him that for the rest of his life he would be "an object of contempt to all honest and well-thinking men"; but the fact remained that Chaffers had won.

A week later, Sir Travers Twiss resigned from all his various distinguished posts. His wife had vanished to the Continent, and, as far as we know, he never saw her again. The *London Gazette* published a paragraph saying that Lady Twiss's presentation to the Queen – which had taken place three years earlier – had been "cancelled" – which was the Victorian way of saying that it hadn't really

happened at all, and the case remains an apparently unsolved mystery.

But it is easy enough to read between the lines: If Lady Twiss *had* been Marie Van Lynseele, she would presumably have fought to the last ditch. The court was already inclined heavily in her favour. Her foster-father, M. Jastrenski, had testified that she *was* Marie Van Lynseele, and many other witnesses had declared on oath that they knew Marie Gelas, and that she was *not* Marie Van Lynseele. It was a foregone conclusion that Chaffers would be found guilty and sent for trial.

What probably happened is that Marie Van Lynseele – or Gelas – had bribed various people to appear in her favour, but that she realized a trial would be a more serious matter; perhaps her witnesses refused to testify at a criminal trial, because they were afraid of the penalty for perjury. She decided the game was up, and vanished. If she was innocent,

why did she tell her husband that she owed Chaffers the £50 for legal fees contracted on behalf of a maid, when she later testified in court that it was *her* will that Chaffers drew up?

Homosexual brothel

On the other hand, there remains the other possibility: that, persecuted by Chaffers, realizing that she had ruined her husband, no matter what the outcome of the case, Lady Twiss's nerve snapped and she fled. The case made upper-class Victorians aware how vulnerable they were to blackmail. A man like Chaffers didn't need any *evidence* that Lady Twiss was a prostitute. He only had to say so in court, and even if he was found guilty of libel, her reputation would never recover from the scandal.

It also made the Victorians aware that they needed a law to prevent people like Chaffers extorting money by threats: hence the statute of 1873 against "de-

"EDDIE", the Duke of Clarence (right), was one of the clients at a homosexual brothel raided by police in 1889. Oscar Wilde (inset) was a famous fellow client.

Radio Times/Quartet

Radio Times Hulton

Mary Evans

Radio Times Hulton/Quartet

RAVISHING . . . Lady Warwick (right) was certainly one of the great beauties of the age. Husband (top left) and lover Beresford (centre) no doubt thought so too! Below: Her home, Warwick Castle.

manding money with menaces". It cost Sir Travers Twiss his career, but his case had changed the law.

Unfortunately, a change in the law was not quite the answer. When a crime suddenly attracts public attention, criminals everywhere wonder whether this is not a new source of income. The Victorian poor had always been the prey of rich debauchees; there were few working-class girls who could refuse the offer of five shillings for the use of their bodies. Now the poor began to retaliate by exerting blackmail on the seducers.

Oscar Wilde was blackmailed by some of the working-class youths he slept with; when a homosexual brothel in Cleveland Street was raided by the police in 1889, the whole affair was quickly hushed up when they realized that one of the chief clients was the Duke of Clarence, the grandson of Queen Victoria. "Eddie" — as the Duke was known — was packed off on a world cruise, and endless possibilities of blackmail were averted.

But it was not only the lower classes who indulged in blackmail. Aristocrats could play the game just as ruthlessly. One

of the most famous — and notorious — of Victorian aristocrats was Lady Warwick, known universally as Daisy — the song "Daisy, Daisy" was written with her in mind. The ravishingly beautiful Daisy married the future Earl of Warwick in 1881 and became mistress of Warwick Castle and a huge fortune. She soon found her husband's passion for hunting and fishing a bore, and began to take lovers.

Sexual promiscuity

For several years she conducted a passionate affair with the dashing Lord Charles Beresford — in the Victorian age there was nothing to stop you having love affairs provided you were discreet about it, and avoided "scandal". When Lord Charles finally broke it off she went to his closest friend, the Prince of Wales, to beg him to help her get back a certain compromising letter.

Edward, Prince of Wales, was the son who had alienated Queen Victoria through his affair with an actress, and ever since that time he had devoted his life to sexual promiscuity with the energy of a Casanova. He took one look at Daisy, and dragged her towards the nearest bed. Daisy was willing enough; for although the Prince was no longer young or handsome — he was fat and inclined to wheeze — she saw he was a valuable ally. As to Prince Edward, he was genuinely in love with the delicious Daisy.

In 1893 her father-in-law died, and Daisy became mistress of a fortune. She immediately had Warwick Castle relandscaped, filled it with expensive carpets and furniture, and gave huge weekend parties that were famous for their extravagance. The socialist press attacked her for wasting so much money when the poor were starving; as a result she went to see the famous left-wing editor, W. T. Stead, and immediately became converted to socialism. She had the double pleasure of being immensely rich and being known as the defender of the poor.

As the years went by, Daisy's beauty

173

faded and her fortune dwindled. In 1912 she realized that she was close to bankruptcy. And then she had her inspiration. She would write her memoirs, make sure they were scandalously frank, and sell them to a publisher for some huge sum — £100,000 was her first estimate. In 1914, she contacted a journalist and writer named Frank Harris — now known chiefly as the author of the semi-pornographic *My Life and Loves*.

Harris was not only an editor, a novelist and a Don Juan; he was a completely unscrupulous blackmailer, and he instantly saw the enormous possibilities of

her scheme. All she had to do was to make sure she included the love letters of the Prince of Wales — later King Edward VII, who had died in 1910 — and then ask the Palace how much it was worth to suppress the book.

Two years earlier a Tory Member of Parliament, Charles du Cros, had lent Daisy £16,000, and he now wanted his interest on the sum. Daisy also happened to know that he wanted a knighthood, and that he had an attitude verging on adoration for King George V, Edward's son. She sent for du Cros, told him about the memoirs, and mentioned that she had

letters from the late King in which, among more intimate and scandalous matters, he had given his frank opinion of such people as the Kaiser and the Tsar of Russia.

Du Cros rushed to see George V's A.D.C. and his solicitor. The solicitor suggested that he had better ask Daisy how much she would take to suppress the book. Daisy said £85,000 — but told du Cros that he would have to see her

INVOLVED in the proposed scandal of Daisy's memoirs — though on opposite sides — were Charles du Cros (below) and the notorious hack Frank Harris (inset).

Radio Times Hulton

Radio Times Hulton

"partner", Frank Harris. Harris had fled to Paris, escaping his creditors; du Cros saw him at the Ritz Hotel, and was told that they would settle for a mere £125,000.

But the Establishment had its own way of dealing with blackmail. Instead of paying up, George V's solicitor asked for a court injunction to prevent Daisy publishing the late King's letters. Daisy at first found it incredible – to drag the affair into open court; but there she was mistaken. The Establishment co-operated admirably. The case was heard in chambers – a closed court. Edward VII's name was not mentioned; it was simply a matter of preventing the publication of "certain letters". The letters had to be handed over to the court. The injunction was granted, and the court also ordered that the letters were to be destroyed.

Two-way mirrors

This was not quite the end of the story. Before the letters were handed over, Frank Harris went to stay with Daisy Warwick at her house, Easton Lodge – she had been forced by debts to move out of Warwick Castle. He asked to see the letters – and when Harris left for America, the letters went with him. In order to get them back, Daisy had to pay Harris for them. She was the loser all round . . . Her

CONFIRMED SOCIALIST William Stead (left) converted Daisy to the defence of the poor – for a time. Edward VII (right) saw only her more obvious charms.

only consolation was that du Cros, feeling sorry for her, took over £50,000-worth of her debts.

Since Daisy's time the art of blackmail has been turned into an exact science – particularly by the espionage and counter-espionage services of all the major countries. In the West, we hear a great deal about the techniques of the Russian secret service, the K.G.B. – for example, how they blackmailed the American army sergeant James Harris, who appeared in the Rudolph Abel case, or of the pressure they brought to bear on the homosexual naval clerk, Vassall. But there can be no doubt that the C.I.A. and Britain's M.I.5 are just as skilled in its uses.

A favourite technique with both sides is to lure a diplomat – or member of the government – into a sexually compromising position. The Russians are credited with the discovery of the use of two-way mirrors for this purpose – the English and American method was cruder, using a picture or photograph with tiny holes in it, usually in the pupils of the eyes, with the camera concealed behind it.

The invention of transistors enabled the C.I.A. to perfect a whole new range of "bugging devices". One of these was a tiny pill that emitted a radio signal. The girl who has been chosen as the decoy swallows a pill that makes a "bleep" noise. Another pill – which emits a "bloop" – is concealed in the food of the victim, so he swallows it. Agents are then able to follow the couple with radio receivers, and when their receivers pick up simultaneous bloops and bleeps, they can assume that the bellies of both parties are in sufficiently close contact to warrant a sudden intrusion.

Blackmail is the least documented of all crimes for an obvious reason: if a blackmailer is caught by the police, it is in everybody's interests to make sure that the case receives no publicity. And in most civilized countries, it is generally agreed that when a victim reports blackmail to the police, he will not lay himself open to criminal charges, even if he is being blackmailed for a crime he has committed. Although this is a convention, not a law, it is seldom broken – the only exception being in cases involving treason. Slowly, very slowly, society is learning to combat the blackmailer. The day may yet come when blackmail, like piracy, is no more than a relic of the past.

THE ONLY WAY OUT

Captain Alfred Loewenstein was not accustomed to being crossed. He had made himself one of the richest tycoons in Europe by playing hard and winning. In fact there seemed to his enemies to be no weaknesses in his formidable armour . . . until a nameless blackmailer probed the secrets of his empire . . .

ᴛᴏ the entourage who followed him from his limousine, over the tarmac at Croydon airfield, near London, and up to his private, three-engined plane, there appeared to be nothing amiss with Captain Alfred Loewenstein. The tycoon—one of the best-known, yet most enigmatic, men in Europe—was his usual confident and aggressive self. He was flying to Brussels to conclude another of the deals which had made him a multi-millionaire, and his staff were prepared to work on documents on the plane.

Yet the night before—on July 3, 1928—Loewenstein had learnt from a private detective in his employ that a blackmailer was about to publish a 5000-word paper which would destroy his personal reputation and business career. The tycoon knew the identity of the blackmailer—a bitter rival he had refused to pay money to—and had told him to "go ahead and do your worst".

Now the man was going to do just that. Before the day was out the world's

HE HAD EVERYTHING . . . Loewenstein (right) seemed impregnable. But there was no defence against blackmail, and he knew it when he boarded his plane (below).

Radio Times/Quartet

newspapers would learn of the crooked inner workings of the International Holdings Company—the firm which handled his investments, stock market speculations, loans to governments, and his mining, hydroelectric, and artificial silk combines. They would learn that what they had long suspected was true: while the financial "milk" remained within the company, the "cream" was skimmed off and kept by Loewenstein himself.

Corrupt practices

More than that, they would learn of the unscrupulous way he had disposed, or tried to dispose, of such reputable competitors as the Dreyfus brothers, who had legitimately defeated him in his ambition to control the firm they had founded, British Celanese . . .

They would learn that he had staged a large-scale jewel robbery at his palatial villa at Biarritz, on the south-west coast of France, and then collected some £½m.-worth of insurance money. . . . They

would learn of the savings he had taken from the pockets of small investors and put in his own.

Worst of all, they—and every stockbroker and banker in Europe and North America—would learn that Loewenstein had no intention of ending his corrupt practices. He was too deeply enmeshed in his own double dealings for that. He could not stop, he could not retreat, he could only go on. And, once the truth about him was out, no one in power could allow him to do that.

Had he been able to confide in anyone —one of the aides or secretaries who entered the plane with him—he might have agreed to meet the blackmailer's terms. The money the man wanted, a half a million pounds or so, meant little to him. But pride, and the knowledge that once the first payment was made there would come another, and another, stopped him from taking the "weak" way out.

He would sooner kill himself than give in to such a villain. He would sooner die

than be exposed as a cheat, a criminal, and a fraud. Then, temporarily shrugging off such untypically pessimistic thoughts, he stood in the plane's cabin as the sun began its slow, evening slide towards the horizon.

Perfect conditions

Everyone he needed for the trip was with him. There was Arthur Hodgson, his personal secretary and right hand, sitting at a table taking papers and files from the brief-case that was as much a part of him as his soft voice and unflappable manner. The two girl secretaries were at their tables, typewriters in front of them, ready to take dictation or type out the letters he had already composed. Fred Baxter, his valet, was seated with his kit of brushes, combs, coat-hangers and shoe polish in a box by his side.

LOEWENSTEIN was ruthless with his competitors, and on the way to Dunkirk (below) he took the tough way out himself.

Aerofilms

The plane—one of a fleet owned by Loewenstein—was commanded by his number one pilot, Captain Donald Drew, who had previously worked with Imperial Airways. He and co-pilot Robert Little had the important task of getting the millionaire safely to Brussels in time for a business dinner—one that could add further assets to his expanding empire.

Before the take-off commenced, Captain Loewenstein—who had been commissioned in the Belgian army during World War One—went forward to speak to Drew. A native of Belgium, and the son of a successful banker, Loewenstein had the accent and excitability of the "continental".

"Remember, I must be dining at my house by nine o'clock."

"No problem, sir," replied Drew. "It's a two-hour flight and the conditions are perfect."

"Even so," continued the tycoon, "I don't want you to fly high. If bad weather comes on you must fly straight through it—don't try to rise above. As you know, I have a fear of great heights."

Drew nodded. "You needn't worry, sir. I shan't take her above 4000 feet. We'll not be out of sight of sea or land."

Gambling splurges

Satisfied, Loewenstein returned to the cabin with its thick, maroon carpet, luxurious armchairs, indirect lighting, and silk curtains. The plane—a Fokker VII—had been modified to his own specifications. One of its prides was the heated and well-equipped toilet—the door of which faced the entrance to the plane. The door—like many of the products of Loewenstein's mind—had more than one function.

When the plane was on the ground it was kept closed so that the lavatory was discreetly hidden from anyone entering or leaving the machine. During a flight, however, it was opened so that it shut off the rear of the fuselage from the cabin—so adding to the effect of exclusiveness and privacy.

Shortly after 6 p.m.—with the summer afternoon dying around it in an explosion of mauve, red, and gold—the Fokker taxied into the wind and took off in the direction of the Kent coast, then across to Dunkirk, and on to Brussels. As soon as the plane left the ground, Baxter the valet opened the toilet door. For the next two hours the world of Alfred Loewenstein was self-contained.

In the cockpit Captain Drew handed the controls over to co-pilot Little and relaxed with a thriller he was reading. In the cabin Arthur Hodgson shuffled papers and read through the voluminous and complicated memos which his employer had asked him to prepare for their forthcoming meetings. The secretaries clacked away at their machines. Baxter put his head back and dozed. Only Loewenstein had nothing to do but think, reflect, and brood.

Unlike some men with his influence and riches, he was not in constant need of sex and mistresses. A devout Roman Catholic, he was happily married and devoted to his wife and 18-year-old son. Living well had never been a problem to him. His main and family home was in Belgium, a mansion on the outskirts of Brussels. Whatever other capital he visited, he always took over an entire floor of one of the leading hotels—the Ritz in London, the George V in Paris, the Adlon in Berlin.

In Biarritz alone he had some 50 villas at his disposal, and filled them with friends whenever he went on one of his periodical gambling splurges at the casino there. It mattered nothing to him what he lost, for he was obtaining interest on the £12m. he lent to the Belgian government in 1926, and the £35m. he lent to France a few months later.

The basis of his fortune had been founded immediately after World War One. He invested the money left him by his father and reaped a rich harvest as inflation made paupers of some men and millionaires of others. His financial activities made him famous—or infamous—in banking and stock exchange circles. But the general public had still to hear of Captain Loewenstein—the man who boasted he had "half Europe in my pocket and the other half clambering to *get* in"!

Tantrums

By the early 1920s, however, his name was appearing in the social columns and sports pages as well as in the financial sections of the Press. Rugged-looking and well-built, he disguised and made nonsense of his congenitally weak heart by becoming one of the leading amateur sportsmen of his day.

He boxed, he swam, he fenced, he played golf and tennis. He was trained and coaxed by his own team of professionals until, in the end, it was they who were learning from him. He was an expert gymnast, could ride a horse as if born in the saddle, and was a frequent competitor at horse-jumping shows held at London's Olympia.

He was a popular and much-followed racehorse owner, and in 1927 thousands of admiring punters backed Easter Hero—the favourite and owned by Captain Loewenstein—in its unsuccessful attempt to win the Grand National Steeplechase. Only one thing sullied his public image: his temper, which grew fiercer and more out of control each time he lost it.

His tantrums when losing on the golf-course or tennis-court made most sportsmen reluctant to play with him. And his rages were not confined to sporting spheres. In 1926 he assaulted one of his private secretaries (the man had had the temerity to alter the phrasing in a letter dictated by Loewenstein), knocked him to the ground, and hit him while he lay.

A few weeks later he and a friend drove to the Biarritz casino for a night's gambling. His companion—dressed in sports jacket and flannels—was refused admission and asked to return wearing evening dress. "How dare you insult a friend of mine!" screamed Loewenstein at the bemused doorkeeper. "Friends of mine are allowed in anywhere—dressed in any way they please!"

Bunching his fist, he struck the doorman on the jaw, breaking several of the employee's teeth. Charges were taken out against Loewenstein by both men, and he was fined at the local court for "assault and conduct prejudicial to the general peace". His self-esteem had received a beating, and that only made his disposition

FAVOURITE HAUNT of the Belgian banker was the casino at Biarritz where he squandered vast sums. The French government owed him so much . . .

touchier, his frenzies more manic.

Perhaps it was looking back on all this that sent what his staff thought was a "hot flush" running through his body. The English coastline had fallen behind when Loewenstein suddenly tore off his coat, shirt collar, and tie. Red-faced and seemingly gasping for breath, he opened the window on his left and put his head halfway out. The Goodwin Sands were just below him, and in anyone else it could be taken that he was admiring the view.

That was certainly the first thought that came to Robert Little as — while flying the plane — he glanced over his shoulder to inspect the people in the cabin. Through the glass panel in the cockpit door he saw that they were all busy with something — all except Loewenstein, who now put his head back in and slumped as if exhausted.

Undue effect

Little then considered that, as the plane was flying so low, the millionaire was possibly suffering from the feeling of being "too near the water or the ground". Either that or the slight loss of oxygen content was having an undue effect upon him. But Loewenstein had given his orders, and Little knew better than to query them — let alone contradict them.

The Fokker flew on at 4000 feet and Little returned to his duties as a pilot. If anything *was* wrong with the tycoon, then his valet or personal secretary could well take care of it. But those in the cabin — fearful of Loewenstein's growing bouts of fury — did not like to mention the fact that he seemed to be in discomfort. Until he raised the subject, they would let it safely and peacefully alone.

Paralyzed

Five minutes went by and Loewenstein suddenly got out of his armchair, strode down the cabin, and opened the door to the toilet and the rear of the plane. Again no one thought there was anything unduly significant — or ominous — about it.

A further 10 minutes passed before Loewenstein's absence caused the first flutter of panic. Looking up from his paper work, and seeing that his boss was still out of his seat, Arthur Hodgson went back to speak to Baxter. He shook the valet by the shoulder and asked him what could be keeping their employer.

Baxter muttered that he didn't know, but he'd go and take a look. He knocked, then reopened the door and peered inside the fuselage. For a moment he couldn't see anyone. There was no one standing by the wash-basin with a towel in hand, or combing his hair in the mirror. He looked again before the truth hammered him. It was starkly clear that Loewenstein was no longer on the plane!

He turned speechlessly to the rest of the entourage, his face the colour of the clean white shirt he was wearing. Hodgson hurried forward to confirm what the valet's expression told him. He then went back to his seat, sat for a moment with his mind paralyzed, and forced himself into action. Taking up a pencil he wrote three words in his notebook: "The Captain's gone."

With the others watching him as if he was about to throw himself under a bus, he hoisted himself to his feet and moved into the cockpit. Silently he gave the note to Drew, who was still deep in his murder mystery. The pilot read the three scribbled words, looked up, and said bewilderedly: "How do you mean — 'gone'?"

Hodgson wrung his hands. "He must have . . . fallen out."

"But how?"

"The outside door — it seems to be open!"

It took Drew only seconds to see that Hodgson was not lying, that he hadn't gone mad. He ran through the cabin and into the toilet area. There the outside

WHEREVER he travelled, Loewenstein always stayed in the best hotels — and occupied a whole floor! Below: The Ritz in London (left) and the Adlon in Berlin.

Staatsbibliothek Berlin, Radio Times

door – the one facing the lavatory seat – was slightly open and shaking in the slip-stream. The gap was not more than a few inches – but the door could have been blown back once Loewenstein had fallen through it.

Or had he fallen? Had he thrown himself out deliberately? Or had he – incredible thought – been pushed? These possibilities raced again and again through Drew's head as he returned to the cockpit, took over the controls from Little, and brought the Fokker down almost to sea level.

There was no sign of the tycoon – no body lying spread-eagled on the flat grey surface of the sea. The three possibilities – accident, suicide, murder – again confronted Drew as he headed the plane towards northern France and landed on the beach near Dunkirk. There the crew and staff attempted to make some sense of

what had happened – or what they thought had happened.

But with the secretaries weeping hysterically, and with Baxter and Hodgson in a state of shock, it was impossible to find any clues, make any sense, put forward any positive explanation. This difficulty arose again when the French police were called in, and the British Air Ministry sent a team of experts to examine the plane's outer door – which could be operated from the inside by a handle.

Mortal sin

The experts soon established that it would be possible for anyone to open the door in mid-air – to an extent of some two feet. That fact, obviously, ruled out two possibilities. It would be practically impossible for a man of Loewenstein's build to fall through such a narrow space. It would be practically impossible for

LUXURY – millionaire style. The sumptuous interior of Biarritz casino.

anyone to have sneaked into the fuselage from the cabin and forced a man of Loewenstein's strength from the plane.

That only left suicide – and that answer was officially accepted when, two weeks later, the millionaire's body was found by a trawler off the coast of France. There was no sign of a struggle having taken place, and Loewenstein had been alive when he hit the water. In fact he had not been killed by the fall: he had drowned.

By his last action – the one mortal sin that a Roman Catholic can commit – Captain Alfred Loewenstein had defeated the man who was going to expose and disgrace him. To the tycoon, death was preferable to shame and dishonour. Whether it was weak or strong, he had taken what for him was the only way out.

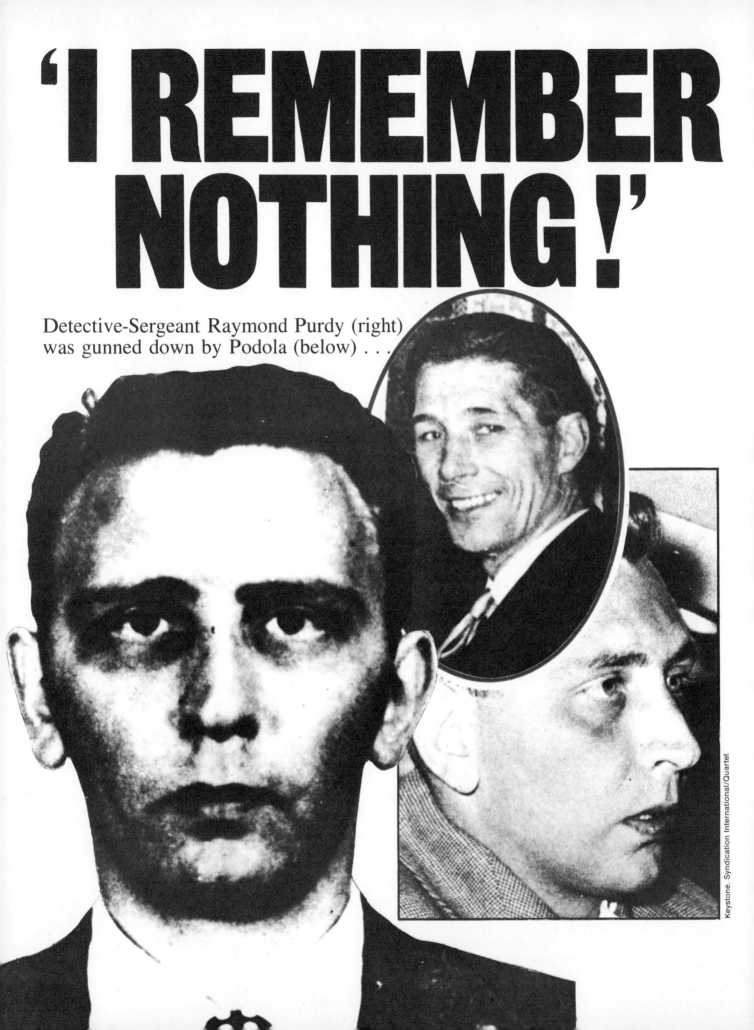

'I REMEMBER NOTHING!'

Detective-Sergeant Raymond Purdy (right) was gunned down by Podola (below) . . .

Keystone. Syndication International/Quartet

BLACKMAILERS DON'T SHOOT was the title of one of Raymond Chandler's early short stories. That maxim is usually accurate – but not always, as Raymond Purdy, a 40-year-old London detective with 19 years of police experience behind him, found out on the afternoon of July 13, 1959.

It was a fatal lesson. Guenther Fritz Erwin Podola, the German blackmailer he had cornered in the entrance to a block of flats in South Kensington, drew a 9mm. automatic and shot him through the heart at point-blank range. Purdy was dead as he hit the ground.

Two months later, Podola stood in the massive dock of No. 1 Court at the Old Bailey. Many other killers – Crippen, Smith, the "Brides in the Bath" murderer, Bywaters, and Thompson – had stood there before him and been the subject of notorious trials. Podola's trial would also be notorious, but for reasons which overshadowed the blackmail and, to a degree, even the shooting of the detective.

For he was the first prisoner, accused in a British court of murder, to claim he was unfit to plead because of hysterical amnesia. Apart from some minor "windows of recollection", he claimed he could remember nothing of his life prior to waking up in hospital after his somewhat violent arrest.

Legal history

Mr. Justice Edmund Davies, red-robed and grey-wigged, entered the court at 10.30 on the morning of September 10. First he dealt with the sentencing of two youths, convicted the previous evening. Then Podola was escorted into the dock. He looked pale but alert, and he gripped the dock rail as the clerk of the court asked: "Are you Guenther Fritz Erwin Podola? Is that your name?" "Yes, that's right," Podola answered.

The judge nodded to Podola to sit down and, as he did so, the defending counsel, Mr. Frederick Lawton, Q.C. and Recorder of Cambridge, rose to his feet to voice the plea that would make legal history. "It is my duty to inform Your Lordship," he said, "that I have evidence available which raises a preliminary issue. It is an issue which my learned friend Mr. Maxwell Turner – prosecuting counsel – has informed me will be contested. It is to the effect that this man has completely lost his memory for all events before July 17 – the day he found himself in hospital."

Several questions were involved, Mr. Lawton went on. In the circumstances, should the defence open the case instead of the prosecution doing so? Was it up to the prosecution to prove "beyond all reasonable doubt" that Podola had *not* lost his memory? Or was it the less onerous task of the defence to prove "on the balance of probabilities" that he had? And, Mr. Lawton went on, "is loss of memory reason in law why a man should not be tried?" The authorities, he added, were not clear on these points.

Mr. Turner, rising to speak in his turn, said: "The case for the Crown is in two parts. Firstly, it is that this amnesia is not genuine amnesia but feigned. That is the main issue. Secondly, if the jury were to find the amnesia is genuine, then I shall submit that, even if a person is suffering from loss of memory, it is not a matter which can give rise to a finding of unfitness to plead. There are two stages. One is a matter of fact; the other of law."

At the end of all the submissions the judge ruled that, before the actual murder trial, another jury would have to decide whether Podola's loss of memory was genuine or feigned. It was up to the defence, not the prosecution, to prove – on "the balance of probabilities" – that the prisoner was not shamming. A jury of 10 men and two women was sworn in.

ATTRACTIVE model Mrs. Verne Schiffman had nothing to hide. When Podola tried to blackmail her she went to the police. He was a clumsy operator.

Popperfoto

Podola had come a long way since, on that July 13 afternoon, at the height of London's hottest summer for half-a-century, he picked up the phone in a callbox at South Kensington Underground Station and tried to put the bite on Mrs. Verne Schiffman, a 30-year-old American model, for 500 dollars . . .

In understanding the issues involved in Podola's loss-of-memory trial, it is helpful to know something of his earlier life, the killing, his arrest and what happened between the arrest and his court appearance. Podola, 30 at the time of his trial, was the only son of a Berlin barber. In 1951, as a result of an affair with a childhood friend named Ruth Quant, he became the father of a son, Micky.

The following year he emigrated to Canada. The Canadians deported him in July, 1958, after he had been in trouble with the police for theft and house-breaking. He sailed for Bremerhaven on a ship named *Seven Seas,* which was to play an important part in the cross-examination over the question of his memory. For a time he worked with a metal-refining firm near Stuttgart, and then, in May, 1959, he flew to London with a three-month British visa.

In London, Podola paid £5 for a 9mm. automatic and some ammunition. He began hanging around the Soho clubs where he gave his name as Mike Colato, flashed his gun around and earned a quick reputation as "a big mouth".

"Just call me Mike," he used to say. "If you know anyone who's planning to pull a job and needs help, tell him I'm his man." As far as is known, nobody took him up on the offer: Podola's trigger-happy air put them off. One significant event did occur during this period, however. A mutual acquaintance took him to Portsmouth and introduced him to a Ron Starkey. Mr. Starkey was to prove the critical figure in the question of whether Podola's amnesia was real or feigned.

Complete file

To keep himself in money, Podola resorted to housebreaking with an eye to possible blackmail as an extra source of revenue. At the beginning of July, he burgled a South Kensington flat after forcing the front-door lock with a piece of celluloid. From the flat, rented temporarily by Mrs. Schiffman, he stole jewellery worth £1785, a £535 mink stole and three passports—Mrs. Schiffman's, her daugh-

ter's and a friend's.

Four days later Podola began his clumsy blackmail attempt with a special delivery letter in which he masqueraded as an American private detective named Levine. "I was hired five years ago to check on your behaviour," he wrote. "I have a complete file with pictures and tape recordings. For 500 dollars I will hand it over and report to my client that you have been leading a blameless life."

Mrs. Schiffman went straight to the police, who arranged to tap her phone. The following Monday afternoon Podola called her to discuss the pay-off, representing himself as "a Mr. Fisher speaking on Mr. Levine's behalf". "Keep him talking as long as possible," the police had instructed Mrs. Schiffman.

Meantime, Post Office engineers had traced the source of the call as Knightsbridge 2355X, a phone box in South Kensington Underground Station. At Chelsea Police Station, less than half-a-

OUTSIDE the apartment block where Purdy was shot, police experts discuss immediate tactics for finding the killer. Shattered pane (inset) has its own grim eloquence as a reminder of the tragedy.

UXP 739

Popperfoto/Quartet

mile away, Detective-Sergeants Raymond Purdy and John Sandford piled into a police car. Podola—although, at that time, they did not know this was his real name—was still talking to Mrs. Schiffman when they seized him.

As they went up to the street, however, he broke free and, after a chase, was cornered in the hallway of the new block of flats in Onslow Gardens. "We are police officers and we are taking you to Chelsea Police Station," Purdy told him. While Sandford tried to raise the porter to help keep an eye on the prisoner while he went to fetch the police car, Purdy told Podola: "Sit on the window sill and behave yourself."

Podola put his hands on the wide marble ledge and eased himself on to it in a sitting position.

Very frightened

There was no reply to the porter's bell. Sandford called out: "I don't think there's anyone in." Purdy turned his head towards him. At that moment, Sandford saw Podola slide off the window ledge and put his right hand inside his jacket. "Look out," he shouted. "He may have a gun." It was too late. Podola fired, Purdy crumpled to the floor and the gunman ran out into the street and freedom.

Once he was recaptured it looked as if it would be an open and shut case. There was a trained police eye-witness of the shooting. There was a police description of the killer—about 5 ft 10 in., slim, brown wavy hair, age about 30, wearing light sports jacket, light grey trousers and suede shoes. There were two clear palm prints on the window ledge. Furthermore, the gun could be identified from the bullet which had killed Purdy.

But, firstly, who was the gunman? With the help of the Canadian police he was identified within 24 hours through his palm prints as Guenther Podola. And, then, where was he? Actually, he was holed up only half-a-mile away in the Claremont House Hotel in South Kensington, where he had registered three weeks earlier as Paul Camay, a photographer from Montreal.

For three days he stayed locked in his room, listening on his portable radio to the news bulletins about the hunt for Purdy's killer. The only time he opened his door was one night to sneak up to the hotel attic where he hid his gun and ammunition, later found by the police wrapped up in a copy of *The Times*, dated the day of the shooting.

On the morning of Thursday, July 16, Podola's picture was published in the newspapers. That afternoon, following a tip-off, detectives accompanied by a police dog named Flame burst into Room 15 at the hotel and arrested Podola. It was Albert Chambers, a 16½-stone detec-

Syndication International

tive-sergeant, who threw himself at the door and twisted the handle.

The door, which was unlocked, opened violently and struck Podola over the left eye. It catapulted him over a chair, and he ended up lying on the floor with his head in the fireplace. Chambers and two other detectives, fearing he might be armed, threw themselves on top of him. Podola struggled for a moment, then—according to later police statements—"appeared to lapse into unconsciousness".

FINGERPRINT experts take evidence from the wood frames of the door where the killer had stood hours before. There was no problem in identifying Podola . . .

Podola was taken to Chelsea Police Station and a police surgeon, Dr. John Stranahan, called. He found the gunman shivering. He appeared "very frightened, dazed and exhausted". "I could not get him to say anything," Dr. Stranahan testified later, "but he would obey simple

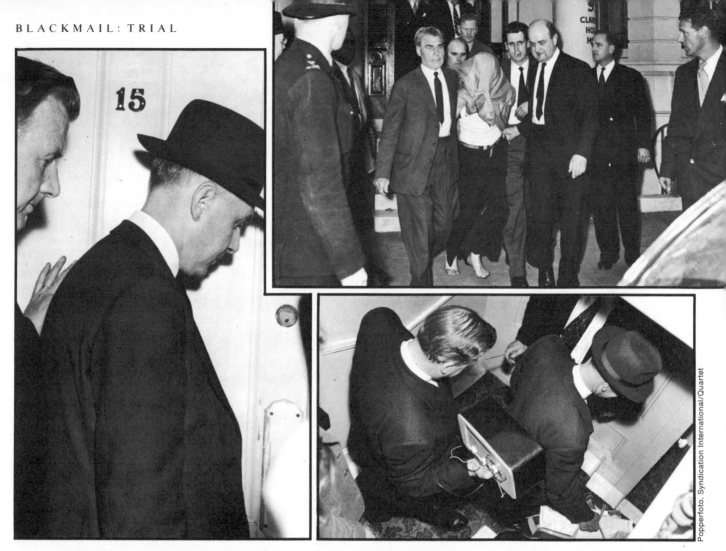

Popperfoto. Syndication International/Quartet

commands like: 'Open your mouth.' " The surgeon was called back again at midnight. He found no change in Podola's condition and ordered that he should be admitted to nearby St. Stephen's Hospital.

Podola was kept in a ward at the hospital, handcuffed to his bed and screened from other patients, from the early hours of July 17 until 2.30 p.m. on Monday, July 20, when he was taken to Chelsea Police Station and charged with Purdy's murder. Dr. Philip Harvey, the hospital's consultant physician, saw him at 2.15 a.m. on the night of his admission and reported: "He is suffering from gross disturbance of consciousness and only partial awareness of his surroundings."

Lumbar puncture

In the late afternoon of that same day, Podola underwent a lumbar puncture to establish from cerebral fluid in the spine whether he had suffered brain damage. The fluid showed traces of blood, consistent with bruising of the brain. According to Podola, it was at the moment of the lumbar puncture, when someone reassured him "this won't hurt", that his memory began to revive. But, apart from several "windows of recollection", he couldn't remember anything about his

TENSE MOMENT . . . Police (left) burst into Podola's hotel room, grabbed him and (top) escorted him to a waiting car. Later (below) they took his things.

life before that point.

Yet, as he grew stronger, he asked the police officers to play cards with him. "There is a game with a banker where you add up to 21," he said. The policemen assumed he meant pontoon. When they played it, Podola not only understood the game but introduced them to a new variation. At one point he also asked: "Are we playing for money? I usually play for a few cents a time."

On another occasion, when his guards were playing chess, Podola laughed loudly when one of them was trapped into losing his queen for a pawn. He also shook his head over one move and nodded approvingly at another. He said he would like a game himself and played with one of the doctors, who asked him: "When did you learn to play chess?" "I have been playing it since I was young," Podola replied. Had he learned to play in Germany? "I have played it everywhere," he said.

His words, and the question of whether it is possible for someone to lose his

memory yet retain skills acquired in his earlier life, were to become a point of considerable controversy at his trial. The prosecution would claim, however, that his greatest blunder was the tone of the letter he wrote from Brixton Prison to Ron Starkey, the man he had been introduced to by a mutual friend. Starkey sent a note from Portsmouth on August 28, saying: "Dear Mike, Is there anything I can get you in the way of tobacco or eats? If so, drop me a visiting card and I will come to see you. Best of luck, Ron."

Salient points

The nature of Podola's reply, according to the prosecution, showed that he was malingering, because he remembered Starkey quite clearly as an old acquaintance. By the time Podola came to trial he had been examined repeatedly by six experts in mental illness. Their findings were weighted substantially in his favour. Four believed he had genuinely lost his memory against two who thought he was shamming. But it was Podola himself, in the witness box, who would be what Mr. Justice Davies described as "the king-pin of the case, the most important of all the 27 witnesses".

He began to give evidence at 11.30 a.m.

on the third day, dressed in a light grey suit, white shirt and dark-blue spotted tie. In all he was under examination and cross-examination for three-and-a-half hours. It is not possible to give all of his evidence. Some of the salient points, however, were:

His memories of Ruth and Micky.

Podola: I see an oval table with a birthday cake in the middle and a little candle indicating it must be the first birthday of the child, and I see a girl sitting on the other side of the table holding a baby in her lap . . .

Mr. Lawton (defending): What is the name of the girl?

Podola: Well, I think Ruth.

Mr. Lawton: How do you know it is Ruth, or why do you think it is Ruth?

Podola: I just feel it is right.

Mr. Lawton: What is the name of the baby?

Podola: Well, Micky.

Mr. Lawton: How do you know that?

Podola: The same way. I just feel it is.

His game of cards in the hospital.

Podola: . . . they gave me the cards to play around with and, after a while, I had a picture more or less in my mind of how you could play a game with a card. I

asked them if they knew something like making up 21s. The policeman said: "How do you call it?" I said I did not know how you call it but you have to make up 21s, that is all.

His game of chess in the hospital.

Podola: . . . we started off playing, you know, and at first I had to think about the moves, but then they just came naturally.

The names of Ruth and Micky had been mentioned in Podola's diary, found in his possession when he was first arrested. The diary also contained references to the *Seven Seas,* the ship on which Podola had been deported from Canada. When Mr. Turner, the prosecutor, dropped the name *Seven Seas* into his cross-examination without warning, it brought from Podola an improbable reply which must have done a lot to damage his credibility in the eyes of the jury.

Mr. Turner had been asking some routine questions about Podola's reading habits in prison. Suddenly he inquired:

"Does *Seven Seas* mean anything?"

INSIDE the courtroom Maxwell Turner, Judge Eustace Davies and Frederick Lawton (left to right) wrestled with Podola's memory. Outside crowds waited.

Podola: *Seven Seas,* yes.

Mr. Turner: What does it mean?

Podola: One fellow was talking about a ship by that name yesterday in Brixton.

Mr. Turner: Yesterday, a fellow in Brixton, about a ship called *Seven Seas*?

Podola: Yes.

Mr. Turner: How did the subject of the *Seven Seas* come up?

Podola: He told me a story of being deported from Australia and he was reeling off a few ship names that are on that run.

Mr. Turner: What other names did he reel off?

Podola: If you tell me the names . . .

Mr. Turner: I want you to give me the names.

Podola: He mentioned the boat he was on, but I forget the name.

Mr. Turner: Why do you remember the *Seven Seas*?

Podola: Because you brought it up. You brought up the name and asked me if I remembered it and I said: "Yes."

To everyone in the packed and tense courtroom it seemed for a moment as if Podola had almost been trapped in a situation that would destroy his claim to be an amnesia victim. But Mr. Turner's

main attack was still to come—on the subject of the letter Podola had written to Starkey. The text read:

"Dear Ron, Thank you for your card. I was very pleasantly surprised to hear from you. How are you keeping yourself these days, old boy? I reckon you heard about the mess I am in, the papers must be full of it.

"I find it awfully nice of you to write, and now you want to come all the way up to London to see me. Well, Ronny, you don't need a special visiting card and you can see me any day, Monday through Saturday, from 10 a.m.-11.30 a.m. and 1.30 p.m.-3.30 p.m. Naturally I'd appreciate anything in the lines of smokes or eats but it really isn't necessary. It'll give me a boost though. However, Ronny, if you should be able to dig up a bunch of old magazines or other reading matter I'd sure be glad and grateful if you would bring them along.

"Well, old man, there isn't much doing around here as you can imagine. The food isn't bad but it lacks variety. The same goes for each day of the week. You do the same things each morning and there is no change in the routine.

"But I don't want to bore you. I got into this thing and I'll have to see it through no matter what. It sure was nice to hear from you, Ronny, and I'd get a kick out of seeing you. Thanks again, and keep your ears stiff.

Cordially yours, Mike.

Fulsome letter

Podola had admitted telling a fellow prisoner he thought Starkey must be "some kind of a crackpot", but thought he would write in the hope Starkey might bring him cigarettes. Why, Mr. Turner wanted to know, had Podola written such a fulsome letter instead of a simple one? Why, in writing to a "crackpot", had he dropped in words like "old boy" and "old man" and addressed this presumed stranger by the diminutive "Ronny"? Why had he turned down cigarettes?

Podola explained that the style of the letter had been dictated by the need to convince Starkey that he, Podola, knew and remembered him.

"You couldn't possibly write to some-

HEADLINE NEWS . . . The murder of a police officer has always evoked a sense of outrage in Britain. Purdy was given a guard of honour at his funeral (inset).

one and touch them for a few cigarettes and say: 'Give me the cigarettes and get going'," he told the court. Besides, he added, if he had not pretended to remember Starkey, the letter "would not even go out of the prison".

Mr. Turner: What do you mean by the phrase: "I got into this thing"?

Podola: I got into it. Nobody else. It is me who got into it . . . I have heard the evidence in this case and that is all there is to it. It must have been me who was in that place when that gun was shot.

More significant

Most of the remaining six days of the memory trial were taken up with highly technical medical evidence. It was broadly accepted that there was not necessarily any conflict between Podola's remembrance of old skills and his "windows of recollection" on the one hand, and, on the other, hysterical amnesia resulting from the traumatic experience of the shooting and his subsequent arrest. The real issue was on whether he was shamming or not, and on that the defence and prosecution witnesses did not see eye to eye.

In his summing-up, however, the judge

Syndication International. Popperfoto/Quartet

found the letter to Starkey more significant than the medical evidence. According to the defence, he said, it was simply "a gushing letter", the kind you write if you want to make a touch. According to the prosecution, it bore unmistakable evidence of having been written to a man of whose existence and identity Podola was perfectly aware.

"I sedulously abstain from expressing my view of this letter," the judge told the jury, "but this I say to you: if I had the privilege of exercising the functions you are called upon to discharge, I think I would begin my deliberations by coming to a conclusion about where the truth lies in regard to that latter."

The hands of the courtroom clock stood at 3.59 p.m. when the jury finally retired on the eighth day of the trial. At 7.20 p.m. they returned to ask the judge to clarify the question of "beyond reasonable doubt" and "on the balance of probabilities". Five minutes later they came back a second time with their verdict: "Podola is not suffering from loss of memory."

New word

The actual murder trial which followed occupied only a day-and-a-half. The prosecution case was overwhelming, and, with Podola sticking to the claim that he couldn't remember what happened, there was little that Mr. Lawton could do to defend him. As he explained to the judge: "May I bring to Your Lordship's attention my professional difficulties which may make it difficult for me to give very much assistance to the court . . . I have no instructions from the defendant."

He did try the only manoeuvre open to him by trying to plant a doubt in the minds of the jury that the gun might have gone off by accident. Podola also made a statement to the jury from the dock, which meant that he was not under oath and could not be cross-examined. The statement was written on a piece of paper.

It said: "Your Honour, ladies and gentlemen of the jury. I stand before you accused of the murder of a man. Throughout the course of this trial I have listened to the various witnesses, and I understand the accusations. The time has now come to defend myself against these accusations, but I cannot put forward any defence. The reason is that I have lost my memory for all these events. All I can say in my defence is that I do not remember having committed the crime which I stand accused of.

"I do not remember the circumstances leading up to the events in connection with the shooting. I do not know whether it was me, or whether it was an accident, or an act of self-defence. I do not know whether at that time I did realize that the man was, in fact, a detective. I do not

know whether I was provoked in any way. For these reasons I am unable either to admit or deny the charge against me. Thank you."

It took the new jury only 37 minutes to find Podola guilty, and he was sentenced to death. The trial that had made legal history was over. Podola appealed, but the appeal was dismissed, the court making the point that: "even if the loss of memory had been a genuine loss of memory, that did not of itself render the appellant insane so that he could not be tried on the indictment, and no other ground for alleging insanity was put forward." Podola was hanged in Wandsworth Prison at 9.45 a.m. on November 5, a dramatic four months after the killing.

During his first summing-up, Mr. Justice Davies had said: "The name of Guenther Podola is assured of a secure place in the legal history of this country." He not only made history. He also gave a new word to the language of the law and police—Podolatry, leaning over backwards to be fair to a prisoner, particularly a foreign prisoner.

Nevertheless, around the Podola case a few important and unanswered questions

A DEMONSTRATION against Podola's execution . . . It had no effect. The girl (inset) is Ruth Quant, his ex-mistress.

still hang in the air. Where did he get the psychiatric knowledge that enabled him to dupe mental experts for weeks on end? Intelligent as he was, why did he not simply play dumb instead of revealing his knowledge of Ruth and Micky, the *Seven Seas*, chess, pontoon and his belief that he would be able to drive a car, given the chance?

Why, too, when he had all the time in the world to think about what he was doing, did he write such a gushing letter to Starkey when a simple one would have raised no problems for him? Is it possible that his explanation might have been genuine—he felt he could not make a touch without first convincing Starkey he remembered him?

Above all, why, if it was false, did he cling right to the end to his amnesia claim? It could not, as it turned out, save him—and it also prevented him from putting forward any other kind of defence which might, at least, have spared him from the hangman's noose.

Popperfoto. Syndication International/Quartet

BODIES IN THE BAGGAGE

The suitcase (bottom) was found at a London railway station. It contained the legs of a young woman whose severed torso had already been discovered. Pathologist Sir Bernard Spilsbury (below) was called in to join the search for a killer who stored away his victim like pieces of unwanted property . . .

G. K. CHESTERTON suggested that the ideal place for a secret society to meet would be an open balcony overlooking a public square. The same kind of wild logic seems to inspire those murderers who use trunks for the disposal of the corpse. The ideal solution to the murderer's problem would be to make the body disappear into thin air; next on the list, to hide it where it could never be found. Putting it in a trunk, where it is sure to be discovered, is no way to conceal a murder.

The policeman and the pathologist, on the other hand, are bound to experience a certain satisfaction when a killer chooses this method of disposal. It gives them a sporting chance. For unless the murderer has the coolness and foresight of a master chess player, he is almost certain to have left a dozen clues that will eventually reveal his identity.

This was the view held by the Chief Constable of Brighton when, on June 17, 1934, he was called to the Brighton left-luggage office to examine the nude torso of a woman that had been found in a plywood trunk. Railway clerks could recall nothing about the man who had deposited the trunk there on Derby Day—June 6th —the busiest day of the year. But there seemed to be an abundance of clues.

Sir Bernard Spilsbury examined the remains. They were of a young woman in her early twenties. The head, arms and legs had been removed; but the torso suggested that the girl belonged to the middle or upper classes. She had a good figure, with no slack flesh, and the muscles were well developed, suggesting plenty of exercise. The golden brown of the skin also indicated that she spent much of her time in a warmer climate than England. At the time of death, she had been four months pregnant.

Important clues

An alert sent out to all other cloakrooms in England led to the discovery of the legs in a case at King's Cross station in London. Each had been severed at the thigh and the knee, and they confirmed the view that the girl had been athletic and well-proportioned. The conclusion that the trunk had been left by a man was reached by weighing it; only a strong man could have lifted it without help.

There were two important clues. On a sheet of brown paper—in which the body had been wrapped—there was the word "ford". It looked as if it was the second half of a place name, like Guildford or Watford. In the trunk, there were two newspapers. The copies of the *Daily Mail* dated May 31st and June 2nd were of an edition that was circulated only within fifty miles of London. When a porter recalled helping a man to carry the trunk on Derby Day, it began to look as though a solution was near.

Secret affair

For the man had travelled on the train from Dartford to Brighton. A girl who had travelled in the same third class compartment was able to give a rough description of him. But of the five cheap day return tickets that had been issued on that day, not all could be traced, and the police eliminated all those they were able to contact.

Although the police were able to trace the makers of the trunk and suitcase, they were unable to give any useful information as to where or to whom these had been sold. No shop owners came for-

CAREFUL PLANNING had gone into the murder of Beatrice Devereux (bottom) and children by husband Arthur (below), but leaving the bodies in a trunk was fatal.

All Fleet Fotos

THE WAREHOUSE in Harrow where Devereux stored the trunk containing the corpses of his wife and two children. He reckoned without his mother-in-law!

ward with any recollections of either piece having been bought from their shop in the weeks leading up to Derby Day. So here the trail petered out.

Spilsbury estimated that the girl had been dead since May 30, a week before it was left at the station. The man obviously had plenty of spare time, as well as a home where he could conceal a body for a week without fear of discovery. That again suggested a man of leisure. The fact that it had taken him a week to dispose of the body indicated that the crime was not premeditated. And so the police could reconstruct most of the story. A well-to-do man, strong and athletic, has a secret love affair with a girl of his own class. He lives in Dartford, which is on the south-eastern edge of London, part of the "stockbroker belt".

She gets pregnant; on May 30, she calls on him to ask him what he intends to do about it. There is a quarrel, perhaps a fight, and he hits her on the head with

some heavy instrument – the head was never found, but the body bore no marks of violence – or perhaps fell on top of her against a piece of furniture. Her death shocks him; he spends several days thinking on what to do with the body, then decides to dismember it, and deposit the trunk at Brighton. He travels on a third class day return, so as not to attract attention. And, in all probability, he leaves the country as soon as he has disposed of the body.

Careful searches

Sherlock Holmes would have had no difficulty solving the problem. He would have ordered a check on all ports, to establish which resident of Dartford had left the country immediately after Derby Day. He would have investigated the sports clubs in the Dartford area, and the riding stables. And the murderer would probably have been arrested boarding the *train bleu* to Cannes . . .

The British police had less luck. Careful searches of left-luggage offices revealed the corpses of three children and much stolen property, but no further clue to the Brighton trunk murderer. And

from that day to this, the crime has remained unsolved. This can be attributed to luck rather than careful planning. But the case remains the interesting exception that proves the rule: that a trunk is the worst possible place to hide a body.

Wishful thinking

A study of the history of trunk murderers suggests that in many cases, the murderer has a subconscious desire to be caught. It can certainly be argued that the act of hiding a body in a trunk bears an interesting resemblance to the ostrich's attempt to hide by burying its head in the sand. In short, this is an example of Jean Paul Sartre's psychology of "magic" – wishful thinking – that we have already encountered in the case of passion-killers. This can be seen clearly in one of the earliest cases of trunk murder in England: that of Arthur Devereux. It is a story of weakness, self-deception and wishful thinking that would have appealed to Stendhal, whose *Scarlet and Black* is based upon just such a true-life murderer.

One warm summer day in 1898, a pretty girl named Beatrice Gregory was strolling in Alexandra Park, Hastings, when she fell into conversation with a polite and neatly dressed young man. His name was Arthur Devereux, and he was a chemist's assistant. Beatrice was on holiday with her mother, and the holiday atmosphere no doubt made her more susceptible to romance; she saw Arthur Devereux every evening for the remainder of her holiday. Her mother liked him too. Arthur Devereux was "different" — imaginative and ambitious. When he talked about the future, it seemed marvellous and exciting, and she longed to share it. When he proposed, she accepted at once.

Pretty and feminine

Mrs. Gregory was less than happy about the engagement. There was something of the born loser about her, and she was afraid it had rubbed off on her daughter. She found it hard to believe that the future could be as glorious as Arthur painted it. And after a few months of marriage, Beatrice began to share her mother's misgivings. The truth was that, emotionally, Arthur was something of a child. He had wanted her because she was pretty and feminine; it never struck him that there is a practical side to marriage. He found the penny-pinching of married life on a chemist's assistant's wages less romantic than he had expected. He became gloomy and preoccupied.

Then a son was born. It made things more difficult for Arthur; yet oddly enough, he didn't seem to mind. He adored his son, whom they named Stanley. For a while, it looked as if the marriage was going to be a success after all. Then fate intervened, and Beatrice discovered she was again pregnant. The news plunged Arthur into depression. He spent more time than ever cuddling and playing with his son. When his wife produced him twin boys, Lawrence and Evelyn, it seemed the last straw. His affections were already fully engaged; he had no interest in the new arrivals.

Morphine bottle

During the course of the next two years, the Devereuxs moved to a flat in Kilburn, north-west London. Beatrice was now undernourished. Arthur was still working as a chemist's assistant, but the wages were poor. He was an embittered man who felt that his wife had trapped him, and he daydreamed of how easy life would be without Beatrice and the twins. One day in 1905, he decided to do something about it.

The murder was carefully planned. First, he asked the landlord if, when the tenants in the flat below moved out, he could take over the extra flat. Then he

IMPRESSED with Maria Vere Goold, Madame Levin lent her a small sum — and paid for it with her life.

brought home a large tin trunk. A few days later, on January 29, 1905, he brought home a bottle of morphine, and somehow induced his wife to swallow most of its contents — perhaps leading her to believe it was a medicine for her cough. Both she and the twins were dead by the next morning. Devereux placed them in the trunk, arranged for it to be taken to a warehouse in Harrow, then moved — with Stanley — to another part of London.

Mrs. Gregory called at the Kilburn flat, and found it empty. She succeeded in getting a letter forwarded to Arthur, but his reply was strangely non-committal. He said that he had sent Beatrice on holiday, and that he would prefer that her mother should not try to contact her. Mrs. Gregory's intuitions warned her of the worst. She heard about the furniture van, traced it to the depository in Harrow, and finally succeeded in getting an order authorizing her to open the trunk.

Twenty-four hours later, with the story of the discovery of the three corpses in all the newspapers, a worried Arthur Devereux prepared to move on again. This time, he went to Coventry, where he found another job with a chemist. Inspector Pollard, the man in charge of the case, had little difficulty in finding him; it was simply a matter of making a nation-wide check on chemists who had recently hired a new assistant with a 6-year-old son. When Pollard called to arrest him, Devereux blurted out: "You're making a mistake. I don't know anything about a tin trunk." Pollard had not mentioned it.

Fantasy world

At the Old Bailey, Devereux's defence was that his wife had killed herself and the twins, and that he had lost his nerve and concealed the body in the trunk. But

LEA (The Sphere)

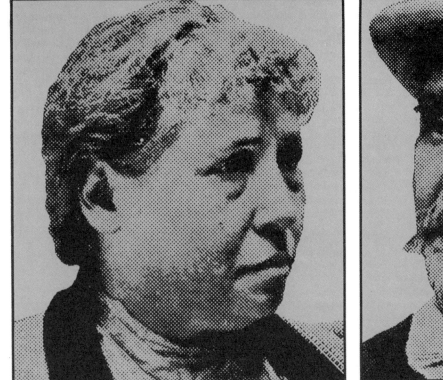

LEA (The Sphere)

THAT'S NO LADY . . . Maria Vere Goold (above) had no official title, but she studied all the arts of aristocratic conduct. Her husband (right) acquiesced.

there was one fact that undermined his story. On January 22, 1905, he had replied to an advertisement for a job at Hull, with a telegram: "Will a widower with one child, aged six, suit?" But at that time, Beatrice and the twins were still alive. On August 15, 1905, Arthur Devereux was hanged at Pentonville prison.

An alienist — which is what psychiatrists were called in those days — had found Arthur Devereux to be sane, but it is difficult to agree with this conclusion. Is it sanity to live completely in a world of

MONTE CARLO: it was at this world-famous resort that Maria carried out her brutal murder of Madame Levin. Was it some kind of twisted revenge for the latter's refusal to part with more money?

fantasy, and to commit a murder without the slightest chance of escaping the penalty? Devereux adored his son; did it not strike him that, in killing his wife, he was risking leaving his son an orphan?

He knew his mother-in-law well enough to know that she would never rest until she had traced her daughter; and he must also have realized that a trunk containing three corpses will soon begin to attract attention by its smell. If he had been sane, he would have taken Stanley and simply left his wife. But he wanted Beatrice to vanish, to disappear like the lady in a conjurer's cabinet. Wishful thinking, to that extent, is surely a form of insanity?

Sexual charms

The Monte Carlo trunk murder, which took place two years after Devereux's execution, raises the same questions in an even more acute form. The killer was an adventuress called Maria Vere Goold, who had assumed the title "Lady Vere Goold". Her husband, an alcoholic and weak-minded Irishman, *was* in line for a baronetcy; but his wife was anticipating.

Maria's career had been even more remarkable than that of her fellow countrywoman, Maria Manning, hanged in 1849 for the murder of her lover. Both were hard, calculating women, who used their sexual charms unscrupulously. Maria Goold—born Girodin—had lost two husbands in suspicious circumstances when she met her third husband, Vere Goold, in London. Goold had little money, but that didn't worry the adventuress; she was used to living on credit and borrowed money.

Mumbled answers

In their first year of marriage, Vere Goold exhausted the patience—and the purses—of all his close relatives. In Monte Carlo, in the early months of 1907, they tried gambling with what was left of their money, and lost it. Various dishonest expedients—like obtaining a ring from a jeweller "on approval", and then pawning it—kept them going a little longer, until Maria succeeded in making the acquaintance of a rich old Swedish lady, Madame Levin, who was impressed by the aristocratic Vere Goolds. But she proved to be tight-fisted with money. She lent Maria forty pounds, but declined to part with any more. In fact, she pressed relentlessly for its return.

On Sunday August 4, 1907, "Lady" Vere Goold invited Madame Levin out to the Villa Menesimy, where they were living in considerable poverty. And as the old lady sat talking to "Sir Vere Goold", whose mumbled answers suggested he was drunk again, Maria crept up on her from behind, and dealt her a crashing blow with a heavy poker. Mrs. Levin collapsed, Maria produced a knife, and drove it into her tormentor's throat. Then she proceeded to hack off the head and limbs of the victim, and to pack them into a large trunk. A niece who was staying with them returned later that evening and found the place covered with blood. Maria explained that her husband had had a fit, and vomited blood.

It is not clear what Maria had in mind. They left Monte Carlo for Marseilles that evening, taking the trunk with them. In Marseilles, the trunk was labelled "Charing Cross, London", and a luggage clerk was instructed to dispatch it, while Maria and Sir Vere Goold retired to a nearby hotel for breakfast and a sleep.

Cold contempt

The clerk, a man named Pons, observed blood oozing from the trunk. The August heat was also causing it to smell unpleasantly. He went to their hotel, and asked them what was in it. Maria explained haughtily that it was poultry, and ordered him to send it off immediately. Instead, Pons called at the police station, where an Inspector told him that the Vere Goolds could not be allowed to leave Marseilles until the contents of the trunk

CELEBRATED for its casino and scenic beauty, Monte Carlo has also etched itself a place in the annals of crime.

Viollet

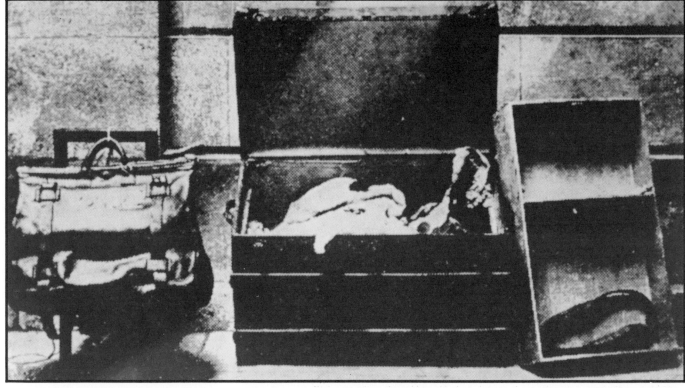

LEA (The Sphere)

had been examined by the police.

Pons returned to the hotel, and found Maria and her husband about to leave. He asked them to accompany him to the police station. With cold contempt, Maria agreed. She took along a carpet bag that had accompanied them to the hotel. In the cab, her façade collapsed, and she suddenly offered Pons ten thousand francs to let her go. He remained immovable. An hour later, the police had found the torso of Madame Levin in the trunk, and her head and legs in the carpet bag.

It was so obvious that Maria was the guilty party that it was she who was sentenced to death, while her husband received life imprisonment. The death sentence was not carried out. While she was in prison in Cayenne, Maria died of typhoid fever. Her husband, deprived of alcohol and drugs, committed suicide. Yet in retrospect, it seems that Maria also subconsciously committed suicide.

Copious bloodstains

What could she gain from the death of Madame Levin? What was to prevent her flitting quietly out of Monte Carlo by night, as she had flitted from so many other cities? Or had a lifetime of crime and calculation finally loosened her hold on reality, as the murder suggests? Once again, the trunk is seen as the symbol of human inadequacy and self-deception.

As to the interesting question of who invented the trunk murder, there is no agreement among historians of crime. Possibly the honour belongs to a Herr Bletry, an innkeeper of Hegersheim,

A FOUL STENCH exuded from the trunk (above) containing Mme. Levin's body, and it aroused the hotel clerk's suspicions.

Germany. When the corpse of a woman was found in a yellow trunk at the Hegersheim left-luggage office, some time in the mid-1870s, the sheet in which the body was wrapped was quickly traced back to Herr Bletry's establishment.

If Bletry was the killer, he was singularly fortunate. Local gossip alleged that the corpse was that of his former housekeeper and mistress, Adèle Brouart, who had vanished some time before. Finally, it was positively identified as that of Adèle Brouart by various witnesses. But while Bletry was preparing to stand trial for his life, Adèle Brouart walked into the police station. . . . The case collapsed, and the police were too discouraged to start all over again. If they had, Bletry would surely have been found guilty.

He tried to explain copious bloodstains in his kitchen with a story of a bleeding nose. The police were fairly certain that the trunk belonged to Bletry's present housekeeper, Franziska Lallemend, but because the other evidence seemed so strong, they had neglected to pursue this line of enquiry. Finally, a strange woman had been seen to arrive at the inn, and had not been seen subsequently. The motive for the crime was probably robbery; but since Bletry was allowed to go free, we shall never know.

A book called *Supernature* by the zoologist Lyall Watson mentions a curious fact that may be of interest to trunk mur-

derers of the future. A Frenchman named Bovis, who was exploring the pharaoh's chamber in the Great Pyramid of Cheops, observed that although it seemed damp, the body of a cat, and various other litter, was apparently undecayed. It struck M. Bovis that perhaps the *shape* of the pyramid might account for this. He made an accurate scale model of the pyramid, and put a dead cat in it.

Cosmic energy

The body mummified instead of decaying. Dr. Watson claims to have tested this himself with a home-made cardboard pyramid (made of four isosceles triangles with the proportion base to sides of 15.7 to 14.94). A dead mouse placed in the pyramid mummified, whereas a mouse placed in a shoe box decayed—and stank —in the normal manner. Even more strange, razor blades left in such a pyramid remain sharp even after much use— a Czech firm has patented the Cheops Pyramid Sharpener.

Dr. Watson's theory is that the pyramid acts as some kind of a greenhouse to cosmic energy, which dehydrates organic matter, and somehow affects the crystalline structure at the edge of a razor blade. So in theory, a trunk shaped like a scale-model of the Great Pyramid should preserve bodies indefinitely—even if dismembered—and prevent smell. On the other hand, it is true that the shape might arouse curiosity in railway cloakrooms. No modification is likely to alter the fact that the trunk is one of the least efficient means of disposing of human remains.

AN EXPERT
SLAUGHTERMAN

London Electrotype Agency Ltd

AT FIRST the attendant at Charing Cross cloakroom paid little attention to the well-built, dark-skinned man who brought a large black trunk for deposit. After all, some 2,000 pieces of luggage were left at the station each day, and in time one traveller came to look much like another. But this particular man seemed anxious to make himself known.

"You must take very great care of my property," he said as he received a ticket for the round-topped, wicker-work trunk. "I shall be travelling later today, and the contents must not be disturbed."

Having issued his instructions the man —who could have been an army officer from his upright stance and short, narrow moustache—strode off into the station yard. He hailed a taxi, and as he was driven away he did an extraordinary thing.

He lowered the window of the cab, put out his hand, and dropped the cloakroom ticket onto the cobbled ground. He was seen to do this by the station shoe-black, whose pitch was nearby the left-luggage office.

The shoe-black helpfully picked up the ticket, and gave it to Mr. Glass, the head of the cloakroom staff. To them, the man appeared to be just another careless traveller, who would later have to identify his trunk by its contents.

Severed head

The porters and attendants then went on with their work, and nothing more was thought about the man, the trunk, or the thrown-away ticket. Nothing, that is, until five days later when—on May 11, 1922 —a peculiar and offensive smell was noticed to be coming from the still unclaimed article.

Mr. Glass examined the outside of the trunk, consulted his immediate superior, and was told to take the box from the rack and place it in an adjoining room. There, in the presence of several mystified officials, a number of keys were tried on the massive brass lock.

None of the keys fitted the lock, and it was then decided to force the lid open with a hammer and chisel. This was duly done and the railwaymen were confronted with several brown-paper parcels tied up with string, a pair of high-heeled shoes, and a leather handbag.

A porter was ordered to open one of the parcels at random and see what it contained. He chose the parcel nearest to him—round-shaped and about the size of a football. He cut the string, unfolded the paper, and found himself holding a woman's severed head!

The horrified Mr. Glass made a phone

A CUT ABOVE the average killer, Robinson (top) carried out everything with military precision. He carved his victim (right) with immaculate skill.

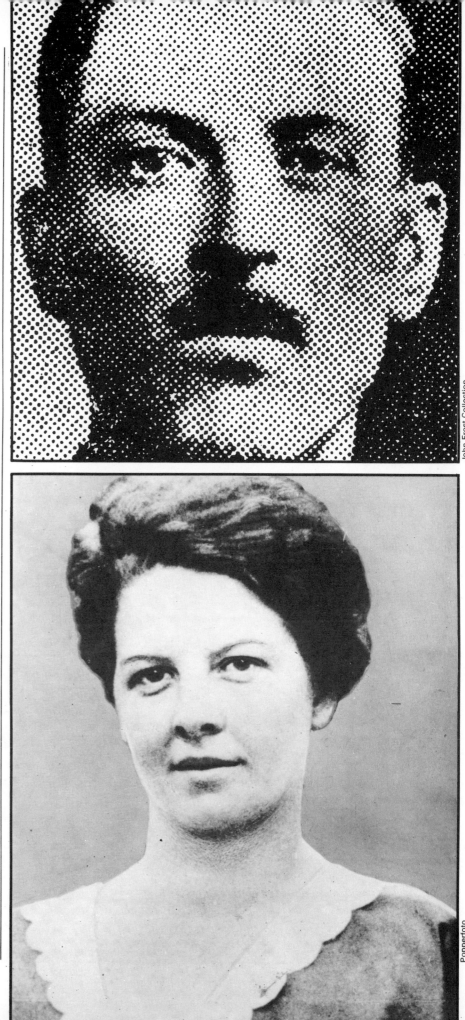

John Frost Collection

Popperfoto

call to Bow Street station, and shortly before 1 a.m. a Detective-Inspector and a police doctor came and took the trunk and its gruesome contents to Westminster mortuary. There it was discovered that the five parcels contained the amputated body of an apparently young woman.

The torso itself lay under some blood-stained clothing—a pair of corsets, a vest, knickers and silk stockings—and the limbs had been sawn off at the shoulders and hip-joints. The remains were examined by the famous Home Office pathologist, Sir Bernard Spilsbury—who, due to his defective sense of smell, could work in conditions which other doctors often found unbearable.

Putrefaction was then in an advanced state, but even so Sir Bernard concluded that the cause of death was: "Asphyxia from pressure over the mouth and nostrils whilst unconscious from head injury and other injuries."

The woman—who had been dead for about a week before the discovery of the body—had been around 35, short, rather stout, and with dark fashionably-bobbed hair. "The clean dismemberment of the parts," added the pathologist, "suggests the work of an expert slaughterman."

TELL-TALE contents of the trunk . . . But even with so many clues upon which to work, the police were in difficulties.

This clue—misleading as it proved to be—was something for the police to work on. The case was put in the hands of Chief Inspector Wensley of Scotland Yard, and after interviewing the cloak-room attendant, he put out the following description of the wanted man:

"Height 5 ft. 7 ins. or 5 ft. 8 ins.; military build; dark, sunburnt complexion; a closely cropped black moustache. Speaks with a slight Midland accent. Believed to be wearing a navy blue suit. Handsome face; features sharply defined; piercing black eyes."

Apart from this, there were other, even more definite leads to follow up. The dead woman's knickers bore a small white

Syndication International

linen tab with the name "P. HOLT" marked on it in block capitals. On another garment there were two laundry marks— H 581 and H 447. And there was also a duster of the kind used in public houses to wipe the glasses clean.

With all this in the police's favour— and with a photograph of the trunk issued to the Press—it seemed as if the case would soon be solved. This false optimism was increased when two of the clues provided speedy and satisfactory results.

First of all a dealer named Ward, who ran a second-hand luggage shop in Brixton Road, came forward and identified the trunk as the one he had sold on May 4.

Mr. Ward told the police that it had been bought by a "distinguished, military-looking gentleman", who had been most particular about the size and the price of his intended purchase.

"I'd like a fair-sized trunk for one journey only," the man had said.

THE CLOAKROOM at London's Charing Cross Station where the "military gentleman" deposited the trunk. It was inevitable that the body would be found.

"I've got this one here," replied the dealer. "It belonged to a family in St. Leonards."

The would-be traveller inspected the trunk and nodded his satisfaction.

"That's fine," he said. "I shall be shipping it abroad and shall put a few clothes and oddments in it. I don't want to pay more than a pound for it."

Very attractive

A bargain was struck at 12s. 6d. To the dealer's astonishment, the customer then hoisted the trunk onto his back and proceeded to carry it away.

"I haven't far to go," the man explained. "Just up the road a bit to where my office is."

This airy reference to an office—which turned out to be opposite the police station in Rochester Row, Victoria—was typical of the coolness of a murderer who cut up his victim in a room overlooking the station and the local police court!

After this promising start, the police were further encouraged when the laundry marks were traced to a Mrs. Minnie Bonati, who had been employed as a cook by a Mr. and Mrs. Holt of Tregunter Road, Chelsea.

Mrs. Bonati was described by her former employers as a friendly, vivacious woman who was "very attractive to men". A short while later the cook's husband, Bernard Bonati, an Italian waiter, was run to earth.

He accompanied the Chief Inspector's men to the mortuary, where he identified the remains of his wife by her teeth formation, and by a crooked index finger on her right hand.

As in most cases of this kind, the husband is the first person to be suspected by the investigating officers. Bonati, however, was able to prove that he and his wife had been living apart for some time.

"She was always fond of dancing and having a good time," he stated. "She went with other men and finally ran off with a lodger we had. After he left her, she sometimes came back to me for money, which I gave to her rather than see her on the streets."

Mrs. Bonati's last address was discovered to be in Limerston Street, Chelsea, where she had last been seen alive at four o'clock on the afternoon of May 4.

She had then been visited by a Receiving Officer who was making enquiries into the many debts she had incurred.

Accomplice

And it was there—and with that information—that the police ran up against a seemingly blank wall. The mysterious "military gentleman" was no nearer to being caught, and for the next few days Chief Inspector Wensley, and his colleague, Chief Inspector Cornish, followed up one false trail after another.

Finally, on May 14, a conference was held at Scotland Yard when the theory was put forward that the murder, or its aftermath, had been the work of two men. No one person, it was argued, could have taken the heavy trunk to Charing Cross station. The murderer must have had help —either from an accomplice, or from someone who did not know what was in the "death box". Then, as every avenue turned out to be a dead-end, three more people gave evidence which was to put a rope around the elusive killer's neck.

A taxi-driver named Waller read about the case, and said that on the morning of

A DEFECTIVE sense of smell helped Sir Bernard Spilsbury (below) to cope with the task of examining Minnie's body.

London Electrotype Agency

May 6 he had been picked up by a man in Rochester Row. He helped his fare put a "very heavy trunk" into the cab, and then drove him to Charing Cross.

Missing agent

Detectives immediately hurried to the office block opposite the police station in Victoria, and stared curiously at the front of No. 86 Rochester Row. On entering the building, they learnt that a Mr. John Robinson—who ran a one-man estate agent's business—had not been seen for several days.

At the same time, other detectives succeeded in tracing the duster which had been found in the trunk. It proved to have been taken from an inn, the Greyhound Hotel, in Hammersmith. There one of the barmaids had a lot to say about Mr. Robinson, who had suddenly stopped visiting the inn to see his wife.

Astounded by their luck, the officers interviewed Mrs. Robinson who was separated from her husband and forced to work in the hotel. She told them how unsatisfactory a spouse Robinson was.

The police officers then went to a house in De Laune street, Kennington, London, S.E., acting upon information supplied by Mrs. Robinson. There they found Mr. Robinson asleep in bed. He was promptly awoken and arrested.

Pathetic story

To begin with, he denied any knowledge of Minnie Bonati, or the trunk, or of recently having been at Charing Cross cloakroom. But at a second interview—and after being kept waiting for a long time at Scotland Yard—he broke down and told the full, somewhat pathetic story of his crime.

According to Robinson (who had been

UNRUFFLED . . . Minnie's husband, an Italian waiter (below), showed little emotion at his estranged wife's death.

John Frost Collection

The Daily Mail

TRUNK CRIME ARREST.

DETECTIVES ROUSE MAN FROM BED.

POLICE SEARCH AN OFFICE

OVERLOOKING A POLICE STATION.

After being roused from his bed in a house in De Laune-street, Kennington, London, S.E., by detectives and questioned at length at Scotland Yard, John Robinson, aged 36, a clerk, was yesterday charged with the murder of Mrs. Minnie Alice Bonati, whose dismembered body was found in a trunk in the cloak-room at Charing Cross Railway Station on Monday, May 10.

Robinson will appear this morning at Westminster Police Court. The charge is one of murdering the woman on May 4 in a block of offices at 86, Rochester-row, Westminster, S.W., which directly overlooks Westminster Police Court and Rochester-row Police Station, where the man is now under arrest.

On arrival at Scotland Yard Robinson was questioned and then detained. Later he was charged. When he had been at Scotland Yard for seven hours he was taken to Rochester-row Police Station.

Detectives from Bow-street, yesterday afternoon visited 86, Rochester-row and took a number of articles, including a

Topix

discharged from the Army in 1923 on medical grounds), he had been "accosted" by his future victim as he left his office late on the afternoon of May 4.

He took her back to his second floor room, where she complained of not feeling well and asked him for a pound. When he refused to give it to her, she became abusive, flew into a temper, and attacked him in the chair in which he was sitting.

Grisly act

"She bent down as though to pick something from the fireplace," he said in his formal statement, "and came towards me. I hit her on the face with my right hand . . . She fell backwards. She struck a chair in falling and fell over it.

"As she fell she sort of sat down and rolled over with her hand in the fireplace . . . I returned to my office about 10 o'clock the following morning. I was surprised to find that she was still there. She was dead. I was in a hopeless position then. I did not know what to do."

Faced with this unenviable situation, Robinson again sat at his desk debating

THE ANSWER to the whole mystery lay in the Greyhound Hotel (below) where the killer's wife worked. Subsequent arrest and conviction were mere formalities.

TRUNK CRIME "DEAD END."

SCOTLAND YARD BAFFLED.

300 STATEMENTS TAKEN AND NO CLUE.

Two conferences were held during the week-end at Scotland Yard by the police officers engaged in trying to solve the mystery of the death of Mrs. Minnie Alice Bonati, whose dismembered body was found in a trunk at Charing Cross Station on May 10.

Two people were interrogated late yesterday afternoon, after which detectives were sent to Brixton to make certain inquiries.

Since the discovery of the body the officers in charge of the case have personally interrogated 120 persons, and in all more than 300 statements have been taken by the police.

Every possible line of inquiry has been exhausted, and Scotland Yard are now at a "dead end."

Inquiries have been made throughout the country with the object of tracing a man named "Jim," a chauffeur who is believed to have been associated with Mrs. Bonati six weeks before her death. This man has not yet come forward.

what his next move would be. He knew the police were only a few yards away, and finally decided to dismember the corpse and dispose of the pieces.

"I went to a big stationer's shop in Victoria Street," he continued, "and bought six sheets of brown paper and a ball of string, for which I think I paid 1s. 9d. . . . I went to a shop in the street nearer Victoria Station, and bought a chef's knife.

"I then went back to my office, and of course I did the job—that is, I cut off her legs and arms. I made them up into parcels and tied them up in the brown paper and string which I had just bought. I finished the job as quickly as possible before dinner."

Robinson's subsequent movements—on the morning of May 6—followed the evidence given by the taxi driver and cloakroom attendant. The knife he used in his grisly act was found where he had hidden it—under a tree on Clapham Common.

After completing and signing his statement, he was charged with murder and was tried at the Old Bailey later that summer. The case dominated the newspapers for the next few days, as thirty witnesses were called for the prosecution, and Robinson himself—who pleaded "not

John Frost Collection

guilty" — spent an hour and a half in the witness-box.

The verdict against him was almost a foregone conclusion, but even so the jury of ten men and two women were puzzled and intrigued by one of the murder's most remarkable features — the almost complete lack of motive. Robinson was duly found guilty, his appeal was dismissed, and he was executed at Pentonville on August

27. The "Great Trunk Murder" as it was called, was not, however, allowed to rest there.

Both at the trial itself, and at the police commission held afterwards, Chief Inspector Cornish was strongly criticized for making Robinson wait for over an hour in a room at Scotland Yard. It was then ruled that such "cat and mouse" tactics would not be used on a murder suspect

THE GREAT trunk murderer was duly executed at Pentonville prison (above), and the case vanished from the headlines. Few "left luggage" slayers ever escape.

again. In more ways than one John Robinson added his own chapter to the story of trunk murders which made such juicy — if bloody — reading for the crime-hungry public between the wars.

ENTERTAINING MR. MANCINI

Popperfoto, Syndication International

Syndication International, LEA

ON a cold mid-December day in 1934, the packed gallery at Lewes Assize Court, in Sussex, England, watched a shifty 26-year-old Brighton waiter known as Tony Mancini stand trial for his life. The case had become sensational, not least because it concerned one of several gruesome murders in Brighton, Sussex, that summer: crimes which had earned the Regency spa the popular title "Queen of the Slaughtering Places".

A large number of girls had unaccountably disappeared from their homes. The torso of one — aged about thirty, and five months pregnant — had been found in a trunk in the left-luggage office at Brighton station. A day later the legs of the same body were found in another box at King's Cross station, London.

Mancini was one of those questioned in connection with the "trunk case number one", although he denied all knowledge of it. But then — six months before the trial — the body of Mancini's mistress, Violette Kaye, had been discovered, doubled up and partly decomposed, in a trunk in his bedroom.

Mancini vigorously denied this murder too; but he was a desperate man with a criminal record, and the facts spoke against him. The affair dominated the newspapers, and among the crowds outside Lewes Court there could have been few people who doubted Mancini's guilt.

But neither the world outside, nor the prosecution at Lewes, and least of all the accused, had reckoned in their forecasts with the astute cross-examination

of the most successful criminal lawyer of the time — Norman Birkett, K.C., who led Mancini's defence. The sordid affair of a down-and-out couple in a seaside resort

SHOWGIRL Violette Kaye had set up a strange relationship with Mancini (seated centre). But their life together in Brighton ended in an unsolved tragedy.

209

SHE LIVED and died at 44 Park Crescent (right). Afterwards Mancini transferred her to new lodgings (left).

became, in Birkett's hands, a bid for the highest principles of justice; it turned out to be the most spectacular legal defence of the lawyer's career.

At the end of his summing-up Birkett fixed his eye on the 12 Sussex citizens who formed the jury: "You are men of the world," he said. "Consider the associates of these people. We have been dealing with a class of men who pay eightpence for a shirt and women who pay one shilling and sixpence for a place in which to sleep. It is an underworld that makes the mind reel. It is imperative that you should have it well in mind that this is the background out of which these events have sprung." He continued: "Now that the whole of the matter is before you, I think I am entitled to claim for this man a verdict of Not Guilty. And, members of the jury, in returning that verdict, you will vindicate a principle of law, that people are not tried by newspapers, not tried by rumour, but tried by juries . . . to decide upon the evidence . . . I claim from you a verdict of Not Guilty."

He had spoken for eighty minutes without a note. A tense silence followed, he added severely: "Stand firm!"

As Birkett sat down the jury cast their minds back for the last time over the sordid events of May and June that year.

How incriminating *was* the evidence against Mancini? Nearly two months passed between May 10, the day on which Violette Kaye had last been seen alive, and July 17, when Mancini was caught on the run. For almost all that time, on Mancini's own admission, Violette's body was kept strapped up in a trunk in his room. Could so depraved a man act so suspiciously and still be allowed to go free?

"Tony Mancini", alias "Jack Notyre", were the Soho names adopted by a man who was originally named Cecil Lois England. He was brought up in Newcastle-on-Tyne, Northumberland, and was educated in Hertfordshire, after which he served two years in the Air Force. Following a spell in prison during 1933 for a petty offence, he got a job at a restaurant in London's Leicester Square, where he fell for an ex-dancer named Violette Kaye. Together they decided to move to Brighton, where they obtained rooms in the basement of 44 Park Crescent.

Mancini soon became dependent on Violette—and although they both worked intermittently for a café called the Skylark, they lived almost entirely off her immoral earnings. He admitted during his trial that when Violette had visitors he would either have to "walk out" or "remain in the other room". They lived in perpetual fear of the outside world; she had also begun to drink heavily and to take drugs. "She was a loose woman, and I knew it," Mancini said. "Strange as it is, I used to love her. We were always on the most affectionate terms. There were no quarrels."

But it seemed that on May 10, at least, they did quarrel—possibly over one of the other waitresses at the Skylark who, it later came out, had taken a fancy to Mancini and went dancing with him. One of Violette's regular clients was a bookie called Charles Moores, who that afternoon sent his assistant, Thomas Kerslake, to apologize for not being able to fulfil a "booking".

Kerslake found Violette, as he later testified, "in a distressed condition over something or other . . . all agitated and twitching". While he was talking to her at the door, he thought he could hear the sound of voices inside. He was probably the last man—apart from the murderer—to see Violette Kaye alive.

The next day Mancini was his normal

chirpy self in the Skylark Café, and he told the others that Violette had gone to work in Montmartre. A telegram was delivered in London the same morning to Violette's sister, who had been planning a holiday with her a few days later. It ran: "Going abroad. Good job. Sail Sunday. Will write. Vi." The handwriting on the original message strongly resembled Mancini's.

On May 14 Mancini became nervous and moved his belongings to another basement at 52 Kemp Street, near the railway station. A fellow waiter at the Skylark helped him there with a heavy secondhand trunk which he had found in the Brighton market. During the days that followed several people complained of a smell, and his landlady pointed to the dark fluid which ran from the bottom of the trunk. Mancini explained that it was French polish, and promised to clear it up.

But time was now literally flowing out. On June 14 Mancini was picked up by the police and questioned about the first torso found in the Brighton left-luggage office. He was soon released—but Mancini caught the next train to London. Meanwhile, his landlady in Kemp Street had opened the trunk and seen the decaying corpse of Violette Kaye. A hue and cry was raised, all ports were watched, and Mancini began to panic.

Greasy little man

In the early hours of July 17, a policeman in Lewisham, South London, spotted him stumbling along the road to Maidstone, Kent, and Mancini gave himself up. "I am the man," he at once admitted. "But I did not murder her. I would not cut her hand off. She has been keeping me for months."

In his statement, later put in evidence by the Crown, Mancini described his return to Park Crescent on the evening of May 10. "She was laying on the bed with a handkerchief tied around her neck and there was blood all over the sheets and everywhere. Well, I got frightened. I knew they would blame me and I couldn't prove I hadn't done it, so I just went out and tried to think things over, what to do . . .

"I hadn't got the courage to go and tell the police what I had found, so I decided to take it with me. . . . There were always men coming to the house . . . I don't know who killed her. As God is my judge, I don't know . . . I am quite innocent, except for the fact that I kept the body hidden."

Mancini was quickly brought before the Brighton magistrates. It was the height of the holiday season and, according to newspaper reports, young men and women in gaudy bathing costumes came and jeered at the little man with the greasy hairstyle and pointed ears as he was taken to court in the Town Hall. Eventually he was committed for trial at the Sussex Assizes in December.

Meanwhile, Mr. F. H. Carpenter, the Brighton solicitor who acted for Mancini, got on the telephone to a friend in London: Mr. A. E. Bowker, the influential clerk to Mr. Norman Birkett. Somewhat under protest, Bowker agreed to accept the brief. Lewes was not on Birkett's circuit, he said, and Carpenter would have to pay an additional "special" fee of one hundred guineas. Besides, the case seemed quite hopeless. He saw little advantage in the defence which he later described as "the flotsam and jetsam that drift, unknown to respectable members of society, along one of the stateliest seafronts in the world". However, a week was finally set aside, and rooms were booked for Birkett on that very seafront, at Brighton's Hotel Metropole.

Deadly effect

Toni Mancini's trial opened in Lewes on December 10 before Mr. Justice Branson, and lasted for five days. Mr. J. D. Cassels, K.C.—later Mr. Justice Cassels—and Mr. Quintin Hogg—the future Lord Chancellor, Lord Hailsham—appeared for the Crown, and Mr. Birkett was accompanied by Mr. John Flowers, K.C., and Mr. Eric Neve.

When Mancini was charged in the customary way by the Clerk of the Assize, he choked as if his throat was filled with sand, and could barely get the words out.

"I am not . . ."

There was an uncomfortable pause, and all in court strained forward as the prisoner attempted pathetically to speak. Finally, he managed a whisper:

". . . not guilty."

Mr. Cassels at once rose to open the

MANCINI returned, on the day after the murder, to the Skylark Café, where he laughed and joked with fellow waiters.

Syndication International

case for the prosecution. With deadly effect, he called witness after witness and calmly amassed the evidence against Mancini. Before he had finished it was clear to many in court that the noose was tightening around Mancini's neck. But although Mr. Hogg continually tugged his sleeve, Cassels did not press his points home. He preferred to let the unutterable speak for itself.

The most damning evidence was the accused's alleged remarks, soon after Violette's disappearance, to three men at a fairground called Aladdin's Cave. It appeared that talk had centred on the question of what to do with troublesome women, and that Mancini had suggested: "What's the good of knocking a woman about with your fists? You only hurt yourself. You should hit her with a hammer, the same as I did, and slosh her up!"

Piece of bone

A charred hammer was, in fact, found among the rubbish at Park Crescent. Although the prisoner denied the statement, he did admit later to Cassels that he had once knocked out a man who had tried to blackmail him. He thus proved that he could be a man of violence.

The hammer became a central exhibit, and the formidable Sir Bernard Spilsbury was called in to give evidence on behalf of the Crown. It was then that Norman Birkett, in cross-questioning Spilsbury— whom he knew well—began to make his presence felt in court. Shrewdly, he drew attention to discrepancies in Spilsbury's statements, and the normally rock-like pathologist began to waver.

He regretted that a vital piece of bone missing from the victim's skull had only been produced on the third day of the trial. He was no longer sure—as he had been at the police court—which end of the hammer, if any, she had been struck with. He admitted that it was conceivable that a depressed fracture such as had occurred to the skull might have been caused by a heavy fall down the basement steps of Park Crescent.

"And, supposing a man had done this horrible thing," Birkett asked the jury later, "don't you think he would have got rid of the hammer?"

No blood was found on the hammer— although the fire would in any case have obliterated it—but small bloodstains were evident on the prisoner's flannel trousers and other clothing. Dr. Roche Lynch, a Home Office pathologist, said that it looked as though the blood had been spattered, as though from an artery. Under cross-examination, however, Lynch admitted that he had not been able to identify the blood group. Birkett later called a tailor to prove that the clothing had not been in Mancini's possession until after the crime had been committed.

"I am not attacking the good faith of either Sir Bernard Spilsbury or Dr. Roche Lynch," said Birkett. "Men may have names and reputations, degrees and distinctions. But high and low, famous and obscure, known and unknown, men are all human and fallible. We have the firm fact clearly proved that those garments on which the greatest stress was laid about blood being deposited from a distance were neither worn by the prisoner nor in his possession until after the death of this woman. The case for the Crown is simply riddled with doubt."

The most telling prosecution evidence was from a pretty 17-year-old, named Doris Saville, whom Mancini had met on a bus when he fled to London, and who claimed that Mancini had asked her to help him with an alibi. However, her story was weakened after she confessed to Birkett that she did not actually know what an "alibi" meant. Mr. Cassels called other witnesses, including the Skylark waitress, to show that there had been quarrels between Mancini and Violette Kaye. Birkett found as many who were able to say that they had been on the most affectionate terms.

COUNSELS for the defence, John Flowers and Norman Birkett, leave court after the opening session of the trial.

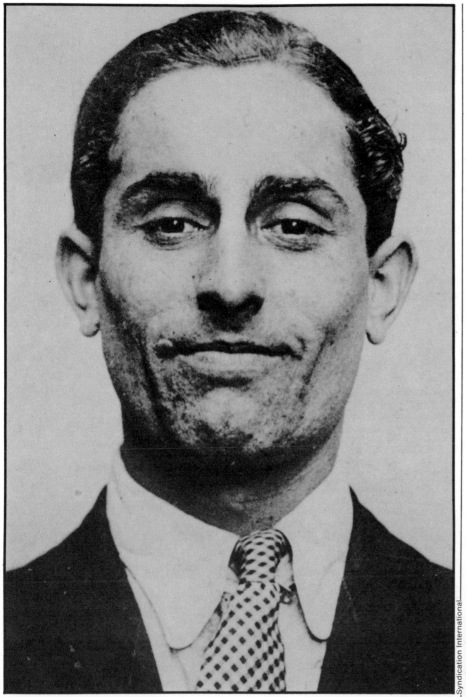

ed into his major speech in defence of Mancini, which he opened with a quotation from the Persian poet Omar Khayyam's *Rubaiyat,* which began: "The moving finger writes, and having writ, moves on." He then asked the jury to look once and for all at Mancini's record, and to understand how a man of this character, "overcome by feelings which may not commend themselves to you", could all too easily commit himself to an irrevocable act of folly.

Birkett next called Mancini to the witness-box, and asked him to repeat his account of the evening of May 10. The prisoner had by this time regained considerable confidence; he was very far from the hunched and speechless figure of a few days earlier.

Lack of motive

"Why did you not go for the police?" Birkett asked.

Reply: "I considered that a man who has been convicted never gets a fair and square deal from the police."

Cross-questioned by Mr. Cassels, Mancini said he thought Violette must have been killed by one or other of the men who visited her.

"Were you not destroying useful evidence then, in disturbing the body and clearing up traces?"

"I did not think of that."

"You were determined no eyes should ever see that body again if you could help it?"

"I knew one day it must come out. I trusted in God, as I do now."

In his closing speech, Birkett did not offer conclusions himself about the way Violette had met her death. But he ridi-

EXPERTS like Dr. Roche Lynch gave damning evidence against Mancini (left). But, for once, they were proved wrong.

Then followed a crucial exchange between Birkett and Detective-Inspector Donaldson of Scotland Yard—who had been in charge of the Mancini case from the time of the first trunk murder. Birkett subtly led him into an extraordinary exposure of Mancini's past record.

"Inspector, this man is a blackguard, isn't he?"

"Yes, sir, I should describe him as such."

"An idle, worthless man without morals or principles?"

"Yes, sir, I think that sums him up."

"With previous convictions?"

"That is so."

"But, Inspector, no conviction or charge of violence?"

"No, sir, none."

Birkett paused for a moment, and then held up a copy of a leading national newspaper, which he passed before the eyes of the judge and jury.

Moving finger

"So this paragraph, which says that the prisoner has been charged and convicted of violence, is completely untrue?"

"Yes, sir, that is so...."

Birkett had scored a tactical point. But he was very far from convincing the jury of Mancini's innocence. He next launched

213

culed the lack of motive in the prosecution's case. Ought not the jury to state clearly that they had not been satisfied beyond all reasonable doubt? "I waited to hear some suggestion when Mancini was in the witness-box as to why he had done it. There has been no word on this vital question."

Human instinct

Lack of motive . . . these were the words ringing in the jury's ears as Cassels wound up for the prosecution. Paying tribute to Birkett's skilful handling of the defence, he, too, concentrated on the main facts of Mancini's character. "Is not such conduct contrary to human instinct and human nature unless there is, for such conduct, the overwhelming reason of guilt?"

Finally, the scrupulous Mr. Justice Branson summed up the evidence before the court. He warned the jury that it was not a court of morals, but a court of law. They did not need proof of motive to convict, he said. "But the fact that there is no express evidence of motive called before you makes it necessary for you to scrutinize with all the greater care the other evidence."

The trial was at an end. The decision could go either way. The judge left the court for lunch in his lodgings, and the jurors retired to their locked room. Outside, the High Street in Lewes filled with people waiting for the verdict, bringing traffic to a near standstill. After two and a half hours, the court at length reassembled. The foreman of the jury then stood up. He stated firmly: "We find him (the prisoner) not guilty."

Mancini swayed in the dock as the Clerk of the Assize asked for the verdict to be repeated. He then stumbled into the arms of the warders. In the corridor his mother swooned on hearing the news that it was all over, that her son was free.

"Go home and look after her," was Birkett's last remark to his client. The following day Birkett dominated the headlines.

The Mancini case was generally acknowledged as his greatest triumph to date. Bowker, who had regretted taking the brief in the first place, agreed that it was equal to any of the defence masterpieces in criminal history. As for Mancini himself, he moved on to a life free from trunks, mysteries, suspicion, and the doubt of his fellow men.

SMALL CROWD gathers outside the court to await the verdict.

Syndication International

HIRED KILLERS

Is money the real motive? Or are there deeper reasons why men offer their services as professional killers? What kind of society do they reflect . . . ?

JUDGEMENT on Floyd Holzapfel (rear centre, above) was sentence of death for his part in the murder of Judge Curtis Chillingworth and wife Marjorie (left).

"I STARTED killing people for pure pleasure when I was eight years old. Then I learned that you could get good money for killing, and so I set myself up in business . . ." The speaker was a 22-year-old Mexican, Zosimo Montesino, whose murder record certainly exceeded a hundred and fifty. His first victim had been a "witch" who had bewitched his parents by giving them a strange brew.

Twelve years later, Zosimo and his chief lieutenants, two brothers named Alcocer, set up an ambush outside the town of Tepalcingo; they had been hired by a local farmer to murder Mendoza Omana, a politician. Mendoza happened to be accompanied by his wife and 3-year-old son; but that made no difference. All three were cut down with shotguns and the father and son killed outright, while the sobbing mother, lying beside the body of her boy, begged two peasants passing by to help her. "We cannot interfere," they said, and walked off.

Casual brutality

Nearly seven weeks later, the killers were arrested in a shanty town shack on the outskirts of Mexico City. They took their capture very lightly, treating it as something of a joke, and Zosimo casually admitted to his hundred and fifty or so contract killings, at prices ranging from £3 to £150. A week later, he alleged that the confession had been obtained from him by torture. "I haven't really killed more than half a dozen people, and that was mostly in self-defence."

Most of us find such casual brutality incomprehensible. It seems more frightening than the more familiar type of murder—the crime of passion or greed or anger. At least these have *personal* motives. To murder a stranger for money seems more depraved. Surely the existence of such monsters is a sign of some profound sickness in our civilization?

Not necessarily. It is a mistake to try to judge Zosimo Montesino in terms that would apply to the average citizen of London or New York. Mexico itself is a weird social paradox. It has the highest murder rate in the world; murder actually accounts for more deaths than disease; yet up to a few years ago it also had one of the lowest rates of juvenile delinquency in the world. In rural areas, the families were very close-knit; a Mexican teenager will put his arm around his mother in public without embarrassment.

On the other hand, because there is so much poverty, life is cheap. It is only in affluent societies that people treat illness and death as a catastrophe. All such societies have high murder rates—it is true of most tropical countries. And nowadays, as Mexico becomes more urbanized—and prosperous—the rate of juvenile delinquency also climbs steadily. It is hardly surprising that Mexico seems to be caught in a spiral of crime.

The theories of the anthropologist Ruth Benedict enable us to understand what is happening. Among American Indians, she observed societies in which there was a high level of kindness and co-operation; she called these "high-synergy societies"; other tribes were naturally mean and self-centred, and she called these "low-synergy societies". Mexico is in process of transition from a high- to a low-synergy

MAD AXEMAN Frank Mitchell (left) allegedly met his match on tangling with the Kray brothers (below, left and right). But their role in his death was unproven.

society. This does *not* mean that it will one day be wholly composed of mean and self-centred people. Civilization may cause a lot of problems; but it also produces a lot of people who care about their fellow human beings. So there *is* reason for optimism.

Most societies *start* as high-synergy societies—when they are primitive—and then they drift towards low-synergy, as they become more sophisticated and civilized. As they slowly become *more* civilized, there is a movement back towards high-synergy, and this appears to be a kind of social law. But when a civilization drifts from high- to low-synergy, it is the poor who feel the effects first—one cheerfully callous student of sociology compared the process to the rats that die first in a plague. *This* explains the existence of people like Zosimo Montesino. It is clear from his confessions that he felt he was living in a wholly vicious and murderous society, where it was a case of kill or be killed.

He told the police: "I don't know why you're making such a fuss about me. I

Both Syndication International

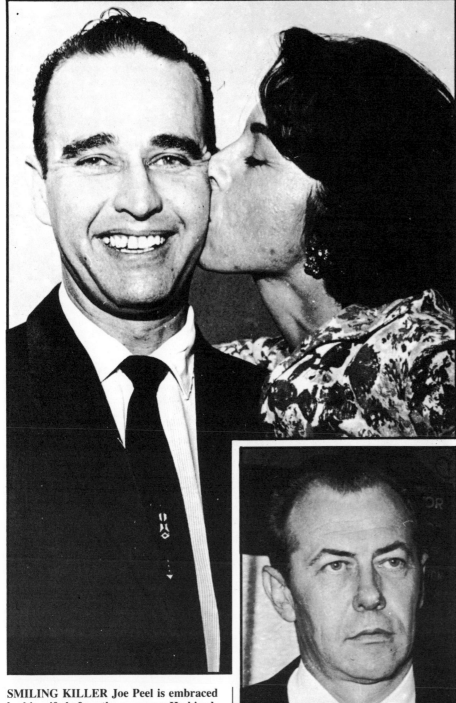

the criminals in brutality. So Zosimo may not have been exaggerating when he called the Mexican police captain a worse killer than himself. But all this adds up to a low-synergy society, where two farm workers can watch a mother and child cut down by shotgun blasts, and walk away saying: "It is nothing to do with us."

If Zosimo is by no means the rule among Mexican criminals, neither is he the exception. Martin Rivera Benitez, nicknamed "Big Soul" in the state of Hidalgo, told police in 1972: "I cannot count the number of people I have killed for money. My fame spread so far that I often had a long waiting list. In order to prove that the job had been done properly, I would cut off the head and show it to the man who had hired me."

In his mortuary in the woods near Jazatipan, twelve headless corpses were found, but these are probably only a small proportion of the people Benitez killed between 1969 and 1972; police believe the victims total more than fifty. "I didn't see anything wrong in killing for money," said Benitez. "If I hadn't done it, somebody else would. And it was better paid than working as a farm labourer." The comment brings to mind the remark of Reggie Kray, the London gangster, to his biographer John Pearson: that in the society in which they were

SMILING KILLER Joe Peel is embraced by his wife before the cameras. He hired Holzapfel and Lincoln (right) to dispose of the man who threatened his ambitions.

know people who have killed more. For example, the police captain Cosme Maldonado. He was a real mass murderer." Zosimo then described at some length how he and one of his gang finally shot Maldonado. "It took 13 bullets to do it, because he was so fat."

Was Maldonado such a mass killer as Zosimo represented him to be? Probably. In the Argentine capital, Buenos Aires, a few years ago, the police got so sick of the crime wave that a special execution squad was formed; they rounded up known gangsters, took them for a "ride", and dumped their bullet-riddled bodies where they would attract attention and serve as a warning to other criminals. Typically, this "rough justice squad" got so out of hand that it had to be suppressed by the police themselves. The moral is a familiar one: in countries with a soaring crime rate and a high level of poverty, where the police are underpaid, they themselves are forced to out-do

born, crime was the *only* way to get out of the social rut in which you were stuck.

Another vital aspect of the psychology of the hired killer emerges in the case of Nestor Mencias Alarcon, the 26-year-old youth who killed Isabel Garcia and her 9-year-old daughter Elvira with a machete. Alarcon claimed he was ordered to commit the murder by his employer, Senora Martinez Anguilar, who was jealous of a long-standing love affair between her husband and the victim. After paying a

217

witch doctor £50—1000 pesos—to be-witch Isabel out of her involvement, the impatient Senora Anguilar ordered Alarcon to kill her—or so Alarçon alleged. Alarcon was paid £55—"That's a lot of money for a man like me," he said.

Senora Garcia's 9-year-old daughter was with her mother, the killer liked her "because she was a nice polite little girl." But as the child saw her mother hacked to death with a machete, she fought with Alarcon and was also killed. The murders, like so many others in Mexico, might have gone unpunished if, said Alarcon, his employer had paid up. But Senora Anguilar lost her temper when Alarcon admitted to kill-ing the child, and called him a sadist. She refused to pay, and Alarcon made the mistake of going on the run, so that he became an automatic suspect.

The police had been convinced that Isabel and her daughter had been killed in a rape attempt. As soon as Alarcon was picked up, he confessed everything, implicating his employer. What is signi-ficant here is that Alarcon claimed he felt obliged to obey his employer's orders simply *because* she was his employer—his social superior.

Criminal mentality

A psychologist who was asked to ex-plain the hired killing of Olga Duncan by Luis Moya and Gus Baldonado pointed out that the killers were Mexicans of poor family, and that they found it easy to obey the orders of a white woman whom they felt to be their social superior. In other words, they felt *absolved* of the crime of murder, in the way that the sol-diers at My Lai felt absolved because they were ordered to massacre Vietna-mese civilians by a superior officer. Soldiers in war generally feel no guilt about killing; dispossessed persons of a "socially inferior" group often feel they are at war with the non-synergic society that surrounds them.

The Mother Duncan case also raises the interesting issue of the psychology of the person who hires the killer. Eliza-beth Duncan had the typical criminal mentality, the outlook that can be seen in murderers like Neville Heath, Marcel Petiot, and George Smith, the "Brides in the Bath" killer; she was a plausible confidence trickster who could become so involved in her own lies that she came to believe them true.

She was also an example of a rarer phenomenon: the female counterpart of A. E. Van Vogt's "right man"—the man with such a paranoid obsession with being "in the right" that he will commit any violence rather than admit that he might be wrong.

Mother Duncan was a "right woman". When she set her mind on something, it

seemed to her that it was one of the laws of nature that she should get it—a religious "right man" would say that it was the "will of God". In her eyes, a woman who had married her son against her wishes had *no right* to be alive. It is tempting to declare that she was insane—and if the definition of insanity is to be out of touch with reality, she was. But if she was in-sane, it was by her own will, her own de-cision. She *wanted* to believe that her wishes were the will of nature, and she had always lived in such a way that she had got away with it.

The same may well be true of the prin-cipal figure in one of the most brutal cases of hired killing in America in recent years. The man behind the crime was a good-looking, smooth young lawyer named Joe Peel, who was a municipal judge at West Palm Beach, Florida. Peel was a "go-getter" whose ambition was to become governor. In 1949, at the age of 32, he seemed well on the way to achiev-ing his ambition. He was well-liked, a member of the social set, and the owner of a number of thriving enterprises such as night clubs. He also found vice profit-able, but his neighbours knew nothing about this:

It was in 1949 that Peel met an ex-convict named Floyd Holzapfel. Hol-zapfel was also good looking and charm-ing, and his criminal record was not too serious—a few incompetent gas station stickups, for which he had served terms in jail. Holzapfel was weak rather than wicked, with a feeling that fate had always dealt him a losing hand, and a strong desire to be liked and accepted.

The chief obstacle to Peel's plans for political eminence was another judge, Curtis Chillingworth, who had had oc-casion to rebuke Peel for legal double-dealing. Peel had good reason to suspect that the judge had learned about his rackets, and that he could not expect to remain a member of the Florida bench for much longer. To Peel's logical and ruth-less mind, the answer was to murder Judge Chillingworth. When he explained the situation to his new right-hand man, Holzapfel was scared, and also shocked.

Social respect

He was basically an easygoing, good-natured man, but his position as Peel's chief lieutenant also gave him the kind of standing and social respect that he had never had before. He allowed himself to be persuaded, but he stipulated that he needed an accomplice. Peel suggested a negro called Bobby Lincoln, who was involved in his rackets. Lincoln was also a non-violent man, with no criminal record, but when a judge asked him a favour, he felt bound to agree.

On June 14, 1955, Holzapfel and Bobby Lincoln went in a boat to the beach

below Judge Chillingworth's house. They expected him to be alone that night—his attractive wife was supposed to be with relatives. Unfortunately for Mrs. Chillingworth, she had changed her plans.

The hired killers knocked on the door, and the unsuspecting judge opened it in his pyjamas. Holzapfel asked if there was anyone else in the house; the judge called his wife. Holzapfel and Lincoln tied their hands with tape, and forced them into the boat. At one point, Mrs. Chilling-worth screamed, and was silenced with a heavy blow from the gun butt.

Undercover man

Once at sea, they put weights around Mrs. Chillingworth's waist. Her hus-band said: "Remember, I love you," and she answered: "I love you, too"; then they tossed her overboard. She sank immediately, without screaming. At this point, the judge managed to fling himself overboard, and began to swim with his feet. He was moving away from the boat when Holzapfel began battering him with a rifle butt. Then the anchor rope was looped around Chillingworth's neck, and the anchor tossed overboard. The corpses were never recovered.

But in killing a man as distinguished as Judge Chillingworth, Joe Peel had over-reached himself. Police began an inten-sive investigation into his disappearance; it was a long job, and in the meantime, Holzapfel had a chance to commit an-other murder. This was of a crook named Lew Harvey, suspected of being an in-former. Harvey was also forced into a boat, shot in the back of the head, and dumped in the canal with a block of con-crete attached to his legs.

A few days later, the body floated to the surface. On the night he was "taken for a ride", Harvey had felt nervous, and had given his wife the number of the car in which Holzapfel and Lincoln col-lected him. The police soon traced the car to Holzapfel; they now had a strong suspicion that this was how Judge Chil-lingworth had disappeared, and that Peel and Holzapfel were the men behind it.

An acquaintance of Peel's, an insur-ance salesman named Jim Yenzer, was hired by the police to act as an under-cover man. Yenzer's inside information had soon got Holzapfel into so much trouble that he was sent to trial for an attempt to hijack arms from a group of Cuban revolutionaries. He was finally set free; but his faith in Peel's friendship —and his generosity—had been heavily eroded; Holzapfel began to mutter threats. Peel now approached the police informer Jim Yenzer, and offered him $2000 to murder Holzapfel. Yenzer agreed, but kept putting it off. Since the police were now paying constant attention to Holzapfel's affairs, his boss persuaded him to flee to Rio de Janeiro, with a promise to support him indefinitely. Shortly thereafter, Yenzer also went to Rio de Janeiro, commissioned by Peel to murder the hired killer of Judge Chillingworth—and by the police to try to get a confession out of Holzapfel.

He did not succeed immediately, but he *did* succeed in persuading Holzapfel it was safe to return to Florida, and during a two-day drinking session in a motel in Melbourne, Florida, Yenzer and another undercover agent finally got Holzapfel to describe the murder of the Chillingworths in detail, while other police agents listened in the next room with a tape recorder. It had taken five years of unremitting police work. As a result, Holzapfel was sentenced to die—although sentence was not carried out—and Joe Peel and Bobby Lincoln each received life imprisonment.

What emerges very clearly from the study of hired killers is that money is seldom the basic motive. In 1973, an American publisher brought out a book called *Killer,* the anonymous autobiography of a "hit man", who is identified on the title page only as "Joey". According to Joey, he has thirty-eight "hits" to his credit, and rates as one of America's top hired killers. Born in the Bronx,

Joey became involved in the rackets from childhood. At the age of 16, he was asked if he would kill a man. He accepted the job, and shot the man in the back of the head in the street.

"Then the realization came to me that I was a made individual. I was a force to be reckoned with. A lot of people who had looked at me as being a snot-nosed wise-ass kid would now be speaking of me in different tones. The job paid $5000." It is significant that he mentions the money last.

What is more important is the feeling of "being somebody". Joey's autobiography may or may not be authentic—an anonymous book is bound to be open to doubt—but there can be no doubt that these blood-chilling pages are an accurate reflection of the psychology of the hired killer. The money is only secondary, even in mob-killings.

All of which makes it clear that it is inaccurate to speak of "hired killers"; it would be more exact to speak of "cat's-paw killers". In the great majority of cases, the true psychological motivation

LONELY COTTAGE by the sea was the peaceful home of Judge Chillingworth and his wife. From there they were led down to the beach and cold-bloodedly drowned.

is to be found in one man's dominance over another. The murders committed by the Charles Manson family are an archetypal example of "cat's-paw" murders, and the Manson case also raises one of the basic legal problems of the cat's-paw murder. Manson's defence—and the defence that his supporters have been making ever since—is that he did *not* order Tex Watson, Susan Atkins and the others to commit murder. They may have thought he did, but that does not make him guilty. In Manson's case, it is almost impossible to believe that he was not closely involved, because his "family" committed at least three sets of murders, but in a more recent case, there is room for doubt.

On the night of February 19, 1972, the home of Black Power leader Abdul Malik—also known as Michael X—burned down near Port-of-Spain, Trinidad. Police investigating what looked like a case of arson discovered the corpse of a man buried in the garden. It was Joseph Skerrit, a 25-year-old barber and disciple of Michael X. Further digging finally revealed the body of Gail Ann Benson, the pretty 27-year-old daughter of a British Member of Parliament. She had been stabbed 7 times, and buried alive.

Gail Benson, it soon transpired, had been the mistress of another of Michael X's close associates, Hakim Jamal. It was believed that she had disapproved of Michael X's influence over her lover, and had tried to cause a rupture between the two men. This, said the police, was the motive for her murder. Skerrit was murdered because he happened to witness it. Jamal was also subsequently murdered by Black Power members in the U.S.A.

Disturbing possibility

Michael X escaped to Guyana, in South America, but was arrested there on March 1, 1972. In Trinidad, three 'lieutenants' were arrested and accused of the actual murder. Of these, Edward Chadee and Stanley Abbott were found guilty, whereas the third, Adolphus Parmassar, turned Queen's evidence, and thus escaped conviction. It was his evidence that really convicted Michael X, who was sentenced to death as the man who gave the orders, although he claimed to have been at home at the time of the murders.

And it must be admitted that, on present evidence, there is no clear proof that Michael X ordered the executions. He was hanged on 16th May 1975; his lawyers were given no time to appeal.

The cat's-paw killer is a social phenomenon, the product of a painfully evolving society. If Ruth Benedict is correct, world civilization will one day become a unified high-synergy society. When that happens, the hired killer will be no more than a relic of the savage past.

Bill Shrout

MOTHER DUNCAN'S DEVOTION

Los Angeles Times. AP/Quartet

MIDDLE-AGED Mrs. Elizabeth Duncan, an outwardly respectable divorcée, devoted mother of a successful grown-up son, went shopping in the downtown area of Santa Barbara, California. Like so many other women among the 59,000 people of this opulent Pacific coast city, careful spender Mrs. Duncan was keeping alert eyes open for a bargain. But her quest, that December day in 1958, was not for a new chic hat, a becoming housecoat or a memorable evening gown. She was out to buy the services of a killer who would "eliminate"—as she delicately put it— her newly-acquired daughter-in-law.

Many women like to have the company of a friend on a shopping spree and Mrs. Duncan was no exception. With her as she bustled along Santa Barbara's State Street was her close friend and confidante, Mrs. Emma Short. To the casual passer by they appeared to be no more than two rather nice, mature citizens, Mrs. Duncan nearly sixty, her friend Emma in her seventies.

But their animated, low-voiced chat was about purchased death. Mrs. Short fully shared her friend's secret and for a homely old pensioner she was remarkably complacent about it. Her only re-action, as she could later recall it, was that, although she was keeping Mrs. Duncan company, "I didn't approve of her plan to kill her daughter-in-law".

Twisted woman

The "market-place" to which their dangerous mission took them was a seedy, run-down beer parlour on State Street, called the Tropical Café, owned by an illegal Mexican immigrant, Mrs. Esperanza Esquivel. Wily Mrs. Duncan had chosen it carefully. Mrs. Esquivel lived in fear that the police would discover that she had no legal right to be living and operating a business in the United States; already, on a quite separate brush with the law over the alleged receiving of stolen property, Mrs. Duncan's lawyer son, Frank, had represented the Mexican family's interests.

As Mrs. Duncan saw it, Mrs. Esquivel owed her a favour and, moreover, she seemed the likely sort of person to know drifting, café-haunting customers ready to offer their services as hired killers.

It was all incredibly cold-blooded yet it all fitted the psychopathic personality of Elizabeth Duncan. For, despite outward appearances, she was a dangerously twisted woman. In the course of her life she had had many husbands—probably 20 or more, but even she was not certain —some taken in legal marriages, others bigamously. She had married most of them in the hope of acquiring their money, for she was also a diligent, if not very skilful, confidence trickster.

The only man who had brought her any

221

lasting joy was Frank Low who had fathered her son, Frank, in 1928. She quickly tired of Mr. Low and illegally "married" a Mr. Duncan, whom she also deposed in favour of yet another "husband", but she raised her son as Frank Duncan. Young Frank she doted upon and wrapped in a suffocating mother love, obsessed with the anxiety that he would one day leave her.

Major quarrel

"Frank," she told her own doctor, who was concerned about the effects on the boy of her neurotic obsession, "will never leave me. He would never dare to get married." Surprisingly, in view of this crushing maternal weight, Frank Duncan showed remarkable independence. An intelligent, lively-minded boy, he did well educationally, made his way through law school and ended up as a successful lawyer with bright prospects.

Somehow he survived the embarrassment of being followed around from court to court by his energetic, clinging mother and listening to her vigorous and sustained applause every time he won a case. Lawyer-colleagues, gossiping together while juries deliberated, expressed the private view that the sooner Frank Duncan found himself a wife and escaped to complete personal freedom the better off he would be.

In the few quiet moments of meditation that he could snatch for himself, Frank began to think along similar lines. He was more than ready to throw off the yoke that bound him and, in 1957, he and his mother had their first major, stand-up quarrel. In his exasperation he ordered her out of their apartment. She, prepared to go to any lengths to remind her son of his permanent servitude, responded by taking an overdose of sleeping pills.

Loving Mother Duncan survived, but her action was to have terrible and far-reaching results for herself and three other people. For she was taken to a nearby hospital and there given into the care of a dark-haired attractive nurse, Canadian-born Olga Kupczyk, 29-year-old daughter of a railroad foreman.

Olga was one of the first people Mrs. Duncan saw when she emerged, pallid and shaken, from her coma. And Olga was almost the only person in the hospital, even including his mother, to whom Frank paid immediate attention on his first bedside visit to the patient. The attraction was mutual and the devastated mother, watching the alarming, affectionate glances between son and nurse, now saw that her worst fears were being realized. Her rival, long dreamed of with dread, had taken human shape and soon Mother Duncan would no longer be Frank's only and eternal love.

Within a few months the web that was being spun between the three principals in the drama tightened with the disclosure that Olga had become pregnant and a hesitant Frank found it necessary to inform his mother that he was considering marrying the girl. Mrs. Duncan, now restored to normal, angry health, was driven into a frenzy of rage, saw the nurse and told her with vehemence: "I'll kill you before ever you marry my son. You are not a fit person to live with my son."

Determined as he seemed to lead his own life, Frank Duncan was nevertheless still too conscious of his mother's vulnerability to make a decisive, precipitate break. Accepting the quite exceptional patience of his betrothed, he secretly married Olga but, from his very wedding night, left her at a late hour each day to return home and sleep at his mother's apartment. Later he remarked, ruefully, "Quite frankly, I was going back and forth like a yo-yo."

Screaming tirade

But it was impossible to under-rate a woman of such tenacity as Elizabeth Duncan. Within a day or so she had learned of the marriage and determined that it would not last. Her first move was to insert an advertisement into a local newspaper declaring: "I will not be responsible for debts contracted by anybody other than my mother, Elizabeth Duncan on, or after, June 25, 1958. Frank Duncan."

The advertisement came as a surprise to Frank but, still anxious to dampen the fires of fury, he felt it unnecessary to do more than to admonish his mother for interfering in his private affairs. As far as Mrs. Duncan was concerned, he had no private affairs and she presented herself, without warning, at Olga's apartment and launched into a wild tirade which was ended only when Olga summoned the help of her landlady who persuaded Mother Duncan and her son to leave.

Clearly, poor Frank had not launched himself upon wedded bliss but his mother was only yet in the early stages of her campaign to separate husband and wife. Her first improbable scheme was to kidnap Frank, while he was visiting his bride, and whisk him away to a hideout in Los Angeles. She even bought some rope with which to secure her rebellious son and confided her plan, inevitably, to her good friend, Emma Short. But in her more lucid moments even Mrs. Duncan was forced to acknowledge that the scheme was preposterous and she abandoned it.

What she could not, or would not,

AUTHORITIES uncover the body of Olga Duncan (right). Hired killer Luis Moya (left) was one of the two men who contracted to dispose of her for a fee.

abandon was her vitriolic hatred of Olga. She assured Mrs. Short that she would disfigure Olga with acid but then, on second thoughts, proposed that she should strangle Olga with Emma Short's assistance. The idea was that Mrs. Short should induce Olga to come to her home where Mrs. Duncan would hide in a cupboard. When Emma Short had invited Olga to take a comfortable seat, with her back to the cupboard, Mrs. Duncan would spring out and strangle the girl.

As the monumentally acquiescent Mrs. Short later explained: "The idea was that she should then hang her up in the cupboard until the evening. Then she would put a blanket around her, tie her with a rope and put a stone to the rope and take her to the beach in a car and throw her over the wharf." According to her own narrative, Mrs. Short's response was curious. "Do you realize," she told her bloodthirsty friend, "what you are trying to do? She will never stay in my apartment all night!"

Faced with Emma Short's reasonable objection to being saddled with the annoyance of a corpse in a cupboard, Mrs. Duncan turned her mind towards

EXACT details of the crime and location of the body were provided by Augustine Baldonado (below), the second of the amazingly incompetent killers.

more businesslike and better-organized methods of disposal. She would put the "job" out on hire and, for a mutually agreeable sum of money, hand over the technical details of her daughter-in-law's death to a third party. And so it was that the two old ladies, Elizabeth and Emma, found themselves in the steamy premises of the Tropical Café on State Street.

Apprentice killers

Mrs. Duncan turned her glib tongue to the immediate task of convincing the Tropical's owner, Mrs. Esquivel, of her problem—adjusting the facts to suit the situation. Her daughter-in-law, she confided, was blackmailing her and unless she could be removed, her son, Frank, might well be the victim of Olga's wrath. Perhaps Mrs. Esquivel had some friends who might not object to "removing" a bothersome person?

Mrs. Esquivel, adopting the view that the customer, however eccentric, was always right, knitted her brows in thought and finally pronounced that there were

SMILING contentedly, Mrs. Duncan gazes at her grief-stricken son during the trial. Her friend Emma Short (right) knew about the murder but said nothing.

"a couple of boys" but whether they would be available or not she did not know. Perhaps if Mrs. Duncan could return the following day she would introduce them to her?

Mrs. Duncan duly returned with the imperturbable Emma still tottering in her wake, and was introduced to two unemployed young men, Luis Moya, Jr., 21, and his inseparable companion, Augustine (Gus) Baldonado, 26. Both were drifters, who had been in and out of the hands of the police, but neither of them had any history of violence.

Almost certainly they had never met any matronly old body with such a persuasive tongue as Mrs. Duncan before and they solemnly sat down at one of the café's grubby tables with her and discussed her proposition as others might discuss a real estate deal.

For once, Emma Short was excluded and left to sit on her own, sipping coffee at an adjoining table. But the trio of Mother Duncan and "the boys" moved swiftly to the heart of the matter. As young Moya subsequently reported: "After we got down to brass tacks we just started making suggestions of how much money it would be worth to her to eliminate her daughter-in-law, and when it could be paid and how much, and there were suggestions made of how to get rid of her body. At first Mrs. Duncan just wanted to pay $3000, but I finally boosted the price up to six . . . She agreed to pay $3000 right away and then the remainder after Mrs. Olga Duncan was eliminated."

Mother Duncan was full of suggestions for the actual commission of the

"elimination". Once again, it involved rope, with the addition of sleeping pills and a final neat touch of acid "to disfigure her in general and her fingerprints . . ." Finally, "the boys" agreed to accept the assignment and promised to proceed as quickly as possible to fulfil it.

There remained, of course, the question of money. Mrs. Duncan omitted to mention that, far from having $6000 at her disposal, she had not the remotest chance of laying her hands on the initial $3000, or anything like it. But Moya and Baldonado were among two of the most gullible apprentice hired killers in criminal history. They listened to Mother Duncan's promises, finally accepted a ludicrous cash advance of $175 and naively agreed to receive the balance after the "contract" had been completed.

Mrs. Duncan left the café in high spirits, informing reliable old Emma on the way back home, "I think they are going to do it."

Moya and Baldonado wasted no time. They hired a 1948 Chevrolet for $25,

borrowed a ·22 pistol from an obliging friend and bought some ammunition to fit it. Soon after 11 p.m. on Monday, November 17, 1958, they drove to Santa Barbara's quiet suburban Garden Street and parked outside number 1114, the house in which Olga Duncan lived.

They waited to ensure that all was quiet and then young Moya went into the building, up the stairs and knocked on Olga's door. She appeared in housecoat and slippers and politely Moya launched into the killers' well-rehearsed script. Frank, her husband, he said, was downstairs in the car. "I met him in a bar and he's pretty drunk and has quite a large amount of money with him and he told me to bring him home. But I need help to bring him up."

Immediately Olga offered that help and followed Moya back down to the street. Baldonado had meanwhile stretched himself out on the back seat of the car, face downwards, to simulate the drunken, passed-out form of Frank Duncan. Moya opened the car door and Olga put her head in, reaching towards what she took to be her inert husband. As she did so, Moya struck her a blow on the side of the head with his pistol and pushed her on to the car floor as the suddenly active Baldonado dragged her towards him. In a moment the car door had shut and Moya was driving fast away towards the beach.

But the two young hoodlums had not made a very professional start to their killer careers. Olga, who was only dazed, came to her senses, began to scream and struggled to escape from the fast-moving car. Baldonado grabbed at her and tried to quieten her but she was a well-built, strong young woman and she fought against him valiantly.

"I can't hold her," the breathless Baldonado gasped and, as he was forced to brake at a stop sign, Moya leaned back across the front seat and struck viciously several more times at Olga's head with the pistol. Quiet at last, her blood spilling into the car, she slid to the floor.

Damaged mechanism

Now the second part of the makeshift plan worked out by the two killers began to go wrong. They had intended to dispose of the body somewhere around the Mexican border but, shaken by events, they changed their minds and decided instead to head for the mountains, south of Santa Barbara, and rid themselves of their victim with the utmost speed. Thirty miles down Highway 150 they found a darkened roadside culvert, parked beside it and, seeing that the road was deserted, dragged Olga Duncan out of the car.

She was still breathing and Moya drew his pistol once again, this time to put a final, despatching bullet through her head. But the use of the gun earlier as a club

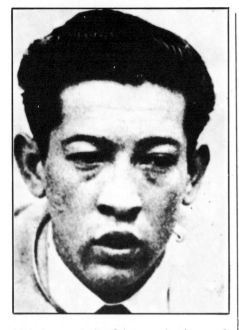

had damaged the firing mechanism and, while Moya struggled with it in vain, Baldonado bent over the reviving woman in the darkness, searched for her neck and strangled her. When she had ceased to move, Moya picked up a rock and used it to deliver the *coup de grâce*.

So pathetically inept were the two young murderers that they had brought no tools with which to dig a grave and conceal the body. Both jumped down into the culvert and began scrabbling the dirt away with their bare hands, gouging out, after much sweated effort, an insecure and shallow pit into which they slid their victim's bloodied body.

Cryptic question

Blood dominated their thoughts as, at last, they drove back to Santa Barbara, for there was blood everywhere. It saturated their clothes, it lay in thick pools on the car seats and it seeped and trickled between their feet. Back in the city they spent anxious hours getting rid of their bloodstained clothes and tearing out the blood-covered seat coverings. They had accidentally started a fire in the car with a lighted cigarette, they explained to the Chevrolet's owner.

For a time it looked as though the clumsy murder might escape detection. A distraught Frank Duncan, calling at Olga's apartment and finding lights blazing and doors unlocked, summoned the police, but their best assessment was that this was a missing-person case. No doubt Mrs. Olga Duncan would return, or be traced, before long. No one came forward to offer any useful information, not even Emma Short who knew the almost certain answer to the mystery.

Two days after the murder, Luis Moya telephoned Mrs. Elizabeth Duncan at her home and reported that the "contract" had been duly carried out. "You don't have to worry about her any more," he said before coming to the principal reason for his call: "Are you going to be able to accomplish your end?" Mrs. Duncan was in no doubt as to what that cryptic question meant. The labourers now wished to make it clear that they were worthy of their hire but, worthy or not, Mrs. Duncan had no money for them and no intention of meeting the full bill.

She had her story well prepared. "The police have been up to the house asking about Olga's disappearance," she explained. "So I can't draw any money out of the bank." She had a little money — around $200 — and that would have to suffice for the moment. A few days later she met the two boys, accompanied by faithful Emma Short, and handed over an envelope to Moya. On opening it later he found it contained only $120.

ALL THREE killers (this page) were slated to die on the same day — in the gas chamber at San Quentin, California, but Mrs. Duncan appeared unperturbed.

Infuriated by what was now clearly a rather nasty con-trick, the two killers began to pester Elizabeth Duncan for their pay-off to such a wearing extent that she decided to indulge in a piece of table-turning blackmail. She told the police that *she* was being blackmailed by two Mexicans, whose names she could not reveal but who were threatening to kill her and her son, Frank. Her theory was that once the killers heard of her action they would quietly leave town and she would be rid of them, just as she was now rid of her daughter-in-law.

It was Mother Duncan's last and clumsiest move. The police, by now aware of the bad blood that had existed between mother and daughter-in-law, began to look more closely at Mrs. Duncan's wide-ranging activities. They questioned Emma Short, because of her known close association with Elizabeth Duncan, and at last old Emma began to talk. Astonished policemen sat wide-eyed as they heard her tell of the "contract" meeting at the Tropical Café and her explanation that she had not thought it necessary to pass on the information before murder was committed.

Side by side

From that point on, events moved swiftly to an inevitable climax. Baldonado and Moya were picked up and Baldonado dictated a confession which included precise details of the roadside grave of Olga Duncan. Mother Duncan's arrest followed as a matter of routine and by the time they came to talk to her at length the police were convinced that she was one of nature's pathological liars. Almost nothing she said rang true — except her blinding devotion to her son.

All three, the female instigator and the two hired killers, were found guilty and sentenced to death. Mrs. Duncan still had hopes of survival and her lawyer son repaid her distorted devotion by fighting, after a long series of appeals, for a final stay of execution. But even his energy and skill could not prevail against the course of the law and the murder trio went to the gas chamber at San Quentin on August 8, 1962. Moya and Baldonado died together, strapped into death chairs placed side by side.

Mother Duncan died alone. Her son could not be with her for, up to that final, eliminating moment, he was still pleading her case. Her last words, as the door of the glass and steel gas chamber was opened, were: "Where is Frank?"

All UPI

UPI

The Argus/Quartet

UNFRIENDLY FAVOUR

Marthinius Rossouw (left) smiled confidently as he stood in the dock accused of the murder of his best friend at the lonely spot marked A (above). "Sure I killed him", Rossouw confessed, "but only because he asked me to . . ."

THERE HAVE been few moments of excitement in the High Court of Cape Town, South Africa, as intense as that moment on September 12, 1961, when a tall, slim man of 23 took his place in the prisoner's dock. The court was crowded and there was not a vacant seat in the spectators' enclosure. For months, the whole of South Africa had been buzzing with gossip about this young man who claimed he had killed a friend—at the friend's request.

The Court Registrar rose and addressed the prisoner: "Marthinus Rossouw, you

are charged with the crime of murder in that upon or about the twenty-fourth day of March, 1961, at or near Vissershoek, in the District of Bellville, you did wrongfully, unlawfully and maliciously kill and murder Dietrich Joachim Gunther von Schauroth. How do you plead?" Quietly, the young man replied: "Not guilty."

As outlined by the Attorney General, Willem Martin van den Berg, the basic facts of the case were straightforward. The body of Baron von Schauroth (he had inherited the title from his late father,

a German settled in South Africa) had been found by a lonely roadside, shot twice in the back of the neck. Near the body was an uncut diamond of about four and a half carats—which suggested either that the baron had been killed during some illicit diamond transaction, or that the motive of the murder was simple robbery which had been only partially completed before the killer fled.

A trail had led to Rossouw, who was known to be a close companion of von Schauroth and had been with him earlier on the night of the killing. When questioned by the police he had made a series of conflicting statements. Eventually he was arrested and the evidence, said the Attorney General, would point conclusively to the fact that he had killed the baron in order to rob him. It apppeared, from the way the prosecution presented it, an open-and-shut case of straightforward murder for personal gain.

Early to the witness-stand came one of the State's most important witnesses, Jacob Michael van Eeden Beyleveld—a private detective having nothing to do with the investigation, but who had happened to be in a hotel bar at a place called Milnerton, five miles north of Cape Town, on the evening of March 24. He recalled two men, whom he did not know, sitting at the bar a few feet apart, and he had sat upon the bar stool between them.

"One of the men," the witness testified, "was dressed in a brown curduroy jacket and green corduroy trousers and he introduced himself to me as von Schauroth, a sheep-farmer from South-West Africa, who was having a short holiday at the Cape. His wife, he said, usually gave him Friday night off to do as he pleased."

Bulging pocket

What really intrigued Beyleveld was the behaviour of the other man at the bar. "He kept walking in and out of the bar," the witness told the jury, "and I said to von Schauroth: 'I wonder what's wrong with that chap. It looks as if he wants to stay in the bar for a drink but can't afford it.' Later he butted in and talked to von Schauroth, and I thought it odd that my conversation should be interrupted by a stranger. After a while he introduced himself to me as Rossouw and asked me to have a drink with him; but I said: 'No thanks, brother, I'm going home.'"

After a while, von Schauroth produced a £5 note with which to pay for drinks for Beyleveld and himself and, Beyleveld said, "I could hear a rustle as he felt in the pocket. It might have been letters or money. His pocket was bulging."

At 7.30 p.m., von Schauroth and Rossouw left the bar, separately, and a few minutes later Beyleveld heard a car drive away. It was a curious story, and as Beyleveld left the witness-box the jury were left to ponder on the mysterious charade of two friends, von Schauroth and Rossouw, playing at being strangers to each other.

But the jury had little time for their thoughts to take root. Almost at once the Attorney General announced a crucial turn in the evidence. During his period of arrest awaiting trial, Rossouw, he said, had been visited by his wife. As she was leaving, he handed her three paperback books. One of the guarding policemen spotted Rossouw slipping an envelope

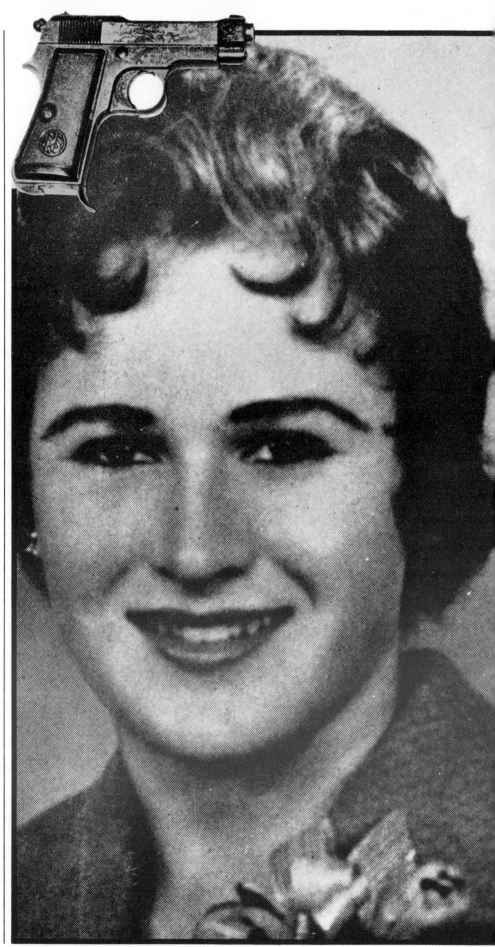

into one of the books and confiscated it. The envelope was found to contain a letter to Rossouw's wife, Johanna, and this letter the Attorney General would now read to the jury. A sudden burst of sobbing from Johanna, sitting next to Roussouw's mother, heightened the expectation of what was to follow.

"Dearest darling," the Attorney General read dispassionately, "I do not know what will happen to me . . . If I am lucky I shall get a few years' imprisonment but, dearest, if it so happens that I am condemned to death, remember that in spite of all our troubles I always loved you.

"Tell our children one day that their father was a murderer . . . Your own husband has shot Dietrich von Schauroth, a baron of standing throughout South Africa. It was also a bitter experience for me, but I released him from his troubles. He had money but no happiness. . . ."

However, there was more than that to Rossouw's communication, the Attorney General said. He took up the envelope and read the scrawl on the back: "Remember the Friday evening of the 24th day of March, 1961; your husband shot Baron Dietrich von Schauroth dead. Relieved him of his troubles."

There was total silence in the courtroom, disturbed only by occasional sobs from Rossouw's wife. The members of the jury stared at the prisoner, his head sunk on his chest, his thick crop of brown hair tousled from constant patting by his nervous hands. The Attorney General let the silence hang for a monent before going on to call his next witnesses — among whom soon came Colleen von Schauroth, the murdered man's wife.

Throwaway line

Colleen stepped timidly into the witness-box, an attractive, well-built girl of 20 with soft eyes and full mouth. She wore the sadly bewildered air of a young woman who had not yet reconciled herself to the knowledge that the two years of marriage to her 36-year-old husband had ended with such brutal suddenness.

Yes, she told the Attorney General, she remembered the afternoon of March 24 quite clearly. She and her husband had been lying in bed, reading, when "at about half past five he dressed hurriedly and said he was going out on business. He didn't return that night and the next day I was told he was dead."

She was shown a Beretta pistol, recovered from the sea close to the shore after the killing, and agreed that it had belonged to her husband. He had never normally carried it with him, she stated,

DESPERATELY tired of life . . . ? The baron and his pretty young wife, Colleen, showed every sign of happiness. But the latter's evidence still seemed ambiguous.

and she did not see him pick it up when he left her on that last afternoon.

Asked about her husband's finances, Colleen remembered that, on the Monday before his death, von Schauroth had counted out some £2000 in cash—mostly in £10 and £5 notes. "I don't know what he did with the money," she added. "It was not unusual for him to count out his money. He always put his notes into bundles of £100 and kept a record on a piece of paper of how much he had. He had brought with him from Karasburg [in South-West Africa, where he had been working on a sheep farm] between £5000 and £6000 in cash."

She told the jury that Rossouw often visited her husband and she knew that, from time to time, he had asked her husband for money and his requests had been met. Mr. Wilfrid Cooper, the leading defence counsel, asked her a question that sounded, at the time, like a throw-away line—but on which so much of the case was to focus. Did she know that her husband had insured his life heavily? No, Colleen replied, she had no idea.

However, when von Schauroth's insurance broker was called, the significance of Mr. Cooper's apparently casual question became increasingly clear. The broker testified that, in May 1960, he had insured von Schauroth's life for £110,000, on five policies with initial, total premiums of £1902. On top of that, in November 1960, von Schauroth had purchased a short-term policy for £70,000.

The result was that the baron, with those policies, plus earlier policies worth £21,000, was a very heavily protected man. There was a total amount of £201,000 available for his beneficiaries if he should die, other than by his own hand, during the policy periods.

The judge, Andries Beyers, Judge-President of the High Court's Cape Division, showed some signs of restlessness at this line of evidence. "Why is this relevant?" he demanded. "This is not an insurance case." But the prosecution was well aware of the direction the defence was taking—and the Attorney General at once made it known.

Unusual companion

"The defence allegation," he told the judge and jury, "will be that von Schauroth insured himself and then virtually committed suicide!"

That gossip was transformed into fact when Mr. Cooper opened the case for the defence. Wasting no time, he told the jury that Rossouw admitted killing von Schauroth, but would plead that von Schauroth had asked him to do so.

Contrary to what he might have liked people to believe, the baron, said Mr. Cooper, was broke and unable to meet his debts. If he tried to escape from his prob-

lems by committing suicide his insurance policies would be void. But if he died by some other means, his wife would be well provided for by the insurance companies, and he could depart from his life without leaving her destitute.

On the eighth day of the trial Mr. Cooper called Rossouw to the witness-box and quickly established the basic details of his background: born in Cape Town, the third of five children of a fitter on the State Railways, himself apprenticed as a railway workshop fitter in Pretoria at the age of 16. It seemed clear that the jury thought him an unusual companion for a man of aristocratic stock with the right to call himself "baron".

Rossouw said he had first met the baron, in January 1961, while travelling among diamond diggers. He recalled that

FAMILY OF FORTUNE . . . The house where von Schauroth lived with his wife (above) was a curious amalgam of styles which only the rich, perhaps, can permit themselves. It was built by the victim's father (far right) and his uncle (right).

"as soon as I saw him I knew he was a man of standing". Rapidly these two men, from quite different social strata, had become close friends—with the generous baron constantly displaying bulky wads of notes and insisting upon picking up the bills for liquor and food. "He would not even let anyone pay for a round of drinks," Rossouw remembered.

It was after only a few meetings, Rossouw told the court, that the baron made a startling proposal. "He suddenly said to me in a bar: 'I'll give you £5000 if

you'll shoot someone for me.' I thought he was joking. I laughed and said: 'Well, you had better bring him along. Why don't you tell me who he is?' He said: 'It might be anyone – my mother-in-law, my wife or even my child.' I thought it was his sense of humour.''

But, as Rossouw told the story, it turned out that the baron did not intend it to be a joke, even a sick joke. One evening, as they were parting, von Schauroth handed him an envelope which contained a cheque for £1150 and a letter which read:

Debt settlement

"I, the undersigned, hereby give to Marthinus Rossouw, cheque No. CA 11 358158, post-dated to July 3rd, 1962, signed by U. von Schauroth, for the sum of £1150, which my brother owes me. I

233

give it to him for services rendered. (Signed) D. von Schauroth."

The "U. von Schauroth," Rossouw explained, was the baron's younger brother, Udo. The cheque, now to be made over to Rossouw in this curious way, was in settlement of a debt owed by Udo to the baron. But for what, the accused man was asked, was this complex system of payment meant to be a reward? "He said it was for accompanying him on his business trips as his bodyguard," Roussouw replied.

Bizarre masquerade

Mr. Cooper steered his client to the day of the murder. He and von Schauroth had met in Cape Town, and then driven out to the hotel in Milnerton where the earlier witness, private detective Beyleveld, had met them in the bar. There, said Rossouw, they had acted as strangers, occupying bar stools separated by a vacant stool, because the baron "had said we must pretend we did not know each other".

"And why was that?" the judge inquired. Rossouw, looking haggard and tired, as though the strain of his six months in custody and now the trial were proving too much for him, muttered that he did not know. "You didn't ask him?" the judge persisted. "I thought," the accused man replied, "that he wanted to conduct business with someone, and I had to keep watch."

Rossouw explained that his constant flitting in and out of the bar, which Mr. Beyleveld had commented on to von Schauroth, was occasioned by visits to the toilet, "and because I was in a hurry to leave. I 'phoned my wife and promised her that I would come home.

"When I returned to the bar I took up a place next to von Schauroth and said, 'Good night, mister,' as I wanted to attract his attention and tell him we must leave. He turned to me and said, 'Good evening, sir,' I replied 'Good evening, sir, my name is Rossouw.' He said, 'My name is von Schauroth' and he then introduced me to Mr. Beyleveld."

After this bizarre masquerade he and the baron left the bar separately, met together outside the hotel and drove off in von Schauroth's car towards Killarney, a small township a few miles north-east. "You have just said you telephoned your wife and told her you were coming home and now he drives you to Killarney," the judge intervened. "Wasn't it time you asked him what he was doing?" "No," Rossouw responded, "I never asked questions."

At Killarney, Rossouw continued, they had one drink each and again returned to the baron's car, with Rossouw in the driving seat. Von Schauroth commanded him to drive "in the direction of" Malmesbury, another town still further north-east "and so I just drove on. He sang a German song and then he became serious. He said that

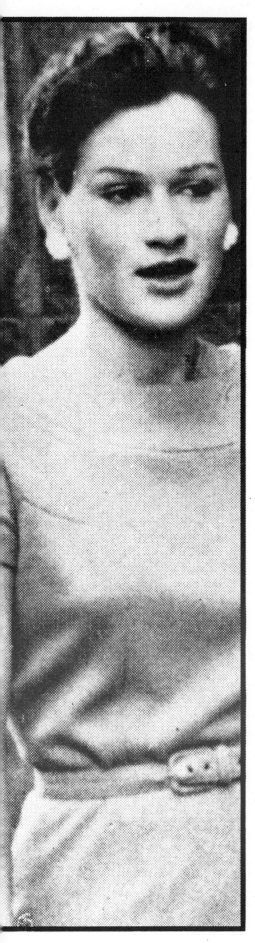

he was not happy with his wife. He was tired of life. Then he slapped me on the back and said, 'Don't worry. Don't forget that tonight you have to shoot someone for me.'"

Rossouw paused and seemed suddenly drained of all energy. It was evident that he was finding it an effort to continue with his narrative. Finally he overcame the worst of his nervousness and, in a lowered voice, went on: "At the old Malmesbury road, when we came to some white oil drums, he told me to turn the car round. I did so and stopped. He took out a pistol and loaded it with two cartridges, using a handkerchief, and gave it to me.

"He got out of the car and stood at the spot where his body was later found and looked towards the trees. Then I got out of the car and walked towards him with the revolver in my hand. Suddenly he turned to me and said, 'I want you to shoot *me*!' I was stunned and I said, 'I can't do it; I will not do it!' He pleaded with me and said, 'You *must* shoot me.'"

Two sharp clicks

Once again Rossouw's voice petered out and his face was parchment pale. Mr. Cooper urged him on and he struggled to resume. "He said there would be no witnesses. He wanted it to look like a diamond transaction. He said that he could not shoot himself because his wife would not get the insurance money if he committed suicide. He told me he was insured for £200,000. Calling him by the name I always used, I said, 'Dieter, you're ridiculous. I can't do it.' He replied, 'I'm tired of life and unhappy with my wife. So you see, Marthinus, you *must* shoot me.'

"He said, 'Go to my bank manager and say to him "I am the man von Schauroth promised £5000" and he'll pay you £5000.' I said, 'I don't want your money.' Then he said, 'Well, shoot me.' Then he turned his back on me, but I turned him round and took his hand and I said, 'Well, goodbye, friend, we shall meet again.'"

"What happened then?" Mr. Cooper asked. Rossouw looked briefly around the courtroom, with strained anxious eyes. Then, in a voice turning hoarse with apprehension, he whispered: "I shot him. I shot him in the back of the neck as he told me to. His arm jerked out and nearly struck me. I closed my eyes. I heard him fall on the ground."

Unconvincing

Mr. Cooper studied his client and let the silence intervene for a second or two. "But there were two shots," he insisted. "Yes," Rossouw agreed. "He jerked with

THE HAPPY COUPLE gave no outward sign that anything was wrong. But why did von Schauroth keep a Beretta, and how did the gun come into Rossouw's hands?

the first shot and then I shot him again. On the second shot his arm jerked out." Did he touch the body, touch the pockets? No, he declared, he touched nothing. "What light was there?" the judge asked. There was moonlight, he said.

The Beretta pistol, with which the murder was committed, was handed to Rossouw. Then rivulets of perspiration erupted on his forehead as he grasped the gun butt. He seemed at first not to hear Mr. Cooper's instruction to demonstrate how the fatal shots were fired. Then slowly he raised the Beretta and squeezed the trigger. The two sharp clicks of the empty revolver sounded unexpectedly loud in the hushed court.

And after the shooting, he was asked, what then? Rossouw spilled out the events, as if in relief at having recounted the worst of the ordeal. He drove von Schauroth's car back to Milnerton, abandoned it, took a bus and eventually made his way to Sea Point, on the Atlantic coast near Cape Town — where he threw the gun and the remaining bullets into the sea. He did not go to the bank next day to collect the £5000 the baron had said would be waiting for him. Then, before he could do anything else, he was arrested.

Now it was the judge's turn to probe Rossouw's story and briskly he pointed out that "in your letter to your wife, you did not tell her that von Schauroth asked you to shoot him." No, Rossouw hastily replied, he did not want to. The judge pursued his points: "The man was the best friend you ever had. He was generous to you. Why did you not try to dissuade him from taking his life?"

Oh, but he did, Rossouw insisted. But the baron had begged him to shoot him and would not listen to anything said to him. And had he looked to see if his friend was really dead or, for all he knew, had he left him there on the ground, wounded? Dully, Rossouw replied: "I was sure he was dead."

In his cross-examination, the Attorney General hammered away at some of the central points in Rossouw's story. It was odd, he thought, that Rossouw — who knew the baron well enough to know that he used more than one bank — had not asked to which bank he should report to collect the promised £5000. Rossouw's answer sounded unconvincing. "That was what he told me," he said. "To go to the bank. And I knew of one bank where he had most of his dealings."

"Is the only reason he gave you that you must shoot him, the fact that he was unhappy with his wife?" the Attorney General asked. "No, he could not do it himself because his wife would not be able to get the insurance money; and he said he was tired of life." — "But he took her out regularly, and they appeared to be happy. Why should he sacrifice his life to give his wife insurance money if he was unhappy with her?" – "He never showed that he was unhappy or annoyed. He always laughed and was friendly."

Again, the judge joined in the exchanges, pressing home an earlier question: "Why, in the letter to your wife, did you not say you had shot him at his own request?" – "I said on the envelope, 'I released him from his troubles.' " – "If your story is true, why did you not give the police your present version of it right from the beginning?" – "He told me to wait a day or two." – "What? Is that the reason you did not tell this story? Because the man who is dead said you must wait a day or two?" – "He said I must wait awhile – if they catch me." – "When did he tell you that?" – "That same night."

Illegal buying

"I cannot follow you. You are asked why you didn't tell the police that you killed the man out of friendship, and you say it was because he asked you to wait a couple of days. Do you really expect me to take this answer seriously? You had better think of a better answer." – "I didn't want to tell them that I'd killed him."

The judge paused for a moment on receiving that reply. "Yes, that I can understand," he commented drily. Still, the judge was not finished, and he sup-

plemented the Attorney General's cross-examination with more questions of his own. These produced from Rossouw a new version of the reason for the payment of £1150 for "services rendered".

It had, the prisoner now said, been in return for putting the baron in touch with diamond-selling contacts. But had he not earlier said it was for acting as von Schauroth's bodyguard? Yes, Rossouw agreed, but for a bodyguard to be around when the baron was dealing with diamond contacts because "he was doing illegal diamond buying". And what about the diamond found beside the body? Had he put it there? No, Rossouw pleaded, he had not. The baron must have done it.

In his summing-up the Attorney General told the jury: "I ask you to find that Rossouw shot von Schauroth in order to obtain his money. It would then be a cold-blooded murder, with robbery as the motive. But even if you should find that von Schauroth did ask Rossouw to shoot him, there is, in my submission, still no question of extenuating circumstances.

"The crime is not against the dead man alone. It is a crime against the community, against the State. Whatever

THE EVIDENCE was all available. The murder weapon, together with the bullets fired into von Schauroth's body (below), made Rossouw's defence doubly difficult.

opinion you may have of the character of von Schauroth, the law demands that no person shall take another person's life."

The jury were out for precisely one hour and returned with a verdict of guilty. Asked, "Do you find there are any extenuating circumstances?", the foreman replied: "We have been unable to find any." Standing quite still and betraying no sign of emotion, Rossouw heard the judge announce his agreement with the verdict, and deliver the sentence of death by hanging. Johanna Rossouw clutched at her husband's hand, mute with despair.

Technical defences

There was a lengthy post-trial fight to save Rossouw's life, but it was in vain. On June 19, 1962, the baron's friend and killer walked firmly to the scaffold, singing the hymn, "Nearer my God to Thee". Despite the trial verdict, the insurance companies' legal advisors felt that there was some truth in Rossouw's story of the murder-by-agreement, and contested payment on von Schauroth's policies on that ground.

In June 1963 the companies announced that the estate of the dead baron "has approached us for a settlement, conceding our right, based on technical defences, to repudiate the claims." As a result, the statement added, the estate had accepted a final settlement, covering all claims, of £10,000 and legal costs.

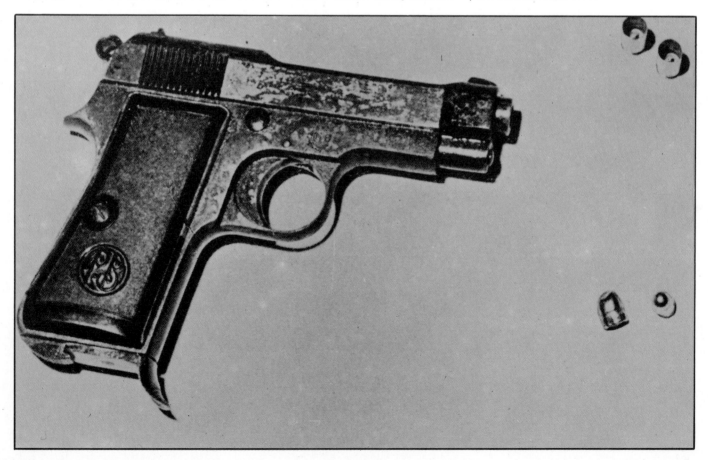

EASY PREY

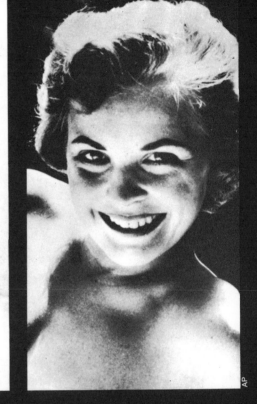

HE was a monster who specialized in pretty young models. He liked to tie them up, to photograph their frenzied struggling. Then he choked them. But did Harvey M. Glatman act out his horrible fantasies in a total vacuum? Is it not possible that one or two of his victims (from left: Shirley Bridgeford, Ruth Mercado, Judy Dull) unknowingly fanned the flame of his unspeakable craving for sexual humiliation and violent death . . . ?

THE pretty German girl led the man through the hole in the hedge. Between the hedge and the fence behind it there was room for the two of them to lie down. She held out her scarf to the man. "Tie my wrists. I am your captive princess. Make me know that I belong to you." When he had tied her, he tugged off her skirt, then her stockings, suspender belt and transparent panties.

As he was unbuckling his trousers, a knife fell from his belt. The girl began to pant. "Cut me a little. Flick the blade against my flesh." Then, as he began to make love to her: "Harder, please. Cut me . . ." She began to whine and moan like an animal. Suddenly, she gasped: "Now. Kill me. Please kill me . . ." And the man, too excited to disobey, drove the knife into her throat.

"Afterwards, I took her handbag," said Guido Benedetto Spimpolo, the killer of Marlene Puntschuh, "I cut it up, and threw the pieces down the lavatory on the train . . ."

His story sounded incredible: he described how, on June 7, 1969, Marlene Puntschuh had picked him up in the Piazza Barberini in Rome, and less than a quarter of an hour later she was begging him to kill her. But a search of her hotel room revealed a diary that left the police no doubt that Spimpolo was telling the truth. Marlene Puntschuh, a bank clerk

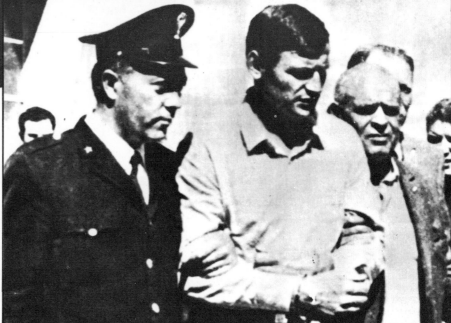

Popperfoto

"PLEASE KILL ME!" begged pretty model Marlene Puntschuh in her ecstasy . . . and her lover Guido Spimpolo, too excited to disobey, cut her throat.

from Stuttgart, was a masochist who dreamed of being tied up and tortured by virile lovers.

Every year she came on holiday to Italy, looking for muscular, sunburnt men who would help her to act out her strange fantasies: Marlene was the born victim. Guido Spimpolo, the ex-waiter with the body of a giant and muscles of a weight-lifter, was a born conqueror of female hearts; and when their eyes met on the

Piazza Barberini, killer and victim instantly recognized one another, and drew together instinctively.

It was in his classic study *The Criminal and the Victim* (1949) that Dr. Hans von Hentig argued that, in many murder cases, the victim may be as responsible as the murderer. But nearly 30 years earlier, in 1920, the novelist Franz Werfel had written a novel called *Not the Murderer, but the Victim is Guilty*. It sounds absurd; but what Von Hertig and Werfel both had in mind was a fact well known to police officers: that people often behave in such a way that they seem to invite violence.

Sexual games

When, for example, we hear about a case of child murder, we are inclined to think in terms of an innocent child lured to its death by a lust-crazed maniac; but in many cases it is the child who invites the adult to play sexual games—and then, perhaps, becomes frightened and begins to struggle; there are cases on record of children who have made a habit of falsely accusing men of exposing themselves.

In the same way, many women who accept lifts from total strangers on dark nights are fully aware of the risk they are running, and may be considered to be playing a kind of Russian roulette with fate. A case in point occurred in Kingsport, Tennessee in August 1970, when a 22-year-old nurse's aide allowed herself to be picked up outside the local supermarket by two men in a car. They parked near a quarry, and one of the men, Harley Phillips, ripped off her clothes, and raped her twice.

They drove to a tavern, and the other man went in to get beer and food, but the girl made no attempt to escape from the car. They slept in the open overnight, and Phillips cut her with a knife and talked about killing her. She was raped again. After another day of terror, rape and threats of death, the three spent the night in a barn, and she allowed the other man to have intercourse with her voluntarily—this was the man whose invitation she had accepted in the first place.

After being made to promise solemnly that she would not report Phillips to the law, she was finally allowed to go home. She told the full story to a girlfriend, who immediately called the police, and in 1972 Phillips was sentenced to 18 years in jail. Undoubtedly the girl was the victim of a sadist; but it is equally clear that her ordeal was at least 50% her own fault. A girl who drives off with two strangers cannot be entirely unaware that they have sex on their minds.

This obvious type of "collaboration" between the victim and the criminal is only one aspect of the complexities of victimology; the relationship may be more subtle. Everyone has known married couples who seem to bring out the worst in one another; the husband may be an irritable bully, the wife an inefficient whiner whose reaction to her husband's bullying is an attack of self-pity and still more inefficiency. Everything he does makes her worse, and everything she does makes him worse.

Family murders

About four-fifths of the murders committed in England are "family murders", in which victim and killer are related, or at least known to one another, and a large number of these are cases in which the victim-murderer relation already exists.

But there is one aspect of "victimology" that has so far been totally neglected by the criminologist: the question of the "born victim": the person who seems to be "destined" for murder. The reason for its neglect is obvious: to speak of a predestined victim sounds more like crystal-gazing than science, yet this is not necessarily true. We recognize that a woman can be responsible for her own murder if she habitually wears low-cut dresses, behaves in a generally provocative manner, takes off her clothes without drawing the curtains, picks up strangers in bars, and it is surely equally conceivable that a woman's whole *personality pattern* could place her in the high-risk bracket where murder is concerned.

Such born victims are more often women than men, for the obvious reason that a man is less likely to be the victim of

a sexual attack. These women often have a pathetic air of accident proneness. It is certainly difficult to analyse such cases in terms of pragmatic psychology, yet you have only to read about them, or even see a photograph, to feel that there *is* such a thing as a born victim, even if they are lucky enough to avoid actually being murdered.

Anyone who has read a biographical sketch of President Kennedy—with his childhood illnesses, his accident proneness, his wartime misadventures—feels that this *was* the type of president to be killed by an assassin's bullet. The same applied to his brother Robert. On the other hand, Lyndon Johnson somehow didn't *look* accident prone; a kind of invulnerability was a part of his total personality.

The same was true of De Gaulle, who was the subject of several assassination attempts, and Hitler survived a bomb blast that went off within a yard of his legs, although other generals in the same room died from it. Yet President Kennedy was killed by a bullet fired by a hopeless marksman from a rifle with inaccurate sights. Moreover, the assassin Oswald's own career shows him to have been accident *and* failure prone, and his subsequent death while in police hands underlines it.

It would be easy for speculations of this kind to turn into absurd hypotheses and preposterous guesses. However, the psychologist Carl Jung developed a valuable concept called "synchronicity" which could be defined as "a coincidence that is not a coincidence". Jung himself described, for example, how he happened to notice that the number on his streetcar

ticket was the same as the number on a ticket for a concert that evening; and then, to make the coincidence doubly unlikely, someone gave him the same phone number later the same day.

Since President Kennedy's death, many writers have pointed out the number of strange similarities between the assassinations of Lincoln and Kennedy: both were shot in the head from behind, both succeeded by a southerner called Johnson, both advised by their secretaries against the visit that led to the assassination, and so on. There is also the extraordinary fact that ever since Lincoln, who was elected in 1860, *all* presidents elected at 20-year intervals have been assassinated or died in office: Garfield, 1880, Mc-Kinley, 1900, Harding, 1920, Roosevelt, 1940, Kennedy, 1960.

Evil omens

Sceptics may accuse us of credulity for taking notice of "coincidences"; but, on the other hand, all science has advanced by a process of observing such matters—for example, comets were once thought to foretell catastrophe—until someone noticed that they reappeared *regularly*.

It would certainly be wrong to make too much of this inherent "victim proneness"; but it would also be stupid to pretend it did not exist. One of the most obvious cases is the Black Dahlia affair. Elizabeth Short once remarked to a friend: "I guess something sure hexed me, and nothing anybody or anything can do can help . . ." Yet when one considers her drifting, self-pitying life, it is also clear that it was partly her own fault.

The "born victim" is often a person suffering from a *deficiency of vitality*, who

A BORN VICTIM? It is hard to read the story of President Kennedy's early years without feeling that for him assassination was somehow inevitable.

is largely aware that her bad luck *is* her own fault, yet takes this as simply another form of bad luck, instead of recognizing that she *could* change it. Such a person often prefers to live in a world of fantasy and shrinks from facing the real world: so that the impact, when it finally comes, may be brutal.

A typical case involving such an "escapist" victim occurred in Vancouver in 1949. The body of a woman was found in False Creek on November 9. She had been strangled, beaten, then thrown—unconscious but alive—into the water. Missing panties indicated that the motive was rape. She was identified as Blanche Fisher, an attractive spinster who looked at least 10 years younger than her actual age, 45; she had failed to return home from the cinema the previous evening.

She had been a pretty, shapely woman; why, then, had she been unmarried? Was she having a secret love affair, as she often hinted to her fellow assistants in the store where she worked? Who was the man who, she claimed, had been trying to persuade her into a secret marriage? As detectives investigated her background, they realized they were facing a dead-end, for Blanche Fisher had no secret lover; no man had asked her to marry him. Her only outings were to the church she attended, and to the cinema. She preferred romantic films, and she was an enthusiastic reader of movie-fan magazines. While she lived her quiet, virginal life, she dreamed of excitement, of masterful lovers . . .

Women's panties

A month later police picked up a man who was prowling the streets wearing only a raincoat. He was 34-year-old Frederick Ducharme, who lived on a houseboat. When police went there, they found half a dozen pairs of women's panties on a clothes-line, and in the living room Blanche Fisher's shoes and watch. Ducharme finally confessed to her murder, claiming she entered the car willingly, then refused to let him make love to her.

What *is* certain is that he forced her back on to his boat, then beat her, raped her and tortured her with a knife before throwing her overboard. Like the unfortunate "Black Dahlia", Blanche Fisher had the *mental outlook* of a victim; unlike Marlene Puntschuh, she did not literally beg to be murdered; yet something about her certainly brought out the worst in her killer.

Two other cases afford interesting parallels to the Blanche Fisher and the Dahlia murders. In March 1972 the nude body of a girl was found leaning against a tree near Wells, in Maine. It was covered with more than 200 cigarette burns, had a deformed upper lip, due to a series of healed scars, a cauliflower ear, and a deformed

right arm, which had been broken and then allowed to heal without splints.

The girl, later identified as 19-year-old Constance Corcione, had died as a result of choking on her own vomit, and the injuries indicated that she had been beaten and tortured for many months before her death. Once she was identified, it was not difficult to piece together her story. A year before, she had been a pretty girl. The parallels with the Dahlia, Beth Short, are interesting; Connie, like Beth, was also born in Cambridge, Massachusetts, and her father had also deserted her mother, leaving her to bring up the family.

Connie ran away from home again and again, leaving for the last time in July 1970 and moving in with the family of a musician named Richard DiMarzo, in Revere, Mass. DiMarzo had a wife and children. He was a man of violent temper.

It was he who had apparently beaten and tortured Connie for almost two years.

On her eighteenth birthday, a family friend had called on Connie at her home in Lynn, and the girl had pulled down her slacks and showed enormous bruises all over her thighs and hips. These had been inflicted by DiMarzo, and the friend threatened to kill DiMarzo if he ever touched her again: yet it was *after* this that Connie actually moved in with DiMarzo. Presumably she was DiMarzo's mistress—medical examination revealed that she had had sexual intercourse shortly before death, apparently without force.

The DiMarzos had moved out when the

TIED UP and crying, Mrs. Bridgeford (below) died in the desert near San Diego. Judy Dull (right) and Ruth Mercado were Glatman's other model-victims.

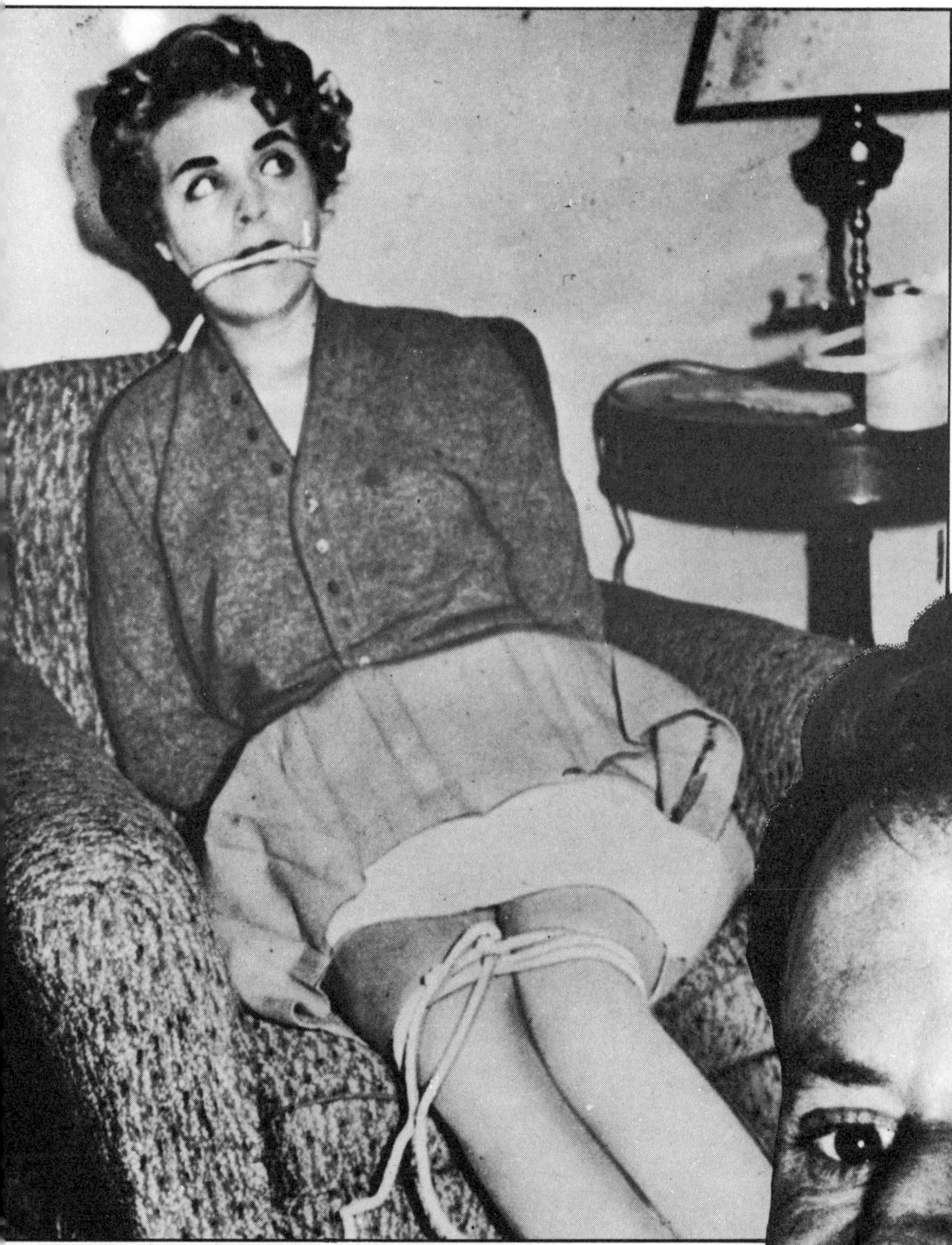

police called at the house, but in an up-stairs room the police found over 200 cigarette butts and other evidence that this was where Connie had been kept and tortured. Many teenagers had been in and out of the house during the period Connie was there; one of them testified to having heard DiMarzo's 3-year-old daughter saying: "You beat up Connie, and you even killed her." DiMarzo had been seen leaving the house with a four-foot-long carpet bag, sagging at both ends, which he had put into his car. That was the last the DiMarzo family saw of Connie.

DiMarzo was already being held on a $15,000 bond on a rape charge; he was later sentenced to life imprisonment for the first degree murder of Constance Corcione. But the mystery still remains: *why* did the girl stay with a man who tortured and beat her, even if she was a

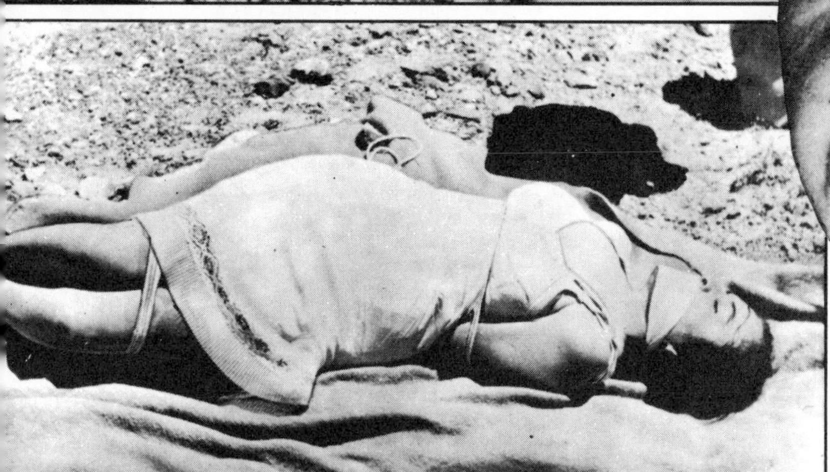

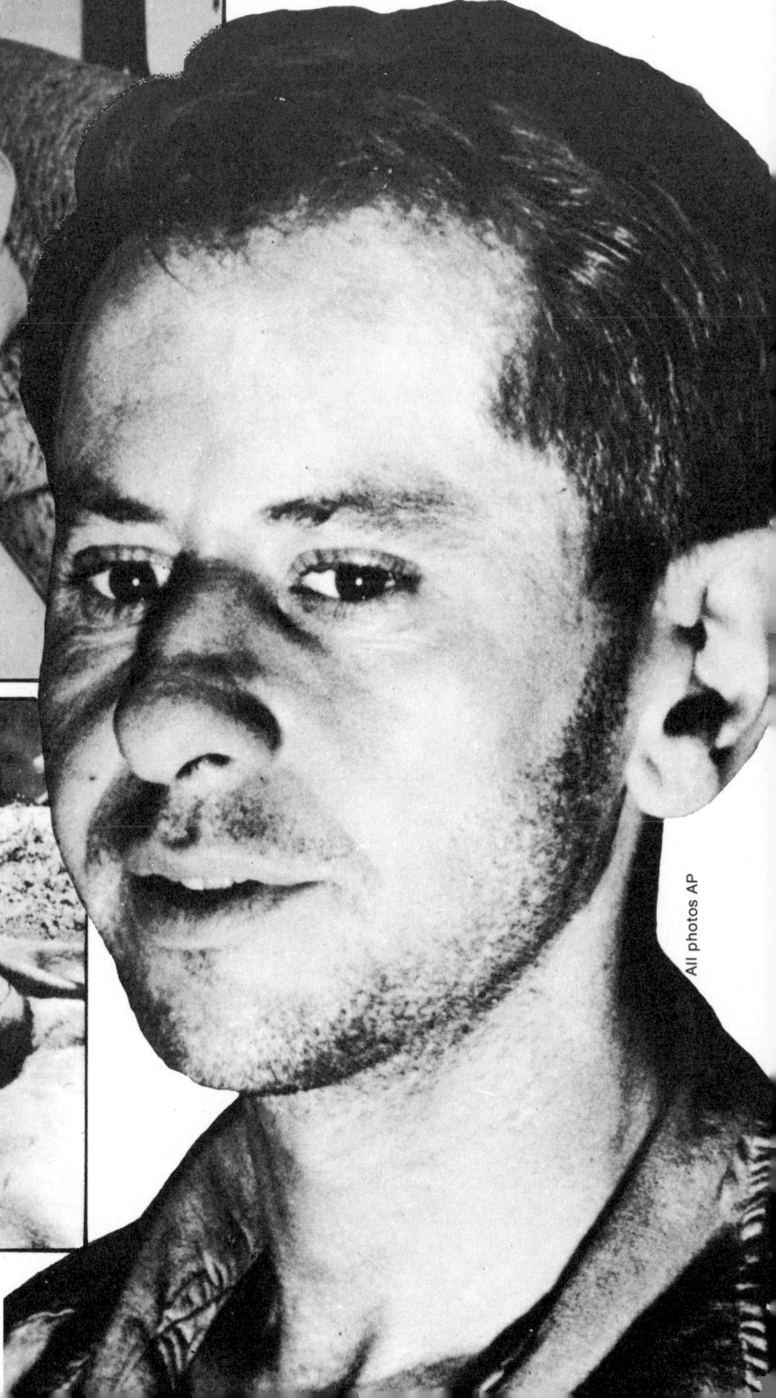

All photos AP

masochist? She can scarcely have enjoyed having her arm broken, and her lip cut off. This victim undoubtedly "collaborated" with her killer.

In June 1972 a pretty Red Indian girl was standing on a pavement in Phoenix, Arizona, looking for a taxi, when a man in his mid-fifties suddenly grabbed her and forced her into his car. After stunning her with a blow, the man, LeRoy Satchel, drove her to his trailer outside the town. There he gagged and tied her, then cut off her clothes with a pair of scissors. When she fought, he bit her, drawing blood.

Rape and torture

When she woke up, her ankles were chained, and the chain ran over a pulley in the ceiling. For three days the girl remained Satchel's prisoner; between periods of rape and torture she was left upside down, suspended over the bed. A neighbour became suspicious, or may even have seen the suspended body through a window; the police were notified, and called at the trailer.

At first Satchel tried to bluster, but the police soon had him under arrest, and the girl freed. He was found guilty of rape and kidnapping, and sentenced to over 200 years in prison. It was revealed that he had served an eight-year sentence for the "manslaughter" of another Indian woman, who had been treated in a similar manner, and that, in 1971, he was suspected of the murder of another Indian woman whose body was found buried near his trailer; however, lack of evidence had led to his release.

It would seem that the Indian girl who escaped was *not* the "victim" type—she might well have died eventually

if the police had not arrived. The three days of torture and ill-treatment would have killed most girls; she had courage, and she lived.

A final illustration of the difference between the victim and non-victim can be seen in the case of the rapist Harvey Glatman. Glatman was a 30-year-old TV repairman of Los Angeles; he was also an enthusiastic amateur photographer. On August 1, 1957, a pretty 19-year-old model, Judy Ann Dull, left her apartment in West Hollywood, hired by a slightly built, jug-eared young man who called himself Johnny Glynn and who had told her that he had a "job" that would only take a couple of hours.

"Glynn" took Judy Dull to his room in Melrose Avenue, Hollywood. She stripped naked and he took two photographs. Then he produced a gun and raped her twice. She promised never to tell anyone and begged him to let her go. "Glynn"—or Glatman—made her dress, and took several "bondage" pictures of her with a gag in her mouth, her hands tied and her dress pushed up. Late that night he drove her out to the desert north of Indio, took more flashlight photographs, then strangled her with a rope and buried her in a makeshift grave.

On March 8, 1957, a 24-year-old divorcee, Shirley Bridgeford, went out on a "blind date" with a man she had met through a lonely hearts club. The man was Glatman; he drove her to the desert near San Diego, raped her, took photographs of her tied up and crying, raped her several times more, then strangled her and left the body covered with brushwood.

On July 23 Glatman called on a 23-year-old Latin girl, Ruth Mercado, another model. He forced his way into her apartment in the Wilshire district of Los Angeles, tied her up, raped her several times and took photographs, then drove her out to the desert near San Diego. He took food and drink along, and spent most of the next day raping the girl and taking

photographs of her. Ruth Mercado was altogether less the victim type than Judy Ann Dull or Shirley Bridgeford; when she begged Glatman to let her go, to feed her pet parrot, he was strongly tempted to. "I liked her." But finally he decided she had to die, and killed her on the second night.

On October 27 Glatman picked up another model, Lorraine Vigil, a 27-year-old Latin girl, and asked her to come to his apartment to be photographed. She didn't like the look of him, and suggested taking a chaperone, but he dissuaded her. He drove fast out to Santa Ana, turned down a dark side road, then produced a gun. When he tried to tie her, she screamed and struggled. The gun went off, burning her thigh, and Glatman looked dazed, saying: "I've shot you." Still struggling, they rolled out of the car. And at this moment a police motorcycle arrived; Harvey Glatman was soon in custody. He admitted the killing of the three girls and on September 18, 1959, was executed in the gas chamber. "I only want to die," he had written to the appeal judge.

The victim type

Even the photographs of Glatman's four victims show clearly that Judy Dull and Shirley Bridgeford were "victim" types, that Ruth Mercado was altogether less of a victim, while Lorraine Vigil was emphatically not the victim type. It is true that this *could* be a matter of chance, due to circumstances, or perhaps to the camera, but, comparing the photograph of Judy Dull with that of Ruth Mercado, it is difficult to believe.

What emerges then, is the interesting suggestion that to be a "victim" is an attitude of mind, and that the same is true of being a non-victim. (In the celebrated dictum of the British crime writer, F. Tennyson Jesse, women can be put into two clear categories: those who will end by being dismembered and left in a trunk at some baggage office—and those who won't.) In a miserable person, the "inner pressure" is low; in a happy person, it is high. And low pressure induces accident proneness as certainly as driving on a flat tyre induces punctures.

Eckermann once remarked to the poet Goethe: "You were born with a silver spoon in your mouth. But supposing you hadn't been born lucky?" Goethe replied contemptuously: "Do you suppose I would be such a fool as to be born unlucky?" Is it possible that Goethe, with his poet's insight, had glimpsed a truth that is now beginning to reveal itself to the modern criminologist?

SHROUDED BONES were all that remained of the women Glatman raped and strangled, as the police found when they uncovered the shallow graves.

THE BLACK DAHLIA

From the top of her raven-tressed head to the tip of her black patent shoes, her sombre sexiness was indelibly blazoned on the soul of any man who knew her. Miss Elizabeth Short knew a lot of men. At least one man too many.

ON the chill, blustery morning of January 15, 1947, a sobbing, hysterical woman frantically flagged down a passing police patrol car in a suburb of Los Angeles, California, and screeched out an incoherent stream of words. When the patrol car crew had managed to calm her a little she pointed with shaking fingers to a nearby, garbage-strewn vacant lot. The police car leapt forward, turned on to the lot, and there the officers immediately understood the woman's behaviour.

What she had seen, and what the policemen now saw for themselves, were the nude halves of the corpse of a young woman. The body had been crudely cut in two at the waist, and each half tied with ropes. Deep into one thigh the killer had carved the initials "BD".

It was a sickening sight, but the repulsion which the hardened police officers felt was deepened when pathologists examined the body in detail and found that it had been revoltingly mutilated. What was even more hideous was the fact that most of the injuries had been

A SICKENING SIGHT met the horrified gaze of the police: Elizabeth Short's hideously mutilated body. Her injuries had obviously been inflicted while she was still alive. Her mother (below) had often been unable to cope with her young family. . . .

inflicted before death – probably while the victim was suspended, head down, by ropes or wires. She might, indeed, have been still living when her murderer began the incisions to sever her body.

It was clear that the girl had not been long dead when the passing woman came across the dismembered corpse. The immediate theory was that she had been killed somewhere nearby, and the remains tipped on to the lot from a car. The police were puzzled by the incised initials "BD", and there were no obvious clues to identification. But, as a matter of routine, the police took fingerprints from the few fingers that had escaped mutilation. These were sent to the Federal Bureau of Investigation in Washington, D.C., for checking against the millions on file.

The Los Angeles police knew only too well that the print check was an outside chance. To their satisfaction, a message came back from the F.B.I. within hours stating that the prints matched those on file for 22-year-old Elizabeth Short, born in the small town of Medford, Massachusetts, who had a police record as a juvenile delinquent.

Her mother, Mrs. Phoebe Short – who was separated from her husband – was then traced. She had the task of trying to identify the body. So thoroughly had the killer carried out his work that she was

All photos UPI

La Times

unable positively to say that what she looked upon had once been her daughter. But she *was* able to produce a letter which Elizabeth had written to her a few weeks before from San Diego. Detectives went immediately to the address and learnt that Elizabeth Short had left there six days before the discovery of her body. Since she had taken no luggage with her, it seemed as though she had intended to return, and had gone to Los Angeles for no more than a brief visit.

Slowly the police built up a picture of Elizabeth Short, her life and her background. One fact was beyond any doubt and dominated all others: she had been tall, graceful, and exceedingly beautiful, with milk-white skin and a mass of raven hair. She was the kind of girl upon whom all men's eyes focused when she walked into a room; if ever any girl was instantly desirable, that girl was Elizabeth.

Great Depression

However, there was little of beauty in her background. She had grown up in an unhappy home and was only six when, in 1931, her parents separated and her father moved to California. He took one child of the family with him, and left his wife to look after Elizabeth and their other three children.

It was the period of the Great Depression, and Phoebe Short often found herself unequal to both making a living and bringing up the youngsters.

Often alone and miserable, without much close contact with her mother, Elizabeth's one main ambition began to grow into an obsession: the moment she was old enough she would leave home

THE TIDE TURNED in Elizabeth Short's life when she met Army Air Force Major Matt M. Gordon Jr. (above). But he was killed in action . . . and the Black Dahlia was born. Many men felt driven to confess to the spectacular murder; one, Joseph Dumais (bottom far right), was arrested, but released to a psychiatrist.

and make a new and independent life for herself.

The opportunity came in 1942, when she was not yet 17. With the United States engulfed by world war there were plenty of job opportunities for young women. Elizabeth decided to seize one of those opportunities for herself — but as far away and as different from Medford as she could make it. She chose Miami.

It seemed to her that the "sun city" was tailor-made for her ambitions. She was already well aware of her physical appeal; there was an air base near Miami, and at week-ends there was no shortage of young servicemen enjoying their brief leaves on the Florida beaches.

The only information the police could obtain about her life in Miami was sketchy — but it was enough to show that it had finally added to her unhappiness and loneliness. She had taken a job as a waitress. For a time it seemed that she had found her hoped-for young lover. But the romance languished when the man went off to the war. Then, while she worked and counted the days to his return, he died on a distant battlefield.

It was a blow from which Elizabeth Short did not recover. She took to drink, and she took to men — any men. She became so promiscuous that word of her

readiness to go to bed with anyone who would buy her drinks and a meal swiftly spread around the Miami bars.

Eventually, almost inevitably, the police caught up with her, and, found drinking with soldiers in a café, she was arrested as a juvenile delinquent. The authorities decided that, since she was in need of care and protection, she should be sent home to her mother. They gave her a rail ticket to Medford and a small amount of subsistence money and put her on a train.

She stayed aboard the train as far as Santa Barbara, and there she got off and found herself another job as a waitress. In the distraction of war no one had checked to see if she had reached home and the custody of her mother, and Elizabeth stayed in Santa Barbara until 1944. But once more, as though she were singled out to be one of nature's chosen victims, the fates were unmerciful to her.

Having got over her first sad love affair, she formed an attachment for an Army Air Force major. It seemed like the turning of the disastrous tide of her life, and, as though to confirm her own good intentions, she returned, in 1944, to her mother in Medford, to await the major's homecoming from the Far East and the marriage which was to follow.

Home was no happier than it had been in the past, but this time, at least, she could look forward to settling down to a new life with a husband to whom she could devote herself. On the morning of August 22, 1946, when it seemed so certain that her major would soon be back from the war, the front-door bell rang and Elizabeth answered it. A taciturn postal messenger handed her a telegram addressed to herself. Excitedly she tore it open. The message inside was from the mother of the major. Cryptically, it said: "Have received notification from War Department my son, Matt, killed in air crash."

Zombie-like trance

In a zombie-like trance, Elizabeth screwed the telegram into a tight-knit ball of paper, tossed it aside and went straight to the nearest bar. There she drank until her lovely grey-green eyes were cloudy with alcohol and her tall, elegant frame sagged over the edge of the bar. The barman became embarrassed by her tipsy monologue in which she declared: "Some people have a hex on them, y'know what I mean? Some people can't never get the breaks, and nuthin' they can do will give 'em the breaks. Y'listenin' me, now? Why'd things happen to me, this way?"

The next day she decided that there was nothing to keep her in Medford any longer, and she set out for California, this time to the place for which her

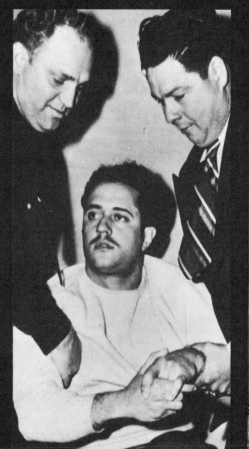

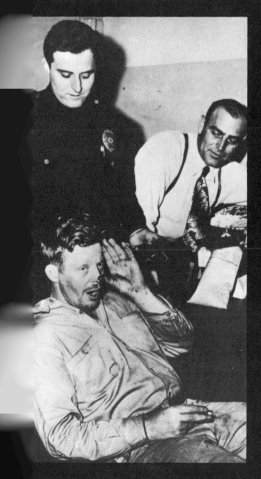

All photos UPI

poise and stunning looks seemed to be so perfectly fitted: Hollywood. The major studios had not yet been overtaken by the TV revolution, and the feeling in the movie capital was that business would be as it always had been, booming. Every day there were calls for "extras", and Elizabeth Short joined the casting lines successfully. For her there was regular and reasonably well-paid work.

She had heard that there were producers and casting directors who were prepared to give a photogenic girl a chance in pictures, for "a consideration". Elizabeth was only too ready to oblige, especially when she was sufficiently anaesthetized with liquor, and she devoted her spare time to going to bed with almost all men who invited her, even though most had no more than tenuous associations with the studios.

Black stockings

She had learned that in Hollywood it was as well to establish some kind of particular identity. Her method was to match her raven hair by dressing totally in black: black sheath dresses, black stockings and underwear, black shoes, even a jet black ring. In its own strange way the ploy worked, and someone named her the "Black Dahlia". The title stuck, she used it herself, and few men who passed in and out of her life were unaware of it.

She took, and discarded, lovers the way most women accept and discard clothing fashions. Some of them she lived with for brief periods. With one man she formed something more than a passing attachment, for in the few effects found after her death was a note addressed to her which read: "I might be gone before you arrive. You say in your letter that you want us to be good friends. But from your wire you seemed to want more than that. Are you really sure what you want? Why not pause and consider just what your

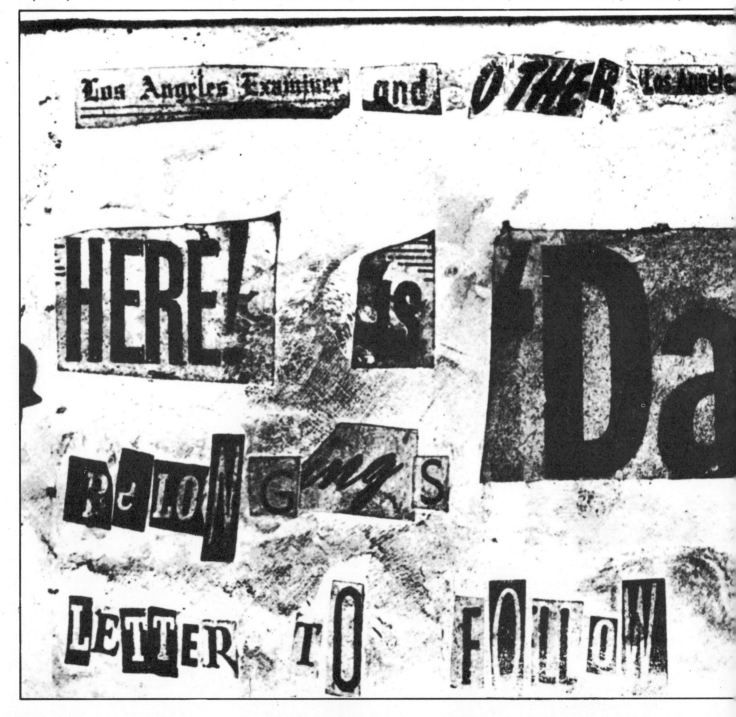

coming out here would amount to? You've got to be more practical these days."

No one would ever discover where "out here" was, and certainly one thing that the Black Dahlia seemed incapable of achieving was practical behaviour. In any case, as the Hollywood movie empire declined into an era of uncertainty it was clear that stardom was not waiting around the corner for Elizabeth Short, and, no longer earning anything like a regular income, she drifted south to San Diego and resumed her career as a waitress.

Her drinking continued unabated, and men pursued her as readily as ever. One man with whom she established a brief liaison was tall and red-haired and reported as having been seen with the Black Dahlia in a San Diego bus station a few days before her dismembered body was discovered. The man was traced by the police and admitted that he had been with the girl. He declared that he went on a drunken binge with her, took her afterwards to a motel and then drove her to the Biltmore Hotel in Los Angeles.

"She said she was going to meet her sister at the hotel," the man told detectives. "I left her there. That was the last time I saw her, and I have no idea what happened to her afterwards or where she went." The police accepted his story; in any case, the man was able to prove that, at the time when the Black Dahlia must have been murdered, he and his wife were visiting friends.

For the authorities the trail set by Elizabeth Short ended at the front entrance to the Biltmore Hotel. She had become lost in the city sprawl; somewhere she met the man who was to so brutally slay her. Her clothing had totally disappeared, and extensive searches — including examinations of drains and sewers — failed to produce any garment that could be traced to her.

From the moment that the news of the severed corpse discovery appeared in the newspapers the police were overwhelmed by supposed "confessions" and reports of suspects. The anxiety of so many men to "confess" to such a deed said a great deal about individual mental states, but told the police nothing that was relevant to their inquiries. One man, at least, had an unusual motive for presenting himself as the killer. His wife, he said, had deserted him. He hoped that if he could make himself notorious, and have his picture in the papers, she might return.

Hysterical cases

One person sent the police a message, composed of pasted-up letters cut from a magazine, offering to meet them and provide them with information. He signed himself "Black Dahlia Avenger". Detectives waited at the proposed rendezvous but no one turned up. One woman walked into a police station and announced: "The Black Dahlia stole my man, so I killed her and cut her up."

Tired-eyed but patient officers chatted to the eager woman, and discreetly mentioned one or two facts about the murdered girl's corpse that could only have been known to the killer. From the woman's response, it was clear that she was no more than another hysterical case.

In the midst of such confessions there was one curious and baffling event. A Los Angeles newspaper received a note which read: "Here are Dahlia's belongings. Letter will follow." Enclosed with the note were Elizabeth Short's birth certificate, address book, and social security card. No letter followed and fingerprints, clearly visible on the envelope and note, were forwarded to the F.B.I. — but they matched none on file. Detectives spent long days searching out men named in the address book, but none of the interviews produced a positive murder lead.

Calls promising information were made to the Los Angeles police from all parts of the United States, and some of the

CURIOUS AND BAFFLING, this note (and the package with it) was never followed up. The killer had made a gesture and turned away — perhaps to new victims.

callers were asked to appear in person. But officers discovered nothing of value.

One development, however, looked promising. U.S. army investigators arrested a 29-year-old corporal, just back from 42 days' leave, who had talked loudly and convincingly about having known the Black Dahlia, and having been with her a few days before her body was found. There were bloodstains on his clothing and, in his locker, newspaper clippings about the murder. He seemed to possess a lot of circumstantial evidence about some of the injuries to the body, and he insisted: "When I get drunk I get rough with women." However, on closer examination, he, too, was found to be an unbalanced personality and recommended for psychiatric treatment.

The gory facts

Despite all the time and energy that the police spent on such confessions, they were helped by one important factor in the case: some of the mutilations of the body were so foul that no newspaper had written about them in any detail. This served in eliminating false confessions, since it was clear that none of the would-be "murderers" knew the full, gory facts.

As a variation on the theme of most of the confessions, one man later came forward and announced that, although he

THE MYSTERY surrounding her death has helped keep alive the memory of the Black Dahlia: this beautiful young victim who seemed so destined for suffering.

had not murdered the girl, he *had* helped to dismember her body. The murderer, he said, was a friend of his. He did not, or could not, identify him—and, as in other offers of "information", his statements did not conform to the facts known only to the police.

Almost certainly someone, somewhere in Los Angeles, knew the identity of the killer. The police considered it hardly credible that he could have committed such an atrocious crime without leaving some clues behind. The killing and mutilation might have taken place in a deserted warehouse, or some remote building—and yet there was no evidence of the girl being seen with a man just before her death. It seemed unlikely that she might have gone to meet her end, in a place conveniently designed for it, without even being observed by a passer by.

In fact two bartenders reported having served her with drinks, two or three days before her death, when she was in the company of a woman. These reports gave rise to rumours that she had been murdered by a lesbian acquaintance. But there was neither direct evidence nor

even remote indications to suggest that she was homosexual.

Then there were those who claimed that the murder was the work of a madman driven by motives similar to those of Jack the Ripper—the unidentified nineteenth-century killer who disposed of prostitutes in the East End of London. Perhaps, they argued, the Black Dahlia murder was a case of a man wishing to rid the world of a woman of easy virtue.

The bald fact was that the killer was never found, and his motives, therefore, remain undisclosed. For some time the police inquiries continued and—for a long time after—the "confessions" flowed in.

These—and the nickname she was given—have kept alive the memory of the young victim who seemed so destined for suffering. The most important is that her murderer knew her, and had probably been out with her several times before.

From the address book, sent anonymously to the local newspaper, one page was missing. It had apparently been removed because it contained the name and address of the Black Dahlia's "friend", who turned out to be her murderer. Was the person who posted that book to the newspaper the killer himself? The odds are that it was. And that, having made his "gesture", he turned his attention to other women—and perhaps other victims.

LETHAL LAWYERS

Perhaps the most unlikely killers of all are lawyers. The risks involved are too great, as they well know. Nevertheless, criminal history shows up some sinister exceptions to the rule.

Earl Rogers (left) a compulsive gambler and brilliant criminal lawyer. He saw clearly into the twists of the criminal mind.

IT is an amusing paradox that many of the qualities required by a good lawyer are those that are required by a good criminal: enterprise, coolness, and the courage to take risks. All three are demonstrated in the famous Earl Rogers story of the Gun Trick. Earl Rogers was one of America's greatest—and in some ways most lethal—criminal lawyers. He was a vain man, a bad loser, and a heavy drinker. But he also had the quality of a real-life Perry Mason.

It was on a hot August day around the turn of the century that three men sat around a table in a gambling joint in Catalina Island, California, playing poker. One of them was a professional gambler named Yeager, also known as the Louisville Sport. The other two young men were business partners, Al Boyd and Harry Johnson. They proposed to buy a cigar store together—mostly with Boyd's capital—but the way this game was going, they'd soon have no capital left. Johnson wanted to cut their losses and quit; Boyd, a compulsive gambler, wanted to continue playing, convinced he could win back everything he'd lost. But the point eventually came where he had nothing left but his gold watch.

Suddenly, there was the sound of two shots. Yeager's hat jumped off his head and rolled across the room, and the Louisville Sport slumped across the table. An ace that he had just dealt off the bottom of the pack lay in front of him, stained with the blood that ran from the hole in his forehead. Harry Johnson rushed to the door, holding a gun. "He shot him. My God, he shot him!" he cried, handing the bartender the gun, which was still smoking. Sitting at the table, his partner looked drunk and bewildered.

Two hits

Later, Al Boyd appeared in court, charged with the murder of the Louisville Sport. The chief witness against him was his partner, Harry Johnson. Johnson was young and blond, and he looked honest and reliable. The jury liked him. But Earl Rogers was convinced that Harry Johnson had shot the gambler.

Questioned by his lawyer, McComas, Johnson told the story of the gambling session. Al Boyd had lost everything but his watch. He begged the gambler to advance him $100 on the watch, so that he could continue gambling. Yeager said the watch wasn't worth two bits, and laughed at him. In a rage, Boyd pulled his gun and shot Yeager. Then he threw the gun down. Johnson picked it up and ran to the door . . .

Doublecrossing

Under further examination, Johnson admitted that he had an arrangement with the Louisville Sport. He would get a percentage of his friend's losses as a payment for steering him into the game. This admission worried Earl Rogers. If it was true, it meant that Johnson had no conceivable motive for shooting the gambler. He was going to get his cut anyway. Rogers grilled Johnson as to why he hadn't told about this "arrangement" at the preliminary hearing. Johnson flushed and said he was ashamed of what people would think.

Rogers pointed out to the jury that this

SHEER FOOLISHNESS cost John Barbot his life; Below: St. Christopher's and Nevis Islands and (inset left) Frigate Bay, where the supposed duel took place.

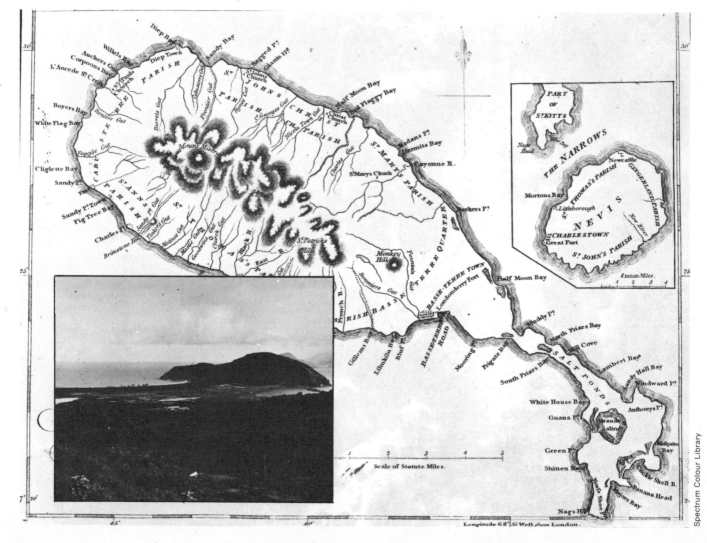

Spectrum Colour Library

Mary Evans

open-faced young man had been double-crossing his closest friend, but he could tell they weren't too indignant about this: California was a rough place, and business was business.

It was clear that Johnson was unworried by the tactics of the defence lawyer. He answered all questions promptly and in a clear voice. Apparently without much hope, Rogers took him slowly and carefully over the events of those last few minutes. The bloodstained table was in court; so were the three chairs at which they had been sitting, and the gambler's hat, with two bullet-holes in it. Rogers made Johnson sit in the chair he had occupied at the time of the murder — to the left of Boyd — and describe again how Boyd had held out his gold watch towards the Louisville Sport and begged for a hundred dollars.

Yell of fear

"And then what happened?" he demanded. Came the answer: "Boyd pulled his gun and shot him, quick as a flash." Rogers pounced. "How could he pull his gun 'quick as a flash' if he already held his watch in his right hand? Show me how he did it." Johnson became nervous and unsure. He repeated his story — how the gambler had fallen, dead, how Boyd had tossed the gun under his chair. "But if Boyd tossed the gun under your chair, he must have had to turn towards you, with the gun in his right hand. For a moment, the gun must have been pointing *at* you. What did you do?" "Nothing," replied Johnson. "I just sat there."

As he heard this statement, Rogers' hand darted into his pocket, and came

out holding a gun. He pointed the weapon straight at Johnson's stomach. With a yell of fear, Johnson jumped backwards, the chair falling over. The court was in uproar; several officers tried to grab Rogers, under the impression that he really intended to shoot the witness. Rogers looked slightly astonished at the commotion. When it died down, he explained smoothly that he was only trying to show the jury that Johnson's story was unlikely. *No* man would sit still as another man swung a gun on him, even for a fraction of a second.

Double-think

The jury took the point, and Johnson was now badly rattled. Rogers continued the cross-examination. "What did you do then? You handed the gun to the bartender? Then what did you do?" "I went to the washroom," said Johnson. Question: "To wash the powder burns off your hands?" Johnson stammered confusedly: "Did I? Did I?" In effect, he had confessed to the murder. At least, that was how the jury saw it. Boyd was found not guilty. Johnson vanished, saving the District Attorney the trouble of charging him with murder.

This was the first time "the gun trick" had ever been used in a court of law; later, Rogers used a number of variations of it. He knew it was a risk — that he might not only lose the case, but face a citation for contempt of court. But such "trivialities" never bothered him. He had the instinct of a gambler, and he enjoyed taking risks.

Rogers possessed another quality in common with the professional crook:

CONTEMPORARY PRINTS of the duel scene tended to include witnesses "of standing". In fact, the only version of what happened came from Barbot himself.

what George "1984" Orwell called "the art of double-think". It can be seen in the case of his defence of a clumsy murderer called Mootry, who had killed a man in a drunken brawl. In a moving speech, Rogers told the jury: "You cannot convict a man like Mootry on the word of a pimp, a prostitute, and a policeman." Mootry was acquitted. As he came up to Rogers, his hand extended, Rogers snapped: "Get away from me, you slimy pimp. You're as guilty as hell." Rogers argued that it was his job to get his client acquitted, whether he believed in his innocence or not. This ability to live by two contrasting kinds of morality can also be found in most professional crooks: the need to convince himself that, although he may be breaking the laws of society, he is not breaking his own moral code. Under the circumstances, it is not surprising that most lawyers who have committed a crime usually manage to persuade themselves of their innocence.

Impetuous type

This is illustrated by the case of John Barbot, whose trial in the year 1753 is described in a rare pamphlet, printed shortly after his execution. John Barbot was a young lawyer, son of a wealthy father, who "sowed his wild oats" soon after qualifying for the Bar, and left his father to clear up an enormous pile of debts. In 1749 his father packed off the crestfallen young man to the island of St.

Christopher (now St. Kitts) in the West Indies. Barbot was a likeable, if impetuous, type. He soon made friends with a man of his own age, Dr. James Webbe, who helped him to find contacts in the town of Basseterre. It was a slow, difficult business; but Barbot enjoyed life in the islands, the warm climate, the Negro slaves, the cheap rum. After three years there, he was established as a professional man with a good practice and a small fortune of about £800.

Mere fraction

In the autumn of 1752 some of Dr. Webbe's creditors distrained for debt. Webbe owned an estate called Bridgwaters, on the island of Nevis; this was seized and offered for sale. Webbe was frantic; he was afraid the estate would be sold for a mere fraction of its value by his creditors. With the help of John Barbot, he tried to get the sale deferred, but it was no good. It came up for sale in November. Webbe hoped it would fetch at least £4500, but not many people *had* that much money. He and Barbot agreed gloomily that it might go for as little as £2000. Then Barbot had an idea. He could raise £800; in land sales, it was customary to pay a third deposit, and the rest within three months. His £800 meant he could bid up to £2400. Then it would be a question of persuading his father in England to let him have the remainder of the cash.

Angry words

The next morning, he and Webbe attended the sale. The creditors were being represented by a solicitor called Matthew Mills, an old inhabitant of the island, who was universally liked. Barbot and his client immediately encountered a setback. The conditions of the sale were read aloud: one third of the money on deposit, and the remainder to be paid within a month. If it wasn't paid, the deposit was to be forfeit. This was bad news; it would take at least a month for a letter to reach England. Barbot stood up and indignantly objected; the conditions were unreasonable and illegal. There were some angry words, and Matthew Mills accused him of trying to waste time, and of "boy's play". Barbot roared indignantly that he expected to be treated "like a gentleman", and Mills said he considered that he had done so.

Then the bidding began. The sum went up to just over £2000. Next, to the general amazement, John Barbot joined in, and offered £2200. Everyone in the room knew he didn't possess that kind of money. There were more heated words, but it was finally agreed that Barbot could have the estate if he paid the deposit and signed the contract.

Barbot was so upset that his hand shook when he tried to write out an undertaking to pay the remainder within a month. He asked the marshal's attorney, Cottle, to write it out for him. When the attorney handed over the paper, Barbot could hardly believe his good luck. Either by accident or design, Cottle had made the bill payable within *three* months. However, just as he was about to sign, Matthew Mills looked over his shoulder, and indignantly pointed out that he was being given too much time to pay. More heated words followed, and Mills

POISONER OR PLAYBOY? Greenwood, pictured here with his second wife, had a keen eye for the ladies. But that did not make him a calculating criminal . . .

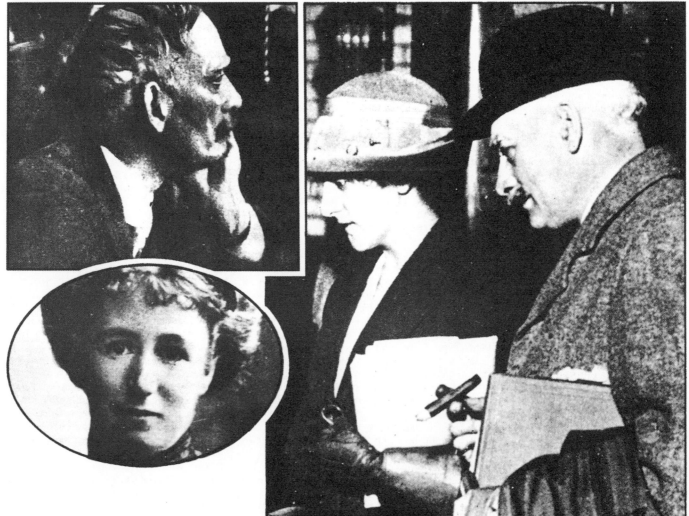

Llanelli Public Library. Topix/Quartet

A FREE MAN . . . Greenwood (above) is released after being found not guilty. Left (top to bottom): his daughter Irene, Marshall Hall, and the family doctor . . .

called him an impertinent fellow. Barbot lost the argument, and the contract was changed again.

Outside, in a fury, Barbot went up to Mills and asked him what he meant' by being so rude. Mills, although usually known as a peaceable man, was still angry. He told Barbot that if he wanted "satisfaction", he knew where to find him. Duelling was forbidden, but the law was not strictly observed. If two men intended to fight, they kept the duel a secret, so that if one of them was left dead the other had a chance of escaping the law.

Rendezvous

Barbot brooded on his wrongs. It looked as if he was going to lose all the money he had managed to save. He decided to take up the offer of "satisfaction". He wrote to Mills, asking for an opportunity to "rendezvous with pistols". After some discussion, they agreed to meet on a beach at Frigate's Bay, St. Christopher, early one Sunday morning. By way of providing himself with an alibi, Barbot stayed with Dr. Webbe on the island of Nevis that weekend. This meant that he had to hire a canoe and some Negro rowers to take him across to St. Kitts. He left the doctor's house soon after midnight on November 26, 1752. A rainstorm soaked him to the skin, but he found his way to the beach, located the canoe, and was rowed across to Frigate's Bay. Mills rode up, and they saluted one another.

For what happened next we have to take the word of John Barbot. He claimed they placed themselves on either side of the road, raised their pistols, and then, at a signal, fired. At least, Barbot fired. Mills groaned: "You have killed me," and sank down to the ground. He died

within a few minutes. By that time, Barbot was out at sea again, and Mills's Negro boy had run to the nearest house to bring someone to his master. The canoe was seen by a passing boat—the occupants of which recognized Barbot—and he was also spotted as he stepped ashore on the island of Nevis. Later that same day he was arrested.

It was at this stage that Barbot, quite incomprehensibly, insisted that he knew nothing of the death of Matthew Mills. He knew that Negroes could not be called on to give evidence in court. Therefore, all the evidence against him was circumstantial. A week before the duel he had been heard to say that either he or someone else would soon be dead. The day before the duel he had been practising shooting pistols at a barrel in Dr. Webbe's garden. Various people had seen him—from a distance—after the death of Mills. But all this did not *prove* he was the man who killed him . . . or so Barbot decided.

Legal skulduggery

It was an utterly gauche defence. Most people present in the court were hard-headed settlers who had achieved a position in the community through the puritan ethic of work and commonsense. They *knew* Barbot was guilty, and if he had pleaded that Mills was killed in a fair fight, there might have been at least a 50 per cent chance they would have acquitted him. But they couldn't countenance this legal skulduggery and talk about "circumstantial evidence".

Barbot's defence exposed him to

Llanelly Public Library. John Frost Collection

another danger. The prosecution called a doctor who alleged that the bullet wound —in Mills's right side—proved that Mills was not in "a posture of defence" when he received it. The prosecution also said that Mills's pistols were not ready to fire. In other words, they were suggesting that Barbot shot him without even waiting for him to prime his pistols. That would be coldblooded murder. Barbot should have countered this. He could at least have pointed out that a wound in a man's right side *is* consistent with a "posture of defence"—if Mills had his own pistol held out at arm's length, with his right side turned towards Barbot.

Moving speech

Instead Barbot called various witnesses to try to prove that he was not the man who had been seen leaving Frigate's Bay. The jury would not accept this, found him guilty, and the judge sentenced him to death. Now, when it was too late, the lawyer decided to tell the whole truth. He made a long statement in which he told the story of the quarrel and the duel. But it made no difference. He was executed at Basseterre on January 20, 1752,

after delivering a moving speech of repentance on the gallows. He confessed that it was his hot temper that had brought him to his "sad predicament". But he was wrong. It was his lawyer's capacity for "double-think" which had lethally backfired on him.

England has had only two notable murder cases involving members of the legal profession. One was of Major Herbert Armstrong—the other, which took place a year earlier, in 1920, was of the lawyer Harold Greenwood, and it ended in his acquittal. Greenwood was a Yorkshireman, who came to Kidwelly, in Carmarthenshire, Wales, in 1898. He was a bluff, cheerful man, but the local Welsh didn't like him much. There were rumours that, for a married man, he was too interested in the opposite sex. But his wife, Mabel, was well-liked in the area.

Beautiful pink

In her forties, Mrs. Greenwood began to suffer from fainting attacks. The doctor diagnosed a weak heart, complicated by the usual emotional upheavals of "change of life". However, Mabel Greenwood continued to attend various

local functions, women's meetings, and so on. During the second week in June 1919 many people thought she looked pale and ill. On the evening of Saturday, June 14, a friend thought she looked "a beautiful pink"—an unusual colour for the usually pale Mrs. Greenwood.

Bilious attack

After lunch the following day, Mrs. Greenwood began suffering from diarrhoea. The doctor sent her a bismuth medicine for stomach trouble. However, she became worse as the evening went on. A nurse who had been sent for advised Greenwood to fetch the doctor, but he said he was unwilling to wake him. The nurse finally went herself. Mrs. Greenwood died in the agonies of a bilious attack in the early hours of Monday morning. Dr. Griffiths certified that the death was due to heart disease. She was buried in the local church.

The town was immediately full of

A LUCRATIVE PRACTICE . . . Greenwood was a highly successful lawyer, as his luxurious house shows. It was later converted into a Nonconformist chapel.

Llanelly Public Library

rumours; both the nurse and the vicar were suspicious of the circumstances of Mrs. Greenwood's death. And when, four months later, Greenwood married 31-year-old Gladys Jones, daughter of the proprietor of the *Llanelly Mercury,* the police finally decided to take action. When they informed Greenwood that the body of his wife was to be exhumed, he replied cheerfully: "Just the thing." But when he was told that the inquest proved that Mrs. Greenwood had died of arsenic poisoning, his only comment was: "Oh dear!"

Contradictory evidence

He was brought to trial in June 1920, defended by Marshall Hall. The prosecution alleged that he had put arsenic weed killer into the Burgundy which his wife had drunk with the Sunday lunch. From the beginning, the evidence was contradictory. The housekeeper said that no one else had touched the wine, but Greenwood's daughter Irene said she had drunk it at both lunch and supper. The parlourmaid stated that Greenwood had spent half-an-hour before lunch alone in the china pantry; Irene Greenwood testified that her father was outside cleaning the car at this time.

The defence suggested that *if* Mrs. Greenwood had died of arsenic poisoning, it was possible that Dr. Griffiths had put it in the medicine in mistake for bismuth. Another doctor gave evidence that the amount of arsenic found in the body—a quarter of a grain—was not enough to cause death; people can have as much as two and a.half grains in the body without ill effect. He thought that the doctor's tablets had contained too much morphia, and that this had killed her. The doctor, who earlier had agreed that the tablets contained morphia, now insisted they had contained opium.

In all the confusion, it was clear that Greenwood could not be found guilty. The jury's verdict was that, while they were satisfied that Mabel Greenwood had absorbed a dose of arsenic just before her death, it was by no means certain that it had been the *cause* of death.

Unmerited publicity

The day after his acquittal Greenwood gave a lunch for the reporters who had covered the trial, and joked about the absence of Burgundy from the table. But

TENSE MOMENTS in court . . . Greenwood is cross-examined about his actions on the day of the supposed murder. He stood up well to the arduous legal barrage.

public opinion still accused him of administering small doses of poison to his wife. His practice declined, and he died eight years later, living in a Herefordshire village under the name of Pilkington, his health completely broken. Whether or not he murdered his wife, there can be no doubt that the gossiping tongues of Kidwelly killed Harold Greenwood.

The fact is that, among the professions, lawyers are among the least likely to turn killer—and that when they do their crimes receive an almost unmerited amount of publicity and criticism. Perhaps they know the ins and outs of the law too well to commit murder. For every murderer who "gets away with it", there are dozens who don't, and who are either imprisoned for life or executed. As Charles Dickens once said, "The law is an ass"—but not when it comes to protecting the lives, freedom, and reputations of those who make their income from it.

A MANIA FOR KILLING WEEDS

ON New Year's Eve 1921, three police officers entered the offices of Major Herbert Rowse Armstrong, lawyer and leading citizen in the small Welsh market town of Hay, Breconshire. Small, dapper, and bespectacled, the Major rose from his desk to greet his visitors. They took a statement and told him that he was under arrest on a charge of attempted murder.

The moment of truth had arrived for Herbert Rowse Armstrong as, shocked and unsuspecting, he protested his innocence. But his surprise was nothing to that of the townspeople who received news of his arrest with open-mouthed disbelief. The parlours and public bars buzzed with rumours and gossip, and the hotels filled with press reporters.

The Major had been prominent in local affairs since coming to Hay in 1906. He was clerk to the local magistrates, was a churchwarden, and was keenly interested in the Territorial Army. His insistence on being addressed as "Major" and his passion for wearing an army officer's overcoat were regarded by some as eccentric. But his high social position was undeniable, and he lived in fine style in a large house with servants, at Cusop, a mile outside the town.

A mouse at home

Although he was much respected, everyone knew that Major Armstrong was a mouse in his own home. His wife, Katharine, wore the trousers. She subjected her husband to constant nagging and humiliation. He was not allowed to smoke or drink and was often bullied in front of the servants: "If the master is late, how can you expect the staff to behave?" she railed at him on one occasion. On another she called him away from a tennis match, proclaiming that it was his bath night.

Katharine Armstrong was a cranky hypochondriac, yet, despite all the henpecking, her husband always treated her attentively and with courtesy. The Major

MILITARY PRECISION characterized the Major's movements. The murder of his wife was so skilful that no one ever suspected that he had been responsible.

Robin Odell

258

found comfort in various activities outside the home, and one of these was gardening. Apart from the usual gardening jobs, he had a mania for weed killing; he spent a lot of time treating the dandelions around his house with arsenic from the local chemist.

In July 1920, Katharine—who was usually unwell for one reason or another and treated herself with a host of proprietary medicines—became really ill. She complained of heart pains and experienced delusions. By August, her condition had deteriorated badly, and the family doctor was making frequent visits. Dr. Tom Hincks was unable to prevent a continuing decline in her health, and before the end of the month she was certified and sent to an asylum.

Katharine improved at the asylum, and after several months the Major brought her home. But by the middle of February 1921 she was again very ill, and within a few days died an agonized wasting death. Major Armstrong noted his bereavement in his diary: February 22 — K died".

New zest for life

Dr. Hincks made out a death certificate to natural causes, and Katharine Armstrong was laid to rest in Cusop churchyard. The card on her husband's wreath bore the words, "From Herbert and the Chicks." The Major's grief was apparent, and the people of Hay were moved by the manner in which he read the lesson in church on the Sunday after the funeral.

A short while later, the Major, following his doctor's advice, went on holiday. He travelled to Italy and Malta, where the change of climate seemed to dispel his sorrow. His diary suggests that he had quite a lively time. Whereas previous diary entries had been on such riveting matters as when he weeded the rosebeds and what clothes he sent to the laundry, he now noted engagements with a succession of women. One intriguing entry read, "April 15 — Billeted with Miss B."

The Major evidently had a new zest for life, and when he returned home he smoked and drank openly. He took up dancing lessons, attended the local dances, and started to gain a reputation as a ladies' man.

Major Armstrong was enjoying his new-found freedom, but there was one cloud on the horizon. While he had been furthering his image as an officer and a gentleman, his rival lawyer across the street, Oswald Martin, had been steadily building a successful legal practice. This had been done largely at Armstrong's expense, and the Major was niggled. Although the two men maintained a polite professional relationship, there were mounting undercurrents.

This relationship became further strained in September 1921 over a property deal. Martin was acting for the purchasers, and Armstrong for the vendor, in what should have been a straightforward conveyance. But for reasons which were not clear at the time, Armstrong would not complete the deal and kept hedging. Eventually Martin became exasperated by the endless delays, told Armstrong that the deal was off, and requested the return of deposits amounting to £500.

The Major's unexpected reaction was to invite Martin to tea at his house. No doubt thinking that this was some sort of peace offering, Martin accepted and

ALWAYS DAPPER and correct, the Major (right) seemed to be a pillar of respectable society. Below: his ill-fated wife and two of the children.

All Robin Odell

drove up to Armstrong's home after work on October 26, 1921. Martin had offered to give his host a lift, but the Major declined. "No, I have something to do at the house, so must go there before you."

The two men took tea, which had been set out for them in the drawing-room by the maids. While they chatted, the Major handed his guest a buttered scone with an apology. "Excuse fingers," he murmured. The meeting was a friendly one, and after about an hour Martin took his leave and returned home.

Poison symptoms

Later that evening Martin was violently ill with stomach pains, vomiting and diarrhoea. His wife called Dr. Hincks, who diagnosed a bilious attack. One of the sick man's visitors was his father-in-law John Davies, who was also the local chemist. Davies was a shrewd man who knew about poison symptoms, and he saw more than just biliousness in his son-in-law's illness. He also recalled having sold arsenic on numerous occasions to Major Armstrong, who said he wanted it for killing weeds.

Davies discussed his suspicions with Dr. Hincks, and they agreed to send a sample of Martin's urine for analysis. With this they also sent a box of chocolates which Martin had received anonymously the previous month. His brother's wife had been ill after eating one, with symptoms remarkably like his own.

Martin recovered after a few days and by chance met Armstrong in the street. The Major asked him how he was, and he replied that he was getting better. Then Armstrong said, "Although it may sound queer, you will soon be ill again."

Whilst the outcome of the analysis was awaited, a war of nerves developed with Armstrong constantly telephoning Martin and asking him to tea. Martin was hard put to find adequate excuses, and the strain took a toll of his nerves.

Then came the news that arsenic had been found in both the urine and the chocolates, and events speeded up. Scotland Yard officers arrived in Hay to start enquiries which were conducted discreetly so as not to alert the Major. But the evidence quickly mounted, and

THE BEDROOM (below) was for Mrs. Armstrong's private and exclusive use. The timid Major was not allowed access without Katharine's gracious permission.

the order was given to arrest Armstrong on a charge of attempting to murder Oswald Martin.

By this time the police had become suspicious about Katharine Armstrong's death, and her body was exhumed from its grave on January 2, 1922. The grisly job of opening the coffin was done in a small cottage close to the churchyard.

The roles reversed

Dr. (later Sir) Bernard Spilsbury, the pathologist, came down from London to perform the post-mortem. He commented on the remarkably well-preserved state of the body considering it had been in the ground for nearly a year. Spilsbury returned to London with numerous bottles containing pieces of tissue from the body, which were needed for analysis.

On the same day that his wife's grave was opened, Major Armstrong made his first appearance in the tiny court-room at Hay. The police-court proceedings probably rank as one of the town's greatest events. And the irony of the situation was missed by very few—here was the man who normally sat as an official of the court now being placed in the dock to face justice.

Robin Odell

THIN-LIPPED and already looking like a tough, determined character, Katharine poses for a wedding portrait. Below: the house she shared with her killer husband.

The Major, wearing a regimental tie and his officer's overcoat, remained calm throughout, and at times seemed to be conducting the proceedings. He interrupted the magistrates when they were trying to fix the next hearing: "The court should be fixed at a time to coincide with the train service," he remarked.

Reputation shattered

There was a feeling that the attempted murder charge was merely a prelude to further sensation. Everyone in Hay knew that the Home Office did not order an exhumation without good reason, and the outcome of the post-mortem on Katharine Armstrong was eagerly awaited. They were not disappointed—her body was riddled with arsenic.

The people of Hay could hardly bring themselves to think that their solicitor had poisoned his wife. But Major Armstrong was duly charged with her murder, and the attempted murder of Oswald Martin was relegated to second place.

The Major's once-proud reputation was shattered in the police court, where details of his philanderings and venereal disease were revealed. It emerged that he was being treated for syphilis with injections of an arsenical preparation. He had quizzed the doctor about arsenic, asking what a fatal dose was. The doctor answered, "Two or three grains," to which Armstrong replied, "Would not one be sufficient?"

When he was arrested and searched, various papers were found in Armstrong's pockets. There were some letters and a packet of white powder which turned out to be a lethal dose of arsenic. There was also a scrap of paper written in Armstrong's hand, which recorded the progress of his syphilis. He noted that he first saw a sore on November 23, 1921, so probably contracted the disease while his wife was in the asylum.

One of the highlights of the police-court proceedings was the appearance of a mysterious woman who was referred to as "Madame X". She appeared briefly in court, acknowledging that she had written three love letters found in Armstrong's pocket.

All Robin Odell

"Madame X", whose identity was kept out of the case at the time, was a 50-year-old widow who lived at Bournemouth. Her name was Marion Glassford Gale, and she had first met Armstrong when he was stationed near her home during World War One. They met several times and corresponded. In August 1921, the Major proposed marriage.

Suspicions of second will

Marion was uncertain about saying yes. She had a strong sense of responsibility to her mother and a niece, both of whom she looked after. Her affair with Armstrong was inconclusive. In her letters she grumbled about her miserable life and chastized Armstrong for not taking more interest in her. "Why this heavy silence?" she asked him in one letter, ". . . don't you want to see me?" she questioned in another.

"Your loving Marion", as she signed herself in her letters, was shocked when she heard that Armstrong had been arrested. She told the police that he ". . . was to me everything that a gentleman ought to be".

But Armstrong the gentleman was also sufficiently unscrupulous to forge his wife's will, thereby illegally gaining her money for his own use. Mrs. Armstrong made a will in June 1917. It contained 13 clauses, and the main provisions were for her three children. There were small be-quests to her sister and housekeeper, and an annuity of £50 for her husband, who was one of the four executors.

On the day of his wife's funeral, the Major remarked that his wife had left everything to him in a second will made a few weeks before she was admitted to the asylum. This will, written in Major Armstrong's handwriting and witnessed by two servants, made no provision for the children, and there were no other bequests. Major Armstrong was both the sole beneficiary and executor.

The police were suspicious of the will, and they questioned the two servants who had witnessed the document. It was immediately clear that the witnessing

procedure had been improperly carried out. Police enquiries also brought to light the true state of Major Armstrong's financial and business affairs—they were, as an officer put it, "in one hell of a crooked mess".

Armstrong had been borrowing without permission from one client to lend to another, and was on the verge of insolvency. As a result of this, he coveted his wife's money. The small annuity she had provided for him was totally inadequate—he needed the lot. So he wrote out a new will in his favour, forged his wife's signature on it, and duped the two servants into putting their signatures on a piece of paper whose purpose they did not understand.

Desperate insolvency

This charge was not put to Armstrong at his trial, but he was asked about the circumstances in which he drew up the second will. He said airily, "I think one does things rather more irregularly for one's own family."

The suspected signature on this will was later studied by a document examiner, and compared with the genuine signatures of both Major and Mrs. Armstrong.

THE LOCAL DRUGSTORE (below) was situated in Hay's main street (bottom). It was here that the Major purchased the arsenic for his "weed-killing" activities.

It was clear that Mrs. Armstrong's supposed signature on the second will had far more in common with her husband's signature than with her own.

For many years one of the great mysteries of the Armstrong case has always been the property sale which brought the Major into conflict with Oswald Martin. It has long been thought that this rivalry, allied with a dislike for Martin, constituted sufficient motive. But the bungled murder attempt on Martin contrasted so sharply with the careful way the Major disposed of his wife that it suggests there were other reasons.

Recent research has underlined the fact that Armstrong was involved in a desperate struggle to remain solvent. His affairs were inextricably mixed with a landowner client who owed him £4500. It was for this client that the Major was involved in the property deal which placed him and Martin in confrontation.

Stalling campaign

At the time of Martin's intervention, completion of this deal had already been delayed for more than a year. Pressed to explain the incessant delay, Armstrong would only speak of "difficulties" which he would soon clear away. There were problems about mortgages, and Armstrong was conducting a stalling campaign hoping that they would be overcome.

Successful completion of this deal would gross £4500 and make good the money owed to Armstrong by his client. The Major would be saved from bankruptcy and disgrace. But failure to complete spelled disaster—he would lose both his client and his money. Even the £2278 gained by forging his wife's will would not save him from ruin.

When Oswald Martin was asked by the two farmers involved at the purchasing end of the deal to handle the matter for them, he cared for nothing other than clearing up a mess. He began to hustle Armstrong. Why had the matter been delayed so long? When would completion take place?

The game was up

The Major, as he had done for so long, played for time—hoping that the mortgage difficulties preventing completion would be cleared away. But Martin was not to be put off by vague promises—he wanted action. He fixed a date by which Armstrong must complete, or the deal would be called off.

Armstrong must have had nightmares at the thought of going bankrupt in a small town like Hay. Tongues would wag,

LUCKY ESCAPER Martin strolls in town with his wife. Only Armstrong's desperation and resulting incompetence saved Martin from a painful death . . .

All Robin Odell

fingers would point – his proud reputation would be shattered. He resolved to stay Martin's hand by poisoning him. In the confusion that would follow, he would find a breathing space enabling him to hold on to the deal.

The prospect of poisoning Martin did not worry him. After all, he was experienced in the art, and he alone knew the secret of his wife's demise. But he was so desperate that everything that he did went wrong. He succeeded only in putting Martin in bed for a few days, and his intimidating telephone calls and remarks about "another attack soon" only drew attention to himself.

On the day he was arrested Armstrong had in his pocket a tiny packet of arsenic. No doubt he hoped to lure Martin into a lethal trap. But the game was up, and that packet of arsenic, which he tried to conceal from the police, was as good as his own death warrant.

Major Armstrong murdered his wife because she nagged him unmercifully, and he forged her will to help finance his newly-won freedom. For 10 months this was a "perfect murder". He had almost a year of philandering before his neglect of business matters caught up with him. His only hope of salvation from this situation lay in holding on to an already protracted property deal.

Total ruin

When Oswald Martin appeared on the scene demanding completion, ruination stared Armstrong in the face. His attempt on Martin's life was not an act of pique against a rival, but the action of a desperate man to save his reputation. The road to total ruin was then short and swift.

When he stood in the dock at Hereford Assizes in April 1922, he failed to give a convincing reason for having arsenic on him when arrested. That lethal packet of poison damned him.

He was not without courage at the end.

He conducted himself with dignity and exhibited good manners to all around him. He made gifts to the lawyers who had defended him, and wrote a letter of thanks to another of his legal defenders.

Because of his size, the little Major was given a long drop of eight feet eight inches. Before he faced the hangman's rope, he was visited by the prison governor. "I don't like this hanging business, Armstrong," he said. The Major replied, "Yes, I am sure it must be most unpleasant for you."

Major Herbert Rowse Armstrong met his fate at Gloucester Prison on May 31, 1922 – the only lawyer in Britain ever to face the scaffold.

EXHUMATION . . . Katharine Armstrong's body is carried into Church Cottage after the exhumation from the grave in Hay churchyard (opposite). Dr. Hincks, the local doctor, and Sir Bernard Spilsbury, the pathologist (inset).

All Robin Odell/Quartet

AN OLD MAN'S MONEY

William Marsh Rice was a financial genius who, during his long life, accumulated vast wealth. Whenever a man does that he brings down upon his head the envy and greed of others less successful than himself. So it was that one lawyer carefully plotted the destitution and death of a millionaire.

OCCASIONALLY he licked his lips nervously; the jagged scars on his throat were a constant reminder of how, in his fear, he had tried to kill himself in prison. But his voice was clear and steady as he told the New York court about the night he murdered the benevolent multimillionaire who had befriended him and given him a home. He described how, in September, 1900, he had crept furtively into the bedroom where the old man was sleeping and placed a towel containing a chloroform-soaked sponge over his face. He had then waited in a different part of the house for 30 minutes—long enough for his victim to die of lung congestion.

Not long after his arrest he had tried to lie his way out of any blame and, in his cell at the Tombs, had been so terrified that he had slashed his throat with a penknife. Now he was confidently telling the truth, for he no longer faced the threat of execution.

More evil

Charles F. Jones, 27, from Houston, Texas, had found sanctuary in a new role —as a prosecution witness. He had been given a guarantee of "some immunity"— and subsequent events showed that he had almost certainly been promised his freedom—if he would co-operate with the State. The People's Prosecutor explained to the jury: "If it were not for the fact that many criminals squeal on each other, many crimes would go unpunished."

The prosecutors considered that Jones, although he had actually done the killing, had merely been acting under the domination of a far more evil and dangerous man —a 41-year-old lawyer called Albert T. Patrick. So it was Patrick who had been indicted with the first-degree murder of the financial genius William Marsh Rice.

On March 26, 1902, the trial—which had lasted more than two months—was reaching its climax. The evidence against Patrick, particularly that given by medical experts, was so overwhelming that the jury had little hesitation in finding him guilty. Under New York law this made the death sentence mandatory. Patrick was condemned to die in the electric chair early in May, 1902.

Most people then thought that this was virtually the end of an amazing story of treachery and forgery, of greed and cold-blooded viciousness. But it was only the end of the first act. For Patrick, with all the scheming brilliance of his depraved mind, was still determined to cheat the executioner.

Exceptional flair

The amazing tangle of intrigue which culminated in the murder of 84-year-old William Marsh Rice was described by the Prosecutor, James Osborne, when he opened the trial in January, 1902. He explained to a crowded court how Rice had left his native New England in the early 1830s to seek his fortune in the frontier state of Texas. He was a man with an exceptional flair for making money. He speculated in oil and in land. He opened a chain of stores and hotels. He became a multi-millionaire.

Rice had married twice, but there had been no children. It was a will left by his second wife, Elizabeth, which had precipitated the events which eventually led to his death. Elizabeth Rice had died in 1896. In her will she tried to leave half his money—her share of it, as she considered—to her relatives. She claimed that this was correct, as they were both citizens of Texas—where the law treated man and wife as equal partners over money and property.

Plausible rogue

Rice considered this to be savagely unfair, and although he had spent comparatively little time in New York since 1865, he insisted that the city was his home. New York had no community-property law. He instituted a Federal Court suit against the executor of his wife's will—aiming to have it declared void. For he had very clear ideas about where he wanted the bulk of his money to go. Texas had been so good to him that he wanted the State to have a permanent memorial to him—a corporation which would not seek profits, but which would be dedicated to the advancement of science, literature and art. It was to be called the Rice Institute.

The issue over the will was therefore a straightforward one. If Rice was a citizen of Texas at the time of his wife's death, her relatives got half his money. If he was a citizen of New York, almost the entire estate would eventually go to the Rice Institute. It was this issue which

Associated Press

brought Albert T. Patrick into the story.

Patrick, an impeccably dressed and fine-looking man with a neat ginger beard, shifted uncomfortably on his courtroom seat as Mr. Osborne, the Prosecutor, described his background for the benefit of the jury. Patrick, said Osborne, had been employed by the executor of Elizabeth Rice's will to defend the action being brought by Rice. He was a plausible rogue—a man of great charm who could inspire the confidence of others. But in Texas, where he had initially practised, he had won himself an unsavoury reputation as a sharp operator.

"The man Jones will tell you how Patrick made his acquaintance—and what transpired from there," said Mr. Osborne.

Charles F. Jones avoided looking at Patrick as he went to the witness box. He took the oath and explained how he had become the confidant and only companion of the multi-millionaire. He had been working as a storekeeper in a Texas

PLOTTERS . . . Charles Jones (above) performed the murder but lacked the brains to plan it. The mastermind behind the slaying was Albert Patrick (opposite).

hotel owned by Rice. The old man had chatted to him there and, taking a liking to him, had engaged him as his personal clerk. A year later, in 1897, he and Rice had moved together to New York City, where they shared an apartment in Madison Avenue. In their behaviour they were more like father and son than employer and employee.

"Now let us come to the month of November, 1899," said Mr. Osborne. "Do you recall somebody coming to the apartment?"

Jones nodded towards Patrick. "He did."

"And what did he say to you?"

"Well, he didn't tell me his name, not his real name. He said he was called Smith and that he wanted to see Mr.

Rice about some cotton business."

"And did he see Mr. Rice?"

"No, Mr. Rice was in bed, and I didn't think it was right to disturb him."

Patrick returned to the apartment later—this time admitting his true identity—and told Jones he would make it worth his while to help clinch the business of the will. All Patrick needed was a letter, on Rice's stationery and apparently with Rice's signature, in which Rice admitted he was a citizen of Texas. Patrick offered to pay Jones $500 if he could provide that sort of letter.

Draft will

Jones, whose salary was $55 a month, was interested. He prepared the forged letter, but refused to hand it over to Patrick when Patrick would not give him the money. However, Patrick—with his charm and promises of rich rewards to come—stayed on friendly terms with Jones and soon learned all about Rice's business. Jones let him go through all Rice's private files and papers, and showed him a copy of a will which Rice had made in 1896.

"Was there any discussion between Patrick and yourself about a further will?" asked Mr. Osborne.

"Yes, in the February—or perhaps it was the March—of 1900," said Jones.

Patrick had shown him a draft of a will, arranging the disposal of all Rice's property, which had been drawn up by Patrick. All the friends and relatives who had been named in Rice's 1896 will were to receive bequests—more generous ones, in fact, than Rice had intended. The rest of the estate was to be divided between Patrick and the Rice Institute.

Too close

Patrick then persuaded him to copy the will on Rice's typewriter—putting his own name down as a witness. The 1896 will was not to be destroyed because, as Patrick pointed out, the relatives and friends would then see that they would do better under the later one—and be as eager to sustain it as he was himself. Jones was not named as a beneficiary.

"He told me I was too close to Mr. Rice and that someone might claim the will had been executed under duress," he told the court. "He said I would be well taken care of."

How would they get Rice to sign the forged will? That was a problem they discussed at length. Finally they decided to resort to forgery. But more than one copy of Rice's signature was needed. One went on a general assignment, purported to have been executed by Rice on September 7, 1900, which transferred all his property to Patrick. This document said that there were two conditions—Patrick was to pay Rice an income of $10,000 a year as long as Rice should live. After Rice's death, Patrick was to erect a monument costing not less than $5000 over his grave.

Another signature went on a will dated June 30, 1900—witnessed by two of Patrick's friends—in which Rice purported to leave nine-tenths of his property to Patrick. One more went on an assignment giving Patrick possession of all Rice's stocks, bonds, and other evidence of indebtedness in his safe-deposit boxes at two New York banks. This document also revoked an earlier order permitting Rice's own lawyer access to the boxes.

Meticulous care

Four cheques—the $250,000 total value of which would have exhausted the money Rice had in New York banks—also bore phoney signatures. Then there was a further signature—on a letter, apparently written by Rice to Patrick in the August, directing that his body after death should be cremated.

INCREDIBLE that Patrick, a lawyer of considerable experience, should think he could get away with forging a paper as inexplicably generous as this one . . .

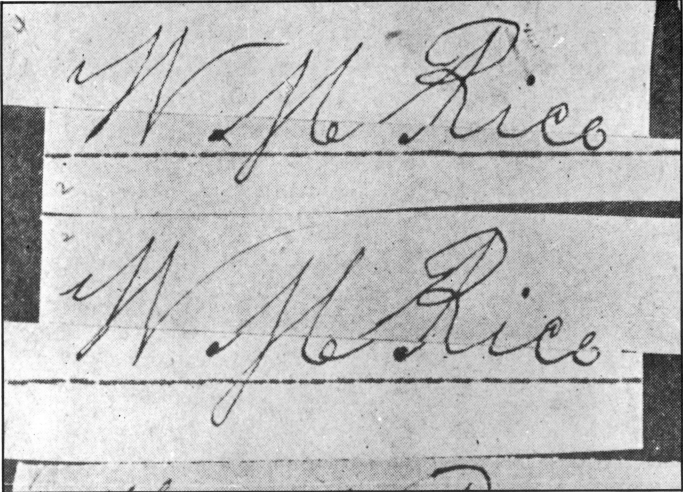

Nigel Morland

ALL ALIKE . . . These are the forged signatures. Genuine ones tend to vary slightly; these are almost identical . . .

All these signatures, traced from genuine ones supplied by Jones, had been drawn with meticulous care. Patrick had even asked for a bottle of the ink used at the Madison Avenue apartment—pointing out that it would never do to use the wrong ink.

Cheques which Rice really had signed were also intercepted by Jones and forged ones for the same amounts were substituted. These forgeries were put through the banks in the normal way and paid. The reason behind this exercise was that Patrick anticipated that, if any of the forgeries putting money into his own pocket were suspected, the "genuine" forged cheques could be produced for comparison.

Agent and friend

But why should it be believed that Rice should wish to lavish so much generosity on a man like Patrick—a man who was employed to fight him over a will he resented so violently?

Again, Patrick had worked out the answers. The official story would be that he had met Rice while trying to settle the business of the Texas will, and had struck up a friendship with the old man. That was why he got Jones to type some 20 letters to Rice's business associates in which Rice apparently referred to Patrick as his lawyer, agent, and friend.

Also, to indicate that he carried on an active correspondence with Rice, he told Jones to send to him, at his office, a series of empty envelopes which had Rice's return address boldly on them. This was the mesh being drawn around the unsuspecting Mr. Rice who was still regarding Jones as his most trusted friend.

Undisguised contempt

There was one more character who, unwittingly, was to play an integral role in the murder—an ancient and doddery doctor called Walter Curry. Patrick, working through Jones, had arranged for Curry to become Rice's personal physician—for, although the doctor was honest and kind, Patrick was confident his eyesight and judgment were blurred enough to make him an unwitting accomplice.

While Jones was giving this evidence, Patrick regarded him through his clip-on nose spectacles with undisguised contempt. But the contempt gave way to anxiety as Prosecutor Osborne led Jones into a conversation which had taken place in August, 1900.

"About that time did you have a discussion with him about the state of health of the deceased?"

Jones hesitated. "Do you mean . . . ?"

"The question is a very simple one, Mr. Jones. Do you, or do you not, recall having any discussion in the early part of August about Mr. Rice's health?"

"Yes, sir, I do."

"Then please tell the court about it."

"Patrick asked me how Mr. Rice's health was, and I said he was better than he had been. Then he said: 'Don't you think Rice is living too long for our interest?'"

Mr. Osborne repeated the words. "'Living too long for our interest.' I see. And what was your reply to that?"

"I said: 'It does seem that way.'"

"And was any suggestion made about how this position might be . . . er . . . corrected?"

"Patrick said that, if I let him in one night, he would put Mr. Rice out of the way. I said that, if anything like that was to be done, Dr. Curry would have to do it, but he told me that Dr. Curry wouldn't do a thing of that kind."

Nigel Morland/Quartet

There was a discussion about the use of chloroform, and they studied a magazine article, provided by Patrick, about the effects of chloroform. Patrick told Jones to obtain some and to find out casually from Dr. Curry if it would be difficult to tell if a person had died as a result of chloroform. Curry informed Jones that it would be hard to tell—particularly so if the heart were affected. Patrick also instructed Jones to start dosing Rice with mercury to "break him down". Jones, having persuaded Dr. Curry that he needed mercury tablets for himself, acquired a bottle of them.

Very sick

On September 1 Jones started giving Rice two tablets a day, assuring him that they were good for him, and Rice immediately started to suffer from diarrhoea. Patrick provided stronger mercury tablets, and Rice's condition worsened. Jones called Dr. Curry, but did not mention dosing Rice with the mercury.

About 10 days before Rice died on September 23, a friend of his, a Mrs. Van Alstyne, called and recommended that bananas were good for stomach troubles. Rice took her word and ate nine of them—making himself very sick

and "clogging his stomach". Jones gave him an extra large dose of mercury "to clear him", and Patrick told him later: "It was silly to have given him the mercury pills. If he had been left alone he might have died from eating the bananas."

Specific instructions

The important thing was that they had now established with Dr. Curry that Rice was thoroughly unwell—and that was paving the way to the night of the murder. On that night, however, Patrick broke the news that he would not be doing the killing—but would be leaving it to Jones. At first, Jones refused. But, after "considerable persuasion", he agreed to "do the job".

Rice was already asleep when Jones returned to the Madison Avenue apartment after his meeting with Patrick. All Patrick's instructions were specific, and Jones knew exactly what to do. He made a "cone" out of a towel and dropped a sponge saturated with chloroform into it. "I put the cone by my own face to test it and got a very strong effect from it," he said.

He then poured a little more chloroform on to the sponge and crept into the bedroom of the sleeping man. Gently,

A MISSING "L" lay between Patrick and Rice's vast wealth. So anxious was he to get his hands on the money that all precautions were dispensed with . . .

so that he would not disturb him, he placed the cone over Rice's nose and mouth and then hurried from the room. Half an hour later he was able to telephone Patrick with the coded message: "Mr. Rice is very ill." That meant Rice was dead. Jones next called Dr. Curry and he arrived at the apartment at the same time as Patrick.

Dr. Curry then entered the witness stand, and he identified a death certificate he had signed. It said: "Cause of death— old age and weak heart; immediate causes —indigestion followed by collacratal diarrhoea with mental worry."

Cremated

He testified to having had an extensive experience in the use of chloroform, having attended more than 40,000 medical and surgical cases while a Confederate Army surgeon during the Civil War. He stated that its smell would have lingered in the room for four or five hours. He would certainly have noticed it if it had been used. There was no evidence of it either in the room atmosphere or on the body.

The next to be summoned to the murder scene were the undertaker, Charles Plowright, and the embalmer, John S. Potter. They both gave evidence that Patrick had insisted that the body was to be cremated "as soon as possible" — and Potter identified the forged "cremation letter" which Patrick had given him as an authorization to show to the officials at the crematorium.

So far the killers were completely in the clear. They would probably have remained in the clear — as far as any murder charge was concerned — if Patrick had not been so eager to get his hands on Rice's money as quickly as possible.

A little queer

If he had waited two days, his forged "cremation letter" would have ensured the disposal of Rice's body — and the final medical evidence would have rested on the safe opinion of Dr. Curry. But the very next morning a paying clerk at the private banking house of S. M. Swenson and Sons found there was a stranger at his window — presenting a cheque for $25,000 which had apparently been signed by Rice.

The old clerk studied the cheque carefully because of the large amount involved, and satisfied himself that it really was made out in the handwriting of Rice's secretary, Jones. He was familiar with Jones's writing and knew that he usually wrote Rice's cheques.

But, as he told the court, the signature "W. M. Rice" was, in his opinion, "a little queer". Then he noticed that the name of the payee on the face of the cheque was "Abert T. Patrick", but the endorsement on the back was "Albert T. Patrick".

Uneasy

He sought the advice of another clerk, Walter O. Weatherbee, and, after comparing the signature with genuine ones, they were not prepared to declare it was a forgery. But Weatherbee suggested that he should not accept the cheque because of the wrong endorsement. There would have to be a new endorsement which corresponded with the name of the payee on the face of the cheque. This was explained to the stranger, who left and returned later with a second endorsement on the cheque, "Abert T. Patrick".

However, the clerks were still uneasy and showed the cheque to one of the bank's proprietors, Eric T. Swenson, who instructed them to telephone Mr. Rice and get his authority before accepting the cheque. Jones answered the telephone and assured them that everything was in order. Still Swenson was not satisfied. He wanted to speak personally to Rice.

For a while Jones hedged with him, saying that it was not possible for Mr. Rice to come to the telephone, before finally admitting that Rice was in fact dead. Swenson asked the stranger to identify himself, and he gave his name as David L. Short — "a friend of Mr. Patrick". This was the same David L. Short who had acted as a "witness" to Rice's signature on the forged documents held by Patrick.

Flame of suspicion

Soon Patrick, alerted by Jones, was telephoning the bank. But Swenson refused to discuss the matter over the telephone. Patrick hurried to the bank and told Swenson it was a pity that the bank had not seen fit to certify the cheque since it was Mr. Rice's intention

THE RICE INSTITUTE now stands just outside Houston, Texas — certainly a more fitting monument than a false legacy "left" to an unscrupulous lawyer.

Associated Press

that it should be paid.

Swenson replied that, as a lawyer, he should know the bank could not pay once it had knowledge of Rice's death. There would have to be an administration of Rice's affairs to establish to whom the money belonged. Patrick insisted that there would be no administration, for Rice had left no property in New York.

He also told Swenson that he had another of Rice's cheques on the bank for $65,000 and an assignment of all Rice's bonds and securities. Then, adding the final drop of fuel to Swenson's flame of suspicion, Patrick added that the body was being cremated the following day.

Curt telegram

As soon as Patrick left the bank, Swenson consulted his lawyers — suggesting that the business was so strange that it rated an urgent investigation. They called in the New York City Detective Bureau and the District Attorney.

None of Rice's relatives had been told about his death. However, with an official investigation starting, Jones began sending them telegrams — advising them that the cremation would take place at 10 o'clock the following morning. Rice's own lawyer heard the news and sent a curt telegram to Jones, ordering him to delay the funeral arrangements.

An autopsy showed that all Rice's organs were sound — except for his lungs. They showed a congestion "as though from some gas or vapour". On October 4 Patrick and Jones were arrested on charges of forgery and were locked in the Tombs. Three months later Patrick's family secured his release on bail — but he was immediately rearrested on a charge of murder.

Impartial

Patrick's "not guilty" plea was based on the argument that Jones was an "incredible liar" and that Rice had died a natural death. That was why Prosecutor Osborne had assembled a most impressive team of medical witnesses for the prosecution. The first was Dr. Hamilton Williams, coroner's physician for the borough of Manhattan, who testified about the autopsy on Rice. Cause of death, in his opinion, was intense congestion in the lungs caused by some "irritant" gas.

The Defence Attorney fought hard to stop the jury believing the possibility of chloroform having been administered. He put a series of searching questions to Dr. Williams. If chloroform had been administered in the manner described by Jones, would not parts of Rice's face have been blistered? Would there not have been some inflammation and congestion of the eyes? Dr. Williams shook his head. "Not necessarily," he said. "It would depend on the degree of the

liquid saturation, and whether any of the liquid was brought into contact with the face or the eyes."

So the medical experts continued with their evidence for day after day, and, despite gruelling cross-examinations, they refused to be shaken. Six handwriting experts followed each other into the witness box to swear that Rice's signatures on the questioned documents were forgeries. They had been traced from genuine signatures. Enlargements of the forged signatures and genuine ones were displayed in court, and the experts used them to provide a wealth of evidence which supported their opinions: the questioned signatures showed "a cramped and unnatural writing" . . . "breaks in continuity, retouchings, and pen-lifts".

Judge Goff, Recorder of the County of New York, was meticulously impartial in his summing-up — reviewing the evidence and outlining the law without giving the jury any indication of his personal opinions about Patrick's innocence or guilt. However, the jury took little time to find Patrick guilty of first-degree murder. That was on March 26, 1902. His attorneys filed the customary motions for a new trial and in arrest of judgment. These were overruled, and on April 7 Patrick was told he would die in the electric chair.

However, for the next six years Patrick stayed in prison while his friends used pressure and legal ploys to secure his release. This expensive exercise finally met with success — on November 28, 1912. Governor John Dix, just before the expiration of his term of office, granted Patrick an unconditional pardon. Dix explained that "the hostile atmosphere which surrounded the defendant when he

was tried precluded a fair trial", and added, "there has always been an air of mystery about the case".

Dix stated that Patrick's release had been recommended by the State Superintendent of Prisons and, as an additional reason for his surprising action, said: "In 1910 the Medico-Legal Society of New York published a brochure of their researches and concluded that the condition of Rice's lungs as found on post-mortem could not have been caused by chloroform."

There were violent protests about the governor's decision, and many people suspected corruption. None of that mattered to Patrick, who considered his 12 years' imprisonment punishment enough. As for Jones — the man who had actually committed the murder — he had been given his full freedom shortly after Patrick's conviction. Like Patrick, he was never heard of again by the general public.

Today, three miles from the centre of Houston, Texas, stands the famous Rice Institute which received an endowment of some ten million dollars under the 1896 will signed by William Marsh Rice. Fifteen hundred pupils, who are charged no tuition fees, qualify from there every year with degrees such as Bachelor of Arts, Bachelor of Science, Master of Arts, and Doctor of Philosophy.

If Patrick's lethal scheme had succeeded, there would be no Rice Institute. Instead, William Marsh Rice would have had some type of monument — "costing not less than $5000" — on his grave.

THE MONUMENT EXISTS, too . . . built on the campus of the Rice Institute — but not by courtesy of Albert Patrick.

Associated Press

MONSTERS

There are a few men who seem driven by some terrible inner compulsion to commit violence against women . . .

"BECAUSE they did not know his identity, they called him the "Monster". It was a fitting epithet, for his crimes were of a diabolical type." These words from Lord Birkenhead's *Famous Trials* refer to Renwick Williams, a "Ripper" who terrorized London during the year 1789. And how many murders did this "monster" commit? None. He was a commonplace sexual pervert who derived satisfaction from slashing women's clothes with a knife. On a few occasions he accosted a girl and asked her to smell a bunch of flowers. The ones who were incautious enough to accept the invitation had a sharp instrument—hidden among the flowers—jabbed into their faces.

An unpleasant character, certainly; but not, by modern standards, a "monster". Psychiatrists call such men "piqueurs" and recognize that they are suffering from sexual frustration and an inferiority complex. The piqueur is usually obsessed

THE FIRST ripper succeeded in terrorizing the girls of London even though he stopped short of murder. He satisfied himself (left) with buttock cutting. (Below) A suggested protection!

Mary Evans

273

FIFTY POUNDS
REWARD.

Horrid Murder!!

WHEREAS,

The Dwelling House of Mr. TIMOTHY MARR, 29, Ratcliff Highway, Man's Mercer, was entered this morning between the hours of Twelve and Two o'Clock, by some persons unknown, when the said Mr. MARR, Mrs. CELIA MARR, his wife, TIMOTHY their INFANT CHILD in the cradle, and JAMES BIGGS, a servant lad, were all of them most inhumanly and barbarously Murdered!!

A Ship Carpenter's Pæn Maul, broken at the point, and a Bricklayer's long Iron Ripping Chissel about Twenty Inches in length, have been found upon the Premises, with the former of which it is supposed the Murder was committed. Any person having lost such articles, or any Dealer in Old Iron, who has lately Sold or missed such, are earnestly requested to give immediate Information.

The Churchwardens, Overseers, and Trustees, of the Parish of St. George Middlesex, do hereby offer a Reward of FIFTY POUNDS, for the Discovery and Apprehension of the Person or Persons who committed such Murder, to be paid on Conviction.

By Order of the Churchwardens, Overseers, and Trustees,

JOHN CLEMENT,
Ratcliff-highway,   VESTRY CLERK.
SUNDAY, 8th, DECEMBER, 1811.

SKIRVEN, Printer, Ratcliff Highway, London.

with some part of a girl's anatomy—her breasts, buttocks, or thighs. He mingles with a crowd, selects an attractive victim, then gets close enough to jab her with a sharp instrument—often an ice pick. By the time the girl realizes what has happened, he has vanished.

For the modern reader, the most surprising thing is that a piqueur should have caused such terror in London—a terror comparable to that caused by Jack the Ripper a century later. Prostitutes tried to keep their pimp in sight; respectable women went out only with a male escort. Many of the stories about the "Monster's" exploits were exaggerated; but, in fact, he was a dangerous man. His knife had inflicted deep and painful wounds, and some of the victims had badly scarred faces. London was seized with panic. Crimes springing from sexual abnormality were almost unknown; they couldn't even begin to understand what could drive a man to attack strange girls. The age of Sex Crime lay nearly a century and a half in the future.

Obscene suggestions

Then, in January 1790, the "Monster" committed the attack that led to his downfall. In St. James's Street there was a tavern run by a man called Porter. His two attractive daughters, Sarah and Anne, were popular barmaids. But on several recent occasions Sarah had been upset when a strange man had sidled up to her in the street and muttered obscene suggestions in her ear.

At 11 o'clock on the night of January 18 the two girls were returning from a ball when. Sarah recognized the foul-mouthed stranger on the corner of St. James's Street. He was apparently drunk. He shouted, "Oh, there you are," and gave her a blow on the side of the head. Sarah told Anne to run: "that dreadful wretch is behind us."

As they reached the door of the tavern, he caught up with them, and slashed at their buttocks with a knife. The girls screamed and rushed inside—but not before they had both seen the man's face clearly. Their dresses and underclothes were soaked with blood, and when they undressed, they found they had long slashes on their buttocks—one of them four inches deep.

Six months later, the girls were walking in St. James's Park with their mother and a male friend when the "Monster" walked past them. He obviously recognized them, for he turned and stared. Anne Porter cried: "That's him. That's the man who attacked us!" The man with them then hurried after the "Monster". He tracked him to a nearby house, banged on the door, and demanded to know the identity of the man who had just gone in. The "Monster" appeared with apparent

astonishment, handed over his visiting card, and asked what all the fuss was about. He even agreed to accompany the young man to the house where the Porters lived. At that Anne and Sarah promptly screamed and fainted.

In spite of his protests, he was arrested, and in due course appeared at the Old Bailey, where crowds flocked to see the infamous Ripper. The judge had to explain to the jury that this was an extremely baffling case, the first of its kind ever heard in England. There was simply no law to deal with a man who slashed ladies' buttocks without apparent motive. On the other hand, there were plenty of laws to deal with damage to property.

So Renwick Williams was charged with damaging the ladies' clothes. The blood-stained dresses and underskirts were produced in court—with ten-inch rents to prove that the "Monster" had ruined valuable property. Williams was duly sentenced to six years in jail, and ordered to produce £400 as a surety for future good behaviour. After that he disappeared from the criminal scene.

Strangely enough, the next wrongdoer to earn himself the nickname of the "Monster" was also called Williams; but in his case, he deserved the title. He slaughtered two families with a frenzy that suggests temporary insanity. Thomas De Quincey has described the case—with magnificent suspense, but considerable inaccuracy—in an appendix to his famous essay "On Murder Considered as One of the Fine Arts".

Frenzied blows

The scene was the Ratcliffe Highway, in the East End of London, not far from the streets where Jack the Ripper would later kill and mutilate six women. The year was 1811. Towards midnight on December 7, Timothy Marr, who kept a hosier's shop, sent out the servant girl to buy oysters. Twenty minutes later, she returned to find the house locked up. There was no reply to her knocks, but she thought she heard stealthy footsteps inside. Neighbours broke in, to find a scene of bloodshed.

The apprentice boy lay at the foot of the stairs, his head beaten to a pulp by frenzied blows that had sprayed his brains on to the ceiling. Behind the counter lay Timothy Marr; his wife Celia was in the doorway, face down; both had

their heads battered and their throats cut. In the basement, the baby had been assaulted with the same fury, its throat also slashed. Nothing of value seemed to be missing from the house.

Sledge hammer

The murders caused panic, not only in London, but all over England. Old ladies in remote parts of Wales had heavy bolts put on their doors. Eight days later, the hysteria increased when there was another mass-slaughter within a few hundred yards of the Marrs' house. This time it was a publican called Williamson, who ran the King's Arms. Shortly after 11 p.m. a lodger named John Turner heard the front door slam heavily. Being of a nervous disposition, he sat up in bed and wondered if the unseen murderer had entered the house. He stole slowly downstairs, and saw a man bending over a prostrate body on the floor. In the room beyond, two more bodies lay.

TERROR again struck Londoners in 1811 when the notorious John Williams slaughtered the Marr and Williamson families. Pictures (opposite) show the murderer himself on the rack; the Marr residence (top right); John Turner's escape from the King's Arms; and the reward notice which was pasted up throughout the East End of London. Map figures show: 1. The Marrs' house; 2. St. George's Church, whose wardens offered a large reward; and 3. The King's Arms.

Turner crept back upstairs, knotted some sheets together, and clambered out of the window. As soon as he was safely on the pavement, he began to shout "Murder, murder!" By the time a crowd had broken in, the killer had escaped out of a back window and scrambled up a muddy bank. Williamson, his wife Elizabeth, and the servant girl, Bridget Harrington, had all been killed in the same violent manner as the Marrs. A 14-year-old girl who had been asleep in a bedroom was unharmed.

The Marrs had been murdered by a kind of sledgehammer called a maul. It was not until after the second mass-murder that this was identified—by initials on its handle—as belonging to a Swedish sailor. The sailor had a perfect alibi, being at sea at the time of the murders; but he had left his tools in a common lodging house, where a man named John Williams now fell under suspicion.

On the morning of the Williamson murders, he had returned to a room he shared with other lodgers, and shouted at them to put out the candle. The next morning, someone noticed that his shoes were muddy, and that he was washing muddy socks. There was blood on his shirt—which Williams explained as the result of a brawl.

A search of the house revealed a pair of heavily bloodstained trousers at the bottom of a privy. The pocket of his coat was also bloodstained, as if it had held a knife, and the knife itself was found hidden in a mouse hole. Williams—a fresh-faced man who didn't look in the least like a murderer—was arrested. But before he could be tried, he hanged himself in jail. His body was buried at a cross-roads near the scene of the murders, and a stake was driven through his "monstrous" heart.

Deeper understanding

It is understandable why De Quincey and his contemporaries refer to him as Williams the Monster. The murders were ostensibly motiveless—although it seems probable that a small sum of money and a few other objects were taken. But robbery could hardly explain the ferocity of the murders, or the killing of the sleeping baby. Neither was there any apparent connection between the victims and the killer which might justify a theory of revenge-murder. It is not surprising that the Ratcliffe Highway murders obsessed the imagination of the nineteenth century, until they were finally eclipsed by Jack the Ripper, 77 years later.

But although criminologists still have no idea of what turned Williams into a homicidal maniac, they have an altogether deeper understanding of the psychology of "monsters" in general. One of the most important insights is owed to the work of the Austrian zoologist, Konrad Lorenz. Lorenz did some of his most valuable work with jackdaws. He quickly discovered that, when a jackdaw is first born, it looks around for some object on which to fix its affections. Normally, the nearest object would be the mother. But if there is no mother available, the baby will attach itself to whoever—or whatever—happens to be around. (This is known to zoologists as "imprinting".) One baby jackdaw decided that Lorenz was its mother, and expressed its devotion to him in embarrassing ways. For example, it waited until he was dozing with his mouth open, and then deposited a load of chewed-up worms on his tongue.

Remarkably tough

This need for a mother (or father) is so great that a baby peacock has been known to fall in love with a tortoise, and a baby monkey with a stone. But experiments soon showed that if the baby is denied *any* kind of parent-figure during the first weeks of its life, it becomes incapable of affection, and develops into what could be called a psychopath. That is to say, it may learn to become a part of a community, but it never learns the basic rules of give and take.

Most humans enjoy "giving" because they relish giving pleasure to someone they love or like. The psychopath is "disconnected"; he doesn't love anybody. He looks coldly at other human beings and calculates what he can get out of them. He can hate, but he doesn't know how to love. Of course, this condition can be produced in perfectly normal people by long periods of emotional strain; but its effect slowly wears off. In the man who is a psychopath through childhood deprivation of affection, it never wears off.

Even so, living creatures are remarkably tough. In a remarkable series of experiments with monkeys, the American Professor Harry Harlow discovered that a newly-born monkey can become passionately attached even to a wire dummy, particularly if the dummy is fitted up with some kind of feeding mechanism that gives milk. The baby will snuggle up to the dummy when it needs comfort. As it gets older, it turns into a fairly normal young monkey, capable of giving affection like any other. Which seems to demonstrate that the mother-substitute doesn't need to *do* anything—just to be there.

However, by far the most serious cause of affection-starvation in children is over-crowding. As soon as overcrowding occurs in any animal community, the infant mortality rate soars, and "psychopathic" babies begin to develop, as an increasing number of babies are actively rejected by mothers who can't cope.

This might seem to raise the question

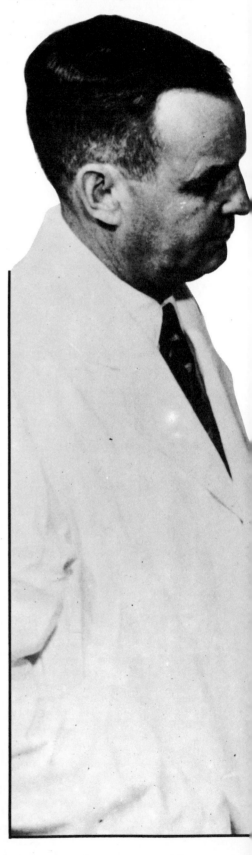

DUMMY MUMMY . . . Professor Harry Harlow (below left) showed, through his experiments with monkeys, that babies have no problem in adopting a substitute if the real mother is missing—so long as there is a parent figure available.

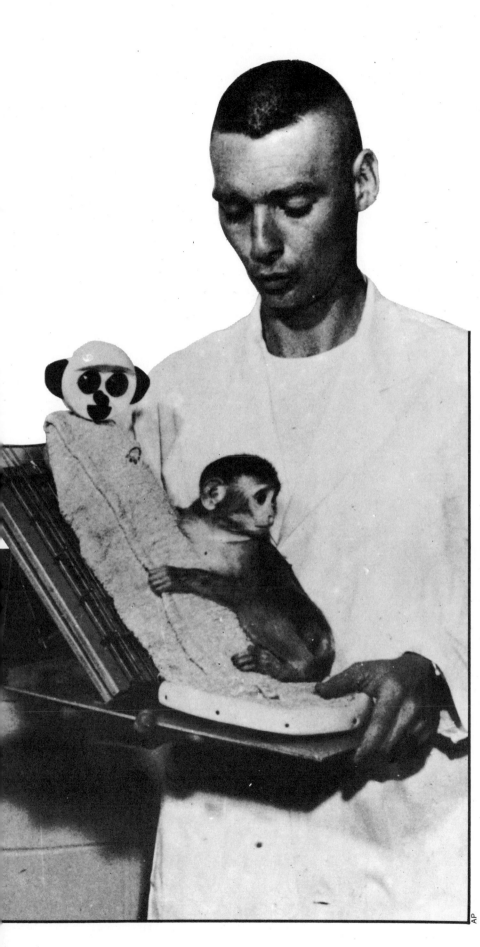

of why there were not far more psychopaths in Thomas De Quincey's London. Surely it was as overcrowded and disease-ridden as many modern cities? But this is not altogether true. London—and Paris and Berlin—may have been overcrowded, but the capital was still a fairly *small* place. Indeed England itself was full of vast open spaces. Moreover, the people who lived in its crowded tenements had deep roots in the community; they were often poor, but they felt they *belonged*.

Symbolic violation

A study conducted among American immigrant communities in the 1930's showed that the first generation of Poles, Croats, etc., were remarkably stable, living in communities with other immigrants from their own country and speaking their own language. It was in the second generation that mental instability began to appear—as the young Pole or Russian Jew found himself torn between two cultures. The rate of mental sickness among Negroes who lived in Harlem—in an all-black community—was far lower than among better off Negroes who moved to partly white neighbourhoods.

All this makes it clear why there were so few psychopaths in the early nineteenth century; why Renwick Williams caused universal panic; why the Ratcliffe Highway murderer became a legend of horror. It is not known what gave Renwick Williams his compulsion to stab women in the buttocks, or what produced John Williams's outbursts of murderous fury. But such people are no longer a mystery. Sexual frustration can take many forms, from stealing ladies' underwear from clothes lines, to jabbing strange women with an ice pick—and they are all clearly forms of substitute rape—a symbolic violation.

Renwick Williams, the "Ripper", was unmarried. Many witnesses described him as polite and "gentlemanly", yet he seems to have been only a tailor's assistant. The picture that emerges is of a shy, withdrawn, rather intelligent man, a social misfit, with a fetish about buttocks, and overpowering sexual desires that could burst out—usually when he was drunk—in the form of a longing to slash and rip the object of his obsession.

Foreign seaports

This description also fits John Williams to a remarkable degree. Although only an ordinary sailor, he was better educated than the average seaman, wrote a good hand, and dressed well. Disliked by most men, he was a favourite with women. A fundamentally weak person, he was inclined to bursts of violent rage when drunk. He had probably been drinking heavily before he killed the Marrs and the Williamsons; some deep frustration

GATEHOUSE STREET

TRENCHES

BODY FOUND HERE

MONSTER'S VICTIM Miss Gladys Hosking (above) relaxes on the beach. Shortly after this photograph was taken she became headline news when her lifeless body was found near the U.S. army camp.

suddenly exploded into psychopathic violence that left him exhausted and strangely lethargic—but temporarily free of his obsessions. Modern case histories of similar types suggest that he may have committed other murders, perhaps in the slum quarters of foreign seaports.

The modern parallel that suggests itself is the case of Edward Joseph Leonski, the man whose crimes terrorized the city of Melbourne, Australia, in 1942. His first victim was a 40-year-old domestic help, Ivy McLeod. She was found in a shop doorway on May 3, 1942, her clothes ripped to shreds, her face battered and lacerated, her body bruised; she was strangled, but there was no sign of rape.

Yellow mud

A week later, the body of a slim brunette, Pauline Thompson, was found on the steps of an apartment house, the clothes torn and the face unrecognizable. Melbourne suddenly realized that it was harbouring a ripper-type killer, and there was panic. Mrs. Thompson, a policeman's wife, was strangled but not raped.

Scarcely a week had passed when, on May 19, the body of another woman was found lying in the yellow mud near an American army camp. Her clothes had

been ripped off and she had been beaten and strangled—but again, not raped. She was Gladys Hosking, a 41-year-old secretary. This time, however, there was a clue. An Australian soldier had seen an American serviceman plastered with yellow mud near the scene of the crime. Police searched the camp, and quickly found a tent with yellow mud on the flap. "Crime chemist" Alan Dower found it to be identical to the clay in which the body had been found.

Shy manners

The occupant of the tent, Private Joseph Leonski, was a baby-faced, blue-eyed giant, universally liked for his gentleness. The strange thing about him was that when he was drunk, his personality changed completely; he began to talk gloatingly about violence; then, if the mood was on him, he offered to fight anybody in the bar. He was a real-life Jekyll and Hyde. After each killing, he was horrified, and screamed in his sleep. His description of the killing of Gladys Hosking was typical.

He fell into conversation with her as she walked along; his shy manners and appealing face convinced her she had nothing to fear. He had no conscious intention of harming her; he was merely lonely and homesick. He found her voice soothing; when it was time for them to separate, he suddenly experienced an insane desire to "keep her voice". The

violence took over like an epileptic fit; when it had passed, she was naked and bruised—and dead.

Leonski was hanged quickly—to satisfy Australian public opinion—and little is known about his psychological history. But what *is* on record is revealing. His mother had been a professional weight-lifter from Poland, an immensely dominant woman whose two unhappy marriages had made her bitter. She undoubtedly loved her son; but had she, during those vital early months of his life, treated him as an irrelevant nuisance? She felt she had to be hard and tough to face the world; she had no tenderness to give to a baby. Eddie developed into a gentle, shy boy, with definite artistic leanings. He drew, played the piano, and won prizes at school. But he was always afraid of girls. Almost any snub or rebuke could make him burst into tears. So again, there is the same basic pattern as in the other two "monsters": the misfit, the "outsider", not really at home with other men, and burning with frustrations that found total violent release only when drunk.

Repressed hatred

The three murdered women were not the only ones Leonski had attacked; three others came forward to tell of being strangled into unconsciousness by him, and a fourth woman related an attempt to rape her in her apartment. Leonski was a virile male; he wanted a woman badly;

UMBRELLA

HAT

SCHIZOID SADIST Joseph Leonski turns his back to the camera (top right) as he boards an army vehicle after a day spent in court listening to the evidence against him. The "gentle giant" was nearing the end of a life tormented by sexual desires and repressions whose origins probably lay in the influence exerted on him by his extraordinary and domineering mother. Unlike the common, calculating type of criminal, Leonski had made no attempt to dispose of the bodies or of other traces of his "work", as the scene of Gladys Hosking's murder (above) clearly shows. Police witnesses at the trial (right) arrived laden with bundles of clothing and other exhibits.

but young women scared him. Equally, he didn't know what to *do* with the middle-aged women he killed; the need for sex got mixed up with his repressed hatred of his mother.

It is not true that all "monsters" are split personalities who kill in a frenzy. Many psychopaths are simply "cold" — Ian Brady, the Moors murderer, is an example. (Interestingly enough, his mother deserted him almost as soon as he was born.) But in most cases, the basic cause can be traced back to very early childhood.

Perhaps when this psychological trait is something that *every* mother and father knows about and takes steps to prevent, "monsters" will again become as rare as they were in the days of Renwick Williams.

All Herald Sun

DUMPED in doorways . . . Mrs. Ivy McLeod (left) was found at the shop entrance (below left) and Pauline Thompson on the house doorstep (right).

Herald Sun

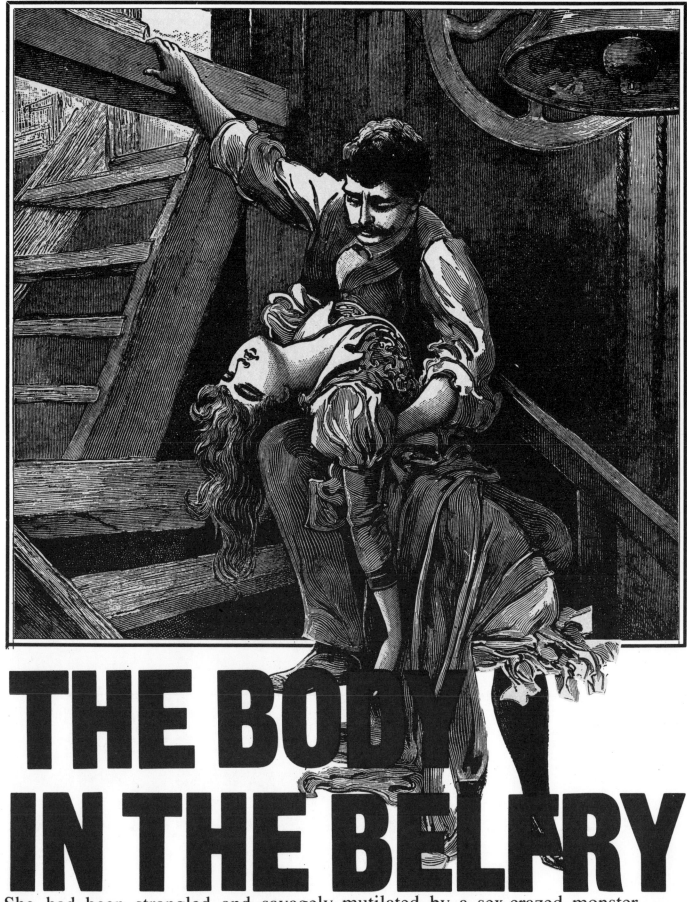

THE BODY IN THE BELFRY

She had been strangled and savagely mutilated by a sex-crazed monster . . .

Granger Collection

WILLIAM Henry Theodore Durrant did not look like a monster. Indeed, to all outward appearances, he was, at 24, a paragon of the kind of ostentatious virtue much in favour in his time. He was studying for the respectable profession of medicine, he was assistant superintendent of the Sunday School at Emanuel Baptist Church, San Francisco, and was particularly admired for such traits of filial devotion as always kissing his mother upon leaving and returning home.

He was a tall, slim young man, with a pale complexion that gave an extra luminosity to his blue eyes and made him noticeable in a crowd. He was, in fact, the kind of young man, apparently heading for a comfortable and secure future, whom most mothers of late nineteenth-century daughters would have welcomed as a prospective son-in-law. The only hint of criticism directed against him was that—for such a well-bred man— he wore his hair rather long.

But beneath the skin of Theo Durrant —who was so proper and polite at church meetings—stirred a darkly brooding, unstable, inner being. He was tormented by sex to such an extent that, secretly, even the most perverted sexual relationships seemed tame to him. He once told a fellow student: "I have no knowledge of women." But he finally rectified that ignorance in a way that went beyond sadism.

Brown eyes

It was 18-year-old Blanche Lamont— born in Montana but living with her uncle and aunt on West 21 Street—who stepped out into San Francisco's swirling, misty air on Wednesday, April 3, 1895, to unwittingly offer herself as the monster's first victim.

She, like Durrant, was tall and extremely pale. But what most excited attention, and gave her an especially delightful feminine quality, were the incredibly long eyelashes that swept demurely over warm, brown eyes. She was the kind of girl who was in no doubt about her attractiveness

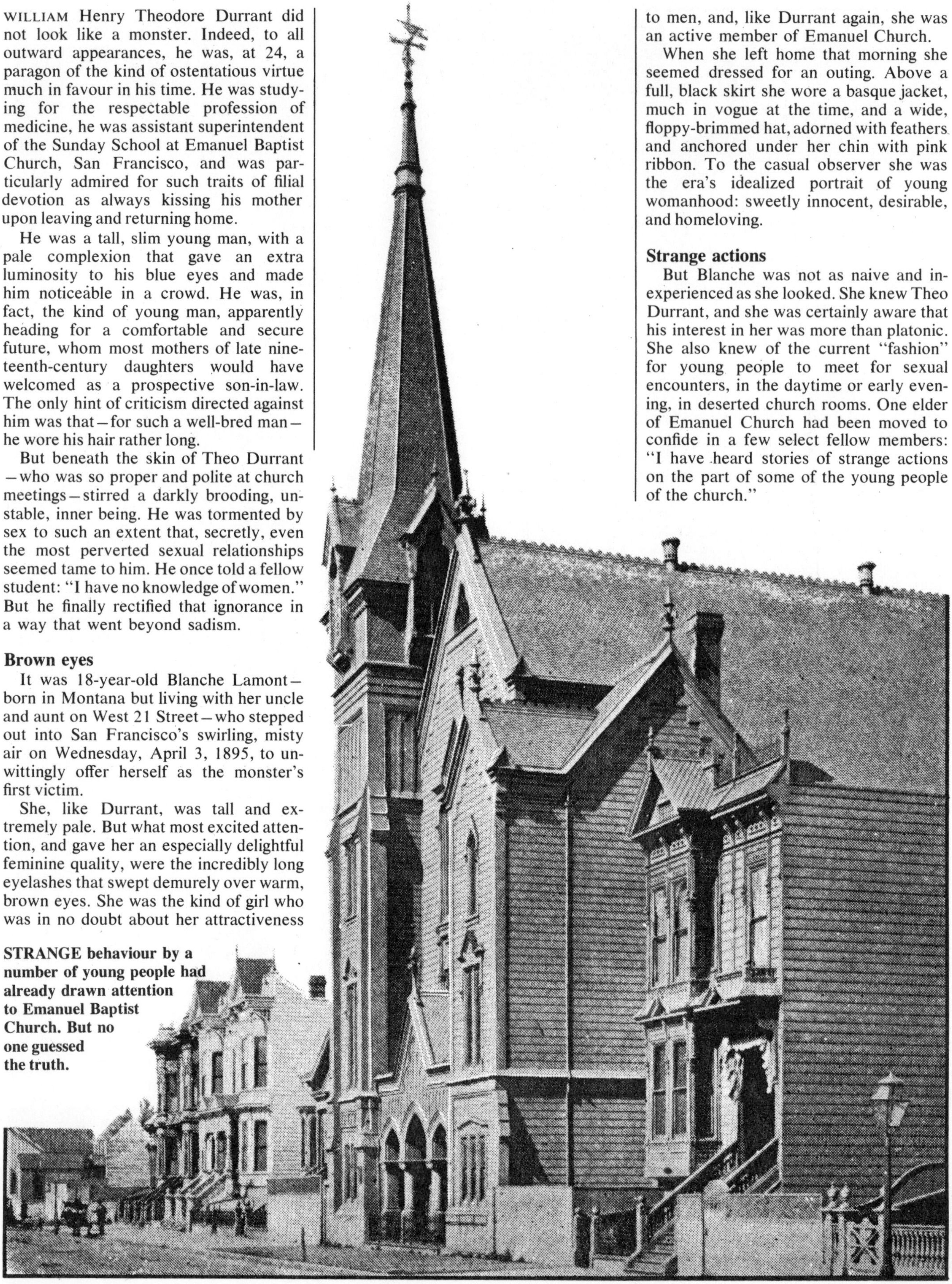

STRANGE behaviour by a number of young people had already drawn attention to Emanuel Baptist Church. But no one guessed the truth.

to men, and, like Durrant again, she was an active member of Emanuel Church.

When she left home that morning she seemed dressed for an outing. Above a full, black skirt she wore a basque jacket, much in vogue at the time, and a wide, floppy-brimmed hat, adorned with feathers and anchored under her chin with pink ribbon. To the casual observer she was the era's idealized portrait of young womanhood: sweetly innocent, desirable, and homeloving.

Strange actions

But Blanche was not as naive and inexperienced as she looked. She knew Theo Durrant, and she was certainly aware that his interest in her was more than platonic. She also knew of the current "fashion" for young people to meet for sexual encounters, in the daytime or early evening, in deserted church rooms. One elder of Emanuel Church had been moved to confide in a few select fellow members: "I have heard stories of strange actions on the part of some of the young people of the church."

McDade Collection

McDade Collection

At 8.15 a.m. Blanche met Durrant at the junction of Twenty-first and Mission Streets and, with his arm about her shoulders, he guided her on to an electric streetcar. They made a handsome couple, and it was not surprising that afterwards other passengers remembered them. Even the busy car conductor, Henry Shellmont, paid them so much attention that he could later recall: "He was fooling with her gloves which she had removed. He seemed to be talking very sweetly to her."

They rode some distance on the car, with Durrant talking continuously and quietly into Blanche's ear. Then, at Polk Street, they parted—Durrant to go to Cooper Medical College and Blanche to the Normal School, where she was studying to be a teacher. But that was only the prologue to their day. By two in the afternoon Durrant was back, impatiently waiting on a corner near the Normal School, carefully watched by old Mrs. Mary Vogel—who lived nearby and whose fear of burglars kept her attention riveted on any loiterers.

Full-bodied figure

Suddenly, Durrant spotted Blanche leaving the school and "ran like a boy" towards her, as Mrs. Vogel remembered. They boarded a cable car, noticed this time by May Lannigan, one of Blanche's fellow students, who said: "It was the man's hair which attracted my attention as it struck me as unusual to see a gentleman with such long hair."

Later the two were observed walking purposefully towards Emanuel Church. By that time the wind had turned blustery and revealed Blanche's full-bodied figure or, as one middle-aged eye-witness, Mrs. Elizabeth Crosset, delicately put it: "Her clothes blew considerably around her limbs—her form—her dress."

Mrs. Caroline Leak, another elderly observer, saw Blanche enter the church

FEMININE and sexy, Blanche Lamont was undoubtedly in search of excitement when she entered the church with Durrant. Instead, she was brutally slaughtered.

first, followed by Durrant. Mrs. Leak was the last person to see Blanche Lamont alive. From within the large, wooden building of the church, on Bartlett Street, no sound came. The door had closed and what was happening within was secret.

Just before five o'clock, George King, Emanuel's 19-year-old organist, arrived for a brief practice session on the music for the forthcoming Easter service. But, before he had played more than a few introductory bars, he was interrupted by the sound of footsteps. Turning from the console, he was surprised to see Durrant coming from the direction of the staircase that led up to the belfry tower.

Theo Durrant seemed paler than ever and, conscious of King's puzzled look, he hastily explained: "I have been fixing a gas jet upstairs and breathing some escaping gas. Would you go to the corner drugstore and fetch me a Bromo Seltzer?"

When George King returned from his errand of mercy, Durrant looked and sounded much better, and the two men left the church together. A few hours later Durrant returned for the evening prayer meeting and the first person he met was an anxious Mrs. Tryphena Noble, the aunt with whom Blanche boarded.

"Ah, Mrs. Noble," Durrant inquired, "is Blanche here tonight?" Indeed, no, the aunt replied, she had not returned home to dinner and her absence was most worrying. "Well, I regret she is not with us," Durrant said. "I have a book called *The Newcomes*, by Thackeray, for her, but I will send it to the house."

Oddly, Mrs. Noble waited several days before she notified the police of Blanche's disappearance. Along with others known to be her friends, Durrant was questioned

and volunteered the curiously ungallant suggestion that perhaps she had wandered from the moral path and "gone astray".

A few days later he attempted to pawn some woman's rings. The offer was turned down by the pawnbroker, and a week afterwards there came by post to Mrs. Noble three of Blanche's rings, wrapped in newspaper. Across the margin of the paper was scribbled the name: "George King".

As the days of Blanche's disappearance progressed, another member of Emanuel Church, 21-year-old Minnie Williams, began to show signs of agitation. "I know too much about the disappearance of Blanche," she told a friend. "I think she has met with foul play."

Mutilated body

At eight o'clock on the evening of April 12, a homeward-bound claims adjuster, named Hodgkins, saw Durrant and Minnie arguing outside the entrance to Emanuel Church. Mr. Hodgkins was so concerned about Durrant's aggressive manner—"it was unbecoming to a gentleman"—that he intervened to restore the peace. As he walked on, however, he saw Minnie take Durrant's arm and the two of them enter the church. Once more, as in the case of Blanche Lamont, the church door closed upon a seemingly affectionate young couple.

At 9.30 Durrant, gaunt and dishevelled arrived at the house of one of Emanuel Church's members for a meeting of the Christian Endeavour group. Before the proceedings began he announced, distractedly, that he must wash his hands. By the time the meeting ended, at 11.25, he was chatting amiably with the rest of the devout gathering and appeared to be his normal, polished self. As the members left he excused himself, saying that he must return to the church, where he had "left something".

283

The following morning some of the members of the Ladies' Society—who were decorating Emanuel Church for the Easter services—decided to adjourn for a rest to a side room used as the church library. In the room was a cupboard which, for some reason, one of the women opened. As she did so she gave a spine-chilling scream and threw back the door so that her companions could share her terror.

Fearfully, they peered inside. There, on the floor, they saw the mutilated and half-naked body of Minnie Williams. Some of her underclothes had been forced far down her throat. She had been stabbed in each breast, and the arteries of her wrists had been slashed, causing her blood to cascade over the cupboard walls.

A necrophiliac?

On Easter Sunday the San Francisco *Chronicle* reminded the police—who had been called immediately upon the discovery of Minnie's body—that Blanche Lamont was still missing. So detectives returned to Emanuel Church and began a thorough search of the building. They found that the door to the belfry tower—a tower which had no bell, and which church officials rarely ascended—seemed to have been recently forced. They thrust the door open and piled up the staircase.

There, on the dust-covered floor of the southeast corner of the tower, lay Blanche's naked body. There were deep bruises on her throat and it was clear that she had been strangled. Her head had been placed on two wooden blocks to hold it in position—in the way medical students were taught to place the head of a body for post-mortem examination—and her hands had been crossed on her breast, as if in preparation for burial. Her clothes were stuffed out of sight behind the belfry's wooden beams.

Medical investigation suggested that Minnie had been a cooperative party to sexual intercourse before her murder. But the findings in the case of Blanche were more ominous and horrifying. She had, it was stated, "not parted with life and honour without a struggle", and a sexual outrage "had probably occurred after death". If that was so then her murderer was also a necrophiliac.

Once the dreadful news of the murders was out and capturing the daily headlines, it did not take long for all those observers of Durrant with Blanche and Minnie to hurry forward with their accounts. And, since Theo Durrant had almost gone out of his way to advertise his association with the two girls, he was swiftly put under arrest.

Once more, paler than ever, seemingly shocked that such allegations should be made against an ardent churchgoer, Dur-

rant protested his innocence. But it was all in vain. On the grounds that there were more witnesses who had seen him with Blanche Lamont than with Minnie, the state decided to try him for Blanche's murder.

He was put on trial on July 22, 1895, and although the evidence was circumstantial, it was strongly so. It took the jury only five minutes to find him guilty—one of the swiftest verdicts ever returned in a major murder case. He was sentenced to death by hanging and, after long legal wrangling, the Supreme Court finally confirmed the sentence on April 3, 1897. The prisoner then announced that he would "die like a Durrant".

Certainly Durrant the monster made the most of his last days in San Quentin. He held press conferences in his cell and was ever ready with quotable material for the eager reporters. "It is not so awful to go to such a death," he announced to them on one occasion. "Such a death as mine may be the means of abolishing capital punishment in this state." When pressed by his spiritual adviser to prepare himself for the next world by purging his conscience in this, he declared: "No, no! I will not confess the murders because I am not guilty."

In the death cell he became a Catholic convert—largely because, his Baptist minister disclosed, "I have not been successful in concealing my conviction of his guilt", and because the minister regarded Durrant as a "psychological monster". Durrant also announced that he was suffering from nightmares and hallucinations—the kinds of manifestations that suggested there were two Durrants: one outwardly normal, the other abnormal and beyond human control.

Having denied the murders, he naturally offered no details about them, and there was no direct information on one especially intriguing point: why, after the gory and brutal killing of Minnie Williams, had the police found no trace of blood on his clothes and no evidence that he had burned, or otherwise destroyed, any clothing?

It was supposed that he had probably stripped off his clothing before the killings as a prelude to sexual intercourse. This theory was reinforced by one church member, who came forward to say that on one occasion Durrant had appeared before her in the church naked—or, as she blushingly put it, "in his birthday suit".

On the morning of the execution, January 7, 1898, Theo Durrant walked calmly up the steps to the scaffold, in the white-walled execution chamber. Then, imperiously holding up his hand, he commanded the executioner, Amos Lunt: "Don't put that rope on, my boy, until after I talk." He paused until the reporters were ready with pencils and notebooks.

"To those who wish to me to say some-

thing," Durrant intoned, "I wish to say this: that I have no animosity against anyone but those who have persecuted and hounded me to my grave, innocent as I am. I forgive them all. They will receive their justice from the Holy God above, to whom I now go to receive my justice, which will be the justice given to an innocent boy who has not stained his hands with the crimes that have been put upon him by the press of San Francisco. I forgive them all, for I do not hold anything against them for it.

"I do not look upon people now as enemies. I forgive them as I expect to be forgiven for anything I have done, but the fair name of California will forever be blackened with the crime of taking innocent blood, and whether or no they ever discover the committors of these crimes matters little to me . . .

"They must consider for themselves, who wished to start up a sensation, that I am innocent. I say now this day before God, to whom I now go to meet my dues, I am innocent . . ."

It was clear that Theo Durrant's last words were far from over. But the hangman, Lunt, had grown increasingly nervous as the speech continued. Suddenly, on the last "I am innocent", he slipped the noose deftly over Durrant's head and sprang the trap.

Well-endowed meal

As soon as he had been pronounced dead, Durrant's body was placed in a black coffin and carried into a side room where his parents were waiting to hold a short vigil beside the remains.

Later, a convict named Williams, acting as attendant to the bereaved, asked gently if perhaps some tea would help to ease the strain, and Mrs. Durrant warmly accepted his offer. Williams was of English extraction and the "tea" with which he returned was—in true English fashion—a well-endowed meal, with meat and other solids.

Drawing their chairs up to a table within three feet of the coffin, Mr. and Mrs. Durrant fell upon the food. Discreetly, the prison officials withdrew. As they did so they heard the dead man's mother say to her husband, with a certain mournful relish: "Please, papa, give me a little more of the roast."

ATTRACTIVENESS to women was one of Durrant's great assets, and one pretty court spectator (above right) even gave him a bouquet of flowers. Contemporary prints (far right) show (top to bottom) the discovery of Blanche's body; his farewell to his parents; the final march to death; and Mr. and Mrs. Durrant's tasty meal beside their son's body. Portraits (right) show Durrant and Minnie Williams.

NOW FOR THE FIGHT IN DALLAS TEX

THE NATIONAL POLICE GAZETTE

THE LEADING ILLUSTRATED SPORTING JOURNAL IN AMERICA.

Copyrighted for 1895 by the Proprietor, RICHARD K. FOX. The Fox Building, Franklin Square Publishing, Printing and Engraving House, New York City

RICHARD K. FOX,
Editor and Proprietor.

NEW YORK, SATURDAY, OCTOBER 5, 1895.

VOLUME LXVI.—No. 944.
Price 10 Cents.

DURRANT'S MYSTERIOUS FRIEND.
THE "SWEET-PEA GIRL" OF SAN FRANCISCO WHO SUPPLIES THE ALLEGED MURDERER WITH FLOWERS.

FINDING THE BODY OF BLANCHE LAMONT.
[View on the top landing of Emanuel Baptist Church tower, San Francisco, where the searchers came across the nude body of one of Durrant's victims.]

PARTING FROM HIS PARENTS.
[Durrant's last interview with his father and mother just before his execution.]

THE MARCH TO DEATH.
[Murderer Durrant, closely following his spiritual adviser, ascending the steps of the scaffold.]

FEASTED BESIDE THEIR DEAD SON.
[Mr. and Mrs. Durgant eating dinner in a private room of San Quentin prison, California, while within a few feet of them was the coffin containing the remains of their son who had just been hanged.]

Granger Collection

McDade Collection

Culver

THE MAIDS OF HORROR

Everything appeared to be cut and dried. The brutally slaughtered bodies had been found, along with the murder weapons, and the two killers had immediately confessed to the crime. Yet something, surely, was wrong. These were not hardened criminals; they were not even psychopaths. They were two ordinary housemaids. What had driven them to hack their employers to death?

THE newspapers had called them "the monsters of Le Mans", "the diabolical sisters", and "the lambs who had become wolves". But as Christine Papin, 28, and her sister, Lea, 21, took their seats in the courtroom of the provincial French town of Le Mans on the morning of September 20, 1933, it was difficult to believe that these were the girls who had inspired those black headlines.

They were impassive. No emotion showed on their peasant-like, but not coarse, faces; they kept their heavy-lidded eyes on the floor. It was almost as if they were in a trance or under heavy sedation. On their way to the dock they moved like robots.

And yet they were charged with a double murder which has been described as "one of the most awesome recorded occurrences of motiveless ferocity"—a crime which "shocked France, baffled psychiatrists, and has yet to be satisfactorily explained".

The men and women in the public seats were hushed as they heard—from the principals this time, not from the columns of their daily newspaper—the macabre details of the crime committed in a middle-class home in Le Mans on a dark winter's evening nearly eight months earlier.

The date was February 2, 1933. Monsieur René Lancelin, an attorney who had been away on business all day, was due to

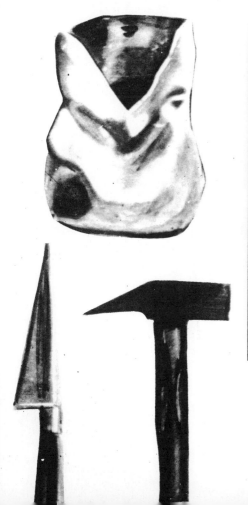

BLOOD RED staircase (above) leading to the servants' room where Christine and sister Lea lay huddled together in a single bed. The landing is where the bodies of Madame and Mademoiselle Lancelin were left, horribly mutilated. The weapons used by the "monsters of Le Mans" were a knife, a hammer, and a severely battered pewter pot (left) and all three were found beside the lifeless bodies.

THE SCENE awaiting Monsieur Lancelin on arrival at his house (below). The front door was locked and the only light came from the maids' room. Inside, his wife and daughter lay hacked to pieces.

meet his wife and 27-year-old daughter Geneviève, for dinner at the home of a friend. "They were not there," he told the court. "After waiting for a while, I tried to telephone my home. There was no answer. I excused myself and went to the house.

"The front door was locked from the inside and the house was in darkness except for a faint glow from the upstairs room occupied by the two maids, Christine and Lea Papin. I was unable to get in so I called the police."

Deep wounds

The story was then taken up by the police inspector who arrived in response to M. Lancelin's call and forced his way into the house. The ground floor was deserted, but on the first-floor landing . . .

"The corpses of Madame and Mademoiselle Lancelin were lying stretched out on the floor and were frightfully mutilated. Mademoiselle Lancelin's corpse was lying face downward, head bare, coat pulled up and with her knickers down, revealing deep wounds in the buttocks and multiple cuts in the calves. Madame Lancelin's body was lying on its back. The eyes had disappeared, she seemed no longer to have a mouth and all the teeth had been knocked out.

"The walls and doors were covered with splashes of blood to a height of more than seven feet. On the floor we found fragments of bone and teeth, one eye, hair pins, a handbag, a key ring, an untied parcel, numerous bits of white, decorated porcelain and a coat button."

That was not all. There were more discoveries — a kitchen knife covered with blood, a damaged pewter pot and lid, a blood-stained hammer. But where were the maids? The police found them, naked and huddled together in a single bed, in their room. Christine, the elder, immediately confessed to the crime.

In the horror-struck courtroom, she kept her eyes downcast as her words — spoken in a sullen, dull monotone — were recalled.

"When Madame came back to the house, I informed her that the iron was broken again and that I had not been able to iron. She wanted to jump on me. My sister and I and our two mistresses were on the first-floor landing. When I saw that Madame Lancelin was going to jump on me, I leaped at her face and scratched out her eyes with my fingers.

"No, I made a mistake when I said that I leaped on Madame Lancelin. It was on Mademoiselle Lancelin that I leaped and it was her eyes that I scratched out. Meanwhile, my sister Lea had jumped on Madame Lancelin and scratched her eyes out in the same way.

"After we had done this, they lay and crouched down on the spot. I then rushed down to the kitchen to fetch a hammer and a knife. With these two instruments, my sister and I fell upon our two mistresses. We struck at the head with the knife, hacked at the bodies and legs, and also struck with a pewter pot, which was standing on a little table on the landing.

"We exchanged one instrument for another several times. By that I mean that I would pass the hammer over to my sister so that she could hit with it while she handed me the knife, and we did the same with the pewter pot. The victims began to cry out but I don't remember that they said anything.

"When we had done the job, I went to bolt the front door, and I also shut the vestibule door. I shut these doors because I wanted the police to find out our crime before our master. My sister and I then went and washed our hands in the kitchen because they were covered with blood.

"We then went to our room, took off all our clothes, which were stained with blood, put on a dressing-gown, shut the door of our room with a key and lay down on the same bed. That's where you found us when you broke the door down.

"I have no regrets or, rather, I can't tell you whether I have any or not. I'd rather have had the skin of my mistresses than that they should have had mine or my sister's. I did not plan my crime and I didn't feel any hatred towards them, but I don't put up with the sort of gesture that Madame Lancelin was making at me that evening."

No regrets

Lea Papin confirmed her sister's statement. "Like my sister," she said, "I affirm that we had not planned to kill our mistresses. The idea came suddenly when we heard Madame Lancelin scolding us. I don't have any more regrets for the criminal act we have committed than my sister does. Like her, I would rather have had my mistresses' skins than their having ours."

The murders had been triggered off by the iron mentioned in Christine's statement. Lea had damaged it at some time during January. On February 1, the day before the killings, Madame Lancelin had deducted five francs from her month's wages to pay for the repair. Then, while the maids were ironing in the otherwise empty house on February 2, the iron fused, putting out all the lights. "What will Madame do to us when she gets back?" Lea had asked anxiously.

It seemed certain that, on her return, Madame Lancelin had been irritated and might have raised her hand to one or both of the sisters. But how could such a trivial incident have led to such savagery — two healthy women having their eyes gouged out and then, blinded and in agony, battered almost beyond recognition with the hammer and pewter pot, and finally their bodies further mutilated with a knife?

Even the judge found it difficult to credit both the story and the lack of emotion of the two sisters as it was related. Lea, looking very much the younger of the two, her dark coat buttoned to the neck, her hands thrust deep into her pockets, gazed vacantly in front of her.

Christine still gazed rigidly at the ground. She might have been asleep but for a strange smile, almost of contentment, that strayed across her lips.

Barely audible

The judge, speaking quietly and calmly, as if to two children, went over the salient facts with them again, almost as if seeking reassurance that he had heard correctly the first time. He said to Christine:

"You knocked Madame Lancelin down with a blow from a pewter pot. As she cried out, your sister came running. What did you say to her?"

"I told Lea to tear her eyes out."

A murmur of horror ran through the listeners in the public seats. The judge then asked Lea: "When your sister saw that Madame Lancelin wanted to get up again, did she say to you: 'Tear her eyes out'?"

"Yes," replied Lea in a barely audible voice.

"You came rushing up. You knocked her out by banging her head against the floor and then you tore her eyes out. How?"

"With my fingers," Lea replied in a flat, matter-of-fact voice.

There was a renewed hubbub in the public seats. "Death to them!" someone shouted. "Death to them!" The judge threatened to clear the court if there was any further disturbance.

Drunkard father

As peace was restored, he resumed the interrogation. What, he wanted to know, had happened after Lea had torn out Madame Lancelin's eyes and helped to batter her to death?

"I slashed her body with the knife," she responded.

"Have you any excuses for your action, any explanation, any regrets?" asked the judge.

Lea made no reply. Nor did Christine when the same question was put to her.

Could there be anything like a deep-rooted resentment of their lives as maids to account for the ferocity of their sudden assault? That suggestion, too, led the court nowhere.

Christine had gone straight into domestic service on leaving her convent school. Lea had followed her after being brought up in an orphanage (their father was a drunkard). They had worked

FLANKED by gendarmes (right), Lea Papin stares grimly at the judge while sister Christine, head bowed, stares stonily at the ground. Pictured (above) is a general view of the court in session during the trial and (left) the outside of the Palais de Justice at Le Mans. The courtroom was always packed with eager spectators fascinated by this bizarre story of monstrous murder. They were not disappointed by what they heard and saw: there were sensational and horrific confessions from both girls as well as a succession of gory exhibits. The verdict of guilty seemed inevitable.

together and changed jobs frequently before joining the Lancelins. Changing employers had been motivated by nothing more sinister than better wages, and all their references spoke of them as "willing, hard-working, and honest".

Both agreed that they had been well treated by the Lancelins. They were sufficiently well paid to have saved 24,000 francs; they ate the same food as the Lancelins; they even had electric heating in their room—considered something of a luxury for servants.

"What *did* you have against the Lancelin family?" the judge asked, sounding almost desperate in his anxiety to find some clue that would explain the sisters' violent action. "There has been mention of the social hatred of the employee for the employer. But this was not the case. You have said that you suffered from no feeling of inferiority, that 'a servant's profession is as good as any other'. Did you love your employers?"

Lea answered: "We served them and that was all. We never talked to them."

Totally indifferent

With that avenue of exploration apparently closed, the court turned to the personal relationship between the two sisters. Were they lesbians? It wasn't merely the fact that the police had found them naked in bed together after the killings. They had always lived what seemed an odd life for two young girls.

They spent nearly all their spare time together in their room, never going to the cinema or to dances. They had no friends of either sex. In fact, they seemed totally indifferent to everything except their work and each other.

Why had Madame Lancelin and her daughter gone home unexpectedly when they were due to meet M. Lancelin at a friend's? The parcel which the police found on the first floor had contained meat. Why had Madame Lancelin—or her daughter—taken the parcel upstairs instead of, as would have been normal, taking it straight to the kitchen?

Could it be that the mistress and her daughter suspected an illicit relationship, and had caught the maids in a compromising situation—and that this had sparked off the horror?

Evidence to support this theory came from Christine's behaviour during the seven months she and Lea had been in prison awaiting trial. She, like Lea, had ceased to menstruate. When they were separated and placed in separate cells, she at first wept, then screamed threats, and howled like a dog.

Once, like a distraught lover, she cried all night for her "darling Lea". Another time, she rolled on the ground, screaming obscenities. "It seemed she was tormented by sexual desires," said a warder.

She begged for Lea to be reunited with her. When they were kept apart, she went on hunger strike and became so violent that she had to be placed in a strait-jacket. Finally, they were allowed to meet for a brief reunion. Witnesses gave two slightly differing accounts of the meeting, both bizarre and both suggesting there was more—at least from Christine's point of view—in their relationship than mere sisterly love.

One version claimed that, as soon as Lea entered the cell, Christine leaped upon her and hugged her so hard they had to be forcibly separated before the younger girl choked. Then, as they sat on a bed, Christine tried to tear Lea's blouse off and to kiss her on the mouth, pleading with her: "Say yes to me, Lea, say yes to me."

Hysteria

In the second version, Christine, in a fit of hysteria, pulled her skirts up above her thighs, and, apparently in a paroxysm of sexual desire, begged her sister: "Come to me, Lea, come to me." Both accounts agreed that, for her part, Lea had remained calm and passive.

The medical evidence for the prosecution discounted this behaviour. The director of the lunatic asylum at Le Mans, in a joint report with another doctor, declared: "Christine and Lea are in no way depraved. They are not suffering from any mental illness and are in no way labouring under the burden of a defective heredity. From an intellectual, affective, and emotive point of view, they are completely normal."

Three other doctors appointed to examine the sisters came to the conclusion "there is no question of an attachment of a sexual nature".

The exact nature of the relationship between the two girls proved a point on which the judge was anxious to satisfy himself and the jury. Once again he spoke almost like a parent trying to coax the truth out of a couple of reluctant youngsters.

Sexual relationship?

There were, he pointed out—somewhat hesitantly as if choosing his words carefully—several strange aspects to the life they lived in the Lancelin household. They never indulged in the kind of social activities that most young people enjoyed. They had no boy friends, and on breaking down the door of their room, the police found them in the same bed.

"I am bound to ask you," he said, "whether there was anything sexual in your relationship?"

Christine answered that they had merely been sisters. "There was nothing else between us," she shrugged.

And that was basically that. They had committed two brutal murders which, for their ferocity, were virtually without parallel in modern times . . . they had confessed . . . they were, despite their grim crime, sane and normal girls according to all the medical opinion produced by the prosecution.

In prison, awaiting trial, Christine had often said stoically: "I shall be punished—my head cut off, even. *Tant pis!*" Now it looked as if her prediction would be fulfilled.

The slender basis of the defence plea of not guilty was that the two sisters were not, in fact, sane and normal girls. In support of that contention, however, the only witness of distinction they could produce to try to refute the overwhelming medical evidence amassed by the prosecution was a Dr. Logre, a well-known psychiatrist of the era

All Keystone

LA TRAGÉDIE DE LA RUE BRUYÈRE, AU MANS
×× ××

LES DEUX SŒURS CRIMINELLES
PRÉCISENT DEVANT LE JUGE D'INSTRUCTION LES CIRCONSTANCES DE LEUR FORFAIT

LEBRUN E DERNIER A «DETTTE»

— On a procédé , dans la Galerie e de France, en bert Lebrun, pré- lique, aux opéra- et dernier tirage n nationale « la u profit des qua- tions de mutilés : sées », « l'Union erre », « les Plus », les Ailes bri-

, qui était accom- nt-colonel Bonas- n militaire, a été t, gouverneur de ance, et par les urs ainsi que par président des .

nalités présentes, mment : M. Miel- ensions, le maré- Renard, préfet de préfet de police,

emercia tout d'a- de la République u honorer de sa réponie du cer-

 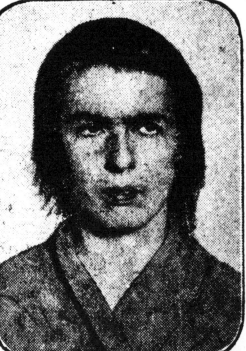

Hier soir dans les couloirs du Palais de
LEA à gauche) **et CHRISTINE**
(Photos

Un n qui dé en

Bordeau comparait Gironde l Bressand, millions fut arrêté l'inculpati faux et u

L'instru cier minis dans sa que de n taient en pour se l bourse.

Rosset-E Me Jean de, et M. soutient l'accusé p rapelle se notariale.

Il achet de temps Après la et fut cit

The prosecutor's case was simple. Christine and Lea Papin were fully responsible for their actions. They had committed a crime which he described, in a ringing phrase, as "the most horrible, and the most abominable, recorded in the annals of justice." And nobody need look beyond sheer bad temper for a motive.

The defence restricted itself to the plea that psychiatry was a complicated and incompletely-understood science. The question of whether the sisters were of sound mind was still a matter of debate.

The argument carried little weight with the jury. At 1.25 a.m., after 100 minutes, they brought in their verdict. Both sisters were guilty. From the public benches came an audible sigh of relief and a ripple of applause.

Christine showed her first sign of emotion when the judge sentenced her to death. She slumped to her knees for a moment before her lawyer helped her back to her feet. Lea, for whom the jury had found extenuating circumstances in the way she was dominated by her sister, received a sentence of ten years' hard labour. Neither sister appealed.

Later, however, Christine's punishment was commuted to a life sentence of hard labour. But she served only four years, during which she refused to work and showed signs of insanity. She was finally transferred to a psychiatric hospital where she died in 1937. During that time she never once asked for Lea who, when her own term of punishment was over, was released to live in obscurity.

3f50
AU POUVOIR DES FORCES OCCULTES PAR ACHEFF

LA VÉRITÉ SUR LE CRIME INEXPLIQUÉ DES SŒURS PAPIN

EDITIONS STYLEX

FIELD DAY for the press . . . . Details
of the trial provided reporters with
plenty of headline copy (left). Le Mans
prison (this page) is where the two sisters
were _____ while awaiting trial and
where treatment was _____

Mansell

THE SOUND OF GUN-FIRE

WHEN you consider that firearms were invented in the fourteenth century, it seems strange that it has taken so long for the gun to achieve its present pre-eminence as a murder weapon. The pistol — probably invented around 1450 in Pistoia in Italy — is certainly one of the quickest and most efficient methods of taking life — its chief disadvantages being that it is noisier than the knife, and a great deal less discreet than poison. This undoubtedly explains why the entry of the firearm into criminal history was relatively late and unspectacular. The Middlesex County Records for the year 1602 contain the following entry:

"On the highway at Howneslow, Co. Middx, Francis Kimber (a Gentleman of London) assaulted Wm. Peverell with a certain instrument called a pistol, which he, the said Francis, with his right hand pointed at the said William's beast and

put him into great fear and terror."

No further information is given, but it is clear that the writer was not at all familiar with the properties of pistols.

Pistols certainly came as a boon to highwaymen, who, prior to the 16th century, used swords and knives as their only weapons of intimidation. James Shaw, a highwayman, who was armed only with a sword: "robbed several coaches and single passengers, and that with very great inhumanity, which was natural, he said, from his method of attacking . . ." Shaw got the victim to hand over his wallet by holding a sword to his throat, solving the problem of pursuit by hamstringing the victim's horse, or slashing the muscles at the back of his victim's knees.

By 1720 — the year in which Shaw was executed — England had been engulfed by a crime wave. The pistol had revolu-

tionized the art of robbery. In one three-week period there were 25 major highway robberies around London, and people in coaches and sedan chairs were robbed in broad daylight in crowded streets.

The law tried to halt the epidemic with sheer barbarity; the gallows at Tyburn were in use from morning till night, and even women and children were executed for stealing a few pence.

Old methods

When someone asked a notoriously strict judge, Sir Francis Page, after his health, the old man quavered jocularly: "Oh, I keep hanging on, hanging on." But it made no difference; the crime wave continued until it was finally halted by the creation of an efficient police force more than half a century later.

Yet in spite of the highway robbers, surprisingly few murders were committed

295

with guns. Most people preferred to stick to the old methods—knives, hatchets and bludgeons. Dick Turpin, the famous highwayman, committed a murder—his only one—with a pistol: but that was of a man trying to arrest him. And ten years later, a party of smugglers added a curious episode to the history of firearms in one of the most gruesome murder cases.

A Customs officer named Galley, travelling in company with a shoemaker named Chater, made the mistake of stopping for a drink in the Hampshire village of Rowland's Castle. As soon as the word got around that there was a Customs officer at the inn, the local smugglers moved in. Galley was tortured with a pair of spurs, his testicles were squeezed until he fainted, and then he was whipped to death.

Mistrust

Chater was also tortured, but no one was willing to take on the responsibility of killing him. Finally, someone suggested that they should put a loaded gun to his head, tie a long string to the trigger, and that all fourteen of the smugglers should pull the trigger. If they had gone through with it, it would have raised an interesting point of law: whether fourteen men can all be convicted for the same murder. But they decided against it; instead, they threw Chater down a well —alive—and buried him with stones. By that time, half the smugglers had got tired of the whole thing and gone home; so only seven were eventually tried and executed for the murders.

The mistrust of firearms persisted even into the nineteenth century. The two most widely publicized crimes of the 1820s were William Corder's murder of Maria Marten in the Red Barn, and the murder of William Weare by Thurtell and Hunt. Corder shot his ex-mistress, Maria Marten, with a pistol, and although (as he confessed) "she fell and died in an instant", he then stabbed her several times with a carving knife. When Thurtell and Hunt—two "sporting gentlemen"— murdered the crooked bookmaker, William Weare, in 1823, they began by discharging a pistol in his face. The bullet glanced off Weare's cheekbone, and the wounded man ran away. Thurtell flung him to the ground and cut his throat with a penknife, then jammed the pistol against his head with such force that it smashed the skull, filling the barrel with blood and brains.

When Thurtell was executed in 1824 (Hunt escaped with a sentence of transportation), street hawkers were selling a poem that does not mention the pistol:
"They cut his throat from ear to ear
   His head they battered in.
   His name was Mr. William Weare—
   He lived in Lyons Inn."

If criminals were unhappy about the use of firearms, the police disliked them even more. If a man was killed with a knife or a bludgeon, the murder weapon could be produced in court and the jury convinced that it had inflicted the wounds; but a gun was a different matter. The bullet might have been knocked out of shape against a bone, and in any case, it was almost impossible to prove which gun had fired it.

Fortunately, there were a few men who took a less defeatist attitude. One of these was Dr. Joseph Bell, the man who inspired Conan Doyle with the idea of Sherlock Holmes. On August 10th, 1893, an ex-army tutor named A. J. Monson went out shooting with his employer's son, a youth called Cecil Hambrough.

As Cecil was climbing over a dyke, there was a shot and he fell dead. Monson claimed that the boy's gun had exploded accidentally. But when it was discovered that Monson had insured Hambrough's life, he was arrested and charged with murder. The key factor was whether Hambrough really had accidentally shot himself at close range or whether Monson had shot him from a few feet away. According to Monson, Cecil had been carrying the gun over his shoulder, and had stumbled and blown off the back of his head.

Dr. Bell brooded on the question. Shotguns are notoriously unpredictable weapons. Finally, Bell took a twelvebore shotgun to the morgue in Edinburgh, and fired it into the skull of a corpse. What he observed enabled him to say confidently in court that Cecil Hambrough could *not* have been shot with his own gun; he was shot from a distance of between six and nine feet from behind.

Bell's evidence should have hanged Monson, but the defence managed to confuse the issue with such a mass of financial evidence that Monson was acquitted on a Scottish verdict of "Not Proven". Nevertheless, Dr. Bell had proved that, where guns are concerned, no pathologist needs to acknowledge defeat.

At the time Dr. Bell was firing shotguns at cadavers in Edinburgh, another firearms expert ran a gun shop near Charing Cross station; his name was Ted Churchill, his shop was conveniently close to Scotland Yard, and he was often summoned there to give his opinion in cases involving guns. When Ted Churchill wanted to find out how far the bullets from a certain gun would damage a human skull, he tested the gun by firing at a sheep's head. And it was Ted Churchill's evidence that hammered the last nail into the coffin of a swindler and murderer called Samuel Herbert Dougal.

Dougal was what the sensational press would now call a sex maniac. His libidinous appetite was truly extraordinary—on

one occasion, he had seduced a mother *and* her three daughters. His career in the army had been reasonably successful, although two wives had died under somewhat suspicious circumstances. After his discharge, however, Dougal found it difficult to continue to live in the manner he preferred; seduction cost money.

He tried his hand at forgery, was caught, and served a prison sentence. Then he had the good fortune to meet a middleaged spinster named Camille Holland, who soon allowed herself to be seduced. Miss Holland was rich. In 1899, Dougal and "Mrs. Dougal" moved into rooms in Saffron Walden while Dougal carried out negotiations to buy a property called Moat Farm near Clavering—with Miss Holland's money. The landlady took a great liking to the sweet, gentle-mannered "Mrs. Dougal"; then her lodgers moved into Moat Farm, and she saw no more of the lady.

Identical crack

At Moat Farm, Dougal was now living alone—although he had a succession of young female visitors. Four years went by, and then in March 1903, a police officer called to question Dougal about the missing Camille Holland. Dougal explained that he had never married Miss Holland because he was in the process of divorcing his previous wife. Miss Holland, he said, had left him for another man in 1899, not long after moving into Moat Farm.

The police found the story unlikely; they knew that Dougal had made determined attempts to seduce a servant girl shortly after moving into the farm, and there had been quarrels between husband and "wife". The police began digging in the garden, and they continued digging, in spite of Dougal's threats to sue the Chief Constable for damaging his crops. The moats that gave the farm its name were drained, but no body was found in the black mud.

Then the police heard about a ditch that had been filled in on Dougal's instructions. They found the man who had superintended the work, and dug where he suggested. Soon the police were looking down at the badly decomposed body of Miss Holland. The pathologist's report showed that she had died from a gunshot wound in the side of the head. A bootmaker identified the boots on the corpse as having been made for Miss Holland. Now it was up to Ted Churchill.

No revolver had been found, but there were a number of ·32 calibre bullets found at the farm. Churchill fired some of

MAD SLAYER Howard Unruh killed no less than thirteen people (above right). Police (top) inspect his arsenal. Unruh (right) was found criminally insane.

Unruh's Residence

1. John P. Pilarchick
2. Orris Smith
3. Clark Hoover
4. James Hutton
5. Mrs. Rose Cohen
6. Maurice Cohen
7. Mrs. Minnie Cohen
8. Alvin M. Day, Jr.
9. Mrs. Helga Zegrino
10. Thomas Hamilton
11. Mrs. Emma Matlack
12. Mrs. Helen Wilson
13. John Wilson

UPI, AP, Acme

these bullets into sheep's heads. In court, he was able to demonstrate not only that the bullet found in Miss Holland's skull was a somewhat distorted ·32, but that it must have been fired by someone sitting beside her—probably in a car. He had been able to produce a crack in the sheep's skull practically identical with that in the head of Camille Holland.

Throughout the trial, Dougal had been cheerful and ironically polite; but as Churchill gave his evidence, his *sang froid* disappeared. He recognized this was the end—and indeed it was; he was executed on July 8, 1903. As the trap was about to open, the chaplain whispered urgently: "Guilty or Not Guilty?", and from the hood that covered Dougal's head came a muffled reply: "Guilty."

Hooded man

The man who, more than any other, was responsible for turning ballistics into a science was not Ted Churchill, but his nephew, Robert Churchill, who took over the family gun shop in 1910. The affair that first brought him to public notice was the case of the "Hooded Man".

In the early hours of October 9, 1912, Inspector Arthur Walls, of the East-bourne police, saw a burglar crouching on the portico of a house in South Cliff Avenue, and called to him to come down. Instead, the burglar fired two shots, and Walls fell dead. Not long afterwards, the police discovered the identity of the killer: he was George Mackay, alias John Williams, a petty crook.

Mackay was betrayed by a "friend", Edgar Powers, who was in love with the burglar's beautiful mistress, Florence Seymour. At the instigation of the police, Powers persuaded the girl to lead him to the revolver with which Walls had been killed—she had helped Mackay bury it on the beach.

Churchill's task was to try and prove that the bullet that had killed Walls had been fired from this revolver. At that time, there was no sure way of proving that a particular bullet had been fired from a certain gun—more than ten years were to pass before this became possible with the comparison microscope. But Churchill devised a way of showing the jury that the rifling on the bullet corresponded closely to the rifling inside the barrel of the gun.

He poured wax into the gun and made a "cast" of the inside of the barrel. In court, he produced enlarged photographs of the bullet, and of the wax cast; the jury could see how closely they corresponded. Mackay, known in the press as "The Hooded Man", because the police kept him hooded on his journeys to court—they were still searching for witnesses to identify him—was convicted of the murder, and hanged in January 1913.

Before he died, he was allowed to kiss his newly-born child. He placed a piece of prison bread in the baby's mouth, saying: "Now no one can say your father never gave you anything."

It was in June 1914 that a young Bosnian called Gavrilo Princip fired the two shots that led to the outbreak of the First World War. Archduke Ferdinand of Austria was visiting Sarajevo with his duchess. Serbian patriots wanted to register their protest about the Austrian occupation of Bosnia. Shortly after 10 a.m. on June 28, 1914, a bomb was thrown at the Archduke's carriage, but it missed, wounding several spectators instead. An hour later, the Archduke left the town hall, and remarked to his wife: "I've got a feeling there may be more bombs around."

He was mistaken; the weapon that Gavrilo Princip concealed in his pocket was a Browning revolver with six shots

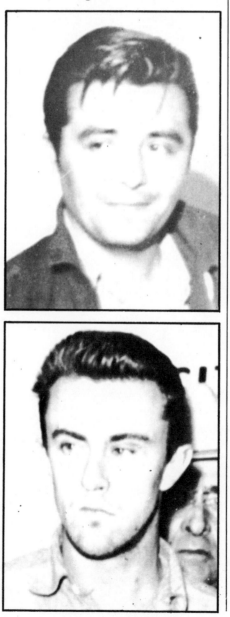

in it. The car approached Princip—and then turned off into another street: modern history hung in the balance. Then someone shouted that the car had taken the wrong turn; the route had been revised. It backed, and proceeded past the young Bosnian—who drew his revolver, and fired twice at close range. One shot killed the Archduke, and the other, his wife.

Princip was seized, but the decisive tragedy of modern history had taken place, and the rest followed inevitably—Austria's declaration of war on Serbia, Russian mobilization, the Kaiser's declaration of war on Russia . . .

Social parasite

Those two revolver shots also launched the world into a new epoch: the age of guns. The 1914 war was the first time that vast numbers of men actually handled guns. Before the war, most guns were owned by farmers or sportsmen; now everybody learned how to use them. An early Spencer Tracy film called *They Gave Him a Gun* put its finger on what happened: the servicemen came back from Europe, and found a new world that had already forgotten the war and the men who fought in it.

There were no jobs for the returning heroes; life was hard. So many of them decided to make use of what they had learned in the army, and suddenly, the police were faced with the greatest crime wave since 1720. But this time it was not just in England, but in America, France, Italy, Germany . . . The petty criminal who had never stolen anything larger than a watch discovered that it was just as easy to walk into a bank and point a gun at the cashier.

And the Americans, with an innocence and optimism that now seem stunning, decided to reform their country by banning all alcoholic liquor, and thereby produced an entirely new breed of social parasite called the mobster; fifty years later, in spite of numerous Acts of Congress and Commissions of Enquiry, America is still as securely in the mobsters' hands as it was in Al Capone's.

In most of the countries of the world, the authorities have achieved some sort of control by banning the sale of guns to private citizens. In America, financial interests—known as the "gun lobby"—continue to prevent a measure that would probably cut the crime rate by 75%.

America's gun problem is not so much social as psychological. The past 25 years have seen an alarming increase in mass murders committed with guns, and the majority of such cases have taken place in America. On December 30, 1950, a young psychopath named William Cook stopped a car driven by Carl Mosser; Mosser's wife, three young children and family dog were also in the car. Cook brandished a gun, and made the Mosser family drive around Texas for 72 hours; then, when the wife and children became hysterical, he killed them all.

On September 6, 1949, a 28-year-old ex-G.I. named Howard Unruh walked out of his house in Camden, New Jersey, carrying a German Luger pistol, and, in the next twelve minutes, killed thirteen people at random. Captured after a siege of his home, Unruh declared: "I'd have killed a thousand if I'd had enough ammunition."

In January 1958, Charles Starkweather took his girlfriend Caril Fugate on a murder rampage across Nebraska, and had shot and killed ten people—mostly strangers—before he was captured a couple of days later. In Lathrup Village, Michigan, in August 1968, a family of six called Robison were all "executed" by an unknown killer with a ·22 revolver.

GUN CRAZY slayer William Cook and his victims, the Mosser family. Facing page: Perry Smith (top) and Richard Hickock who shot up the Clutter family.

In October 1970, John Linley Frazier "executed" the family of Dr. Victor Ohta at his home near Santa Cruz, California, and threw the five bodies into the swimming pool. On November 7, 1973, a family of nine—four adults, three teenagers and two young children—were all shot through the head by unknown killers at their home near Victor, California . . .

It would be possible to list dozens— even hundreds—of such cases that·have taken place in America—the only English parallel is the case of psychopath, Peter Manuel, who killed two families with a gun in late 1956 and early 1957—but one more will suffice. On November 15, 1959, two ex-convicts named Perry Smith and Richard Hickock broke into the home of the Clutter family near Holcomb, Kansas, and slaughtered all four in the course of robbery.

In 1966, Truman Capote's reconstruction of the crime, *In Cold Blood,* broke best-selling records in America, although it failed to achieve the same success in other countries. Obviously, Capote had touched on some strange, dark nerve in the American psyche. If we understood this, we should understand something important about the mysterious lure of gun violence in America. That lure can only be quashed by outlawing the gun.

Radio Times, Savoy Hotel/Quartet

MME FAHMY

Glamour, wealth, a beautiful woman and one of the greatest lawyers the British courts had ever produced —the trial of Madame Marguerite Fahmy (below) for the murder of her husband (left) in their Savoy Hotel suite had all the ingredients for a sensational trial. No one was disappointed.

THE TRIAL of Marie-Marguerite Fahmy for the murder of her playboy husband Prince Ali Kamel Fahmy Bey, which opened in London's Central Criminal Court on September 10, 1923, had all the elements of a drama of powerful passions. The accused was an attractive and sophisticated 32-year-old Parisienne brunette of slender height and striking beauty.

Her late husband, ten years her junior, was an abnormal and vicious young Egyptian of considerable wealth and worldly possessions, who was widely believed to have treated her with disgusting cruelty. He held the nominal post of attaché at the French Legation in Cairo and had obtained his princely title in return for making gifts to various Egyptian charities.

Prince Fahmy's death, which his wife admitted she had caused by shooting him, had taken place during the night of

Syndication International, Radio Times Hulton/Quartet

THE DAILY MIRROR, Tuesday, September 11, 1923.

GERMANY SEEKING NEW CONFERENCE WITH FRANCE

The Daily Mirror

NET SALE MUCH THE LARGEST OF ANY DAILY PICTURE NEWSPAPER

No. 6,194. Registered at the G.P.O. as a Newspaper. TUESDAY, SEPTEMBER 11, 1923 One Penny.

SAVOY SHOOTING : MME. FAHMY'S TRIAL OPENS

Mme. Said, sister of the dead man, with her husband, Dr. Said (centre), and Abdul Faath Razal Bey, an Egyptian lawyer, representing Mme. Said.

Sir Henry Curtis Bennett, K.C., one of the counsel engaged for the defence.

Mr. Cecil Whiteley, K.C., who held a watching brief, arriving at the Old Bailey.

Said Enani, the dead man's secretary, said the couple were not very happy.

A new portrait, received from Paris last night, of Mme. Fahmy, who is charged with the murder of her husband, Ali Kamel Fahmy Bey (inset), a wealthy young Egyptian.

The large crowd that waited outside the Old Bailey in the hope of gaining admittance for the opening of the trial. Many fashionably-dressed women were present

Passionate letters, descriptions of life in an Egyptian palace, and an account of frequent quarrels between the dead man and his wife, figured in the evidence and examination of Said Enani, secretary to Ali Kamel Fahmy Bey, at the opening yesterday of the trial of Mme. Marie Marguerite Fahmy on a charge of murdering her husband by shooting him at the Savoy Hotel. In his opening address, counsel for the prosecution stated that after marriage Mme. Fahmy always slept with a pistol close at hand.

302

Daily Mirror

the previous 9-10 July in the Savoy Hotel in London, where they occupied a luxurious suite of rooms. At the inquest which followed the killing, the coroner's jury returned a verdict of wilful murder against Madame Fahmy.

Mr. Justice Rigby Swift presided at the trial. He was the youngest judge on the High Court bench, having been only 46 at the time of his appointment three years previously, but he had already made his mark by his effective handling of jury cases. The prosecution was led by Mr. Percival Clarke, son of the famous Victorian advocate Sir Edward Clarke. Marguerite Fahmy was represented by two leading King's Counsel, Sir Edward Marshall Hall and Sir Henry Curtis Bennett, though in fact the defence was to be entirely handled by Marshall Hall, who had taken Sir Edward Clarke's place as the most popular and sought after defence lawyer in the country.

Incompatible

Opening the case for the Crown, Mr. Percival Clarke said that Fahmy Bey had inherited great wealth from his father, an engineer. He became infatuated with the accused, then Madame Laurent, a divorcée, whom he first met in Paris in May of the previous year. He followed her to Deauville, where she became his mistress, and they lived there and in Egypt and Paris. In December, Marguerite became a Moslem and there were civil and religious marriage ceremonies. Prince Fahmy returned to Cairo where he was later joined by his wife, who had remained in Paris, but at no time were they happy. Their natures seemed incompatible.

At the beginning of July 1923, the couple came to London and put up at the Savoy Hotel, accompanied by a secretary, valet and maid. On July 9 they had some disagreement because the wife wanted to go to Paris to have an operation which the husband wished to have performed in London. At supper in the hotel restaurant that night there was a violent quarrel during which Madame Fahmy, it was alleged, said to her husband: "You shut up. I will smash this bottle over your head."

When the band leader came to her table and asked if there was any particular tune she would like to be played, she replied, "I don't want any music — my husband has threatened to kill me tonight!" The polite maestro bowed gravely and said, "I hope you will still be here tomorrow, madame." After supper Fahmy twice asked his wife to dance, but she refused, though she danced once with his secretary Seid Ernani.

They went upstairs to their suite about 1.30 a.m. A violent thunderstorm was raging at the time. Shortly afterwards a luggage porter was passing the door of the suite when Fahmy came out in his pyjamas and said to the porter: "Look at my face! Look at what she has done!" The porter saw a slight red mark on his cheek. Then Madame Fahmy, who was in evening dress, came out and, speaking hurriedly in French, pointed to her eyes; the porter told them to go into their rooms and not create a disturbance in the corridor, and then continued on his way.

Hearing a whistle, the porter looked back and saw Prince Fahmy stooping down, whistling and snapping his fingers at a little dog which had come out of their suite. A few moments later the porter heard three shots in quick succession, and running back to the suite saw Madame Fahmy throw down a pistol. Her husband was lying on the floor bleeding from his head. "Oh, sir," said Madame Fahmy when the manager was summoned, "I have been married six months which has been torture to me. I have suffered terribly."

The police and a doctor were sent for and the wounded man was removed to hospital where he died shortly afterwards. Marguerite was then taken into custody.

Seid Ernani was the first to give evidence for the prosecution, corroborating details of his late master's life and marriage. Cross-examined by Marshall Hall, he denied that he had any influence over Prince Fahmy which would have made his wife jealous.

Sickening flattery

"Was he in the habit of beating women?"

"He would dispute with them," the secretary replied, "but I have never seen him beat them."

"You have known of his intimacies with many women?" Marshall Hall continued.

"Yes," the witness agreed.

"You said that you tried to dissuade the prince from marrying her?"

"Yes."

"Did you say he was an Oriental, and passionate?"

"Yes."

"You were very much attached to Prince Fahmy?"

"Yes."

"Was he infatuated with her at that time?"

"Yes, very much in love with her."

Marshall Hall then quoted a letter written in French from Egypt by the Prince to Marguerite in terms of sickening flattery. The translation read in part:

"Your image pursues me incessantly . . . Torch of my life . . . your head so haughty and majestic, brightly encircled by a crown which I reserve for it here. Yes, this crown I reserve for you on your arrival in this beautiful country of my ancestors."

"Everybody thought he was a prince, then?" Madame Fahmy's counsel asked.

"We always refer to our ancestors," was all the secretary could say.

"But they do not all wear crowns?"

"No."

Divorce condition

Answering further questions, Seid Ernani said that it was in Cairo that the question of marriage first arose. Fahmy first suggested that she live with him, and then suggested marriage. Two of the stipulations in the contract were that Madame Fahmy would not be obliged to wear Egyptian clothes and that she would have the right to divorce her husband. She adopted the Moslem religion because Fahmy's mother had left him a large legacy on condition that he married a woman of that faith.

"When the religious ceremony took place, did Fahmy decline to allow the divorce condition to be inserted?"

"Yes."

"After the religious ceremony, then, he could divorce her, as she was a Moslem, at a moment's notice and she could not divorce him, and he had the power to take three wives if he liked?"

The witness agreed that this was so. Marshall Hall then turned to the prince's treatment of his wife.

"Were people always set to watch her when she went out?"

"They were lately," the witness again agreed.

"On February 21st was there a very serious scene? Do you know that he swore on the Koran to kill her?"

"No."

"Do you know that she was in fear of her life?"

"No, I never knew that."

"On the 23rd, did Fahmy take her on his yacht at Luxor?"

"Yes."

"Were there six black servants on board?"

"Yes."

"I suggest that from that moment Fahmy began to treat her with persistent cruelty?"

"I cannot say cruelty. He was a bit unkind."

Training

"The day he arrived at Luxor, did he smack her face, tell her she must not leave the yacht, and then kick her?"

"I have not seen him kick her. I knew he locked her in." Further pressed by Marshall Hall, the secretary was obliged to admit that he remembered an incident when Fahmy struck his wife a violent blow on the chin and dislocated her jaw.

To drive home his point Marshall Hall went on to read from a letter which Fahmy had written to his wife's younger sister:

"Just now I am engaged in training her. Yesterday, to begin with I did not come in to lunch nor to dinner and I also left her at the theatre. This will teach her, I hope, to respect my wishes.

"With women one must act with energy and be severe – no bad habits. We still lead the same life of which you are aware – the opera, theatre, disputes, high words, and perverseness."

"When you came over from Egypt," counsel continued, "his treatment of his wife was the talk of the ship?"

"They were always quarrelling," replied the secretary.

"Do you know that he locked her in her cabin for 24 hours and that the captain had to have her released?"

"I don't know that."

"Was not the Madame Fahmy of 1923 totally different from the Madame Laurent of 1922?"

"Perhaps."

"From a quite entertaining and fascinating woman she became miserable and wretched?"

"They were always quarrelling."

"Did she say that you and Fahmy were always against her, and that it was a case of two to one?"

"Yes."

Notorious relationship

Marshall Hall went on to suggest to the witness that Prince Fahmy was a man of vicious and eccentric sexual appetite, and that he had a homosexual relationship with Seid Ernani which was notorious in Egypt. He showed the witness a coloured cartoon which had appeared in an Egyptian newspaper depicting Prince Fahmy, his secretary and a friend as "The Light, the Shadow of the Light, and the Shadow of the Shadow of the Light".

While agreeing that he and his employer were represented in the cartoon, the witness loyally denied any unfavourable reflection on his or his master's morals. The judge then asked to see the cartoon, and when he had examined it he remarked that it did not reflect on anybody's moral character, except perhaps the artist's.

It was a masterly cross-examination. Marshall Hall did not attack the secretary's character, though he got very near to it at the end. Had he done so, this would have entitled the prosecution to attack that of Madame Fahmy, and it was of vital importance to her counsel's case that she should not be exhibited as an habitually loose woman. As it was, the secretary admitted enough to impress the jury by creating an atmosphere of intense sympathy for the accused woman, who had been in the power of this decadent Oriental millionaire.

The porter, night manager and assistant manager of the Savoy Hotel followed the secretary into the witness box. In cross-examining the assistant manager, Marshall Hall again showed his characteristic skill and incidentally his knowledge of the French language. According to this witness, Madame Fahmy had said to him in French immediately after the shooting, "Monsieur, what have I done? I have lost my head."

The actual words used by Madame Fahmy were, *"J'ai perdu la tête."* Marshall Hall put it to the witness that the real meaning of the phrase was not "I have lost my head", but "I was frightened out of my wits". The witness agreed, and this interpretation was not challenged by the prosecution.

Painful complaint

Robert Churchill, the gunsmith and firearms expert, testified that the weapon used in the killing was a .32 Browning automatic of Belgian manufacture, capable of holding eight cartridges. Prosecuting counsel asked him: "Is it a weapon that continues to fire when the trigger is pressed, or does the trigger require pressure for each shot?"

"The trigger has to be pulled for each shot," the witness replied. "It is automatic loading, but not automatic firing." The gunsmith added that the pull of the trigger was 8¼ pounds. It was not a light pull. The pistol had a safety grip and a safety catch and was not the sort to go off accidentally. Churchill was cross-examined at length about the mechanism of the weapon by Marshall Hall who suggested that, when the pistol was tightly gripped, a very small pressure on the trigger would discharge each shot. The witness agreed that this was so and also explained that after one shot had been discharged through the barrel it would immediately be replaced by another. An inexperienced person might thus easily reload the weapon, believing that in fact he had emptied it.

Dr. Gordon, who had been attending Madame Fahmy and had made arrangements for her to go into a London nursing home for her operation on the day after the killing, testified that he was called to the scene of the tragedy and asked Madame Fahmy what she had done. "I have shot my husband," she replied. She was in a white evening dress trimmed with beads, and was very dazed and frightened.

"Did you see any marks of bruising on her arms?" asked the prosecutor.

"She showed me a scratch on the back of her neck about 1½ inches long, probably caused by a finger nail. She told me her husband had done it."

Asked by Marshall Hall in cross-examination whether the marks on her neck were consistent with a hand clutching her throat, the doctor said they were.

"When you visited Madame Fahmy for her illness, did you see her husband?"

"No. He was in the next room, and a black valet was outside Madame's door."

Questioned about the nature of Madame Fahmy's illness, Dr. Gordon agreed that she was suffering from a painful complaint which might have been caused by the conduct she alleged against her husband. The published accounts of the trial are silent on the nature of this conduct, but it may well be that Prince Fahmy forced his wife to have anal intercourse and may conceivably have communicated a venereal disease to her in the process.

After police evidence of the accused's arrest, the prosecution case was closed and Marshall Hall opened his defence with a speech to the jury, to whom he submitted that it would be impossible justly on the facts to find "this poor unfortunate woman guilty" of either murder or manslaughter. She was "perhaps a woman of not very strict morality", he went on, because they had heard that she had been divorced and had lived with Fahmy before their marriage.

There was no doubt, however, that although they were infatuated with each other at the beginning, she had made a terrible mistake in her estimate of his character.

"We know that women are sometimes very much attracted to men younger than themselves," Marshall Hall told the jury, "and he went out of his way, with all his Eastern cunning, to make himself agreeable and acceptable to her. But this was a man who enjoys the sufferings of women. He was abnormal and a brute. After marriage all restraint ceased and he developed from a plausible lover into a ferocious brute with the vilest of vile tempers and a filthy perverted taste. It makes one shudder to consider the conditions under which this wretched woman lived."

New evidence

Coming to the night of the tragedy, Marshall Hall recounted how Fahmy had called his wife into his bedroom and pointed to a heap of money on the table. She asked him to give her the French money, about 2,000 francs, for her travelling expenses to Paris for her operation. He told her she could not have it unless she agreed to a suggestion he made, apparently for abnormal sexual intercourse. She refused and he spat in her face, telling her to go to the devil. He then followed her outside into the corridor, catching her by the neck and tightening his grip on her so that she feared she would be strangled.

Thanks to the judge's intervention, Marshall Hall went on, "a new and wonderful piece of evidence" had come into his hands. This was the report of the prison medical officer, who was also the governor of Holloway Prison where the accused was taken after her arrest. He was called

Daily Mirror

The Daily

NET SALE MUCH THE LARGEST OF ANY

No. 6,195. Registered at the G.P.O. as a Newspaper WEDNESDAY, SEPTEMBER 12.

MME. FAHMY'S SECRET

Mme. Fahmy and, inset, Ali Kamel Fahmy Bey, of whose murder she stands accused.

Dr. E. F. Gordon (on left), who had attended Mme. Fahmy, was one of the principal witnesses yesterday.

Mr. Arthur Mariani, night manager of the Savoy Hotel, who gave evidence.

Remarkable allegations regarding the dead man were made by counsel at the trial of Mme. Fahmy at the Old Bailey yesterday. He declared also that Mme. Fahmy had given her lawyer in Egypt a sealed document not to be opened till after her death.

as the first witness for the defence, and he described how Madame Fahmy, when she was admitted to Holloway, had three abrasions on the back of her neck apparently caused by a man's hand.

Marshall Hall intended to call the accused next, but before he did so he informed the judge that it was necessary to discuss a point of law in the absence of the jury. When the jury had accordingly been sent out, the leading defence counsel said he had been told by the prosecutor, Mr. Percival Clarke, that he proposed to cross-examine Madame Fahmy to show that, as she was a woman who lived an immoral life, she would therefore be a woman of the world well able to look after herself. "The only effect of that," observed Marshall Hall, "would be to prejudice the jury unfavourably towards this woman. We know the effect of these suggestions."

Legal discussion

"Sir Edward has said she was an immoral woman," the judge remarked, "but he has said it in such a way as to give the impression to everyone who listened to his speech that she was an innocent and most respectable lady. It is a difficult thing to do, but Sir Edward, with all that skill we have admired for so long, has done it." Mr. Justice Swift then ruled that the evidence so far did not justify Mr. Clarke in asking Madame Fahmy about her relations with any other men, but with regard to the dead man he might ask anything he liked.

When the jury returned to court, the judge said he did not propose to inform them of the legal discussion which had taken place, and added: "I must now give instructions that you are not to be allowed access to any newspapers until the trial is over. I am sorry to deprive you of them. It must be very boring to be shut up all the evening without even a newspaper, but I am bound to do it."

Then the prisoner was called to testify in her own defence. Slowly and carefully —through the medium of an interpreter, since she knew no English—Marshall Hall took her through the tragedy of her life with Prince Fahmy until the three fatal shots were fired. She said she had married her first husband M. Laurent in April 1919 and had divorced him a few months later for desertion. On the subject of her second husband's treatment of her, she said that his black valet was always following her about and used to enter her room when she was dressing. When she complained to her husband, he replied: "He has the right. He does not count. He is nobody."

She described how one day in Paris, when her young sister Yvonne Alibert was present, he had threatened her with a horsewhip, seizing her by the throat and

305

throwing her backwards. He only stopped when her sister, who had a revolver in her hand, told him to desist. After the scene on the yacht, she described how Ali Fahmy had taken the Koran and sworn on it that he would kill her. Later she wrote to her French lawyer that she had been held literally prisoner on board the yacht for three days and that on her arms were "the marks of my husband's gentleness".

Final scene

In further replies to her counsel, she said that she had never fired a pistol till the night of her husband's death. Fahmy himself had given her the Browning .32 loaded, saying, "It is all ready to fire." She had often seen him unload the pistol by opening the breach and taking out a cartridge. On that dreadful night, when he had tried to strangle her and she had been in an agony of fear, she had tried to do the same thing. But her hands had not been strong enough to pull back the breach cover fully, and she had struggled to extract the bullet by shaking the weapon in front of the window. While she was thus engaged, somehow the first cartridge went off and the bullet spent itself harmlessly out of the window.

"After the cartridge had been fired," she said, "I thought the revolver was not dangerous." However, unknown to her, the second cartridge had automatically come up into position.

"I know nothing about automatic pistols," she said, as her counsel handed the weapon to her. At first she shrank back from it, but eventually she took it in her hands. She tried, but was quite unable to pull back the breach cover.

"Why did you assent to come to London when you were so frightened?" Marshall Hall asked her.

"I had to come to London for family reasons," she replied. "I had always hoped he would change. Every time I threatened to leave him, he cried and promised to mend his ways. I also wished to see my daughter who was at school near London."

With a sob punctuating every phrase, she told the story of the final scene.

"He advanced and had a very threatening expression. He said, 'I will revenge myself.' I had taken the revolver in my hand . . . I went out into the corridor in front of the lift. He seized me suddenly and brutally by the throat with his left hand. His thumb was on my windpipe and his fingers were pressing on my neck.

"I pushed him away, but he crouched to spring on me, and said, 'I will kill you.' I lifted my arm in front of me and without looking pulled the trigger. The next moment I saw him on the ground before me. I do not know how many times the revolver went off. I did not know what had happened.

"I saw Fahmy on the ground and I fell on my knees beside him. I caught hold of his hand and said to him, 'Sweetheart, it is nothing. Speak, oh, please speak to me!' While I was on my knees the porter came up."

Marshall Hall asked her two final questions in his examination-in-chief.

"When the pistol went off, killing your husband, had you any idea that it was in a condition to be fired?"

"None," the witness answered emphatically. "I thought there was no cartridge and that it could not be used."

"When you threw your arm out when the pistol was fired, what were you afraid of?"

"That he was going to jump on to me. It was terrible. I had escaped once. He said, 'I will kill you. I will kill you.' It was so terrible."

Mr. Percival Clarke began his cross-examination by asking if her father was a cab-driver in Paris. Immediately the judge intervened. "Does it matter whether he

WORLD'S GREATEST . . . That was the verdict of many people after Sir Edward Marshall Hall's masterly performance in the sensational trial of Mme. Fahmy.

was a cab-driver or a millionaire?" he asked the prosecutor. "I don't want a long inquiry into the lady's ancestry or into circumstances which may not be admissible."

Counsel did not pursue this line. Instead he asked the witness, "Can I correctly describe you as a woman of the world, a woman of experience?"

"I have had experience of life," Madame Fahmy answered sagely.

Asked whether she had not gone to Egypt with the idea of marrying Prince Fahmy, she said that she had arrived at no decision but had merely "accepted to be his *amie*".

"Were you not very ambitious to become his wife?"

"Ambitious, no," replied the witness. "I loved him so very much and wished to be with him."

Asked what she did when her husband was cruel, she said, "Once only I boxed his ears when he had beaten me very much. I was always alternating between hope and despair," she went on. "Some days he would be nice and I had new confidence in him, but the next day he would be bad again, and it was always the same." Their physical relations she described as "being never quite normal". She added that when she went out to buy new dresses, her husband's secretary Seid Ernani was always sent with her and she had to undress before him.

"Why did you not have him to protect you if you feared your husband?"

"He was not my friend. He obeyed my husband's orders, not mine."

"Did you think that he was in league with your husband to ill-treat you?"

"Sometimes I have thought so, because I noticed each time I told him something he immediately went to my husband and told him what I said, and did whatever he could to make matters worse."

On the whole Madame Fahmy stood up well to this cross-examination, particularly when she was asked about the pistol. "I never intended to shoot it out of the window," she said. "I just wanted to get the ball out, and I tried to pull the thing back but I had not the strength to do it. As I was shaking it, it went off and I felt perfectly certain it was safe."

Important letter

"Did you not think that when you got rid of the cartridge you were depriving yourself of the only defence left to you if your husband assaulted you?"

"I never wanted to kill my husband," the prisoner answered between sobs. "I only wanted to prevent him killing me. I thought the sight of the pistol might frighten him. But I never wanted to do him any harm. I never did . . . I never noticed that I had pressed upon the trigger . . . I saw my husband lying on the ground before I could think or see what had happened."

Marshall Hall had kept one important piece of evidence in reserve for re-examination. This was a letter Madame Fahmy had written to her lawyer, accusing her husband of being responsible should she disappear. It read in part:

"Yesterday, January 21, 1923, at three o'clock in the afternoon, he took his Bible or Koran — I do not know how it is called — kissed it, put his hand on it, and swore to avenge himself upon me tomorrow, in eight days, a month, three months, but I must disappear by his hands. This oath was taken without any reason, neither jealousy, nor a scene on my part."

LONDON-MANCHESTER AIR MAIL CRASH: FIVE DEAD

The Daily Mirror

NET SALE MUCH THE LARGEST OF ANY DAILY PICTURE NEWSPAPER

No. 6,198   Registered at the G.P.O. as a Newspaper.   SATURDAY, SEPTEMBER 15, 1923   One Penny.

SUMMING UP IN FAHMY TRIAL: VERDICT TO-DAY

Sir Edward Marshall-Hall, whose dramatic final speech for the defence was in striking contrast to the quiet reply of Mr. Percival Clarke (inset) for the Crown.

Mr. Justice Rigby Swift had not concluded his summing-up when the Court adjourned yesterday, the fifth day of the trial.

Mme. Fahmy, the Frenchwoman charged with the murder of her husband. The verdict is expected to-day.

Daily Mirror

"Is that letter true?" asked Marshall Hall, holding it up.

"It is the exact truth," Madame Fahmy answered with conviction.

After the prisoner's sister, maid, and chauffeur had been called to corroborate the catalogue of Prince Fahmy's cruelties, Marshall Hall began his closing speech to the jury on the fourth day of the trial. "She made one great mistake, possibly the greatest mistake any woman of the West can make," he said of his client, "she married an Oriental. I dare say the Egyptian civilization is, and may be, one of the oldest and most wonderful civilizations in the world. But if you strip off the external civilization of the Oriental, you get the real Oriental underneath. It is common knowledge that the Oriental's treatment of women does not fit in with the way the Western woman considers she should be treated by her husband."

Marguerite Fahmy's defender went on to make the jury's flesh creep with his description of the subtle means by which the prince had enticed her into his "Oriental garden", after which she was constantly watched by his retinue of black servants. "Why was this woman afraid?" he asked the jury and went on to supply the answer. "Was she afraid that some of the hirelings of this man would do her to death? The curse of this case is the atmosphere which we cannot understand — the Eastern feeling of possession of the woman, the Turk in his harem, this man who was entitled to have four wives if he liked for chattels, which to us Western people with our ideas of women is almost unintelligible, something we cannot deal with."

Marshall Hall had not finished when the court adjourned. He resumed his speech next morning with a reference to the storm on the night of the killing. "You know the effect of such a storm when your nerves are normal," he told the jury. "Imagine its effect on a woman of nervous temperament who had been living such a life as she had lived for the past six months — terrified, abused, beaten, degraded."

Theatrical performance

The advocate went on to stage what was perhaps the most remarkable theatrical performance of his professional career when with the pistol in his hand he described the shooting in detail, imitating Fahmy's stealthy crouch as he advanced on his wife. "In sheer desperation — as he crouched for the last time, crouched like an animal, retired for the last time to get a bound forward — she turned the pistol and put it to his face, and to her horror the thing went off."

As he spoke the last words, the great

advocate held up the pistol and pointed it for a moment at the jury. Then he paused and dropped the weapon so that it fell with a clatter on the courtroom floor, just as it had fallen from the prisoner's hands in the corridor of the Savoy Hotel. The effect of this demonstration was chillingly dramatic, yet Marshall Hall always said afterwards that the final touch was an accident and that he had not meant to drop the pistol at all.

He concluded with two references. The first was to what the prosecutor's father Sir Edward Clarke had said in another sensational Old Bailey trial. "To use the words of my learned friend's great father many years ago in the Bartlett case, 'I do not ask you for a verdict—I demand a verdict at your hands.'"

His second reference was to a modern best-selling novel by Robert Hitchens called *Bella Donna*, in the final scene of which a Western woman goes out of the gates of an Oriental garden into the dark night of the desert.

"Members of the jury," he said, "I want you to open the gates where this Western woman can go out, not into the dark night of the desert, but back to her friends, who love her in spite of her weaknesses—back to her friends, who will be glad to receive her—back to her child who will be waiting for her with open arms. I ask you to open the gate and let this Western woman go back into the light of God's great Western sun."

Marshall Hall pointed to the skylight where the bright English September sun was streaming in and suffusing the court with its warmth and brightness. With this final dramatic gesture, he sat down.

Strong protest

In the face of this superb pleading, it took the jury little over an hour to reach their verdict—not guilty of murder, and not guilty of manslaughter. The cheering which greeted the result was so great that the judge immediately ordered the court to be cleared. The prisoner broke down when she was discharged, the climax to an ordeal in which she had not been able to understand a single word of the concluding speeches and the judge's summing up. "Oh, I am so happy, I am so thankful," she sobbed as she stumbled from the dock supported by two wardresses. "It is terrible to have killed Ali, but I spoke the truth. I spoke the truth."

Marshall Hall's oratory in defence of Marguerite Fahmy drew a strong protest to the British Attorney-General from the leader of the Egyptian Bar, who accused the advocate of "allowing himself to generalize and to lash all Egypt and indeed the whole East".

This was unfair, as indeed Marshall Hall himself pointed out. "Any attack I made was on express instructions, re-ceived through Egyptian sources on the man Ali Fahmy, and not on the Egyptians as a nation," he wrote to the Attorney-General. "If my instructions were, as I believe them to be, accurate, anything I said about that person was more than justified. The only thing that I remember saying that might be misunderstood was that it was a mistake for Western woman to marry Eastern man, and his idea of his rights towards a wife were those of possession instead of mutual alliance."

It must be remembered that these were the days of plays like *The Sheik* and *The Garden of Allah* and stories which roman-ticized the sexual allure of the East. As the English *Daily Mirror* wrote in an editorial at the time, the moral of the Fahmy trial for most people had little to do with the circumstances in which the fatal shot was fired, but bore chiefly if not solely upon the undesirability of marriage which united Oriental husbands and Western wives. The editorial continued:

"Too many of our women novelists, apparently under the spell of the East, have encouraged the belief that there is something very romantic in such unions.

"They are not romantic.

"They are ridiculous and unseemly; and the sensational revelations of the trial which terminated on Saturday will not be without their use if they bring that fact home to the sentimental naive girl."

For Sir Edward Marshall Hall the

ORIENTAL TWIST . . . Having achieved acquittal on the charge of killing her husband Ali (right), Mme Fahmy broke into films—playing an Egyptian wife!

Fahmy trial remained perhaps his most outstanding and widely known forensic triumph. Letters of congratulations poured in to him from all over the world. One of them was addressed simply to "Marshall Hall, the Greatest Lawyer on Earth". The Post Office delivered it safely to his chambers in the Temple.

Radio Times Hulton

AN AFFAIR OF STATE

Picture postcards reflect public opinion after the gunning down of Gaston Calmette, influential editor of the political newspaper *Le Figaro*, by celebrated beauty Henriette Claretie. But soon the mass killings of World War I overshadowed the Calmette case—and influenced its outcome.

HATRED, jealousy, personal passions and political intrigue, low envy and high treason, all these things contributed to the murder of Gaston Calmette, editor of *Le Figaro*, the most influential newspaper in France.

But before them all came love: love of the intense and dangerous kind enjoyed by high society in the heyday of Paris before World War I.

Madame Henriette Claretie was a beautiful woman, full-figured and wasp-waisted, with large eyes and an alabaster complexion. Hardly surprisingly, she made a deep impression on M. Joseph Caillaux — France's Minister of Finance and Premier-to-be — when they met at a reception at the Elysée Palace.

Love-letters

With another chance meeting at a wedding reception a few weeks later, they fell passionately in love. But there was one small obstacle to complete fulfilment. They were both married.

Removing Henriette's husband from the scene turned out easier than expected. Her marriage to the writer Leon Claretie had been breaking up for some time, hastened by his insensitivity at home and violence in public. Within a few months, their marriage was annulled.

Easing the Minister's wife out of the marital bed was a different matter altogether. Stubborn and almost pathologically jealous, Madame Berthe Caillaux's distrust had hovered like a thundercloud over her husband since the day they walked up the aisle. Her neurotic suspicion of any woman who came within a mile of the Minister poisoned their entire relationship. Their marriage had all the spontaneity of a jail sentence, yet there was no question of her retiring to make way for Henriette.

Like all insanely jealous people, Berthe Caillaux could only be completely satisfied by being proved right. The illicit affair had been going on for more than a year — matched by Berthe Caillaux's mounting suspicion — when evidence of her husband's adultery fell, almost literally, into her lap.

One day, while the Minister was away, Henriette's maid visited Berthe Caillaux on "a private and delicate mission". Claiming to be driven by conscience and impelled by the noblest sentiments — in reality, a desire for payment — she handed to Berthe Caillaux a bundle of love-letters she had stolen from her mistress. With a kind of gratified horror, Berthe Caillaux recognized the handwriting of her husband, the Minister. The letters were explicit, erotic, conclusive.

When her husband returned home, Berthe Caillaux threatened a scandal. "I'll make you pay!" she stormed. "I have influence. I'll publish the letters."

While Henriette vanished out of harm's way to the Riviera, the lawyers took over. Berthe Caillaux's price for her husband's freedom was punitive: a substantial cash settlement, plus backbreaking alimony. In return, she agreed to destroy the letters.

With his new-found happiness assured, Joseph Caillaux gladly agreed to the terms and a few months later he and Henriette were married in one of the capital's most glittering social events. The President of the Republic gave a banquet in their honour. But at that point, everything started going wrong. The trouble was not personal retribution, but political malice.

Despite his professional integrity, Joseph Caillaux was an unpopular public figure. As Minister of Finance, he had incurred the fury of the rich by introducing income tax. He was also a pacifist, desperate to prevent war at any cost, particularly with France's powerful and aggressive neighbour, Germany.

Between 1911 and 1912 — while Premier of France — he pursued a policy of compromise and appeasement which cut right across sabre-rattling public opinion. It was only too easy for vengeful opponents — who had never forgiven him for cutting their profits — to fan public prejudice and smear him as "the most hated man in France".

Joseph Caillaux bore the public abuse with patience. What was more difficult to stomach was the sustained and virulent attack launched against him in *Le Figaro* by the editor, Gaston Calmette. Over a period of 14 years, Calmette wrote nearly 150 articles, virtually accusing Caillaux of betraying his country.

Betrayed

As the campaign mounted in hysteria — with threatening hints of "exposure" and "professional ignominy" — Minister Caillaux began to suspect that personal rather than patriotic motives were behind it.

Caillaux decided to dig deeper into the private background of editor Calmette. As a former Premier, he was not without influence. Locked doors were opened. Silent people talked. What Caillaux anticipated was evidence of some personal peccadillo. What Caillaux discovered was so horrifying it transcended all petty, individual motives. There are some things in life which are too dangerous to know. He had stumbled on one of them. The month was February, 1914.

Calmette soon got wind that Minister Caillaux had been investigating his activities. How much had he discovered? There was no way of finding out, but it was a perilous situation. Caillaux had to be stopped, and editor Calmette knew exactly how. In his desk drawer, Calmette had a "trump card". It was a despicable card, but Calmette decided to play it.

The first Caillaux heard of the plot was when M. Paul Painlevé, the Minister of Education, came to see him privately. Painlevé had close contacts, inside *Le Figaro*, and information had leaked. "I can hardly bring myself to tell you," he said, "but I understand that Berthe Caillaux, your first wife, has handed over certain compromising letters to the editor of *Le Figaro* and that he intends to publish them. They could be very damaging."

There was no doubt what the letters were. They were Caillaux's love-letters to Henriette, the ones Berthe had undertaken to destroy. Her jealous malice had been simmering all these years. Now she had betrayed him.

Caillaux was trapped; caught between his secret knowledge of Calmette's activities and his protective instincts towards his lovely wife. On the way home, his bitterness increased as he thought of Calmette's malevolent plan. There was only one answer. Unfortunately, it was a stupid and reckless one.

Black-metal revolver

A few days later, a brown-paper parcel arrived at Caillaux's home, clearly addressed to the Minister. For some inexplicable reason, Henriette opened it . . . and found herself staring at a black-metal revolver and a box of ammunition. The couple had a furious row. Caillaux was angry that his wife had opened the parcel. Henriette was dissatisfied with his evasive explanations for buying the weapon.

At last, the story came out. Rather than expose his wife to scandal, Caillaux admitted that he planned to shoot editor Calmette. Deeply moved, Henriette calmed him down. "What does it matter?" she asked. "We're married now, after all." Caillaux reminded her of some of the phrases in the letters . . . "I am burning to touch your sweet little body" . . . "I cannot live without the happiness that our secret hours of love bring us".

He was a public figure, Caillaux pointed out, a Minister of the Republic. At the time he had written the letters, he had been married to someone else. Henriette had been his mistress. Apart from humiliating her, the scandal would damage the reputation of the government and wreck his own career. Caillaux refused to hand over the revolver. "If Calmette publishes the letters," he said, "I shall kill him."

The following day was March 16, 1914. After a sleepless night, Henriette woke to find her husband had already left. Still half-asleep, she went down to the breakfast-room. In a flash, she was wide awake. Lying on the table was that morning's issue of *Le Figaro* . . . and right across the front page was a reproduction of one of Caillaux's love-letters to her.

Henriette rushed to her husband's desk and tore open the drawer into which he had put the gun. It had gone. There was

no time to waste. She had to stop her husband from carrying out his foolhardy threat. Calling a cab, she drove first to the Ministry of Finance, but her husband was in conference with the Prime Minister, M. Gaston Doumergue, and unable to see her. Not bothering to wait, she continued to the offices of the Chief Justice, M. Fernand Monier, where she pleaded for him to intervene and prohibit further publication of the letters.

"In a democracy, any paper can publish what it pleases," he told her unctuously. Henriette returned to the Finance Ministry, but by then her husband had left. "Where has he gone?" she asked. "He didn't say," was the reply.

Confused and distraught, Henriette stood alone outside the Ministry. It was then that the solution came to her. She may have failed to stop her husband from leaving . . . but at least she could try to get to editor Calmette ahead of him. First, she must make a small purchase.

He wanted to destroy us

Just after 4 p.m. the doorbell rang in the shop of Georges Fromentin, master gunsmith. Henriette stood at the counter. "I would like to buy a revolver," she said. Fromentin recognized her immediately and pointed out, as politely as possible, that only a few days earlier he had sent a gun to her husband. "Never mind," said Henriette, "I'll have that one." She pointed to a 6·35 mm. Browning pistol. "And please load it for me."

Fifty minutes later, Henriette walked into the *Figaro* building at 26 Rue Drouot and asked to see the editor. She was shown to his outer office, where the secretary told her the editor was busy. Refusing to give her name, Henriette said she would wait. The secretary was overawed by this commanding and strong-willed figure and let her take a seat. Five minutes later, tired of waiting, Henriette handed her card to a passing office-boy and asked him to give it to Calmette.

At that moment, Calmette was just saying goodbye to Paul Bourget, the poet. He stared at the card in disbelief, then showed it to Bourget. "You cannot receive this woman!" said the poet. "She is the wife of your greatest enemy!" Calmette smiled thinly. "Maybe she wants to suggest a truce," he said. Bourget shook hands and Calmette walked into the outer section, introduced himself and ushered Henriette into his private office.

There could have been little time for pleasantries. The door had barely shut behind them before five shots echoed in rapid succession. The staff rushed in.

SOCIETY BEAUTY Henriette Claretie (above) shot down Gaston Calmette (left), influential editor of *Le Figaro*, to protect her politician husband.

René Dazy

Henriette was standing there, quite calm, the revolver still in her hand. At her feet lay Calmette, covered in blood and choking to death. As they carried him out, he gasped his last words: "Forgive me for causing a disturbance."

Police swarmed into the building from the street. Henriette offered no resistance. "I shot Calmette deliberately because he wanted to destroy my husband and me," she said. At least she had forestalled her husband—or had she? When Caillaux was told of her arrest, he was not on his way to *Le Figaro* with his pistol in his pocket. He was back at the Ministry with the Premier.

Traitorous secrets

Four months passed before Henriette was brought to trial. In that time, a single shot, fired far from France, had captured the world's headlines. In the dusty Balkan town of Sarajevo, a political terrorist named Gavrilo Princip assassinated Archduke Franz Ferdinand, heir to the Austro-Hungarian Empire. It was the fuse that began World War I. Austria-Hungary prepared to invade Serbia.

As war fever swept Europe, secret pacts were revealed and mighty nations took sides. Above everything loomed the menace of France's old enemy, Germany.

In the streets of Paris, crowds lit bonfires and chanted "To Berlin! To Berlin!" In this hysterical atmosphere, the mere suggestion of pacifism or compromise was tantamount to high treason.

The atmosphere of a great trial frequently reflects public feeling outside the courtroom. When the trial of Henriette Caillaux opened on Monday, July 20, 1914, the excitement of a *crime passionnel* had given way to a more dangerous and prejudiced mood. Henriette faced not only judge and jury but also the hostility of a mob who regarded her as the executioner of a patriot, a man who had stood out against the appeasers.

Even without this bitter undercurrent, the trial had everything . . . illicit love . . . illustrious names . . . jealousy . . . a hint of political intrigue. The whole of France was agog. Reading the French newspapers of July 1914, nobody could have guessed the world was plunging towards catastrophe. The trial dominated everything.

Yet only Minister Caillaux knew the one fact that could alter the whole balance of the case. The guilty secret of the editor of *Le Figaro*. It formed a strange and tortuous link between that single shot at Sarajevo and the five bullets which killed Gaston Calmette. But even to save the life of his wife, dare he use it?

More than 500 people—including the cream of French society—packed into the largest criminal court in Paris for the opening day of the trial. Extra seats had to be provided. Most of the people had come to gape at Henriette, and they weren't disappointed. The four months in jail had taken their toll. She was a shadow of her former self.

There was no doubt of her guilt. The only possible defence was justification, an almost hopeless task for Henriette's counsel, Maître Fernand Labori. The climate of opinion was against them; far worse was to come.

The first witness was M. Henri Latzarus, an assistant editor of *Le Figaro*. He was cross-examined by Maître Maurice Chenu, representing the Calmette family. Cleverly playing on the public's hostility to Henriette and her husband, he put into words what was at the back of everyone's mind . . .

Chenu: Madame Caillaux claims that M. Calmette had pursued her husband with unreasoning hatred. What were his motives for this campaign?

Latzarus: Purely patriotic. My late chief could not stand idly by and watch the interests of our beloved France entrusted to a man who had betrayed his country.

Chenu: Have you any proof?

René Dazy

René Dazy

EMBITTERED WIFE. Mme Gueydan (left) gives evidence of her ex-husband's infidelity. Her politician husband, Caillaux (right), hides his face.

Latzarus: Yes, incontrovertible documents. I took them out of the murdered man's briefcase.

Chenu: Where are they now?

Latzarus: In the hands of the President of the Republic!

Public prejudice had been triumphantly vindicated. Henriëtte had not killed editor Calmette because of a few indiscreet love-letters, but because he threatened to expose her husband as a traitor. Henriette's defence of justification was wrecked before it even started. She was as good as guillotined.

But the prosecution had reckoned without Minister Caillaux. As he walked towards the witness-box, he had already made up his mind. To protect Henriette, he would reveal Calmette's secret. Or at least part of it. He paused for a moment, bowed respectfully over his wife and kissed her hand.

Henriette's eyes were full of tears as her husband turned towards the jury, his birdlike face tight and drawn. "I want to do everything possible not to sully the memory of a dead man," he said. "But it concerns my honour and the life of my wife. Calmette has accused me of betraying my country to the Germans.

Therefore I am forced to tell the truth. *Le Figaro* has accepted treasonable money, German money!"

Maître Labori lost no time in capitalizing on Caillaux's accusation. Calling the publisher of *Le Figaro*, Georges Prestat, to the witness-box, he forced him to admit that several German financiers were on the newspaper's board of directors.

The next step was to dispose of the "traitor" smear on Minister Caillaux. Labori demanded that the incriminating documents be produced in court, "if, in fact, they exist". The ball had landed right in the government's court. In confusion, the President adjourned the trial until the following day.

The next morning, a chastened public gallery — so eager to believe the worst of Minister Caillaux — heard the Public Prosecutor, M. Herbaux, say:

"The government has authorized me to announce that no such documents exist, that *Le Figaro* possessed no papers that could in any way cast a shadow on the honour of M. Caillaux and that nothing of this kind has been handed over to the President of the Republic."

With the lowering of the emotional temperature, Maître Chenu was quick enough to seize on the point that the trial was now back to Square One. Once again, the question of justification revolved round the love-letters, coupled with one

vital factor: Had editor Calmette intended to publish them as part of a legitimate political campaign, or for reasons of personal malice?

Maître Chenu decided to go in for the quick kill. He called Madam Berthe Gueydan-Caillaux, Minister Caillaux's first wife and "the wronged woman". No actress from the *Comédie française* could have surpassed Berthe in the skill with which she turned the courtroom into a theatre. Pointing dramatically at Henriette, she said: "That woman bewitched my husband. One day he even fell on his knees and confessed that he had been tempted to creep up to my bed and murder me!"

Cunning evidence

This was the stuff the public had been waiting for . . . the despised Minister Caillaux revealed as a marital monster. Once again the pendulum of opinion swung against Henriette, sitting pale and emaciated in the dock.

Berthe had waited a long time for this moment, and she was not to be deprived of a second's relish. Slowly, as if loath to contribute to Henriette's misery, she admitted that, yes, she still possessed some of the love-letters she should have destroyed. Under the mildest pressure from the judge, and with simulated reluctance, she opened her handbag and handed several sheets of notepaper to

Maître Labori. "If I must," she cried, "I shall give the letters to the defence!"

It was a trap. The letters had been carefully selected. They were mawkish but innocuous, hardly the reason for pumping five bullets into the editor of *Le Figaro*. The anguished way in which Berthe handed them over also served to divert suspicion from her as editor Calmette's source of supply.

Maître Labori was caught. If he read the letters he would both weaken his case and expose Minister Caillaux to ridicule. If he refused to read them, the public would suspect the worst. Purely as a calculated risk, Labori decided not to read them. He had only one more manoeuvre left. And it all depended on Minister Caillaux. If editor Calmette could be exposed as a hypocrite — or worse — Henriette might be saved from the guillotine. Caillaux would have to substantiate his earlier accusation that Calmette had been helping a hostile power.

Conflicting loyalties

It was a conflict of loyalties Caillaux had been trying to avoid since the trial started. He spent a sleepless, anguished night. Outside his window, he could hear the sounds of a nation preparing for war. Conscripts marched through the streets. Vehicles rumbled over the cobbles. He could hear snatches of patriotic songs from cafés and bars, the occasional shout of "To Berlin! To Berlin!"

All hope of conciliation between the nations had passed and nothing could stop the coming conflict. Serbia had already mobilized, backed by promises from Russia. Austria-Hungary was on the brink of invading the Balkans and Germany was loading its guns.

High on a wave of belligerent patriotism, France was prepared to fight to the death. It was essential to maintain public morale and faith in the country's leaders. The secret that only Minister Caillaux knew could destroy that confidence overnight. It was not a matter of individual lack of integrity or corruption in high places, but of complete betrayal.

Caillaux felt that to reveal the enormity of editor Calmette's crime at this crucial moment could vitiate the whole war effort, even contribute to the defeat of France. Was it too high a price to pay for his beloved wife's life? When he went into court the next day, he had still not made up his mind. Within hours, the decision was out of his hands.

Throughout the day, opposing counsel wrangled over the love-letters that had been produced like a conjuring-trick from Berthe's handbag. Finally, Berthe won her appeal to have them read in court. As expected, they were coy and absurd. By the late afternoon, it seemed that Henriette's case was irretrievably lost.

Just before the court adjourned, a note was passed to Caillaux. It was from a Count Karolyi, who had just arrived in Paris from Hungary. "I must see you," it said, "I have vital evidence I wish to submit to the court."

That night, Caillaux met the mysterious Hungarian count. The evidence Karolyi handed over was political dynamite. Among the documents was a copy of editor Calmette's will and papers proving beyond a shadow of doubt that he was a traitor. The truth could no longer be hidden. Caillaux immediately contacted Maître Labori and, with a heavy heart, agreed to present the incriminating documents to the judge immediately the hearing began the following day.

There was a puzzled silence as Caillaux, looking tired and haggard, mounted the witness-stand. The first document, Calmette's will, revealed why the editor had been such an implacable opponent of the Minister's income-tax policies. For years, he had been salting away tax-free money, including the interest on a huge legacy left to him by a wealthy mistress. The French, however, are a thrifty race and have a grudging regard for those who manage to hang on to their money. Calmette's conduct had been reprehensible, certainly, but hardly damning.

But Minister Caillaux had not finished; under visible strain, Caillaux continued shakily: "In this court, there has been endless talk of patriotism. For months, my own loyalty to my country has been questioned by *Le Figaro*. For months, my wife and I have been libelled. The legal representative of the Calmette family has repeatedly used the word *la patrie*. I will now lay before the High Court the proof of what patriotism meant to Calmette."

As the President of the Court, M. Albenel, studied the sheaf of documents, the silence seemed interminable. At last, he spoke. In a tight, colourless voice, he said: "It is my duty to reveal to you the significance of these documents."

"A bullet was too good"

The papers included a secret contract between Calmette and the Austro-Hungarian government in which the editor agreed to write anti-French propaganda for the government's official news-agency in return for "certain payments". Other papers included certificates of payment and copies of the treasonable articles. In the pandemonium which greeted the news, one voice rang loud and clear from the public gallery: "A bullet was too good for him!"

The verdict was inevitable. Not Guilty — by a unanimous vote. The date was July 28, 1914. Even before the crowds swarmed out of the court, news had already reached Paris that Austria-Hungary had invaded Serbia. The holocaust had started. Russia at once moved to Serbia's aid. Germany declared war on Russia, and France, together with Britain, in the Triple Entente — marched into Belgium. On August 4, Britain declared war on Germany.

For months, *l'affaire Caillaux* had dominated the French newspapers to the exclusion of everything else. Now it was forgotten. Within a week, Henriette Caillaux's five shots — passionate, patriotic or foolhardy — had been swallowed up in a lunatic, four-year fusillade which was to kill nearly 10,000,000 men and maim another 6,295,512.

SIGHTSEERS jam the Paris streets to watch the funeral procession of editor Calmette. His initials adorn a black drape (right on picture).

MURDEROUS FAMILIES

Both UPI

She was young, delicate and beautiful. Yet she lived under the shadow of death. For her own mother was one of the "black" sisters who, like others before them, turned murder into a family business. One day, Mommy struck . . .

ONE OF the most bizarre cases in criminal history is also the earliest British murder case of which there is a detailed record. And the details are so incredible that they sound like the plot of a horror film. Anyone who knows the highlands of Scotland realizes that there is something frightening about those great tracts of bleak hillside and boggy valleys—a touch of the emptiness of the Sahara Desert. In the year 1400, the whole of Scotland was like this, from John O'Groats to the border. "Glasgow" means "dark glen", and it was little more than that; even the city of Edinburgh, later the seat of the royal family, was hardly larger than a modern country town.

Reign of terror

It was in the reign of James I of Scotland that the people of Galloway were subjected to a reign of terror. Travellers were vanishing—so many of them that the natives at first suspected packs of wolves. But there were no wolves—in that bleak country they would have starved to death. And even wolves would have left behind some sign of their presence—bloodstained clothing, or the bones of a horse. There were no such signs; the travellers had simply vanished.

Alarmed by the situation, the king sent his officers to investigate the natives. Several suspicious looking tramps were arrested, and hanged just to be on the safe side. A number of inn-keepers fell under suspicion, and were also executed. But the "vanishings" went on. They continued for so many years that some people reached the conclusion there were supernatural forces at work—werewolves, or perhaps the Devil himself.

One day, a man and his wife were returning from a village fair, both riding on the same horse. Suddenly, a wild-looking man leapt out of the bushes at the side of the road, and seized the horse's bridle. The horseman was well armed; he pulled out his pistol, and fired. There was a yell, and suddenly the horse seemed to be surrounded by savages. The man drew his cutlass and slashed at them, spurring his steed. His wife screamed as she was pulled off from behind him. One of the creatures slashed her throat with a knife. The man was dragged to the ground. And, at that moment, rescue belatedly arrived.

A crowd of about 30 people, travelling from the same fair, came round the corner. What they saw stunned them. The woman's clothes had been torn off, and someone had disembowelled her. Others were tearing at her flesh, and apparently eating it. It was like watching a pack of hunting dogs tearing a deer to pieces. The husband was still holding off other attackers with his cutlass. Someone gave a shout. Within seconds, the cannibals had vanished at incredible speed.

UNIMAGINABLE . . . That is how the terrifying savagery of the Bean family must have appeared to the artist who drew this nineteenth-century print. He has pictured Sawney Bean and one of his daughters as "civilized" beings in genteel dress. In reality, they were more as James I had described them — wild beasts.

J. Allan Cash

The woman was dead, but her husband —and the horse—were alive, the first living creatures to survive an attack from the human wolves in 25 years. It now became clear why travellers had vanished without trace. The wife's body had already been dragged a considerable distance off the road. If any traveller had passed by the spot 24 hours later, he would have noticed nothing—for by that time the bloodstains would have been indistinguishable from the brown grass and heather.

The news was carried immediately to the king in Edinburgh. Within four days, he was in Galloway, with a troop of 400 men. They went to the place on the road where the woman had been killed. There were plenty of rocks and thickets where the murderers could have hidden to waylay travellers. They then set out across the moorland, in the direction taken by the fleeing murderers.

In a short time, they arrived at the seashore. The scene was dominated by tall cliffs, and below them the sea pounded on the rocks. They waited until the tide went out, then rode along the beach, looking for any sign of habitation. There seemed to be nothing; they noticed some caves, but none of them big enough to shelter a large gang. Discouraged, they turned and went back.

Sickening smell

At this moment, however, two of the hunting dogs began barking at a small crack in the cliff face. Someone clambered up to examine it; it hardly seemed wide enough to admit a human being. But the dogs had now gone inside, and were still barking and howling with excitement— as if they had sighted their quarry. The king sent some men to the nearest village for torches, while a few of his soldiers ventured into the rocky cleft, and called out that it seemed to go deep into the cliff. Finally, the torches arrived. Led by the almost hysterical dogs, the men squeezed through the crack, and followed the winding, narrow way. A sickening smell came from inside.

Quite suddenly, the tunnel opened out into a cave. In its recesses, they could see crouching human figures, dazzled by the torchlight. In the corners, there were piles of money and jewels. And, hanging from the ceiling, objects that were easily recognizable as parts of human beings —arms, legs, torsos.

Cornered in their den, the wild creatures were prepared to fight; but they were quickly overcome by the men in armour. The soldiers counted their prisoners and discovered that a family of 48 beings was crowded into the cave. It became clear why the cave-dwellers had flung themselves on the murdered woman with such ravenous appetite. They were cannibals,

and the unappetizing lumps of flesh were part of their larder. They ate it raw. It must have seemed a luxury for them to be able to eat fresh meat.

The soldiers buried the limbs and torsos in the sand. The savages were taken to the Tolbooth in Edinburgh (which is still standing), then to Leith. By this time it had been established that the head of the family was a man named Sawney Bean, who had been born in East Lothian, not far from Edinburgh. As a youth, he had run away with a woman, and for 25 years they had been living in the same cave. The woman had been fertile, giving him eight sons and six daughters; these, in turn, had produced eighteen grandsons and fourteen granddaughters.

Leith was their place of execution. There was no trial, "It being thought

STILL STANDING (above) the Tolbooth prison in Edinburgh is a grim reminder of the past. The entire Bean family was imprisoned here before being executed.

J. Allan Cash

needless to try creatures who were even professed enemies to mankind," recorded the chronicler, John Nicholson, of Kirkcudbright. The barbarity with which the Beans were executed was typical of the period; the men's hands and feet were chopped off and they were left to bleed to death. The womenfolk, having been made to watch this, were then burned alive in three fires. "They all in general died without the least sign of repentance," wrote Nicholson, "but continued cursing and vending the most dreadful imprecations to the very last gasp of life."

In executing them without trial, the king recognized that they were wild beasts; it is a pity he could not have ordered them to be killed as cleanly as such. Civilized culture is only skin deep, and there are well-authenticated cases of human babies who have been brought up by wild animals; there have been several such instances recorded in India. In one of the most remarkable, a "wolf-child" was captured by hunters at the age of two, and taken back to civilization.

Carnivorous species

Like Kipling's Mowgli, he had been brought up by wolves since babyhood— presumably his parents were killed by them, and the baby acquired the smell of the animals, which would be enough to protect him. But the child remained a wolf for the rest of his short life. No amount of civilized training could make him behave like a human being.

There is a central lesson to be learned from the Sawney Bean family; it applies to all "murderous families"—which explains why they are so rare in the history of crime. When people reach the extremes of desperation, they turn away from human society, and in so doing place a gap between themselves and the rest of humanity. They look upon other human beings as a farmer looks on his sheep and pigs—as a *different species*. It makes no difference whether they do this instinctively, as the Beans did, or intellectually, as Charles Manson's followers did. In a fundamental sense, they cease to be human.

It is shocking to read about Sawney Bean's family disembowelling a woman and eating her flesh in front of her husband. But it is no worse than what Manson's followers did to actress Sharon Tate and the LaBiancas. It is definitely not "sadism", any more than the Jewish butcher is sadistic when he cuts the throat of a *kosher* animal and drains off its blood. It is basically the attitude of one carnivorous species to another. The same is true of the Bender family. They were not murderers so much as butchers.

There is a paradox in the idea of a family banding together to commit murder. Members of a family feel close to one another. They are aware of one another as human beings. In that case, they are bound to be aware of their neighbours as human beings. Unless they feel desperate—fighting with their backs to the wall against the rest of society—they are unlikely to combine together for purposes of slaughter. Families like the Beans, the Benders, the Mansons, are a million-to-one-chance accidents. In almost every case, the reasons for the accident are completely different. But they can be roughly classified into three groups: sadism, gain, and resentment.

Apart from the Beans, British criminal history has two cases of murderous families which fall into the first classification, sadism. They both occurred at the same time, and in the same place:

London in the mid-eighteenth century. Elizabeth Brownrigg was a midwife who treated her servant girls—supplied to her from the Foundling Hospital—with such barbarity that one of them died from the beatings. She and her husband and son were tried for the offence, and Mrs. Brownrigg died on the gallows, to the howling of an indignant mob.

Badly beaten

A few months later the London crowds had an even more sensational case to gloat over, when a mother and her daughter, both called Sarah Metyard, were tried for murder of two servant girls. Like the Brownriggs, the Metyards were given to sadistic ill-treatment of their hirelings. The mother was a

milliner who lived in Bruton Street, and in 1758, five girls were handed over to her from various foundling hospitals; these included a sickly child called Anne Naylor and her sister.

Anne worked badly, and was beaten and half-starved. She tried to run away twice, and Sarah Metyard decided to tame her by cruelty. The girl was badly beaten, then made to stand upright, with her hands tied behind her back to a door handle so she couldn't sit down. After three days without food, she was allowed to crawl into bed—whereupon she expired of exhaustion. The other girls were told to go and wake her; when they said she wouldn't move, the younger Sarah Metyard, a teenager, flung herself on the body and beat it with a shoe. She

The Kitchen where the floor Girls were employed & often whipped and tortured. | M.ᵣˢ Brownrigg in the Cell, Newgate. | The of the

Mary Evans

soon realized that the child was dead.

For a while, the two women panicked. They decided that the best plan was to conceal the body. They locked the attic door – where the child lay – and told the other girls that Anne had run away again. That seemed to satisfy them – all except the younger sister, who had noticed that Anne's shoes and clothes were still in her room. During the next two months, she voiced her suspicions. The Metyards, who were already half insane with worry about the decomposing body behind the attic door, decided she had to die too.

They duly strangled her and hid the body. After this, they set about the gruesome task of disposing of Anne's remains, chopping them up, and wrap-

under the Stairs where one lay & where both were fined on Sundays.

ping the members in two bundles. An attempt to burn one of the hands made so much smell that they took the corpse out into the street, and tossed it over a wall on to the grate of a sewer. The watchman found it there next day, and the local coroner was called to look at the pieces. Since they were so decomposed, he gave it as his opinion that the body had been dug up from a churchyard. The pieces were buried, and no one suspected the Metyards. Presumably they disposed of the second body more efficiently – it was never found.

Psychological question

Four years went by and young Sarah Metyard ceased to be her mother's favourite. All the evidence indicates that Mrs. Metyard was a violent, foulmouthed old woman who felt the world had treated her badly. A lodger called Mr. Rooker felt sorry for the daughter, and invited her to come and be his servant. The girl accepted, in spite of her mother's objections; within a short time, she was Mr. Rooker's mistress. Her mother was enraged; she called at Mr. Rooker's house every day and screamed abuse through the front door. He tried moving out to the western suburb of Ealing; but the old lady traced him, and continued to make a nuisance of herself.

One day, he let her into the house, hoping to cajole her into a less hostile mood; but she flew straight at her daughter and beat her. Angry words passed – some of which puzzled Mr. Rooker. When they had got rid of the old lady, he asked Sarah what she meant about "killing". Sarah told him everything. Mr. Rooker decided this was the ideal way of getting his revenge on the mother. He assumed the daughter would not be brought to trial, since she was still under age. He was mistaken. The Brownrigg scandal had made the officers of the law sensitive. And both Metyards had taken part in the disposal of the body. They were tried together, and executed at Tyburn in July 1768, one year after Elizabeth Brownrigg.

It is a psychological question of great interest whether crimes like these should be labelled sadistic. The motive behind them seems to be less a desire to inflict pain than a need to inflict "just" punishment; probably Mrs. Metyard, like Mrs. Brownrigg, would have been outraged if anyone had accused her of *enjoying* hurting Anne Naylor. The same is certainly true of America's worst case of calculated ill-treatment, the Ocey Snead

SLAUGHTERING SERVANTS seems to be a speciality of women. The notorious Mrs. Elizabeth Brownrigg (left) appeared to be a respectable member of society. The truth is that she was a vicious sadist who had a twisted sense of justice.

affair, which involved three highly respectable sisters.

The sisters were Caroline, Mary, and Virginia Wardlaw, daughters of a Supreme Court Justice of South Carolina. Virginia, the clever one of the family, became head of Montgomery Female College in 1900. Her two sisters lived nearby. Caroline was married to a Colonel Martin, and had a daughter named Ocey, a quiet, gentle girl; Mary, separated from her husband, had two sons, John and Fletcher. One day, John ran away with a pretty student from his aunt's college. He was pursued and dragged back. Two days later, there were screams from the Wardlaw house on the campus: John was found writhing on the ground, his clothing burning. He died shortly afterwards, and the coroner agreed that the death was suicide. But his mother benefited by an insurance policy worth $12,000.

Starvation

There was much local gossip about the incident, and the sisters decided to separate. Mrs. Martin went to New York with Ocey and was joined there by her husband. One day, the landlady heard groans; she burst open the door, and found Colonel Martin writhing on the floor, and Ocey – filthy and in rags – on a bed in the corner of the room. Colonel Martin died shortly afterwards; his death was assumed to be from natural causes – and the widow benefited from a policy for $10,000.

Virginia Wardlaw had now changed her job; she was principal of a women's college at Murfreesboro, Tennessee – where the other two sisters joined her. The women seemed to be dominated by a pathological meanness. They proceeded to starve Ocey to death. A doctor who called was shocked by the filth and bareness of the house. Another doctor quickly diagnosed Ocey's complaint as starvation, and threatened to get the police. The sisters told him that it was none of his business – Ocey was now married to her cousin Fletcher. This turned out to be true. But the doctor still caused trouble, and the three sisters – who now habitually wore black – left the college hastily.

With the benefit of normal food, Ocey immediately revealed that she was no invalid – indeed, she blossomed and became pregnant. But then the three deadly sisters descended again. Fletcher was completely under his mother's thumb, and allowed himself to be sent to Canada. Once more, the sisters began to starve Ocey to death. When the baby was born, they immediately handed it over to a foundling hospital, telling Ocey it was dead. And on November 29, 1909, at a house in East Orange, New Jersey, the police were called in to another "suicide".

Ocey had drowned in her bathtub, in

MOTHER AND AUNT OF THE BATHTUB VICTIM.

MRS CAROLINE WARDLAW MARTIN

a few inches of water. As soon as the police discovered that she had been insured for $32,000, they arrested the "sisters in black". Virginia Wardlaw starved herself to death in jail. Ocey's mother was sentenced to seven years in prison, although the prosecution declared she was insane. The third sister was found not guilty. In jail, it soon became clear that Mrs. Martin *was* insane; she died in an asylum in 1913.

No account of family murder would be complete without a mention of the strange case of Russell Colvin, which took place in New England in 1812. Two brothers, Stephen and Jesse Boorn, hated their brother-in-law Colvin, not only because they suspected that their father meant to leave him his farm, but because he made excessive sexual demands on their sister Sally. Some time later, as they were clearing a field of rocks, Colvin and the brothers began to quarrel. Colvin's son ran back to the farm in a panic. Later, his uncles told him that his father had "run away up the mountain", and threatened to kill him if he mentioned the quarrel.

Seven years after this, in 1819, Old Amis Boorn, the uncle of the brothers, had a dream in which Russell Colvin appeared and told him he had been murdered, and his body buried near the farmhouse (which had meanwhile been burned). Charred bones were found in a field; the brothers were arrested, and confessed to the murder. They were sentenced to hang. Then, to everyone's amazement, Russell Colvin turned up again. He *had* gone off up the mountain. No one has ever answered the question of why the brothers made such a circumstantial confession; it remains one of the greatest psychological puzzles in the history of crime.

In today's society the phenomenon of the lethal family—the family that stays together slays together—is not likely to occur. With the increase of social communications, and the "shrinking" of the world, it is no longer so possible for families to hide in hills and backwoods—or in city tenements even—without their presence being known to the authorities.

Once they are officially on record their murderous activities (if indeed they plan any) are severely circumscribed. They have become part of the human family in general, and are guarded against turning on their kind.

MURDEROUS MOTHER Mrs. Caroline Martin starved her own daughter almost to death and then finished her off by drowning her in the bathtub. Allegedly she was helped by sisters Virginia and Mary. The latter (inset) was acquitted in court, but all three sisters were probably insane.

New York Historical Society

THE BLOODY BENDERS

Travellers would stop at the lonely Bender shack for a welcome meal or a drink—and to gaze at the beautiful, passionate-looking girl who served them. They little suspected that, behind the curtain which divided the cabin in two, stood a man ready to crush their brains with a heavy hammer. As they settled comfortably in the carefully placed chair, the hammer rose and struck . . .

MA BENDER and husband William were reputed to be the initiators of the idea of murdering hungry guests. Seen together (left) they appeared to be normal, simple folk. But anyone who sat at their table was in the most mortal danger (above). The curtain hid the murderer.

AP

DINNER AT HOME with the Bender family (top). No one knows how many innocent travellers ate their last meal in the company of Kate Bender. When one of the men of the family had battered their guests' skulls, Kate would finish them off by slitting their throats with her knife (below). Then they callously dropped the bodies into a pit.

Culver Pictures

Kansas State Historical Society, Topeka

ON March 9, 1873, Dr. William H. York left Fort Scott on horseback for his home in Independence, Kansas. He never arrived there. Nearly three weeks later a local newspaper gave a brief account of his mysterious disappearance and the story was quickly picked up by other newspapers in the state. There was considerable speculation that he might have been murdered, as it was known that he had been carrying a large sum of money, and a posse was formed to find him.

The posse was led by his brother Colonel A. York who followed the trail, it was said, "with the tenacity of an Indian and the devotion of a saint". Rivers were dragged, possible spots for an ambush thoroughly searched, and the route Dr. York must have travelled was taken from town to town. There were no signs anywhere to show how he had met his death, or even that he had been murdered. He was traced as far as Cherryvale in Labette County, about 50 miles from the south line of the state, and no farther. There the trail ended.

Cherryvale in 1873 was a small railroad town. About two miles south of it was a modest frame house where travellers could buy a meal or a drink. It stood about 100 yards back from the Osage trail which ran to east and west in front of it. Over the door was a sign marked "Grocery". The single room, which was all the house was, was divided into two by a curtain. One half served as a store and eating place, and the other half as a living-room and bedroom for the Bender family who owned it. The house was sparsely furnished with two beds and some sticks of furniture.

Steel eyes

The Benders had moved into the house in March 1871. John Bender, who was about 60 years old, and his son, John Jnr., aged 27, were large, coarse-looking men. The daughter Kate or Katie was 25. Mrs. Bender was hysterically described in an early newspaper account as 42 "with iron grey hair, ragged at the ends and thin over her temples. Her eyes were steel-grey and hard".

On April 3, 1873, some of the posse rode out to the Benders' home and asked if they had seen or heard anything of the missing Dr. York. The family said that they were ignorant of his whereabouts. A few days later, however, another bunch of men rode out and asked the same questions. The Benders, believing that they were under suspicion, then

PROFESSOR KATIE . . . the sensual serving girl at the Bender store satisfied her intellectual pretensions by lecturing on spiritualism (above) or setting herself up as a doctor of genius (below). But her patients never returned home.

hastily abandoned their store and fled.

Their disappearance was discovered by a horseman riding in from the prairie who galloped into town and soon returned with the posse.

Terrible smell

A terrible smell permeated the house, which was where the posse started to search. Rods and levers were pushed into every crack and hollow to see if the flooring was loose or hollow — but both it and the walls seemed solid. It was only when the beds were moved that the men saw a slight depression in the floor which turned out to be, on closer examination, a trap door.

Beneath it was a small pit about five feet in diameter and six feet deep. The bottom and sides looked damp. One of the men climbed into the pit and probed the bottom with a rod to see if anything was hidden. He could find nothing. But as he climbed out he saw that his hands, where he had been groping the ooze, were covered with blood. This was the source of the mysterious smell.

The search moved to the back of the house, where there was a half-acre orchard.

"Boys, I see graves yonder in the orchard!" called Colonel York.

Heavy metal rods were then driven into the ground. As they were withdrawn it was seen that they were matted with hair and putrefying flesh. Shovels were used to carefully scrape away the soil, and within a few minutes the first body had been uncovered. It had been buried on its face and some of the flesh had dropped away from the legs. It was only covered by a shirt which was torn in places and thick with damp and decay.

As soon as it was disinterred it was laid on its back, and Colonel York numbly identified the body as that of his brother. The rear of his head had been smashed in. The skull had been driven into the brain, and to make quite sure that the victim was dead, his throat had been cut right through to the spine.

By nightfall seven more bodies had been found. Five graves contained only a single body. But buried in the sixth was

Prof. Miss KATIE BENDER

Can heal all sorts of Diseases; can cure Blindness, Fits, Deafness and all such diseases, also Deaf and Dumbness.

Residence, 14 miles East of Independence, on the road from Independence to Osage Mission one and one half miles South East of Norahead Station.

KATIE BENDER.

June 18, 1872.

Culver Pictures

Kansas State Historical Society, Topeka

325

Photographed by Julius Ploetz
...nendence Kas. May. 9th 187...

Kansas State Historical Society, Topeka

BENDERS' BOOT HILL . . . Searchers found six graves near the Bender family home. One of the bodies was that of a little girl interred alive with a dead victim.

a man and a little girl. Some of the corpses were in the last stages of decomposition, but others were not so far gone that they could not be identified.

Among those subsequently identified were two men from Cedarville, who, on different dates, had apparently stopped off at the Benders' for a meal. One had been contesting a land case in Independence, and the other was a horse trader who—because of decomposition—could only be recognized by his silver rings.

A third man had been missing since December 5, 1872. He had been travelling to Independence to live there. His sister could only identify him by his clothing. The fourth and fifth victims were a Mr. Longcor and his 18-month-old daughter. His wife had recently died and he was leaving for Iowa. The sixth and seventh bodies were the unidentified remains of two men.

In every case the skull had been smashed in from behind and the throat of the victim cut. The only exception was the Longcor child, who had been suffocated. As there were no marks on her body it was assumed that she had been thrown alive into the grave, and her father's body dropped on top of her.

Badly mutilated

But the horrifying discoveries were not at an end. The remains of a second child victim were found the next day. This time it was the body of a small girl of about eight. She had been so badly mutilated that her sex and age could only be guessed at. After she had been exhumed someone cut off her golden hair and wove it into a wreath. Her breast bone had been driven in, her right knee wrenched from its socket and the leg doubled up under the body.

In the search party was a grocery store owner named Brockman, who had been a partner of the Benders for two years. He was a close friend of theirs and, like them, German. He was immediately suspected of being an accomplice. To make him confess, a rope was thrown over a beam and he was strung up.

According to an eyewitness his eyes were starting out of his head and he was nearly dead when he was cut down. "Confess! Confess!" the crowd screamed. Brockman swore that he was innocent, and again he was jerked to his feet and again his face convulsed.

Once more he was let down and revived. This time he did not appear to understand what was wanted. It was an eerie sight. "The yelling crowd, the mutilated and butchered dead, the flick-

327

ering and swirling torches spluttering in the night wind, the stern set faces of his executioners . . ."

For the third time he was hoisted aloft, and this time he was only released when he was unconscious. Gradually he revived and was permitted to stagger away, his innocence accepted.

After this, several rewards were offered for the capture of the Benders — particularly of Kate who was generally credited with being "the leading spirit of her murderous family". But descriptions of her were wildly conflicting.

One was that she was a "large, masculine, red-faced woman", and another that "Her hair was a dark, rich auburn. She had deep, greyish-blue, or dark-grey, eyes. She was over medium height, some five feet six or seven inches tall, slender, well-formed, voluptuous mould, fair skin, white as milk, rose complexion.

"She was good-looking, a remarkably handsome woman, rather bold and striking in appearance, with a tigerish grace and animal attraction, which but few men could resist."

Rapacious greed

"She was a fluent talker, gifted with fine conversationalist powers, but she did not display any educational advantages of a high order. She used good English with very little, if any, German accent."

Apart from her rapacious greed for money, and the ruthless manner by which she achieved it, she had longings to be a great lecturer. She had an inflated reputation as a medium and gave talks in the nearby towns on spiritualism.

Certainly she fascinated men — including her father's old partner, Brockman, who was very much in love with her and who thought that she was going to marry him. She encouraged his belief, but postponed their marriage until Easter Sunday 1873 when, so she said, the planets would be in the right conjunction for them.

Meanwhile, she milked him of money and jewellery and possibly persuaded him to be an accessory to the Bender murders — although this was never more than a suspicion. Certainly he was brutal enough. Later on his daughter died of the treatment she received from him, and Brockman was indicted for her death.

A more bizarre sexual relationship is the incestuous one she enjoyed with her brother John. According to one of the many lynching stories, Kate confessed that she and her brother had been living together as man and wife and that they both had gonorrhoea. If true, this would explain Brockman's fights on several occasions with John Bender over his sister — when he accused the younger man of being his "rival".

Clearly whatever the truth, Kate was an attraction when the Benders opened

for business. As their store was on the outskirts of town they must have needed someone — or something — to pull the customers in. Otherwise why should travellers have stopped there when they had just started their journey, or had only two short miles to go to end it?

To stimulate business, Kate served meals while her mother cooked. The food was placed on a table close to the dividing curtain — so that when the traveller was sitting down the back of his head could be clearly seen from the other side.

As he was eating, one of the Bender men would come up behind the curtain. Then, when the victim's head was pressed against the curtain, he would strike at the base of the skull with a heavy stonebreaker's hammer, and crush in the skull.

As travellers were constantly coming to the house, it was necessary to get the body quickly out of sight — and it was hastily dropped into the pit. According to legend, it was Katie Bender herself who leaped in after them and cut the victims' throats. Later, when it was dark, the bodies were buried in the orchard.

Stories of travellers who realized how near they came to being "planted" in the Bender orchard substantiated the known facts. One man, believing Katie's inflated claims as a healer, rode out to the Bender store with a friend to see if she could cure his neuralgia.

After examining him, Katie said that she thought that she could. As it was dinner time she invited them both to stay for a meal, and seated them close to the curtain. Both men had noticed the hard scrutiny they received from the Bender men, but dismissed it as nothing more than curiosity.

Melodramatic stories

When they sat down to eat the two male Benders disappeared. For some reason the two travellers could only put down to "intuition", they got up from the table and took their meal over to the counter to eat.

Until then, Katie Bender had been charming and affable to them. But now she began to abuse them and call them names. This added to the men's growing suspicions, and they hastily left the store. They saw with some relief two waggons going by on the trail and hitched lifts. Later, they were ashamed of their frightened behaviour and thought that they must have exaggerated the whole incident.

More melodramatic stories flourished of Katie Bender stalking her victims and of her efforts to get behind them. According to these a gust of wind inevitably blew up her apron to show the hidden hand beneath it gripping a large knife.

In two years the Benders earned themselves $5000, plus money they got from

the sale of the victims' waggons and horses and the pieces of jewellery, such as rings and watches, which they had worn. It was said that they had accomplices to help them dispose of the goods — including such "innocents" as the young men who came courting Katie Bender.

Another account stated that Brockman was their accomplice. The loot was allegedly disposed of — in part at least — through his store without arousing suspicion. Some goods were certainly disposed of by the Benders themselves, and late in April 1873 John Bender was noted to have sold a watch, some clothing, two mules, a shotgun, and some pistols.

Lynch mob

In spite of the posses and vigilante committees which scoured the countryside for the Benders — and the state and private rewards that were offered for their capture — they were never officially caught. The waggon in which they had escaped was found abandoned and bullet-ridden, as if they had been apprehended and put to death by a lynch mob. This seems to be the fate accepted by most people.

Despite this, stories persisted of the Benders — particularly of Kate, of how she ended her days as a white-haired old lady, or a whore, or a society queen. According to another and contradictory account, a band of Gypsies saw the Benders lynched by a posse of armed men. Equally colourful is the version that after the family had been killed, their bodies were split open to stop them from swelling up and floating to the surface of the river into which they were thrown.

The exact truth was never established. Unlike other lynch mobs, the men who wreaked vengeance on the Benders dare not boast openly of what they had done. For the several thousand dollars that the Benders had made from their killings disappeared along with them.

In 1884, in an attempt to end the conjecture, Dr. York's family offered $2000 for proof that the Benders were dead. But the reward was never claimed. So the legends continued. One had it that an ear of red-coloured corn found growing on the Benders' land was stained from the blood of the victims they buried there.

A more realistic reminder of the inhuman savagery of the bloody Benders can be seen today in the Bender Museum in Cherryvale. It is a wreath of woven, golden hair taken from the body of the little girl who — most probably — was befriended by Kate and then brutally murdered by her when her back was turned.

WANTED NOTICES were pasted throughout the state offering handsome rewards for information about the Bender family. All in vain: they were never heard of again.

GOVERNOR'S PROCLAMATION.

$2,000 REWARD

State of Kansas, Executive Department.

WHEREAS, several atrocious murders have been recently committed in Labette County, Kansas, under circumstances which fasten, beyond doubt, the commissions of these crimes upon a family known as the "Bender family," consisting of

JOHN BENDER, about 60 years of age, five feet eight or nine inches in height, German, speaks but little English, dark complexion, no whiskers, and sparely built;

MRS. BENDER, about 50 years of age, rather heavy set, blue eyes, brown hair, German, speaks broken English;

JOHN BENDER, Jr., alias John Gebardt, five feet eight or nine inches in height, slightly built, gray eyes with brownish tint, brown hair, light moustache, no whiskers, about 27 years of age, speaks English with German accent;

KATE BENDER, about 24 years of age, dark hair and eyes, good looking, well formed, rather bold in appearance, fluent talker, speaks good English with very little German accent:

AND WHEREAS, said persons are at large and fugitives from justice, now therefore, I, Thomas A. Osborn, Governor of the State of Kansas, in pursuance of law, do hereby offer a **REWARD OF FIVE HUNDRED DOLLARS** for the apprehension and delivery to the Sheriff of Labette County, Kansas, of each of the persons above named.

In Testimony Whereof, I have hereunto subscribed my name, and caused the Great Seal of the State to be affixed.

[L. S.]   Done at Topeka, this 17th day of May, 1873.

THOMAS A. OSBORN,
Governor.

By the Governor:
W. H. SMALLWOOD,
Secretary of State.

Kansas State Historical Society, Topeka

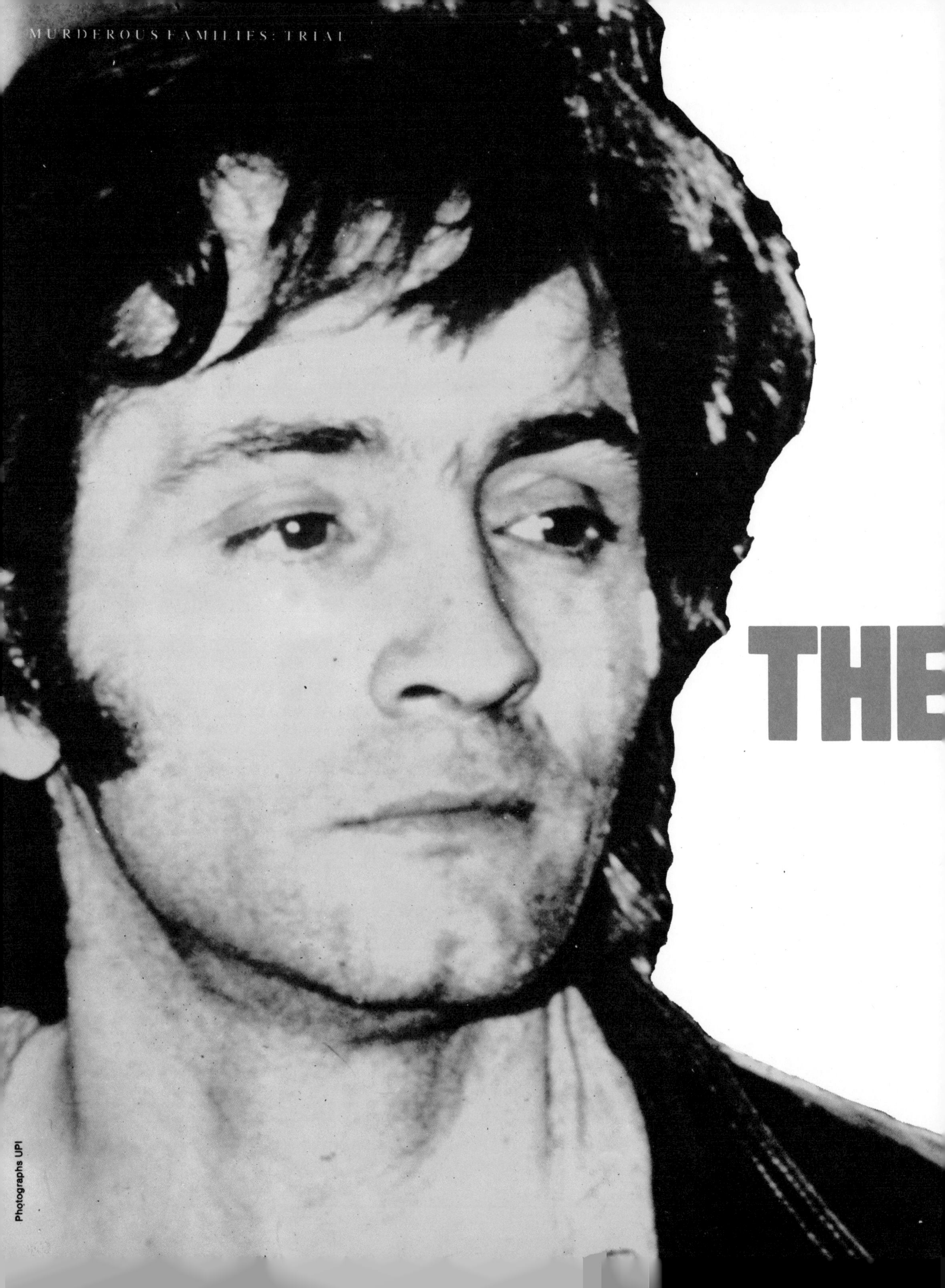

Photographs UPI

THE

UPI

MANSON FAMILY

UPI

Beautiful actress and film star Sharon Tate and six others had been savagely murdered during two nights of terror in Hollywood in the summer of 1969. Now three young girls and a 35-year-old man were on trial. But Manson and his "harem" behaved as if they were on a Sunday picnic!

Los Angeles Times

WHEN Charles Manson entered the Los Angeles courtroom for the first time his presence seemed to evoke, among the waiting newsmen and spectators, a strange mixture of misgiving and complete revulsion. Charged, along with three female members of his "family", with the savage murder of Hollywood actress Sharon Tate and six others in August 1969, it was the revulsion which held sway in people's minds. But the disquiet was there too, as the memory of Manson's weird outbursts to the press invaded the courtroom. "I'm at the other end of your society," he had asserted.

Now, as the audience stared at this curious figure of horror and tragedy their fascination was not untinged with fear. When he turned to face them, a gasp of shocked astonishment went round the court. For 35-year-old Manson, pale but composed in blue prison denim, his dark hair flowing like a prophet's round his intense, wiry face, had branded in blood on his forehead the symbol of the outcast: an X, put there because "I have X-ed myself from your world".

Even before the 9½-month trial began Manson provided reporters with plenty of headline copy. He clearly intended to be the star of the proceedings, and made an early attempt to be allowed to conduct his own defence so that no "interfering" lawyer could come between him and his "public". Judge Charles Older, however, decided otherwise. Manson, it was argued, was incapable of safeguarding his own procedural rights and must, therefore, be represented by a defence team.

With stubborn perversity the defendant then proceeded to interview more than 60 hopeful attorneys before settling on three. It would be difficult to imagine a group of lawyers less likely to work well together than this strange, ill-matched trio.

First, there was Ronald Hughes, 35, a onetime conservative turned hippie who had flunked the bar exam three times be-

MURDER SCENE . . . Police (top right) watch over the house where the murder of Sharon Tate and friends took place. Two of the victims were Polish writer and director Frykowski (top left) and his girlfriend Abigail Folger (above). Panel (opposite) shows Manson with his family.

fore passing and had never tried a case in his life. In his favour was that he had met Manson previously—and, at the latter's insistence, he agreed to appear in court wearing a beard.

Hughes did not see the end of the trial through. He disappeared suddenly while on a short camping trip in north California and was later found drowned. The trial had to be adjourned for 2 weeks while a replacement—Maxwell Keith—familiarized himself with the case.

Then there was Irving Kanarek, 52, whom Manson brought in. Kanarek was a well-known attorney in Los Angeles and he hoped that his legal skills would be able to reduce Manson's infamy in the eyes of the court and the general public. Not many people shared his optimism and even Manson himself must have had his

own doubts and felt uncertain about the outcome.

The third member of Manson's team was Daye Shinn, 53 a former used-car salesman, who sometimes earned his living by arranging immigration papers for wealthy clients seeking foreign maids.

To Manson's fury, the public defender's office assigned a fourth defence lawyer to the case—in a necessary effort to ensure a modicum of sanity and competence in dealing with the complexities of what was obviously going to be a gruelling and lengthy legal ordeal. This was the young but highly skilled Paul Fitzgerald who, at 33, was soon to reveal how much better than his older colleagues he had mastered the art and science of courtroom crossfire.

Fitzgerald soon became the unofficial defence leader. But he often found himself aligned not only against the prosecution case—admirably led by Vincent Bugliosi—but also against Hughes, Kanarek, and Shinn—whose courtroom techniques frequently undercut his own efforts. Kanarek, in particular, sometimes seemed actually to assist incompetent prosecution witnesses, leaving them more confident and impressive than when they started.

"It's like living in a concentration camp," Fitzgerald remarked. Even Prosecutor Bugliosi was dismayed by some of the defence "tactics". "This isn't a trial," he blurted at one point, "this is a laugh-in comedy!"

There was nothing amusing, however, about the prosecutor's opening remarks on the first day of the trial, in which he referred to the full horror of the Tate murders. The quiet tone in which he outlined the case against Manson—and the three young members of his harem accused with him—belied the savage story

333

Los Angeles Times

of hatred and blood lust to which the jury of seven men and five women listened in awestruck silence.

Patiently and with commendable clarity, Bugliosi explained that two of the girls on trial—Susan Atkins, 22, and Patricia Krenwinkel, also 22—had been involved both in the murder of Sharon Tate and house guests on the night of August 9, 1969, and in the murder of Mr. and Mrs. Leno LaBianca in Los Angeles on the following night. The third girl, Leslie Van Houten, 20, was on trial only for the LaBianca murders.

Violent death

Two others, said Bugliosi, were involved. One of these, Charles Watson, was in a Texas jail fighting extradition and would be tried later. The second, 21-year-old Mrs. Linda Kasabian, was the only defector from the Manson "family" and would, later, give a detailed account of the events on the two murder nights.

First, however, Bugliosi wanted to implant in the minds of the jury his own version of what happened to the victims. He began with a brief account of what he called "Manson's mind". He told of the defendant's passion for violent death and his bitter hatred for the "establishment". Son of a prostitute, Manson seemed destined for some kind of career in crime. As a young boy, he was frequently in court for juvenile delinquencies and later he graduated first to car theft and then to pimping—which culminated in a ten-year jail sentence.

Armed, continued the prosecutor, with a grudge against society and a fanatical interest and belief in hypnotism and the occult, Manson began to see himself as a kind of messiah. A messiah who, just as in the Bible, was the creator of a new way of life. The poor and the dispossessed—particularly if they were young girls—were offered a place where they could feel accepted.

But, Bugliosi added, Manson's messianic ravings were not about love but about hate, violence, lust, sexual depravity, and ritual murder.

Bugliosi talked briefly about the Manson "family" and the quasi-hypnotic effect which he exercised over its members so that they would, apparently, obey his every wish with unquestioning devotion. Then he mentioned one of the most absurd—and for that reason frightening—of the influences which had motivated Manson's behaviour: his devotion to the Beatles, who spoke to him "across the ocean". One song in particular, called *Helter Skelter,* whose lyrics seemed unexceptional to the normal ear, had been given a weird interpretation by the defendant.

According to him, Bugliosi asserted, the words signified a black uprising against the whites. Manson would escape from it by leading his followers into the California desert—where they did have a hideout—and then recreate a paradise of sex and drugs. First, however, the family would precipitate helter-skelter by fostering the idea that it had already arrived. That is why they scrawled the words PIG and WAR in blood on the walls of their victims' homes.

The murders themselves, the jury were

HOME ON THE RANGE . . . The Manson family home was an abandoned cabin once used as a movie set. Described at his trial as a "human vegetable", Charles Watson (right) was chosen to lead the band sent to attack Tate household. There were many helpers (opposite) to choose from.

told, had not been directly conducted by Manson. Like some demoniac general he had sent out his troops to kill the pigs, the "enemies". To a tense courtroom Bugliosi spelt out the murderous happenings. He told of the approach to Sharon Tate's rented house in Hollywood and how Charles Watson, armed with a .22 calibre rifle, had led Susan Atkins and Patricia Krenwinkel into the house, leaving prosecution witness Linda Kasabian on watch outside.

In the temporary absence of her husband, film director Roman *Rosemary's Baby* Polanski, eight-months pregnant Miss Tate had invited round former boyfriend Jay Sebring, writer Voityck Frykowski and his lover, coffee heiress Abigail Folger. It was, said Bugliosi, a quiet, intimate evening of drinks and talk. The arrival of the Manson family signified not merely an end to the get-together, but an end to their lives. One by one the guests were brutally hacked to death.

Frykowski alone was shot twice, hit at least 13 times on the head with a blunt instrument, and stabbed no less than

Los Angeles Times

CHAINED and manacled, Manson, now condemned, is led away to San Quentin's death row. The ageing hippie — he was thirty-five — had no trouble persuading unhappy youngsters to join him. Susan Atkins, Linda Kasabian and Leslie Van Houten (right) were just three of them.

51 times. Sharon Tate, the jury heard, heavy with her unborn child, was left until last. Then, to the "music" of her pleas — as one of the murderers later described it — her frantic pleas to save the child, she too was stabbed repeatedly in her neck, breast, back — and womb.

The murder of Mr. and Mrs. LaBianca on August 10, in which Leslie Van Houten also took part, was of similar brutal savagery, said the prosecutor. Only Linda Kasabian, he stated, had balked. She, as a relative newcomer to the Manson family, was the only one who was unaware of the purpose of the August 9 mission — and only fear had led her to accompany the murderers on the second night's outing.

For Prosecutor Bugliosi, this was the crucial point of his case. Only if he could establish that Mrs. Kasabian — who was originally indicted but later promised immunity in return for her testimony — was not legally an accomplice to the murders, could this key witness be considered reliable and trustworthy. Otherwise his case would be seriously weakened. For it would undoubtedly be argued by the defence that Kasabian was merely trying to save her own skin and was as guilty as the rest.

Girlish figure

Thus her story would be seen as presenting tailored evidence designed merely to convince the jury of her own innocence. Ultimately Judge Older would decide the issue. Much depended on the young mother's performance in court, and it was a tense moment when, in July 1970, she stepped for the first time into the witness box.

She was a girlish figure in her simple blue and white dress and blonde pigtails. It was difficult to believe that someone who looked so unremarkable could have been involved at all in crimes whose bloodiness and cruelty had horrified the world. As Bugliosi approached her, she glanced nervously round the packed courtroom. For a moment her eyes rested on the three accused girls, each of whose foreheads now bore the X mark of the outcast. They grinned at her with a kind of unconcerned maliciousness. Then she turned to Manson, her lips set firm in determination as if trying to prove to herself that he no longer had control over her actions.

For seconds she held his fierce stare and only turned away when, in an obvious attempt to frighten her, Manson drew a thin forefinger across his throat. But Linda Kasabian did not falter, and her composure drew a quick smile of relief from Bugliosi. He knew from that moment that she would adhere to her evidence.

Under the prosecutor's questioning, Kasabian told how she had first joined the Manson clan shortly before the murders. "I felt like I was a blind little girl in a forest. I took the first path," she said. It was not a surprising statement from a girl who had run away from a broken home as a young teenager and by the age of 20 had had two husbands, two children, and lived in at least 11 drug-orientated communes. To her, Manson was the bountiful giver of life and happiness; she loved him and believed "he was the Messiah come again".

Then, as she began to reveal details of the Tate murders — which had been inspired by Manson's jealousy of the rich and famous — the courtroom grew silent. Audience and jury strained forward to hear every word of her narrative, and held their breath at peak moments as if in the presence of a great dramatic performance. She related how, left on guard outside the Tate home, she suddenly became aware of what was happening inside: "Then all of a sudden I heard people screaming saying 'No, please, no!'"

"What kind of screams?" snapped Bugliosi.

"Loud, loud."

"How long did they last?"

"Oh, it seemed like forever, infinite. I don't know."

She went on to describe how the dying Frykowski had crawled out of the house towards her: "He had blood all over his face . . . and we looked into each other's eyes for a minute — I don't know however long — and I said, 'Oh, God, I am so sorry. Please make it stop.' And then he just fell to the ground into the bushes."

Upraised knife

Entering the house, the witness continued, she saw Watson beating one of the victims on the head. "And then I saw Katie — Patricia Krenwinkel — in the background with the girl, chasing after her with an upraised knife . . ." Watson, she said, was screaming: "I'm the Devil. I'm here to do the Devil's work!"

By the time Linda Kasabian had finished her testimony several members of the audience were in tears, and the jury looked suddenly fatigued and pale. Even Judge Older was visibly moved, and Bugliosi, whose probing, intelligent questions — continuously interrupted by literally hundreds of objections from the defence — had provided a framework for her story, was trembling with emotion and fury.

Mrs. Kasabian herself stood up well to the harrowing ordeal, though at the end of her testimony she, too, was clearly exhausted. The pressure on her had been enormous. For, apart from the

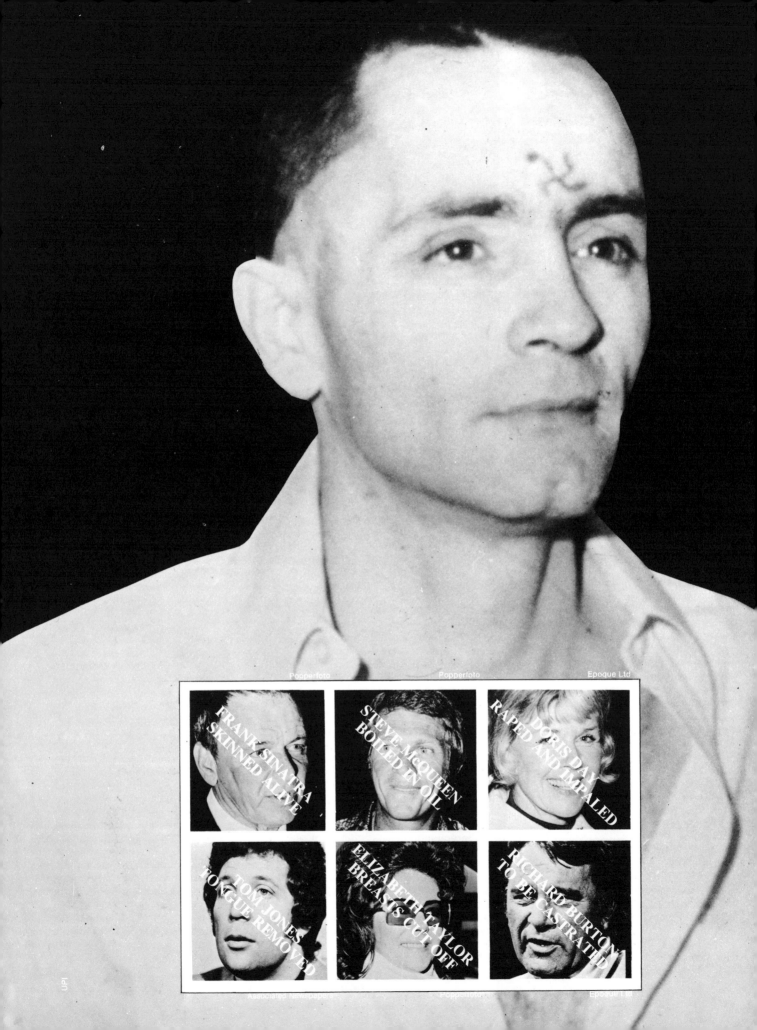

Popperfoto Popperfoto Epoque Ltd

FRANK SINATRA
SKINNED ALIVE

STEVE McQUEEN
BOILED IN OIL

DORIS DAY
RAPED AND IMPALED

TOM JONES
TONGUE REMOVED

ELIZABETH TAYLOR
BREASTS CUT OFF

RICHARD BURTON
TO BE CASTRATED

Associated newspapers Popperfoto Epoque Ltd

extraordinary obstructionist antics of the defence, she also had to face continuous pressure from the four accused. Once, Susan Atkins fixed her eyes upon Linda's. "You are killing us," she breathed. "I am not killing you," came the reply. "You are killing yourselves."

Undaunted, Mrs. Kasabian continued, for ten days, to pour out her narrative and face the barrage of often absurd questions flung at her by the defence.

The latter's tactics were simple. Their whole method lay in attempting, by any means possible, to discredit Mrs. Kasabian as a reliable witness. Kanarek, in particular, was persistently belligerent. He made the witness go through her story detail by detail in a vain effort to secure an admission from her that she was involved in the killings—thus rendering her whole testimony suspect. When this failed he tried a new tack.

"Have you ever taken hallucinogenic drugs?"

"Yes."

"LSD, for example?"

"Yes."

How many trips had she made on LSD? "Oh, about 50, I guess."

At the time this looked like a rewarding line of questioning, and Kanarek followed it up by delving into her sexual life with the Manson family. Mrs. Kasabian admitted that drug-induced orgies were frequent—and pleasurable. What happened during an orgy? Kanarek wanted to know.

"Everybody made love to everybody else. We all shed our clothes and we were lying on the floor, and it was like it didn't make any difference who was next to you."

Did she know who was the father of her second child—the one conceived during her time with the Manson family?

"No," she replied, "I couldn't be sure."

It was more sensational material for newsmen, and exciting entertainment for the spectators—many of whom had come, no doubt, in anticipation of hearing just such confessions as these. But, in the end, Kanarek's probings and innuendos were in vain. Judge Older stuck to his ruling that Linda Kasabian's testimony was in order and acceptable as evidence.

Even so, Bugliosi had never intended to

CHARLIE'S HATE LIST. It was rumoured that Manson kept a secret list of future targets with graphic details of how he was going to "deal" with them. The full story never emerged but certain prisoners who shared jail cells with members of the Manson family on trial testified that the hate list was a frequent source of conversation amongst them. Most of the hatred seemed to be directed at the rich and famous (left) for whom Charlie invented crude tortures.

rely entirely on Mrs. Kasabian. He then called a further 84 witnesses, and presented some 300 exhibits, in his effort to prove that Manson—in spite of the fact that he was not personally present at the killings—was "as guilty as sin"; and he took four months to present the prosecution case. At the end of this marathon there came another unusual twist.

The four beleaguered and bickering defence lawyers finally managed to reach some kind of uniform agreement between themselves. Before a stunned court they promptly announced that the defence rested. In short, there would be no defence at all. The reasons for this curious procedure—or lack of it—were not, on examination, difficult to understand.

Manson had devised a curious and almost satanic means to escape the law. He had persuaded—the word seems totally inadequate—the three girls to take the stand, "confess" that they were responsible for the murders, and declare their "master" innocent. Manson would then confirm their story and proceed to tell the world about his divine "mission".

Life story

Appalled, the lawyers refused to let them do it. When the girls insisted—backed by the judge, who ruled that they had a right to testify—the legal team declined to ask any questions. The girls countered by demanding to tell their stories verbatim, whereupon the jury was removed so that they could later be presented with a written version with the inadmissible portions edited out. Then the girls objected once more, and refused to testify unless the jury was present. It looked like stalemate—and a difficult decision for the judge.

Unbelievably, the situation was rescued by Manson himself. He suddenly sprang up, asked to take the stand, and talked for fully 90 minutes about his origins, his "family", and his beliefs. It was, possibly, the most remarkable testimony ever heard in a United States court. And though it did nothing to allay the horror of his actions, it did much to explain them. Occasionally in tears, but more often restrained and seemingly sincere, Manson began with the story of his life, and ran it through to the "end".

"I have stayed in jail," he stated, "and I have stayed stupid and I have stayed a child while I have watched your world grow up. And then I look at the things you do and I don't understand. Most of the people you call the family were just people that you did not want, people that were alongside the road; I took them up on my garbage dump and I told them this: that in love there is no wrong.

"I have done my best to get along in your world, and now you want to kill me. I say to myself, 'Ha, I'm already dead,

have been all my life . . .' What you want is a fiend. You want a sadistic fiend because that is what you are. You only reflect on me what you are inside of yourselves, because I don't care anything about any of you. If I could I would jerk this microphone off and beat your brains out with it, because that is what you deserve. You kill things better than you.

"I don't care what you do with me. I have always been in your cell. When you were out riding your bicycle, I was sitting in your cell looking out the window and looking at pictures in magazines and wishing I could go to high school and go to the prom. My peace is in the desert or in the jail cell, and had I not seen the sunshine in the desert, I would be satisfied with the jail cell much more over your society."

There was an almost tangible silence as everyone hung on Manson's words. For the next few seconds the weird, merciless killer held the whole court under his fanatical spell. Then as nothing more came from him, Bugliosi stepped into the gap determined to normalize the strained atmosphere with a blast of ridicule:

"You say you're already dead, don't you, Charlie?"

"As anyone will tell you," Manson retorted, "you are dead when you are no more."

"You think you've been dead for close on 2000 years, don't you?"

This was an allusion to Manson's expressed belief that he was Christ incarnate, and the defence promptly objected. Judge Older sustained the objection, but Bugliosi pressed on.

"Just who are your children, Charlie?" he demanded.

"Anyone who will love me," Manson replied quietly, and then stared fixedly at the judge for several seconds.

Finally he stepped down, shuffled over to the accused girls and whispered: "Don't testify."

They didn't. And neither did Manson when offered the chance to repeat his story before the jury. "I've relieved all my pressure," he told the judge.

In his summation, Bugliosi called Manson "one of the most evil, satanic men who ever walked the face of the earth". The jury agreed, and all four defendants were found guilty and later sentenced to death—which, in the legal situation of the time, meant they would be kept alive and waiting in Death Row.

As a murderous family unit they were no more. Whether they were eventually executed or not, the essential thing was that they were kept apart from each other. And that Manson—so named, he said, because he was the "son of man" —was no longer the all-powerful, all-vengeful patriarch.

THE LADYKILLERS

One alarming theory about the Ladykillers is that they murder to make their presence felt. There are many cases to support this, few more spectacular than that of the haunting necrophiliac Reginald Christie, the notorious killer of Rillington Place. Christie was a weakling and a hypochondriac. He may have killed as many as seven women and a baby. Some of the bodies were found in a cupboard by a tenant at the house where Christie had lived. By then, another (presumably innocent) resident of the same house had been hanged for two of the murders.

LADYKILLER CHRISTIE . . .
Victims like 26-year-old Miss Hectorina MacLennan (above) were boarded up in a hidden cupboard. Gradually, the stripping of the house revealed more bodies (top).

Popperfoto

THE three doctors called in to pronounce upon Henri Désiré Landru's mental condition were agreed upon one thing: the man, despite the ten women he was said to have murdered, was not mad. The first medical expert, Dr. Vallon, faced the crowded court at the lady-killer's trial and stated:

"I already had to examine the accused in 1904, when he was being charged with obtaining money by false pretences. I found him then in a state bordering on the psychopathic, but he was not mad. Perhaps he was on the borderline, but not beyond it. I find now that Landru is perfectly lucid, perfectly conscious of what he is doing. He is quick and alert in his mind. He is easy and facile in repartee. In short, he must be considered responsible for the acts of which he is accused."

The second doctor, Roques de Fursac, added: "There is no trace of obsession. In examining Landru's personality, we have found him to be normal in every way." While Dr. Roubinovich said: "We were struck by his subtlety and presence of mind. His psychology is what might be called that of the 'transportee'. Transportation is always before his eyes as a nightmare which threatens him . . . The transportee has to live, and his past means that he cannot be choosy about the means he employs to keep himself alive. He will use any means to avoid being caught and sentenced afresh, to avoid transportation. Landru was in this position in 1914."

Lack of feeling

Landru—whose criminal and sexual career had been under police surveillance for some twenty years—was jubilant when he heard this. "The crimes of which I am accused could only be explained by the most pronounced insanity," he asserted. "The doctors say I am sane—therefore I am innocent."

Said to be "completely lacking in moral responsibility", Landru displayed an ambivalent attitude towards women, whom he courted like any other men and later killed with a brutal lack of feeling that branded him as a monster without humanity or heart.

If murderers derived their interest, like butterflies, from their rarity value, then Landru would belong to the rarest and strangest of species, the lady-killer. A surprising statement, perhaps, if you consider that over fifty per cent of all murder victims are women. But this is because the commonest type of murder is the family quarrel, in which the husband kills his

THE BRIDES IN THE BATH murderer, George Smith, with four of his wives. The lucky ones were deserted. The alternative was drowning in the bath.

MURDER CASTLE: He built a house riddled with secret passages . . . and killed 27 women. H. H. Holmes was one of America's most remarkable murderers.

wife in a fit of rage or jealousy. Much lower on the list—but still providing a high proportion of the crime figures—is the sex murder. The sex killer has the mentality of a hungry fox; women are chickens, who are protected from him by a screen of social conventions; like a fox, he waits for his opportunity to slip under the wire and help himself.

Landru, however, was not a sex killer in this sense. On the contrary, he belongs to the very small group of killers who chose to make a poor living (Landru "earned" about £100 [$250] a victim) by the destruction of gullible women. He was possessed by a strange, morbid compulsion—the same compulsion we can see in the case of the French "werewolf", Martin Dumollard, of George Joseph Smith, the British Brides in the Bath murderer, of H. H. Holmes, the American mass-killer, of the wife poisoner George Chapman, of the Hungarian Bluebeard Bela Kiss—perhaps even in the case of Jack the Ripper himself.

Killer of children

In order to understand the nature of this compulsion the question must be asked: Why are these lady-killers called "Bluebeards"? The original Bluebeard, the 15th-century Marshal of France, Gilles de Rais, who fought beside Joan of Arc, was not a killer of women, but of children. Noted because of his glossy blue-black beard, he was a sexual pervert, and also thought he could use the children's blood in the making of gold. But it was the French writer of fairy stories, Charles Perrault, who created the popular version of Bluebeard the lady-killer in the late seventeenth century. One of his more macabre stories tells how a young girl, Fatima, marries the rich landowner Bluebeard, and one day looks into a secret

room—to find there the bodies of his previous wives. Although Perrault wrote the tale from the Gallic viewpoint, many countries have similar legends of wife-killers—Cornwall has a story of a giant called Bolster who killed his wives each year by throwing rocks at them. The folk-imagination understands these dark male compulsions to destroy women—and also the woman's half-frightened, half-fascinated attitude towards it, which in some cases leads her to invite assault and violence upon herself.

A modern crime

The strange thing is that all the known cases of real-life Bluebeards are fairly modern. Of the hundreds of criminal cases contained in such compilations as *Lives of the Most Remarkable Criminals* (1735), *The Newgate Calendar* (1774), and even Camden Pelham's *Chronicles of Crime* published as late as 1886, there are no "lady-killers". Highwaymen, pirates, cut-throats, housebreakers galore; but no lady-killers. Why should this be? If folk-legend had been obsessed by Bluebeards for centuries, why, up until then, should there have been no real-life Bluebeards?

The work of the psychologist Abraham Maslow suggests a fascinating explanation which, if correct, throws an entirely new light on this question, and on the history of crime. Maslow's basic theory, first published in 1942, is known as "the hierarchy of needs" or values. It was intended as a counterblast to Dr. Sigmund Freud's theory that man's basic needs are sexual—not to mention Karl Marx's theory that his basic needs are economic, and Alfred Adler's theory that the basic human urge is the Will to Power.

Maslow pointed out that if a man is starving he has *no* other strong urge except the urge to eat, and he cannot imagine any higher bliss than having large and regular meals. But as soon as he achieves regular meals, he begins to brood on security—the need for a roof over his head. If he achieves this, he now begins to think about sex—not just rape, but a mate to settle down with. And when a man has got a home, a good job, and a happy family, what is the next thing he wants? Respect and admiration, to be accepted socially, to be liked—and if possible envied—by his neighbours. This is the stage at which men join rotary clubs, and wives form coffee groups and worry about keeping up with the Joneses. At this stage, the urge for *self-esteem* becomes paramount, and this explains the penchant of some killers—Heath is a classic example—for dressing-up as heroes and officers.

Once all these needs are satisfied, what then? According to Maslow, the highest level of all can emerge: the creative urge

343

—what, in more old-fashioned days, we would have called his "spiritual drives". But this is not restricted to the emotional and egotistical need to write symphonies, compose plays in blank verse, or build cathedrals. Anybody who wants to do a job *well*, just for the sheer pleasure of it, is expressing the creative urge. From this it can be seen that Maslow's hierarchy of needs is a kind of ladder. If you are stuck on the bottom rung, then Marx's materialistic theories will strike you as true. If you are stuck on the next rung, it will be clear that the psychoanalyst Freud was right when he said there is nothing more important than sex. On the next rung, the Austrian analyst Adler's Will to Power — and self-esteem — will seem the profoundest truth about human nature. All are partly right; none is wholly right.

Food and territory

Maslow's theory is borne out by the history of crime. In primitive societies, food and "territory" are the most important things, and if a man commits a murder, it is likely to be for one of these two reasons or drives. Until a hundred years ago, for instance, most people in Europe and America were living at mere subsistence level. These were the conditions under which Burke and Hare, the two Edinburgh body-snatchers, committed their murders in 1828, and it is not surprising that they killed human beings for the sake of the few pounds paid by Dr. Knox of the medical school for the corpses. *This* is basically the reason that *The Newgate Calendar* is so full of footpads and burglars and highwaymen. And why there are so few rapists. Society was still stuck on the bottom rung of Maslow's ladder.

The Victorian age rolled on; the tide of prosperity spread slowly across Europe. Most of the famous British Victorian murders were still for gain; but the age of middle-class murder had arrived, bringing in the domestic dramas of such killers as Constance Kent who butchered her four-year-old half-brother, mass-poisoner William Palmer, wife-poisoner Dr. Edward Pritchard, Madeleine Smith, the Scottish girl who disposed of an unwanted and awkward lover. Then, in 1888, the savage and apparently motiveless murders of five London East End prostitutes, by the unknown killer nicknamed Jack the Ripper, signalled the beginning of a new age — the age of sex crime. Society, by virtue of its progress and growth, had reached the next rung of Maslow's ladder. By the 1940s, sex crime, once the rarest of all reasons for murder, had become commonplace. It still is; but already, the next age has begun — the age of what could be called "the self-esteem murder". Why did the London gangster-brothers Ronnie and Reggie Kray commit murders in

front of a crowd of witnesses? The answer sounds astonishing: to *impress* the London underworld. The element of pride, of self-esteem, becomes increasingly common among murderers, whatever the motive appears to be. Multiple sex killer John Reginald Halliday Christie loved exerting his authority as an English war reserve constable; Heath posed as "Group Captain Rupert Brooke"; Arthur Hosein — kidnapper of Mrs. McKay, wife of an executive of the London *Sun* — set himself up as a "gentleman farmer"; Charles Manson saw himself as leader of a world revolution. Typical of this new trend in murder is the statement of 18-year-old Robert Smith, who made five women and two children lie on the floor of an Arizona beauty parlour and shot them all in the back of the head: "I wanted to get known — to get myself a name," he stated afterwards.

There is one major consolation in all this. If society can get past the stage of the self-esteem killer, the murder rate should drop steeply. The next rung up the ladder is the purely creative stage, and creativity and murder are usually incompatible. Whether that stage will ever be reached in our overcrowded world is a matter for speculation; but if Maslow's theory is correct, there is ground for hope.

Masked inadequacies

As for Landru — the prototype and most quoted example of the 20th-century lady-killer — a brief examination of his adult sexual career reveals that he is a typical self-esteem killer. His Paris childhood certainly provides no hint of his subsequent "anti-women" activities. He was a sunny, good-natured child, liked by everyone, and adored by his parents (as his name — Désiré — hints). His father was an ordinary workman — a stoker. When Landru left school, he went to work in an architect's office — and his old friends immediately noticed the change. He became "stuck up", and he lost no opportunity to mention that he was a white collar office worker. He had achieved middle-class status — which, in the French provincial society of the 1890s, meant considerably more than it would today. For the rest of his life, Landru played this part of the member of the professional classes: he posed as lawyer, doctor, engineer, businessman, accountant — anything that boosted his ego, masked his inadequacies, and made him feel "talented" and a "gentleman".

Unfortunately for Landru and his future victims, society had no special place for the intelligent but mercurial young man. In the army — where he did military service — his record was excellent. Then he returned to civilian life, married the cousin he had got pregnant, and faced the

task of making a career for himself and providing security for his family. But the prospect of a lifetime in an office bored him, and he was too unstable to stay in any one job for long. Attempts to launch his own businesses invariably failed. His natural charm and alertness suggested petty fraud and false pretences as a means of tiding his wife and four children over bleak periods. And it was with the enthusiasm of someone who has finally found his niche that he turned to crime — a more exciting, more "creative", way of living than office work. Experience showed him that elderly widows were particularly gullible, and eager to give him the keys to their hearts and deposit boxes. Being a confidence trickster — especially such a well-loved and successful one — appealed to his vanity, to his intelligence, even to his artistic impulse (for, as Thomas Mann, the German Nobel Prize-winner pointed out in his novel *Felix Krull — Confidence Man*, the confidence trickster has a touch of the artist about him). Inevitably there were periods in gaol; and when, in 1912 (when Landru was 43) his father committed suicide, overwhelmed by his son's disgrace, the con-man entered a new phase of his career. He determined to throw all scruples to the wind and make an audacious career of murder.

It is a curious fact that — with one borderline exception — the life-styles of all the best known lady-killers resemble Landru's in certain basic respects.

Johann Hoch, born in Strasbourg in 1860, was intended for the ministry, but left Germany — for undisclosed reasons — and went to the United States. There he advertised in German language papers for widows without children, "object, matrimony". This technique was very like Landru's. He represented himself as a wealthy businessman or a man with a respectable position in a commercial company. He married the woman — if necessary — parted her from her money, and decamped. Unlike Landru, he appeared to prefer poison when it came to despatching his brides. He was married some thirteen times — unlucky number as far as his "wives" were concerned — and poisoned six of his brides. He was executed in Chicago in 1906.

Carefree scale

H. H. Holmes, perhaps the most remarkable American criminal of the 19th-century was also born in 1860, the son of a postmaster. Determined to rise in the world, he studied medicine, then became a swindler. His first known murder was of a store-owner, a Mrs. Holden, in Chicago. Holmes duly became owner of the store. He then built a house, riddled with secret passages, and proceeded to murder women on a large and carefree

Photographs AP

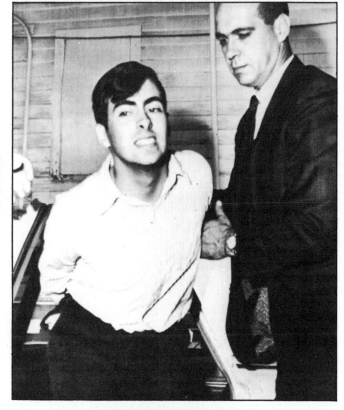

TO MAKE A NAME for himself, Robert Smith, aged 18, made five women and two children lie down, like spokes in a wheel, on the floor of an Arizona beauty parlour. Then he shot them all twice, in the back of the head. He was a typical case of the "self-esteem" murderer. "I wanted to get known," he said.

FATAL FAME . . . the cost of Robert Smith's bid for attention: Clockwise: Toddler Debra Sellers, Glenda Carter, Mary Olsen, Bonita Sue Harris, who was seriously wounded, Carol Farmer, and the Sellers baby, Tamara Lynn. Mrs Sellers, who was killed, is below. Centre: Robert Smith arrives in court.

scale. The motive was not sexual, for most of the girls had been his mistress for some time before they "vanished". At least eight women disappeared after entering his "murder castle", and he later schemed with a man named Pitezel to swindle an insurance company. In the end —as often happened with Holmes' friends—Pitezel and three of his children were killed. Mrs. Pitezel was also on the murder list, but Holmes was arrested before he could eliminate her. In all, he confessed to 27 murders.

George Chapman—actually a Pole called Klosovski—was executed in 1903, having been found guilty of poisoning three wives. Chapman's English was poor, and the early part of his life was spent abroad, so altogether less is known about him than about other notable lady-killers.

Son of a carpenter, he spent much of his life trying to "better himself", setting up in various businesses, including those of barber and publican. (He was in Whitechapel in London's East End at the time of the Ripper murders, and has been suspected of being the Ripper.) There is no evidence that he was ever involved in swindling and the motive for the poisonings has variously been put down to sexual lust, craving for security and money, and sadism.

George Joseph Smith, the infamous "Brides in the Bath" murderer was a Londoner, born in 1872. He was in and out of reformatories and gaols from the age of nine. After a two year sentence for receiving stolen goods, he embarked on the career of a swindler of widows and unmarried females. He married and

345

LEADER of a world revolution? Charles
Manson wasn't short on self-esteem.
He had a "happy family", and impressed
them by instigating a rampage of murder.

authorities had been notified of his death
in action during the First World War.
Later stories, however, told of him en-
listing in the French Foreign Legion
under the name of Hofmann, and of being
spotted by a New York Homicide Squad
detective emerging from the subway
station in Times Square.

One other thing that the lady-killers
—the men who mask their loathing of
women with love—have in common is
the so-called "hypnotic power" which
they have wielded over their victims. This
again can be explained by the way in
which they carefully chose as their
"wives" women who wanted—needed—
to be subjected to the power of a "superior" man. These eager and willing victims
—the "murderees"—cannot wait to meet
a man who is going to mistreat them,
both physically and emotionally, and then
strip them of their pride, their dignity,
their money and their possessions. Without such women—who seem to draw their
killers towards them—the Landrus and

deserted an unspecified number of women
before deciding to drown Bessie Munday
in 1912. When his third "wife" drowned
in her bath, a newspaper report aroused
the suspicions of a relative of a previous
victim. Protesting his innocence to the
end Smith was executed in 1915.

Frederick Deeming, born in England
about 1853, was a confidence swindler
who specialised in cheating jewellers by
pretending to be the manager of a diamond mine. For reasons of gain, he also
posed as a millionaire, and as "Sir
Wilfred Lawson" and "Lord Dunn". He
was a braggart and a remarkably inventive
liar. In 1891, he murdered his wife and
four children, and buried the bodies under
the floor in a rented house. He then went
to Australia with a new wife, who was
soon murdered and buried under another
floor. Posing as Baron Swanston, he had
persuaded another girl, an heiress, to
marry him when the discovery of his

second wife's body led to his arrest.
Three houses in which he had previously
lived in South Africa also proved to have
girls buried under the floors. He declared that the ghost of his dead mother
urged him to murder women. Despite
this "defence", he was executed in 1892.

Bela Kiss, an amateur astrologer and
Hungary's most spectacular lady-killer,
claimed a total of at least twenty-four
victims. When he joined the army in 1916,
the new tenant of his house opened seven
petrol drums and found them to contain
bodies of women preserved in alcohol.
Kiss proved to be well known in the red
light district of Budapest—a man of immense physical strength and boundless
sexual appetite. He had advertized for
ladies to share his rural seclusion in
Cinkota; the ladies vanished, and their
valuables provided Kiss with more funds
for excursions to the city brothels. By
the time his victims were discovered, the

other Bluebeards would have no one to
abuse, take advantage of and fleece.
Their "hypnotism"—George Joseph
Smith was reputed to have "eyes that
could make a girl do anything"—would go
for nothing simply because there would
be no one on whom they could successfully practice. Every Landru has to have
a Madame Cuchet—his first widow victim—and but for her, and those like her,
he would be no more than another eccentric possessed with "strange" ideas about
the sexes and the roles played by men
and women in the marriage game.

Lady-killers are to be abhorred, and their
victims pitied. But compulsion can be a
two-way process: the compulsion to
kill and to be killed. Lock up the lady-
killers by all means, but also educate
their "wives", teach them to beware of
men like Smith, men like Landru, who are
too smooth, too polite, too charming—
and, underneath it all, too deadly.

GREED

Keystone

A SINGLE OBSESSION DROVE MARTHA MAREK TO CHOP OFF HER HUSBAND'S LEG, TO POISON HER OWN CHILDREN...TO MURDER FOUR TIMES

THE real greed-murder is, strangely enough, the rarest of all murders. Because to be *that* greedy is basically a pathological condition. For the psychologist, the greed murderers are among the most fascinating of all types of killer.

The case of Frau Loewenstein-Marek, who was born around 1904, is a prime example of this illness. Martha Loewenstein was a dazzlingly beautiful young girl who worked in a dress shop in Vienna, and whose background was miserably poor. She was a foundling, who had been adopted and brought up in the slums of Vienna. When she went to work in the dress shop, she was so efficient, and carried herself so well, that the woman

who owned the shop presented her with smart dresses.

One day in the early 1920's, she met a rich man who lived alone in a villa in the nearby city of Mödling. He was so impressed by Martha's charm and firmness of character that he invited her to become his ward. Suddenly, the life of poverty was behind her; Cinderella was adored and spoiled by her elderly Prince Charming.

Yet there were drawbacks. She would have preferred a younger admirer, and this explained why she experienced fits of depression and irritability. Her kindly benefactor, Moritz Fritsch, cheered her up by telling her that he intended to leave

her the house and a part of his fortune. A year later, at the age of 74, Fritsch died peacefully. His ex-wife was infuriated to learn that he had left the house to a girl who had been his ward for less than five years; but her son persuaded her against having the body exhumed.

Fraulein Loewenstein soon married a handsome engineer, Emil Marek, with whom she had been carrying on a secret affair before Fritsch's death. Cinderella should have lived happily ever after. Unfortunately, there were problems. Although young and handsome, Emil had not yet established himself in a career; and the money left by her benefactor proved to be less than she had expected.

347

At this point, Martha and Emil Marek concocted a plot that must be unique in the annals of crime. Emil took out an insurance policy for $30,000 against disablement or accident—which was easy enough for an obviously healthy young man.

A week later, they went into the garden, and Emil started to cut down a tree. After this, he sat down, closed his eyes, and allowed Martha to hack off his leg with the razor-sharp axe. Then she went back into the house. Emil cried out, and the servants rushed out, and found him bleeding to death. Martha "conscientiously" applied tourniquets and Emil was then rushed to hospital.

Preposterous scheme

It was a preposterous—to say nothing of painful—scheme. For how does a man accidentally chop off his leg below the knee while swinging an axe? Naturally, the doctors—and the police—were curious. Close examination of the amputated stump revealed that it had taken three separate blows to sever it, and the Mareks were accused of fraud. Martha promptly made things worse by trying to bribe an orderly to testify that he had seen a doctor tampering with the wound.

The Mareks then appeared in the dock, but the magistrates were unconvinced by the medical evidence—or perhaps they thought Emil Marek had suffered enough. The case against the couple was dismissed, and the insurance company settled for a relatively small sum—by dropping hints that they were thinking of having Moritz Fritsch's body exhumed. For some reason, Frau Marek did not like the idea.

It was the beginning of a long run of bad luck for the Mareks. An attempt to set up a radio business in Algiers was a failure. An ambitious engineering scheme —that might have made Emil's fortune— fell through because of the scandal of the trial—which followed them to North Africa. When the Marek's returned to Vienna, they had two children, and were so poor that Martha had to sell vegetables in a street market. Not long after, Emil Marek died in a charity ward of "tuberculosis", and a month later their small daughter, Ingeborg, also passed away.

Free of such "encumbrances", Martha's luck turned. She moved into the home of an elderly relative, Susanne Loewenstein, and cooked for her. Before long, Frau Loewenstein died, leaving the house and her money to Martha. But Martha still hadn't learned how to live modestly and without attracting attention.

She was extravagant, spent the money, and then took in a few selected lodgers. These included an insurance agent, and an elderly lady named Kittenberger, together with her son. The insurance agent arranged to insure Frau Kittenberger for $1000, with Martha as the beneficiary. Soon Frau Kittenberger conveniently died.

The insurance money did not last for long, and once again, Martha resorted to fraud. She arranged for a removal firm to call one night, and take her paintings and tapestries into storage. She then reported them stolen, and claimed the insurance. The detective sent to question her— Ignatz Peters—had also been on the earlier "amputation" case. Suspicious from the start, he checked around the city's removal firms, and quickly found the one that had stored Martha's valuables.

For a second time, Martha was arrested and charged with fraud. The announcement of her arrest led Frau Kittenberger's son to approach the police and assert that his mother had died of poison. Ignatz Peters immediately went to work. Four corpses were exhumed: Emil Marek, their daughter Ingeborg; Frau Loewenstein, and Frau Kittenberger. All were found to have been poisoned with thallium, a rare metallic chemical element discovered in 1861.

Then Peters recalled that Martha had a second child, a son. He traced him to where he was boarded out in a poor district of Vienna. He was also suffering from thallium poisoning—although the symptoms looked like tuberculosis. His mother had been paying him visits and bringing him food. The boy was hurried to hospital, and his life was saved.

Martha Marek, accused and found guilty of four murders, was duly sentenced to death. This was in December 1938, when Hitler had reintroduced beheading as a means of execution. The headsman was more efficient than Martha had been. He accomplished his task with one clean swing of the axe.

Peculiar character

Beyond all doubt, Martha Marek was sane; no one ever suggested otherwise. Yet what can be said of a woman who can poison both her children, and who poisoned one of her victims—Frau Kittenberger—for a mere $1000? She was clearly an obsessional character of a very peculiar type. Her greed and obsession with money was almost a physical disability, like colour blindness.

The case records reveal nothing about Martha Marek's psychological problems; but a significant amount can be deduced from her history. She was a bastard, brought up by a foster mother, whom Ignatz Peters described as "fat and vulgar". Her later development strongly suggests that she did not receive affection

TO THE GUILLOTINE: Macabre man's uniquely macabre moment. Faced with the basket which awaits his head, Weidmann doesn't flinch. Above: His last victim.

Photos Keystone

A FAMILY OF EIGHT was murdered by Jean Baptiste Troppmann . . . and he was only 20 years old. He buried his victims in a field, and was arrested by accident.

in her early years. It is now a well-known fact that the first months of a child's life are of vital importance. Baby animals who are deprived of parental affection during this period become *incapable of giving affection* later. It is as if something inside them has starved to death. The same happens to human beings.

It can be inferred that Martha Loewenstein was affection-starved during this important period. Added to that, she certainly belonged to the group of "high dominance females" who, in order to achieve sexual satisfaction, need to settle with a man who is even more dominant.

Martha Loewenstein married a man who was undoubtedly of merely moderate dominance. *She* dominated him — for it is impossible to imagine a high-dominance male allowing his wife to chop off his leg merely to collect a thousand dollars. He would have suggested insuring *her* and chopping off *her* leg.

After five years as the ward — and probably mistress — of an old man, she wanted a passionate and violent young lover. Emil Marek failed to satisfy her, physically or psychologically. So she killed him, and administered poison to the two children of the union.

It is tempting to say that the basic motivation of the crimes was her dread of poverty — something to be sympathized with. But if that was really her basic motivation, she would have carefully conserved the money Moritz Fritsch left her — and the later legacy from Susanne Loewenstein. In fact, it is clear that she was thoroughly spoilt and undisciplined. Instead of being grateful to Fritsch when she became his ward, she indulged in tantrums and black moods that would have led a less patient man to throw her out.

Frau Marek became a killer through an unusual combination of character traits: high dominance, inability to feel, with its

inevitable self-centredness, and pure — or impure — greed. Strictly speaking, this does not constitute insanity. Yet today alcoholism is recognized as a kind of disease, even though it is agreed that the alcoholic is not insane. Martha Marek was suffering from a compulsion similar to alcoholism, if more complicated. Her curious mixture of compulsions can be seen, in varying degrees, in all greed-criminals, whether they are killers, or only robbers or swindlers.

One thing is clear: the greed criminal is suffering from a kind of violent, unquenchable thirst, similar to that of the alcoholic. The result is that the crimes of the greed criminal have a weird air of irrationality.

It can be seen that most of the greed killers were also swindlers and confidence tricksters. But here again, there is a distinctly irrational element. The ordinary confidence swindler — like "Count" Victor Lustig, the man who, in 1925, "sold" the Eiffel Tower to a group of scrap metal tycoons — has a touch of bravado and humour about him; and a man with a sense of humour is basically sane. But the greed criminal is slightly paranoid; he

has delusions of grandeur, and he lies to impress people.

This is true of the most spectacular mass murderer of modern times, the Frenchman Dr. Marcel Petiot. The greed crimes for which Petiot was executed began, strictly speaking, in 1941, and by the time they terminated, in 1944, he had killed at least 63 people. But Petiot had prepared for murder with a career of petty theft.

Born in Auxerre in 1897, he stole from classmates at school, and later from letter boxes. After a brief career in the army — from which he managed to get himself discharged as mentally unstable — Petiot qualified as a doctor at the age of 24. There is a strong possibility that he was a sadist. As a child, he had a reputation for amputating the tails of cats with scissors; women patients whom he "treated" after hours in his surgery were heard to cry out in pain.

In 1928, by virtue of his persistent canvassing, he was appointed mayor of Villeneuve. Shortly afterwards his housekeeper became pregnant and then vanished. Two years later another woman patient was killed and robbed. Petiot was suspected, but his chief accuser — who was also one of his patients — died suddenly, and Petiot signed the death certificate. In spite of being mayor, he was in trouble several times for absurd petty crimes — robbing a gasmeter, stealing from a bookshop. He also trafficked in drugs.

It was the war that gave Petiot his opportunity to rise above petty crime. A Jew named Joachim Gubsinov wanted to escape to England with his wife and children, and Petiot offered him an "escape route" in return for a large sum of money. Gubsinov duly raised two million francs on his fur business, and called with his wife and children at Petiot's lonely house in the Rue Lesueur. Petiot gave them lethal injections, claiming that they were a protection against typhoid. Then he went into the next room, and through a secret window, watched the Gubinsovs die.

Overstoked fire

Petiot lived — with his family — in the Rue Caumartin. The house in the Rue Lesueur was his execution chamber. But one day in March 1944, he overstoked the fire that consumed the bodies. The house went up in flames and a fireman who burst into the basement rushed out, shouting: "The place is full of bodies!" Petiot, who came up in time to see what was happening, accosted a police officer and whispered: "I am a member of the Resistance. Those bodies are the remains of traitors against France." The police believed him and let him go. By the time they realized — from identification papers found in the house — that the victims were mostly Jews, Petiot was nowhere to be found.

But his vanity was his undoing. In October of 1944 – after the liberation of Paris – he wrote a letter to a newspaper claiming that he had been framed by the Gestapo, and that he was an officer in the Resistance. The handwriting was checked against that of Resistance officers, and Petiot was discovered to be hiding under an alias of Captain Henri Valéry; he had been in the Free French Forces for six weeks. He was guillotined on May 26, 1946.

It is true that Petiot's case was complicated by sadism; nevertheless, he is a typical example of the greed killer. There was the usual inability to form meaningful human relationships (his wife was a pale, docile girl, 15 years his junior, whom he married to silence gossip about his affairs and sexual perversions), the curious tendency to petty crime – as if he was unable to resist any opportunity to steal – and the vanity that made him so determined to become mayor. Above all, there was the decision to use murder – and not his talents as a doctor – to gain riches and rewards.

Criminal instinct

One of the world's strangest greed killers was another Frenchman – a young homosexual named Jean Baptiste Troppmann, who was obsessed by the idea of gaining money without legitimately working for it. Unlike most greed killers, he was never accused of the usual petty crimes; but the criminal instinct was certainly there. He was a student of poisons, and developed one that he claimed was undetectable. When he was 20, in 1869, he met a rich provincial businessman, Jean Kinck, and decided that this was his key to wealth.

An early attempt to con his new friend into parting with money was a failure. But Kinck was finally taken in by a story about deposits of precious metals near the mountains of the Upper Rhine. He set out with Troppmann, and was poisoned over a meal – his body being hidden in a heap of stones.

Troppmann then persuaded Madame Kinck to send him a cheque for 5500 francs. The local postmaster in Alsace, however, refused to cash it, and Troppmann decided that his only way of obtaining the wealth he needed – so that he would emigrate to America – was to slaughter all eight members of the Kinck family – including the youngest of the children.

He therefore arranged a meeting in Paris with Madame Kinck, and all her sons and daughters. He then lured them to the open countryside, where he brutally and sadistically stabbed them to death. His next move was to

Both Keystone

Roger Viollet

MONSTER MAYOR ...
a mass-murderer unparalleled in modern history. He killed 63 people, most of them Jews. The belongings of his victims, stacked above, were court exhibits poignant in their horror. Petiot was a doctor ... who dealt only in death. His home (top) was an execution chamber.

Keystone

Roger Viollet

DEATH for the death-doctor. He was guillotined in 1946, after being held in the prison pictured above (inset). "I am a member of the Resistance. They are bodies of traitors against France."

flee to Le Havre, where luck was against him. A policeman mistook him for a sneakthief, and when he tried to arrest him, Troppmann leapt into the harbour. The Kinck family papers were found on him. He was executed—fighting frenziedly—in January 1870, still under 21 years of age.

As far as the homicidal-cum-sexual greed criminal is concerned, France has an unenviable lead over Britain, other European countries, and the United States. Her most enigmatic greed killer, however, was a German: Jerome Weidmann. This case began in 1937 when Jean Belin—the Paris-based police officer who had arrested the French Bluebeard, Landru—was investigating the disappearance of a young American dancer, Jean de Koven. She had last been seen with a good-looking and apparently rich young man known as "Bobby".

On September 8, Belin learned that a hired car driver named Gouffy was found shot in the back of the head on the Orléans road. He, too, had driven off with a good-looking young man who appeared to be rich. Shortly afterwards, the naked body of a dead man named Leblond was found in the back of a car at Neuilly. He also had last been seen with a good-looking young man.

On November 20, 1937, an estate agent, a M. Lesobre, was found in the cellar of a house with a bullet in the back of his neck. His secretary's description of the young man with whom he had left the office suggested that this was the same killer. Apparently the man chose his victims for the little money they carried with them.

The police were searching for the murderer when Belin next heard about the disappearance of a young man named Frommer. He had been friendly with a foreigner called Sauerbrey, who lived in a house in the St. Cloud forest near Paris. Two detectives called on Sauerbrey, who invited them into the house. Suddenly he turned round with a gun in his hand, and began shooting. His aim was poor. He only grazed one of the policemen, and the other knocked him out with a hammer.

When gendarmes searched the grounds, they found the corpse of Jean de Koven under a foot of earth. She had been killed for her traveller's cheques; there was no evidence of sexual assault. Frommer's body was then found in the cellar; he had been shot in the back of his head. Sauerbrey subsequently said that his real name was Jerome Weidmann and admitted to being the notorious "mass killer". After his confession, Weidmann repented, publicly and noisily, and went to his death without flinching.

Mad recklessness

His basic motivation, however, remains a mystery. Why should he have killed so casually for such absurd sums of money—at most, a few hundred francs? The evidence suggests that he killed out of a kind of boredom, as boys pull the wings off flies.

All this explains why greed killers, and greed robbers in general, are the subject of inexhaustible interest to the criminologist—as unpredictable and exceptional as man-eating tigers, but far more difficult to understand. The only thing that is clear is that all of them suffer from a form of schizophrenia.

Whether the target is a train—stopped and robbed of the valuables it carries—a bank with rich deposits, or a lonely and frustrated widow, there is one element present in the greed criminal's behaviour and mentality. He—or she—does not countenance the possibility of failure or of being caught. In that alone lies madness, recklessness, and the greatest aid to the police in the tracking down of the offender, and his ultimate imprisonment or execution.

THE KIDNAPPERS

THEY TRADE in human anguish . . . the highest-priced of all commodities. They are a generation of criminals who belong to modern times . . . to the times in which it has become possible for the criminal to infiltrate the habitat of the rich and famous, and take human hostages. And, because their victims are rich and renowned, the list of great cases reads like a "Who's Who" of fame and fortune. There was the Lindbergh baby, the Peugeot child, and Mrs. Muriel McKay . . .

IT WAS not until the second half of the nineteenth century that professional criminals thought of seizing a human hostage and holding him for ransom. In the days when crooks lived in slums, and the rich resided in great houses or country estates, criminals seldom had a chance to encounter the children of the rich. Then came the age of industry and factories. Men acquired fortunes overnight, and many evildoers brooded on how to separate them from their wealth.

It was in the United States, where the rich and the poor rub shoulders, that the first notable modern case of kidnapping occurred. It was conceived in the summer of 1874 when two men made a habit of driving past the home of Christian Ross, a once moderately successful Philadelphia grocer who had recently become bankrupt. The men stopped and spoke to Charley Ross, aged four, and Walter Ross, aged six, as the children played innocently on the sidewalk. On July 1 the children asked their new friends to buy them fireworks for the Fourth of July celebrations.

The men agreed and invited the youngsters to hop into the buggy. A few streets away, they gave Walter 25 cents and sent him to a nearby shop. When the little boy returned, the buggy had vanished, and his brother Charley with it.

The howling Walter was then taken home by a neighbour, and Christian Ross hurried to the police. Everyone was baffled. Why, they asked, should anyone steal a four-year-old baby?

The mystery was solved two days later when the Rosses received a scrawled and badly spelled letter; it said "you wil hav two pay us befor you git him", but did not mention any sum. Such a thing had never been heard of in North America before. Indignation swept the country. Thousands of police joined in the search for "little Charley Ross". No one bothered about search warrants as they burst into any premises that might conceal the missing child. On July 6, Ross received a letter asking for $20,000, and threatening to kill the child if the hunt was not called off. He was told to insert an advertisement in the *Philadelphia Ledger* saying he was ready to negotiate. Instead, he tried to drag out the correspondence, hoping that the kidnappers would provide a clue to their whereabouts.

The men expressed their impatience at his tactics, and he countered by stating publicly that he was "damned if he would compound a felony." His wife, however, was so shattered by the ordeal of waiting that he changed his mind, and agreed to pay $20,000 which he had managed to borrow. Ross went to an appointed rendezvous, but no one appeared to collect the money. So month after month dragged by. There were more appointments, more correspondence, but still no sign of the missing child. The grim story ended six months later, on December 14, 1874, when a burglar alarm sounded in the home of a rich New Yorker, Holmes Van Brunt; it meant that burglars had broken into the summer residence belonging to his brother, next door.

Dying confession

Van Brunt and three other men duly crept up to the house with shotguns, and waited. When, an hour later, the burglars came out, Van Brunt ordered them to halt. Instead, they started shooting. The Van Brunt party fired back with their shotguns, and both burglars fell. One of them gasped out a dying confession: his name was Joseph Douglass, and he and his companion, William Mosher, had kidnapped Charley Ross. The boy would be returned alive and well within a few days. . . . Then Douglass died.

The confession was undoubtedly genuine, for the police already knew that Douglass and Mosher were the men they wanted: another crook had informed on them. But no sign of flaxen-haired Charley Ross was ever found. A third man named William Westervelt was tried as an accomplice, and sentenced to seven years' imprisonment, although there was no real evidence against him—a sign of how much frustrated anger had been aroused by the kidnapping.

The age of kidnapping had arrived; but fortunately for parents and relatives it got off to a slow start. This was partly due to the death of poor Charley Ross, for in February 1875, the Legislature of

"THE FOX": A manic egoist, with a sadistic desire to make a parent suffer. A grudge drove him to arrange a rendezvous with horror. Edward Hickman was hanged in San Quentin.

Pennsylvania passed a law defining kidnapping, setting the penalty at a maximum of 25 years' solitary confinement and a fine of $100,000. It is a measure of how much horror was excited by the Ross affair. There is also a certain irony in it. The word kidnapping was originally coined in England about two hundred years earlier, and the kids who were "nabbed" were usually sent to America as cheap labour on the tobacco plantations; now America was forced to enact the first law against the crime.

At about the time of the Charley Ross kidnapping, a country on the other side of the globe was being forced to give serious thought to the question of how to stamp it out. In Greece, as in Corsica and Sicily, kidnapping was a long-established custom, and brigandage was looked upon as an almost respectable occupation.

Complete amnesty

In 1870, however, the whole system backfired, and nearly caused the occupation of Greece by England. On April 11, Lord Muncaster, an Irish peer, together with his wife and a distinguished party of tourists, set out to see the ancient battlefield at Marathon—the site of the Athenians' victory over the Persians, around 490 B.C. A group of soldiers warned them about brigands and started to escort them back to Athens; but the soldiers were too slow, and the carriages rushed on ahead. A band of brigands, led by the notorious Arvanitákis brothers, swooped down and seized them, then forced them to run at top speed over rough countryside. Negotiations with the authorities followed, and the females—including a six-year-old girl—were released, together with Lord Muncaster. Four men, including an Italian nobleman,

Count Alberto de Boÿl, remained as hostages. The ransom demanded was £50,000. Alternatively, the brigands sought a complete amnesty. Previous hauls had made them rich; they wanted to be able to return to society.

When he heard of the outrage, King George of Greece was so upset that he offered to hand himself over to the brigands as a hostage. For the next ten days, however, negotiations dragged inconclusively on. The Greek government categorically refused to grant an amnesty. But Takos Arvanitákis, the brigand chief, said there had to be one—otherwise the prisoners would be killed. Troops drew up near the ravine where he held the four prisoners, while negotiators tried to persuade the brigands to take the ransom and withdraw over the Turkish border. Then something went wrong. The troops, unable to resist taking a potshot, opened fire. The brigands fled towards the village of Dilessi, and on the way, the four captives were callously murdered. Seven brigands, including one of the leaders, were killed; six more were captured. Takos and seven others escaped into Turkey.

Invasion threat

The furore that followed was tremendous. England burst into roars of rage. The British said that if Greece couldn't cope with her own brigands, England should invade the country and do it for them. The Russians promptly stated that, in the event of hostilities, they would go to war to help Greece. "Investigating commissions" were set up; dozens of men who had helped the brigands were rounded up. Fifty eventually went on trial, but most were released. The "Dilessi murders", as they were known, became the scandal of Europe, and Greece lost face badly in the eyes of the world. The government was brought down. One of the brigands was extradited from Turkey and beheaded. Takos himself was finally shot two years after the killings. And in Greece, at least, kidnapping ceased to be a more-or-less acceptable custom.

In the United States, on the other hand, its popularity was growing. In June 1907, in the Italian district of New Orleans, seven-year-old Walter Lamana went off trustingly with a man who offered him his hand. His father soon received a demand for $6000, and it gradually became clear that the kidnappers were the Mafia, or "Black Hand". The organization already ran the Italian part of New Orleans as Al Capone was to run Chicago 20 years later. The publicity aroused by the kidnapping led many Italians to admit that they had been paying "protection money" for years. One of the gang was arrested—Frank Gendusa. Under questioning, he admitted to being involved in the kid-

ELLERY PARADE; SEAFORTH

BODY FOUND HERE

FIRST KIDNAPPING in Australia. The parents of eight-year-old Graeme Thorne (right) had just won £100,000 in a lottery when he vanished. Discarded belongings (below) led police to find Graeme's body near a beach (above). A rug in which the body was wrapped identified the kidnapper, who was arrested in Ceylon (far right), and charged with murder.

napping, but said he didn't know where the child was. Other members of the gang were then taken into custody. One of them, Ignazio Campisciano, was captured by a posse, who used a time-honoured method to induce him to talk: they bound his hands, put a noose round his neck, and pulled it tight over the branch of a tree. Campisciano broke down, and led them to a dirty swamp, where wrapped in a blanket, was the body of the missing boy. The child had kept crying for his mother, he said, and one of the men had strangled it. (In fact, Walter had been killed with a hatchet blow.)

Four of the kidnappers went on trial, including Tony Costa, who had actually abducted the youngster. They were found "Guilty without capital punishment", and for a while, it looked as if the angry crowds of New Orleans would take justice into their own hands and lynch them—as they had done in 1890, when nine members of the Mafia were acquitted of the murder of the Chief of Police, and were subsequently dragged from their cells and killed by a mob. But the crowd was persuaded to disperse quietly.

The trial of two other accomplices—Nicolina and Leonardo Gebbia—had to be postponed for another four months because public feeling ran so high. The Gebbias were both found guilty; Leonardo was hanged, and his sister sentenced to life imprisonment. The man who actually killed Walter Lamana was never caught. But at least his crime had one beneficial result: the power of the Black Hand in New Orleans was crushed and broken.

Major undertaking

It was slowly becoming clear, to the police and the general public, that the surest way of dealing with kidnappers—and of lessening the danger to their hostages—was to pay the ransom, then let the police take up the trail. The value of this method was proved in 1909, in Sharon, Pennsylvania. On March 18, a man drove up to the local school and explained that he had been sent to collect Billy Whitla, the eight-year-old son of a wealthy attorney; his father needed him immediately at the office. The boy was allowed to go and that afternoon Mr. Whitla received a ransom note demanding $10,000. No doubt recalling the Ross case, Whitla declined to co-operate with the police. He delivered the ransom according to instructions, and his son was safely returned. Skilful police work, aided by luck, located the room where the boy had been held by a man and a woman. Detailed descriptions of them led to the arrest of James H. Boyle and his wife within six days of the kidnapping. Both were sentenced to life imprisonment.

But it was in the 1920's, the Bootleg era, that kidnapping became a major criminal undertaking in the United States. Possibly the Sicilian gangsters recalled how lucrative such activities had been in their homeland. For these gang-snatches, children were no longer the automatically chosen victims. The gangsters realized it was just as easy to kidnap a rich business man—and it aroused less public indignation.

Machine-Gun Kelly

Even when it became a crime punishable by death, the crooks didn't seem to be deterred. One of the classic police investigations into such a "snatch" occurred in 1933. The millionaire Charles F. Urschel was sitting on the porch of his home in Oklahoma City, playing cards with his wife and another couple. Suddenly, two men with Tommy guns appeared. When Urschel and his friend refused to say which was Urschel, they were both bundled into a car and driven away. A few hours later, the friend reappeared; he had been released by the kidnappers when they established his identity. Edgar Hoover, Director of the F.B.I., personally took charge of the investigation.

Urschel, so he told the agents, was driven for 12 hours, then taken to a house, where he was blindfolded. He was made to write a ransom note. Then, for the next eight days, he was kept tied up in a dark room. But he kept his wits about him, and noted that aeroplanes flew overhead at 9.45 every morning and 5.45 every afternoon—all except Sunday, when a heavy storm apparently prevented the 5.45 from passing that way. The following day, he was driven a further distance, then put down at a railroad station and released. His ransom of $200,000 had been paid.

The aeroplanes were the only clue the authorities had to go on. Hoover's men studied hundreds of airline schedules. Since the drive had taken about 12 hours, they assumed that the hideaway must be within about three hundred miles of Oklahoma city. Next, after hours of painstaking research, they located an air route that crossed a certain point in Texas at 9.45 each morning and 5.45 each afternoon. They were even able to verify that on the Sunday, a heavy storm had caused the plane to turn off its usual route. The town in question was called Paradise. And in Paradise, they discovered, lived the mother of Kathryn Kelly, wife of a gangster named Machine-Gun George Kelly, who was prominent on their list of suspects for the kidnapping.

Posing as state surveyors, F.B.I. men then called at the house. One of them asked for a drink of water. It tasted bitter with minerals, just as Urschel had described it. A few days later, the F.B.I. swooped at dawn, and found Harvey Bailey—identified as the second kidnapper—with a Tommy gun at his side. Another accomplice, Albert Bates, was

Central Press

Both Central Press

Popperfoto

Popperfoto

863 FK75

Central Press

THE PEUGEOT CASE: Little Eric
Peugeot, aged four (foreground), was the
son of the French automobile millionaire.
He was kidnapped while out with his
nurse and the family chauffeur (left).
World attention was focused on the
episode, reconstructed above by police.
Kidnappers Raymond Rolland (top left)
and Pierre Larcher (top right) held young
Eric in a house near Paris threatening to
kill him unless a £35,000 ransom was paid.
To the anguished parents, the money was
a trifle. The ransom demand was met by
M. Peugeot, and Eric was returned unharmed. The kidnappers were arrested
two years later, living in a ski resort with
a beauty queen and a striptease dancer,
and sentenced to 20 years' imprisonment.

MRS. McKAY was the wife of a senior figure in newspaper management. She was abducted by two brothers who lived at Rooks Farm (above).

traced when he got into a fight in Denver, Colorado; the money the police found on him was from the kidnap ransom—the bill numbers of which had all been noted. For a few months, Machine-Gun Kelly became the latest Public Enemy Number One. He even wrote letters threatening to kill Urschel.

Then, in October, a girl in Memphis, Tennessee, confided to a schoolfriend that her "parents" were not actually her parents; they had "borrowed" her. A policeman who heard this story from his child made cautious investigations. There was another dawn raid, and as the armed policemen burst into his bedroom, Machine-Gun Kelly threw up his hands and yelled "Don't shoot, G-men!" It was the first time Hoover's men had been called G-men, meaning Government men, and the name stuck. As for Kelly, he died 21 years later in Leavenworth Penitentiary.

Lindbergh laws

Before the snatching of aviator Charles A. Lindbergh's son in 1932, America's most famous—and horrible—kidnapping case was that of "The Fox". This was the signature on the ransom note sent to Perry Parker, father of 12-year-old Marian Parker. Parker was a Los Angeles banker; and Marian had been abducted from her school one day in December 1928. During the next few days, Parker received more letters, signed "The Fox" or "Fate", and it was clear that the sender had a sadistic desire to make the parents suffer. Finally, Parker kept his rendezvous with the kidnapper; he could see Marian sitting stiffly beside him in the car. He handed over the money, and the man drove off, promising to let Marian out at the end of the street.

When Parker reached her, she was dead; her legs had been hacked off, and her eyes propped open with wire. Her legs were found in a nearby park. But the shirt in which they were wrapped gave the police the vital clue; it led them to 20-year-old Edward Hickman, who said he wanted the $1500 ransom money to go to college. He also had a grudge against Parker, whom he considered responsible for a prison sentence he had received for forgery. Hickman proved to be an almost manic egoist, revelling in the publicity. He was hanged in San Quentin jail in 1928.

After carpenter Bruno Hauptmann's execution for the murder of the Lindbergh baby, in 1935, the kidnapping "boom" came to an end. As a result of the case, laws known as the "Little Lindbergh Laws" came into operation in various states. These made it a capital offence to commit kidnapping—even if it did not involve a removal across state lines—if any physical harm came to the victim. In New York State, some time later, a man was convicted of kidnapping for forcing a young girl—whom he subsequently molested—to accompany him from the street and onto the roof of a nearby building. Even the sending of a ransom note could mean a maximum penalty in a federal court of twenty years' imprisonment, or a fine of $5000, or both.

In 1960 Australia had its first child kidnapping case. Eight-year-old Graeme Thorne was the son of a travelling salesman of Sydney; his parents had recently won £100,000 in a lottery. Graeme's corpse was found near a beach a month after his disappearance, and scientific examination of the rug in which the body was wrapped finally led the police to the house where he had been taken—and eventually to Leslie Stephen Bradley, a married man with three children, who was arrested on board a ship bound for England.

Symbolic damages

England's first kidnapping case occurred in December 1969, when Mrs. Muriel McKay, wife of a senior Fleet Street newspaper executive, disappeared from her home in Wimbledon, South London. Nine years earlier in France, however, another snatch had taken place which gained almost as many world-wide headlines as the McKay story. Little Eric Peugeot, aged four, the son of the Paris automobile millionaire, Raymond Peugeot, was taken from the playground of a fashionable golf club on the outskirts of the city.

His captors—Raymond Rolland and Pierre Larcher—were two small-time crooks who wanted money in order to indulge their taste for nightclubs and blondes. They demanded £35,000 from the Peugeot family—a mere trifle to M. Peugeot, who handed over the ransom himself. Fortunately for him and his wife, the kidnappers kept their word and Eric was returned a short while later unharmed. It was not until October 1962, however, that Rolland and Larcher—who had been captured living it up in a ski resort chalet with a Danish beauty queen and a striptease dancer—were put on trial.

They were each sentenced to the maximum sentence under French law of 20 years' imprisonment. And the Peugeots—who had recovered some £10,000 of the ransom money—were awarded the symbolic sum of one franc damages. A small price, some people thought, for the agony and torment they had suffered. But the truth is that no parent—or lover, or friend, or relative—can ever be adequately compensated for the distress they undergo in such circumstances. One franc or a million, it does not erase the memory of the event. Especially if, as is usually the case, the kidnapping ends in the physical death of the victim, and the mental death of his family.

CR ATURES THAT THIRST FOR BLOOD

Vampires have fascinated the so-called civilized world for centuries and doctors have even made efforts to discover if they exist. Why is man so attracted to these creatures? What kind of human fantasy do they seem to represent?

"WITHIN stood a tall old man, clean-shaven save for a long white moustache . . . His face was a strong—a very strong—aquiline, with high bridge of the thin nose and peculiarly arched nostrils; with lofty domed forehead, and hair growing scantily round the temples, but profusely elsewhere. His eyebrows were very massive, almost meeting over the nose . . . The mouth was fixed and cruel-looking."

Bram Stoker's description of his legendary Count Dracula is a remarkably accurate sketch of the original Dracula—the great Wallachian warrior whose terrible perversions earned him the name of Vlad the Impaler. After his murder in 1476, he was buried in the monastery of Snagov—now in Rumania; yet the grave has never been discovered. It seems to lend weight to the legend—mentioned by Irishman Stoker—that Dracula belongs to the legions of the undead and of vampires.

National sport

Voivode Dracul—Count Dracula: the word is actually a title, derived from the Rumanian word *dracoul,* meaning devil (which, in this case, might be better translated "the terrible one"). And there is no doubt that he was a sadistic psycho-path *and* a national hero. When he came to the throne in 1456, Wallachia (today part of Rumania) was weak and divided. Rival noblemen kept the country this way by squabbling among themselves. Wallachia was menaced by Turks and Hungarians, and its trade was strangled by German merchants, who controlled all the customs posts. Added to this, the murder of its kings had become almost a national sport—there had been 20 of them in less than 40 years.

Dracula had seen his own father murdered and his favourite brother buried alive. So when he acceded to power, he

All New York Graphic Society

acted with brutal decisiveness. His enemies among the noblemen were murdered, and their families systematically exterminated, in case someone contemplated revenge. The Saxon merchants were seized and impaled *en masse*. When Turkish ambassadors failed to show him the respect he demanded, he had their turbans and clothes nailed to their bodies —making sure the nails were short, so death would be slow.

All this may sound like the typical savagery of an uncivilized warrior. But there is definite evidence that he was a pervert who derived sexual satisfaction from torture. On one occasion, he invited all the poor and sick people of the area to dine in the palace at Tagoviste, then had it boarded up and set on fire, so they were all burned alive. He had men blinded, maimed, and boiled. When the Hungarians kept him prisoner, from 1462 to 1474, he vented his sadism on animals.

Victim's blood

But his favourite method of torture was impalement on a long, pointed pole. The victim was placed on it so that his own weight and his death struggles gradually forced the point through his body. One print shows Vlad dining among the spiked bodies of men and women, and the positions of the victims reveal agonizing and ingenious variations in the methods of impalement.

The German chronicles that describe these tortures make particular mention of his practice of drinking the victims' blood. This was why Bram Stoker chose Vlad as the model for his own sinister Transylvanian nobleman. When Dracula speaks of the exploits of his heroic but cruel ancestor to solicitor Jonathan Harker, he is obviously speaking of himself—and of Vlad the Impaler.

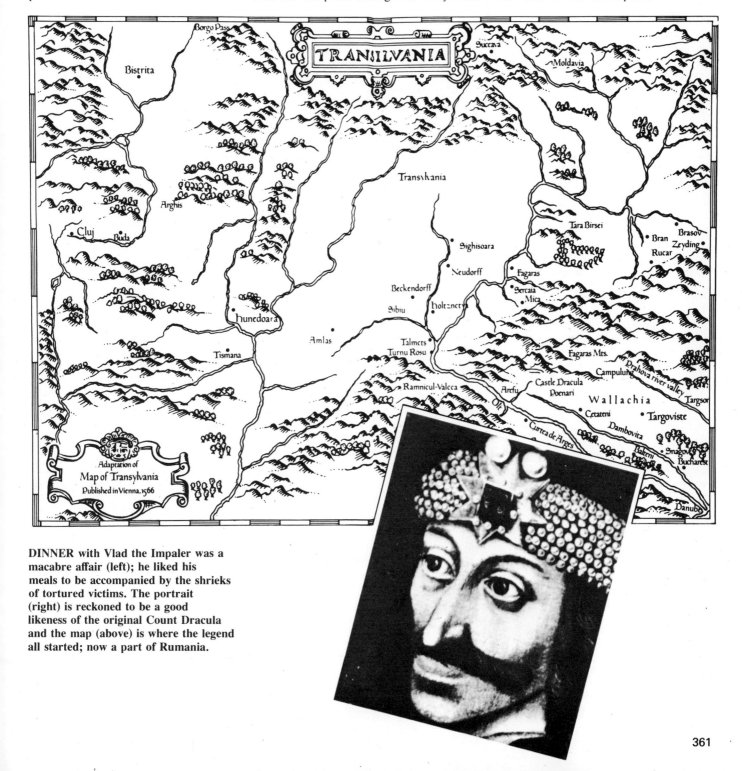

DINNER with Vlad the Impaler was a macabre affair (left); he liked his meals to be accompanied by the shrieks of tortured victims. The portrait (right) is reckoned to be a good likeness of the original Count Dracula and the map (above) is where the legend all started; now a part of Rumania.

How did the imagination of Bram Stoker come to transform the historic Vlad into the supernatural Dracula—the most famous vampire in world literature? This is an intriguing question, for Stoker—who put his inspiration for Dracula on a nightmare following a supper of too much dressed crab—was not a particularly imaginative man. A huge, gentle Dubliner, he became secretary to the actor Sir Henry Irving at the age of 30, and for the next 30 years worked like a drayhorse for his talented but eccentric employer. When Irving died a pauper, Stoker—already famous as the author of *Dracula*—churned out second-rate horror novels that reveal just how little imagination he possessed. On his death the death certificate bore the word "Exhaustion".

Stoker was a typical Victorian gentleman—courteous, chivalrous towards women, basically rather puritanical. And yet *Dracula* is a masterpiece of horror, full of instinctive insights into perversions and cruelties. Its author would have been shocked if someone had told him that his novel was replete with sexual overtones and rape fantasies; yet no one who reads *Dracula* can fail to be aware of them. Was this a case of Freudian repression—or was it something altogether more sinister?

Primeval fear

The Swiss psychologist Jung believed that below the ordinary memory of each individual there is a deeper layer of the unconscious mind, the collective or "racial" unconscious, which has been passed on to us by our remotest ancestors. This racial memory contains certain primordial images or symbols, which Jung calls "archetypes"—for example, father-figures, mother-figures, giants. From the moment Dracula first made his fictional appearance in 1897, he exercised the same curious fascination.

The book has never been out of print, and in the form of plays and films, the story has been seen by millions. (Stoker would have been a very rich man if he had lived a few years longer.) All this suggests that Stoker had stumbled on one of the Jungian archetypes and given it a new life. But had he merely given shape to some primeval fear, some imaginary bogyman? Or is it possible that there *is* some kind of reality behind the idea of the vampire?

There were stories about vampires in ancient Greece and Rome, but they were significantly different from the modern vampire. The Romans believed in a creature called the Lamia, a beautiful woman, who seduced men and then ate them. In his humorous classic *The Golden Ass,* Lucius Apuleius describes how the witches of Thessaly, in northern Greece, were in the habit of chewing pieces off newly dead male corpses. These legends obviously spring from man's ambiguous feelings towards women—a mixture of fear and masochistic desire. Being eaten alive—or having vital organs gnawed off—by women is a masochist's daydream.

But the later vampire is not a masochistic fantasy; it is definitely sadistic. Perhaps the strangest thing about it is that the legend swept across Europe like an epidemic during the early eighteenth century. It seems to have started at the village of Meduegna, near Belgrade, Yugoslavia. A young soldier named Arnold Paole had returned from active service in Greece in 1727, and he told the girl to whom he was engaged that while away he had been attacked by a vampire. The record does not specify whether this was a male or female vampire; but he said he had found its grave and destroyed it.

DRAB and uninteresting, at least in appearance, Bram Stoker nevertheless had enough intuitive insight to begin a cult based on violent sexual fantasies.

Some time after returning to his native village, he died after a serious fall. A month later, however, people began to see him around the village. Some of those who saw him died soon after; finally, there was a decision to disinter the body. It was found to be perfectly preserved, and there was dried blood around the mouth. Paole's corpse was burned—as were the bodies of four of the people who had died since his burial.

The reports of the "walking dead" ceased for a time—six years. Then there was a fresh outbreak, which writers on the case attributed to the death of someone who had been bitten by one of the "vampires", and who duly became a vampire after his (or her) death. There were further investigations, undertaken by three surgeons from Belgrade—Johannes Flickinger, Isaac Seidel, and Johann Baumgartner.

On January 7, 1732, these three, together with a lieutenant-colonel and a sublieutenant, signed a document at Meduegna in which they described the opening of several graves, and the finding of another 15 vampires—bodies which looked as if they had been freshly buried, with ruddy cheeks. Significantly, the majority of these creatures were young or fairly young women, and there were three children among them.

All this may have been pure superstition and hysteria; if so, then it induced a wave of similar panic in Hungary, Rumania, and other Slavonic countries. So many cases of vampires were reported that they began to attract the attention of European travellers, who brought reports back with them. Then in 1746 the French author Dom Augustin Calmet popularized the subject in his *History of Apparitions and Vampires.*

He cited a case which took place in the village of Haidam, on the Austro-Hungarian frontier, and which was investigated by a commission on the orders of the Emperor Charles VI. The Count de Cadreras, of the Alexandetti Infantry, made a deposition at Freibourg University in 1730 verifying his own part in the investigation—how he had ordered the corpse of an old farmer to be dug up, and had found it to be completely fresh.

Buried alive

The farmer had been dead for ten years. Yet only a few evenings before, he had appeared to his family at their dining table, touched his son on the shoulder, and then gone out. The son, as though stricken by the plague, had died the next day. The Emperor's commission verified these facts by taking depositions throughout the village.

Rationally, what is to be made of these strange events? Some writers ascribe them to hysteria, which seems unlikely—the accounts appear too circumstantial. Others believe that the stories about vampires originate from a few genuine cases in which people had been accidentally buried alive, so their bodies were found in life-like positions when they were exhumed. This is obviously a possibility. However, serious students of the occult are inclined to accept another and more bizarre explanation.

There are, in occult literature, thousands of well-authenticated cases of "apparitions of the living"—that is, of a living person who may be seen in a place many miles from where his physical body happens to be at the time. In many such accounts, the person himself is quite unaware that his "apparition" has been seen miles away, although he may have been *thinking* about the place at the time.

There is also another phenomenon, equally well-attested, called "projection of the astral body". This occurs when a person feels himself to be leaving his physical body and floating around in the air above it—or even travelling somewhere else. This cannot be dismissed as mere superstition; both the English and American Societies for Psychical Research have investigated hundreds of such cases, and found evidence for accepting them as genuine.

Scalding liquid

Such findings have led some writers on vampirism to advance the theory that vampires may be some kind of "astral projections", endowed with a malign power to suck vitality (rather than blood). Everyone has had experience of people who seem to "drain one of energy"; perhaps vampires are disembodied forces who have the same enfeebling effects.

Whether or not vampirism is a supernatural phenomenon, there can be no doubt whatever that it *is* a sexual perversion, and one that has been encountered by most psychiatrists. And it is regarded by them as one of the most puzzling of all the sexual deviations. Most sexual perversion springs from frustration. Unlike animals, whose physical appetites are governed by natural cycles, human sexual desire is present all the year round. In certain people—particularly young men—it may become a kind of scalding liquid that causes the same kind of inner discomfort as a violent need to urinate.

The inner pressure becomes so great that it can be released by almost anything that has sexual associations; a sexually frustrated male may find female shoes or underwear as exciting as a naked woman. After a few experiences of experimenting with such objects, he may begin to find them *more* satisfying than a naked woman —or at least they become an essential element in his sexual experiences.

This is known as fetishism, and is fairly harmless and widespread. If a frustrated male brings himself to a sexual climax with fantasies of ill-treating his sexual partner, he may develop into a sadist; if the fantasies are of *being* ill-treated, into a masochist.

Dead cats

It is easy to see how men who have access to the corpses of women might become necrophiles—lovers of the dead. In fact, most recorded cases of necrophilia concern mortuary attendants. But there have been cases in which a man has become a grave robber to satisfy this craving. British writer Montague Summers quotes the classic case of necrophilia in his book *The Vampire in Europe* —that of Sergeant François Bertrand,

sentenced to a year's imprisonment in 1849 for robbing graves in and around Paris and violating female corpses.

Bertrand, who was 27, was known as an admirable soldier. He admitted that at an early age he had sexual fantasies which involved torturing and raping girls. He was, in fact, an attractive man, who had no difficulty finding mistresses, many of whom wanted to marry him. But "normal" sex was never as satisfying to him as his fantasies.

At the age of 24, he began sadistically maltreating animals, and also cutting open the bodies of dead dogs and cats. A year later he happened to be walking through a cemetery with a friend, and saw a half-filled grave in which a young woman was buried. (In those days, many people were interred without coffins.) He later returned to the grave in a state of wild excitement, dug up the corpse, and proceeded to beat it with a spade in a kind of frenzy. Someone heard the noise and he ran away.

RELICS of Count Dracula remain to fire the imagination of those seeking to give the story some kind of basis in the real world.

Both New York Graphic Society

STOKER, a normally unimaginative Victorian, created a masterpiece replete with rape fantasies and sexual overtones. Freudian repression — or something more sinister?

Two days later he dug open the same grave with his hands, and tore open the belly of the corpse — at which he enjoyed intense sexual satisfaction. The experience convinced him that it was dead women he wanted, rather than live ones. He made a practice of digging up corpses — preferably of young women who had been newly buried — and of violating them, after which he often tore them to pieces. Afterwards he always felt ashamed and vowed never to do it again.

Obsessed women

The curious thing about Bertrand — who once swam an icy pond in midwinter to get into a cemetery — is that he was not a violent or brutal man. He disliked obscene talk, always treated women with chivalry, and refused to have affairs with married women. His social personality was reasonable and presentable. Under the surface, however, there was another personality, a kind of vampire or werewolf, that took over when he was possessed by sexual desire.

This is what makes *Dracula* such a remarkable book. Written by a rather puritanical Victorian, who adored his wife and was never unfaithful to her, it reveals that, somewhere inside him, Stoker possessed an alter-ego that understood all the nauseating violence and perversion of Sergeant Bertrand.

What is, perhaps, even more surprising is that the literature of sexual abnormality is full of examples of women who have been obsessed by blood. Psychologist Wilhelm Stekel describes a woman who could only become sexually excited by making small cuts on her lover's body and sucking the blood, and cites in detail the case of another woman completely obsessed by fantasies of smashing her lovers to a pulp and drinking their blood.

On the other hand, it is equally clear that women recognize a sexual significance in the idea of the vampire. The legendary vampire is not brutal; he doesn't inflict pain or commit rape; but he masters her completely, and draws her soul to himself so that it eventually joins him in death. The masochistic element is always strong in a woman's sexual response. Psychiatrist Magnus Hirschfeld records the case of a patient who was normally sexually frigid, but whose favourite fantasy involved lying naked on a butcher's slab, while the butcher prodded her all over deciding where to cut.

At a certain point the butcher would insert his finger into her sexual organ; she would then achieve a violent climax. Here the masochistic element, the desire to be a victim, can be clearly seen. And, as in the case of Sergeant Bertrand, the woman's fantasies had made her incapable of normal sexual response.

It seems possible, therefore, that the concept of the vampire is a Jungian "archetype", which lies concealed in the "racial unconscious" of each of us. This in turn raises the question: why, in that case, should the idea be so relatively modern? It is true that there are recorded stories of vampirism dating back three thousand years; but the idea of the Dracula-type vampire has possessed the European imagination only since the strange epidemic of the 1730's.

Strange cases

The answer to this may lie in the concept that the patterns and types of crime change slowly from age to age. When civilization was crude and barbarous, crime tended to be purely economic — committed for food, or money, or perhaps land. The eighteenth century, the age that saw the publication of Calmet's book on vampires, was also the age of Baroque civilization. And, from the criminologist's point of view, it marked the beginning of the age of modern crime — of sex crimes, crimes of jealousy and violence.

Suddenly, the criminal records are full of strange cases of sadistic violence: men like Sergeant Bertrand, like Andrew Bichel, a Bavarian "ripper" who tore open the women he killed, like Vincenzo Verzeni, an Italian murderer possessed by a craving to eat women, or like the French sexual pervert Victor Ardisson, another necrophile, who slept with the mummified head of a 13-year-old girl — or like that almost symbolic figure of murderous violence, Jack the Ripper.

In all this disturbing history of ferocity there is one ray of comfort. Although Dracula remains as popular as ever — and there is even a revival of interest in the original *dracoul*, Vlad the Impaler — the typical murders of our time are crimes of self-esteem, like the Moors murder case, or the murders of the Manson clan.

They may often be sadistic, but they tend to be more cerebral than the overpowering urges that gripped Sergeant Bertrand. Whether this is an advantage is open to question. But from the criminologist's point of view, it is a significant change — perhaps even the prelude to an age in which men cease to be prey to urges of irrational violence. And in which vampires — traditionally without a mirror image, allergic to garlic, terrified of crucifixes, and unable to exist in daylight — will remain in their Transylvanian graves.

Only a stake through the heart, it was said, could kill them. But they can also die of rational thinking — leaving only their human imitators for the police and psychiatrists to contend with.

To the festering slums of the New World they came— first the immigrants, ther
he violent parasites fattening on the hard work of their industrious brothers . .

THE PROTECTION
RACKETS

IN the year 1880, an English clergyman named Rose was travelling with two Italian companions through Sicily. They were about a mile from the railway station of Lecrera when, quite suddenly, they found themselves surrounded by bearded, rough-looking men who carried knives and carbines. This was the gang of a notorious brigand, Leoni, whose name was feared all over Sicily.

The gang released Rose's companions, who were told to go to the Italian authorities in Palermo and report that the Rev. Rose was being held for a ransom of £5000. The authorities were concerned, but penurious; they reported the incident to the British Consul, and forgot it. A few weeks later they received a parcel containing one of Mr. Rose's ears.

The British government, stirred by the clamour in the newspapers, decided to pay the ransom; but before they had completed the endless formalities the brigands had grown impatient, and sent another ear, together with a note saying that if the ransom still wasn't paid Mr. Rose would be chopped up piecemeal.

The British were now enraged; they paid the £5000 and recovered the earless Mr. Rose; and they also made such threatening noises that the Italian government sent an army into the mountains. There was a bloody battle, Leoni himself was killed, and most of his men captured. The British newspapers congratulated themselves for forcing the inefficient Italians to do something they should have done years ago, and the affair was almost forgotten.

Small and evil-looking

But not entirely. For the most dangerous of the gang had escaped, together with six companions. His name was Giuseppe Esposito, and he was a small, evil-looking man with a cruel mouth and a low forehead. Friends in Palermo smuggled Esposito on to a ship bound for the United States, and he landed in New York and made his way to New Orleans with a few selected followers. There, under the name of Radzo, he rented a house in Chartres Street, bought himself a boat—probably with his share of the clergyman's ransom—and dredged for oysters. He was so confident that he was a free man in America that he called the boat *Leoni* and flew the bandit's flag from the mast.

But respectability bored Esposito; he had been a bandit for too long to enjoy making money legitimately. There were no mountains here to hide in, but there were plenty of wealthy Italians in New Orleans. Giuseppe Esposito called on some of them, and explained that he needed money to finance a fleet of boats; when they asked what guarantee he could offer in return for a loan, Esposito would casually take out a revolver and cock it,

peering down the sights. Then, with slow deliberation, he would pull the trigger. The hammer clicked on an empty chamber. Pretending not to notice the trembling of his startled host, he would say deliberately: "Protezione"—protection.

It is possible that Giuseppe Esposito was not the originator of this popular euphemism, but he was certainly one of the first of the American "gangsters" to employ the method. In fact, he got his "loan" from Italian grocers and restaurateurs who understood the value of Esposito's good will, and he proceeded to organize his local "Black Hand gang" along the same lines as the great Leoni.

He began by deposing the leader of the local Mafia, Tony Labruzzo, who lacked Esposito's casual ferocity. Then he bought a fleet of boats and ships, and conducted elaborate piracy operations on the Mississippi and in the Gulf of Mexico. With his brigand's instinct for a hide-out, he had huts constructed in the depths of the swamps. He intended to conduct his protection racket along Italian lines: that is, to kidnap anyone who refused to pay, and hold him for ransom—the Italians with their regard for property, would only use vandalism as a last resort.

However, Esposito was never to achieve his ambition to become the Leoni of Louisiana. His deposed rival, Tony Labruzzo, told the Italian Consul that Leoni's chief lieutenant was in New Orleans, and the Chief of Police, Thomas Boylan, kept Esposito under surveillance. He learned that two New York detectives, James Mooney and D. Boland, had been hired by the Italian government to find Esposito.

For weeks two of Boylan's best men, the brothers David and Mike Hennessy, shadowed Esposito, and one day, when they received the word to pick him up,

THE FIVE POINTS GANG (named after New York neighbourhood, above) was one of many in close alliance with the bosses at Tammany Hall (top), whose protection and vote-buying rackets flourished in the slums.

they quickly moved in on their quarry as he walked across Jackson Square, pushed guns into his ribs and rushed him to the police station. It had to be done quickly: the Mafia were capable of storming the jail. Early the next morning Esposito was taken down river, and put on board a ship for New York.

Deported to Italy, he was tried, and sentenced to life imprisonment—in irons. But before he went on trial, Tony Labruzzo, the man who had betrayed him, was already dead, shot down in the street by a Mafiosi. The Black Hand knew that if it was to maintain its

All Museum of the City of New York

stranglehold on the Italian community it had to gain a reputation for absolute ruthlessness and terrible efficiency. The two Hennessy brothers left New Orleans; but Mike was killed in 1886, and David in 1890, both by Mafia gunmen.

Of course, Esposito was not the inventor of "protection". It had been known on the border of England and Scotland as far back as the sixteenth century, when bands of wanted men, led by local chieftains, extorted a "second rent" – or "mail" – from local farmers by threatening to burn their farms and destroy their crops; this was the origin of the word "blackmail".

In Sicily and Corsica – both islands with a violent history – brigands maintained themselves by extorting food and other necessities from the population. But "protection" was rare for an obvious reason: the wealthy citizens lived in the towns, where they were fairly well protected by the police, and the brigands were in the mountains. In Naples, there was a flourishing secret society called the Camorra, which certainly included "protection" among its many activities, and in Sicily, the original Mafia was basically an alternative to the police, providing quite genuine protection and other favours for those who paid a certain sum. In its early stages, it was a "protection racket" only in the same sense as is Securicor.

Dead Rabbits, Plug Uglies

In America, gangs had always abounded; in the early nineteenth century, the New York slums were full of outfits with names like the Dead Rabbits, the Plug Uglies and the Five Points. These specialized in burglary, theft from docks and warehouses, receiving stolen property, intimidation of prostitutes and all the usual extra-legal activities of slumdwellers with more than the customary share of dominance.

The same was true of San Francisco, Chicago and other fast-growing towns – Los Angeles was, at this time, a tiny and peaceful village with no law enforcement problem. Politicians discovered the use of gangs to bully voters, and by the 1850s, the New York gangs and the Tammany Hall bosses were in close alliance. A man about to enter a polling booth was likely to be stopped by a man with a cosh and asked how he intended to vote. If he mentioned the wrong name, he never got inside; the roughneck would do the voting instead.

In the 1860s, the Chinese in the goldfields near Marysville, California, organized themselves into secret societies called "tongs"; the first two were known as the Hop Sings and Suey Sings, and they came into violent conflict when the mistress of a Hop Sing member was stolen by someone from the Suey Sings. The girl was only handed back after many men on both sides had died. The tongs moved to railroad construction camps, then to the larger towns—the chief of which was San Francisco, known for its brothels and gambling houses.

Traffic in girls

The average Chinese in America were a docile and well-behaved people—too docile in many ways, for the whites preyed on them unmercifully. Their two chief necessities were opium—which had been introduced into China by the British—and girls. There was a flourishing traffic in girls, who were glad to get away from the terrible poverty of their own land to the relative luxury of sharing a cellar with 20 other "slaves".

The tongs were probably the first large-scale protection racket in America, and this was largely because they organized the lives of their fellow citizens in this foreign country, and got them to pay a proportion of their wages. If a Chinaman established himself enough to want to bring his wife to America, the tong demanded a certain payment.

The tongs had a simple way of enforcing their will: murder. Their assassins preferred hatchets—hence the term "hatchet man"—but also carried a silk rope around the body, like the Thugs of India. Their "protection" was genuine, like that of the Mafia in Sicily. In San Francisco in 1875, a hatchet man named Ming Long, of the Kwong Dock Tong, came upon Low Sing, a member of the Suey Sing Tong, holding the hand of a pretty "slave girl" named Kum Ho, and split his skull with a hatchet.

Before he died, Low Sing gasped out the name of his killer to the head of his tong. Formal challenges were sent, and the next day at midnight the deadliest hatchet men of both tongs met in a certain street in Chinatown, and fought earnestly and bloodily until the police—mostly Irish—arrived with their whistles and night-sticks. No one was killed—although some died later. The Suey Sings were held to have won, because they had injured a large number of the enemy.

Payment was made to Low Sing's relatives; Ming Long was formally ejected from the tong, which meant that he was fair game for any hatchet man, and fled to China, where the tongs did not exist. The historian of San Francisco, Herbert Asbury, points out that both the tongs and chop suey were invented by the Chinese in America.

The Italians were the next great wave of immigrants to arrive in New York, fleeing from political troubles at home. The first generation settled down to hard work, running shops, restaurants and small businesses, and eventually many became prosperous. It was then that new arrivals like Giuseppe Esposito began to prey on these more successful countrymen, and the "protection racket" as we know it today came into being. The rise of the gangs was very slow, and most non-Italian Americans knew very little about them until the year 1890.

A life in chains

After Esposito had been deported back to Italy—and a life in chains—two New Orleans brothers named Charles and Tony Matranga decided that there were better ways of making money than in the saloon business. Inspired by Esposito's efficient take-over of New Orleans crime, they settled down to the business of organizing the gangs, and extorting "protection" from their fellow Italians.

Many Italians in New Orleans worked in the docks at the fairly reasonable wage of 40 cents an hour. A rich and influential family named Provenzano had a monopoly of the unloading of fruit ships from South America. Charles Matranga approached them, and suggested that, in future, they might like to obtain their dock labour through him. Naturally, the labourers also paid the Matrangas a "kick back" for their good services.

The Matrangas had discovered what Esposito knew: that a few "dominant" human beings can always lead a large number of non-dominant ones by the nose. In those days, zoologists knew very little about animal dominance, and had certainly never heard that precisely 5% of any animal group is "dominant". Most human beings make the very natural assumption that most other human beings

THE TONGS had a simple way of enforcing their will: murder. Their gangs fought pitched battles in San Francisco's Chinatown, while in New York the Short Tail Gang (right) plotted more violence in the docklands. . . .

Museum of the City of New York

love their independence and will fight for it, and it is true that all animals, including humans, will fight grimly for their own "territory".

But it is also true that in any casually chosen group of 20 men, one is a leader, and can impose his will on the other 19. Dictators like Stalin, Hitler and Mussolini owed their power to this biological peculiarity; and so did the Matrangas. If there had been any concerted resistance, no doubt they would have gone back to keeping a saloon and brothel. But their army of labourers handed over 10 per cent of their wages without protest; the Provenzanos paid the Matrangas for their services as a labour exchange, and suddenly the latter were on the road to being rich.

New Orleans masters

One day it struck them that the reason the Provenzanos didn't mind paying them "protection" was because they were making such an excellent income from the fruit ships they unloaded: after all, the labour force belonged to the Matrangas. So the Matrangas told the Provenzanos that from now on they would cease to act as middle men. Instead, the Matrangas would take over the loading and unloading of the ships. To underline the point, Provenzano managers and foremen were badly beaten up, the Provenzanos gave in to the blackmail, and the Matrangas, still slightly astonished at the ease with which it had all been accomplished, were masters of all the Italian casual labour in New Orleans.

But the Matrangas made the mistake of carrying on their war against the Provenzanos; they began to harass their grocery business. In desperation, the Provenzanos hired their own gunmen, and there were clashes in the streets. David Hennessy, one of the brothers who had captured Esposito, knew and liked the Provenzanos. He had an intense dislike of the Matrangas' organization of murder and extortion, which had killed his brother Mike in Houston, Texas, five years after Esposito's arrest.

When he was appointed chief of police, Hennessy decided he would stamp out the Mafia. One morning in 1890, a truckload of Provenzano men were on their way to work at a dock that had still not been taken over by the Matrangas. Suddenly, men with shotguns appeared out of the darkness and began firing indiscriminately. Since they were using buckshot, the darkness made no difference; two men were killed, and many others wounded.

Hennessy decided this was the last straw, and he began collecting evidence of Mafia activity in New Orleans. An anonymous letter warned him that he would be killed if he continued, but he ignored it. He corresponded with the Rome police, asking for names and photographs of some of Esposito's old gang. In April 1890, the Provenzanos retaliated by ambushing Tony Matranga and two of his henchmen. They succeeded in wounding them. Matranga identified two of his assailants as Joe and Pete Provenzano.

The police had no alternative but to arrest them, and their trial was set for October 17. David Hennessy declared publicly that he would appear in the witness stand for the Provenzanos, and make their trial the opportunity to divulge information about the Mafia in New Orleans.

He never reached the court room, for at midnight on October 15, 1890, Hennessy turned into Basin Street, and three men jumped out of a doorway, to riddle him with bullets. The dying man pulled out his own revolver and succeeded in firing four shots at the fleeing assassins; but he died as he reached the hospital.

This was too much—to shoot down a chief of police who was doing his best to stamp out organized crime. It was a direct confrontation between the criminals and the rest of society. Hennessy's investigations had disclosed that, in Sicily, the Mafia was stronger than the police, but it should never happen in America. Feeling against Italians became so intense that they began to be afraid of venturing outdoors during daylight; many were attacked in the street.

Eleven strong suspects

Hennessy's files quickly provided the police with 11 strong suspects. The 11 men were arrested the day after the police chief's murder. One of them was a man called Antone Scaffide. On the day after his arrest, a young man named Duffy walked into the jail and asked to see Scaffide. When the prisoner was brought out, Duffy suddenly produced a revolver and fired. The bullet only wounded Scaffide. Asked why he had done it, Duffy said that if there were more men like him in New Orleans, the Mafia would soon cease to exist. Naturally, his sentence was light.

Twenty-one Italians were eventually arrested, including Charles Matranga, and a 14-year-old boy who was accused of signalling Hennessy's approach to the killers. The law-abiding citizens of New Orleans sighed with relief—it looked as if justice would be done after all. The trial of nine of the Italians, including Matranga, was set for February 1891, but soon the citizens began to suspect that Justice was not going to have it all her own way. The Matrangas could afford expensive lawyers, and a great battery of legal talents was lined up for the defence.

The evidence at the trial was overwhelming. Many witnesses came forward to say they had seen some of the defendants running away from the scene of Hennessy's murder. One defendant broke down and confessed to being present at a meeting of the Mafia when Hennessy's death was decreed. It ought to have been an open and shut case. But halfway through the trial the judge ordered the acquittal of the 14-year-old boy, and also of Charles Matranga. The jury retired; when they returned, their verdict was that four of the accused were not guilty, and that they were unable to agree about three others, including Scaffide. It was obvious that the jurors had been either bribed or intimidated and that the same applied to many of the lawyers on the case.

The flag of Italy

The Italian colony added insult to injury by holding parties in the street to celebrate the acquittal of the nine—which everyone expected to be a prelude to the dismissal of the case against the others. A gang of Sicilians tore down an American flag, trampled it in the mud, and then hung it upside down below the flag of Italy.

For the citizens of New Orleans, that was the final indignity. In the morning newspapers of March 14, advertisements requested "all good citizens" to attend a mass meeting that evening, and to come "prepared for action". It was signed by 61 prominent citizens. That evening, a seething crowd filled Canal Street. The 61 citizens appeared, and some of them spoke briefly from the pedestal of a statue of Henry Clay, declaring that it was necessary for the people to take justice into their own hands. The men led the crowd to a gun store and handed out rifles. Then they marched to the prison.

The prison governor locked all prisoners in their cells except the Italians, who were told to find hiding places. The execution squad, led by William Parkerson, a well-known public figure, broke open a wooden door at the back of the prison, stationed armed guards there, then went deliberately through the jail, seeking out 11 Italians who were believed beyond doubt to be guilty of the murder. (Oddly enough, this list did not include Charles Matranga.)

These 11 men were dragged out and killed—nine shot, two hanged. Then, in good order, the "avengers" marched out. The mob dispersed quietly. It was the end of Mafia power in New Orleans. There was an attempted revival in 1900 when the "Black Hand" kidnapped the child Walter Lamana and killed him. But when the gang members were arrested and tried, this second "rebirth" also came to an end.

Sadly, this was only the beginning of the story of the Mafia and protection rackets. In the 1970s the story is still unfolding and it seems as if organized crime—like the poor—will always be with us.

WITCHCRAFT

The Papal Inquisition started it all, but Joan of Arc was hardly the only heretic to burn at the stake. Thousands of lives have been claimed through the ages by witch-hunters . . . and by "witches", "werewolves", and "vampires". Or were their crimes simply those of sadistic sex-maniacs?

National Film Archive

MOST forms of crime have a history so remote that it is impossible to say when they first occurred. But in the case of witchcraft murder, it is possible to be more precise. In the year 1242, two of the Pope's Inquisitors were staying in a house in Avignonet, in the south of France. They were in the Languedoc area to root out heretics. Unfortunately for them, their host was secretly in sympathy with the heretics. In the middle of the night, a dozen men with axes were admitted to the house. They burst into the bedroom, and slaughtered the two monks and their servants, hacking at the bodies until they were almost unrecognizable. Then, ignoring the mutilated corpses, they divided the booty.

The reason why this is regarded as the first witchcraft murder is because the heretics who committed the outrage belonged to a sect called the Cathars who, among other things, believed the Old Testament God was a demon. The killing of the Inquisitors made the Pope determined to stamp out the heretics at all costs. A bloody crusade followed. Cathars were dragged from their homes and burned. In 1244, two hundred of them were burned on a gigantic bonfire at Montségur, and that was almost the end of them. The survivors, however, scattered over a large area, some taking refuge in remote Swiss valleys.

The Inquisition, which had been formed specially to eradicate them, pursued and burned them wherever they could be cornered. But these survivors were no longer accused of heresy—of holding false Christian doctrines. They were accused of a new and strange crime: conspiring with the devil, or, as it soon came to be known, witchcraft. The killing of the two Inquisitors at Avignonet was the signal for four centuries of horrible torture and thousands of deaths. If the two Inquisitors had not been killed, it is probable that the world would never have heard the word "witch".

Of course, there were witches before the persecution of the Cathars. There is the Witch of Endor, in the Bible. But although Exodus says "Thou shalt not suffer a witch to live", no one really minded witches. They were useful old crones who gave you lotion for your backache or told your fortune by looking into a bowl of water. They were as much an accepted part of life as a witch-doctor in an African tribe. The murder of the two Inquisitors changed all that. From then on, people began to look on witches as if they were poisonous snakes.

Pact with the devil

Even so, the horrors started slowly. Between 1347 and 1400, a "mere" 67 people were burned for witchcraft in France. And the first full-scale witch-hunt took place at Arras, France, in 1459 and 1460. Once again, the Inquisitors were looking for heretics. They arrested a feeble-minded woman called Deniselle Grenières, and under torture, she admitted to making a pact with the devil, implicating five other people. One managed to commit suicide in prison; the rest were burned alive. Then, in the manner that was to become so familiar, the whole thing snowballed.

There were more arrests, more tortures, more confessions. The jails were so crowded with "witches" that the domestic business of the town almost came to a standstill. Finally, good sense prevailed; two archbishops declared the witchcraft assertions to be "nonsense", and the prisoners were released. In 1491, the Parliament of Paris declared that the Inquisition had acted "in error", and condemned such methods of "persuasion" as crushing limbs and putting feet into a fire.

Mounting hysteria

Unfortunately, this was the last time good sense prevailed. The hysteria mounted, and became tinged with sadism. At Neisse, in Silesia, the executioner made an oven in which he roasted witches; in 1651, 42 women and young girls were roasted to death in it, and in nine years, he roasted over two thousand, including two babies.

Franz Buirmann, the witch-seeker of Cologne, was a murderer on a scale that anticipated Hitler's extermination camps. In one small village alone, he burned 150 people. He decided he wanted to sleep with a woman named Peller, who rejected

THE WITCH-FINDER GENERAL:
Matthew Hopkins ordered hundreds of deaths in England. He was motivated more by sadism than religious zeal.

him. Buirmann had her arrested as a witch; within hours, she was being tortured, with every hair shaved off her body. The torturer's assistant was then allowed to rape her. Buirmann looked on, and stuffed a dirty rag into her mouth. Then she was burned alive in a hut full of straw. The same kind of thing was happening all over Germany at the time. By comparison, England was fairly civilized. At first, torture was forbidden here, and witches were hanged or strangled, not burned alive.

The great witchcraft scare in England began with an attempted murder. The intended victim was no less a person than the Edinburgh-born King James I (1566-1625), who in 1597 wrote a treatise, *Demonology*, which advocated severe measures against witchcraft. (An interesting point this, as it suggests something that few modern historians are willing to admit: that perhaps some of the witches *were* guilty, that perhaps they *could* really cast magic spells, just as witchdoctors in Africa can summon rain by means of outward mumbo-jumbo.)

The case started when a Scottish gentleman named Seaton heard rumours that his young servant, Gilly Duncan, was a witch. He had noticed that she was often out all night. So, without worrying about the legal side of the matter, he had her seized, and all her clothes stripped off. After that he examined her carefully

THE WEREWOLVES: Sole evidence that they existed was from murder suspects who said they had turned into wolves. Below: The "true story" of a witch.

The moſt wonderfull

and true ſtorie, of a certaine Witch named *Alſe Gooderige of Stapen hill*, who was arraigned and conuicted at Darbie at the Aſiſes there.

Is alſo a true report of the ſtrange torments of Thomas Dirling, *a boy of thirteene yeres of age, that was poſ-ſeſſed by the Deuill, with his horrible fittes and terrible Apparitions by him vttered at* Burton vpon Trent *in the Coʋntie of* Stafford, *and of his maruellous deliueran̄ce.*

from head to foot for "devil's marks" (which, among other places, were said to be found inside the lips of the vagina), and tortured her by crushing her fingers and strangling her with a rope.

She consequently "confessed", naming several people, including an elderly gentlewoman, Agnes Sampson, and John Fian, a schoolteacher who was also the secretary of the Scottish Earl of Bothwell, the King's cousin. Under torture, they admitted to being witches, to being in the service of the devil, and to using witchcraft in an attempt to kill the King.

When King James was sailing back from Denmark with his bride, 15-year-old Anne of Denmark, they claimed to have raised a storm that almost sank his ship. The odd thing was that James's ship *had* almost been sunk in a violent storm. Fian later withdrew his confession, and was allowed to go free. Two other women were burned—one while still alive—and a third released because she was pregnant.

Certainly, it sounds like the usual superstitious bigotry: unfortunate innocent people tortured by fanatics until they confessed to patent absurdities. This, of course, was done in direct accordance with the law—which, from very early times, made witchcraft a punishable offence. It was held to be so in such states in antiquity as Rome, Greece, and Persia, and the Christian church also roundly condemned it. Indeed at the

373

beginning of Christianity witchcraft was treated as a crime by the ecclesiastical and civil courts of every "God-fearing, Christ-loving" land. To start with, however, the penalties were relatively light. In Anglo-Saxon England the Archbishop of Canterbury, Theodore (925-40) prescribed periods of fasting and penance for witches lasting from one to ten years. Under Athelstan (c. 894-939), grandson of Alfred the Great and King of the West Saxons, murder by witchcraft was punishable by death—although the accused was able to clear himself (or herself) by Trial by Ordeal, whether by fire or water. Such Ordeals continued until they were banned by the Lateran Council in Rome in 1215, and disappeared from England four years later.

In the thirteenth century, however, it was still held to be "extreme heresy" to involve oneself in a personal pact with the devil. On the continent of Western Europe, there were widespread hunts, persecutions, and torture sessions inflicted upon those thought to be on the side of Satan. In 1563 the mania flourished again in England with the introduction of the Second English Witchcraft Act, and was heightened even more by the much harsher act of 1604—which resulted in a relentless persecution of alleged heretics which did not end until the beginning of the eighteenth century.

Worship of Satan

In England the usual punishment for witches (male or female) was death by hanging, or a period in the pillory if the offence was not held to be a serious one. In Scotland and on the Continent, however, witches were burned at the stake—and the popular belief in witchcraft grew as more and more prisoners confessed under torture to the worship of Satan, to "image-magic", and to damaging property or hurting people by spells cast at a distance.

At the time, the American colonies were bound by much the same witchcraft laws as those of the parent countries. In New England the most generally known "devil-worship" cases were those at Salem in 1692, when 20 people were executed for the crime of witchcraft through accusations later discovered to be false. There, such proceedings were prohibited by Governor Phips in the following year—around the same time that the witchcraft trial craze began to die out in Britain.

Back in 1584, in his sceptical book, *Discoverie of Witches,* author Reginald Scot had boldly declared that there were no such things as "magical people" or "magical spells". A hundred years later, other scholars, lawyers and magistrates were adopting his opinion, and Sir John Holt—the English Lord Chief Justice

Prado, Madrid

THE GOOD BOOKS rise from the fire, while the heretical ones burn. Witch-hunter St. Dominic looks on. He helped to lead the battle against the Cathars.

from 1689 to 1710—summarily dismissed every witchcraft case brought before him—thus influencing the carriage of justice in other courts.

In England the infamous "witch-finder general", Matthew Hopkins, had been responsible for several hundreds of deaths in the eastern counties between 1645 and 1646. Eventually, however, he shed too much blood. People began to realize he was motivated more by sadism than genuine religious zeal. He therefore retired, and died a year later thoroughly discredited. His influence continued for some time however—the last English execution of a witch being that of the notorious Jane Wenham in 1712—who was later granted a pardon. Finally, the Witchcraft Act of 1736 prohibited further prosecutions for witchcraft, and removed the offence from the British list of statutory crimes—an example followed by most other European countries.

The brave monster

Before this took place, however, France was the scene of some of the most depraved and disgusting black magic practices—intensified, some people thought, by the fact that witchcraft and Satan-worship *was* illegal. Had there been no laws to break, then the perverse villains might well have turned their evil in other directions, and so saved the lives of countless men, women, and children.

It was children who were the "speciality" of probably the most inhuman monster of all—a man whose atrocities are well and substantially documented. The crimes of Marshal Gilles de Rais—one of Joan of Arc's former comrades-

in-arms—were so atrocious that the evidence was, until recently, kept hidden in the original Latin. Gilles de Rais (or Retz) was one of the richest men in France—in fact, in Europe, and his fortune was increased when, at the age of 16, he married one of the wealthiest heiresses in France. He was still only 25 when he fought bravely at the side of Joan of Arc and won himself military honours. After the coronation of the Dauphin in 1429, he retired to his various estates, and proceeded to waste his vast fortunes in extravagance.

Craved satisfaction

He continued to maintain a large private army, although he no longer needed it. He had always been an excitable, violent person who got pleasure out of watching others suffer. After one battle, he had ordered all prisoners to be slaughtered—and now he found peace too tame. The sadistic impulses, which had found outlet in war, craved new satisfactions. In 1432, he began killing children. It was easy enough to find victims; after the war, France was full of children without parents, wandering around and begging for food and shelter. De Rais's pleasures were particularly vicious. After sexually assaulting the children—usually committing sodomy—he had them strangled, then hacked to pieces or disembowelled. He admitted to getting more pleasure from the mutilations than from the sex that preceded them.

His vast fortunes began to ebb away, and he sold some of his land. He then hired a team of alchemists to try to make gold—the blood of children being an important element in these ceremonies. So the murders went on. But like Matthew Hopkins, de Rais's bloodlust was becoming too obvious. In May 1440, he committed an absurd act that was bound to cause him trouble. He had sold one of his favourite castles; now he regretted the sale, and decided to get the castle back. In the course of regaining it, he marched into the estate's church, and had a priest imprisoned. For a long time, the Bishop of Nantes, Jean de Melestroit, had been looking for an opportunity to have de Rais arrested: not because of the evil rumours about vanishing children, but because he wanted to seize the marshal's lands. The "nuisance-monger" was arrested, and his estate at Machecoul was searched. In a tower there, officials found 40 bodies or fragments of bodies. About the same number were discovered at Champtocé, another estate. The evidence indicated that he had tortured and murdered more than 300 children.

When he appeared in court, 36-year-old de Rais was at first arrogant, dismissing the charges as frivolous. Then, suddenly, the horror of his past life appeared to strike him. He confessed to everything, and expressed deep repentance. The testimony of the dozens of parents called was heartrending. But perhaps the strangest thing about the whole case was that when Gilles sobbed and publicly repented of his sins, many of the parents sobbed with him and forgave him. On October 25, 1440, the mass child-murderer was excommunicated, and the following day, was strangled and burned, together with two servants who had helped him with his deeds.

Equally common and widespread as the medieval belief in "black witches", was the belief in vampires and werewolves. The accounts of these are often so circumstantial that they cannot entirely be put down to imagination. Towards the end of 1521, for instance, three men were tried by the Inquisitor General of Besançon on a charge of being werewolves. The evidence alleged that a traveller was attacked by a wolf, and that when he followed the wounded animal, it led him to a cottage, where he found the wife of one Michael Verdung dressing her husband's wounds.

Verdung confessed (no doubt under torture) implicating two other men, Pierre Bourgot and Philibert Mentot. Pierre claimed that he had sold his soul to the devil 20 years earlier, had attended witches' Sabbaths, and had changed himself into a wolf many times. He said that in this state, he had eaten a four-year-old girl and found her flesh delicious, and had copulated with female wolves, with whom he had had as much pleasure as with his wife. The other two made similar confessions, and all three were burned.

Insane delusions

The case of Gilles Garnier, which took place half a century later, suggests that many so-called "werewolves" were in fact, sadistic sex maniacs—who, like de Rais, were suffering from insane delusions. In the Dôle area, in 1573, there were a number of cases of savage attacks on children. Gilles Garnier, an unsociable peasant who lived with his wife in a dilapidated hut, was arrested, and confessed to being the "wolf" responsible for the outrages. At his trial Garnier gave details of other similar attacks. One of them was made on a ten-year-old girl, whom he stripped and ate; (he said he enjoyed the flesh so much that he took some of it home to his wife); another on a twelve-year-old boy, whom he was prevented from eating by the approach of strangers. Shortly before his arrest, he claimed, he had strangled a ten-year-old boy and eaten part of his body.

**BLOOD-LUST killed Frau Meiner . . .
Police look for more victims of modern "werewolf" Peter Kurten, who killed nine people in Germany between 1913 and 1930.**

Garnier's confessions were believed and he was duly burned alive.

The evidence in Garnier's case, however, raises questions such as: how does a wolf "strangle" a boy? In most of the werewolf trials, there was usually no doubt about the murders and attacks being committed by the accused man, but the only evidence that he actually changed into a wolf was his own confession.

Such was the case in the most celebrated werewolf trial of all, which took place at Cologne in 1589. The accused was a multiple sadistic murderer named Peter Stube. For 28 years, Stube committed his attacks. Occasionally he killed livestock, or even men. But—significantly—most of the victims were women and girls, and these he invariably raped. Obviously, Stube was a sex maniac—even though he claimed that the devil had given him a magic belt by which he changed himself into a wolf. According to the trial evidence, he had had incestuous relations with his sister and daughter, and had attacked two of his daughters-in-law while in the form of a wolf.

The horror—and universal interest—excited by the case was reflected in the penalty. Stube was sentenced to have his skin torn off with red hot pincers, before being beheaded. Apart from the confessions about the magic belt, Stube's career sounds very much like that of the

Both Fox Photos

German mass murderer, Peter Kurten, who was executed in 1931.

Kurten's career was almost as long as Stube's—from 1913 to 1930—although he spent much of this time in prison. In 1913, when he was 30, he broke into a hostelery in Cologne—the site of Stube's crimes—and strangled and sexually assaulted a 13-year-old girl he found asleep there. In 1929, he began his reign of terror in Düsseldorf, and in ten months, committed eight murders. The victims included a man, as well as women and children. The methods used included strangling and stabbing. Kurten had a sexual climax as he murdered—stimulated by the sight of blood.

If Kurten had been born a few centuries earlier, he might now be one of the famous "werewolves" of history. So might Joseph Vacher, a French murderer, who raped and disembowelled 14 women and boys in country areas of southeast France in the 1890's. Both Vacher and Kurten were driven by a violent sadistic urge that they could not understand. But

AT WITCHCRAFT TRIALS the accused were pre-judged. The verdict was against them—and the sentence. The only winners were the accusers and the court.

in the sixteenth century, they would have assumed it was a demoniacal urge sent from the devil, and would probably, when caught, have confessed to all manner of Satanic messages and impulses.

Closely linked to the legend of the werewolf is the legend of the vampire—in eastern European folklore a dead person who leaves his or her grave to prey, by means of blood-sucking, upon the living. To begin with, vampire tales suddenly swept across Europe, from Greece to Hungary, Silesia and Poland, in the second half of the seventeenth century. These stories always alleged that a man—or woman—was seen walking around after death, and that neighbours became anaemic, and sometimes died. When the man's grave was opened, he was found to look fresh and rosy; sometimes there was fresh blood on his mouth. The body had to be burned, or beheaded, or reburied with a stake through the heart. No historian has ever been able to explain *why* these stories became so widespread and popular; it remains an unsolved mystery.

Indeed it is this feeling of the inexplicable that has made so many people—especially in more recent times—scoff at the existence of witches, warlocks, and witchcraft. What they cannot see and touch does not, to them, exist. This dismissal of the unseen and the unknown—and the denial of other powers and other forces—was lambasted as far back as 1822 by the English writer Charles Lamb, in his *First Essays of Elia*.

Invisible world

"We are too hasty," he said, "when we set down our ancestors in the gross for fools, for the monstrous inconsistencies (as they seem to us) involved in their creed of witchcraft . . . Once the invisible world was . . . opened, and the lawless agency of bad spirits assumed . . . maidens pined away, wasting inwardly as their waxen images consumed before a fire . . .

"Corn was lodged, and cattle lamed . . . whirlwinds uptore in diabolic revelry the oaks of the forest—spits and kettles . . . danced . . . about some rustic's kitchen when no wind was stirring—(these) were all equally probable where no law of agency was understood . . .

"That the intercourse was opened at all between both worlds was perhaps the mistake, but, that once assumed, I see no reason for disbelieving one attested story of this nature more than another on the score of absurdity.

"There is no law to judge of the lawless, or canon by which dreams may be criticized."

THE BLACK DOG OF DEATH

In the 20th century, a weird ritual killing sets one of murder's most fascinating mysteries. A legend comes to life . . . and claims as its victim a man who seems to have been singled out for this fate. In a haunted corner of England, scene of a horrific St. Valentine's Day killing, the powers of witchcraft seem to live on.

Mary Evans

AT a time when the roll of those dying by another's hand had mounted to millions, the murder of one solitary, lonely individual seemed of little account. So it was that few outside the tiny English village of Lower Quinton paid much heed to the news that, in the chill dusk of February 14, St. Valentine's Day, 1945, the mutilated body of 74-year-old Charles Walton had been found beneath a willow tree.

In a world at peace, the discovery would have warranted immediate front page attention – for the manner in which the aged recluse had died was both revolting and deeply mystifying. He had been pinned firmly to the ground by his own hayfork, driven savagely through his neck and then down into six inches of soil. Across his throat and chest had been crudely scratched the sign of the Cross, and from the wound still hung Charlie's own long-handled hedge-trimming hook.

At first the local police were bewildered by the brutality of the killing, and its apparent lack of motive. Then a curiously sinister chain of events began to unroll. First, a heavy curtain of silence descended over the village. None of its 450 inhabitants would talk in any detail about Charlie or the circumstances of his death; none could offer any kind of lead except that "it couldn't have been anyone here who did it". Second, and most extraordinary of all, one word began to whisper its way under the thatched roofs and along the narrow, twisting lanes: "Witchcraft!"

It was a word much used in the past in Lower Quinton. The village lies in Shakespeare country, between Stratford-on-Avon and Chipping Norton, in Warwickshire, and there is little doubt that William Shakespeare drew upon boyhood memories of local gossip about witches and black magic while working upon such plays as *Macbeth* and *A Midsummer Night's Dream*.

A headless woman

Lower Quinton, like several other medieval villages, had its own fearful legend – the legend of the black dog. Over the decades, it was said, this strange animal, larger than most dogs and with unearthly, burning eyes, appeared from nowhere and disappeared into nowhere. Few had doubts about what its appearance portended: someone was about to die.

One nineteenth-century student of the legend, a Warwickshire parson named the Reverend Harvey Bloom, had recorded a frightening story about the black dog

Topix

VILLAGERS thought he was "odd". But was Charlie Walton (ringed) the same person who featured in the frightening folk-tale of the haunted ploughboy?

THE FAMILIAR half-timbered look of victim Walton's home (arrowed) acts as a reminder that this is Shakespeare country, home of many a witch's tale.

in his book, *Folk Lore, Old Customs and Superstitions in Shakespeareland.* In 1885, he wrote, a ploughboy encountered the dog nine times on successive days at dusk. The boy told his tale to fellow farm-workers and they scoffed at his vivid imagination. On the ninth day, however, the dog turned into a headless woman who glided hair-raisingly past him with a faint rustle from her silk dress. The next day the boy's sister died.

That boy, identified by name in the book, was – Charles Walton. No wonder that the villagers, remembering the story of Charlie and the dog and drawing a straight connecting line between it and his brutal death, preferred to keep silent and lessen the risk of further visitations. This might be 1945, and the climax of a war in which modern technology was playing a devastating part, but in Lower Quinton no march of history could dim respect for ancient and inexplicable powers.

Charlie Walton himself had fitted closely into the pattern of the shadowy world of the unknown. To the local inhabitants he was "odd". He liked the company of the birds that sang around the village and its meadows more than he liked the company of people. As he worked at his various field-labouring tasks, he would talk to the rooks and jackdaws, and he claimed he could follow the meaning of

every sound they made. Quiet and withdrawn, he had spent his whole life in Lower Quinton, rarely going more than a mile or two away. In his final years, he lived in the centre cottage of a row of three where his niece, Miss Edith Isabel Walton, looked after him.

He was never seen in the village pubs – and not to be at least an occasional caller at these two centres of village social life marked a man out as "peculiar". Not that Charlie Walton was a teetotaller; far from it. He drank a great deal of cider and sometimes bought 12 gallons at a time. But he always took the cider home, often trundling his supplies in a wheelbarrow with as much speed as his rheumatism would allow, and drank alone behind closed doors.

Two-pronged hayfork

The village thought he "had money", not only because of the cider he bought but because he was known to have a bank account – a most unusual status for a casual labourer in those days. When he worked he earned only around 1s. 9d. (8½p. or $0.20) an hour. Some of the local gossips assumed, therefore, that he was a sorcerer whose money came from "fees" paid for magical services rendered.

Wednesday, February 14, 1945, was a surprisingly mild day, a forerunner of what was to be an early spring followed by a long summer. It was just the day, Charlie Walton decided, to make a start on some hedge cutting he had promised to do for one of the local farmers, Alfred

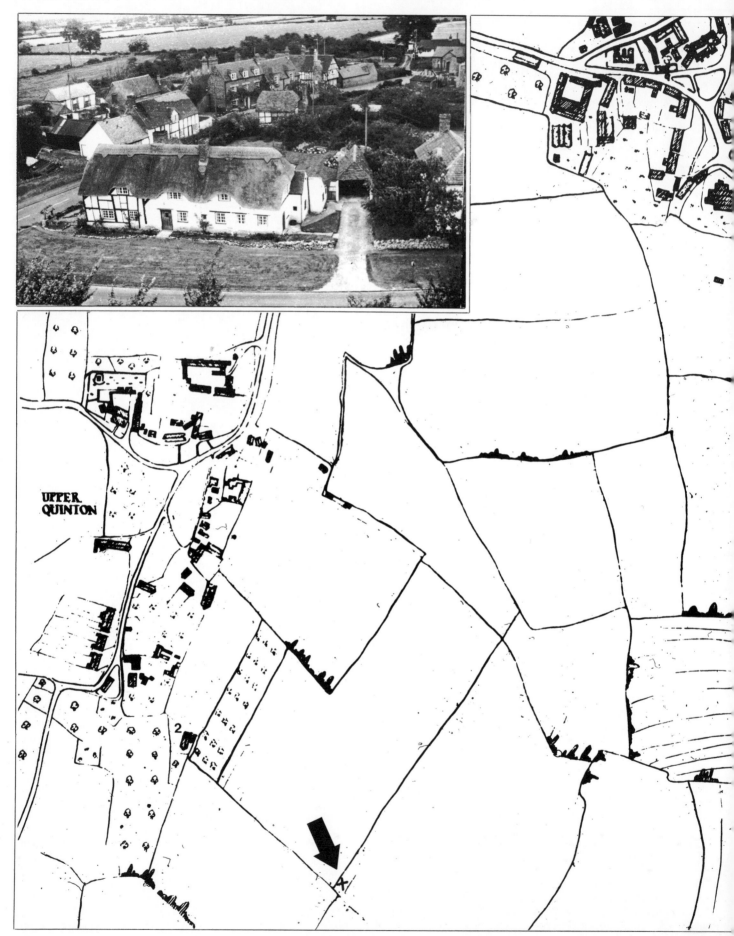

"X" MARKS THE SPOT where the strangely-impaled body of Charlie Walton was found. Was this a witchcraft killing? What happened after Walton left his cottage (marked by the figure 1 on the police map)? How did he meet the fate which was to so frighten the search party from Potter's farm (2)? In the local pub (3), "silence fell like a physical blow" when questions were asked. Indeed, the whole picture-postcard village (inset) was shrouded in silence. Cottage doors were slammed, and beneath thatched roofs there were only frightened whispers. "Innocent witnesses seemed unable to meet our eyes," recalled a detective. There was sullen opposition to police. "We don't talk much about it . . ." The villagers refused to yield a single secret . . . however tenacious or distinguished the inquirer. Not for Scotland Yard's famous Fabian, not for the intrepid Margaret Mead, would the people of Lower Quinton unburden themselves of their innermost fears . . .

Potter. Shortly after nine, he set off with his walking stick, his two-pronged hayfork and his trimming hook, and made his laborious way to the slopes of Meon Hill, a little over a mile from his cottage. He told his niece he would be home at four to make his own tea.

That was the last that anyone, apart from his murderer, positively saw of Charlie Walton alive. Just after midday, Farmer Potter, making the rounds of his fields and inspecting his sheep and cattle, *thought* he saw Charlie slashing hedges about 500 yards away. Certainly it appeared to be a man working in shirt sleeves, and he could not think who else it could be, except Charlie. Although at that distance it was not possible to make out the old man's familiar flowing moustache and sun-varnished features.

At six in the evening Miss Edith Walton returned to the cottage from her war job in a neighbouring factory. She was immediately worried by the absence of her uncle, who was a meticulous time-keeper and never came home later than his announced time. Quite naturally, thinking of his unsteady, rheumatic legs, she feared he had suffered a fall. She called in at the cottage of a neighbour, Harry Beasley, and together they went to The Firs, Mr. Potter's farm.

Shock and abhorrence

Alfred Potter—as puzzled as Miss Walton—took a flashlight and lit the way from his farm to the middle of a group of five fields on the lower slopes of Meon Hill where he had last seen Charlie.

Quite suddenly the sharp snapping of fallen twigs under the men's boots ceased, and the beam of light came to rest on a patch of ground close by a willow. Then the light flashed back into Edith Walton's face and Potter's voice, trembling with shock and abhorrence, cried: "Stay there! Don't come any nearer. You mustn't look at this!" Bracing themselves, the men brought the flashlight beam back to bear on the hideous sight of old Charlie Walton, impaled and bloodily marked with the Cross, his moustache-draped mouth drawn back in a final grimace of terror and desperation.

Leaving Potter to guard the corpse, Beasley took Miss Walton home and summoned the police. When they arrived it took the combined strength of two policemen to release the deeply-embedded hayfork from Charlie's body—which was then lifted on to a five-barred gate and carried down to the village. There a brief examination disclosed that the old man had not died without a struggle. His bony, tanned arms were scratched and torn, and there were large bruises and blood on his head.

Charlie's walking stick, found close to the body, was bloodstained. All the in-

dications were that he had been felled by a blow from his stick, and then lain helpless on the ground, watching in agony as his assailant stood over him and delivered the pitiless death thrust. Disconcerted by the mysterious circumstances, the Warwickshire police asked Scotland Yard for assistance. They promptly received it in the person of Detective Superintendent Robert Fabian, one of Britain's finest detectives and so familiar to the public that he was known simply as "Fabian of the Yard". With him came his extremely able partner, Detective-Sergeant Albert Webb.

Prisoners of war

A first move by Fabian and Webb was to implement a suggestion from the local police and arrange for the questioning of the 1043 enemy prisoners of war being held in a camp at Long Marston, two miles from Lower Quinton. There Detective-Sergeant David Saunders, a multilinguist from the Yard's Special Branch, was called in as interpreter for the interrogation of the men, who included Italians, Germans, and Slavs.

For a while it looked as though the murder hunt might quickly produce a quarry. Some of the prisoners, not averse to turning stool pigeon on a comrade, reported seeing an Italian frantically trying to wash blood from his jacket. The man was found and his coat sent to a forensic laboratory in Birmingham, some thirty miles away. The resulting report, however, brought police hopes to an abrupt end: the blood was rabbit's and it seemed that what the Italian had been trying to conceal was the fact that he had slipped out of camp and gone poaching.

One of the many frustrating features of the case for Fabian and his partner was that, unwittingly, Farmer Potter and his little search party had churned up the ground in going to and from the body and obliterated what might have been crucial footprints in the damp earth. Less excusably, the local police had added to the disturbance of the murder scene in carrying the body away.

From the village itself came neither word nor hint. So, day after day, Fabian gloomily tramped the slopes of Meon Hill, looking for just that one sign that would point his investigation in a positive direction. Then, one evening as dusk was closing in, a large black dog scuttled past him and was lost in the darkening woods. A moment later a boy came walking over the hillside and Fabian asked: "Looking for that dog, son?" The boy gaped: "What dog, mister?" "A black dog,"

POTTER'S FARM (inset) was one of the places where Charlie Walton worked. He was cutting hedges for farmer Potter (left) when he was last seen alive.

FABIAN OF THE YARD: Even this indefatigable sleuth was powerless. In the end, to his great regret, he went back to Scotland Yard empty-handed.

said Fabian, and without a word the boy raced off as though the Devil himself was at his heels.

That night in the Gay Dog the indefatigable Fabian attempted, as usual, to strike up a conversation with the silent "locals" and mentioned the odd incident of the black dog. To his surprise someone answered and, for the first time, he heard the legend of the dog, the headless woman, and the ploughboy whose sister died. "We don't talk much about it," said his informant, grudgingly. "Nobody has spoken about it for years; not since afore the war, anyway." The rest of the farmhands in the bar sat tight-mouthed, and Fabian noticed that some looked embarrassed and turned back to their pints of beer and other subjects.

New and sinister

A few days later Fabian mentioned the dog and the pub story to a colleague in the Warwickshire police force who was interested in local legends. The colleague showed him a book he had just acquired, the Rev. Harvey Bloom's book. Fabian was astonished when, idly turning the pages, he came across not only the account of the black dog legend, as the man in the pub had related it, but also the one important item the man had left out: the name of the ploughboy, Charlie Walton.

This opened up a new and sinister line of inquiry and, unreal as it would have seemed in other circumstances, Fabian felt he had to pursue it. In another book, entitled *Warwickshire,* by Clive Holland, he read of an actual murder, in 1875, which closely followed the pattern of Charlie Walton's killing. At Long Compton, a village only a few miles from Lower

383

Quinton, and reputedly a centuries-old centre of witchcraft, John Haywood, a feeble-minded lad had killed an 80-year-old woman, named Ann Turner, with a hayfork.

At his trial Haywood declared that there were 16 witches in Long Compton at the time and he said of Ann Turner: "Her was a proper witch. I pinned her to the ground before slashing her throat with a billhook in the form of a cross." There had been many cases throughout the history of witchcraft in England, and particularly Warwickshire, of suspected witches being impaled by hayforks. It was, in some ways, the equivalent of driving a stake through the heart of one of those mythical creatures, the vampires, as in Bram Stoker's fictional story of Count Dracula. In England, too, February was a much favoured month for ritual killing, and probably bore some link with ancient blood-letting festivals which took place at that time.

Fertility rite

The central purpose of such blood-letting—usually it was animals' blood—was to replenish the fertility of the soil. Subsequently a Birmingham woman claimed, in a newspaper interview, that she knew the name of Charlie Walton's killer and that the murder had, indeed, been part of a fertility rite. "Three or four survivors of an ancient cult live in the locality, but the actual murderer was a woman who was brought by car from a different part of the country," she said. Although she refused to be more specific the police did believe that there were "black magic" groups active in and around the area.

Meanwhile, Fabian and Webb found that the barrier of silence in Lower Quinton effectively kept them from real contact with the villagers. They suffered some remarkably bad luck, or "warnings" as some of the village people termed it. One of their police cars had the mis-

A POLICEMAN'S VIGIL: For 19 years, Detective Alec Spooner made pilgrimages annually to the murder hill (top), where even the graffiti speak of witchcraft.

fortune to run over and kill a black dog (normal size and "natural") in one of the winding, concealed country lanes. That was enough to convince the villagers that any word from them to the police might bring far worse visitations upon their community.

Despite this, Fabian and his colleagues took 4000 statements—from the P.O.W.s, passing tinkers and gypsies, Allied soldiers and airmen stationed in the area. The Royal Air Force shot aerial photographs of Meon Hill, and men of the Royal Engineers trudged through meadows and copses with their mine detectors. They brought to light a great deal of metallic garbage, but no murder clue.

In fact all the detectives' endeavours were in vain. People in surrounding villages spoke darkly of a witches' coven, formed at the turn of the century and still active around Meon Hill. But in Lower Quinton the sullen opposition to the detectives hung heavily in the air. Fabian later wrote: "When Albert Webb and I walked into the village pubs silence fell like a physical blow. Cottage doors were shut

in our faces and even the most innocent witnesses seemed unable to meet our eyes."

All this had a profound effect upon Fabian and Webb, whose inherent sense of duty would not normally let them rest until they had examined every possibility in an investigation. But, in the end, even they, with all their stamina, were forced to admit that they could make no progress. They were powerless against the solidarity of the picture postcard village, with its lovely Saxon-Norman church which displayed a sixteenth-century coat of arms prayer reading: "God love our noble Queen Elizabeth. Amen!"

Along the grapevine—the only open line of communication—it was "suggested" to Fabian that perhaps an outsider had killed Charlie for his money. After all, it was asserted, he carried a bulging money belt. But there was nothing to support this and, in any case, why would a thief risk time and capture by going through the hideous death ritual? Shaky old Charlie Walton could have been laid low by one swift blow from behind and, even if he survived, never have seen his attacker.

Primitive island

Finally, and to their everlasting regret, Fabian and Webb called it a day. They returned to Scotland Yard and other crimes that lacked black magic undertones and overtones. Life in Lower Quinton returned to normal, and if the villagers had any concrete evidence they steadfastly refused to yield it up. Later, the adventurous and energetic American anthropologist, Margaret Mead, paid a visit to the village, no doubt rightly regarding it as a strangely primitive island in a sea of so-called Western civilization. But she, to whom other "backward" peoples had readily opened their mouths and minds, went away unrewarded.

There was one person, however, who could not turn his back on the scene, and for whom the case held a totally absorbing fascination. He was Detective Superintendent Alec Spooner, of the Warwickshire Criminal Investigation Department, on whose "manor" the killing had occurred.

Every year for 19 years, on the murder's anniversary, he went to Meon Hill and there kept watch, not attempting to conceal his presence. His theory as he explained it, was: "If the murderer is about, he wants the crime forgotten. My return shows him that it has not been forgotten and this may wear him down."

In 1964 Alec Spooner retired from police work and was not seen again on Meon Hill. The Lower Quinton murder file was not closed but put away, awaiting a concluding paragraph. Almost certainly it will never be written.

THE WITCHES OF SALEM

During early colonial days in America all but a very few men believed in the actual existence of demons and witches, and harbored many superstitions that had been handed down from the Middle Ages —

TODAY most people laughingly dismiss witchcraft as a superstition of the ignorant. But in seventeenth-century Europe and America, witches, defined by the English judge Lord Coke as persons who had "conference with the Devil to consult with him or to do some act," were taken very seriously. Witches were women—the male equivalent was warlock—and as a result of their dealings with the Devil were commonly believed to be able to perform supernatural acts.

AROUND THE WORLD, witch-hunting was a major occupation. A 1647 woodcut (left) shows British witch-finder Matthew Hopkins. In America, several women were hanged at Gallows Hill, Salem (below). But Tituba (far right) never faced trial because she repented.

The penalty for being proved a witch was death, and in the few years of Oliver Cromwell's rule in England many unfortunates accused of witchcraft perished on the gallows—60 being hanged in a single year in Suffolk, a county which the notorious witch-hunter Matthew Hopkins pronounced to be infested with witches.

The panic on the subject was the natural result of Puritanical teaching acting on the mind and predisposing the ruling authorities to see Satanic influences at work in the community, expressed through the supernatural phenomena of witchcraft.

The seeds of the superstition crossed the Atlantic with the Pilgrim Fathers, and at a time when it was beginning to disappear in England it flourished alarmingly in the state of Massachusetts—which in 1692 was the scene of the most celebrated witch-hunt and witch trials in history. It all happened in the small rural community of Salem Village, since renamed Danvers, situated near the old port of Salem a few miles to the northeast of Boston.

The Rev. Samuel Parris, a local preacher, had previously been engaged in trade in the West Indies before accepting a call to the parish of Salem Village. He had brought back a married couple with him from Barbados, slaves called John and Tituba, whose presence undoubtedly lent prestige to the parsonage. Tituba, who was half Carib and half Negro, spent a good deal of time with the two children in the household, the Parris' nine-year-old daughter Betty, and her cousin Abigail Williams, who was two years older.

During the winter of 1691-92, a group of eight girls, including Abigail and Betty, mostly teen-aged, used to meet in the kitchen premises of the minister's house in the company of Tituba. It was later assumed that Tituba had stuffed their impressionable heads with tales of African or West Indian magic, and had even practised it with them—although no credible evidence of this came to light in the subsequent trials which were documented in great detail.

Tituba's activities do not seem to have gone beyond fortune telling and possibly what another New England divine, the Rev. Cotton Mather—who had made a

Mary Evans

Mary Evans

study of witchcraft and written a book about it—described as "little sorceries", practised with sieve and scissors and candle.

I N THE YEAR 1692 SOME YOUNG GIRLS OF DANVERS, A VILLAGE NEAR SALEM, MASSACHUSETTS, BECAME SO FRIGHTENED READ-ING BOOKS ON WITCHCRAFT THAT THEY BELIEVED THEMSELVES BEWITCHED. ————

These sessions ended by driving Betty, Abigail, and a 12-year-old girl named Ann Putnam into what was evidently a hysterical illness. Abigail and Ann, in particular, moaned and shrieked for no apparent reason, grovelling and writhing on the ground and occasionally acting as if they believed that they had been transformed into animals.

The symptoms soon spread throughout the child population in Salem Village, and as a result it was concluded by the adult community—led by Parris and other clergymen in the area—that the girls were bewitched. Eventually, in February 1692, Abigail and Ann were able to name three of their tormentors. The first of these was Tituba; the other two were an elderly pipe-smoking hag named Sarah Good, and a moderately well-to-do married woman named Sarah Osburne, who owned some property.

The two Sarahs seem to have been unpopular in the settlement and were certainly disapproved of by the Puritan leaders of the community—Sarah Good, because she had become something of a tramp who begged from door to door, and furthermore did not go to church, and Sarah Osburne, because as a widow she lived in sin with her overseer before marrying him as her second husband.

The three women were now arrested and brought before two magistrates, John Hathorne and Jonathan Corwin, who were sent out from Salem Village to examine the accused in a public session at one of the local churches which had been borrowed for the purpose. Both the Sarahs denied everything. Asked why she did not attend church, Sarah Good replied

that she had no suitable clothes. Further questioned as to what she said when she went away muttering from people's houses, she answered confidently: "It is the commandments I say. I may say my commandments, I hope."

As for the unfortunate Sarah Osburne, she had been dragged from her sickbed and had to be supported by two constables during her interrogation. She was obviously very ill, and the most the magistrates could get out of her was that she was "more like to be bewitched than that she should be a witch."

After the two Sarahs had been taken off again to prison, the extraordinary Tituba was brought in. She produced an imaginative confession in which she said just the kind of thing her Puritan accusers wished her to say. She talked about red cats and red rats. These cats and rats, she declared, could talk to her and in fact had said to her: "Serve me." She went on to tell of "a Thing" which she could only describe as "something like a cat"—it had a woman's face and it had wings, and it was Gammer Osburne's creature. These and other shapes, she said, told her to pinch Betty and Abigail, but "I would not hurt Betty—I loved Betty." They also told her to attack Ann Putnam with a knife. Ann and Abigail were then fetched into court in Tituba's presence and they began to moan and whimper.

"Who hurts the children now?" asked magistrate Hathorne.

"I am blind now," Tituba cunningly answered. "I cannot see." Thus the slave made it clear that second sight was not for a witch who had repented and renounced her calling.

No doubt Tituba's confession saved her life, and she was never arraigned. Meanwhile the list of suspect witches quickly grew, largely on the accusation of Abigail and Ann—though other girls occasionally joined in, and some of the accused followed Tituba's example by confessing.

It is noteworthy that none of those who confessed and implicated others was executed. Only those who steadfastly protested their innocence in the event suffered. Among those in this category were George Burroughs, a minister of religion, Martha Corey, who was a church member in good standing, and Rebecca Nurse, an invalid of unsullied reputation.

Not even children escaped, since Dorcas Good, the five-year-old daughter of the pipe-smoking Sarah, was also hauled off to prison.

There were also a few old villagers —such as the tavern keeper Bridget Bishop and Susanna Martin—who had been suspected of witchcraft in the past, and they were likewise taken into custody.

The Governor of Massachusetts, Sir

William Phips, appointed a special commission of seven judges, presided over by the Governor's Deputy, Chief Justice William Stoughton, to sit in Salem Village and try the suspects. It might be expected that the two Sarahs would be tried first, but this was not possible. Sarah Osburne died in prison before she could be brought into court again, while Sarah Good's case was put back until the delivery of her child—since she was pregnant at the time of her arrest.

Consequently the first to face a formal trial was Bridget Bishop, against whom there was already considerable local prejudice. Not only had she been suspected of practising sorcery in the past, but she was regarded as a flashy dresser and an unsatisfactory tavern keeper.

LOOK! SHE HAS TAKEN THE FORM OF A YELLOW BIRD!

E VERYONE WAS SO FRIGHTENED THAT THE UNLUCKY PRISONERS COULD NOT HOPE FOR A FAIR TRIAL. THE HYSTERICAL RAVINGS OF THE "BEWITCHED" GIRLS WERE ACCEPTED AS TESTIMONY. ————

Her "red paragon bodice" set her style, as did her "smooth and flattering manner" with men, and it was a long standing complaint that she permitted young people to loiter at unseemly hours in her tavern, playing at "shovel-board" and disturbing the sleep of decent neighbours.

Her trial, like that of most of the others, was a travesty of justice, since the record of the pre-trial examination before the magistrates was accepted by the court as consisting of proven facts, rather than something to be tested. In the words of Cotton Mather, describing the court procedure in Bridget's case, "there was little occasion to prove the witchcraft, this being evident and notorious to all beholders."

Poor Bridget, who like all the other

HER CRIME was probably running a rowdy tavern. But Bridget Bishop was hanged as a witch on Gallows Hill (top). Sheriff Corwin reported back that she had been executed (below). Other Salem "witches" were to live.

Brown Brothers

The Mansell Collection

defendants in the subsequent trials was denied the aid of defence counsel, got off to a bad start. While walking under guard from Salem prison to the court she cast a glance at "the great and spacious meeting-house", and at once a great clatter arose within. Those sent to see what the woman's evil eye had done reported that "they found a board which was strongly fastened with several nails transported to another quarter of the house."

Four male witnesses testified that she haunted their beds at night, sometimes coming in her own form, sometimes like a black pig and in one instance with the body of a monkey, the feet of a cock, and the face of a man. Three children of these witnesses pined away and died, they swore, because being good men they had virtuously repelled her advances.

Testimony to the effect that Bridget's own husband thought she was a witch was given by a female witness named Elizabeth Balch, who described how she had once seen a quarrel between them. Bridget was riding pillion on horseback behind her husband when the latter spurred his horse to a pace that nearly threw her. Bridget thereupon lost her temper, and they had words. She was a "bad wife", said her husband; "the Devil had come bodily to her . . . and she sat up all night with the Devil." What particularly struck Mistress Balch, who was riding beside them, was that throughout this tirade Bridget did not once open her mouth to defend herself.

Other witnesses, who had searched Bridget's house in Salem, found in the cellar some dolls made of rags and hog's bristles, into which pins had been stuck. When she was confronted with these objects, Bridget could give the court no "reasonable and tolerable" explanation.

Both immediately before her trial and immediately afterwards, Bridget was physically examined for witch marks by a jury of matrons—who were equipped with pins which they stuck into any part of her body that looked at all unusual. On the first occasion the women discovered a "witch's tet" between "ye pudendum and anus"; on the second, three hours later, this "tet" had withered to dry skin.

DEATH WAS THE USUAL PENALTY FOR WITCHCRAFT IN THOSE DAYS, AND THE CONDEMNED PERSONS WERE SENT TO THE GALLOWS.

The court jury found Bridget Bishop guilty and the judges condemned her to death. Ten days elapsed before the sentence could be carried out, since it had to be legalized by reviving an old colonial law which made witchcraft a capital offence. Then on June 10, 1692, High Sheriff George Corwin took Bridget to the top of Gallows Hill and hanged her from the branches of a great oak tree.

The court did not sit again for nearly a month. The reason for the delay, which was kept from the public, was a difference which occurred among the judges as to the credence to be given to spectral evidence. At least one member of the commission was impressed by the fact that, had such evidence been held inadmissible, Bridget Bishop would have been convicted for little more than wearing scarlet, countenancing "shovel-board" in her tavern and getting herself talked about—no doubt all offences, but hardly capital ones even in those harsh days.

Since witchcraft involved theological as well as legal considerations, Governor Phips referred the question to a committee of 12 ministers of religion in the Boston region. Unfortunately the committee, to which the historian Cotton Mather acted as secretary, equivocated. While advising that conviction should in future be based on evidence "certainly more considerable than barely the accused person being represented by a spectre unto the afflicted", at the same time it praised the "sedulous and assiduous endeavours" of the magistrates and judges who had in practice disregarded nearly all other evidence.

The committee went on to "humbly recommend the speedy and vigorous prosecution of such as have rendered themselves obnoxious."

First to be tried was Rebecca Nurse, an old invalid lady, almost totally deaf. The jury had before them a petition signed by more than a score of respectable inhabitants of Salem Village, testifying to her unwitchlike character, piety and the extraordinary care she had lavished on the Christian upbringing of her children.

"I am innocent and clear and have not been able to get out of doors these eight or nine days," Rebecca protested. "I never afflicted no child, no, never in my life."

One of the witnesses against Rebecca was a certain Deliverance Hobbs, who had herself confessed to being a witch and repented with the result that her life was spared. When Deliverance came into court, Rebecca was said to have turned her head towards her and exclaimed: "What, do you bring her? She is one of us."

However, after deliberating on these matters, the jury brought in a verdict of not guilty. Ann Putnam, Abigail Williams, and several other girls were in the court house, and they immediately set up a howling and wailing, twisting their bodies as if convulsed.

When the din had subsided somewhat, Chief Justice Stoughton addressed the jurors. "I will not impose on the jury," he said, "but I must ask you if you considered one statement made by the prisoner." The judge then repeated what the accused was alleged to have said to Deliverance Hobbs. "Has the jury weighed the implications of this statement?"

Neither the foreman nor the other jurors could remember exactly what Rebecca had said. Rebecca was thereupon questioned again and asked to explain herself.

THEY LIVED and died here . . . Salem, the New England village where Puritans held their famous trial of witches.

The Mansell Collection

The Bettmann Archive

Unfortunately Rebecca, as she herself put it afterwards, was "something hard of hearing and full of grief", and consequently did not give a very satisfactory answer. The jury again retired and this time brought in a verdict of guilty.

On trial with Rebecca Nurse were Susanna Martin, the pipe-smoking Sarah Good, and two other women who had been denounced as witches, Elizabeth How and Sarah Wild, the latter by the nefarious Abigail Hobbs and the former by a family named Perley from Ipswich who claimed that their ten-year-old daughter had been "afflicted" by Goody How. "Did I hurt you?" asked Elizabeth How, when she was confronted with the child and took her hand. "No, never!" the little girl replied. "If I did complain of you in my fits, I knew not that I did so."

The tale of Susanna Martin's spectral misdeeds was recited at length. A neighbouring farmer swore that she had cast a spell upon his herd of oxen because he refused to hitch his ox cart to haul her some staves. "Your oxen will never do you much service!" Susanna was alleged to have said, with the result that the oxen took fright and plunged into the sea.

Another neighbour told an unlikely tale of a phantom puppy which sprang at his throat as a result of Susanna's witcheries. Like Bridget Bishop, Susanna was also said to have molested honest men in their bedchambers, "scrabbling at the window", hopping down from the sill and boldly getting into bed.

All four women were found guilty, and along with Rebecca Nurse, they were hanged on Gallows Hill.

Four men were condemned in the immediately following trial. They included the Rev. George Burroughs who was charged with seducing girls to witchcraft by offering them "fine cloathes" and subsequently biting them. The girls had toothmarks all over their arms and Burrough's mouth was prized open when it was established to the satisfaction of the jury that his teeth were responsible for the marks.

FIGHTING for her life . . . a woman accused of witchcraft faces the court in Salem. But eventually, the hysteria that swept the village was to die down.

Then there was the case of the octogenarian Giles Cory who had incriminated his wife Martha—though his testimony had amounted to little more than an expression of wonder that Martha should linger by the fire to pray long after he expected her in bed, and one of annoyance that when the examinations were going on before the magistrates she had hidden his saddle to prevent him from riding to court. ("Nevertheless," she commented later, "he went for all that.")

In due course he, too, was arrested and charged with witchcraft—having apparently been denounced by some of the girls in their fits. However, when brought to court he remained more or less speechless and steadfastly refused to plead to the indictment. "I am a poor man and cannot help it" was all he would say.

Under English criminal procedure, an accused person who "stood mute" and refused to plead was subjected to *peine forte et dure*—in other words he was tied to the floor of his cell and heavy weights were placed on his chest until he consented to plead "guilty" or "not guilty".

The result was that Giles Cory was pressed to death by the sheriff in an open

391

field beside the jail. His only recorded utterance as rock after rock was piled on his chest was to cry out "More Weight!" Such a revolting punishment was never afterwards carried out in America.

Although only 19 people in addition to Giles Cory were executed for witchcraft in Salem in 1692—a number small by contemporary European standards—nevertheless about 400 people were arrested and crammed into the local jails. Others fled to the safety of other states, abandoning their property and livelihood. However, a reaction set in quickly and the popular hysteria died down as suddenly as it had begun.

In October 1692, Governor Phips cancelled the special commission and re-manded the prisoners in custody on witchcraft charges to the ordinary courts, which acquitted the majority. The rest were pardoned.

Afterwards all concerned with the witch-hunt sought to make amends as best they could. A day was set aside for public mourning and prayers for forgiveness. "We walked in clouds and could not see our way," declared the Rev. John Hale, who had testified against Bridget Bishop. "And we have most cause to be humbled for error . . . which cannot be retrieved." Judges and juries made public repentance, expressing their "deep sense of sorrow" to the survivors of their victims and their heirs.

No execution for witchcraft ever again

ARRESTED . . . The witch-hunters swoop on yet another woman as the purge goes on. But after the Salem trials, no witch was to be executed in America.

took place in Colonial America. Sanity gradually prevailed in place of madness, and the spirit of enlightenment and rationalism eventually triumphed over ignorance and superstition—though not entirely. Ideological witch-hunts still occur in the United States, being carried out with Puritan zeal by such campaigners as Anthony Comstock (1844-1915), and the late Senator Joseph McCarthy.

The Puritan spirit which sent the Salem witches to the gallows is not altogether dead in the land of the free.

JEALOUSY

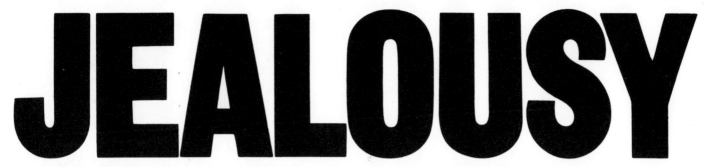

IT CAN be stronger than the love it so often accompanies. Jealousy is the most potent of human emotions . . . and often the most potently poisonous. The green-eyed monster, as Shakespeare called it, is something of a mass-murderer . . . with a spectacular style in killing. But is a passion-crazed person insane?

Popperfoto

IN THE annals of homicide, there are few truly unique crimes. Most types of murder have been committed before, and will be committed again. Yet there is a bizarre and ghastly originality about the murder committed by a middle-aged Victorian lady named Christiana Edmunds in 1871. In the second part of the nineteenth century, Brighton, in southern England, was a highly respectable seaside town, much favoured by the retired middle classes. Christiana Edmunds was a bad-tempered, sharp-tongued virgin who lived there

with her aged mother. Her exact age is not known, but descriptions of her bring to mind lyricist W. S. Gilbert's lady who could "very well pass for forty-three in the dusk with the light behind her".

Life for the waspish Miss Edmunds was unexciting, and she had few male acquaintances. Predictably, she was subject to attacks of headaches and other neurotic ailments. One day when the headache was exceptionally severe, a new doctor was called in, the charming and popular Dr. Beard. He divined correctly that Miss

THREE'S A CROWD . . . so one man had to die. Caught in an emotional whirlpool, Edith Thompson persuaded her lover (left) to kill her husband (right).

Edmunds needed affection and attention rather than aspirin. He only intended to be kind; but his manner was so captivating that by the time he left the room, Miss Edmunds was wildly infatuated with him. A short while later she began to write to him long and emotional letters. He was too good-natured to rebuff her, and pen-

CRIME PASSIONEL . . . and the atmosphere in the courtroom is one of decidedly Gallic melodrama. Flanked by police, Pauline Dubuisson, said to be a nymphomaniac, shot her lover. Right: Her lawyer's eloquence helps to save her neck . . . the sentence is life imprisonment, for non-capital murder. The victim's fiancée (foreground) gave evidence at the trial . . . the last one at which photographers were allowed under French law.

ned kindly replies. At this point, Christiana Edmunds became convinced that Dr. Beard was willing to marry her – or would be, if he hadn't already happened to be married. Mrs. Beard was younger and more attractive than Miss Edmunds; the benevolent Dr. Beard would not abandon her by choice.

One day Christiana Edmunds called on Mrs. Beard for tea, and presented her with a box of chocolates. In the Victorian era, chocolates were not sealed in cellophane; the confectioner often provided the box himself, and put the chocolates in by hand. So Mrs. Beard was unsuspicious when her visitor opened the box and insisted that she should eat a chocolate with her tea. She bit into a chocolate cream, which was so bitter that she instantly spat it out. Miss Edmunds was apologetic; she said it must be the fault of the confectioner. Mrs. Beard

pretended to agree; but as soon as her husband returned home, she told him that his "mad female admirer" had tried to poison her. Dr. Beard agreed. He called on Miss Edmunds and told her firmly that their acquaintance must come to an end immediately.

Outrageous story

Miss Edmunds was lucky; she had escaped being arrested as a poisoner. But she was too hysterical to see it that way. She collapsed with nervous prostration. All she could think of for days was that Dr. and Mrs. Beard suspected her of attempted murder, and might well be repeating their "outrageous story" to their acquaintances. Tortured by this conviction, she conceived an extraordinary scheme for vindicating herself. If someone else – someone totally unknown to her – should die of a poisoned chocolate from

the same confectioner, it would prove that the chocolates were to blame. Her next problem was how to insert poison into chocolates that were still in the shop. She overcame this difficulty by accosting a small boy in the street, and asking him to go and buy her half a pound of chocolates. With considerable care, she put strychnine into them. Then she found another small boy to take them back to the shop and explain that they were not the kind she wanted. The unsuspecting assistant changed them. A few days went by, and no one died. Miss Edmunds got impatient, and sent another youngster to buy chocolates. Still nothing happened. She had obtained the strychnine in March 1871, and as April passed, and then the first week of June, she began to despair of her plan. Gradually, however, people started to purchase the poisoned chocolates; some felt sick, and complained to

spent the rest of her life in Broadmoor — the State institution for the criminally insane, built in 1863 in Berkshire. There she exercised her bad temper and imperious manners on the other prisoners, and regarded herself as the social leader of the place. If it had not been for her curious mistake in tearing out the wrong page of the poisons book, she might have lived on into old age as a respectable, if discontented, member of Brighton society.

Violent infatuation

On one issue, however, there is no doubt. Christiana Edmunds *was* insane. Dr. Beard was telling the truth when he said she might lose her reason if he rejected her. For her behaviour — offering to testify at the inquest, sending for the poisons book, and tearing out the wrong page — was typical of the attention-seeking lunatic. Another strychnine poisoner, the Glasgow-born Victorian women murderer, Dr. Neil Cream, drew the noose around his own neck by writing letters in which he accused other people of the crimes he had committed in both Chicago and London. Like Miss Edmunds, he also approached the police and offered to testify at a time when no one suspected him. This curious kind of exhibitionism, directed at self-destruction, is also manifested by the great majority of "jealousy-killers".

This suggests an unorthodox conclusion: that most people who kill out of jealousy are insane, and should be treated as such. The French have always recognized the *crime passionel* as a special category, amounting to second-degree murder. But the English and the Americans are inclined to take a moralistic standpoint. They feel that passion is no excuse for murder. Self-control is what counts, and the person who gets carried away by sexual jealousy deserves all he gets. This view is based on logic, but not upon fact. The court that rejected Miss Edmunds's plea of insanity felt that a wicked and selfish woman *could* value her reputation so highly that she would commit murder to make people think well of her. And no doubt such a person could exist. The fact remains that Miss Edmunds was insane rather than wicked. Her mother suspected it before she met Dr. Beard; and her violent infatuation for the doctor suddenly brought it out.

Where English law is concerned, the problem lies in the definition of insanity. In 1843, a young schizophrenic called Daniel M'Naghten, decided to murder Prime Minister Sir Robert Peel — the founder of the British police system — whom he was convinced was persecuting him. He mistook Peel's private secretary, Edward Drummond, for the Prime Minis-

All Popperfoto

the confectioner that the sweets were bitter. But it was not until June 12, 1871, that a four-year-old boy accepted a chocolate cream from his uncle, and died within half an hour of strychnine poisoning.

The result was all that Miss Edmunds could wish. The story was picked up by newspapers all over England. The confectioner's chocolates were examined, and some were found to contain strychnine. No one doubted that it was an unfortunate accident; nevertheless, it created panic.

Curiosity aroused

Meanwhile, Dr. Beard failed to call on Miss Edmunds to apologize for doing her an injustice. She wondered how she could best remind him of the "insult" he had paid her. She even went to the local police, and offered to give evidence at the inquest about her own experience of bitter chocolates. But the officers were too busy to bother with her. They were fully occupied with routine enquiries at chemist's shops. All recent purchasers of strychnine were checked; all were able to prove they had a legitimate reason for wanting it. All, that is, except a "Mrs. Woods", of Hill Side, Kingston, Surrey, who could not be traced. But since the coroner had by then recorded a verdict of accidental death on the little

boy, this hardly seemed to matter. Or it didn't until the chemist told the police that his register had been borrowed, ostensibly by the coroner. And that the date on which this had happened was *after* the inquest. Their curiosity aroused, the police examined the register more closely, and found that a page had been torn out — the page before "Mrs. Woods'" entry. A messenger had apparently called at the shop with a letter signed with the coroner's name.

Now "Mrs. Woods" came under suspicion, and it was not difficult to trace her, and to identify her as Christiana Edmunds. The police got hold of a specimen of her handwriting — which was identical with the signature of Mrs. Woods. Officers questioned hundreds of small boys, and found the ones who had bought the chocolates and returned them to the shop. Without further ado Christiana Edmunds was arrested. She was tried in January 1872, and her defence pleaded insanity — a plea which the court refused to accept. Dr. Beard's letters to her were read aloud. They seemed unnecessarily affectionate, and the doctor explained that he was convinced Miss Edmunds would lose her reason if he rebuffed her. Gossips took a less charitable view, and as a result his practice suffered. Miss Edmunds was found guilty and sentenced to death. She was reprieved, however, and ter, and shot him in the back in Whitehall, killing him. At his trial the prosecution presented witness after witness to prove that he was sane, and his chances of acquittal looked slim. But a brilliant defence saved him—and also changed the course of legal history, by establishing that a criminal who does not know the nature of his act is not guilty by reason of insanity.

In that sense, however, Christiana Edmunds was not insane. She was not suffering from delusions; she intended to kill. Obviously, there is something wrong with the M'Naghten definition of insanity. It doesn't require delusions; just a strange kind of blindness. Sanity depends on how you *react* to a chal-

lenge. The twentieth-century French novelist Marcel Proust gives a graphic example of this. Suppose you are standing in a crowded street, talking to someone about how much you hate crowds. Your companion says he quite agrees—and then pulls out a revolver and proceeds to shoot the passers-by. It is not his hatred of crowds that makes him insane: you may hate them just as much yourself. It is his *reaction* to his hatred: what he thinks permissible. Judged by this standard, most of the famous jealousy killers were at least partly insane. This certainly applies to Britain's three most notorious cases: Mrs. Pearcey, Edith Thompson, and Ruth Ellis.

The Pearcey case is now half-forgotten.

and doesn't even appear in the Notable British Trials series. Mrs. Mary Pearcey was a handsome, well-built young woman of 24, who lived in the Kentish Town area of north London. She was the mistress of two men: a Mr. Charles Creighton, who supported her, and a furniture remover called Frank Hogg. But it was Hogg with whom she was truly in love. A working man with educational and social aspirations, he had attended a Polytechnic, and had cards with his name printed on them.

Unlucky creature

He seemed to be above the slum environment in which he lived with his young wife and baby. As for his wife, Phoebe, she was an ailing, unlucky sort of creature. Hogg had married her because she was three months pregnant with his child, and ever since her marriage, Phoebe Hogg had been worried about her husband's interest in the handsome Mrs. Pearcey.

On Friday, October 24, 1890, Mrs. Pearcey invited Phoebe Hogg to her house for tea. Phoebe arrived with her baby in the pram at about half past three. She was never seen alive again. Late that evening, her body was found not far away in Crossfield Road, Hampstead, with the throat cut from ear to ear. The baby carriage, saturated with blood, was found in nearby Hamilton Terrace, St. John's Wood, and the corpse of the 18-month-old girl was discovered later on building land nearby. When reports of the murder appeared in the newspapers the next morning, Phoebe's sister-in-law Clara called on Mrs. Pearcey, and asked her to accompany her to the morgue to see the corpse. Mrs. Pearcey went, but she found the sight upsetting.

A Detective Inspector who was in the morgue considered her behaviour "very suspicious", and his men duly went to search Mrs. Pearcey's home. Mrs. Pearcey didn't openly object to this, and while the search progressed, she sat down at the piano and burst into song. The police found bloodstains all over the place; when they asked Mrs. Pearcey what she'd been doing, she went on singing: "Killing mice, killing mice, killing mice."

After that the trial was a straightforward affair. There was no doubt about Mrs. Pearcey's guilt. Neighbours testified to hearing screams coming from the

Popperfoto

HISTORIC CASE: The last woman to be hanged in Britain was Ruth Ellis (right). In the London of the 1950's, her lifestyle was judged to be both glamorous and immoral. She shot her lover (top) with a Smith & Wesson .38 revolver outside a bar in fashionable Hampstead, London. Left: the leader of a protest against her execution.

Syndication International

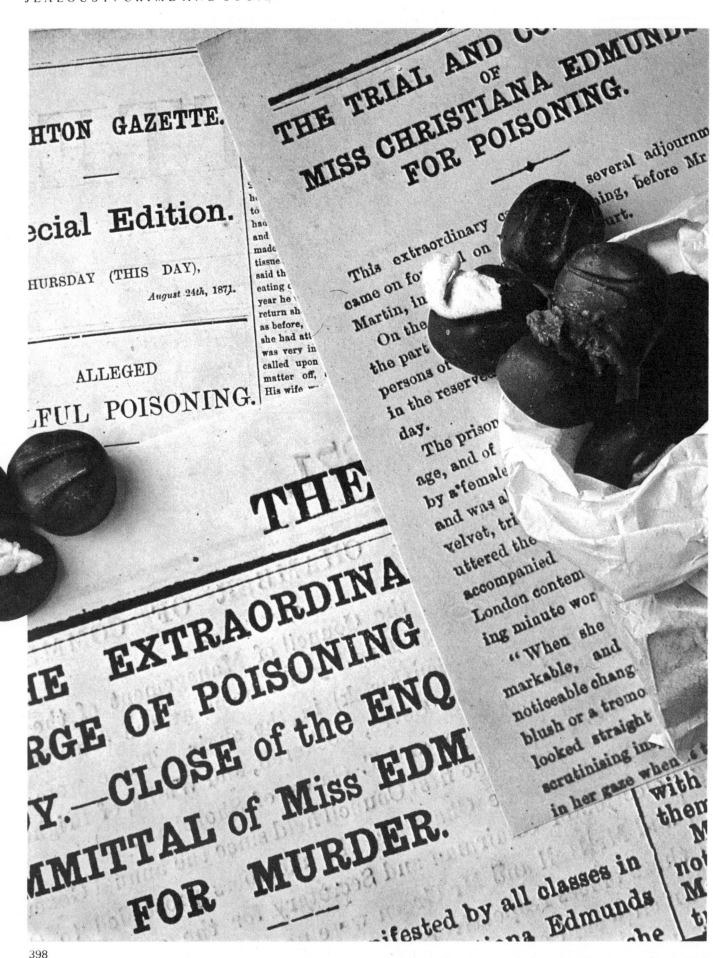

house around teatime on the Friday afternoon. The curtains had been drawn all day, Mrs. Pearcey having told a neighbour that her brother had died. Medical evidence showed that Phoebe Hogg had been knocked unconscious with three violent blows on the head before her throat was cut. Mrs. Pearcey then placed the body in the baby carriage, and put the baby on top of it—by this time, she had probably suffocated the child, although this was not definitely established. She covered both bodies with a black shawl, and then set out pushing the baby carriage past her victim's house, on towards Hampstead. In spite of the dark, several people saw her. It was early, and the streets were crowded with Friday shoppers. She dumped the body of the mother in Crossfield Road, then went on a mile to Finchley Road, where she threw out the baby, then another mile farther on to leave the baby carriage.

Curious conduct

Her curious conduct while the police were searching the house suggests that, at the time, she wanted to be thought insane. In fact, she pleaded innocence, in the face of all the facts, and maintained her innocence to the gallows. Everything about the crime, however, points to insanity. She obviously planned it—hence the story about her dead brother and the drawing of all the curtains—but there wasn't a chance in a thousand of her getting away with it. She could have smothered the unconscious Phoebe; instead she cut her throat, so drenching the house with blood. Then, instead of waiting until midnight, when the streets would be quiet, she walked along the busy Prince of Wales Road, where she was immediately recognized by several acquaintances. Mrs. Pearcey, however, was not insane within the meaning of the M'Naghten rules; there were no delusions. Yet she was so obsessed by the thought of Frank Hogg that she couldn't think straight. Under the circumstances, to describe her as sane is merely a quibble.

Emotional fantasy

Neither Edith Thompson nor Ruth Ellis were quite so obviously obsessional. Both lived in a strange, twilight world of emotional fantasy. The defenders of Edith Thompson say that the whole scheme for killing her husband was pure make-believe, and that even the great pathologist, Sir Bernard Spilsbury, agreed that her story of administering powdered glass ("big pieces, too") was absurd.

CHOCOLATES, tea and strychnine were served to begin an extraordinary chapter of crime for Christiana Edmunds, a waspish virgin insane with jealous love. Her bizarre murder-plan was unique.

THE RESPECTABLE seaside resort of Brighton was favoured by the retired middle classes in Victorian times. Here in West Street was the fatal sweetshop. The child victim lodged in the arrowed house.

This is probably true; but her letters reveal that it was she who first thought up the notion that her husband should die, and she who kept urging her lover, Frederick Bywaters, to kill him. On the other hand, her distress when it actually happened was obviously real: the frenzied cry of "Don't, oh don't!", and her sobs as she rushed to find help. It is the completely self-contradictory nature of her impulses that suggests she was caught in the same emotional whirlpool as Christiana Edmunds and Mrs. Pearcey. As for Bywaters, he was half-insane with jealousy when he stabbed Percy Thompson—convinced that the woman he loved was being virtually raped by her sex-hungry husband. Like Thompson himself, he was a victim of Edith's strange fantasies.

On the surface of it, the Ruth Ellis case seems a classic *crime passionel*. Ellis, a 28-year-old, shot her ex-lover David Blakely outside the Magdala public house in Hampstead, North London, in April 1955. She was incensed, so she claimed, by the fact that he was having an affair with another woman. On closer examination her "motive" ceases to make sense. Although Ruth Ellis and David Blakely had been passionate, if quarrelsome, lovers for two years, both had slept with other people. At the time she killed Blakely, Ruth Ellis was living with one man, sleeping with another, and married to a third. Clive Gunnell of England's Westward Television, who was with Blakely when he was shot, has stated that Ruth Ellis—who had had a miscarriage two weeks before committing the murder—was basically a kind of exhibitionist: "She wanted to be famous." Or notorious. It begins to sound altogether more like the "exhibitionism" of Neil Cream and Christiana Edmunds.

A British jury found Ruth Ellis guilty, and, despite a widespread public outcry, she was hanged—the last woman to die on the gallows in England. The 1951 case of Pauline Dubuisson, which has many similar features, reveals the altogether more flexible attitude of the French. In France, the penalty for a *crime passionel* may be as little as a few months in prison; the penalty for capital murder is death. When 24-year-old Pauline Dubuisson's former lover was found shot through the head in his Paris apartment, it certainly seemed to be a *crime passionel*. Pauline had turned on the gas tap and lay unconscious by the stove. Closer investigation revealed that she had bought the gun weeks before, and had made several threats against medical student Felix Bailly's life. This made it a capital murder charge.

Pauline Dubuisson proved to be a tempestuous character. Her diary revealed such a lurid sex life that the police described it as her "orgy book". During the war she had been the mistress of a German colonel and held nude orgies with soldiers; after the liberation of France indignant neighbours had shaved her head. She was undoubtedly a nymphomaniac, sleeping with as many men as possible and recording their lovemaking techniques. She had an affair with Bailly which ended when he went to study in Paris. In any case, he was tormented by jealousy at her infidelities. In Paris, he became engaged to a less volatile girl. Pauline heard about it, and went to see him in Paris; she later claimed they again became lovers for a while. Then Felix told her their relationship was finally over. This was the point at which she bought the revolver, and announced her intention of shooting him. She found him in his apartment early one morning, and shot him in the back of the neck.

Lasting sentiment

The French jury decided that, whatever the motive was, it was not straightforward jealousy. Pauline was too emotionally mixed up for that. But neither was it an ordinary premeditated murder. The jurors therefore compromised, and found her guilty of non-capital murder, which involved life imprisonment. In France, Ruth Ellis would have received the same benefit of the doubt. For jealousy—described by Shakespeare as the "green-eyed monster"—can sometimes be as strong, if not stronger, than the love it so frequently accompanies. "I can't really love him because I'm not jealous of him," women sometimes say. Pauline Dubuisson took this a stage further when she stated, "I wanted to force myself to love other people, in order to persuade myself I was capable of having lasting sentiment for Felix."

The subject is as complex, dark, and contradictory as the workings of the human mind itself. But to the seventeenth-century French aristocrat and moralist, La Rochefoucauld, there was no mystery about jealousy at all. He summed up and dismissed the emotion in his famous book of *Maxims,* when he wrote: "In jealousy there is more self-love than love."

MURDER HOUSE: A woman's throat was cut, and her baby murdered, behind carefully-drawn curtains in this house. The murderess then placed both bodies in the baby's pram, covered them with a shawl, and wheeled them through the streets before dumping them. Not long after the murders, Priory Street was tactfully re-named Ivor Street. It was later completely redecorated.

THE ALIBIS

They come in all shapes and sizes: iron-clad, watertight . . . and dangerous. Like the alibi concocted for sex killer Raymond Morris by his trusting wife, "to save him trouble"—and to free him for more fiendish attacks on children.

CHRISTINE
DID YOU SEE HER HERE ON SAT. AUG. 19? IF SO TELL THE POLICE
Evening Mail

Syndication International, UPI

A CASE that would have taxed the ingenuity of Sherlock Holmes took place in Montana in September 1901. The body of an old man named Dotson was found in his cabin, near Helmsville, with a bullet in the heart. On the opposite wall, a gun had been rigged up in a wooden frame, with the muzzle pointing at the dead man. A string ran from the dead man's hand, through a metal ring in the wall, to the trigger of the gun. It looked like a clear case of suicide. A note beside the body seemed to confirm this. It read: "It warnt my son Clint done that Cullinane murder. Clint lide to save me. I done it." It was signed Oliver Dotson, and friends verified that it was in his handwriting.

The "Cullinane murder" had taken place on August 5, 1899. A prospector named Gene Cullinane had been found shot dead in his cabin, not far from Dotson's place. A few days later, sheriff's officers arrested Clint Dotson, and two other men named Oliver Benson and Ellis Persinger. Benson and Persinger admitted robbing Gene Cullinane, but alleged that it was Clint Dotson who had shot the prospector twice in the heart. Benson and Persinger were sentenced to ten years in prison; Clint Dotson received life.

Now it looked as if Dotson might have been innocent after all. He had what amounted to a double alibi. He was behind bars at the time of his father's death, so there could be no question that he might have forced his father to sign a false confession. Old man Dotson seemed to be offering his son a kind of posthumous alibi for the time of the murder . . .

A strange problem

Undersheriff John Robinson, the man who had sent Clint Dotson to jail, went to interview Persinger and Benson. Were they quite sure it was Clint who had killed the prospector? They insisted they were absolutely certain; they had *seen* him do it. That left the undersheriff with a strange problem. Why had the old man confessed to a crime he did not commit? He was certainly an alcoholic; but had never been weak in the head.

He checked with the prison governor at Deer Lodge jail, where Dotson was serving his sentence, and learned that one of Dotson's closest friends, a robber named Jim Fleming, had been released from prison only a few weeks earlier. Sheriff Robinson decided he had to talk to Fleming. But first he adopted one of Sherlock Holmes's favourite expedients, and put on the worst fitting clothes he could find.

Then he made his way to the distant ranch, fifty miles from Helena, where Fleming's girlfriend lived. He introduced himself as an ex-convict from Deer Lodge, and explained that he was looking for his old friend Jim Fleming. The girl believed him. She told him that Fleming would be back in a few days, and invited him to have a cup of coffee. They had a friendly talk, and soon she mentioned a matter of $50,000 that Clint Dotson had got when he robbed Union Pacific. It seemed that she was expecting a share of the money.

This is what Sheriff Robinson wanted to know. Now he had his motive for murder. He rode back to Helena, and made intensive inquiries to find out if Jim Fleming had been seen with old man Dotson at any time; soon he found what he wanted – someone who had seen them together just before the old man's death. Robinson went back to the ranch, lay in wait for Jim Fleming, and arrested him.

Incredible viciousness

The sheriff had nothing to go on but guesses; nevertheless, he played his suspect as a skilful angler plays a big fish. He told him that he had been talking to Clint Dotson in jail. He spoke as if he knew all about the Union Pacific robbery. "Clint didn't do that stick-up. He didn't have anything to do with it. There ain't no fifty thousand dollars." And then he hinted casually that he knew Fleming had been drinking with old man Dotson just before his death. He knew because Clint had told him . . . Suddenly, Fleming saw himself surrounded by pitfalls of treachery. So when Robinson said: "Would you like to make a statement?" Fleming said: "Yes, I sure would." The story he told revealed such incredible viciousness that even the veteran sheriff was shocked.

Clint Dotson had deliberately planned the murder of his own father, in order to clear himself of the murder of Gene Cullinane. With promises of a share of the $50,000 he had persuaded Fleming to go to the old man's cabin, and get him drunk. When the old man was drunk, it was easy to persuade him to do anything; that was how Fleming had got the note. The old man did it "for a joke". Later, when Oliver Dotson was stupefied with the raw whiskey, Fleming shot him through the heart, and rigged up the shotgun to make it look like an accident.

Fleming was hanged on September 6, 1902, Dotson in April 1904; and the double-alibi murder has come to rank as one of the strangest cases in modern criminal history. Yet if you had asked Clint Dotson if he had an alibi for the murder of Gene Cullinane, he would not have known what you were talking about. It is only in recent years, since the rise of the detective story and the TV thriller, that the word has passed into the language.

The Latin word "alibi" actually means "elsewhere", so it is incorrect to say: "The prisoner has an alibi"; it should be "The prisoner *was* alibi". Oddly enough, it is only in the past fifty years or so that the criminal has given serious thought to the problem of alibis. In less sophisticated days, he committed his murder, and then did his best to be elsewhere when the crime was discovered. The modern criminal has discovered the advantage of persuading the police that he was already "alibi" at the time the crime was committed.

On the whole, most of these attempts have been fairly crude. In *The Three Musketeers*, D'Artagnan puts back the clock half an hour, then draws the attention of his regimental commander to it, to establish that he could not possibly have been present at a certain fight. Real-life alibis have sometimes been as obvious – and absurd. George Joseph Smith, the "Brides in the Bath" murderer, moved into rooms in Highgate, London, on December 17, 1914, accompanied by his new wife, a clergyman's daughter named Margaret Lofty.

The following day, the landlady heard sounds of splashing coming from the bathroom, and hands slapping the sides of the bath – then silence. This was broken by the sound of the organ playing in the sitting room; John Lloyd – alias George Smith – was establishing his alibi. A few minutes later, the front door slammed loudly; then he came back saying "I've brought some tomatoes for Mrs. Lloyd's supper". At this point, the landlady noticed water leaking through the ceiling. Lloyd rushed upstairs, burst into the bathroom, and shouted: "My wife can't speak to me – go for a doctor." Predictably, "Mrs. Lloyd" was drowned.

BATH MURDERER George Smith drowned Bessie Mundy (right) in their Herne Bay home. He also killed Alice Burnham (centre) and Margaret Lofty (top) before learning the hard way that a poor alibi can be worse than none at all. One who got away: Alice Reavil (above).

Both John Frost

But Smith might well have got away with it, if a newspaper report of the death had not been seen by a relative of one of Smith's previous victims. And when George Smith finally appeared in court, and the story of that evening was told by the prosecutor, Sir Archibald Bodkin, the killer found out that a poor alibi is worse than no alibi at all. . . .

Far more brilliant and elaborate alibis than George Smith's have proved just as ineffective. The classic American case —with all those features so dear to the heart of the lover of detective stories—

took place just one year after the execution of the "Brides in the Bath" killer. Frederick Small was an unsuccessful grocer of Portland, Maine, whose matrimonial affairs were pursued by misfortune.

His first wife died in childbirth; his second wife ran off with the president of a baseball team. Small was granted $10,000 damages. In 1911, when he was approaching the age of 45, Small married a third time, Florence Arlene Curry, a girl nearly 15 years his junior. The marriage was not happy; Small seems to have been a coarse and bullying man,

who often beat his wife.

In 1914, Small decided that it was time to retire; they moved to a cottage near Mountainview, New Hampshire. It was on the edge of Lake Ossipee, and Small spent much of his time fishing. The Smalls were not poor, but neither were they as well off as the husband thought they deserved to be. In early 1916, he insured his wife's life for $20,000, and his cottage for a further $3000. The outlay—$1000 or so—was large, for Small's total fortune was less than $5000. But he had plans for re-couping his losses.

Popperfoto

403

The man who had sold him the life insurance was Edwin Conner, who was also principal of the local school. Unlike most of the residents of Mountainview, Conner seemed to find Small pleasant enough, and Small went out of his way to be nice to Conner. They even agreed to take a trip to Boston together, partly to look into some further insurance business, but mainly for pleasure.

On the morning of September 28, 1916, Small phoned his friend and asked him if he could make the Boston trip that day. This was short notice; Conner said it would be difficult. Small insisted. Finally, Conner said he would see what he could do. At two o'clock, a local wagon driver named Kennett was asked if he would collect Small at three-thirty, in time for the four o'clock train to Boston. Kennett deliberately arrived early, because on previous occasions Small had invited him in for a tot of rye whiskey. But this time he found Small all ready, waiting on the back porch. Small opened the door, shouted "Goodbye" to his wife, and they drove off.

Everyone was sympathetic

The two men took the afternoon train, arriving in Boston at eight. There they checked into a hotel, and went to see a play; afterwards they ate supper, and returned to the hotel. The desk clerk was waiting with a message for Small. There had been a fire back at Mountainview, and he was to ring the local hotel. A few minutes later a distraught Frederick Small asked Conner to take the phone and confirm the message. His house was in flames, said the hotel keeper, and he had better hire a car and return immediately; Small's grief seemed enormous and genuine. Everyone was sympathetic.

Back home, as the dawn was rising over the lake, Small viewed the smouldering ashes of his cottage. In a choking voice, he asked the local doctor if someone could search the ruins for his wife's body. An hour later, the doctor rang Small at the hotel. "We've found the body. What do you want us to do with it?" For a moment, Small was nonplussed; then he asked with amazement: "You mean there's enough to be buried?"

There was indeed. For the body had collapsed through the floor of the sitting-room, into the basement, and there were several inches of water in the basement. Mrs. Small still had a cord knotted tightly around her throat. She had a bullet wound in the skull, and the head had been bludgeoned.

Frederick Small was promptly placed under arrest. He insisted that his wife had been alive when he left the house, and asked Mr. Kennett to verify that she had come out on the back porch to say goodbye. The wagon driver replied that,

as far as he could recollect, Small had called goodbye, but there had been no reply. The police found other evidence to indicate that the murder had been carefully planned. In the wreckage there was an alarm clock with wires and spark plugs attached to it. There could be no doubt that it was a timing device.

Small had been too clever. In order to make sure that his wife's body was completely consumed, he used a quantity of a substance known as thermite, a powder made of aluminium filings, metallic oxides and magnesium. It is used in welding, because it produces such an intense heat. The heat was intended to incinerate Mrs. Small's corpse; instead, it burned a hole in the floor, and the corpse fell into the water in the basement.

The evidence suggests that Small killed his wife accidentally, or in a fit of rage. Various witnesses described his violent temper. It is just possible that he might have escaped the gallows with a plea of second degree murder; as it was, he was hanged on January 15, 1918.

It is an interesting question whether Small's ingenuity inspired another fire murder in 1933. On October 25 of that year, Richard Budde, a middle-aged lumberjack of Eagle River, Wisconsin, arrived home from work at six in the evening, and found the doors all locked. As he shouted his wife's name, neighbours came over to see what was the matter. They forced their way in, and immediately smelled smoke; there had been a fire in the bedroom closet — a large wooden cupboard. It had burned through the floor, and the closet door had fallen through into the basement. So had the body of Virginia Budde, which had also been in the closet.

The door was unlocked

This was a baffling problem for Sheriff Thomas McGregor. Why had Mrs. Budde shut herself in the closet and set fire to it? Or was it possible that she had been *put* in there and set alight? On the other hand, the key was still in the lock of the closet door — on the outside — and the door was unlocked. The theory of the coroner was that Mrs. Budde, who had recently been ill, had gone into the closet and committed suicide by setting herself on fire. Burning oneself to death is, oddly enough, a fairly common form of suicide.

Budde had a watertight alibi. He had left for work at eight in the morning — neighbours not only heard him calling goodbye to his wife, but also something about bringing a loaf and some sausages home with him. The local fire chief estimated that the fire must have started about two in the afternoon. *If* Budde had killed his wife, he must have returned home to do so. That was just possible — he worked alone in the woods. But a check on the

amount of wood he had chopped revealed that he had done an exceptionally hard day's work; there would have been no time to rush home and kill his wife — a process that would have taken two hours. Besides, the neighbours would most certainly have seen him.

The pathologist's report seemed to establish Budde's innocence beyond all doubt. Presence of smoke in the lungs proved that Mrs. Budde had been alive when she entered the closet. The fact that the door was unlocked seemed to clinch it. If she had been alive and conscious, she would have simply walked out. The coroner's jury saw no reason to doubt Budde's innocence. His wife's death brought him no advantage; she had not been insured, and there was no rumour of another woman. It was true that the Buddes often fought, but that was nothing unusual. A verdict of death through causes unknown was returned.

At which point — as in the Small case — fate took a hand. The coroner, P. J. Gaffney, was sitting alone in his office after the inquest, with various items of evidence on his desk — Mrs. Budde's half-burnt shoes, fragments of clothing, and the lock from the closet door. By some chance, the lock fell off the desk.

Startled, Gaffney jumped up and picked it up. He noticed that the fall had made the lock spring out. He dropped it again. The lock went back. He tried it several times. Through some peculiar fault, each impact caused it to either lock or unlock. He sat down again, and began to think deeply. This didn't prove anything, of course. But if the closet door, complete with lock had fallen through into the base-

THE BEST-LAID ALIBI — a fire —
went wrong when Frederick Small set
off too hot a flame. It burned through
the cottage floor, allowing the bludgeoned
body of his wife Florence to fall into
the basement . . . and eventual discovery.

All Boston Globe

ment, shouldn't it have been *locked* when it was found? The fact that it was unlocked suggested that it had been locked before it fell.

But if Budde had put his wife in the closet, how had he set fire to her six hours after he left for work? There was no evidence of a timing device. The coroner was a painstaking man. He bought wood, and constructed a closet of exactly the same size and design as the one in which Mrs. Budde had died. He lined it with a flame-resistant material of the same kind that had lined Budde's closet. He allowed the same quarter inch air gap at the bottom of the door. He filled it with old clothes, set them alight, and closed the door. The fire that began at eight in the morning took more than twelve hours to burn through the floor. The fire chief had made a mistake. Richard Budde *could* have started the fire before he left for work.

With this much evidence, Gaffney decided on an autopsy. It confirmed all his suspicions: strychnine was found in Mrs. Budde's stomach. It had been a murder of atrocious cruelty. Budde had given his wife the poison — a large dose, enough to make her unconscious after considerable suffering. Then he had placed her in the cupboard, set fire to her, and then left her to suffocate. There was not enough of the body left to allow the coroner to estimate time of death.

Budde was tried, but there was one thing that the coroner had not been able to establish: a motive. The jury decided that Mrs. Budde could have taken the strychnine herself. They acquitted Budde, who proceeded to drink himself to death. A few months later, in a fit of delirium tremens, he also took poison, in the bedroom where his wife had died. He left a note confessing to the murder. There were many people in Eagle River who

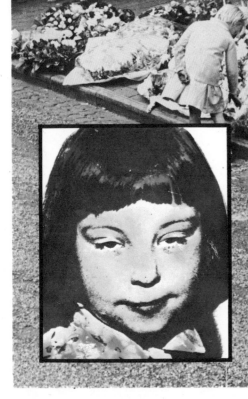

said that it was his wife's ghost who drove him to kill himself. Gaffney was not entirely sceptical. He always claimed that the lock had been in the middle of his desk.

In the long run, the most effective alibis are probably the simplest. Perhaps the most effective method of all is to get someone else to provide it: preferably a wife, who cannot give evidence against her husband in court. Raymond Morris, the English sex murderer, persuaded seven-year-old Christine Darby to get into his car on August 19, 1967; her naked and misused body was found in nearby woods near Cannock Chase, Staffordshire. Morris was among those questioned by the police, because his car fitted the description of the murderer's car.

Morris's wife told the police that her husband had been at home at the time the murder was committed. She had no suspicion he was the killer; she only wanted

HIS WIFE'S ALIBI almost enabled Raymond Morris to kill again. A year later, police caught him trying to re-enact the sex murder of Christine Darby (inset) with a new victim. (Left: Nicholas Baldry, 10, saw Morris abducting Christine.)

to "save him trouble". In the following year, Morris tried to drag a ten-year-old girl into his car; a woman noted the number, and he was arrested; his wife's well-meant loyalty almost led to another murder.

This whole matter of alibis has undoubtedly been exaggerated by the rise of the detective story. Could *you* remember what you were doing on the evening of August 10 last year? Of course not. Neither could I. Fortunately, most criminals are too stupid to realize that nothing makes a detective so suspicious as a "watertight alibi".

All Syndication, International

RAPE

Dean Corll's house (below) in Pasadena was stocked with elaborate torture tools (inset). He was a vicious, homosexual rapist who slew his victims. . . .

AP, UPI/Quartet

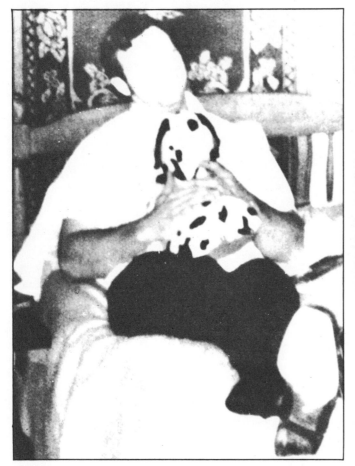

AP and UPI

IF A list was made of the most notorious murderers in criminal history, there would be very few rapists among them. This statement may seem incredible: what about Christie, what about the Boston Strangler, what about Werner Boost, what about Joseph Vacher, the French Ripper? But having named these, even the memory of the criminologist begins to run short of examples. Of course there have been thousands of rapists; but most of them are commonplace criminals whose names are difficult to recall.

A large proportion of the sex killers whose names everyone can recall were not rapists: Jack the Ripper, Neville Heath, the American-born Peter Manuel. Even the man who probably ranks as the most notorious sex killer of all time, Peter Kürten, "the Monster of Düsseldorf", seldom performed the act of rape on his victims; he derived his sexual pleasure from the stabbing or throttling.

This underlines the basic point about sex murderers. When a man is prepared to kill for sex, he is already so abnormal that the ordinary sex act hardly interests him. Most men think they can understand the psychology of the sex killer; but they are wrong. He is not just an oversexed man who has been carried away by desire; he is a person whose desires could not be satisfied by the normal sexual impulse.

The ordinary rapist is a different mat-

CLUTCHING a stuffed dog, Dean Corll (left), the homosexual mass killer, is all smiles. Seventeen-year-old Elmer Henley (right) finally shot him dead.

ter. The United States has over 100,000 rapes every year—which means that about one woman in every thousand can expect to be raped. In Britain, the comparable figure would be about one in ten thousand. But most rapists are not violent. In his book on sex offenders, *The Twisting Lane*, the British writer and sociologist Tony Parker cites a typical case—that of Andrew Brown, a garbage collector in his mid-thirties.

Knock at the door

Brown had no record of previous sexual offences when, one summer in the late 1960's, he committed ten rapes or attempted rapes during a period of four weeks. They were all within 15 miles of his home. In one case—that may be taken as typical—he knocked on a front door and asked the woman who answered some question. She said she couldn't help him, and closed the door. He went round to the back door and into the house, looking for something to steal. The woman was in a bedroom. She told him he could take her jewellery, but he ordered her to lie on the bed.

"You're not going to rape me, are

you?" she asked. "I said I didn't know, because I didn't," Brown reports. She tried to talk him out of it, but after ten minutes gave way. "I had an intercourse with her and then I went. She was crying a bit." In only one case did the girl resist violently, then Brown ran away. He was caught one day after his workmates had been discussing the case, and Brown told them the newspaper reports were exaggerated; one of the men went to the police. Brown was identified and sentenced to life imprisonment.

Paul de River's classic study, *The Sexual Criminal*, makes it clear that the general pattern in the United States is similar. De River quotes a multiple rapist: "Well, I went by this girl's window, or not window, it was a walk, and her shade was up and I saw her and I just went into the building and went into her room. Then I showed her the knife and I told her to keep quiet and lay down. She laid down and I don't remember whether she took her lower underclothes off or not, or whether I helped her . . . Then I had intercourse with her. One thing, I told her to keep her mouth shut, then I left . . ."

What emerges clearly from these and other similar case reports is that the rapist is often in a somewhat confused, indefinite frame of mind. There is no need to disbelieve Andrew Brown when he says: "I said I didn't know (if I was going to rape her) because I didn't." De River describes another sexual offender who was apparently impotent and incapable of having an erection. He explained that he started to rob automobiles because he wanted money.

"The first people I held up I got an idea that it would be nice to undress them so there would be no chance they would follow me . . . When I undressed the first girl I got excited and I started to pet and love her. I tried to assault her but I couldn't get it in . . ."

He claims that this girl—like others—became so excited by his petting that she began to enjoy it. Whereupon the unsuccessful rapist ordered her male companion to have intercourse with her. "It exhilarates me to see that." Later the same evening, he held up another couple, and again petted the girl. He explained: "I wanted to do something for them, and she got hot and I tried to give her relief. I took no money from them."

Horrific case

So the original motive of robbery was forgotten. This kind of confusion seems typical of many rapists. So does the rather apologetic tone, and the slightly prudish wording: ". . . she took her lower underclothes off". In crime fiction, the rapist is usually a hard-eyed monster driven by inhuman lust; in reality, such men are exceptions. Most rapists, like Andrew Brown, are not sure whether they intend to go through with it or not; it often depends upon the attitude of the woman. She may talk him out of it, or frighten him away by resisting, or give in.

But in our present age of violent sex, rape is not restricted to savage and lustful attacks upon women. The most horrific American criminal case of 1973 was undoubtedly that of Dean Corll, the 33-year-old homosexual murderer of Houston, Texas. When he was finally shot dead by a 17-year-old accomplice, Elmer Henley, Corll had tortured and murdered around 30 young men.

Corll's method was to invite the youths —usually hitchhikers—to his house for a party, wait until they passed out (from liquor or drugs), then tie them to a "torture board". He often tortured and raped his victims for days before killing them. From the details that have been made public it is immediately clear that this was no straightforward case of a "sex maniac".

This was some kind of insane ego-assertion, bound up with a deep-rooted immaturity. (One photograph shows Corll cuddling a toy dog.) Compared with Corll, the rape murders of John Christie, the sex killer of London's Notting Hill, are easy to understand.

However, the criminals who make the headlines are usually untypical of the majority of murderers. Jack the Ripper, Neill Cream, and George Chapman were all multiple killers of women, who committed their crimes towards the turn of the century; but they were untypical: the age of the sex criminal still lay a quarter of a century in the future. Again, the crime of Leopold and Loeb—who battered to death a young boy to prove they were "supermen"—was completely untypical of its period—1924; but it is thoroughly typical of our own period.

It is always the strange criminals, the "outsiders", who fill the case history books and set the pattern for the future—while the majority of criminals commit the crimes that *are* representative of the age. So although the most notorious criminals of our own time are egomaniacs, driven by a passion for self-assertion, it is still rape and other forms of sexual offence that dominate the crime statistics.

This explains why so many of the worst sex criminals of the past few decades have *not* been rapists. The Scottish killer Peter Manuel was executed in 1958 for eight murders. Six of these were women. The body of 17-year-old Ann Knielands was without knickers; but she had not been raped. Another 17-year-old schoolgirl, Isobel Cooke, was strangled and stripped almost naked—but not raped.

In a house in East Kilbride, Manuel shot three women—Margaret Brown, her sister Mrs. Watt, and her daughter Vivienne. Mrs. Watt's nightdress was around her waist, and the pyjama trousers of the other two women had been pulled off—but there was no rape. Manuel himself was an egoist who, in the middle of his trial, insisted on conducting his own defence, convinced that he was cleverer than any mere lawyer.

Seduction

Again, in July 1966, sailor Richard Speck entered a hostel for student nurses in East 100 Street, Chicago, tied up nine of them, and then took them into the next room one by one and murdered eight of the nine. (One escaped by hiding under a bed.) None of the girls had been raped. Speck and Manuel were completely unlike the prototype rapist—bemused and slightly apologetic. A few months after the Speck murders, 18-year-old Robert Smith, a college student, walked into a beauty parlour in Mesa, Arizona, forced seven people to lie on the floor, then shot them all in the back of the head.

He explained: "I wanted to get known —to get myself a name." It is the same impulse that can be sensed in the personalities of Manuel and Speck that means that they cannot be classified as sex criminals.

But all this leaves one interesting question unexplored: the psychology of the genuine sex criminal—as distinguished from the apologetic rapist and self-esteem killer. The real sex killer falls somewhere between the two. He differs from the average rapist in being violent and ruthless, and often possesses a touch of sadism. His intelligence ranges from very low to normal—but not above.

An intelligent man does not commit violent rape, no matter how powerful his desires. If he possesses any vitality or charm, he goes in for seduction—which carries no legal penalty. If he lacks both these romantic "musts", then he may release his frustrations with prostitutes, or perhaps with pornography. The majority of sex killers are men who are psychologically inadequate.

The simplest way to illustrate this is through case histories. In the United States, the era of sex crime that followed World War I may be said to have begun with Earle Nelson, the so-called "Gorilla Murderer", who terrorized the North American continent for almost two years. Nelson undoubtedly belongs to the type of the physical degenerate, as his photographs show. Nine months after his birth (in 1897), his 20-year-old mother died of a venereal disease contracted from his father. At the age of ten, he was knocked down by a street car, which made a hole in his head; he was unconscious for six days. For the rest of his life he suffered from pains and acute headaches. In 1918, he was charged with a sexual assault on a child, and sent to a lunatic asylum.

Prospective lodger

Nelson's criminal history was continued in February 1926 when a young man called on his aunt, Miss Clara Newman, in San Francisco; she owned a large house and let rooms, mostly to male lodgers. Unable to locate her, he pushed open the lavatory door—and found the naked body of the 60-year-old woman, the eyes wide open, propped on the seat. Medical examination revealed that she had been violently beaten and assaulted before being killed. (In that sense, Nelson was not a "normal" rapist; there was a sadistic element in most of his crimes.) The "To Let" card, which had disappeared from the front window, suggested that her murderer had been a prospective lodger.

A week later, on March 2, it became clear that the killer-rapist found his victims by knocking on the doors of houses with "Room to Let" signs. Mrs. Laura Beale, aged 60, of San José, was found strangled and violated under circumstances strikingly similar to those of the previous murder. Alarm spread throughout the Bay area; the newspapers began to refer to the killer as "The Dark Stranger" or "The Phantom".

EGOMANIAC Peter Manuel, who slew eight women, sketched the self-portrait (above) two months before his arrest.

Popperfoto

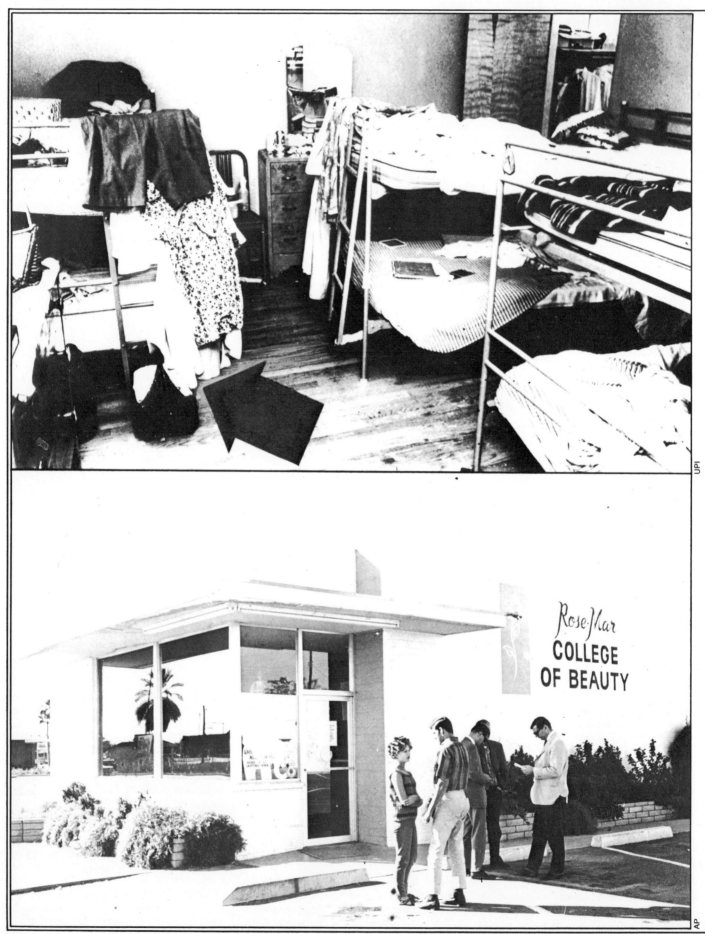

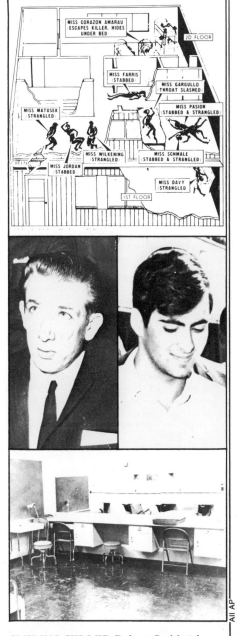

All AP

SCAR-FACED sailor Richard Speck (below centre left) attacked nine student nurses at South Chicago Hospital in July 1966. Seven of them were stabbed and strangled, while another had her throat slashed. Only one, Corazon Amarau, escaped by rolling under her bunk (left arrowed). Later, she helped to identify Speck, who was found in a Chicago skid row hotel with self-inflicted wounds.

SMILING KILLER Robert Smith (above centre right) ordered four women and a child to lie on the floor of Rose Mar Beauty College, Arizona (above and left), then shot them. He told police, "I want to get known". Earle Nelson (right) ranged from Kansas City to Winnipeg, raping and slaying 22 women, before his arrest. He was the notorious "Gorilla Murderer". Nelson was executed in 1928.

His next victim was Mrs. Lilian St. Mary, 63, of San Francisco; her naked and brutally violated body was found under a bed in her rooming house. It seemed obvious that the killer knocked on the door, asked to see the advertised room, made sure he was alone in the house with his victim, then raped and strangled her. The strength and ferocity of the killings led some newspapers to dub him "The Gorilla Murderer".

The method seemed to be foolproof. Before the end of 1926, the number of victims had risen to 15—among them an eight-month-old baby, who was throttled with a piece of rag after his mother, 28-year-old Germania Harpin, had been raped and strangled. In October, Nelson increased his pace and committed three murders on three consecutive days. The only description of the killer came from some old ladies who rented a room to him in South Portland; they said he seemed a polite, pleasant young man. His gallantry included selling them some jewellery stolen from one of the victims.

By the time the police interviewed his "customers", the killer had moved eastwards, first to Iowa, then Kansas City. In April, he killed a 60-year-old woman in Philadelphia, then moved from Buffalo to Detroit, and on to Chicago—bringing his death roll to 20. Then Nelson made his big mistake; he travelled north into

Winnipeg Free Press

411

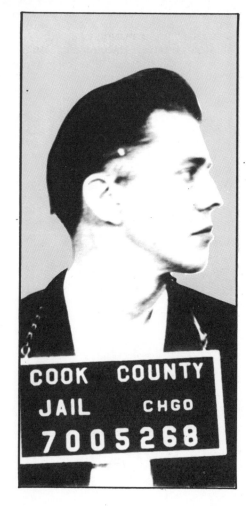

COOK COUNTY
JAIL CHGO
7005268

Canada. In Winnipeg, he found a job as a builder's labourer and a room. Again his landlady found him quiet and likeable; he told her he was highly religious.

The next day, when Nelson had gone out—apparently to work—a 14-year-old girl, Lola Cowan, was reported to be missing. In the afternoon, a man named Patterson returned home and was puzzled by his wife's absence. Late that evening, kneeling down to pray, he found her violated body under the bed. Not long after this, Lola Cowan's body was discovered beneath a bed in the house where Nelson had taken a room; she had been treated so sadistically that the police refused to reveal the details.

These were Nelson's last murders. A few days afterwards he was arrested—having been recognized by a shopkeeper from his description given in the newspapers. He managed to escape from jail by picking the lock; but 12 hours later he was caught. Nelson was tried for his two **Winnipeg** murders, and hanged on January 13, 1928, despite his pleas of insanity and innocence.

Nelson—the killer who hid corpses under beds—was mentally subnormal. The subnormality had the effect of removing the inhibitions that held his sex urge in check. Sexually speaking, Nelson may not have been more "lustful" than most healthy men in their twenties—almost any dominant young male would be happy to spend his life sleeping with a

different girl every night. A judge in an American rape case made the penetrating comment that nature has provided man with a sexual urge that is far stronger than it needs to be for the mere propagation of the species. Possibly civilization is to blame; animals living close to nature are altogether less interested in sex. Nelson is an example of what happens when a man with a powerful libido feels he has nothing to lose.

Against this, there are numerous cases in which a reasonably intelligent man has decided that he can "get away with it", and committed a series of rapes. In Peoria, Illinois, in 1934, a young man named Gerald Thompson made a habit of driving around until he saw a girl walking alone. He then knocked her unconscious and raped her in the back of his car—taking photographs of his victim naked. He silenced the girls by warning them that the photographs would be sent to their friends if they laid any complaints. His career as a rapist was highly successful until he killed Mildred Hallmark—probably because she knew his identity. Skilful detective work then led to his arrest, and officers found a large collection of photographs in his room. He was executed in 1935—before which more than 50 women had come forward in response to a police appeal for previous victims of the Peoria rapist.

Thompson, an after-dark motorist, operated at night; a more recent rapist,

YELLOW automobile rapist James Juricic thought that his forays in search of victims was a worthwhile risk. He got a life sentence.

James Juricic, drove about openly by daylight. He lived alone in a house outside Western Springs, near Chicago—his wife preferred to live in Alabama. He owned a conspicuous large yellow car, and the first of his rapes in the Chicago area took place on April 4, 1970, when he pulled up alongside a 15-year-old girl on her way home from an evening class.

Calculated risk

She was ordered into the car at gunpoint and made to lie on the floor, face down. Later they drove into a garage, and the doors closed electronically. The man blindfolded her and led her into a bedroom. There she was made to strip item by item, and the man raped her. He was recording the "love sounds" they made on tape—and she thought there was an automatic camera rigged up, filming the scene. He then made her dress, and drove her back to the place where he had picked her up; he removed the blindfold and speeded away. After this, there were a series of rapes—in one case, two teenage girls were kidnapped at once. (The rapist told the second one that she was his 56th victim.)

It was clear to the police that the perpetrator must live within a certain area, since the car journeys were usually brief. One victim was able to supply the first five digits of the car licence number; others helped construct an identikit picture. In May 1970, a patrolling police car noticed a yellow vehicle weaving in and out of the traffic—which is an offence; an officer in the police vehicle checked, and found that the first five numbers corresponded with those of the rapist's licence plate, James Juricic, a 38-year-old research worker at Boeing, was arrested. Victims identified him, and he was sentenced to life imprisonment. The interesting point to note here is that Juricic was not a moronic pervert, like Nelson—but an intelligent man who calculated the risk involved in his weekly rapes.

The conditions in our civilization produce the sexual tensions that can lead to rape; so the chance of any steep reduction in the rate of sex crime seems at present unlikely. On the other hand, the increase has been less steep in recent years than in the late 1960s. Even more significantly, there has been a sharp decrease in the rate of sex crime in Denmark since pornography was legalized. This could indicate that, as society becomes more permissive, the unhealthy forces that produce such offences will find release through other channels.

Although Britain and the United States have both experienced a sharp reaction against "permissiveness" in recent years, the general attitudes are still immeasurably healthier than they were 50 or 100 years ago. In which case, there is reason to hope that the time will come when rape is again as rare as it was in the days of the *Newgate Calendar*.

TRIANGLE
OF DEATH

Caught up in the demands of his own perverted
passions, Ivan Poderjay (below) went from one
bigamous relationship to another until
he was finally led to murder.
Freud was fascinated . . .

THERE is one matter on which the professional criminologist and the general public simply do not see eye to eye: the so-called "eternal triangle". For the criminologist, most such cases are elementary, if not downright boring. But the general public has a voracious and apparently limitless appetite for them. And who is to say who is right? The "triangle" murder may be of small psychological interest; but it often contains great drama.

Though it is rare for such a case to appeal equally to both public and criminologist, the murder of Agnes Tufverson achieved this unusual distinction. Her killers were described by Freud as one of the most remarkable examples of sexual perversion he had ever encountered.

"Captain" Ivan Poderjay was not, in fact, a Captain; nor was he, as he declared, a member of Yugoslav Army Intelligence. He was a confidence trickster and professional lady-killer – in every sense of the word.

Born into a poor Serbian family in 1899, Poderjay started his career as a fortune teller in Belgrade, then joined – and quickly deserted – the French Foreign Legion. In 1926, he was cited as co-respondent in a divorce case by a high government official; he subsequently married the ex-wife, got possession of her fortune, and vanished.

Up to the age of 33, Poderjay continued to live off seduction. He was short, plump and losing his hair; but he also had that essential quality of the professional Casanova, the ability to make a woman feel that she was the most fascinating person in the world. He was heartless; but at least his victims escaped with their lives, until, in 1931, he met Marguerite Suzanne Ferrand, a Frenchwoman with a firm mouth and schoolmistressy face.

Jackbooted feet

She was a research assistant in the British Museum. As soon as their eyes met, each knew they had found something they had been looking for all their lives, for the 37-year-old Marguerite enjoyed chastizing men; and Ivan enjoyed being chastized. After crouching naked at her jackbooted feet, Ivan realized that he had found the ideal sexual playmate, a woman whose fantasies were as bizarre as his own.

This was another case of a "catalytic" relationship. If they had never met,

BELTED BIGAMIST . . . Poderjay (below centre) is charged in New York with the least important of his numerous crimes.

Marguerite and Ivan might have pursued their ways harmlessly for the rest of their lives. But together, they entered into a combination as deadly as fire and gunpowder. Marguerite was not shocked to find that Ivan was a confidence man who lived off women; on the contrary, the thought of causing pain to other women caused her deep pleasure. In March, 1932, they were married in London – although Ivan was, in fact, already married to several other "wives".

One year later, in the lounge of a cross-channel ferry, Ivan noticed an attractive woman of about 40 – Agnes Tufverson. She was well-dressed, and she looked distinctly sick. Ivan introduced himself as a Captain in the Yugoslav Army, and advised her to get some air on the deck, where he mentioned casually that he was a millionaire and an inventor.

In subsequent weeks, in London, they saw a lot of one another, and Ivan spent a great deal of money on her – well over £500. But this was not a source of concern to him, for he had persuaded Agnes to allow him to invest $5000 of her money . . .

Back in New York, Agnes returned to her job as an executive at the Electric Bond and Share Company, and she confided to her best friend that she was to

—Bilderarchiv—

AP

Vanished into thin air ... Poderjay's explanation for the disappearance of Agnes Tufverson. Inset shows Marguerite Ferrand, tyrannical sadist.

escorted this trunk to the docks himself, and insisted on staying with it until it was in his cabin on the *Olympic*. He had booked this cabin a week before—a single passage—with instructions that he must have a cabin above the waterline.

No one ever saw Agnes Tufverson again. Some months later, her family began to institute enquiries. These led to the arrest of Ivan and Marguerite Poderjay by the Vienna police, who were astonished to discover that their apartment was filled with instruments of torture and flogging. The police called in Sigmund Freud—the world's most famous psychoanalyst.

Lesbian affair

Freud found the Poderjays fascinating. Marguerite alleged that her true "personality" was a tyrannical sadist named Count John, although she also had two subsidiary female "personalities". Poderjay in turn was psychically "controlled" by a female called Ita, who was the mistress of Count John, and who was having a lesbian affair with one of Marguerite's female personalities; he was also controlled by another two "spirit" girls who were tortured by Count John.

Poderjay admitted that Agnes had not sailed on the *Hamburg*; he told the police she had run off with another man, on the spur of the moment. Her luggage had arrived in Poderjay's flat in Vienna and was still there. The New York police had no doubts whatever as to what had happened to Agnes. On the day he bought the trunk, Poderjay· had also bought 800 razor blades—explaining that they were cheaper in America. He had also bought large quantities of cold cream.

Once on board the *Olympic*, he had spent several days in his cabin. During that time, the police believed, he had carefully shaved the flesh from Agnes's bones until she was only a skeleton. The flesh had fed the fish who follow every liner. The skeleton, greased with cold cream, had also slipped out of the porthole.

Poetic justice

There was no body, and circumstantial evidence was not strong enough to hang Ivan Poderjay. Instead, he was sentenced to five years in prison for bigamy. While he was serving his time, an angry fellow convict, outraged by some bizarre proposition, beat Poderjay so badly that he lost his left eye and eight teeth. It sounds like poetic justice until we reflect that he probably enjoyed it. He returned to Marguerite, moved to Belgrade, and presumably continued to live a multiple

marry a romantic Yugoslav millionaire.

A week later, she received a cable from her· "millionaire", declaring that he had a marvellous opportunity to invest another $5000 for her, and asking her to wire the money. She decided against it, for she wanted Ivan to come and get her, and that is precisely what he did.

In November 1933, Poderjay arrived at her New York apartment with a huge bunch of flowers, and on December 4 they were married. Ivan explained that it was hardly worth cabling his bankers to send money from London; they would

be returning to London in a couple of weeks. In the meantime, they could live on Agnes's money; Agnes agreed.

On December 20 Agnes and Poderjay prepared to leave New York. But instead of sailing as arranged on the *Hamburg,* they returned to their apartment late that night. The next day, Poderjay told the daily help that his wife had decided to sail on ahead, and that he was following her immediately. Their luggage had gone ahead on the *Hamburg*—all except one huge trunk, which had been delivered to the apartment the day before. Poderjay

sex life with Count John and his harem.

This is surely one of the clearest cases in all psychological literature of the "catalyst effect"—that is, of two people, who would be harmless alone, inspiring one another to commit murder. Parallel cases—Snyder and Gray, Bywaters and Thompson, Brady and Hindley, Fernandez and Beck—have been discussed in connection with crimes of dominance.

This is only one type of catalyst effect; there is another, equally familiar to criminologists, that is also fraught with explosive possibilities. In this situation, the murderer and the "catalyst" do not become partners in crime; the "catalyst" inspires the crime, but takes no part in it. This happens when the "catalyst" has a particularly yielding and gentle nature, inspiring a frenzy of desire and protectiveness that may explode into violence.

Violent man

It is illustrated perfectly in the relationship between Cesare Borgia and his sister Lucretia. Lucretia, with her gentle face and weak mouth, was a born "victim"; it was inevitable that she should become her brother's mistress. But from then on, Cesare could not bear the thought of any other man possessing her; one suitor saved his life by fleeing; another became her husband, and was murdered on Cesare's orders.

Borgia was, of course, a "violent man" in A. E. Von Vogt's sense—a man who would rather commit murder than ever admit that he was in the wrong. On the other hand, Crippen, who was also driven to murder by a "gentle catalyst", was basically a non-violent man. His wife Cora was dominant, and Crippen accepted her as "the boss". His typist, Ethel Le Neve, was completely undominant: gentle, yielding, faithful; half a century after the murder, she told crime-researcher Pat Pitman that she was still in love with Crippen. In her company, Crippen felt like a superman. The result: the murder of Mrs. Crippen, and Crippen's execution in November 1910.

Eyeing a sparrow

The case of Dr. Philip Cross bears some basic resemblances to that of Crippen. A retired army doctor, 62 years of age, he lived comfortably with his wife and six children at Shandy Hall, near Dripsey, Co. Cork. His wife was 22 years his junior; they had been married 18 years, and it had been, on the whole, a satisfactory marriage. In October 1886, Mrs. Laura Cross engaged a new governess for the children, a 20-year-old girl

HE DOUBLECROSSED young Effie Skinner (above) who was unaware that he had poisoned his wife. But the doctor (right) was blinded by his lust for her.

named Effie Skinner. Effie, like Ethel Le Neve, was the catalyst type: not particularly pretty, but with something soft and yielding about her. As soon as he saw her, the military, rather forbidding Dr. Cross felt like a hawk eyeing a sparrow. For the first time, he realized that his marriage had been merely satisfactory, never ecstatic. It had never provided him with any real outlet for his male dominance.

One day, as Effie stood talking to him about the children, he bent and kissed her. He was afraid she would tell his wife or leave immediately. But she stayed, and his desire to possess her increased. His wife noticed it, and she took what seemed to her the sensible course: she sacked Effie. The girl was shattered, she went to Dublin, and when Dr. Cross visited her there, she finally gave herself to him. Possession did not cool his desire; he wanted to be married to her, living in comfort in Shandy Hall.

Early in May, 1887, Mrs. Cross began to suffer attacks of vomiting. Her husband told her she had a weak heart. She died on June 1st, and was buried three days later. Less than two weeks after this, he married Effie Skinner in London. At first, he decided that they had better keep the marriage a secret and live separately, but when he got back to Dripsey, he discovered the news had preceded him.

There seemed no point keeping Effie in London, so he moved her to Shandy Hall. Inevitably, there was gossip, and the police finally decided to act. Laura Cross was exhumed, and the coroner found 3·2 grains of arsenic in her body, as well as strychnine. There was no trace of heart disease.

State of shock

The police were also able to trace the firm from whom Dr. Cross had bought arsenic "for sheep dipping". Tried at the Munster Assizes in Cork, he was found guilty on December 18, 1887, and hanged in the following January. Effie was so shocked by the realization that she had been the cause of the murder that she refused to see him in the condemned cell, and Cross's hair turned white overnight.

Of more recent cases involving the "innocent catalyst", the one with some of the most dramatic features is certainly that of Armand Rohart, mayor of Peuplinges, near Calais. In the early hours of May 24, 1967, the mayor of Escalles, near Peuplinges, was awakened by the sound of a motor horn. He found Armand Rohart, one of the district's richest men, collapsed over the wheel of his car.

MILLIONAIRE Armand Rohart (right) is placed under arrest as a result of the tape-recorded evidence supplied by ex-legionnaire, Jacob Kerbahay.

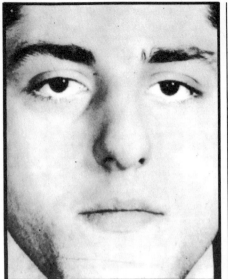

Rohart seemed to be in a state of shock, and was taken to the Lille hospital. Back at Rohart's farm, his brother Jules mentioned that Rohart and his wife Jacqueline had gone off to the beach for a swim that afternoon, and had not been back since.

A search of the beach revealed Jacqueline's body, dressed in a pink bikini and covered in seaweed. Rohart's story—when he regained consciousness—was that he and Jacqueline—who was 45—had waded into the sea up to their necks, holding hands, when a great wave had swept them away. Neither could swim. Rohart had struggled ashore, lost consciousness, and wakened after dark on the empty beach . . .

Dairy maids

Why had a middle-aged man and woman decided to go swimming on a chilly May day? Rohart was quite frank with the police. A few years before, he had had a love affair with the 14-year-old nurse of his children, Odile Wissocq, and she had borne him a child. He had sent the girl back to her parents, and ever since then had been trying to make his wife forget his lapse. They had decided to go to the beach because it was on just such a day, many years earlier, that they had made love by the sea . . .

The story sounded convincing. Certainly, Rohart's grief at the funeral seemed genuine. But the post mortem demonstrated that Jacqueline Rohart had not died of drowning; she had no water in her lungs. Further research into Rohart's background revealed that Odile Wissocq had not been his only lapse. For many years, the rich farmer had exercised a kind of *droit de seigneur* on dairy maids and farm girls. But the affair with Odile had been different. She was the sweet, yielding type, and it was not true that Rohart had broken off with her. They had been seen lying together on a blanket

HOT-BLOODED passions were in play in the DiFede murder case. Both Armando Cossentino and Dr. Joseph DiFede (left and right) had voracious sexual appetites.

It was Armando's jealousy of DiFede's marital rights over wife Jean (centre) that led to the brutal murder. Police (below) remove the shattered corpse.

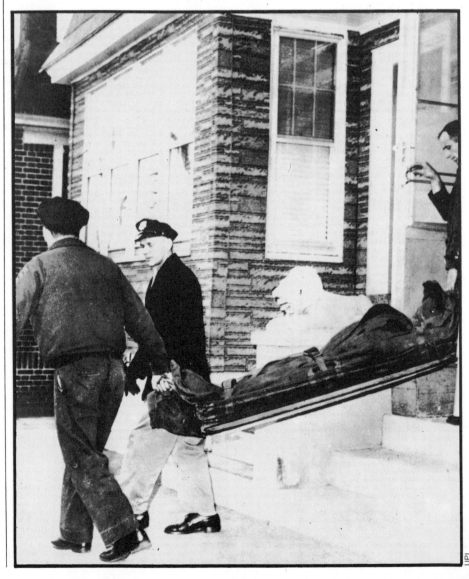

AP

long after she had returned to her parents. But recently, Odile had talked of marrying a younger man; she was a girl who needed a protector, and her status as a mistress was wearing on her nerves.

There was still no reason to charge Rohart with murder. Then, on June 14, an ex-legionnaire named Jacob Kerbahay walked into the local police station with a tape recorder, and played the police a conversation in which Rohart asked him to murder Jacqueline. Kerbahay, who lived in a cottage on Rohart's land, said that Rohart had raised the matter with him earlier. At that point, Rohart's plan was to hide a needle covered with *curare* —the alkaloid used by pygmies on their darts—in her car seat, so it would penetrate her skin as she sat down; she would crash and perhaps break her neck . . .

Perfect plan

Kerbahay didn't like or trust Rohart, so when Rohart called on him again, he decided to tape the conversation for his own protection. Rohart noticed that the tape recorder was turning, but Kerbahay told him he was recording music from the radio, and played it back to prove it— switching to another track.

On Kerbahay's evidence, Rohart was arrested, and the police quickly uncovered the corroborative evidence they needed. On the day before her death, Jacqueline Rohart had been to the hairdresser, and had her hair set in a new style. The fixative would have been washed off if she had been in the sea for any length of time. The body was exhumed, and it was discovered that the fixative was still in place.

Her bloodstream contained a large amount of alcohol, although she normally did not drink, and two weeks after the tragedy two bottles were washed up on the beach, one containing sleeping tablets, the other, traces of ether. Rohart's "per-

DRAMATIC MOMENT captured by the camera: Jean DiFede and lover Armando Cossentino wince in anguish and open desperation as the murder charge is read.

fect murder" plan now became clear.

He had persuaded her to drink heavily, to celebrate their sentimental excursion to the beach. He had anaesthetized her with ether, then carried her body into the sea to drown her. She had woken up and fought him—he had shown the police scratches on his chest, which, he alleged, were made when Jacqueline tried to cling to him.

He had beaten her unconscious, dragged her ashore, and suffocated her with a car blanket or cushion. She had been dead when he took her back into the sea to "drown" her, so no water went into her lungs. Finally, the police discovered that Rohart had insured his wife's life for a million francs—£100,000—not long before the murder. Their case was complete. Rohart was sentenced to life imprisonment.

Terribly injured

When a love triangle is complicated by violent Latin tempers, the result is almost inevitably violence. When Dr. Joseph DiFede was found murdered—apparently by a burglar—on December 7, 1961, the New York police sensed that this crime was less straightforward than it looked. The sobbing widow, 35-year-old Jean DiFede, told how she had been awakened by noises coming from her husband's bedroom. She had looked in, and found him dying, terribly injured.

It was the violence of the murder that troubled the police; someone had hit DiFede with a hammer, knocking out one of his eyes, then stabbed him again and again, covering the room with blood. This was surely no burglar, but someone who *hated* DiFede.

It seemed that there might be many people who felt like that. 38-year-old DiFede was not only a highly successful doctor; he was also an incredible lover, who made no secret of his voracious sexual appetite. His temper was so violent that his wife never dared to object; on one occasion he had been heard to boast that he had 15 mistresses.

In the course of a thorough investigation of DiFede's patients, the police interviewed two Italian youths who lived nearby; one of them had only a temporary visa. What puzzled the police was that although neither of them had regular jobs, they lived in a comfortable apartment, and one of them, 19-year-old Armando Cossentino, ran an expensive car.

Eventually, investigation revealed that while the fiery Dr. DiFede was out with other women, Armando was comforting his plump, long-suffering wife, and clearly, she was his source of income.

The two youths were subjected to long interrogation. Armando, the stronger character, insisted he knew nothing; but his friend finally broke down, and told how he and Armando had gone to the doctor's house to murder him. Armando was only 19, but he was as hot-tempered and strong-willed as Dr. DiFede, and he felt it was time Jean was freed from her husband's domination.

Cossentino was sentenced to death, later commuted to life imprisonment. Jean DiFede, accused of being an accessory— the actual charge was manslaughter—was also sentenced to life imprisonment.

Cases like these lead to a strange but inevitable conclusion: where a "love triangle" is concerned, it is a mistake to speak of the "psychology of the murderer". What is at issue is the *group* psychology of three people. And as absurd as this sounds, the ultimate responsibility for the murder lies with all three—including the victim.

DEADLY DOCTORS

Rapid advances in medicine made doctors powerful and respected men in the nineteenth century . . . but some used their high social position to gratify their lust and greed, like Doctor Deschamps (inset, below) whose misuse of twelve-year-old Juliette Deitsch horrified New Orleans.

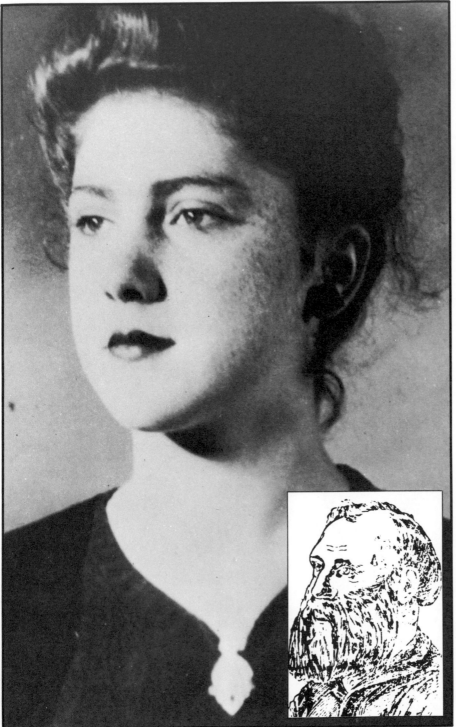

Courtesy of New Orleans Public Library

THE nine-year-old girl was sobbing so violently that her father could not understand a word she said. He shook her impatiently: "Where is Juliette?" The girl controlled herself for a moment. "She's asleep, and the doctor says he's going to die." The father, Jules Deitsch, rushed through the streets to the house where Doctor Etienne Deschamps was lodging. The door of his room was locked. Deitsch ran to the police station, and begged the police to help him break in. "I think my twelve-year-old daughter is in there." She was. When the police entered the room, Juliette was lying naked, on the bed. Beside her, also naked, lay a great hairy man with a beard. Blood was streaming from wounds in his chest, but he was still alive. The little girl was dead.

It was the beginning of one of the most sensational murder trials in the history of New Orleans. For when the body of Juliette Deitsch was examined, it was discovered that she was no longer a virgin, and that she had been carnally abused in other ways. There were even love bites on her body. And, as the evidence made clear, this had not happened just once, but dozens of times over the course of six months or so. Dr. Deschamps was obviously the worst kind of pervert.

How had the respectable carpenter, Jules Deitsch, come to allow his daughter to fall into the hands of the monster? Deitsch had met Dr. Deschamps in 1888, when Deschamps had told him that he was an adept in the occult. He possessed hypnotic powers, and he intended to use them to discover the lost treasure of the pirate Jean Lafitte. All he needed, he said, was the help of a pure young girl to act as a medium.

Deitsch was so impressed by the fifty-year-old doctor that he had no hesitation in entrusting Juliette to his care—in fact, both his daughters—for Juliette's young sister Laurence was fascinated by the doctor, and didn't want to be left out.

Later, Laurence described the "experiments". Juliette would be told to undress and to climb into bed. She was an unusually well developed child for her age, although she had not yet reached puberty. The doctor would also undress, and climb in beside her. He would soak a clean handkerchief in chloroform, and place it over her face.

The doctor always made them promise not to tell their father what had happened. So things had continued until that afternoon of January 30, 1889, when Deschamps had suddenly begun to sob in French: "My God, what have I done?" Then Laurence, who was terrified, was told to run home and tell her father that the doctor was going to die. But the doctor did not die. The stab wounds he inflicted on his chest were too superficial to endanger his life.

It was obvious to everybody that Juliette's death was accidental—to everybody, at least, but the prosecutor. He alleged that Deschamps had deliberately killed the girl because he knew that his sexual abuses would soon be discovered. This was obviously absurd, since killing her was the sure way to discovery. On the other hand, Deschamps was more cunning and calculating than he tried to make out. The police found letters in his room, written by Juliette and signed "Your love forever", and "your little mistress".

Covering his tracks

Juliette, however, was a backward child, and could not have composed them. Deschamps had written them, and got her to copy them out, so that he could claim she had been willing to be seduced. But if she was willing, why chloroform her, as he had on every occasion? Besides, the letters also mentioned a jeweller in the neighbourhood called Charlie, and implied that he had been the man who had originally taken Juliette's virginity. But "Charlie" was proved to be innocent. Again, Deschamps was covering his tracks. Why should he, argued the prosecutor, unless he meant to kill her?

The Deschamps case—which ended with the doctor being hanged—gained nationwide coverage in the American press. This was not simply because of the sensational nature of the crime; it was because Deschamps was a doctor. It is a curious fact of criminal history that doctors who commit murder excite more interest than almost any other type of criminal. The usual explanation for this is that doctors are supposed to save life, not take it. But that supposes that the public are more interested in morality than they actually are. The true explanation is that the doctor is a symbol of middle-class respectability.

In earlier centuries, people felt the same morbid interest in priests who committed crimes—hence the excitement aroused by the trial of Father Urbain Grandier, burned alive in 1634 on a charge of having seduced and bewitched a convent full of nuns.

The great age of medicine was the nineteenth century. It was also the great age of the medical murderer. Yet the company of killers had one distinguished predecessor of the eighteenth century: Dr. Levi Weil, whose strange story helps to explain why the medical murderer was such a latecomer on the criminal scene. Dr. Weil, a Dutch Jew, came to London from Holland in the 1760's—the London of Dr. Johnson, the actor David Garrick and the statesman Edmund Burke.

London then was full of disease, and most doctors were constantly busy. But this Jewish doctor with a foreign accent encountered a certain amount of prejudice, and his practice remained small.

Brother's gang

One day, a merchant asked Weil if he would travel out to Enfield, outside London, to attend to his sister—the regular doctor was ill. Weil drove to the village, attended the old lady—with some success—and then ate supper with her brother, who paid him in cash.

All the way home Weil thought about the house full of money and jewellery and determined to take some of it for himself. In the City, he said goodbye to the merchant—and promptly made his way back to Enfield. When he finally reached home at daylight, he was exhausted, but some £90 richer—more money than he had made in months.

Ironically, Weil's practice began to improve as his income from burglary soared to £500 a month. He kept his surgery open, knowing it was his best disguise. He entered the houses of wealthy patients, "cased the joint", and passed on the information to a gang run by his brother. On one occasion, he heard that an old caretaker who lived near St. Paul's Cathedral had his life's savings hidden in the room.

Other burglars had already broken in, but although they had prised up every floorboard and ripped plaster off the walls, they had been unable to locate the money. Weil was called to the old man's bedside when he was ill. He tried to persuade the caretaker to go into hospital; the

TO SATISFY his lust for the good life Dr. Castaing (centre) poisoned Auguste Ballet (right) after the strange death of his brother Hippolyte (left).

Culver

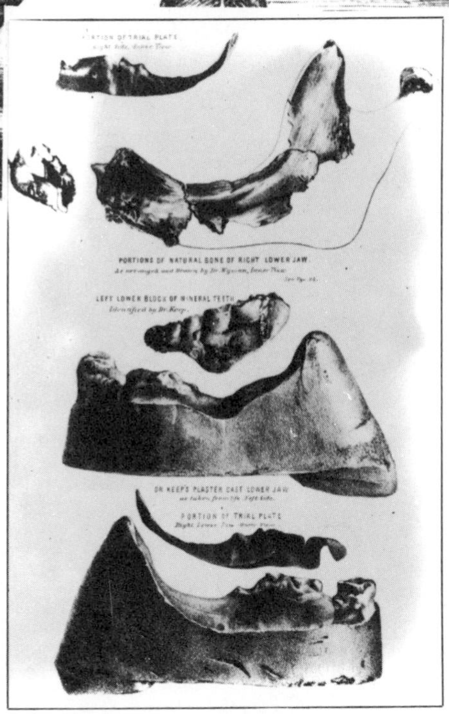

FEARING exposure, Webster clubbed his friend to death (top), but bones found in his medical furnace (above) gave him away.

vehemence with which the idea was rejected convinced Weil that the money was hidden in his room.

The floor and the walls had been explored – so it had to be the ceiling. A great beam crossed the room. Weil examined it when the caretaker was asleep, and found a cavity. Two nights later, as the old man slept heavily from one of the doctor's sedatives, Asher Weil and an accomplice took nearly £3000 from the hiding-place in the beam. The old man never discovered the robbery. He died a few days later. This may have been Weil's first murder.

By then, the gang had swelled to eight. One of the members, a German Jew named Isaacs, tried to conceal more than his share of the booty, and was dismissed. That was Weil's first mistake. Not long after, he made his second.

In the autumn of 1771, the gang – including Weil himself – waited until after dark in the vicinity of a house in Chelsea Fields – in those days, Chelsea was a village outside London. When all the lights were out, they knocked loudly.

The servant who opened the door was overpowered. The lady of the house, a Mrs. Hutchings, fought strenuously, but was tied with her petticoats over her head. In the upper part of the house, the gang burst into a bedroom, and two servants who had been asleep started up, alarmed. One was knocked out; the other, as he struggled, was shot with a pistol. After that, the gang fled with their loot.

Unfortunately for them, the servant, John Slow, died. Now the authorities decided to offer a reward for the gang, and Isaacs, the man who had been dismissed, saw his opportunity for revenge.

He knew that if he turned King's Evidence, he would be safe. Weil was planning his most ambitious robbery so far – of a diamond merchant expecting a consignment of £40,000 worth of jewels – when he was placed under arrest by the Bow Street runners. Six of the gang were tried; two were acquitted for

lack of evidence – a proof that, even in those days, justice was impartial. But Weil and his brother were among those executed at Tyburn on December 9, 1771.

The next notable name in the roll of medical infamy is that of Dr. Edmé Castaing of Paris. At the age of 27, Dr. Castaing enjoyed the good life, and did not look forward to the lifetime of drudgery of a general practitioner. One of his patients was a wealthy man named Hippolyte Ballet, who had tuberculosis. Castaing became friendly with Hippolyte's younger brother Auguste, and learned that the brothers were on bad terms – so bad that Hippolyte had excluded his brother from his will. One evening, as they drank together, Auguste hinted that Castaing might hasten his brother's death, and gain possession of the will.

So, on October 22, 1822, Hippolyte quite suddenly died, to the astonishment of other doctors who had occasionally attended him. A month later, Castaing paid off all his debts, and lent his mother 300,000 francs. The following year, on June 2, Castaing and Auguste Ballet went for a drive in the country, and stopped at a hotel in St. Cloud, where they ate and drank. Then Auguste was suddenly taken ill, and soon died, attended by his friend Castaing and two other doctors. The other G.P.s recognized the signs of morphine poisoning, and they discovered that, even after Ballet had started to vomit, Castaing had gone to

425

a local chemist and bought more morphine. When it was discovered that Ballet had made a will in Castaing's favour, the doctor was arrested.

Castaing was relying on the fact that morphine was very difficult to detect. And he was proved to be right. Although the doctors agreed that Auguste Ballet had shown all the signs of morphine poisoning—vomiting, diarrhoea, heavy breathing, contraction of the pupils—no trace of morphine could be detected in his stomach. The prosecutor asked indignantly if all murderers who used morphine should be allowed to go free, just because medical science was unable to detect its presence. That swung the jury. Castaing was sentenced to death, and executed in December 1823, protesting his innocence.

The next medical murder of any note took place in the peaceful environment of Harvard University, in Cambridge, Massachusetts, more than a quarter of a century later. Like so many medical murderers, Professor John Webster, aged 56, was given to living beyond his means. He frequently borrowed money from a wealthy friend, Dr. George Parkman. But Parkman ceased to be friendly when he learned that Webster's famous mineral collection, which Webster had pledged to him as security for a loan, had also been pledged to another creditor. The angry Parkman threatened exposure. On November 23, 1849, Parkman failed to return home for lunch, and the river was dredged in case he had drowned.

In fact, Parkman had called on Webster in his laboratory, and as he turned to go out, Webster had struck him such a tremendous blow on the back of the head —with a piece of wood—that he died.

AN AFFAIR with a 15-year-old led Pritchard (opposite) to kill his wife and her mother (left and right). He was betrayed by the anonymous letter (below). Opposite, left, the house where he seduced and murdered is now flats.

Later on, Webster alleged that Parkman had been so insulting that he had hit him in a blind rage; but all the evidence indicates a cool head and careful planning. Later the same day, he told an agent who collected his lecture fees that he had repaid Parkman. And that night, behind locked doors, he proceeded to dismember the body and to burn it in his medical furnace.

Two days after Parkman's disappearance, Webster called on his family, and told them that he had repaid Parkman a few hours before his disappearance. Surely this proved that Parkman had been killed by a robber who had concealed the body . . . ? Unfortunately for Webster, the caretaker at the medical school, Littlefield, detested him. Littlefield wondered why the doctor worked all night in his laboratory, and kept his furnace burning all the time. Whenever Webster left the laboratory, he took care to double-lock the door; but Littlefield had a plan. The furnace was built against a wall, and there was a passageway on the other side. With his wife standing guard, Littlefield broke through the wall with a crowbar, shone his torch through—and saw a bone which he recognized as a human pelvis.

At his trial, which lasted eleven days —and got national press coverage— Webster pleaded not guilty. He contended that the bones in the furnace were not Parkman's at all—just the remains of a body they had been using for dissection. But a dentist positively identified the false teeth as Parkman's, and Webster's defence collapsed. Before he was hanged, in August 1850, he confessed to killing Parkman "in a fit of rage".

Weak characters

The murder of Parkman was the beginning of what might be called the great age of medical murderers. It lasted for about a hundred years—from approximately 1855, the year in which Dr. William Palmer of Rugely poisoned his racetrack associate John Cook, to 1954, when Dr. Sam Sheppard of Ohio was found guilty of murdering his wife. Studying the killers, an interesting point emerges. A great majority of the medical murderers were weak characters, given to lying or boasting, and to living beyond their means. And this implies that many of them were drawn to the medical profession to satisfy vanity—the self-esteem urge.

This was perhaps most obvious in the case of the Glasgow poisoner, Dr. Edward William Pritchard. In photographs, he looks a typical Victorian *paterfamilias,* with his frock coat and bushy beard, surrounded by a respectable-looking family. In fact, he was an utterly weak character, a joke among his colleagues because of his incredible boasting and lying. He claimed to be a friend of the Italian patriot

Glasgow March 18th 1865

Sir

Dr Pritchards' Mother in law died suddenly and unexpectedly about three weeks ago in his house in Sauchiehall Street Glasgow under circumstances at least very suspicious His wife died to-day also suddenly and unexpectedly and under circumstances equally suspicious. We think it right to draw your attention to the above as the proper person to take action in the matter and see justice done.

To Hunt Esqr

Yours &
Amor Justitiae

Culver

Guiseppe Garibaldi, although they had certainly never met.

A typical narcissist, he was fond of presenting people with photographs of himself—he even handed one to a stranger he met on the train. He gave lectures—mostly invented—in which he described himself as an intrepid traveller and hunter. He also regarded himself as a great lover, and seduced servant girls and anyone else who would have him. In 1863, when he was 38, a fire broke out in the room of the servant girl in his house; she was found dead, and it seemed clear that she had made no attempt to leave her bed during the fire. Pritchard was widely suspected, but he nevertheless won a claim from an insurance company.

In 1864, he made another servant girl

THE MOST AMBITIOUS of all . . . seven relatives had to die before Hyde (top) could inherit the Swope fortune through his wife Frances (above).

—aged 15—pregnant, but performed an abortion. And it may have been desire to marry her that led him to start poisoning his wife Mary, to whom he had been married for nearly twenty years. In November, 1864, she became ill, vomiting and dizzy. A doctor called in by Pritchard suspected she was being poisoned, and wrote to Mary Pritchard's brother, suggesting she should be moved into hospital. The result was that Mary Pritchard's mother, Mrs. Taylor, decided to come and nurse her daughter. Soon, Mrs. Taylor was suffering from the same

symptoms. She died on February 24, 1865, and Mrs. Pritchard followed her a month later.

Pritchard provided both death certificates, stating that Mrs. Taylor died of apoplexy, and his wife of gastric fever. Someone wrote an anonymous letter to the police, and Pritchard was arrested. When the bodies were exhumed, both were found to be saturated with antimony, which Pritchard was proved to have bought.

Since the 1880s, England has produced her fair quota of medical murderers, while America has produced many more.

Test tube diseases

There was Dr. Milton Bowers, of San Francisco, who almost certainly poisoned three of his wives, but who succeeded in persuading a jury to acquit him in 1888, and lived happily (with another wife) until 1905.

Most ambitious of all was Dr. Clarke Hyde, of Kansas City, who decided in 1909 to poison no less than seven relatives who stood between him and the fortune of Thomas Swope, the millionaire founder of Kansas City. Hyde was married to Swope's niece Frances. In October that year, Swope and his financial adviser James Hunton died—apparently from natural causes. Shortly afterwards, Hyde procured several test tubes of diphtheria and typhoid germs, claiming he intended to take up the study of bacteriology. Five assorted brothers- and sisters-in-law then fell ill, and Hyde told them it was typhoid fever. Chrisman Swope died after Hyde administered a capsule, and other members of the family showed symptoms of typhoid fever.

When Hyde left on a trip to New York, all the patients improved considerably—which confirmed the suspicion of the nurses that the doctor was responsible for their illness. Hyde then made a curious mistake; walking along a lamplit street, he took something out of his pocket, and stamped it into the snow. One of the brothers-in-law saw him, and investigated; he picked up a broken capsule, and recognized the odour as potassium cyanide. The body of old Thomas Swope was exhumed, and cyanide and strychnine were found in it. Hyde was tried and found guilty; but he had money enough to appeal to a whole series of higher courts. In 1917 he was freed.

Since the trial of Sam Sheppard in 1954, there have been no more medical murders in the United States—or, if there have been, they have gone undiscovered. Nowadays, when there is almost no poison or drug that cannot be detected even in the smallest quantities, it looks as if the great epoch of the medical murderer—who mostly killed out of greed and for gain—is over.

THE HUMAN BEASTS

The man who gave his name to the guillotine was only trying to be humane. Yet no method of killing strikes quite the terror into man's mind as death by beheading. Is it the finality of this fate that freezes fear icy-hard? Or does the thought of meeting out decapitation unlock the most raw animal spirit of the inner beast? Was Freud right in his brutally blunt analysis of human behaviour? Was this the key to Eliott Ness's greatest case?

NESS FREUD

GUILLOTIN

Mary Evans. The Plain Dealer. Cleveland

René Dazy

AS THE Duke of Monmouth was about to kneel and place his head on the block, he held out his hand to the notorious executioner, Jack Ketch. "Here are six guineas for you. Pray do your business well. Don't serve me as you served Lord Russell."

He had reason to be nervous. When Ketch had beheaded Lord William Russell — for his part in the Rye House Plot to kidnap Charles II — he had completely bungled the job. After several violent swipes with the axe, Russell was still twitching, and his neck was unsevered. Monmouth, now being executed for his rebellion against James II, was understandably anxious to die less bloodily.

He turned to a servant, and handed him a purse containing more guineas. "Give him that if he does his work well." Then he felt the edge of the axe, and said, sighing: "I fear it is not sharp enough." Ketch was unnerved by all this coolness. He raised the axe, then threw it down, shouting: "I can't do it." The sheriff had to threaten him with dire penalties before he could be persuaded to make another attempt.

The crowd gave a groan

Looking pale and ill, he raised the axe above his head, and brought it down. The crowd gave a groan, and Monmouth jerked with agony; but his head stayed on his shoulders. Now thoroughly demoralized, Ketch made three more attempts, but there was no strength in the blows. The neck was only lacerated. Finally, he threw down the hatchet, pulled out a knife, and sawed the head off. The servant holding the purse pocketed it and walked away. Meanwhile, the crowd booed and threw things.

It was no sinecure, being an executioner in those days. Ketch usually hanged his clients; but he wasn't very good at that either, and most of the condemned men died by slow strangulation. It was preferable, however, to being butchered with a blunt axe, and even when the headman *was* efficient, it was tiring work. In 1746, Jack Thrift had to behead two Jacobite rebels, Lord Kilmarnock and Lord Balmerino. He severed Kilmarnock's head with one clean blow, but it took him three swings of the axe to decapitate Balmerino. There were many officers of the law who felt that somebody ought to devise a swift and infallible method for taking a man's life.

Half a century later, it became an urgent necessity. France rebelled against its rulers. The Bastille was stormed, and its defenders massacred, the king fled and was recaptured: the Terror began. The enemies of the new regime had to be killed by the hundred — by the thousand. How could it be done? The solution was found by a gentle, kindly man, well-

known for his good works: Dr. Joseph Ignace Guillotin.

Dr. Guillotin was a freemason — in fact, one of the founders of freemasonry in France. The freemasons are a benevolent secret society, devoted to the improvement of mankind; but the Church regarded them as wicked atheists. And it was for this reason more than for anything else that Dr. Guillotin found himself in the Constituent Assembly, with an influential voice in the new revolutionary government of France.

Now this gentle humanitarian was horrified at some of the bloodshed he had seen. He loathed those barbarous and primitive instruments of execution, the wheel and the gibbet. He was sickened by the sight of a man swinging from a gallows all day, while the crowd underneath drank beer and made merry. Guillotin foresaw the mass executions that were coming, and he brooded on how they might be made painless and swift: a moral lesson rather than a sadistic spectacle. Some kind of "machine" was needed. He consulted the public executioner, Charles Henri Sanson, and they looked over various old prints and engravings.

As early as 1555, the Italians had invented a beheading machine, in which a heavy axe blade was placed between two upright posts, so that it could be hauled up to the top with a rope, then allowed to fall down the groove on to the neck of a man kneeling underneath. These "sliding axes" had also been tried in Germany, in Persia — even in Scotland. But they'd never really caught on. The blade often got stuck in the groove, or the rope caught. The old manual method was simpler and more reliable.

An agonizing eternity

And now occurred one of those supreme ironies of history. The man who solved the problem was none other than the king himself, Louis the Sixteenth. It was shortly before the flight that cost him his life, and precipitated the Terror. The Assembly had asked Dr. Antoine Louis, the king's physician, to look into Dr. Guillotin's plan. Dr. Guillotin was asked to call on Dr. Louis at the Tuileries Palace, and he took Sanson, the executioner, with him.

As the three men were engaged in examining the sketches of the machine, a stranger knocked and entered. It was the king, dressed in ordinary clothes. He asked Dr. Louis what he thought of the machine, and looked at the drawing. Then he shook his head. "That curved blade wouldn't suit every kind of neck." The king picked up a pencil. "What you need is something more like *this*." He drew a straight, sloping line on the underside of the axe blade. Guillotin looked at the drawing. "Yes, of course, you're right . . ." A few weeks later, the first guillotine was

tried out on three corpses. The king had been right: a curved blade failed to decapitate one of the corpses, but the sloping blade worked perfectly on the other two. Two years later, the king was decapitated by the machine he had helped perfect.

For the next two years — until the Terror ended with the execution of Robespierre in 1794 — the guillotine thudded with horrible, mechanical persistence, and thousands of heads rolled into the basket. As to the good Dr. Guillotin, he continued his humanitarian work. He was one of the earliest pioneers of smallpox vaccination, and his work on the extermination of smallpox undoubtedly

Dazy

MORAL LESSON or sadistic spectacle? The machine that immortalized Dr. Guillotin . . . he would rather have been remembered for his work against smallpox.

saved more lives in Europe than his guillotine destroyed. But when he died, in 1814, he already knew that it would not be his medical discoveries that would immortalize his name, but that triangular blade, with all its association of horror . . .

This raises the interesting question: *why* is it that decapitation strikes us as so sickening and gruesome? Guillotin was right: as a method of execution, it is certainly more humane than hanging,

electrocution or the gas chamber. Hanging is only about 95% certain; a slight miscalculation in the placing of the rope, and the condemned man strangles to death. Men in the gas chamber have been known to hold their breath for minutes before breathing in the cyanide gas. And the criminologist Nigel Morland, who once stepped on a highly charged electric grid, is on record as saying that the last seconds of an electrocuted man must seem to be an agonizing eternity.

Only the guillotine has never failed to carry out its work with perfect swiftness and efficiency. Yet Guillotin is remembered as a monster, because the idea of decapitation touches some deep chord

of horror in the human psyche. It may be because the loss of the head is so final; men can lose an arm or leg and still survive; not the head. Or could it be, perhaps, because our earliest ancestors cut off the heads of their enemies in battle, and often ate the brains? Is the twinge of horror due to some deep racial memory?

Whatever the reason, there can be no doubt that crimes involving beheading always seem more cruel and brutal than other types of crime. And this is absurd. For sheer vicious cruelty, slow poison is probably the most inhuman method of killing. Then there are the murderers who get pleasure from the fear of their victims—like José Marcellino, Mexico's

431

"lover's lane killer", captured in 1973, who admitted: "I liked it so much, to see the males squirm, and the women frightened and crying, that I'd make my threats last a long time . . . I enjoyed the fear of death in their eyes."

By comparison, murderers like Crippen and Patrick Mahon seem decent and sane. Yet it is Crippen and Mahon whose cases are endlessly rehashed by crime journalists under titles like: "Horror of of the headless corpse." Still, no matter what the general public may feel about them, Crippen and Mahon are of scant interest to the professional criminologist. He is concerned with the motivations behind a crime, and it hardly matters to him *what* the killer does to dispose of the body. On the other hand, he finds a criminal like Patrick Byrne, the Birmingham Y.W.C.A. killer, of altogether greater interest.

There is no need to ask why Byrne killed Stephanie Baird—that is perfectly obvious. He was drunk, and he wanted sex. When he had strangled her into unconsciousness, he undressed her and raped her. All that is straightforward, if horrible; but why did he then cut off her head, and commit further sexual acts on the body? Why did he, even then, go out and try to kill another girl by hitting her with a stone? Why did he write a note saying: "This was the thing I thought would never come."

In the course of his confession, Byrne said one thing that provides a key to his strange personality. He said he wanted to terrorize all the women in the hostel "to get my own back on them for causing my nervous tension through sex". This is a curious statement. Even the most stupid man must see that women are not to *blame* for making him sexually excited. A cat may as well blame mice for making it feel hungry.

But Byrne was not trying to be logical; he was trying to explain, in his own fumbling way, what dark forces had suddenly mastered him when he found himself in a room with an unconscious girl. He also admitted to a psychiatrist that he had been indulging for years in daydreams in which he cut up girls with a circular saw. This brings us altogether closer to the heart of the problem, for what we can see so clearly, in Byrne's case, is that when he made his way into the Y.W.C.A. that December afternoon, it was not simply a girl he wanted—ordinary sexual intercourse. It was somehow *all* women, all the women in the world. He was expressing one of the savage, basic frustrations of man.

Craving for gratification

In 1930, Freud published a book called *Civilization and Its Discontents*, in which he advanced a disturbing—and profoundly pessimistic—theory. He suggested that man is not made for civilization, or civilization for man. Man is a carnivorous animal, and his basic instincts are violent and aggressive. Whether we like it or not, it is "natural" for him to go on a raiding party to another village, kill the men, and then drag off the women for his own pleasure, as natural as it is considered for a tiger to eat antelopes.

But this human tiger was also intelligent and gregarious. He learned to live with other human beings in communities, and to create civilization. Every step he has taken into civilization has been a violation of his basic instincts. Culture is another name for suppression of these instincts. The great basic conflict of all human existence, says Freud, is the conflict between the individual's craving for personal gratification and the claims of society. So how *can* man be happy? Unhappiness is a basic part of his condition . . .

Less pessimistic psychologists, like Abraham Maslow, have pointed out that this is a one-sided view. Happiness does *not* mean unlimited self-indulgence. The history of crime and violence reveals to us that the men who *could* indulge themselves without self-discipline—Caligula, Ivan the Terrible, Vlad the Impaler—were

SHOWING HOW he suffocated Bonnie Leigh Scott, while a detective holds the fatal pillows . . . sleepless Charles Melquist was stunned (below, right) at the "guilty" verdict.

Both UPI

not particularly happy men. Long-term happiness must involve self-discipline. Nowadays, there are very few reputable thinkers who take Freud's argument about civilization seriously.

Nevertheless, without fully intending it, Freud *had* expressed the basic psychology of psychopathic killers like Patrick Byrne, Jack the Ripper, Peter Kürten. These *are* men who feel that Man and Civilization were simply not made for one another. Consider, for example, the nature of the male sexual drive. Unlike most women, man is not basically "faithful". Particularly when young and virile, the average man would be perfectly happy to sleep with a different girl every night; even healthy men have their sexual fantasies.

Avenging sexual tensions

Surely, where sex is concerned, civilization is *intended* to torment males, as you might torment a caged tiger by poking it with a stick? Taking it a step further, is a man to blame if he seizes his opportunity to grab a girl and pull her into a dark alleyway . . . ? *This* is what Byrne meant when he talked about "getting his own back on women for causing my sexual tensions", and he was almost paraphrasing Sigmund Freud.

But why the decapitation? This is also easy to explain. Once a man is possessed by this urgency—like a fox in a chicken farm—he is subjected to endless twinges of desire, like electric shocks. He compensates for an increasing feeling of frustration and inferiority

with daydreams in which he dominates the girl completely; and the longer the fantasies continue, the more violent they are likely to become.

Charles Melquist, arrested in 1958 for the sex-murder and decapitation of 15-year-old Bonnie Leigh Scott, near Chicago, admitted to years of fantasizing about naked women, and of tossing them into huge grinding machines. When such a man finally finds himself with his hands around the throat of an unconscious girl, sexual intercourse is not enough. It seems an anticlimax. His overheated desires crave some stronger satisfaction, some ultimate act of violation and possession. And here, the basic human revulsion at the idea of decapitation rises up from the subconscious—the ultimate act of aggression. . . .

What is equally significant is that both Byrne and Melquist were horrified by what they had done. Byrne said he was glad the police had found him; the murder had tormented him for the past two months; Melquist also made his confession in a long, relieved babble, and admitted that he had been unable to sleep after the murder. Not only is their act of violence no solution to the cravings that produced it: the killer recognizes that he is *further than ever* from a solution. Many killers of this type commit suicide.

The pattern can be clearly seen in the case of Jack the Ripper. The early victims—Mary Anne Nicholls, Annie Chapman, Catherine Eddowes—were mutilated in the area of the genitals, indicating that the Ripper's basic obsession was with

SAVAGED: Stephanie Baird was the focus for man's most basic frustrations. By brutally murdering her, Patrick Byrne struck a terror-blow against all women.

the woman's sexual function—perhaps with the womb. The last murder took place indoors; this time, the killer had unlimited time at his disposal, and the victim—Mary Kelly—was not only disembowelled but almost decapitated. Then the murders ceased, and all the evidence suggests that the Ripper committed suicide.

The novelist Zola based a novel on the Ripper crimes—*La Bête Humaine*—the human beast. This goes to the heart of the problem. Such a man has decided to become the solitary hunter in search of prey, rather than a responsible human being. In doing so, he has retreated from society as deliberately as if he had decided to become a Trappist monk. But men like Byrne, Melquist or the Ripper lack the qualifications for becoming hermits; they *need* society. Hence the conflicting whirlpool of urges that may end in suicide.

"Mad butcher"

The case that most clearly demonstrates the complex morbid psychology of "the human beast" took place in Cleveland, Ohio, in the mid-1930s: the curious unsolved case of the Butcher of Kingsbury Run. Between 1935 and 1938, the "mad butcher" killed at least a dozen people, hacking the bodies into small pieces, and removing the heads—several of which were never found.

433

On September 23, 1935, two decapitated bodies were found in the area of Kingsbury Run and East 45th Street, a slum area. Both had been mutilated with a knife; both were men—one, a 28-year-old medical orderly, the other, a 40-year-old vagrant, who was never identified. The fact that both victims were male suggested that the killer was homosexual, and a sadistic pervert. But when, four months later, the headless body of a 42-year-old prostitute was found not far from Kingsbury Run, the police became less sure that they were looking for a homosexual; the woman's body had been hacked as if in a frenzy, and the head was never found.

At intervals during 1936, three more victims were found in the area; all were men, all were headless, and in one case, the head was never found. The killer was obviously possessed by some kind of frenzy; some of the bodies were little more than a pile of mangled pieces.

On February 23, 1937, the victim was again a woman—headless, and in pieces. In June, the dismembered body of a 30-year-old Negro woman was found in a burlap bag under the Lorain-Carnegie Bridge. The ninth victim, a man, was found in July; he had been decapitated and the body hacked in pieces. The head was never found. And in 1938, there were three more victims; a dismembered and headless woman was found on April 8, and on August 17, the "Mad Butcher" (as the press called him) committed another double murder, a man and a woman. In each of these cases, the killer decapitated the victim, and in six of them, the heads were never found.

The man who was then in charge of Cleveland's police department was Eliott Ness—hero of T.V.'s "Untouchables". Ness recognized that the usual methods of detection were of doubtful value here. But he realized that the mad killer was

VICTIM NUMBER TEN: At the riverside in Cleveland, Ohio, the "Torso Killer" struck again. They also called him "The Mad Butcher of Kingsbury Run".

finding most of his victims among prostitutes and down-and-outs. The latter congregated in a shanty-town area in the centre of the city, near the market. One night in August, Ness raided the place, forced its inhabitants to leave, and burnt it down. This had the desired effect of depriving the killer of his victims; there were no more murders.

Ness also reasoned that the "mad butcher" must be of a certain type. He must be big and powerful to overpower his victims. He must own a car, to transport the bodies. He must live alone, and in some quiet area—perhaps an unfrequented *cul de sac*—in order not to arouse the curiosity of his neighbours. And in order to fit this pattern, he must be rich, or at least well off.

Ness's team made painstaking enquiries in Cleveland society and, according to Oscar Fraley, chronicler of the "Untouchables", soon found a suspect who fitted. He was physically huge, homosexual, sullen and paranoid, and well-to-do. Ness had the man brought in for questioning, and for months played a cat and mouse game with him. The man, confident he was cleverer than the police, almost

admitted the murders, and dared Ness to find evidence.

And, finally, while Ness was still searching, he had himself committed to a mental home, where he died a year later. Ness never doubted that this was the torso killer.

Ness's suspect was an intelligent, literate man; he may well have read Freud's *Civilization and Its Discontents*. If so, he could have added a final footnote; that the man who lives as a beast of prey will almost certainly die as one alone and unmourned by his fellow creatures.

A CASE FOR Eliott Ness, hero of "The Untouchables". He has a theory . . . and first he applies the "scorched earth" policy. Soon, he has a suspect, but is the man too smart for the police? He's both intelligent and literate . . . it's a game of cat and mouse.

THE GANGSTERS

Since Sodom and Gomorrah, it has been cities that have bred gangsterism. It was violence, with Asian roots in Hong Kong that first infected the United States, but the Sicilian brand of gun law finally prevailed. And the organized crime that was spawned by Prohibition lives on today.

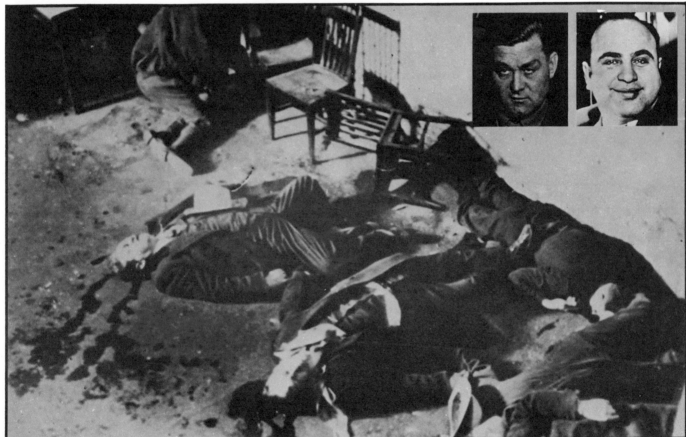

AP/The Bettmann Archive

ON the evening of July 22, 1934, people began to emerge from the Marbro Cinema, on Chicago's West Side. The plain clothes police who were standing around the entrance were tense with anxiety. They were hoping to arrest John Dillinger, America's Public Enemy Number One; they knew he'd gone into the cinema with a brothel madame—who had tipped them off—and another woman. What scared them was that some of the women and children in the crowd might get shot if Dillinger went for his gun. They had reason to worry; last time the Federal agents cornered Dillinger, in a Wisconsin farmhouse, they got so nervous they opened fire on a car full of innocent people, and killed several; Dillinger escaped.

Now, as Melvin Purvis and his agents waited outside the movie theatre, a police car suddenly drew up. The cinema cashier had noticed the plain clothes cops, assumed they were planning to stage a robbery, and rang the local police station. A Federal agent rushed up to the car, showed his identification, and ordered the police to move on fast. A few minutes later, John Dillinger walked out of the cinema with the two women, one of them wearing a bright red dress, so the police could identify her. To Purvis's relief, Dillinger pushed clear of the crowd, and started along an empty stretch of pavement. Purvis yelled: "Stick 'em up, John, you're surrounded." Dillinger went for his gun; dozens of shots sounded, and he crumpled to the pavement.

Most criminologists agree that the

DOOM DAY: An infamous date in the calendar of gangsterism was St. Valentine's Day, 1929 . . . when the notorious massacre took place. Two notorious figures were Bugs Moran (top left) and Al Capone (top right).

death of Dillinger was the end of an era. Capone had been in jail since 1932; prohibition had been repealed in 1933. There were still a few notorious gangsters at large—for example, "Creepy" Karpis and Ma Barker's gang—but never again would the hunt for a gangster produce the nationwide excitement provoked by Dillinger.

It was the notorious Volstead Act—better known as Prohibition—that plunged the United States into its greatest period of lawlessness, starting on January 16, 1920. The puritans and bigots who persuaded the United States Senate to ban all alcoholic drinks thought they were inaugurating "an era of clear thinking and clean living"; in fact, they were allowing organized crime a stranglehold on the U.S.

The Irish and Italian gangs of New York City and Chicago seized their chance to move into the big time. It was the era of Dion O'Banion, Johnny Torrio, Al Capone, Joe Masseria, Salvatore Maranzano, Vito Genovese. On February 14, 1929, five Capone gangsters, disguised as policemen, walked into the garage owned by an Irish gangster, Bugs Moran, lined seven men up against the wall, and mowed them down with sub-machine gun fire.

The "St. Valentine's Day Massacre" shocked the world; suddenly, the U.S. wanted to be rid of its gangsters. A tough but intelligent Sicilian named Charles Luciano—known as "Lucky"—organized the killing of many of the old-style gangsters. He then called a meeting of the survivors, and warned them that the public was sick of gang warfare. In future, he said, there would be a policy of cooperation. Their common enemy was the law; their common prey was the public. A few of the older mobsters—such as Dutch Schultz—preferred to carry on in the old way. After Schultz had eliminated his chief rival, Legs Diamond, he himself was shot down as he sat in a restaurant in Newark, New Jersey, in October 1935. After that, America was more securely than ever in the grip of the mobsters—but the average American knew nothing about it.

Murder incorporated

Quietly and efficiently, Luciano organized "Murder Incorporated", a pool of professional killers who committed murder only when the gang bosses decided someone was stepping out of line. Instead of booze, this new syndicate—sometimes known as the Mafia, sometimes as "Cosa Nostra" ("Our Thing")—dealt in narcotics, gambling, prostitution, extortion, labour racketeering, and anything else that made money.

The general public became intrigued by its existence in November 1957, when the New York State Police stumbled on a business conference of more than 60 top racketeers near the village of Apalachin. All at once, "Murder Incorporated" was world news. There was a national scandal, and a special commission to investigate crime, headed by Senator Kefauver, produced amazing revelations of mass corruption. A top member of the Mafia, Joe Valachi, decided to talk, in exchange for police protection. Some of the more notorious gangsters, including Luciano, were deported. A book about the Mafia,

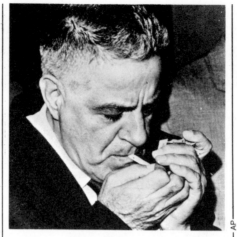

JOE VALACHI, the Mafioso who decided to talk . . . in exchange for police protection. His testimony revealed the workings and methods of the Mafia.

written in 1959, ends with a chapter entitled: "Twilight of the Villains?" The years since then have shown that the answer is: Definitely not.

Soon after the immense success of Mario Puzo's Cosa Nostra novel *The Godfather* in 1971, there were further outbreaks of gang warfare in New York City. Gangleader Joe Colombo was shot and critically wounded at a rally in Central Park; the rival gangster responsible for this shooting, Joe Gallo, was himself murdered as he celebrated his birthday in April 1972; in between these shootings there were a dozen other Mafia executions. Now, forty years after the death of John Dillinger, America is still firmly in the hands of its "mobs". Capone and Luciano have been replaced by another Mafia leader; but there is always a "Godfather" ready to step into the shoes of his predecessor.

Will this ever change? An unprejudiced look at history suggests that the answer is: Probably not. If prostitution is the world's oldest profession, then gangsterism is probably the second oldest. Moreover, scientific investigation suggests that this is more than just plain wickedness; it is a deep-rooted animal instinct. An instinct that is activated and intensified by conditions of overcrowding—not only in present-day communities and cities, but in the living areas of long ago.

This gives an interesting insight into the beginnings of crime—and of gangs. It is known that most of man's earliest cities, some of which sprang up 5000 years B.C., contained overcrowded slums. This may sound strange; after all, the world of those days had a tiny population. So why didn't the people spread themselves out more? The answer is simple. Men built cities for mutual protection; they preferred to be huddled

together. Moreover, these cities were often in river valleys where there was a limited amount of space to expand. The result was inevitable—crime on a large scale. To people from quiet country villages, the wickedness of the cities must have seemed terrifying—as is instanced in the Bible, with its stories of Sodom and Gomorrah, and those godless cities of Mesopotamia that were destroyed by the Flood (which actually took place about 4000 B.C.). The city, therefore, literally created crime—at least, large-scale crime. And, unfortunately, the pestilence soon overflowed into the surrounding countryside; travellers were robbed and murdered; small villages were overrun by robber bands who killed the men, raped the women, and burned the houses.

It can thus be said with some confidence, that the first gangsters appeared soon after the first cities. But at this point, an important distinction must be made. There are two distinct kinds of gangster which, for convenience, can be labelled the bandit and the "true gangster". Bandit obviously means the same as gangster (since a gang is a band); but their motivations are different. To put it simply, the gangster tends to be crueller and more vicious than the bandit. The bandit lives in rural areas; he has space. He may have taken to crime for a variety of reasons; but one of these is *not* overcrowding. He prefers to be a member of a band because being a loner in wide open spaces is a demoralizing business. (Criminal loners often commit far more atrocious crimes than "bandits", because boredom and solitude make them lose their sense of identity.)

Emotional damage

Apart from his criminal activities, the bandit may be a normal human being with normal human emotions. On the other hand, the man who becomes a gangster because of the pressures of an overcrowded slum, has often suffered permanent emotional damage. To begin with, as already noted, overcrowding produces bad mothers and brutal fathers. The true gangster is the product of the slum, and he sees the world as a place to be plundered—if he can get away with it.

The city of Hong Kong offers some gruesome examples of this dating from recent years. Trapped between the sea and steep hills, Hong Kong is one of the most overcrowded cities in the world, and its murder rate has always been high. After World War II, the population quickly rocketed from half a million to more than two and a half million. Consequently, there was a terrifying wave of gang murders—murders so atrocious that the police speak of them as the work of "horror cults".

In 1958, there were more than 900

JOE VALACHI talked about "Cosa Nostra" . . . "This thing of Ours", but the architects of organized crime in the United States were more popularly known as The Mafia. Either way, an Italian expression or a Sicilian one, there was no doubt of the organization's racial origins. That was one reason why "Dutch" Schultz had to die at dinner (left). His death was at the hands of Sicilian "Lucky" Luciano (below), perhaps the biggest ever of the Mafia's bosses. Luciano was eventually caught and imprisoned, then deported after serving a 10-year sentence. Ironically, the action of the American authorities enabled him to die peacefully. He had a heart attack at Naples airport, while waiting for a friend from the United States. His funeral (bottom picture) was magnificently ornate . . .

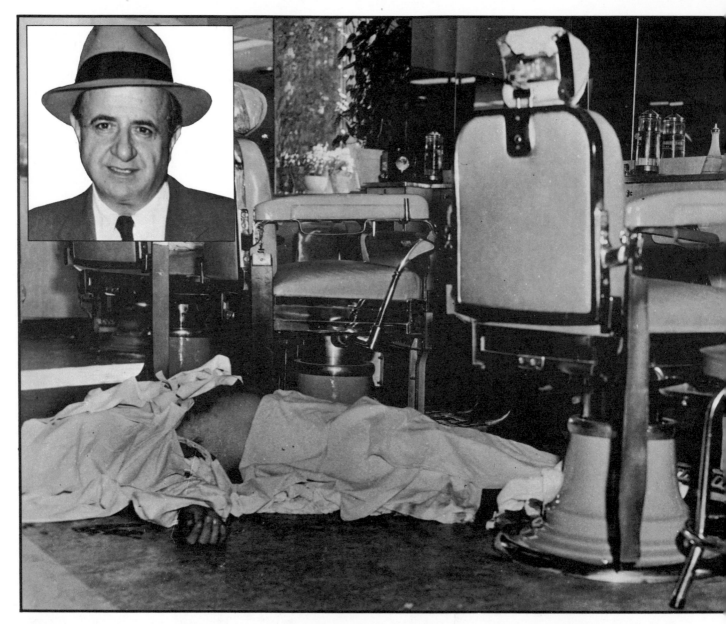

murders—five times the American murder rate, and 150 times the English. These "horror cults" are, in fact, Chinese "tongs", or "Triad Societies". (The earliest tongs were called "Three Harmonies Societies".) Like their American counterpart, the Mafia, they operate prostitution, drugs rackets, protection, and extortion. But their methods of ensuring obedience depend upon terrorism.

For example, in 1958, a rich merchant named Ko Sun Wei, together with four of his family, were horribly murdered in his house in Kowloon. The victims were staked out, with their arms and legs spreadeagled. Three women—the merchant's two daughters and his daughter-in-law—were raped repeatedly, then tortured to death with knives. One woman was still alive when the police arrived, but was unable to speak—her tongue had been cut out.

These were only five among 350 murders that took place in Hong Kong in September 1958. Sergeant Arthur Ogilvie, of the Hong Kong Police, who gives these figures, also mentions that during the riots of 1956, Triad Societies took the opportunity to pillage more than $25,000,000 worth of goods. With a figure of this size involved, it can be seen that crime in modern Hong Kong is an even bigger business than it was in the Chicago of the 1920s. The interesting point here is the verification of observations about overcrowding. It produces true gangsters—men who are adepts in cruelty and violence, because they are unable to experience ordinary human emotions.

Bearing in mind this important distinction, it can be seen that many of the famous criminals and gang leaders of the past 200 years have been bandits rather than gangsters. For example, Australia's most famous criminal, Ned Kelly, was definitely a bandit. Kelly, the son of an Irish farmer and former convict, became Australia's public enemy Number One when he killed three constables at Stringybark Creek in 1877.

From then on, he lived the traditional life of the bandit on the run, moving around the countryside with his gang—which included his brother Dan—and robbing banks. He made himself head and body armour, weighing 97 lb., and was wearing it when the police finally ambushed his gang in Glenrowan. He was only 24 when he was executed in 1880. Asked why he had decided to confront the police at Glenrowan, Kelly made a reply that was to be echoed by many American gangsters of the Bonny and Clyde era: "A man gets tired of being hunted like a dog . . . I wanted to see the thing end."

The most significant feature about Kelly is that he was a man who thought he had

BIG SHOTS: The end came for senior Mafioso Albert Anastasia (inset left) as he sat in the barber's chair at a smart New York hotel. He had become too ambitious. The result: one of the world's most memorable news-pictures. The assassination habit dies hard. In 1971, Joe Colombo was shot in New York's Central Park. Soon afterwards, the rival responsible for the shooting, Joe Gallo (below) was killed while celebrating his birthday at a New York restaurant. Life may be cheap to the Mafia bosses, but death still brings tears . . . for Gallo's wife and daughter (bottom).

N.Y. Daily News photo

NY Daily News Photo

A P

a grievance against the law—and in this he resembles many of the famous "bandits", from Billy the Kid to John Dillinger. Whether the grievance is real or not is beside the point; but it starts the bandit off on the road that leads to the gallows, or the final bloody shoot-out with the police.

Most wanted man

The story of South Africa's most famous "gangster" may be taken as typifying the pattern. William Foster was born in 1886, and his family moved to Johannesburg in 1900. While still under 20, William decided to seek his fortune in German South West Africa. Plodding around in the desert one day, he met two companions who were driving a pack of donkeys. He joined them—and a few miles farther on, all three were arrested and charged with stealing the donkeys. The young men claimed they had found the donkeys wandering in the desert, and were driving them back to the nearest village. William lost his temper with the officious German magistrate. As a result of this, he was sentenced to a month in prison, while his companions were allowed to go free. The injustice of this infuriated him. When he came out of jail, he was aggressive and inclined to drink too much. A series of minor offences led to further prison sentences—and a thoroughly resentful William Foster was ready to become a "complete" criminal.

He fell in love, and wanted money to marry. His first major crime, therefore, was a well-planned robbery of a jeweller. He and two accomplices ran into bad luck and an efficient police force, and each received 12 years' hard labour. Foster's girlfriend Peggy married him while he was in jail, awaiting trial. Nine months later, Foster escaped. In a bank robbery a few months later, two clerks were killed, and Foster's career as a "hunted dog" began. Like Kelly, he had an amazing ability to shoot his way out of tight corners; and, as the deaths piled up, he became South Africa's most wanted man.

Committed suicide

Whenever possible, his wife—who now had a baby daughter—joined him. The tragic end came in September 1914, when Foster and two companions were cornered in a cave in the Kensington Ridge. One of the men committed suicide. Foster's parents, his sisters, and his wife Peggy were then sent for. They agreed to try and persuade him to give himself up, and bravely entered the cave. The parents and sisters came out, with Foster's baby daughter. Then three shots rang out. Peggy had decided to die with her husband.

In the United States, the gangster era began long before Prohibition. New York

Camera Press

GANG MURDER and organized crime . . .?
In Chinese Triad Societies, the flag is
for ceremonial purposes, the sword for
the ritualistic beheading . . . of a cockerel.

was America's first major city, and as early as 1790 it had slums that were as foul and miserable as any in the world. In the hundred or so rooms of the Old Brewery, human beings were packed like rats, and murders averaged one a night. When the district was demolished in 1852, the builders filled numerous sacks with human bones and remains. There were many tough and colourfully-named gangs: the Dead Rabbits, the Roach Guards, the Shirt Tails, the Plug Uglies (which referred to their huge plug or top hats). Then, during the 1840s, Tam-

many Hall politicians discovered that gangsters could be useful allies, threatening rivals and drumming up votes. And it was from this period that the real history of American gangsterdom began.

At the time, most of the gangsters were Irish—and, oddly enough, Chinese. The Chinese were accustomed to their "Triad Societies" at home. When they came to settle in America—mostly on the West Coast—they naturally formed themselves again into "tongs" for mutual protection.

The Chinese were also among the first

to practise gang assassination. In 1897, a rich Chinese gangster, Little Pete— owner of several gambling houses—was sitting in a barber's chair in San Francisco. He had made the mistake of sending his bodyguard out to find the result of a horse race. Two men who had been trailing him for months, awaiting their opportunity, came in and literally filled him full of lead. The killers were never caught. A similar scene was to be repeated half a century later when, in October 1957, Albert Anastasia, one of Murder Incorporated's assassins, was shot in a Manhattan hotel barber's shop.

Black Hand Gang

In the early years of the century, most of America's most formidable gangsters were Chinese. By comparison, the Irish were relatively amateurish and badly organized. But another racial group was slowly achieving ascendancy—the Italians. Fleeing from the poverty of their homeland—and from its chronic political troubles—they also had their tradition of secret societies. The word "Mafia" originally described a Sicilian outlaw who had taken to the hills, covered with low scrub (mafia), to hide from justice (either at the hands of the police, or of the family of someone he had killed).

The Mafia came to New Orleans— under the name of "the Black Hand")— in the 1880's. Almost without exception, mafiosi preyed upon their fellow citizens, who, in turn, were too terrified to appeal to the police of their adopted country. Similarly, the Irish gangsters tended to prey upon their fellow Irish, and the Chinese on the Chinese.

Escape from slums

As the century progressed, the Chinese slowly lost their reputation as gangsters —perhaps because many of them succeeded, through hard work and intelligence, in escaping from the slums—and the Irish, and their bitter rivals the Italians, took over. Then came the double-edged sword of Prohibition. Chicago's crime industry was run by men like the O'Donnell brothers, and the flamboyant Dion O'Banion, who was quoted as saying angrily: "To hell with them Sicilians!"

On November 10, 1924, four men walked into O'Banion's flower store, and unceremoniously gunned him down. The man who arranged the murder commented ironically: "O'Banion's head got away from under his hat." His name was Al Capone. The United States had entered its third and most lethal era of gangsterdom. It is still in the midst of it.

THE CROOKED COPS

They are the men people go to for help in cases of robbery, rape, theft.
But what if the police themselves are dishonest?
Who then ensures that justice is done?

IN NEW YORK, Whitman Knapp (below) led a commission on police corruption. At a news conference in August 1972 he spoke of the "urgent" need for a special state prosecutor to investigate corrupt activities among local police, district attorneys, judges and lawyers. Among witnesses at the hearing were truck driver George Burkert (above left); bearded detective Frank Serpico (centre); and commission investigator Mark Hansen (right).

IN JANUARY 1728, a play called *The Beggar's Opera* became the rage of London. It was written by John Gay, and presented by a manager called Rich; it made Gay rich and Rich gay. What the audiences found so piquant about it was that it was not about tragic kings and queens, but about thieves, highwaymen, prostitutes, and fences. The villain, Peachum, is a receiver of stolen goods who supplements his income by handing over some of his customers to the law. In essence, it was an amusingly realistic portrayal of crime and corruption in eighteenth-century London.

Only three years earlier, Londoners had crowded to watch the execution of the man who served as the model for Peachum—the "thieftaker" Jonathan Wild. In fact, Wild may be regarded as the archetype of the crooked cop. He was *not* a cop—officially the British police force didn't come into existence until the end of the eighteenth century—but he was regarded as a valuable ally of the law. Arriving in London about 1710, at the age of 22, Wild quickly made the discovery that the man who makes most out of crime is not the thief, but the man who finances him.

At this time, there was an extraordinary loophole in the law: a receiver of stolen goods could not be prosecuted. Wild set up as a receiver, and soon became so prosperous that he was able to buy an inn. By the time an Act of Parliament changed the law on receivers, he had already devised a way to operate legally. He would approach men who had been robbed, and offer to buy the stolen goods back from the thief, for a small commission. This was so successful that he set up a shop where people who had been burgled could come to inquire about their property.

Jealous friends

For five shillings, Wild would enter their names on his books; a few days later, in exchange for a reward, he would restore the goods. The peace officers—employed by the City of London—had no objection. Wild was one of their best informers. So long as he helped to send highwaymen and thieves to the gallows at Tyburn, they didn't care what he did.

Wild would probably have died comfortably in his bed if he hadn't overreached himself. He organized some of the robberies himself. Business was so good that he had to store some of the stolen property in warehouses. Jealous confederates finally betrayed him. The law had to act. In May 1725 he was taken to Tyburn—now Marble Arch—in a cart, pelted and jeered at by the mob; there he was hanged on the triangular gallows. It was probably his reputation for betrayal, rather than dishonesty, that prompted the crowd's hostility.

"Wild's system and methods have been copied many times since then, in America and on the Continent, as well as in this country," wrote a biographer of Jonathan Wild in 1937. This was not quite true. Before you can have large-scale official corruption, you must first have a flourishing crime industry. In the London of Jonathan Wild, the crime rate was very nearly as high as in present-day New York—and for a rather odd reason.

Enormous bribes

In the middle of the seventeenth century, a Dutch professor named Sylvius discovered how to distil a powerful spirit from juniper berries. It was called "genièvre"—French for juniper—and then shortened to "gin". The English had always been beer and wine drinkers; but when William of Orange became king in 1689, Dutch gin began to flow into England. In 1690 an Act of Parliament allowed anyone to brew and sell spirits without a license. Thousands of gin shops opened up; the sign "Drunk for a penny, dead drunk for twopence, straw free," became commonplace. The crime rate rocketed, and men like Wild flourished. He was the most notorious "crooked cop" of his time—but there were dozens of others. Gin, crime, and crooked peace officers went together.

However, it is not quite accurate to talk about "police corruption". It is seldom the uniformed man on the beat who gets corrupted. In all the major police scandals—from the "trial of the detectives" in London in 1877 to the widely publicized Knapp Commission Hearings in New York in 1971—the culprits have been plain clothes detectives. There was even a certain amount of corruption among the famous "Bow Street Runners", the forerunners of the modern London police force.

These un-uniformed detectives were known for their high living, and at least two of them left fortunes of over £20,000. That kind of money is not made by honest thief-catching. But the detective has to spend part of his days in contact with crooks, because his job is to obtain information. When he is dealing with small-time crooks, the temptation is small. But the big crook can offer enormous bribes—and his "success" lends him a certain aura of sophistication and authority that may induce a sense of inferiority in a detective earning less than £2000 a year. As if these pressures are not enough, the detective may be induced to compromise himself, and then be blackmailed.

All three of these factors were at work in the events which led to the London police scandals of 1877. The crooks in this case were two highly successful confidence swindlers named Kurr and Benson. Both had mastered the art of seeming to be rich men. Benson, with an excellent French accent, played the part of an aristocrat; Kurr appeared to be a bluff country gentleman who might have stepped out of the pages of a novel by Anthony Trollope.

Their chosen field was sport. And their method of swindling had a certain classic simplicity and originality. Benson, who was living in luxury at Shanklin, Isle of Wight, under the name of Yonge, wrote a letter to the Comtesse de Goncourt, explaining that he was a brilliantly successful sportsman. As a result, he said, bookmakers always shortened the odds when he backed a horse—knowing it was almost certain to win.

All that he wanted of the Comtesse de Goncourt was that she should act as his agent, and place bets on horses for him. He would send her the money, and when the horse won, she would post him his winnings, upon which he would pay her a 5 per cent commission.

The Comtesse could see no harm in this arrangement. She forwarded the cheque to a bookmaker; in fact, the bookmaker was Benson himself. Soon, she received a cheque for £1000 from the "bookmaker"—Benson's winnings. She forwarded the cheque to Benson, who

promptly sent her £50 for her trouble. Naturally, the Countess wanted to invest some of her own money in this apparently foolproof scheme. She gave Benson, and his accomplice Kurr, £10,000 over a short period. She was only one of their victims.

How did Scotland Yard detectives come to be involved with these swindlers? The full story is unknown, but the first one to accept bribes seems to have been Detective Inspector Meiklejohn of the Yard. Meiklejohn was a friend of a man called

Mansell Collection

Mansell Collection

CRIME AND corruption often started in the gin shops so popular in nineteenth-century London. If death didn't claim his victims then, he did so when (left) they were arrested and sent to be hanged. Then they needed drink most.

Druscovitch, who was in charge of the continental branch of the "fraud squad". Druscovitch got himself into some extraneous financial trouble, and urgently needed £60. Meiklejohn introduced him to a "perfect gentleman", who persuaded Druscovitch to accept the £60 as a present. The "gentleman" was Kurr.

Meiklejohn's boss Clarke was then drawn into the web by the "aristocratic" Benson. Benson sent him a message, claiming to have information about a gang that Clarke had recently broken up. He explained that he was too crippled to leave his home on the Isle of Wight; could Clarke call on him? (Benson had previously crippled himself in an attempt to commit suicide in jail by setting fire to his mattress.) This was good psychology. Clarke went to the palatial home at Shanklin, and was introduced to the exquisitely dressed gentleman who lay on a couch, and whose handkerchiefs had coronets embroidered upon them.

Benson explained that he was afraid Clarke was about to be blackmailed; rumours were circulating that he had taken bribes from the gang he had recently broken up. Clarke said indignantly that he had never taken bribes. Of course not, Benson agreed silkily. But unfortunately there was a letter that Clarke had written to one of the gang, arranging a secret meeting. Perhaps it *was* all police business, but it certainly read very suspiciously. Finally, Clarke was not so much

blackmailed as charmed and dominated.

When a fourth Yard man, Detective Inspector Palmer, was drawn into the circle, the swindlers felt they were ready to face the world. And they very soon had to. Benson decided that it was time for a grand *coup*. He told the trusting Comtesse de Goncourt that he had a superb opportunity to invest £30,000 for her. It would bring a huge return. The Comtesse did not have that much in ready cash, so she consulted her lawyer, a man named Abrahams. Abrahams was instantly suspicious, and checked with Scotland Yard on "Mr. Yonge of Shanklin". Druscovitch instantly warned Benson that the Comtesse's lawyer had "smelled a rat".

Used notes

The conspirators launched into action. They hadn't expected to be discovered quite so soon. The loot—well over £10,000—was drawn out of the Bank of England. But in a transaction of that size, the numbers of the notes were known—it would have excited suspicion to ask for the money in old used notes. The police reached the Bank soon after the cash had gone, and Druscovitch was ordered to telegraph the numbers of the notes to all banks in the British Isles.

He conveniently overlooked Scotland – which gave Benson time to get to Glasgow, and change his "marked money" into £100 notes on the Bank of Clydesdale – which had the advantage of being unnumbered, and the disadvantage of being difficult to change outside Scotland. Duly, the detectives were all given their "rewards" – Meiklejohn receiving £500. However, he acted stupidly. He changed one of the notes with a wine merchant in Leeds, Yorkshire. The Leeds police soon found out that a Scotland Yard man had cashed a Clydesdale note, and wrote to another of Druscovitch's superiors, Williamson, at the Yard. Druscovitch intercepted the letter and burned it.

The Clydesdale notes were proving to be more trouble than they were worth. Benson went to Rotterdam and cashed one at a hotel; the Dutch police promptly arrested him. Druscovitch informed the other swindler, Kurr, who sent a cable to the Dutch police, signed "Williamson" (Druscovitch's immediate superior), ordering them to release their captive. They almost did so, but decided to wait for confirmation by letter – which failed to arrive.

Ironically enough, Druscovitch was then sent to Rotterdam to bring Benson back. He was in a gloomy mood; he realized that the net was closing in on him and his confederates. Within a short while, Kurr was also arrested, and he and Benson were tried. Benson got fifteen years, Kurr ten. They then decided that their "bent cops" had not lived up to their side of the agreement in allowing them to get caught – and in retaliation they denounced them.

The result was the "trial of the detectives", which shook the English middle class to its foundation. If its members couldn't trust the renowned British bobby, who *could* they trust?

The feeling in favour of the police was so strong that Clarke was actually acquitted. The other three were put inside for two years. The two swindlers were also satisfied; their sentences were reduced by a third. Benson later committed suicide – after a spectacular swindle practised on Adelina Patti, the Spanish-born coloratura who appeared in concerts in New York from 1850 – by jumping from a high gallery in an American prison, where he had ended up.

Raw material

The scandal created by the trial of the detectives indicates how strongly the British trust their policemen. And, statistically, they are right to do so. Britain has never suffered from the presence of major crime – its murder rate is still one of the lowest in the world. Where there are no large pickings to be made from such activities, there is unlikely to be undue police corruption. In the Scotland Yard affair, only Meiklejohn had the makings of a really dishonest official.

In the United States, however, graft has always been so widespread – starting with the local City Halls – that police corruption is accepted with habitual resignation. From the beginning, the United States had the raw material, the wide open spaces, and the vitality that makes for enormous wealth. Violence – together with the opening of the frontiers – was a part of the way of life. In the original Wild West, the distinction between robbers and lawmen was likely to get blurred. In fast-growing towns such as Chicago and San Francisco, the same thing was true; and there it was actively encouraged by the Horatio Alger "Protestant ethic" of success, which is so basic to American society.

Any society which attaches so much importance to wealth and gain is asking for corruption. One of the first big inquiries into police corruption in New York was in 1893 – inspired by the Rev. Charles Parkhurst, who had discovered that practically every member of the police force had paid "contributions" to Tammany Hall for the privilege of getting his job.

One police captain had handed out $15,000 for his rank. Where did he get the money? From the keepers of gambling houses and brothels. The police chief, Alexander S. Williams, had shares in a brewery, and forced saloon owners to sell "his" whiskey on penalty of being raided. Williams was unable to explain how he had managed to afford an estate on Long Island, complete with a yacht (and its own dock) on his police salary. Although no charges were made against him, he resigned a year later.

French connection

Understandably, then, a deep-seated distrust of the law is a part of American life – particularly among oppressed racial and religious minorities. Herbert Asbury, historian of New York gangs, records that in race riots at the turn of the twentieth century – usually started by white youths – the police would join in on the side of the whites, battering the Negroes with their clubs and arresting them.

From 1894 onwards, there have been major investigations into police corruption about every two decades. In New York, the most recent of these was the Knapp Commission of 1971. In spite of the sensational nature of the revelations, the hearings excited little coast-to-coast attention. The final report which came out in December 1972 colourfully divided "bent cops" into "meat-eaters" and "grass-eaters". Meat-eaters are policemen who "aggressively misuse their power for personal gain"; the grass-eaters "simply accept the pay-offs that come their way". The vast majority of corrupt policemen, said the report, are grass-eaters.

In an area like New York's Harlem, with its illegal gambling, a bent cop could make $1500 a month. If he was transferred to another command, this payment would continue for another two months – giving him time to adjust to his "lower

SWINDLER Harry Benson charged a group of detectives with graft when sentenced himself to 15 years. Another of his "suckers" was star Adelina Patti.

MEIKLEJOHN

WILLIAM KURR.

DRUSCOVITCH.

H BENSON.

E. FROGGATT.

PALMER.

CLARKE.

income". It could explain how, when the police seized heroin, it was likely to find its way back into the drugs market—and how of $137,000 seized from drug traffickers, $80,000 went into the pockets of the arresting officers. In one police precinct, over 68 pounds of "French connection" heroin had vanished from the police laboratory—$7 million-worth at current prices then.

The figures poured out regularly, and no one was very shocked or very surprised. Americans had heard it all before. They *expected* their police to behave like that. They might be roused to protest occasionally if the misbehaviour became too public—as when Mayor Daley's Chicago policemen were seen on television beating up anybody who looked like a demonstrator during the Democratic Convention of 1968. But generally speaking the feeling is that the

CROOKS and cops. Meiklejohn (top left); Kurr (centre); Druscovitch (top right); Benson (centre left); Froggatt (right); Clarke (bottom left); Palmer (right).

police have got a tough job, and that a little brutality and corruption is inevitable—if not, occasionally, necessary.

There is something to be said for this attitude. England has an average of three murders a week; in 1971, the United

States had a murder every *33 minutes*, and the figure shows no sign of declining. With violence on this scale, toughness is regarded as a basic necessity in a policeman or a prison guard. Unless there is some system of public checks, excesses are bound to occur.

When Tom Murton became Superintendent of the Tucker Prison Farm in Arkansas in 1967, he soon discovered that nearly two hundred convicts were listed as having escaped, and had never been caught—a far higher number than would have been expected. Seasoned inmates said openly that there were a hundred or so bodies buried in the prison grounds; men who, for one reason or another, had fallen foul of the "wardens".

Murton dug in an area where the ground had sunk, and quickly unearthed three skeletons. For a few weeks, the scandal drew nationwide headlines; then, suddenly, the authorities ordered that there should be no further digging. Murton was dismissed, and the scandal was allowed to simmer.

Dirty hands

Where tensions *have* increased—in racially mixed areas in both the United States and Britain—charges of corruption and brutality against the police have also increased. In September 1973, a Detective Chief Inspector and five of his staff were charged at London's Old Bailey with manufacturing evidence of drug smuggling against a Pakistani family. The police were convinced that the family was guilty, but there was not enough evidence against them. The prosecution alleged the police strengthened the evidence. The father's five-year sentence was later quashed.

The most interesting feature about such a case is that the newspapers scarcely bothered to report it. For the most part, it rated a small paragraph on an inside page. The English public was apparently as blasé about it as the American public was about the New York scandals of 1971.

As long as there is crime, as long as criminals flourish, police officers will be needed to combat the evil. It is inevitable, therefore, that some of the graft, the corruption, will rub off onto them. You cannot put your hand in a sewer without it coming up dirty. In the words of the lyricist W. S. Gilbert, "The policeman's lot is not a happy one." It was true when he wrote it some hundred years ago: unhappily it is truer than ever today.

PRISON Superintendent Thomas Murton was shocked on discovering 3 bodies buried in crude wooden coffins at Tucker Prison Farm, Arkansas. According to rumour, some 100 bodies were under the ground. Murton said he would resign—and was dismissed. The scandal was buried.

INDEX